TRANSFORMATIONS
Mathematical Approaches to
Culture Change

TRANSFORMATIONS
Mathematical Approaches to Culture Change

Edited by

COLIN RENFREW
Department of Archaeology
University of Southampton
Southampton, England

KENNETH L. COOKE
Department of Mathematics
Pomona College
Claremont, California

ACADEMIC PRESS   New York   San Francisco   London
A Subsidiary of Harcourt Brace Jovanovich, Publishers

ACADEMIC PRESS, INC.
111 Fifth Avenue, New York, New York 10003

United Kingdom Edition published by
ACADEMIC PRESS, INC. (LONDON) LTD.
24/28 Oval Road, London NW1   7DX

Library of Congress Cataloging in Publication Data
  Main entry under title:

  Transformations.

    Includes bibliographies and index.
    1. Archaeology––Mathematical models. 2. Social
change––Mathematical models. 3. Mathematical
anthropology. I. Renfrew, Colin, 1937–
II. Cooke, Kenneth L.
  CC75.7.T7   301.24'01'51   79–10802
  ISBN 0–12–586050–1

PRINTED IN THE UNITED STATES OF AMERICA

79 80 81 82   9 8 7 6 5 4 3 2 1

For John Wilkinson

Le Temps scintille et le Songe est savoir

—PAUL VALÉRY
Le Cimitière marin

Contents

vii

3   RICHARD BELLMAN
Mathematics in the Field of History   83

4   ROBERT ROSEN
Morphogenesis in Biological
and Social Systems   91

II
HIERARCHY AND
SOCIAL SPACE   113

5   IAN HODDER
Simulating the Growth of Hierarchies   117

KENNETH L. COOKE
COLIN RENFREW

14

An Experiment on the Simulation of Culture Changes

V

THE DECISION NEXUS AND EARLY ECONOMIES

15

MICHAEL B. SCHIFFER

A Preliminary Consideration of Behavioral Change

16

ARTHUR S. KEENE

Economic Optimization Models and the Study of Hunter–Gatherer Subsistence Settlement Systems

21 COLIN RENFREW

Systems Collapse as Social Transformation: Catastrophe and Anastrophe in Early State Societies

List of Contributors

Numbers in parentheses indicate the pages on which the authors' contributions begin.

JOHN R. ALDEN (169), Museum of Anthropology, The University of Michigan, Ann Arbor, Michigan 48109

ALBERT J. AMMERMAN (275), Department of Anthropology, State University of New York at Binghamton, Binghamton, New York 13901

RICHARD BELLMAN (83), Departments of Electrical Engineering, Mathematics, and Medicine, University of Southern California, Los Angeles, California 90007

L. L. CAVALLI-SFORZA (275), Department of Genetics, Stanford University, Stanford, California 94305

A. J. CHADWICK (237), (formerly of Downing College, University of Cambridge), 52 Gough Way, Cambridge, England

KENNETH L. COOKE (45, 327), Department of Mathematics, Pomona College, Claremont, California 91711

JEFFREY L. EIGHMY (205), Department of Anthropology, Colorado State University, Fort Collins, Colorado 80521

LUCIEN A. GÉRARDIN (299), Corporate Management, THOMSON-CSF, B.P. 96-08, 75362 Paris Cedex 08 France

JOEL GUNN (257), Division of Social Sciences, The University of Texas at San Antonio, San Antonio, Texas 78285

IAN R. HODDER (117), Department of Archaeology and Anthropology, Downing Street, Cambridge, England

ARTHUR S. KEENE (369), Museum of Anthropology, The University of Michigan, Ann Arbor, Michigan 48109

ERIC V. LEVEL (145), Department of Mathematics, University of Minnesota, Minneapolis, Minnesota 55455

FRED PLOG (221), Department of Anthropology, Arizona State University, Tempe, Arizona 85281

TIM POSTON (425, 437), Département de Physique Théorique, Université de Genève, Geneva, Switzerland

A. COLIN RENFREW (3, 145, 327, 437, 481), Department of Archaeology, University of Southampton, Southampton S095 NH England

ROBERT G. D. REYNOLDS (405), Department of Computer and Communication Sciences, University of Michigan, Ann Arbor, Michigan 48104

ROBERT ROSEN (91), Department of Physiology and Biophysics, Dalhousie University, Halifax, Nova Scotia, Canada

MICHAEL B. SCHIFFER (353), Department of Anthropology, University of Arizona, Tucson, Arizona 85721

RENÉ THOM, Institut des Hautes Etudes Scientifiques, Bures-sur-Yvette, France

E. C. ZEEMAN (463), Mathematics Institute, University of Warwick, Coventry, England

BERNARD P. ZEIGLER (405), Department of Applied Mathematics, Weizmann Institute of Science, Rehovot, Israel

Foreword

It is always very gratifying for the originator of some ideas to see how, in later years, they grow and develop. It is also a source of interest to observe in which medium they are finding favor; which soil is proving receptive and which not. Had it been said, some 6 years ago, that the first book to use catastrophe theoretic methods in a relatively systematic way would be an archaeology book, I would have been rather surprised. However, when I made my acquaintance with the subject through reading C. Renfrew's excellent book, *Before Civilisation,* I gained some insight into why this should be so. There are, in fact, two basic reasons that oppose the growth of catastrophe theoretic methods: The first is the existing paradigm of the exact sciences, essentially that of fundamental physics. Undoubtedly the hard quantitative predictions derived from physical laws provide a stronger tool in physics than the softer catastrophe theoretic methods. And many people still believe in the possibility of extending the exact quantitative methods of physics beyond their natural domain (where physical laws apply) essentially by implementing them with statistical tools and methods, although the validity of such procedures is often quite doubtful. On the opposite side, in many social disciplines, the customary "conceptual" method of explanation, using ordinary language and notions, may frequently appear to be very efficient, up to the point of rendering any mathematical approach unnecessary. The same is true in biology, where "concrete" local causes are frequently invoked, without any appeal to mathematical description.

Indeed, the concept of causality is a very fascinating one, although its real content is frequently very difficult to pin down. In disciplines in which immediate action is needed, such as in medicine, one always looks—in any particular situation—for a local causative agent upon which to act; hence the need to find everywhere a very precise factor deemed to be the principal (or unique) cause of the phenomenon studied. Unfortunately, in many cases, these causal interpretations are bound to fail, because—as pointed out precisely in catastrophe theory models—a very striking or discontinuous phenomenon may be the result of a slowly varying situation which is difficult to comprehend or explain as a whole, and for which one may only hope to define the relevant parameters. On the other hand, archaeology is an interpretative hermeneutic theory, a discipline whose need of social usefulness or immediate applicability is less obvious; it aims to answer a very natural, but gratuitous curiosity of the human mind, namely to know our own past. Hence the use of academic ways of investigation is not biased by the necessity of obtaining immediate results, or profits. Incidentally, archaeology may not in fact be as useless as it seems a priori, for mankind has had to solve many problems in the past very similar to those that now confront it; the only difference is that whereas in the past these problems, like those of scarcity, were on a local scale, today they are at the planetary level.

I feel myself very much in agreement with the author's general philosophy: a constant distrust about "obvious" causality mechanisms, with more emphasis on the global study of a situation. Diffusionist hypotheses—as special cases of too easy a creative agent—are quite rightly submitted to cogent criticism throughout the book. "Replacing anecdote by analysis"— as aptly expressed by C. Renfrew—is the major program of this volume, whose methodological importance cannot be underestimated. Already the late C. H. Waddington, quoting A. N. Whitehead, criticized the too frequent appeal in biology to obvious local mechanisms as "the fallacy of misplaced concreteness." The main interest of the studies presented here is to realize a full spectrum of models, extending from the almost purely quantitative methods of physics, to the purely verbal conceptual explanations. In the middle of this spectrum, catastrophe theoretic models are given an eminent position, exemplifying the use of soft mathematics in situations in which the use of hard quantitative models is not possible, but where the subtle intricacy of conflicting factors may not be easily described in ordinary language. Of course, out of such models, no certain nor definitive conclusions may necessarily be drawn; nevertheless, they dissipate some too obvious illusory explanations, they open new ways of research, and they allow for new ways of thinking. In a discipline such as archaeology could we hope for a better result?

RENÉ THOM

Preface

Those who study man's past are increasingly concerned to understand change and to undertake the explanation of change, rather than simply to reconstruct and narrate past events. Culture change is now widely seen not just as the fortuitous product of individual actions and events compounded together, but rather as the cumulative consequence of processes which operate over long periods in a manner largely unrecognized by the actors upon the historical stage.

To undertake the study of culture process does not, of course, imply that individual human actions and decisions are of secondary significance in history, but it carries the implication that these decisions are themselves made within an environment and a framework far from capricious. One of the most important tasks of anthropology and archaeology is therefore to examine the nature and origin of such early frameworks, to clarify how and in what circumstances the recognizable structures of society—social forms, urban forms, economic mechanisms and mechanisms for decision making, belief systems, regional styles—emerge and develop.

In recent decades mathematics has developed a number of approaches and techniques well suited to the study of the evolution and change of structures. This problem of the emergence of form and of the stabilizing of viable forms, of the processes which life scientists term *morphogenesis,* is a preoccupation of the biologist as well as of the culture historian. Indeed there are several real and striking similarities (as well as some misleading analogies) between the problems facing the biologist and the archaeologist in their search for an understanding of the processes of growth and the emergence of form.

This book, conceived jointly by an archaeologist and a mathematician, is an attempt both to bring contemporary mathematical techniques to bear on the phenomena of culture change, and to formulate the problems of the archaeologist, the anthropologist, and the historian in such a way that they are indeed susceptible to treatment of a mathematical kind. Some of the models outlined here, by contributors who are mostly professional mathematicians or archaeologists, we see as broadly successful attempts at such analysis, albeit preliminary and rather schematic ones. The mathematical models employed or explained include optimization models, dynamical systems, simulation, catastrophe theory, computer-aided transformations of symbols, kladistics, and more.

These are early days, and it is often easier to talk in general terms of mathematical models than it is to formulate specific examples which positively help in the handling of actual data from the past. The task is certainly a daunting one. Yet we would claim that this book does identify and present for consideration a number of central problems and original approaches which later workers will undoubtedly investigate more completely.

William Blake certainly little imagined how close, within two centuries, mathematics—applied both in microcosm to the atom and in macrocosm to the universe—would come to a concrete and objective realization of his vision:

> To see a World in a Grain of Sand
> And a Heaven in a Wild Flower

Biology, aided by mathematics is likewise now yielding a whole series of insights into the nature of human life, of the functioning of the human being as an individual organism, and illuminating our knowledge of human origins. The origins and nature of human society, however, of human culture at the collective level, have yet adequately to be explained and understood. We hope that the mathematical approaches indicated here will prove fruitful in this challenging enterprise of explaining culture change.

COLIN RENFREW
KENNETH L. COOKE

Acknowledgments

We are grateful to the following copyright holders for permission to quote the passages cited:

Faber and Faber Ltd. and Harcourt Brace Jovanovich Inc. for the lines from "Burnt Norton" in *Four Quartets* by T. S. Eliot, and for the lines from *Murder in the Cathedral* by T. S. Eliot.

Faber and Faber Ltd. and Oxford University Press (New York) for the lines from "One Foot in Eden" in *Collected Poems* by Edwin Muir.

Lord William Taylour, for the passage from his book *The Mycenaeans*.

Hachette for passages from Baechler, J., *Les Terreurs de l'An 2000*, 1976, 175–203.

The following have kindly given approval for the reproduction of illustrations as indicated:

Dr. John Bintliff, for Figure 1.14.

Cambridge University Press for Figures 1.8, 1.9, 1.10 and 1.11, from *On Growth and Form*, by W. D'Arcy Thompson.

Gerald Duckworth and Co. Ltd. for Figure 1.5, from *The Explanation of Culture Change*, edited by C. Renfrew.

Mr. Dennis Flanagan, Editor, *Scientific American*, for Figure 1.2, from the article "Numerical Taxonomy" by R. R. Sokal.

Oxford University Press, for Figure 1.7 from *Essays on Growth and Form*, edited by W. E. Le Gros Clark and P. B. Medawar.

Sir Osbert Lancaster and John Murray (Publishers) Ltd., for Figures 1.17, 1.18 and 1.19, from *Drayneflete Revealed*.

Mr. P. Psomopoulos, Editor, *Ekistics*, for Figure 1.15, from the article "Origins, ideology and physical patterns of Arab urbanisation," volume 33, no. 195, Feb. 1972, by A. A. Ismail.

W. B. Saunders for the figure from *Principles of Animal Ecology* by W. C. Allee, A. E. Emerson, O. Park, T. Park, and K. Schmidt (1949).

George Braziller for Figure 1.13 entitled "Plan of Massa Homestead," from *Village Planning in the Primitive World* by Douglas Fraser (1968).

Macmillan for Figure 1.16 "Neanderthal Man in Modern Dress" from *The Races of Europe* by Carlton Coon, 1954.

The woodcuts by M. C. Escher are reproduced by permission of the Escher Foundation, Haags Gemeentemuseum, The Hague. © The Escher Foundation, 1979. Reproduction rights arranged courtesy of the Vorpal Galleries: New York, Chicago, San Francisco, Laguna Beach.

TRANSFORMATIONS
Mathematical Approaches to
Culture Change

I

MATHEMATICS AND CULTURE CHANGE

Nature that fram'd us of four elements,
Warring within our breasts for regiment,
Doth teach us all to have aspiring minds:
Our souls, whose faculties can comprehend
The wondrous Architecture of the world:
And measure every wand'ring planet's course,
Still climbing after knowledge infinite,
And always moving as the restless Spheres,
Will us to wear ourselves and never rest,
Until we reach the ripest fruit of all.

Christopher Marlowe
Conquests of Tambourlaine

1

COLIN RENFREW

Transformations

*Of the chemistry of his day and generation, Kant declared that it was a science, but not Science—**eine Wissenschaft, aber nicht Wissenschaft**—for that the criterion of true science lay in its relation to mathematics. This was an old story: for Roger Bacon had called mathematics **porta et clavis scientiarum**, and Leonardo da Vinci had said much the same.*

D'Arcy Thompson
On Growth and Form (1942, 1)

To know *what* happened in the past is not sufficient: The aim is to understand *why* it happened. Yet despite the great advances in archaeology in recent decades, and in history over a longer period, in providing a wealth of data to describe and reconstruct the human past, there remains a paucity, indeed often an absence, of coherent explanation. The ecological approach, it is true, has brought out and made intelligible some regularities hitherto obscure, and the new willingness to apply explicit models has helped to replace anecdote by analysis. But theoretical archaeology is still young, and generalizations are few.

In order to explain it, it is necessary first to compare and then to go further and to generalize. The central belief that underlies the present book is that mathematics, with its rich store of concepts and languages of a general nature, already offers many of the tools for the job—insights into pattern, growth, and form as relevant to the human world as to nature. To try to look sympathetically at what it has to offer seems appropriate. But the approach is not an easy one: To the nonmathematician, many mathematical concepts and, above all, notations can be daunting. Equally the confusing disorder in which we perceive the past can lend itself to superficial and unsound attempts to systematize. The introductory chapters that follow suggest, from the standpoint of the mathematician and mathematical biologist, several approaches which may be fruitful in seeking pattern and order in man's past. In this first chapter I hope to express, in a rather subjective manner, some of the optimism which I feel about the potential of such approaches.

The aim here is certainly not to dehumanize the human past. Everyone

3

Transformations:
Mathematical Approaches to Culture Change

is very well aware that the use of unfamiliar notations and sometimes difficult concepts at once risks evoking cries of "jargon," and accusations of advocating a dangerous and misleading scientism. The reply must simply be that if the concepts are sometimes difficult, so undoubtedly is the task. Nor is any affront intended to the uniqueness of humankind or of human behavior by the attempt to generalize wherever generalization may be possible, or to analyze whatever patterns and regularities that may be perceived among human activities. No threat is offered to the magic of human experience, to the authentic force and irrationality of the passions: The stars in the sky are not any the less wonderful now that we can estimate their age and their distance from us, or measure the wavelength of their light. Mathematics, it has been well said, is both Queen and Servant of the Sciences, and there will be those, following other approaches, who will prefer her in the second, subsidiary capacity. But her power and authority should not be overlooked, even by those who may yet seek to prevent "the scientific and technological servant from usurping the Throne of History" (Hawkes 1968, 255).

For over a century now there have been two polar extremes to the problem of historical explanation (cf. Harris 1968): explanation as biography versus explanation by lawlike statement. On the one hand there is a tradition running from Carlyle to Collingwood or Croce. In Carlyle's words (1841):

> Ah, Thought I say, is always Thought. No man lives in vain. The history of the world is but the biography of great men.

This view of history in heroic mold, of the story of deliberate human action, sees the essential drama as constituted by the play of ideas in the minds of the actors. As Collingwood (1946, 214) put it in his still influential work, *The Idea of History:*

> For history, the object to be discovered is not the mere event, but the thought expressed in it. To discover that thought is already to understand it. . . . All history is the history of thought.

For the prehistorian and archaeologist such an approach is, however, altogether inappropriate, and to follow it implies embarking on the sort of "imaginative recreation" which leads on to the historical novel and from there to unbridled invention—entertaining perhaps in itself but scarcely meriting critical examination. It is not necessary to be a follower of Marx in order to recognize that the enormous complexity of interactions in any human society cannot adequately be subsumed under the thoughts and activities of a few individuals.

Yet, on the other hand, for more than a century there have been exponents of law and order, desiring to formulate laws for human society, laws possessed of the same rigor as the laws of physics. Auguste Comte (1875, 427) was optimistic:

This sociological recognition of laws perfects the concept in all other provinces. . . . The sense of the presence of invariable laws, which first arose in the mathematical province, is fully matured and developed in high philosophical speculation, by which it is carried on to universality.

Very much the same view still persists in some quarters, apparently undiminished in ardor by the chastening experience of a century of sociology. So it is that some exponents of "an explicitly scientific approach in archaeology" (Watson, LeBlanc and Redman 1971, 163) have insisted that "A scientific theory, formally speaking, is a body of related laws," and that nothing else will do. But unfortunately, observations possessed of the perfect universality displayed, for instance, by Newton's laws of motion, are vanishingly few in archaeology, and this paradigm seems difficult to achieve. Kent Flannery (1973, 51) in his entertaining article, "Archaeology with a capital S"—the title referring back ultimately to the view of Kant with which this chapter is prefaced—has written acerbically of "Mickey Mouse laws":

From a Southwestern colleague I learned last year that "as the population of a site increased, the number of storage pits will go up." I am afraid that these "laws" will always elicit from the response, "Leapin' lizards, Mr. Science!" Or as my colleague Robert Whallon once said after reading one of these undeniable truths, "If this is the 'New Archaeology,' show me how to get back to the Renaissance."

Of course there is much of value in the arguments put forward by Watson *et al*. (1971) or by Fritz and Plog (1970), and by other theorists who are attempting to make explicit the assumptions and the reasoning underlying explanation in history. These authors are responding constructively to the challenge first clearly formulated by Lewis Binford (1962) in his "Archaeology as Anthropology" and repeated 6 years later when he expressed as a goal (Binford 1968, 9): "gaining some understanding of laws of cultural development." But it seems doubtful whether the ideas of Carl Hempel, in the form in which these writers express them, offer the ideal framework for explanation, whatever their logical coherence.

It is not yet clear just what form the explanations ultimately found to be appropriate will have. Unlike very traditional forms of historical explanation, they will not, I think, consist simply of chains of events, purporting an "explanation" by reference to an ever-increasing wealth of specific and contingent detail. On the contrary, most of the contributors to this book would agree that the appropriate path to understanding is generalization, that is, the formulation of general relationships between events and between processes, of which specific individual occurrences and phenomena can be seen as concrete expressions or manifestations. This is not to deny the crucial importance of circumstantial detail, of the analysis of environment, and of the context of events, but to assert that the nub of the explanation lies in the generalization (whether or not this is expressed in the form of a universal law) which, when set beside that circumstantial detail, produces the pattern or the phenomenon which we are seeking to explain.

This search for broader pattern is naturally something common to many historians as well as archaeologists. One appreciates the broad sweep, the masterly ability to see the wood behind the trees, in great historical works such as Braudel's masterpiece (Braudel 1972). For although he is speaking of a specific area at a given period, his analysis proceeds in terms of universals (e.g., "Distance, the First Enemy") combining "What have come to be known as *structure* and *conjuncture,* the permanent and the ephemeral, the slow moving and the fast. These two aspects of reality, as economists are well aware—indeed it is to them that we owe the original distinction—are always present in everyday life, which is a constant blend of what changes and what endures" (Braudel 1972, 353).

The position in archaeology and prehistory today resembles in some ways what it was in the biological sciences at the time that D'Arcy Thompson was writing his illuminating work *On Growth and Form* some 60 years ago. There are regularities which are evident, and others which investigation can easily reveal, yet the more general relationships and in particular the processes which have led to those regularities in form still largely elude us. We may glimpse that there are relationships which may one day find formal expression, just as those of chemistry have done, and following Kant and D'Arcy Thompson we may aspire to express them by means of the precision and the generality of mathematics. But just as the biochemist today, for all the formidable success he has had in analyzing the chemical reactions of life, finds it difficult to predict the structure of more complex organisms, so we still find it difficult to use our insights into the workings of the human individual in order to make significant predictions about the behavior of human societies. Nor is it to be hoped that explicit structures at once so simple and so rich in explanatory power as the Crick–Watson model of DNA will be found for human reactions, to mediate effectively between the molecular level of the individual and the more complex structure of the human group.

In this introductory essay I can do no more than indicate where certain opportunities seem to lie, and to suggest that the deeper understanding of relationships, of forms, and of processes which the mathematician can bring to bear (or which mathematical thinking can offer) may yet allow us to outline why and how human societies have taken the forms and followed the courses of events, the trajectories, which they have.

If altogether simplistic and misleading formulations are to be avoided, it is necessary to distinguish several different levels of analysis, and to give proper attention to the structures of things, whose precise form, while seemingly irrelevant at one level, may be of determining significance at another.

Levels of Analysis

Order in the world may be recognized at different levels and at different scales. The regularities occurring in human societies, which we seek to explain or to model, may either be peculiar to those societies or, alternatively, be expressions of a more fundamental order, of wider application at a greater or lesser scale.

The hierarchy of systems in Table 1.1, with the higher level at the top, implies that the behavior of the entities in each level is in part governed by the regularities of the underlying level. In every case here, the whole is greater than its parts: That is, the behavior at one level is difficult to infer even from a very close understanding of the lower level. For instance, complex molecules, such as proteins, have particularities of structure which cannot readily be predicted from their chemical composition alone. At the molecular level these are mere details, yet at the next level they crucially determine the behavior of the enzyme. In every case listed in Table 1.1 the entities at one level unite to form a higher entity at the next level—from molecule, to cell, to organ, to organism, and so on.

Each level also has its own modes of explanation, often with the formulation of appropriate theoretical entities. (And we should not forget that concepts such as electron or enzyme are theoretical entities deliberately formulated by research workers just as is white dwarf or black hole, all of them difficult to observe directly.) To attempt to do so without reference to the complexities emerging at the new level of the hierarchy may properly be stigmatized as reductionist. At each successive level in the hierarchy, effective explanation becomes more difficult, and new and ingenious ways have to be found of coping with the overwhelming complexity of elaborate organisms. Sometimes it is tempting to use the concepts and regularities that have been found effective at a lower level to model behavior at a higher level, but the risks of oversimplification are great. It is probably true to say

TABLE 1.1

A Hierarchy of Systems and of Fields of Study

Behavior	Field of study
Behavior of human communities	Anthropology, archaeology, history, human geography, sociology
Human personal behavior	Psychology, sociology, proxemics, microeconomics
Primate behavior	Ethology
Behavior of organisms (and populations)	Biology, ecology, animal behavior (demography)
Behavior of living material	Biochemistry, molecular biology, cytology
Molecular behavior	Organic and inorganic chemistry, biochemistry
Atomic and subatomic behavior	Physics, nuclear physics
Properties of space, time, and energy	Relativistic mechanics, thermodynamics

that the task of the prehistorian or historian who seeks to explain his material is more complex and more difficult than that of the physicist.

The distinctions to be drawn here are not simply a question of size. The hierarchy of scale of entities in the world is a familiar one (Figure 1.1), relevant to modeling, but not coterminous with that of complexity.

Explanatory achievement at one level is often followed by the energetic attempt to apply the same techniques at another level, not always with success. The euphoria that followed the widespread recognition of Darwin's theory of evolution, for instance, was responsible for much speculation about sociological laws, such as that quoted by Comte earlier. The development of statistical mechanics, to allow generalization from the behavior of one molecule to that of great quantities of molecules, was likewise a success when applied to gases, tempting to emulate but difficult to achieve for the behavior of living organisms.

It is disappointing, too, that it is at the level of the human individual that modern science has told us least. Modern psychology can make few predictions about human behavior that were not available a century ago. The explanation is perhaps to be found in terms of *Verstehen*—the wealth of insights which the human observer already has through intuition into the human condition—so that many of the potential contributions of psychology are already part of our shared store of "common sense." Indeed one of the difficulties of the archaeologist and anthropologist is precisely to make generalizations about aspects of behavior which, if applied to other entities, would be greeted as highly significant, but when relating to humans appear obvious. It is the absence of such generalizations (even if they can be attacked as "Mickey Mouse laws") which accounts largely for the theoretical weaknesses of our discipline.

Mathematics, "the abstract science of space and number," is particularly suited to handling relationships in a manner both highly general and precise to any required degree. That is what underlies Kant's assertion at the head of this chapter, and what Galileo had in mind when he stated that "the book of Nature is written in characters of Geometry." It is this thought, then, which underlies the optimism of many of the contributors to the present volume. Nor is the undoubted complexity of the real world in itself a valid obstacle to the use of such broad generalizations. As D'Arcy Thompson (1942, 1028) put it:

> Every natural phenomenon, however simple, is really composite, and every visible action and effect is a summation of countless subordinate actions. Here mathematics shows her peculiar power, to combine and to generalise. The concept of an average, the equation to a curve, the description of a froth or cellular tissue, all come within the scope of mathematics for no other reason that they are summations of more elementary principles or phenomena. Growth and Form are throughout of this composite nature; therefore the laws of mathematics are bound to underlie them, and her methods to be peculiarly fitted to interpret them.

All these statements are so far at a very general level, and indeed most of the contributions in this volume are of a very general nature. Some critics will argue that they are mere abstractions, often with little real explanatory power. Certainly Binford (1977, 6) has stressed the need for "middle-range theory," intermediate between the available (and in this sense contemporary) data that are gleaned from the archaeological record, and whatever more general theories and models we may have at our disposal to express our understanding of the dynamics of past culture systems. It has to be admitted that, in this sense, there is little of such middle-range theory in this volume, such as would firmly relate the general ideas and models which are offered to the available archaeological data, and hence open the way to honest hypothesis testing. And of course there is here hardly any systematic presentation of data.

I would argue, however, that at this stage these are not devastating criticisms in themselves. Archaeology (like history) stands much in need of coherent theories, and of theoretical framework which may offer the hope of explaining some aspects of the past. As David Clarke (1968, xiii) rightly observed at the beginning of *Analytical Archaeology:* "Archaeology is an undisciplined empirical discipline." Once we have enough theories and models at our disposal we shall hope to choose between them, in order to reach some agreed framework, and rigorous testing will then be obligatory. But at the present stage, theoretical archaeology is a tender plant: It needs careful husbandry before it can be expected to bring forth abundant fruit. No apology should be needed, then, and certainly none is offered for failing, at this early stage, to test rigorously.

The Tyranny of Darwin

Any discipline must first consider form, and must review the phenomena which are of interest and which it hopes to explain. Yet paradoxically the greatest single contribution in the nineteenth century to the historical sciences and to the study of form, Charles Darwin's *Origin of Species* (1859), was largely responsible for the stultification of explanation of the variety of forms which constitute the very subject matter of archaeology.

The descriptive stage of "botanizing" terminated by Darwin was brought to near perfection for the living species by Linnaeus (1707–1778), and the subsequent refinements of numerical taxonomy have served to confirm many of his insights. Archaeology and ethnography in the nineteenth century were much taken up with systematic description of this kind, as the great ethnographical collections of the world testify.

The first basic concept of the theory of evolution is as valid for artifacts as for species. It simply asserts the gradual and continuous development of form, an unbroken trajectory through time, rather than the sudden and

DISTANCE

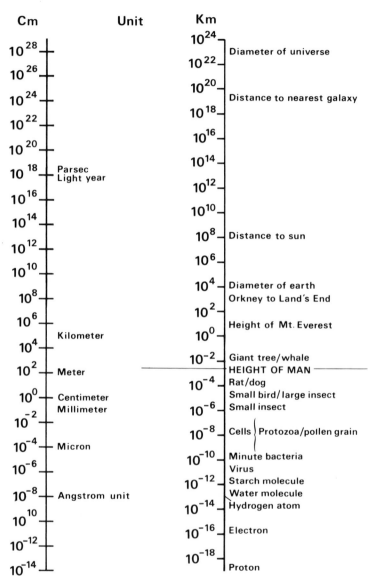

FIGURE 1.1. *Man's place in space and time: The scale of entities in the world.* (T *indicates half-life and* P *indicates periodic time.*)

TIME

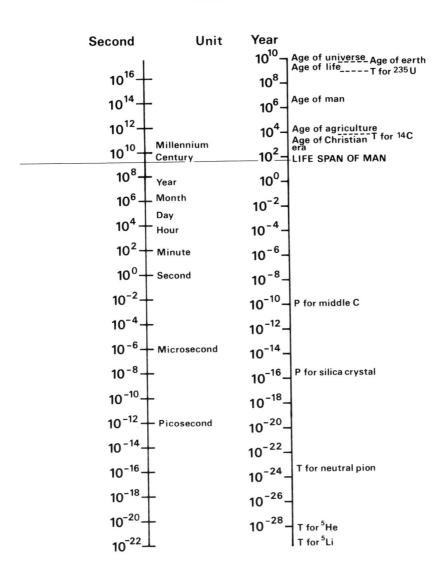

FIGURE 1.1 *continued.*

discontinuous creation of new forms. It was naturally, and effectively, applied to artifacts, and by later writers to the forms of human society. All that has stood the test of time well.

The second fundamental Darwinian principle is more dangerous. It offers an explanation for the affinity between two similar species by tracing back each through the evolutionary tree to reach their common ancestor. It cannot be overstressed that much of archaeology for almost a century has been conducted in the shadow of that great idea, or how seriously it has distorted the archaeologist's understanding of form.

The first basic insight, that forms usually change gradually, and that like goes with like, was exploited to good effect by Flinders Petrie (1899) to give a basic relative chronology for prehistoric Egypt. The same assumptions have been made in recent years to allow chronological ordering by computer seriation (Clarke 1968; Robinson 1951), and the procedure has validity in many cases. Simple linear seriation by matrix ordering has subsequently been criticized on the grounds that there may be more variables operating than time alone, and it is now generally regarded as a special and rather limited case of numerical taxonomy (Sokal and Sneath 1973). There the important mathematical idea of hyperspace, as space of many dimensions, is used to arrange artifacts (or whatever is to be classified) in terms of their similarities to one another, and then often to represent this picture in two dimensions.

But the second principle moves beyond classification to pronounce upon origin. Frequently it is asserted, often implicitly, that the forms most close to each other in appearance (morphologically, in terms of phenotype) are closest in terms of descent (phylogenetically). The kladistic tree (see Bellman, Chapter 3, this volume) or dendrogram of phenotypes (Figure 1.2) is thus imagined to reconstruct the historical path of evolution.

In 1875, Pitt-Rivers in his brilliant essay, "On the evolution of culture," was already arranging artifacts into what seemed a natural evolutionary order and thereby seeking to create what was inferred to be a historical order (Figure 1.3). And the great European prehistorian Oscar Montelius, inventor of the "typological method" (Montelius 1903), used similar insights in arranging the artifacts of the European Bronze Age right across Europe in like manner (Figure 1.4).

This pattern of thinking, I would argue, has dominated much of archaeology for a century, and has only been consistently and coherently questioned in the past decade.

In reality, for societies and for artifacts this second major principle simply does not hold, or rather "convergent evolution" is of greater importance. The analogous forms of society, and the comparable forms of artifacts, which interest us were often not the result of some common origin to be sought a century or a millennium earlier on the evolutionary tree. The

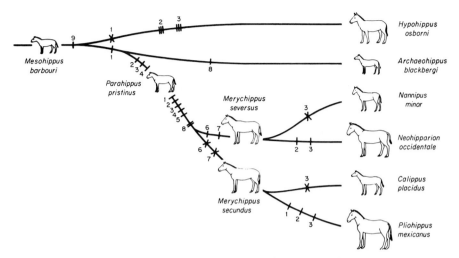

FIGURE 1.2. *Kladistic diagram (cladogram) establishing the branching sequence in an evolutionary tree for fossil horses, using the methods of numerical taxonomy. (After Sokal.)*

basic similarities in form cannot always be traced back to a common ancestor, but often instead emerge quite independently through local evolution, in analogous environmental circumstances. Although ultimately all human societies may have certain common origins (assuming that the human species itself does go back to a common area and period of origin, some Garden of Eden at one of the nodes of a Darwinian kladistic tree), many of the forms that interest us do not go back to this early time. Human social evolution has multiple and effectively independent evolutionary sequences.

In consequence it follows that similarities between phenotypes need not betoken kladistic affinity. Their explanation is thus not to be sought in tracing back to the common origin, and by analyzing the pathways in detail to see how the divergencies occurred. That is an essentially *historical* approach, dealing with a single joint occurrence (where the fundamental process operating is already well understood and implicit to the argument, and where the analysis comes instead through narrating in rich anecdotal detail the circumstances which have brought about the actual outcome). On the contrary, we can see more clearly now that, if there are similarities of form, they may reflect underlying similarities of process, and it is rather these which we seek to understand and to analyze.

The contributions of Darwinian evolution to the understanding of culture change are no doubt immense, but they should not hide from us that the most important and difficult problems demand a very different kind of solution.

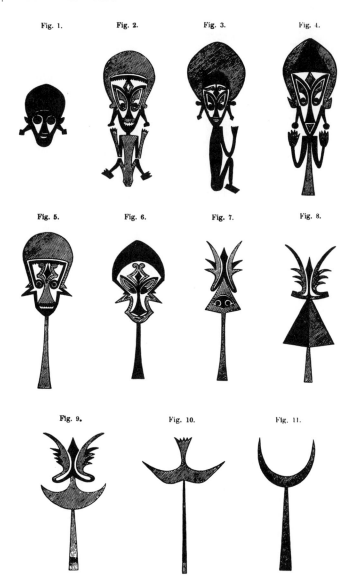

FIGURE 1.3. *Evolutionary sequence for Melanesian paddles, showing the transition of form, as established by Pitt-Rivers in 1875.*

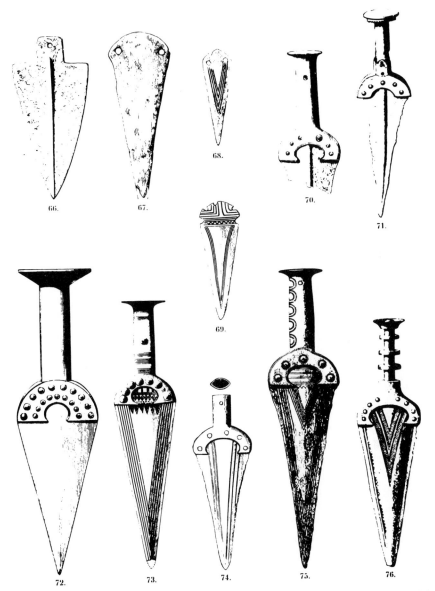

FIGURE 1.4. *Typological sequence for Italian Bronze Age daggers as established by Montelius in 1903.*

Comparative Archaeology

If the arguments in the preceding section are accepted, it may be necessary to suppress our inclinations toward the re-creation of Darwinian family trees, the process which Richard Bellman (Chapter 3, this volume) terms kladistics. Although accepting that this procedure may account effectively for identities of form in certain limited areas of space and time, it does not tell us why some forms seen in one part of the world recur independently elsewhere, whereas others do not.

The first lesson, if we want an *explanatory archaeology*, may be that we have to return first to a *comparative archaeology*, and seek to observe affinities of form in whatever aspect, such as may indicate the working of fundamentally similar general processes. Of course there is nothing initially to tell us that these processes have any real existence, any more than we have a prior knowledge of the laws of nature. But all scientific research is conducted with the ambitious optimism that there *are* regularities awaiting discovery, and that only in seeking them can they be found.

In what follows, two approaches are outlined. Both are comparative. The first is *diachronic,* following the course of a particular culture through time and comparing this trajectory with those of other cultures. The second is *static,* the comparison of structures at fixed points in time in order to see which elements may be invariant to transformation.

Comparing Trajectories: Allactic Form

The search for recognizable forms, identifiable and classifiable structures, among human societies has not been an easy one. Lewis Henry Morgan's division into savagery, barbarism, and civilization (Morgan 1877) was an early attempt, influencing Marx's typology (Marx 1964) of preclass, ancient, oriental, feudal, and capitalist social formations. Archaeologists have long since moved on from C. J. Thomsen's ages of Stone, Bronze, and Iron as meaningful divisions of the past, although today many continue to use the "neoevolutionary" nomenclature of band, tribe, chiefdom, and state (Service 1962), but not without an awareness of the difficulties accompanying some of these terms (cf. Helm 1968). Social anthropologists have been a little more successful in their taxonomy, notably with kinship classifications (Levi-Strauss 1969), so that in this field at least it is generally accepted that identifiable structures may be recognized cross-culturally, without limitations or space (or, perhaps, of time).

Such recognition of form is a helpful, perhaps an indispensable, first step in the analysis of change (*pace* Hill 1970) and recent criticisms of the use of terms such as "chiefdom" have been effectively countered (Johnson 1976, 571; Willey 1974, 150). In the words of Blalock (1960, 12): "The basic and most simple operation in any science is that of classification." The idea of a social form or type implies a cluster of attributes that may be recognized (or rather, for a polythetic classification, most of which can be recognized) in any given member of the class at a given time and place. The entire science of taxonomy is devoted to the comparison of forms in this static way (cf. Sokal and Sneath 1973; Doran and Hodson 1975).

It is curious that, with formal taxonomy so well elaborated, the classification of *types of change* is relatively undeveloped. Common language has a wide vocabulary for change, as wide for dynamical form (the verbs) as it is for static forms (the nouns) or attributes (the adjectives). Melting of solids, boiling of liquids, crystallizing of solutes, all designate changes of state, transformations, but archaeology, indeed the sciences in general have not been so quick or so systematic in analyzing such changes in their own right. The formal analysis involves specifying attributes at a number of successive points in time: It can be made just as explicitly as can a conventional taxonomy of static forms.

It is therefore as legitimate to classify types of change as it is to classify system states, and this allactic approach (*allactic:* of change, pertaining to change; Greek $\alpha\lambda\lambda\alpha\gamma\eta$: change) may be a necessary preliminary to the understanding of culture process. What characterizes a transformation is not solely the initial and final state, but the way the transition occurs.

A few simple allactic forms of this kind are already familiar in general systems theory, where they have been termed "isomorphic laws" (von Bertalanffy 1950, 136):

> For example the exponential law or law of compound interest applies with a negative exponent to the decay of radium, the monomolecular reaction, the killing of bacteria by light or disinfectants, the loss of body substance of a starving animal, and to the decrease of a population where the death rate is higher than the birth rate. Similarly with a positive exponent, this law applies to the individual growth of certain microorganisms, the unlimited Malthusian growth of bacterial, animal or human populations, the curve of human knowledge (as measured by the number of pages devoted to scientific discoveries in a textbook on the history of science), and the number of publications on *Drosophila*. The entities concerned—atoms, molecules, bacteria, animals, human beings, or books—are widely different, and so are the causal mechanisms involved. Nevertheless the mathematical law is the same.

The patterns of decay and growth in question here are seen in Figure 1.5, and the growth equation is of a simple form:

$$X = be^{kt}$$

where X is the quantity or parameter whose magnitude we are observing, t is time, and k and b are constants. For exponential growth, k has positive sign, and for decay negative sign. Birdsell has given an elegant example for growth of this kind in human population after initial colonization of an empty area.

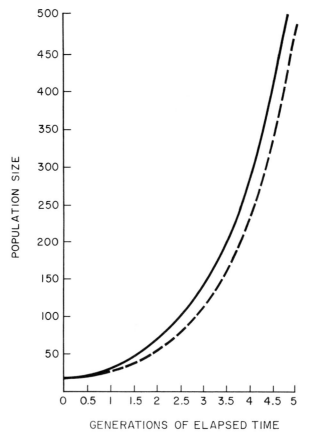

FIGURE 1.5. *Exponential growth: Intrinsic rate of population increase for Pitcairn and Bass Strait islanders. (After Birdsell.)*

A second pattern of very general applicability is logistic growth (Figure 1.6) (von Bertalanffy 1950, 136):

> In physical chemistry, this occurs as the equation of autocatalytic reaction, and in biology it describes certain cases of organic growth. It was first stated in demography to describe the growth of human populations in a limited space of living. It governs also the advancement of technical inventions such as the growth of the railway system in the United States during the last century or of the number of wireless sets in operation.

These patterns are familiar from ecology (Maynard Smith 1974, 18; Lotka 1956, 65). They are commonly observed in human affairs (e.g., Coleman 1964, 45), and an elegant archaeological example has been offered by Eighmy (Chapter 8, this volume).

Several other growth curves have been systematically studied (Table

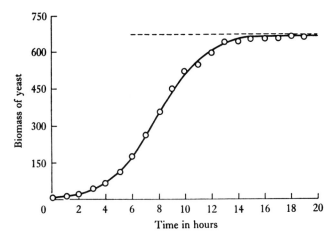

FIGURE 1.6. *Logistic growth: Growth of yeast in a culture. (After Maynard Smith and Allee.)*

1.2) and Medawar (1945) has given the derivatives for one of these, the Gompertz function (Figure 1.7). Other studies of growth have conveniently eliminated the time factor by comparing the sizes at successive times of two entities, establishing the possibility of relationships like that for allometric growth (Reeve and Huxley 1945). It is interesting to note that what are effectively the same relationships as those seen in curves of growth and decay, but using distance rather than time as the independent variable, have already been applied to the archaeology of trade and exchange in studying distance decay effects (cf. Renfrew 1977).

Such patterns have been seized on by sociologists, who have seen in them the basis for "A Mathematical Theory of Social Change" (Hamblin, Jacobsen and Miller 1973). There is little doubt that many processes in human society take such forms, and the analysis can be useful in documenting fundamental features of the process. In such cases, however, it is scarcely enough simply to comment on the regularity. One must also gain insight into why it holds (i.e., offer some explanatory model for it) and into the conditions in which it will or will not continue to hold.

These regularities are of great interest here because of their simplicity: They can readily be expressed by means of a few parameters, and can thus be used to offer paradigm cases for lawlike behavior in the social sciences and in history. Many demographic processes, in particular, can be expressed in this way, although the reality will only conform to a certain extent, and over a limited time span, to so agreeably simple an expression.

Yet comparative archaeology can offer a much richer repertoire of types of change than these, even if they are generally more complicated and cannot yet be expressed with algebraic precision. Such dynamical forms are in fact already quite widely used in archaeology and anthropology, although

TABLE 1.2
The Common Growth Functions and Their More Important Analytical Properties[a]

Function	Equation	Linear form	W $t = 0$	W $t \to \infty$	Point of inflection (W, t)	Specific growth rate	Specific acceleration
1. Exponential	$W = be^{kt}$	$\log W = \log b + kt$	b	—	—	k	0
2. "Monomolecular"	$W = a(1 - be^{-kt})$	$\log \dfrac{a - W}{a} = \log b - kt$	$a(1 - b)$	a	—	$\dfrac{kbe^{-kt}}{1 - be^{-kt}}$	$-\dfrac{k^2be^{-kt}}{(1 - be^{-kt})^2}$
3. Logistic	$W = \dfrac{a}{1 + be^{-kt}}$	$\log \dfrac{a - W}{W} = \log b - kt$	$\dfrac{a}{1 + b}$	a	$\dfrac{a}{2}, \dfrac{(\log b)}{k}$	$\dfrac{kbe^{-kt}}{1 + be^{-kt}}$	$-\dfrac{k^2be^{-kt}}{(1 + be^{-kt})^2}$
4. Gompertz	$W = a\,exp(-be^{-kt})$	$\log \log \dfrac{a}{W} = \log b - kt$	ae^{-b}	a	$\dfrac{a}{e}, \dfrac{(\log b)}{k}$	kbe^{-kt}	$-k^2be^{-kt}$
5. Parabola	$W = bt^k$	$\log W = \log b + k \log t$	0	—	—	$\dfrac{k}{t}$	$\dfrac{k}{t^2}$

[a] The symbol W may be read "size": It usually stands for weight. Logarithms are expressed to the natural base e. Many of the analytical properties may be more simply expressed as functions of W rather than of age, t; but time has been chosen as the independent variable. The Gompertz function (4) and its derivatives are illustrated graphically in Figure 1.1. (After Medawar.)

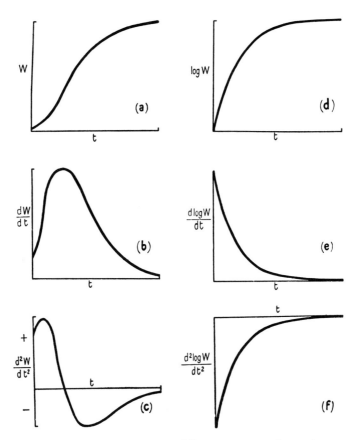

FIGURE 1.7. *Growth curves illustrating different measures of growth rate, taking the Gompertz function as an example (see Table 1.2). The curve of (a) growth; (b) growth rate; (c) acceleration; (d)* specific *growth; (e) specific growth rate; (f) specific acceleration. The curves have been plotted from an equation for the Gompertz function, but the scales of the ordinates have been adjusted to make the height of each graph uniform. (After Medawar.)*

without adequate definition. Gordon Childe was perhaps the most influential expositor with his concept of a "neolithic revolution" and an "urban revolution." The very act of naming these amounts to an assertion that we are in the face of a cross-culturally recognizable process. He went so far as to suggest the underlying interplay of forces for the urban revolution, with particular reference to Mesopotamia (Childe 1950). The most influential among the pioneers in this field was perhaps Julian Steward, whose "trial formulation of developmental regularities of early civilization" (Steward 1955, Chap. 11) was a significant step. But his analysis was presented as a succession of static "eras" ("formative," "regional florescence," etc., including "dark ages") and the really original feature, the succession of *transitions,* was rather rigidly expressed. The insistence on a long and firmly prescribed order of succession invited criticism in terms of "unilineal evolution," yet if we focus instead on the transitions from one era to its immediate successor, his "Table of periods grouped in major eras" (Steward 1955, 189–190) is a pioneering catalog of transformations.

Something of this is already implicit in much systems thinking in archaeology: The idea of homeostasis already takes a dynamic view of stable state, and the "second cybernetics" (Maruyama 1963) begins to focus on processes of morphogenesis. However, the classification of types of change is only now beginning (Poston, Chapter 18, this volume; Thom 1975), and not surprisingly the description is mathematical. Just as von Bertalanffy, Medawar, and others have set out the properties of some relatively simple growth curves, so catastrophe theory has taken on the very much greater undertaking of classifying, with much more ambitious mathematical apparatus, the range of discontinuous changes which underlie some of the basic phenomena of the real world. These may well turn out to be some of the building bricks to be used in the construction of any theory of change in complex systems, such as those of the biological and cultural world.

Empirical study, however, is the necessary preliminary and counterpart of formal analysis and in the final chapter of this book one specific type of change, systems collapse, is examined and its dynamic morphology outlined. An attempt is then made to identify the general underlying processes which generate this specific allactic type in a variety of very different cultural contexts, widely distributed in time and space. The study is, however, an empirical one, to the extent that the recognition of a number of analogous cases suggests a search for the underlying dynamic, rather than the reverse. Its interest, I think, goes beyond the specific case of systems collapse, in that the exercise may suggest a search in the archaeological record for other allactic types. They will not all be discontinuous, nor dependent as this one seems to be on one of the elementary catastrophes. Indeed many allactic forms, such as empire formation by invasion or decline as a result of plague and followed by regeneration, are already well known to history and archaeology, even if often misinterpreted and rarely analyzed explicitly and in detail. Ultimately, however, such examination is what the study of culture process is about. The classification of allactic forms may be one useful approach.

Comparing Structures: Transformations

The systematic study of allactic forms may thus yield a number of stimulating insights. For too long such regularities as the "birth and death of civilizations" have been recognized and accepted without careful analysis, it being assumed without much question that the "superorganic" behavior (Kroeber 1917) of human societies should in some way be analogous to that of living organisms.

The comparison of static forms has likewise often taken place on a rather naive level, its object often being seen, in the manner indicated earlier, as the measurement of the degree of affinity, and hence, it was thought, of a phylogenetic relationship. Only in social anthropology has the careful analysis of forms in terms of their underlying structure been carried very much further (Levi-Strauss 1969). But disappointingly the analysis is often regarded as completed when the structural homomorphism is demonstrated, rather than as leading on to an examination of the underlying processes which have generated the analogous forms. The attractive notion that the classificatory forms seen in human kinship structures or in primeval myths are in some way a direct projection of universal structural features of the human mind perhaps merits more close critical attention than it has received.

It was D'Arcy Thompson who elegantly demonstrated the manner in which certain forms of nature could, with suitable topological transformations, be made equivalent. His transmogrification of a human skull into that of a chimpanzee (Figure 1.8) by a process of continuous transformation, and that of a fish of the genus *Scorpaena* to one of the genus *Antigonia* (Figure 1.9) are brilliant examples of the principle of "topological similitude." In these cases, of course, the species so transformed are indeed phylogenetically related, but I think that the insight and vision which bring out the underlying elements in this way are deeply illuminating.

Equivalent forms are demonstrated again in D'Arcy Thompson's analysis of skeletal forms in terms of cantilevers (Figure 1.10) so that the underlying logic, one might almost say the necessity, of the form is clearly brought out. The elements of one structure are seen to have analogous, although not

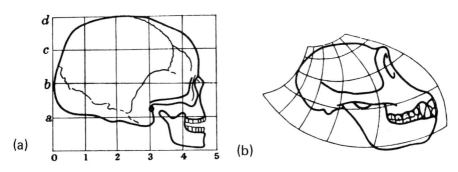

(a)

(b)

(c)

FIGURE 1.8. *Transformation of the human skull (a) to that of a chimpanzee (b) and of a baboon (c), by a simple projection involving the "continuous transformation" of Cartesian coordinates. (After D'Arcy Thompson.)*

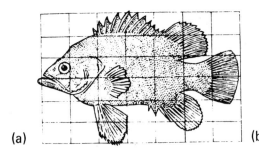
(a)

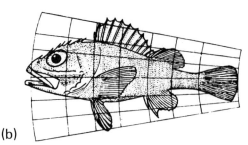
(b)

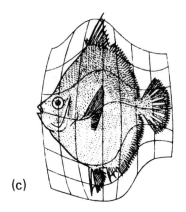

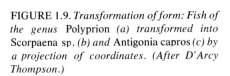

FIGURE 1.9. *Transformation of form: Fish of the genus* Polyprion *(a) transformed into* Scorpaena sp. *(b) and* Antigonia capros *(c) by a projection of coordinates. (After D'Arcy Thompson.)*

(c)

identical, counterparts in the compared structure. And there need now be no explanation in terms of phylogenetic relationship. The common structure, when it can be demonstrated, cannot be explained in terms of a shared history, but rather leads to a consideration of the processes of formation of the two forms and of what these processes may themselves have held in common.

The world is full of formal equivalences of this kind, and they merit the closest attention: They should not be accepted unquestioningly or without wonder. For instance, it is now a truism that the hexagonal packing seen in many cellular organisms (Figure 1.11) and repeated in the honeycomb of the bee may be discerned among many human settlements. This has rightly promoted discussion, and the underlying reasons are now adequately understood in terms of maximizing efficiency, with assumptions akin to those underlying Zipf's law of least effort (Zipf 1949). It is often no trivial question, however, whether the formal analogy lies, like beauty, in the eye of the beholder rather than in the objects of study.

The simple branching "hierarchy" of the branches of a tree or the tributaries of a river serves as a convenient model for analyses of the nervous system and for the structure of many human organizations, and hierarchical structure is another widespread and fundamental form (Pattee 1973) whose significance for human society we have only begun to grasp.

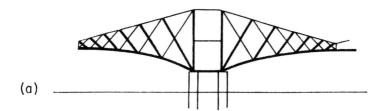

(a)

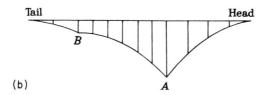

Tail   Head

B

(b)   A

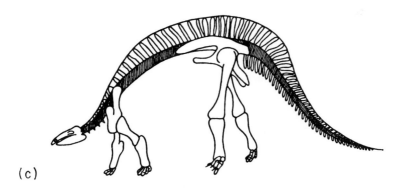

(c)

FIGURE 1.10. *Structural homologies and analogies: (a) Two-armed cantilever of the Forth Bridge–thick lines, compression members (bones); thin lines, tension members (ligaments); (b) stress diagram of the prehistoric reptile* Titanotherium; *(c) diagram of* Stegosaurus. *(After D'Arcy Thompson.)*

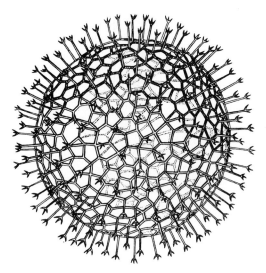

FIGURE 1.11. *The ubiquity of hexagonal structures: The outer skeletal surface of the radiolarian species* Aulastrum triceros *Hkl. (After D'Arcy Thompson.)*

These are all examples in which a deeper formal similarity underlies the superficial resemblances. The social anthropologist may well remark that this kind of relationship is no more than the correspondence of structures with which he is already familiar from his kinship studies. But the mathematician, on the other hand, will see in these general notions just some aspects of the very much wider and well-developed field of topology (Figure 1.12) (Bell 1950, 156):

A *transformation* of one space S into another space S' is the assignment of a correspondence between the objects in S, S' such that to every object in S there corresponds at least one object in S' (as in mapping). The transformation of a subset A of S is the set of all correspondents under the transformation, of all objects in A. The transformation is said to be *uniform*, or *single-valued*, whenever it assigns a unique correspondent to every object in S; it is said to be continuous whenever the transform (the image on the map) of

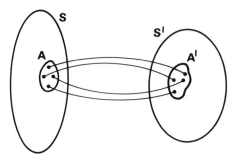

FIGURE 1.12. *Transformation from a space S to a space S'.*

every open set A of S is an open set of S'. The transformation is said to be homomorphic when it is one–one and continuous both ways.

To use the language of topology in this way does not, in one sense, add anything to what we have already seen. But in another sense it brings out the far from trivial importance of such comparisons.

Figures 1.8 and 1.9, for example, are Cartesian transformations of a relatively simple nature, but the approach should also be useful and more revealing when we are dealing with forms that are not phylogenetically related (cf. Woodger 1945).

To take another example, Flannery (1972) has compared the settlements at a number of early farming sites including Nahal Oren in Israel and the compound of the Tiv in Nigeria. It was concluded that the form in many was not unlike that in Figure 1.13. In effect, it is asserted that the plan of village A (or selected elements of it), suitably transformed, is equivalent to that of village B (or elements of it). We tend to generalize this by saying that each is "a circular village of round huts." But this simple and innocuous phase is in fact doing something rather ambitious—it is generalizing from two cases, and extracting from them what is essential to both. To use mathematical language again (Bell 1951, 95):

> *Regularities* and *repetitions* in patterns at once suggest to a modern mathematician the *abstract groups* behind the patterns, and the various *transformations* of one problem, not necessarily mathematical, into another again spell *group* and raise the question, *what, if anything remains the same,* or invariant, *under all these transformations?* In technical phrase, what are the *invariants* of the *group of transformations?*

To place comparison on this footing largely eliminates that rather tiresome controversy about the appropriateness or otherwise of "ethnographic parallels," for example (Ucko 1969). If the forms or processes (whether material or social forms) appear to us as in some sense comparable, it is appropriate to ask what elements of the comparison are likely to be of more general validity, and which are contingent to the cases in question.

It should clearly be understood that the mathematical expressions here are simply being used as an aid to clarity of thought. I am not claiming to have applied topological ideas or the theory of groups to archaeological problems, but merely suggesting that the approach may be fruitful. The idea of transformation, or "transform," has already been used to good effect by Schiffer (1972; Schiffer and Rathje 1973) in application to archaeological material. But each of his examples relates to a single trajectory through time of a set of objects. I suggest in addition that we may usefully compare assemblages on different trajectories in this way.

To take another example, the plan of a Greek city at, for example, Rhodes may be compared with the plan of the city at Priene (Ward-Perkins 1974, figs. 12 and 13). It is not difficult to propose a general model, a highest

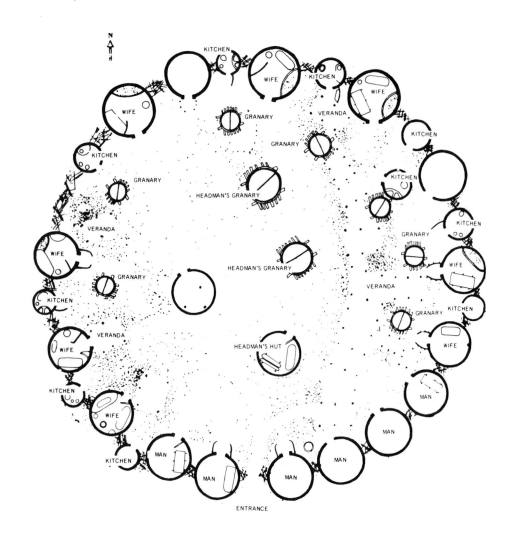

FIGURE 1.13. *A circular village of round huts (Massa homestead, Yagoua, Cameroun, Africa): A widespread form with elements invariant to transformations of time and space. (After Fraser.)*

common factor, for Greek cities of this kind. Of course it may reasonably be remarked that the architects in the same culture may be using the same mental model. But when we compare two cities in different cultures in this way—for instance, Chan Chan (Hardoy fig. 45) in Peru with Ancient Babylon (Lampl 1968, fig. 33)—any correspondences that may be found must have a different explanation.

The comparison proposed by Bintliff (1977), to take another example, between the Minoan palace (the concept "the Minoan palace" already suggesting a measure of invariance among specific Minoan palaces) and the medieval monastery, offers an analogous path to further insights about both (Figure 1.14).

My point here is that a comparison between forms amounts, in effect, to the execution of certain mathematical procedures. A more rigorous ap-

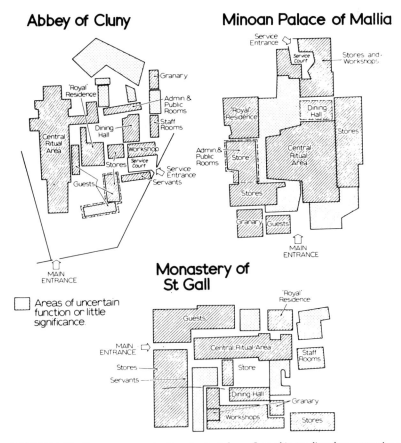

FIGURE 1.14. *Common organizational principles reflected in medieval monasteries and a prehistoric palace in Crete. (After Bintliff.)*

proach here should lead one to distinguish what elements are indeed common in the two analogous cases chose, and what elements may be invariant to transformation in a large number of cases. When invariance of this kind is established it should lead the way to, and certainly demands, further explanation in terms of the analogous processes which must have generated the comparable forms.

Modeling the Past

Comparative archaeology may be the most appropriate procedure for recognizing the regularities we seek to detect and then to explain, but the explanations themselves will be of a different kind. For comparative archaeology must inevitably be *analytical*—an attempt to analyze the rich variety of past forms, and to extract from them some simpler elements of order, just as the natural scientist isolates selected aspects of the world before undertaking explanation. Much explanation, on the other hand, will be *synthetic,* formulating hypotheses of very simple form, and seeking to use these, in different circumstances, to generate the rich variety under examination. Most models, then, are simple, and a good model is one which, although simple in itself, will bring forth a range of varied forms, most of which achieve a close correspondence with part of the observed data. Often the observed data are so varied and confused that a random procedure, a stochastic element, has to be introduced into the model, and this is one of the functions of simulation (see Part IV, this volume).

It has already been stressed that the appropriate theories and models must operate at the right level of analysis, and deal in forms suitable to human society and action. In practice much of the development of theoretical archaeology has involved and will continue to involve the recognition or the formulation of suitable concepts and forms. Through our basic human insight we have some clear ideas about the motivation of the human individual, although it has proved surprisingly difficult to express these coherently and to offer models for individual human action. In Part V several useful notions are developed which may offer some framework for individual human behavior.

The more formidable problem, however, is to explain human aggregate behavior, the behavior of human groups, for their corporate behavior is not often readily predicted from the study of just a few individuals, even the great men of Carlyle and Collingwood. The behavior of large numbers of humans may be considered under two headings. The first concerns those aspects which arise simply because large numbers are involved: This is the atomic approach. The second comprehends those features of behavior which are emergent, exclusive to human groups alone.

The Atomic Level

The ancient Greek ἄτομος means literally "indivisible," and modern Greek τό ἄτομον means an individual or person. In talking of human atomic interactions, then, one is not speaking at the submolecular level of the chemist or physicist. But if we imagine these individuals or "atoms" as fundamentally alike, some aspects of behavior can be seen to arise simply from their group interactions.

Give to these atoms the ability to multiply, and the law of exponential growth can readily be generated (see earlier). If each is deemed to require a specific intake of limited resources, then the growth can be shown to be logistic (Figure 1.6). If the production of these resources requires the use of the land, then a dispersed pattern of distribution may be inferred. Should the resources be mobile, then territorial patterns (Jochim 1976) and prey–predator demographic cycles (Maynard Smith 1974, 19) which have been observed for hunter–gatherers logically follow.

When land is being exploited agriculturally, Zipf's law of least effort (1949) suggests a dispersed distribution, but if economies of scale are postulated for some of the activities of the atoms, there will also be a tendency toward aggregation. Aspects of this tension between attraction–nucleation and repulsion–dispersal are discussed in Chapter 19. These principles alone are already enough to allow geographers to predict a hexagonal lattice of nodes of settlement (although to generate a hierarchy of settlements would require further assumptions). The use in agriculture of crops which demand a varying input of man-hours of work can readily be used to predict the concentric zones discussed by von Thünen (1875).

Should the individuals require commodities not locally available, so that some exchange system is necessary, very simple assumptions of an analogous kind will predict some of the regularities which archaeologists are beginning to detect in the archaeological record.

Simple processes can be readily modeled using these assumptions. The ideas of exponential or logistic growth already mentioned can be given spatial expression, a single parent settlement generating a new settlement by a process of budding off. Simply by assuming that there is an upper limit of size for any one settlement, a pattern of growth in two dimensions may be generated (cf. Hägerstrand 1967) analogous in many ways to cellular growth of living material in three dimensions. Aspects of such models are discussed by Chadwick (Chapter 10, this volume) and Hodder (Chapter 5, this volume). Ammerman and Cavalli-Sforza (Chapter 12, this volume) have used further very simple assumptions of an "atomic" nature to generate their "wave of advance" model for the spread of farming through Europe. Although it naturally, in its initial form, takes no account of ecological diversity, it gives a very satisfying picture to replace the old and very simplistic idea of the migration of peoples.

If different zones of the earth are suitable to different degrees to settlement and exploitation by these human "atoms," then an ecological approach becomes necessary. Grahame Clark (1952) was one of the first archaeologists to show how patterns of human activity, archaeologically documented, are determined by ecological constraints. Indeed the work of his followers, such as Higgs (1972), closely parallels the studies of many human geographers (e.g., Chisholm 1968) in illuminating how hunter–gatherers and subsistence farmers unconsciously order their affairs and activities in accordance with very simple general principles. These demonstrations are among the most successful of theoretical archeology. In each case they reveal patterns which could not be inferred from a consideration of the single individual, of the kind advocated by Croce or Collingwood. Indeed Collingwood (1946, 216) would deny them any place in history: "So far as man's conduct is determined by what may be called his animal nature, his impulses and appetites, it is non-historical; the process of those activities is a natural process." Yet few prehistorians would deny their significance.

Such models may appear as mechanistic to some: Clearly if all the atoms are imagined as behaving in the same way, we cannot expect to account for the richness of human variety. But their very merit is their success in explaining a fairly wide range of patterns by these very simple assumptions. To do more than this implies going beyond the "atomic" view and considering a much greater variation in the range of human behavior.

The Human Dimension

Many of the most successful approaches to archaeological explanation rely on a range of further key concepts, themselves fairly limited in number. The first of these is undoubtedly the phenomenon of ranking—the propensity of human individuals to arrange themselves in a rank order, in terms of a variable which is often termed "prestige," and which involves differential access to resources and a symbolic expression of increasing elaboration.

People of high rank are less numerous than people of low rank, and they exhibit tendencies of mutual repulsion (perhaps because each tends to maximize his potential access to the scarce resources). Using precisely the assumptions which lead to the prediction of central places, a network of what I like to think of as "central persons" can be predicted. Moreover, along with the notion of ranking comes the key concept of hierarchy, and we can predict higher and lower central persons. For various reasons there is a correlation between central persons and central places. The great significance of this correlation between the concept of "central place" (a common enough notion in geography) and what we have termed "central person" has rarely been emphasized. But it was brought out already by the tenth century Arab geographer Al-Muqaddasi. "In my grading system of settlements, the *amsar* are comparable to kings; the *qasabat* are comparable to ministers; the *mudun* are comparable to cavalry men; and the *qura* are comparable to soldiers" (Muqaddasi 985). His scheme (Figure 1.15) has been summarized by Ismail (1972) and counteracts the tendency of Western central theory to stress rigidly economic factors at the expense of political ones (see Chapter 6).

The second family of concepts special to human affairs and of widespread significance embraces the different modes of human exchange trans-

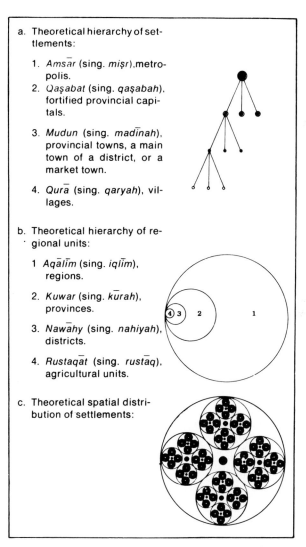

FIGURE 1.15. *Sociospatial hierarchy, as perceived by the tenth century Arab geographer Al-Muqaddasi. (After Ismail.)*

actions. The ideas of reciprocity, redistribution, and market exchange (Polanyi 1957) have proved to be fundamental to any understanding of the growth of complex societies.

Using these two groups of ideas, which express aspects of forms which are peculiar to human societies, some of the most powerful and satisfying models of social development have been created. For instance, Flannery (1968) offered a model for the growth of a state society among the Olmecs by proposing that the status of those chiefs who controlled access to the exotic goods obtained from outside by means of exchange was so positively and progressively enhanced by doing so that their power and authority consistently increased, leading to the emergence of a social organization of very marked centrality. This is a process that can be recognized as significant in the formation of other hierarchical societies also.

A third family of ideas relates to technological advance, again something specific to human society. In the agricultural field, linked with the idea of Boserup (1965) that such advance is the consequence rather than the cause of demographic increase, this has given rise to a whole cluster of interesting theories (cf. Spooner 1972). The consequences of technical advance coupled with exchange developments and with increasingly accentuated social ranking have been used to explain the development of complex society in the Aegean (Renfrew 1972).

The notion of power has so far been only implicit in the discussion, entering it by implication along with the ideas of ranking and prestige. But with it comes the notion of political control and the concept of communication. Wright (1978) and Johnson (1978; cf. Wright and Johnson 1975) have used these key ideas to give an insight into the fundamental nature of complex societies.

Since the 1950s archaeology at last began to use or fashion theoretical concepts such as these which, although of a general nature, are specific to human societies, and critical to any understanding of them (which is not to say that related ideas are without usefulness in other fields). These concepts have grown up in a rather piecemeal and incoherent way. But at last these essential forms seen in human society are being identified, defined, and then used in the explanation of its origins. They are among the entities and variables proper to the analysis of human society (see Table 1.1), the counterpart to the theoretical concepts used by the physicist, the chemist, or the biochemist. They are the building bricks with which general theories of past human behavior are likely to be constructed.

The Problem of Growth

To recognize, by means of comparative archaeology, the forms and processes common to human societies, and then to model these, is already a brave beginning. But so far no very satisfactory models for the growth of whole human societies have been found. Some of the reasons can be detected when the notion of growth is considered more carefully (Miller 1965, 372):

> Growth, a progressive, developmental, matter–energy process which occurs at all levels of systems, involves (a) increase in size—length, width, depth, volume—of the system, and commonly also (b) rise in the number of components in it; (c) increase in its complexity; (d) reorganisation of relationships among its structures—subsystems and components—and their processes including differentiation of specialised structures and patterns of action; and (e) increase in the amounts of matter—energy and information it processes.

But what models can we find which will allow us to describe or simulate processes of growth of this kind—not merely increase in size or number, but rise in complexity and differentiation, and in capacity to process information? This is the problem that besets the culture historian. And it is also, to a large extent, the problem that besets the biologist, which is one reason theoretical archaeology has so much to learn from mathematical biology.

It is useful here to distinguish between quantitative growth, the first of Miller's features, and qualitative growth. Existing models of dynamical systems (e.g., Forrester 1969; Meadows, Meadows, Randers, Behrens 1974; cf. Part IV, this volume) usually set out various feedback loops that are regarded as permanent features of the model. The analysis takes place in terms of the changing rates of flow within the feedback loops and the changing state variables, representing accumulations within the components which the loops link. But my point here is that true innovation, real qualitative growth, creates new loops. The Forrester–Meadows world model is appropriate only to changes in scale, not to model growth in the full sense set out by Miller.

In systems terms we are concerned less with homeostasis and negative feedback than with morphogenesis, mutually amplifying processes, and positive feedback. And it is in the seemingly random and unpredictable features of this growth that we may have difficulty. We cannot easily predict, from the form of the acorn, the placing of the leaves on the oak. Yet it may be some aspect of that placing which will have a determining role in the next stage of the growth process. Maruyama (1963) has stressed that it is not the initial kick but the amplifying process which we should seek to analyze, and can in fact analyze. But the troubling circumstance remains that the direction and place of that initial kick may have a determining importance out of all proportion to the size of that kick. And unfortunately, within the framework of the analysis, the kick may itself be a random event.

If we are using a game theory framework, the position is analogous. Bellman and Marchi (1973) have discussed in these terms a possible approach to the understanding of urban growth. This could easily be generalized to the growth of the entire culture system, if we allow several

games to go on at once at different levels—the culture as a whole "competing" with the environment to maintain its successful adaptation, while the members or classes within the population simultaneously play against each other. But the point I am making is that we shall have to allow the rules to change as the game develops, in a way foreign to the usual treatment of games of protocol. We may find it difficult to predict how these rules will change, but a successful simulation will have to do this, and therefore embody rules for changing the rules. If we can envisage the law code being changed in a systematic way by the state legislature, we must also imagine these metarules themselves being altered, with the passage of time, as Congress, or perhaps the Supreme Court (to continue the metaphor), intervenes.
metaphor), intervenes.

The same observations hold for the two other models which have been proposed for this undertaking. Cooke's approach in terms of directed graphs (Cooke 1973; Bellman, Cooke and Lockett 1970) requires that we assign probabilities (or transition times or costs) to transitions between specified states of systems. Clearly the whole behavior here, the whole future trajectory, is crucially governed by these assigned values. An important aspect of the simulation will be the systematic procedure by which the values are established. The appearance of a major innovation automatically must mean that many of these values have to be changed. Like a new major feedback loop, or a change of certain rules, the change in a set of these values is the equivalent of a change of internal structure.

The matrix of interactions suggested in Chapters 13 and 14 changes in a similar way. We have to indicate, in appropriate positions in the matrix, the strength of interactions between variables. Innovation and structure change are in fact introducing new variables. (It would be possible to suggest that these were already present but with zero interactions in all respects, but this would avoid the point that it is the continuing .growth of the system that determines *which* new variables are in fact introduced.) Imagine a civilization with thermonuclear power but without transistors, and our own with the reverse—it is the precise configuration at one stage in the trajectory which determines the further growth in the next. Which is why, of course, simulation is so useful an approach.

These comments can be summarized as shown in Table 1.3.

There is no easy and instant answer to this problem. Each of the models for growth and change which we can at present put forward succeeds only in generating a certain measure of complexity. Further growth, in the sense of differentiation and integration, is limited by the very structure of the model we have created. Ultimately, we shall hope to generate a model in which the structure created develops its own new rules, and hence shows truly emergent properties.

Such a model will clearly be hierarchically structured, and will incorporate (or generate) a number of thresholds, so that the society modeled will

TABLE 1.3
The Difficulty of Modeling Long-Term Change

Approach	Short-term change	Long-term growth: Morphogenesis
Game theory	Different actual moves, different constraints	Different strategies, different utilities, different rules
System dynamics	Change in values for flow and state variables, and for constants in model equations of state	Change in components of system, new feedback loops, new equations of state
Directed graphs	Transition to successive states	Radical changes in transition probabilities/times/costs. Possible addition of new states
Interaction matrix	Changing strengths of interaction between variables	Introduction of new variables

succeed in transcending the limitations of one level and find itself transformed in the process of succeeding to the next.

These ideas may appear vague at the moment, but the mathematics is
probably already available for the construction of such a general model, and
the computer capacity already sufficient to allow experimental runs or simulations. What is lacking, perhaps, is the further insight into the forms and
structures of human societies, discussed above, which are necessary for
them to be modeled effectively.

La Comédie Humaine

Many of the ideas in the foregoing sections occur again in the chapters
that follow. In each the problem arises of distinguishing the underlying
regularity from the accompanying fortuitous occurrences—the signal from
the noise, the wood from the trees, the structure from the conjuncture (to
use Braduel's terminology). The distinction, inevitably, is always drawn by
the observer, and what appears irrelevant in one frame of reference may
appear crucially significant in another. The first assumption that all scientists
make is that there are regularities which can be found or formulated.

Yet in concluding this subjective review of some of the problems of
explanation of change in societies, it is useful to return again to the human
individual, and recognize human idiosyncrasy within the context of these
generalizations.

Moreover, underlying much that has been written herein is a further
important sustaining assumption. A human individual born to specific conditions at a given time and place will behave in just the same way if born into
those same conditions at a different time and place. We have no reason to
doubt that this has been so for the past 10 or 20 thousand years, and Carleton

FIGURE 1.16. *Neanderthal man in modern dress: MacGregor's restoration of the fossil remains from La Chapelle aux Saints provided with hat, hair, and clothing by the artist. (After Coon.)*

Coon's delightful picture of Neanderthal man in modern dress (Figure 1.16), implying that you would not look at him twice in the street and would have no cause to, applies a fortiori to *Homo sapiens sapiens.*

Of course this generalization need not be true. It is possible that there has been a directional change in man's innate abilities through time over the past 20 or 30 millennia. It is also possible that different human groups at any one time have markedly different innate abilities. Yet despite the racialist views prevalent in some parts of the world today, the evidence for the innate inequality of ethnic groups is not persuasive.

Each generation, then, starts afresh, with the environment which its predecessors have left, and in particular with the inheritance of cultural equipment and experience which the ancestors have been able to hand down. In the words of the Orcadian poet Edwin Muir (Muir 1965, 80):

> *Yet still from Eden springs the root*
> *As clean as on the starting day.*

It is precisely this which makes some sort of science of man possible: Were it not so, generalizations about human behavior would be very much more difficult.

We may therefore, if we wish, think of different societies, at different periods and localities, as being transformations one of another, with the individuals of society *S* transformed into those of society *S'*. The culture heritage and immediate past of each would be different (different trajectories), and so would be the mental sets of the populations, and hence their individual psychologies. But some elements are unchanged.

I find great encouragement in this image of the same group of actors, in different dress, and in different language, yet with the same range of abilities and innate skills, playing their allotted roles in the human comedy on different stages and at different times: the man of action, who may be or become the leader; the man of vision, the priest or seer; the man with patience and ability who will be the craftsman; the belligerent who may become criminal or war hero. To say this is not to deny the ultimate uniqueness of the single individual, nor the impact which certain individuals, Carlyle's "great men," have had upon the course of events, but to assert that in many different societies different men play analogous roles. For the image reminds us that our theories and formulations can validly operate within fairly well-defined limits, and the explanatory task may not be of quite the daunting complexity that one sometimes fears. History may never repeat itself, but underlying the variety it is sometimes true that *Plus ça change, plus c'est la même chose.*

Of several books dealing with the human past one that I have found delightfully illuminating is a frivolous *jeu d'esprit* by Osbert Lancaster, *Drayneflete Revealed* (1949). He takes the imaginary small English town of Drayneflete, and traces its history, as it might be found in a rather conventional and unimaginative guidebook, following the vicissitudes of the local noble family, the Parsley-Fidgets, through the centuries. He illustrates the story with the usual clutter of family portraits ("*La belle Fidget*," by Lely) to be found in any second-rate stately home in England. Figures 1.17, 1.18, and 1.19 illustrate, respectively, Roman Drayneflete, Drayneflete after the Norman Conquest, and Drayneflete at the end of the seventeenth century, and Lancaster offers several more glimpses along the trajectory from Roman times to the twentieth century AD. The joke improves as one compares the whole series.

Although Lancaster would perhaps be appalled to learn it, his illustrations give a perfect example of successive *transformations* along a single trajectory, with a number of fundamental elements (including approximate scale, degree of ranking, a measure of craft specialization, state religion, market economy, conspicuous display of wealth and leisure, etc.) *invariant* to change. Environmental constraints are largely unchanged. A strong, and I think not invalid, insight is offered into what (in this context) are the contingencies of each cultural matrix, so that the basic processes underlying the elements invariant to transformation may be approached.

No doubt Lancaster could have given us the same actors in a series of different societies around the world, where the correspondences could not be felt to be simply the result of historical continuity. That would have stressed even more effectively the underlying unities among the variety of

ROMAN DRAYNEFLETE

FIGURE 1.17. *Time trajectory point A: Sir Osbert Lancaster's reconstruction of Roman Drayneflete (ca. AD 200).*

FIGURE 1.18. *Time trajectory point B: Lancaster's Drayneflete soon after the Norman Conquest (ca. AD 1070). Some elements (e.g., the beggar) appear invariant to temporal transformation.*

DRAYNEFLETE AT THE END OF THE SEVENTEENTH CENTURY

FIGURE 1.19. *Time trajectory point C: Lancaster's Drayneflete at the end of the seventeenth century* AD. *Compare with Figures 1.17 and 1.18: continuity and contingency.*

expressions seen in societies of analogous scale and structure around the world.

The underlying ideas here of structure and invariance are in a broad sense mathematical, although Osbert Lancaster has not expressed them in such a form. Yet the point is a suitable one with which to end this introduction, for it does not follow that mathematical thought is inimical to humane imagination.

Acknowledgments

The following have kindly written to signify their approval of the reproduction of illustrations: the editor of *Scientific American* (Figure 1.2); Sir Osbert Lancaster, and John Murray (publishers) (Figures 1.17–1.19); the Oxford University Press (Figure 1.7); the editor of *Ekistics* (Figure 1.15); the Cambridge University Press (Figures 1.8–1.11), from *On Growth and Form* by D'Arcy Thompson), and Dr. John Bintliff (Figure 1.14).

References

Ammerman, A. J., and Cavalli-Sforza, L. L., 1973, A population model for the diffusion of early farming in Europe, in C. Renfrew (ed.), *The Explanation of Culture Change*, London, Duckworth, 343–358.

Bell, E. T., 1950, *Mathematics, Queen and Servant of Science,* New York, McGraw-Hill.

Bellman, R., Cooke, K. L., and Lockett, J. A., 1970, *Algorithms, Graphs and Computers,* New York, Academic Press.

Bellman, R., and Marchi, E., 1973, The city as a competitive process and games of protocol. (Dialogue Discussion Paper for the Center for the Study of Democratic Institutions, Santa Barbara).

Bertalanffy, L., von, 1950, An outline of General Systems Theory, *British Journal of the Philosophy of Science* 1, 134–165.

Binford, L. R., 1962, Archaeology as anthropology, *American Antiquity* 28, 217–225.

Binford, L. R., 1968, Archaeological perspectives, in Binford, L. R., and S. R. (eds.), *New Perspectives in Archaeology,* New York, Aldine, 5–32.

Binford, L. R. (ed.), 1977, *For Theory Building in Archaeology,* New York, Academic Press.

Bintliff, J. L., 1977, New approaches to human geography: prehistoric Greece, a case study, in Carter F. E. (ed.), *An Historical Geography of the Balkans,* London, Academic Press, 59–114.

Birdsell, J., 1957, Some population problems involving Pleistocene man, *Cold Springs Harbor Symposia on Quantitative Biology,* 22, 47–69.

Blalock, H. M., 1960, *Social Statistics,* New York, McGraw Hill.

Boserup, E., 1965, *The Conditions of Agricultural Growth,* Chicago, Aldine.

Braudel, F., 1972, *The Mediterranean and the Mediterranean World in the Age of Philip II,* London, Collins.

Carlyle, T., 1841, *On Heroes, Hero-Worship and the Heroic in History,* London, James Fraser.

Childe, V. G., 1950, The Urban Revolution, *Town Planning Review* 21, 3–17.

Chisholm, M., 1968, *Rural Settlement and Land Use,* London, Hutchinson.

Clark, J. G. D., 1952, *Prehistoric Europe, the Economic Basis,* London, Methuen.

Clarke, D. L., 1968, *Analytical Archaeology,* London, Methuen.

Coleman, J. S., 1964, *Introduction to Mathematical Sociology,* New York, Free Press.

Collingwood, R. G., 1946, *The Idea of History,* Oxford, University Press.

Comte, A., 1875, *The Positive Philosophy,* trans. Harriet Martineau.

Cooke, K., 1973, A model of urbanisation and civilisation. (Dialogue Discussion Paper for the Center for the Study of Democratic Institutions).

Darwin, C., 1859, *The Origin of Species by Means of Natural Selection,* London, Murray.

Doran, J. E., and Hodson, F. R., 1975, *Mathematics and Computers in Archaeology,* Edinburgh, University Press.

Flannery, K. V., 1968, The Olmec and the valley of Oaxaca, in Benson, E. P. (ed.), *Dumbarton Oaks Conference on the Olmec,* Washington.

Flannery, K. V., 1972, The cultural evolution of civilizations, *Annual Review of Ecology and Systematics* 3, 399–425.

Flannery, K. V., 1972, The origins of the village as a settlement type in Mesoamerica and the Near East: a comparative study, in Ucko, P. J., Tringham, R., and Dimbleby, G. W. (eds.), *Man, Settlement and Urbanism,* London, Duckworth, 23–54.

Flannery, K. V., 1973, Archaeology with a capital S, in Redman, C. L., (ed.), *Research and Theory in Current Archaeology,* New York, John Wiley.

Forrester, J., 1969, *Urban Dynamics,* Cambridge, M.I.T. Press.

Fritz, J. M., and Plog, F., 1970, The nature of archaeological explanation, *American Antiquity* 35, 405, 412.

Hägerstrand, T., 1967, *Innovation Diffusion as a Spatial Process,* Chicago, University Press.

Hamblin, R. L., Jacobsen, R. B., and Miller, J. L. L., 1973, *A Mathematical Theory of Social Change,* New York, John Wiley.

Hardoy, J., 1968, *Urban Planning in Pre-Columbian America,* London, Studio Vista.

Harris, M., 1968, *The Rise of Anthropological Theory,* London, Routledge.

Hawkes, J., 1968, The Proper Study of Mankind, *Antiquity* 42, 255–262.

Helm, J. (ed.), 1968, *Essays on the Problem of the Tribe,* New York, American Ethnological Society.

Higgs, E. S., (ed.), 1972, *Papers in Economic Prehistory,* Cambridge, University Press.

Hill, J. H., 1970, School of American Research Advanced Seminar, *American Anthropological Association Newsletter* 11(10), 13–14.

Ismail, A. A., 1972, Origin, ideology and physical patterns of Arab urbanisation, *Ekistics* 33, 113–123.

Jochim, M. A., 1976, *Hunter-Gatherer Subsistence and Settlement,* New York, Academic Press.

Johnson, G. A., 1976, Review of Moore, C. B. (ed.), *Reconstructing Complex Societies, An Archaeological Colloquium* in *American Antiquity* 41, 569–71.

Johnson, G. A., 1978, Information sources and the development of decision-making organisations, in Redman, C. L. (ed.), *Archaeology as a Social Science.*

Kroeber, A. L., 1917, The Superorganic, *American Anthropologist* 19, 163–213.

Lampl, P., 1968, *Cities and Planning in the Ancient Near East,* London, Studio Vista.

Lancaster, O., 1949, *Drayneflete Revealed,* London, John Murray.

Levi-Strauss, C., 1969, *The Elementary Structures of Kinship,* London, Eyre and Spottiswoode.

Lotka, A. J., 1956, *Elements of Mathematical Biology,* New York, Dover.

Maruyama, M., 1963, The second cybernetics: deviation amplifying mutual causal processes, *American Scientist* 51, 164–179.

Marx, K., 1964, *Pre-Capitalist Economic Formations,* London, Lawrence and Wishart.

Maynard Smith, J., 1974, *Models in Ecology,* Cambridge, University Press.

Meadows, D. H., Meadows, D. L., Randers, J., and Behrens, W. W., 1974, *The Limits of Growth,* London, Pan.

Medawar, P. B., 1945, Size, shape and age, in Le Gros Clark, W. E., and Medawar, P. B. (eds.), *Essays on Growth and Form Presented to D'Arcy Wentworth Thompson,* Oxford, Clarendon, 157–187.

Miller, J. G., 1965, Living systems: structure and process, *Behavioural Science* 10, 337–374.

Montelius, O., 1903, *Die älteren Kulturperioden im Orient und in Europa, I. Die Methode,* Stockholm.

Morgan, L. H., 1877, *Ancient Society or Researches in the Lines of Human Progress from Savagery through Barbarism to Civilisation.*

Muir, E., 1965, *Selected Poems,* ed. T. S. Eliot, London, Faber.

Muqaddasi, 985, Ahsan At-taqasim, edited de Goeje, M. J., *Bibliotheca Geographorum Arabicorum* (1906), quoted by Ismail, 1972.

Pattee, H. H., (ed.), 1973, *Hierarchy Theory, the Challenge of Complex Systems,* New York, Brazilier.

Petrie, W. M. F., 1899, Sequences in prehistoric remains, *Journal of the Anthropological Institute* 29, 295–301.

Pitt-Rivers, A. H. L. F., 1975, The Evolution of Culture, *Proceedings of the Royal Institution* 7, 496–520.

Plog, F. T., 1974, *The Study of Prehistoric Change,* New York, Academic Press.

Polanyi, K., 1957, The economy as instituted process, in Polanyi K., Arensberg, C. M., and Pearson, H. W. (eds.), *Trade and Market in the Early Empires,* New York, Free Press, 243–269.

Rashevsky, N., 1968, *Looking at History through Mathematics,* Cambridge, M.I.T. Press.

Reeve, E. C. R., and Huxley, J. S., 1945, Some problems in the study of allometric growth, in Le Gros Clark, W. E., Medawar, P. B. (eds.), *Essays on Growth and Form presented to D'Arcy Wentworth Thompson,* Oxford, Clarendon, 120–156.

Renfrew, C., 1972, *The Emergence of Civilisation: the Cyclades and the Aegean in the Third Millennium B.C.,* London, Methuen.

Renfrew, C., 1977, Alternative models for exchange and spatial distribution, in Earle, T. K., and Ericson, J. (Eds.), *Exchange Systems in Prehistory,* New York, Academic Press, 71–90.

Robinson, W. S., 1951, A method for chronologically ordering archaeological deposits, *American Antiquity* 16, 293–301.

Schiffer, M. B., 1972, Archaeological context and systemic context, *American Antiquity* 37, 156–165.

Schiffer, M. B., and Rathje, W. J., 1973, Efficient exploitation of the archaeological record: penetrating problems, in Redman, C. L. (ed.), *Research and Theory in Current Archaeology,* New York, Wiley, 169–179.

Service, E. R., 1962, *Primitive Social Organisation,* New York, Random House.

Sokal, R., and Sneath, P. H. A., 1973, *Numerical Taxonomy,* San Francisco, Freeman.

Spooner, B., (ed.), 1972, *Population Growth: Anthropological Implications,* Cambridge.

Steward, J. H., 1955, *Theory of Culture Change,* Urbana, University of Illinois Press.

Thom, R., 1975, *Structural Stability and Morphogenesis,* Reading, Mass., Benjamin.

Thompson, D. A. W., 1942, *On Growth and Form,* Cambridge, University Press, 2nd edn. (First edn. 1917).

Thünen, J. H. von, 1875, *Der Isolierte Staat in Beziehung auf Landwirtschaft und Nationalökonomie,* Berlin.

Ucko, P. J., 1969, Ethnography and archaeological interpretation of funerary remains, *World Archaeology* 1, 262–80.

Ward-Perkins, J. B., 1974, *Cities of Ancient Greece and Italy,* New York, Brazilier.

Watson, P. J., LeBlanc, S. A., and Redman, C. L., 1971, *Explanation in Archaeology, an Explicitly Scientific Approach,* New York, Columbia University Press.

Willey, G. R., 1974, A summary of the complex societies colloquium, in Moore, C. B. (ed.), *Reconstructing Complex Societies, an Archaeological Colloqium* (Supplement to the Bulletin of the American Schools of Oriental Research no. 20), 143–153.

Woodger, J. H., 1945, On biological transformations, in Le Gros Clark, W. E., and Medawar, P. B. (eds.), *Essays on Growth and Form presented to D'Arcy Wentworth Thompson,* Oxford, Clarendon, 95–119.

Wright, H. T., 1978, Recent research on the origin of the state, *Annual Review of Anthropology,* in press.

Wright, H. T., and Johnson, G. A., 1975, Population, exchange and early state formation in southwestern Iran, *American Anthropologist* 77, 267–289.

Zipf, G. K., 1949, *Human Behaviour and the Principle of Least Effort,* New York, Hafner.

2

KENNETH L. COOKE

Mathematical Approaches to Culture Change

The process of evolution, change, or transformation of a culture or a society is a dynamic process. That is, the structures, relationships, and activities within the culture undergo modification as *time* passes. In addition, there may be significant influences due to *spatial* patterns or relationships. Therefore, in order to use mathematical approaches in the description of culture change, it is necessary to find mathematical theories which can describe or simulate structure and organization, which can describe transformation through time, which can take account of spatial or geographic variation, and which can at least in part embody the decision processes in human societies.

In this chapter, we shall give brief introductions to two general categories of mathematical methods that have some or all of these desirable properties and seem to be suitable in some measure for modeling cultural transformations. First, there are methods of dynamical systems theory, in which one attempts to specify the influences causing short-term changes and to derive the long-term behavior therefrom. The mathematics involves the theory of difference equations or differential equations, and the models are ordinarily relevant for large-scale phenomena. The second class of methods is directed more toward discrete entities and the structural relations or patterns among them. The theory of games, mathematical theories of optimization, and graph theory are among the fields included here. Actually, of course, the two classes have close interrelations. Since we cannot cover so wide a field at all thoroughly in the space available, references are provided to many more complete works on modeling and on the mathematics in-

45

Transformations:
Mathematical Approaches to Culture Change

volved. References to work in which applications are made in the cultural or archaeological area are given when appropriate and when known to us.

We shall begin with an elementary discussion of difference equations and differential equations, using very simple examples. Such equations are so basic in dynamic modeling that we think a discussion here is warranted for the benefit of readers unfamiliar with the subject. Furthermore, by means of slightly more complex examples, we then introduce a number of important qualitative concepts: stability, equilibrium points, and periodic behavior. By examples, we hope to demonstrate that from simple models may sometimes emerge broad qualitative principles or an explanation of observations that may, without a model, be poorly comprehended.

From this beginning, we proceed to a study of the modeling of complex systems by simulation. Techniques of dynamical systems theory and structural modeling are described.

In the final sections, we examine probabilistic or nondeterministic models, optimization models, and the theory of games. Other areas of mathematics which have already been widely applied in archaeological or historical studies of a more static kind, such as taxonomic and statistical methods, are not considered here. Also, models of spatial dependence are not emphasized because Chapter 4 by Rosen (this volume) is devoted to this subject.

In a chapter of this kind, it is necessary to make some assumption about the level of mathematical training of the readers. We shall assume in the sections on differential equations, stability and qualitative behavior, and cultural models and dynamic simulations, that the reader has had some introduction to calculus. In the section on randomness and stochastic processes, we assume the elementary concepts of probability theory. The sections on dynamic models and difference equations, and on optimization and the mathematical theory of games, should be accessible to readers with only a background of elementary algebra.

It is our hope that archaeologists may find here some new tools for the difficult task of understanding cultural change.

Dynamic Models and Difference Equations

In order to introduce the use of difference equations in dynamic modeling, let us consider the classical "cobweb" model of economic theory. The object for study is the relationship between the price of a commodity and the supply and demand for it. Introduce functions $p(t)$, $S(t)$, and $D(t)$ to represent these. That is,

$S(t)$ = supply available at time t
$D(t)$ = demand for commodity at time t
$p(t)$ = price of commodity at time t

We assume that the demand increases as price decreases, in accordance with an equation

$$D(t) = c - dp(t)$$

where c and d are certain constants. We also assume that the supplier increases the available amount as the price increases, but that this production increase is not instantaneous but requires a fixed period of time, h. We might then have an equation of the form

$$S(t) = a + bp(t - h)$$

where a and b are constants. As a specific illustration, we could think of the commodity as some farm crop, and h as the time from one planting to the next. Then the number a represents the fixed amount planted even if none can be sold, and b represents the additional amount planted per unit increase in price. The model supposes that the supply at time t depends on the amount planted at time $t - h$, which in turn is governed by the prevailing price at time $t - h$. Consumer demand is assumed to adjust rapidly to price changes, and consequently in the first equation D and p are evaluated at the same time t. For the sake of simplicity, let us assume that as soon as a crop is harvested, a new crop is planted. To complete the model, the last assumption is that in each period the market determines the price in such a way that the demand (consumption) exactly equals the supply. Then $D(t) = S(t)$ and we have the system of equations

$$S(t) = a + bp(t - h)$$
$$D(t) = c - dp(t) \qquad (2.1)$$
$$D(t) = S(t)$$

By replacing D by S in the second equation and subtracting the second equation from the first, we obtain

$$p(t) = \frac{c - a}{d} - \frac{b}{d} p(t - h) \qquad (2.2)$$

Equation (2.2) is an example of a *difference equation* or *recursion equation*. One should think of the independent variable t as taking on successively the values $0, h, 2h, 3h, \ldots$. In this model, there is no need to consider the continuum of times, since only the values of the variables at the *discrete* sequence of times $0, h, 2h, \ldots$ are relevant. What kind of information can be deduced from Equation (2.2)? To simplify the discussion, we temporarily let $(c - a)/d = r$ and $b/d = s$, so that the equation is

$$p(t) = r - sp(t - h) \tag{2.3}$$

Let $p = p(0)$, that is, let p denote the prevailing price at some arbitrarily selected initial time that we call $t = 0$. Then from (2.3) we have, recursively,

$$
\begin{aligned}
p(h) &= r - sp \\
p(2h) &= r - sp(h) = r - s(r - sp) = (1 - s)r + s^2p \\
p(3h) &= r - sp(2h) = r - s(1 - s)r - s^3p \\
&= (1 - s + s^2)r - s^3p
\end{aligned}
$$

It can be seen that

$$p(nh) = [1 - s + s^2 - \cdots + (-1)^{n-1}s^{n-1}]r + (-1)^n s^n p$$

where n represents any positive integer. It is known from elementary algebra that this series can be summed to yield

$$p(nh) = \frac{r}{1 + s} + (-1)^n s^n \left(p - \frac{r}{1 + s} \right) \tag{2.4}$$

Thus, we see that the model assumptions have led to mathematical equations, which in this case have been solved. The solution is given by an algebraic formula for the price at any arbitrary time period nh.

Various consequences can be inferred from (2.4). First of all, if s is less than 1, then the successive powers s^2, s^3, ... become smaller, and in fact s^n approaches zero as n increases without bound. This is expressed by the equations, in the "limit" notation of calculus,

$$\lim_{n \to \infty} s^n = 0, \qquad \lim_{n \to \infty} p(nh) = \frac{r}{1 + s}$$

Thus, if $s < 1$, the prices at successive time points approach a fixed value $r/(1 + s)$. In other words, the price moves to an *equilibrium level* if $b < d$. On the other hand, if $b > d$, then $s > 1$ and s^n becomes arbitrarily large as n increases. In this case, the price as predicted from the model fluctuates more and more widely (in fact, it takes on negative as well as large positive values). For additional discussion of this model, and of economic models in general, see Gandolfo (1971).

Equation (2.3) is called a first-order, linear difference equation. More generally, an nth-*order* linear difference equation has the form

$$a_0 x(t) + a_1 x(t - h) + \cdots + a_n x(t - nh) = b \tag{2.5}$$

where $a_0, a_1, \ldots, a_n, b$ are given numbers, with $a_0 \neq 0$, $a_n \neq 0$, and $x(t)$ is the unknown function that we wish to determine. It is nth order because only n "differences" in the argument or independent variable t occur, that is, $t - h$, ..., $t - nh$. It is linear because each term $x(t - kh)$ occurs with exponent 1. The theory of linear difference equations is well understood. For a discussion, see Goldberg (1958) or Gandolfo (1971).

Many models, however, lead to nonlinear difference equations, as now illustrated by a model for the growth of a population of animals. Consider a species of animal which has a single breeding season once a year, and in which adults live for only one breeding season. For the sake of simplicity, we ignore all interactions with other species. Let $P(t)$ denote the number of adult females at the start of the breeding season in the tth year. Then $P(t + 1) = RP(t)$, where R represents the number of female offspring produced, on the average, by one adult female, which live to their first breeding season. In general, the reproductive rate R will not be a constant for all situations, but rather will be *density dependent*. That is, R will be a function of P. Often, it is expected that the function $R(P)$ will decrease toward zero at very high densities, due to excessive crowding and competition for resources. One of the simplest hypotheses, and one that will be adequate for explanatory purposes here, is that $R(P) = A - BP$ where A and B are constants. The resulting equation is then

$$P(t + 1) = P(t)[a - bP(t)] = aP(t) - bP(t)^2$$

This is a nonlinear equation, since the term $P(t)^2$ appears in it. We will return to difference equations in the section on stability and qualitative behavior, after we have introduced some models in terms of differential equations.

Differential Equations

In the preceding section, elementary examples of the use of difference equations in modeling dynamic (time-varying) situations were given. In these examples, it was assumed that there are discrete time periods, and that changes or jumps in the values of the variables occur from one period to the next. This approach is likely to be approximately true in the biological and economic examples given—a population with discrete nonoverlapping generations, or the supply–demand–price model under the simple assumptions given. In fact, the use of difference equations in economic analysis is widespread, largely because the data are usually only measured at discrete, regular times. However, in many or perhaps most cases of scientific description, the variables are changing continuously with time. As one knows, the appropriate mathematical description is then the differential and integral calculus. A basic concept is that of the *rate of change* of a function of time, given by the derivative of the function. For example, if $y(t)$ is a function representing some variable quantity, then

$$\frac{dy}{dt} \quad \text{or} \quad y'(t)$$

represents its rate of change, the instantaneous change in y per unit change in time.

Instead of difference equations, one now finds differential equations. A differential equation is merely an equation containing a function y and its derivative dy/dt. A basic problem is to *solve* the equation, which means to find all functions that *satisfy* the given equation. A simple example is the equation

$$\frac{dq}{dt} = -\frac{1}{10}q$$

which might describe the quantity q of material of a certain radioactive substance. The equation says that the rate of disintegration, per unit time, is always just one-tenth of the amount of material actually present. It is known that all *solutions* of this equation are functions of the form $q(t) = ce^{-t/10}$, where c can be any number (constant), and e denotes the special number $e = 2.71828…$.

Let us consider one more example, returning to the problem of describing population growth. As before, we let $P(t)$ denote the population of an isolated species at time t, but now we consider time t to vary continuously. Moreover, although the population must at any instant be an integer, we imagine that it can take on all possible values, fractional or even "irrational" as well as integral. This fiction is likely to produce negligible errors if we are dealing with large numbers, and it represents a smoothing of the data that is necessary in order to use the powerful nethods of calculus. Now

$$\frac{dP}{dt} = B - D + M \tag{2.6}$$

where B is the number of births per unit time, D is the number of deaths per unit time, and M is the net inward migration. A particularly simple equation is obtained if we assume that $M = 0$, and that $B = bP$ and $D = dP$ where b and d are constants. That is, the births and deaths per unit time are linearly proportional to the present population. Such an assumption might approximate reality for, say, an insect population when there is an abundance of resources and mating occurs somewhat randomly. The resulting equation is

$$\frac{dP}{dt} = (b - d)P \tag{2.7}$$

and its solutions are known to have the form

$$P(t) = ce^{(b-d)t} \qquad (2.8)$$

Note that we cannot obtain the specific differential equation (2.7) from the law (2.6) until it is known or hypothesized how B and D depend on P. In (2.8), any constant c is permissible. However, if we set $t = 0$ in (2.8), we find that $P(0) = c$, so that c represents the size of the *initial population* (population at time zero). Thus, we could write

$$P(t) = P(0)e^{(b-d)t}$$

This equation describes the law of exponential or Malthusian population growth if b exceeds d.

Equation (2.7) is a linear differential equation. More realistic population models generally involve nonlinear equations. For example, just as in the model in the section on dynamic models and difference equations, we may assume that the reproductive rate decreases as P increases. We might then obtain the equation

$$\frac{dP}{dt} = bP\left(1 - \frac{P}{K}\right) = bP - \frac{b}{K}P^2$$

containing a term in P^2. This equation is called the *logistic equation* and is widely used as exemplifying population growth when there is a natural birthrate b (net births per unit time) and a *carrying capacity K*, which is the maximum sustained population permitted by the equation (see also Chapter 1). This equation can be easily solved for P, by the so-called method of separation of variables. It turns out that every solution has the form

$$P(t) = \frac{Kbe^{bt}}{KC + be^{bt}}$$

where C is a constant determined from the known population at some designated time. Methods of calculus applied to the equation for $P(t)$ show that P rises in the familiar S-shaped growth curve, approaching the limiting value K as t increases. This logistic model has already been successfully tested in relation to population estimates obtained from archaeological data (see Eighmy, Chapter 8, this volume). The same model has been found by Fisher and Pry (1971) to describe a variety of processes in which one material or activity is replaced by another. Note the similarity of form between the logistic equation and the nonlinear difference equation at the end of the preceding section. More complicated models involving differential equations are discussed in the following three sections. Braun (1975) gives a lively introduction to the subject of differential equations.

Stability and Qualitative Behavior

The examples up to this point have been designed to illustrate the use of difference equations and differential equations. Often, the phenomena under study result from the interactions among several variables, and the corresponding models may therefore consist of several difference equations (or differential equations), each of which contains several of the unknowns. When this is the case, the variables may exhibit behavior of a much more complicated kind than what we have shown so far. In this section, we shall illustrate some of the possibilities with examples. Also, it is generally impossible to obtain explicit formulas for the solutions of such sets of equations by the elementary devices of calculus. Consequently, an attempt is made to introduce the reader to some of the techniques used in such cases.

First, we shall explain a well-known model of a two-species ecosystem in which both species compete for the same limited resource. This resource might be food, sunlight, nesting space, and so on, or some combination of factors that ecologists designate as an "ecological niche." Let $P_1(t)$ and $P_2(t)$ denote the respective population sizes of the two species. Assume that each species would grow in logistic fashion in the absence of the other, so that the growth equations would be

$$\frac{dP_1}{dt} = aP_1 - bP_1^2, \qquad \frac{dP_2}{dt} = cP_2 - dP_2^2$$

To take account of the effect of competition, let us introduce terms to reduce the growth rate of each species due to the presence of the other. The simplest assumption is that this reduction of growth rate is proportional to the other species' population. The resulting equations have the form

$$\frac{dP_1}{dt} = P_1(a - bP_1 - uP_2)$$
$$\frac{dP_2}{dt} = P_2(c - dP_2 - vP_1)$$

(2.9)

where u and v are proportionality constants.

Equations (2.9) do not have an explicit solution by means of integrations. Nevertheless, there are methods for extracting much useful information from these equations. One such method is the use of the so-called phase plane. A solution of Equations (2.9) consists of a pair of functions $P_1(t)$ and $P_2(t)$, describing the time evolution of the population sizes. One graphical means of displaying these is to graph the functions, illustrated in Figure 2.1. A second method is, for each value of t, to locate the point $(P_1(t), P_2(t))$ in the P_1, P_2 plane. As t increases, the point moves in the plane, tracing out a curve called an *orbit*, or *trajectory*, as illustrated in Figure 2.2.

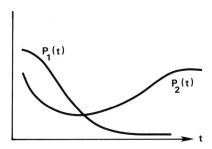

FIGURE 2.1. *Population sizes as functions of time.*

In Figure 2.2, the explicit way in which P_1 and P_2 depend on t is obscured, but, as we shall see, much useful information remains. Usually, an arrow is placed on an orbit to indicate which way the point $(P_1(t), P_2(t))$ moves on the orbit as t increases.

We shall now show how to obtain a picture of the orbits for Equations (2.9) specifically. From Equations (2.9) we obtain by division

$$\frac{dP_2/dt}{dP_1/dt} = \frac{dP_2}{dP_1} = \frac{P_2(c - dP_2 - vP_1)}{P_1(a - bP_1 - uP_2)} \tag{2.10}$$

In Equation (2.10), time t has been eliminated; the equation represents a relationship that must always hold between P_1 and P_2. A useful way to analyze this is to consider the algebraic equations

$$P_1(a - bP_1 - uP_2) = 0, \qquad P_2(c - dP_2 - vP_1) = 0 \tag{2.11}$$

The set of all pairs of numbers (P_1, P_2) satisfying (2.11) can be geometrically represented in the phase plane. It consists of the four lines with equations

$$P_1 = 0, \qquad P_2 = 0, \qquad bP_1 + uP_2 = a, \qquad vP_1 + dP_2 = c \tag{2.12}$$

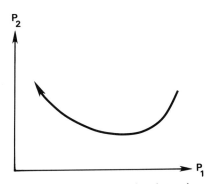

FIGURE 2.2 *Trajectory of population sizes in the phase plane.*

The lines $P_1 = 0$ and $P_2 = 0$ are the coordinate axes. Since b, d, u, and v are positive numbers, the other two lines have (by elementary analytic geometry) negative slopes and positive intercepts on the axes. Depending on the values of the constants, there are four possible geometrical configurations, shown in Figure 2.3. Note that only the quarter of the plane where P_1 and P_2 are greater than or equal to zero is depicted, since negative values of P_1 and P_2 are not meaningful.

Consider Figure 2.3a. From Equations (2.9) we see that at any point on the line $bP_1 + uP_2 = a$, we must have $dP_1/dt = 0$, or $\dot{P}_1 = 0$ if we use the dot for convenient representation of differentiation with respect to t. Above this line, $bP_1 + uP_2$ is greater than a and therefore $\dot{P}_1$ is negative. Similarly, above the line $vP_1 + dP_2 = c$ we have $\dot{P}_2 < 0$, and below it, $\dot{P}_2 > 0$. The signs of $\dot{P}_1$ and $\dot{P}_2$ are shown in the figure for each of the regions created by the two lines. Now observe that in the region closest to the origin, since both $\dot{P}_1$ and $\dot{P}_2$ are positive, P_1 and P_2 must be increasing as t increases. Moreover, since dP_2/dP_1 is positive, the orbit has positive slope. As the line $bP_1 + uP_2 = a$ is approached, $\dot{P}_1$ approaches zero whereas $\dot{P}_2$ remains positive, and therefore the ratio dP_2/dP_1 approaches infinity. In fact, as the orbit crosses the line, it must do so with infinite slope, meaning that it is vertical. Next, in the region between the two lines, $\dot{P}_1$ is negative and $\dot{P}_2$ is positive, and therefore P_1 is decreasing while P_2 continues to increase. It can be shown that the orbit cannot cross the line $vP_1 + dP_2 = c$, and that it must tend toward the point where $P_1 = 0$ and $P_2 = c/d$. In fact, further analysis of this kind can be used to show that all orbits in Figure 2.3a must approach the point $(0, c/d)$. This means that population P_1 becomes extinct, whereas P_2 approaches c/d, its natural carrying capacity in the absence of P_1.

Similarly, from Figure 2.3b one can see that all orbits approach the point $P_1 = a/b$, $P_2 = 0$, corresponding to extinction of the second population. In Figures 2.3c and 2.3d, however, the lines intersect at a point. By simple algebra, this point may be shown to have coordinates

$$P_1 = \frac{ad - uc}{bd - uv}, \qquad P_2 = \frac{bc - va}{bd - uv} \qquad (2.13)$$

It is possible to show that P_1 and P_2 are both positive only in the cases shown in Figures 2.3c and 2.3d. That is, Figures 2.3c and 2.3d show the only cases in which there is an equilibrium situation with both species present. In all cases, the point $P_1 = a/b$, $P_2 = 0$ and the point $P_1 = 0$, $P_2 = c/d$ are equilibrium points. By geometrical reasoning, using the signs of $\dot{P}_1$ and $\dot{P}_2$ in the four regions formed by the intersecting lines, it can be shown that in Figure 2.3c, all orbits approach the equilibrium point given by (2.13). This means that whatever may be the initial size of the two populations, their sizes tend, as time passes, to the values given in (2.13). If any exogenous disturbance were to displace the populations away from their equilibrium

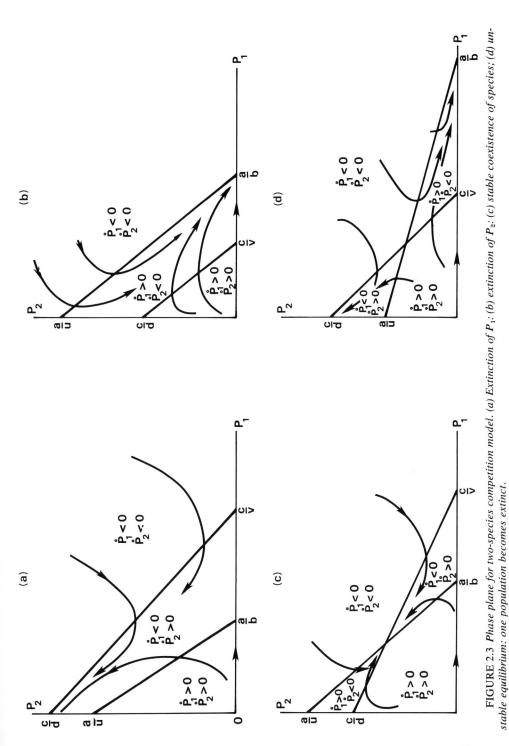

FIGURE 2.3 *Phase plane for two-species competition model. (a) Extinction of P_1; (b) extinction of P_2; (c) stable coexistence of species; (d) unstable equilibrium: one population becomes extinct.*

55

values, they would tend to return to this equilibrium. In short, we say that the equilibrium is *stable* (or *asymptotically stable*). The system has a high degree of stability or homeostasis. The equilibria at $P_1 = a/b$, $P_2 = 0$ and $P_1 = 0$, $P_2 = c/d$ are *unstable* since all orbits originating near these points tend away from them.

In Figure 2.3d, the equilibrium (2.13) is *unstable* and one or the other species becomes extinct, depending on the initial values of P_1 and P_2. (There is one exception. There is a single curve in Figure 2.3d along which the equilibrium point (2.13) is approached. However, there is essentially zero likelihood that a process would start exactly on this orbit. Even if it did, random disturbances would cause the process to follow a different orbit.) The condition for stability is given by the two inequalities

$$\frac{a}{b} < \frac{c}{v} \quad \text{and} \quad \frac{c}{d} < \frac{a}{u} \tag{2.14}$$

or, equivalently,

$$\frac{u}{d} < \frac{a}{c} < \frac{b}{v} \tag{2.15}$$

This condition has a simple biological interpretation, which is most readily understood in case $a = c$, that is, in case the two species have the same intrinsic growth rates. For then (2.15) reduces to $u < d$, $v < b$. This means that the presence of P_2 inhibits the growth of P_1 less than it inhibits its own growth, and also that the presence of P_1 inhibits the growth of P_2 less than its own growth. The two species can coexist only under this condition, according to the model. If, for example, the two species are limited by different scarce resources, condition (2.15) is likely to be satisfied, but if they have identical requirements ($u = d$, $v = b$), then (2.15) will be violated and the more efficient species will eliminate its competitor. This result is the basis for what has been called the "principle of competitive exclusion."

The pair of equations (2.9) is but one of many possible pairs of equations that might be postulated to describe the interactions between two species, and detailed analyses have been made of equations of the form

$$\frac{dP_1}{dt} = P_1 f_1(P_1, P_2)$$
$$\frac{dP_2}{dt} = P_2 f_2(P_1, P_2) \tag{2.16}$$

for a variety of choices of the functions $f_1(P_1, P_2)$ and $f_2(P_1, P_2)$. For further explanations and extensions in the biological context, see Maynard Smith (1974) or Rescigno and Richardson (1973).

Equations of the form (2.16) may also be used as models of interaction between two human groups, rather than between two species. For example, Cooke and Freedman (n.d.) are in the process of analyzing a model for the interaction of two population groups when there is a technological or other factor which gives one group an advantage over the other. The equations may take the form

$$\frac{dP_1}{dt} = P_1(a - bP_1) - g(P_1, P_2)$$

$$\frac{dP_2}{dt} = P_2(c - dP_2) + g(P_1, P_2)$$

(2.17)

The term $g(P_1, P_2)$, which may be given various specific forms, represents *migration* (or *conversion* or *assimilation*) from group 1 to group 2, due to a real or psychological attractiveness of the latter.

There are extensive mathematical works on the nature of solutions of systems such as (2.16) and its generalizations to a larger number of variables. Sometimes general results can be proved that are valid for wide classes of such equations. Whenever this is possible, it is very valuable, since there are at present few generally accepted underlying "laws" which would specify the exact form of the equations. One of the principal objectives of twentieth century mathematical investigations has been to classify the behavior of solutions for large values of t. The positive *limit set* of an orbit is defined to be the set of all points in the phase plane (or phase space if there are more than two equations) which are approached arbitrarily closely by the orbit as t becomes indefinitely large. For example, a stable equilibrium point is a point in the limit set. A closed orbit is its own positive limit set. Figure 2.4 shows

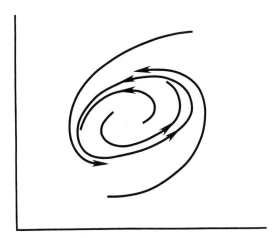

FIGURE 2.4 *Stable limit cycle.*

an example of orbits spiraling around and toward a fixed closed orbit, which is therefore their limit set. Such a closed orbit is called a *limit cycle*.

In modeling some phenomena, it may be desirable to take into account the presence of time delays during the process. For example, when an economic decision is made by policymakers, there is usually a time delay before the policy can be implemented. Thus, the change in the system at a time t may depend on the decision made at time $t - r$ for some constant r. A simple example of an equation to model this situation is

$$\frac{dx}{dt} = f(x(t - r))$$

This equation states that the present rate of change of variable x is a function of the value of x at r time units before. Such an equation is called a delay differential equation. See Driver (1977) or Bellman and Cooke (1963) for the theory of such equations. In discrete-time models, a similar phenomenon occurs if the new value of a variable depends not only on the previous value but also on values several time steps before. The resulting equation will be a difference equation of order greater than one. Equation (2.5) is such an equation in the linear case. Because of space limitations, we must forego discussing the theory of these equations.

Graphical Representations

In the examples in the preceding sections, we were dealing with processes involving only one or two functions of time, and we found that graphical representations were helpful in understanding the processes. However, in trying to describe an evolving cultural system in quantitative terms, we must often use a large number of variables. Even assuming that we have data on the values of all these variables through time, we may still face the problem of representing this information in a useful or vivid way.

Suppose that the system is described by N functions of time, which we label $x_1(t)$, $x_2(t)$, ..., $x_N(t)$. We assume for the moment that these are known to us, at least for a sequence of times t. One way to represent these graphically is to draw N graphs, one for each function. Thus, the ith graph is a plot of x_i versus t. Alternatively, we may draw all N graphs on one set of axes, using different colors or symbols to differentiate one from another. No doubt graphs of this type are familiar to all our readers.

A second kind of representation was illustrated by Figure 2.2, which was designed to depict the relation between two functions $P_1(t)$ and $P_2(t)$. Recall that for each time t, the point with coordinates (P_1, P_2) was located in the plane. If t varies continuously, the point then traces a curve that is a representation of the process. This curve is called a trajectory in the *phase plane*. If t takes on only discrete values, then the points will also be discrete rather than lying on a continuous curve. In this case, a continuous curve sometimes is drawn through the points for greater clarity, but this curve is not really a representation of known data, merely an extrapolation or inference.

If there are three variables $x_1(t)$, $x_2(t)$, $x_3(t)$, one locates points with coordinates (x_1, x_2, x_3) in three-dimensional space and traces the curve that is formed as t varies. In practice, this is hard to visualize, although sophisticated computer programs can be constructed to assist in visualization. If there are N variables with $N > 3$, then abstractly we may conceive of a point $(x_1, x_2, \ldots, x_N)$ with N coordinates, moving in an abstract "N-dimensional space." In practice, of course, this is of no help, and one often has recourse to the idea of looking at planar graphs of two variables at a time, such as the graph of x_1 versus x_2, the graph of x_1 versus x_3, the graph of x_2 versus x_3, and so on.

A third type of representation has been suggested by Herman and Montroll (1972) (also see Montroll and Badger 1974). Their method gives a plane diagram, simple to visualize, that represents a number of variables simultaneously. It is most readily applicable when the variables $x_1, x_2, \ldots, x_N$ are measured in the same unit. For example, x_j might represent the fraction of a total population engaged in the jth activity, or, alternatively, x_j could be the fraction of gross national product coming from the jth sector of the economy. Suppose, then, that each x_j is a number between 0 and 1 and that the sum of all the x_j terms is 1. Construct N rays emanating from the origin of a two-dimensional coordinate system, and separated by equal angles of $2\pi/N$. The length of the jth ray is chosen to be x_j. Now if the ends of the N successive rays are connected, the result is a polygon, or "snowflake." Herman and Montroll used this method to depict the proportion of the labor force in a country devoted to each of several sectors, such as agriculture, trade, manufacturing, and service. For example, if for a certain country the proportions are, respectively, 30, 15, 15, and 40%, we take $x_1 = .30$, $x_2 = .15$, $x_3 = .15$, and $x_4 = .40$. The resulting snowflake is shown in Figure 2.5. Different countries can be quickly compared by comparing their snowflakes. The same method can be used to show a comparison of different cultures, or of the distribution of artifacts at different sites. For example, one could draw a snowflake to represent the proportion of each type of pottery.

Furthermore, a distribution that is changing in time can be represented by drawing the snowflake for each successive time. Since this may be cumbersome if N is large, a simpler approximation has been suggested by Montroll and Badger. Instead of drawing the whole snowflake, we draw only its center of mass. Provided that we place x_1 at angle $2\pi/N$, x_2 at angle $4\pi/N$, and so on, this is the point whose x and y coordinates are as follows:

$$x = \frac{1}{N} \sum_{j=1}^{N} x_j \cos\left(\frac{2\pi j}{N}\right), \qquad y = \frac{1}{N} \sum_{j=1}^{N} x_j \sin\left(\frac{2\pi j}{N}\right)$$

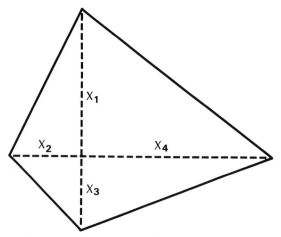

FIGURE 2.5 *Snowflake diagram.*

(*Warning:* The number x_j is the distance of the *j*th point from the origin, not the coordinate of the point.) The point (x, y) now partially indicates the nature of the distribution. However, the representation is only partial since different distributions could yield the same x and y values. By repeating this calculation for each successive time, we obtain a sequence of points (x, y), and when these are plotted on the same coordinate axes, we can visualize the changes that have occurred. For example for the data in Table 2.1, we find the respective centers of mass to be $(.0375, -.0625)$, $(0, -.025)$, and $(-.075, .025)$. These points are shown in Figure 2.6.

In cases in which N is large or there is a great deal of data, a computer could be used to perform the calculations and plot the points one after another on a display screen.

The same methods can be used to compare distributions (of the same attributes) at different geographical locations, by drawing a snowflake centered at each point. With a proper choice of scale, the snowflakes will not overlap and can be visually compared. As observed by Hodder and Orton (1976, Chapter 2), trends in spatial variation of the proportions may yield information about trade and exchange patterns.

TABLE 2.1

	Time t_1	Time t_2	Time t_3
x_1	.30	.20	.10
x_2	.15	.25	.30
x_3	.15	.20	.40
x_4	.40	.35	.20

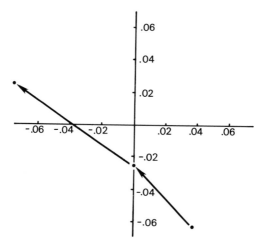

FIGURE 2.6 *Temporal evolution of a system depicted by changing center of mass of its snowflake.*

In the following section, we shall describe methods for constructing mathematical models of the complex interactions in a culture which result in the evolution of the culture. One way to test the efficacy of such models is to compare the snowflake diagrams that they produce with the snowflake diagrams drawn from real data.

Cultural Models and Dynamic Simulations

The study of the dynamics of large systems that contain complex inter-connections or feedbacks among the constituent parts—and certainly evolving cultures fit this description—is in the domain of "systems theory." It is assumed here that the reader is familiar with the basic ideas of systems theory (subsystems, feedback, homeostasis, etc.) as outlined, for example, by Clarke (1968). Many variations of this approach to socioeconomic systems have been proposed, many of these addressed to prediction or decision making in present-day societies. For example, there are large models of energy systems, urban systems, and even "world models." Our objective in this section is to sketch some methodologies which can perhaps be applied to the description of historical or archaeological data.

In any systems theoretic treatment, one must begin with a specific question or problem. There are then two aspects of the modeling process. First, one establishes the *structure* or arrangement of the elements or entities of the system. Second, the system is then studied by actuating the static structure in order to observe the system behavior. In order to describe the structure, two things are necessary. One must isolate or define the most important entities and the relations or processes that connect or alter these entities. Each entity is characterized by certain properties, which should be at least roughly quantifiable or should have distinguishable levels or states. These quantifiable properties are generally called variables since their values may fluctuate as time passes. Thus, one finally seeks to describe the system by a set of variables (functions of time t) that we denote by $x_1(t)\ x_2(t), \ldots, x_N(t)$, where N is the total number of variables to be considered. For example, in a model of a culture, some of the variables might denote levels of production of different products, some might refer to measures of social organization, some to belief systems within the culture, and so on. The problem of clarifying or identifying useful concepts in terms of which the variables can be defined is, of course, a formidable one for the model maker or social scientist. The supply and demand model in the first section is a simple small model in which the designated variables are the supply, the demand, and the price.

After one has chosen the variables, it is necessary to identify or to postulate the interactions among them. A convenient procedure in many cases is to think in terms of the influence that a certain variable may exert on certain other variables. For example, it may be decided that a high level of variable x_1 will, by some process, exert a pressure toward increase (or decrease) of variable x_2. Then, the rate of change of x_2 might, in the simple case of linear dependence, be given by the equation

$$\frac{dx_2}{dt} = ax_1 \qquad (2.18)$$

The more general case $dx_2/dt = a(x_1 - b)$, where b is a constant, can be reduced to (2.18) by a substitution of variables.

Equation (2.18) states that if x_1 is greater than 0, x_2 will increase (if a is positive) at a rate proportional to x_1, but if x_1 is less than 0, then x_2 will decrease at a rate proportional to x_1. More generally, all of the variables may influence the rate of change of x_2, so that the resulting equation takes the form

$$\frac{dx_2}{dt} = a_1x_1 + a_2x_2 + \cdots + a_Nx_N$$

Finally, similar equations may be assumed to be valid for the rates of change of all the variables, and the whole system will be described by a set of N differential equations. For the sake of typographic simplicity, we can take $N = 3$ and write

$$\frac{dx_1}{dt} = a_{11}x_1 + a_{12}x_2 + a_{13}x_3 \qquad (2.19)$$

$$\frac{dx_2}{dt} = a_{21}x_1 + a_{22}x_2 + a_{23}x_3$$

$$\frac{dx_3}{dt} = a_{31}x_1 + a_{32}x_2 + a_{33}x_3$$

Here, a symmetry of form has been achieved by using double subscripts. The number denoted a_{ij} (i,j = 1, 2, or 3) represents the strength of the influence of variable x_j on the rate of change of x_i. The system (2.19) can also be expressed more succinctly, using the mathematical summation notation, as follows:

$$\frac{dx_i}{dt} = \sum_{j=1}^{3} a_{ij}x_j \qquad (i = 1,2,3)$$

This form makes it easy to write the system for N variables, where N is arbitrary:

$$\frac{dx_i}{dt} = \sum_{j=1}^{N} a_{ij}x_j \qquad (i = 1, 2, ..., N) \tag{2.20}$$

It can be shown that the more general form

$$\frac{dy_i}{dt} = \sum_{j=1}^{N} a_{ij}(y_j - b_{ij})$$

can usually be transformed into the form (2.20) by a change of variables.

A similar formulation can be given in terms of difference equations rather than differential equations. In analogy to Equation (2.18) we might postulate that the change in x_2 during a time interval h is proportional to $x_1 - b$, and therefore obtain the equation

$$x_2(t + h) - x_2(t) = a[x_1(t) - b] \tag{2.21}$$

In analogy to Equation (2.19), we than have the following system of difference equations:

$$x_1(t + h) - x_1(t) = a_{11}x_1(t) + a_{12}x_2(t) + a_{13}x_3(t)$$
$$x_2(t + h) - x_2(t) = a_{21}x_1(t) + a_{22}x_2(t) + a_{23}x_3(t) \tag{2.22}$$
$$x_3(t + h) - x_3(t) = a_{31}x_1(t) + a_{32}x_2(t) + a_{33}x_3(t)$$

We can also write

$$x_1(t + h) = (1 + a_{11})x_1(t) + a_{12}x_2(t) + a_{13}x_3(t)$$
$$x_2(t + h) = a_{21}x_1(t) + (1 + a_{22})x_2(t) + a_{23}x_3(t)$$
$$x_3(t + h) = a_{31}x_1(t) + a_{32}x_2(t) + (1 + a_{33})x_3(t)$$

For notational convenience, we may as well replace $1 + a_{11}$, $1 + a_{22}$, and $1 + a_{33}$ by a_{11}, a_{22}, and a_{33}, respectively, and take the following form as the basic one to be used:

$$x_1(t + h) = a_{11}x_1(t) + a_{12}x_2(t) + a_{13}x_3(t)$$
$$x_2(t + h) = a_{21}x_1(t) + a_{22}x_2(t) + a_{23}x_3(t) \qquad (2.23)$$
$$x_3(t + h) = a_{31}x_1(t) + a_{32}x_2(t) + a_{32}x_3(t)$$

In summation notation, we have

$$x_i(t + h) = \sum_{j=1}^{N} a_{ij}x_j(t) \qquad (i = 1, 2, \ldots, N) \qquad (2.24)$$

In these difference equations, t takes on only discrete values $0, h, 2h, \ldots$. Such a formulation might be appropriate when data are available only at discrete times.

The equation sets (2.19) and (2.20) can be written in more compact form by noting that the coefficients can be conveniently displayed in a table, containing N rows and N columns, in which the entry in row i and column j is the strength coefficient a_{ij}. For example, for $N = 3$, this might appear as shown in Table 2.2.

TABLE 2.2

	x_1	x_2	x_3
x_1	a_{11}	a_{12}	a_{13}
x_2	a_{21}	a_{22}	a_{23}
x_3	a_{31}	a_{32}	a_{33}

Moreover, this suggests introducing the *matrix A*, which is the array of coefficients themselves. Thus, we write

$$A = \begin{pmatrix} a_{11} & a_{12} & a_{13} \\ a_{21} & a_{22} & a_{23} \\ a_{31} & a_{32} & a_{33} \end{pmatrix}$$

Furthermore, if we introduce the matrix

$$X = \begin{pmatrix} x_1 \\ x_2 \\ x_3 \end{pmatrix}$$

which consists of one column (often called a *column vector*), then the system (2.20) can be written in the compact symbolic form

$$\frac{dX}{dt} = AX \qquad (2.25)$$

Mathematicians, by defining the concept of multiplying two matrices, have in fact given this more than symbolic meaning. In a similar way, the system of difference equations (2.23) or (2.24) can be compactly written

$$X(t + h) = AX(t) \qquad (2.26)$$

The purpose of this discussion has been to show how the assumption that each variable may affect the rate of change of the others leads rather easily to sets of differential or difference equations. We want now to address the question of how the matrix A is determined and how such equations are solved or such models used. The method of *structural modeling* is one of the simplest and most qualitative modeling schemes. In this method, the time scale is discrete, and the model is equivalent to a set of difference equations of the form (2.22), (2.24), or (2.26). A large part of the modeling effort is directed toward determining the coefficients a_{ij} for the table, that is, the matrix A. Frequently, the coefficients a_{ij} are not assigned absolute values, but only relative values on some rough scale, because of the difficulty of precise quantification of variables in the social system. So, for example, their values might be restricted to be $+1$, -1, or 0, according as the influence is judged to be either favoring increase, favoring decrease, or of negligible effect, respectively. On a slightly more refined scale, they might be restricted to 2, 1, 0, -1, -2. Chapter 13 by Gérardin in this volume describes how appropriate variables might be chosen and values for the coefficients a_{ij} estimated via consultations with experts and contenders in the social process. His chapter gives a number of additional references.

The information in Table 2.2 can also be put in useful graphical form. Represent each variable by a small circle or dot, labeled with the symbol for the variable. For each nonzero entry a_{ij}, draw a line or arc from the circle for x_j to the one for x_i, and place the number a_{ij} beside the arc. In this way, the fact that x_j acts to change x_i is shown. For example, for Table 2.3, we obtain

TABLE 2.3

	x_1	x_2	x_3
x_1	0	1	-1
x_2	-1	1	1
x_3	-1	0	0

Figure 2.7. Such a figure is called by mathematicians a *weighted digraph* (or *directed graph*).

After the table of influences has been constructed (the structure determined), one starts with known or hypothesized values of the variables at a fixed time (called $t = 0$), and then generates successive values by means of Equation (2.24). In this way, the "behavior" or time trajectory of the model is found. Structural modeling also permits the inclusion of time delays or "viscosities" in the action of one variable on another. In any case, the result is equivalent mathematically to a system of linear difference equations with constant coefficients. The objective is to determine the relative direction and magnitude of change of the variables. The method is simple to use, and in graphical and tabular form its meaning is clear to nonmathematically inclined persons. For further details, see Chapter 13 by Gĕrardin, this volume.

Since Equations (2.20) and (2.24) are linear, well-known mathematical theories exist for determining the solutions, although the calculations can become lengthy if N is large. The long-term behavior of any solution is essentially exponential—either exponential growth or exponential decay. Let us briefly outline the nature of solutions for (2.20) or (2.25). As expected, this depends entirely on properties of the matrix A. Associated with each matrix A is an algebraic equation of degree N in one unknown, typically called λ. The coefficients in this *characteristic equation* can be determined directly from A. If each root (solution) of this characteristic equation is a negative number or a complex number with a negative real part (i.e., $\lambda = c$

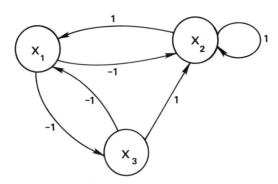

FIGURE 2.7 *Weighted digraph.*

$+ id$ with $c < 0$, $i = \sqrt{-1}$), the matrix A is called *stable*. If each root is negative or zero or is a complex number with zero or a negative real part, then the matrix A is called *semistable*. It is known that if A is stable, then every solution of Equation (2.25) decays exponentially to 0 as t tends to ∞. If A is merely semistable, the situation is more complicated to describe. If A is not even semistable, then at least some solutions grow exponentially (possibly with oscillating sign). See Brauer and co-workers (1970) for further discussion, and Goldberg (1958) for similar considerations for difference equations. Careful mathematical analysis of the method of structural modeling and of weighted digraphs can be found in Roberts (1976), Roberts and Brown (1975), and MacDonald (n.d.).

As we have suggested earlier, in our applications the numbers a_{ij} making up the matrix A may only be known qualitatively or approximately. Often, one is fairly confident of the sign of each a_{ij} but not of its magnitude. It is therefore interesting to ask whether the stability of the system depends only on the sign pattern of the matrix. Let us say that two matrices A and B have the same sign pattern if a_{ij} and b_{ij} have the same sign for all i,j (if $a_{ij} = 0$, then b_{ij} must equal zero). Now call a matrix A *sign stable* (respectively, *sign semistable*) if every matrix B with the same sign pattern is stable (respectively, semistable). Complete characterizations of the matrices that are sign stable or sign semistable have been found (see Maybee and Quirk 1969; Jeffries, Klee and Van den Driessche 1977; Klee and Van den Driessche 1977). Unfortunately, these conditions appear to rule out many situations that one might expect to encounter in modeling, and there appears to be need for mathematical analysis under a more relaxed definition of sign stability.

There are several ways to build models which avoid the limitation of linearity. We have already used the nonlinear logistic equation as a model in the section on differential equations. One possibility is to use the structural modeling approach but to build in mechanisms for changing some of the numbers a_{ij} in a predetermined way when the variables pass designated thresholds. For example, it might be decided that a_{12} should be $+1$ until x_1 reaches a value of 5, and that a_{12} should then be changed to 0. Another method of introducing nonlinearity is described in Chapter 14 by Cooke and Renfrew in this volume. The work of Forrester (1968, 1969, 1971) provides great flexibility in modeling interactions or influences by functional relations of arbitrary form. His formulation is equivalent to a system of differential or difference equations in which the expressions need no longer be linear. Thus, for example, for $N = 3$ the system may have the form

$$\frac{dx_1}{dt} = f_1(x_1, x_2, x_3) \tag{2.27}$$

$$\frac{dx_2}{dt} = f_2(x_1, x_2, x_3)$$

$$\frac{dx_3}{dt} = f_3(x_1, x_2, x_3)$$

in which f_1, f_2, and f_3 may be any designated functions of the variables. Forrester has built up a conceptual system which makes it relatively easy to build specific forms of the functions (perhaps expressed via tables rather than algebraic formulas) to fit particular situations.

With nonlinear systems in several variables such as (2.27), it is generally impossible to produce an exact mathematical solution. Even for the relatively simple model of competition with two variables in the section on stability and qualitative behavior, we found it expedient to use the graphical tools of phase plane analysis. What, then, can be done? One of the standard methods is to search for *equilibrium solutions,* that is, solutions that are not time dependent. Such solutions, if any exist, are constants and will have zero derivatives and must therefore satisfy the equations

$$f_1(x_1, x_2, x_3) = 0, \qquad f_2(x_1, x_2, x_3) = 0, \qquad f_3(x_1, x_2, x_3) = 0 \quad (2.28)$$

This method was used in the section on stability and qualitative behavior to derive Equation (2.13). However, as we saw there, an equilibrium point (x_1, x_2, x_3) is sometimes stable and sometimes not. A standard method of determining this stability question is to "linearize the system near the equilibrium point." See Brauer, Nohel, and Schneider (1970) for a discussion of how this is done. In brief, there is a linear system of the form (2.25) which provides the answer. For this reason, the discussion of linear systems is very important. They provide good approximations for the way that most nonlinear systems behave *near equilibrium.* On the other hand, they provide little information about solutions that do not stay near an equilibrium.

As we have hinted in the section on stability and qualitative behavior, more advanced methods sometimes provide very useful information of other kinds. Often, however, mathematical analysis is inadequate, and one must use methods of numerical analysis to replace (2.27) by a system of approximating difference equations. An approximate solution can then be generated with the aid of a digital computer, starting from any known or assumed initial values of the variables at a designated starting time and continuing to as large a value of t as is feasible. Furthermore, because of the speed and accuracy of modern computers, it is often feasible to do this for many variations of the assumed system structure. In other words, it is possible to *simulate* the real system with a mathematical model and then to trace out the behavior predicted by the model under varying conditions.

As examples of the use of simulation models in archaeology, we mention the work of Zubrow (1975) on prehistoric carrying capacity and of Thomas (1972) on subsistence and settlement patterns. In the latter, the objective is not to simulate the long-term changes in a society, but rather the cyclic seasonal variations in a stable pattern of hunter–gatherer subsistence. Many examples of simulation studies in a variety of fields, and papers on the methodology of simulation, can be found in the journal *Simulation*.

Randomness and Stochastic Processes

The models considered in the preceding sections have been deterministic. That is, given the values of the variables at a specified time, their values are precisely and completely determined at subsequent times by the postulated mechanisms (i.e., by the equations). In applications, however, one rarely has sufficient knowledge to specify all factors in such a complete way. For example, some of the variables in a model may represent fluctuating environmental or exogenous factors such as climate, which cannot, at the present stage of science, be specified in a deterministic way. Consequently, these are regarded as random events. Models that incorporate randomness or probabilistic considerations are called *stochastic models*.

The mathematical theory underlying the treatment of random or probabilistic events is large and deep. Here, assuming only a knowledge of the most elementary notions of probability and of matrix algebra on the part of the reader, we shall give a brief introduction to the concepts of Markov chains and stochastic processes. Suppose that a system is such that at any moment it can occupy one of a number of "states." For example, the weather at a given time and place could be classified as clear, cloudy, or raining (or into a larger number of specified states if so desired). The collection of possible states is called the *state space*. Suppose that over the course of time, the system changes from one state to another. Further suppose that we cannot predict the changes in a deterministic way, but can give probabilities for each of the possible changes of state. We then refer to the system or process as a *stochastic process*. A *Markov chain* is a special type of process with these properties: (*a*) there is a discrete state space; and (*b*) the probability of transition from one state to another depends only on the present state (i.e., on the state currently occupied and about to be left). The second condition is the "Markov property" and it means that the probability of being in state j at a future point in time depends only on the state you are currently in and is independent of the path that led to the current state.

In order to put these ideas in mathematical form, let us suppose that there are k possible states, which we label as states $1, 2, ..., k$. We then let p_{ij} denote the *probability of transition* from state i to state j during one unit of time. The *transition matrix* is the matrix

$$P = \begin{pmatrix} p_{11} & p_{12} & \cdots & p_{1k} \\ p_{21} & p_{22} & \cdots & p_{2k} \\ \vdots & \vdots & \vdots & \vdots \\ p_{k1} & p_{k2} & \cdots & p_{kk} \end{pmatrix}$$

(This may remind the reader of the interaction matrix discussed in the preceding section, but the interpretation is quite different.) Thomas (1972) has modeled the harvesting of piñon nuts by Shoshone Indians using such a transition matrix. He considers three states: good harvest, fair harvest, and failure of harvest. If these are taken as states 1, 2, and 3, respectively, the matrix

$$P = \begin{pmatrix} .08 & .07 & .85 \\ .09 & .11 & .80 \\ .12 & .05 & .83 \end{pmatrix}$$

would indicate that the probability of having a good year followed by a good year is .08, of having a good year followed by a failure is .85, of a fair year followed by a good year is .09, and so on. The idea can be illustrated by a *transition diagram* in which each state is indicated by a dot or circle, and each possible transition is indicated by a directed arc. The numbers p_{ij} can be entered beside the corresponding arc. Figure 2.8 is the transition diagram that represents this matrix.

Not every matrix is the transition probability matrix of a Markov chain. In fact, the sum of all the entries in one row of such a matrix, say row number i, is the sum of the probabilities of passing from state i to every possible state j. Since it is certain that the system must pass to exactly one state (perhaps state i itself), this sum must be exactly 1, by elementary principles of probability. Also, of course, each entry p_{ij} must be a number

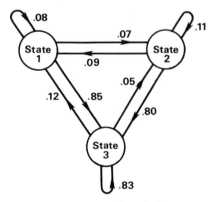

FIGURE 2.8 *Transition diagram of a Markov chain.*

between 0 and 1, inclusive. In fact, a matrix P is suitable as a transition matrix when, and only when, all its entries are numbers between 0 and 1 and the sum of the entries in each row is 1.

The evolution of a system may now be described in the following terms. Suppose that at some initial time $t = 0$, we know the state of the system. After one unit of time, or one step, the system may have moved to another state, and the matrix P enables us to tell the probability of its being in each state. After two steps, there are certain (different) probabilities of being in each state. Although we cannot say with certainty what the state will be after 1, 2, or n steps, we can, as we shall see, determine the probability of being in each of the states. In order to see how this is done, we take $k = 3$ for simplicity and let z_1, z_2, z_3 be the respective probabilities that the system is in states 1, 2, 3 at time zero. (If we know the state of the system exactly at time zero, we take 1 to be the probability it was in that state and 0 for the probabilities of being in the other states.) Of course, z_1, z_2, and z_3 must be numbers between 0 and 1 and their sum must be 1. We form the matrix or row vector

$$z = (z_1 \quad z_2 \quad z_3)$$

A vector of this type, with entries $0 \le z_i \le 1$ whose sum is 1, is called a *probability vector*.

Now observe that $z_1 p_{11}$ is the probability that we started in state 1 and made transition to state 1, $z_2 p_{21}$ the probability that we started in state 2 and made transition to state 1, and $z_3 p_{31}$ the probability that we started in state 3 and made transition to state 1. Thus, $z_1 p_{11} + z_2 p_{21} + z_3 p_{31}$ is the probability that after one step the system is in state 1. Similarly, $z_1 p_{12} + z_2 p_{22} + z_3 p_{32}$ is the probability of being in state 2 after one step, and $z_1 p_{13} + z_3 p_{23} + z_3 p_{33}$ the probability of being in state 3. In terms of matrix multiplication, this may be expressed by saying that

$$(z_1 \quad z_2 \quad z_3)P$$

is the row vector that gives the probabilities of being in each of the three states after one unit of time.

More generally, the following is true. Let $Z_0 = (z_1 \, z_2 \, \cdots \, z_k)$ be the vector of probabilities of being in each of the k states at time zero, and let Z_n be the vector of probabilities of being in the various states after n time steps $(n = 1, 2, ...)$. Then

$$Z_1 = Z_0 P, \qquad Z_2 = Z_0 P^2, \qquad ..., \qquad Z_n = Z_0 P^n \qquad (2.29)$$

where P^n denotes the nth power of the transition matrix P. This result makes it easy to compute the probability vectors Z_n for many time steps. Of course, if k is large, use of a computer for such a calculation is desirable. The matrix P^n is called the *n-step transition matrix*. The product of Z_0 and P^n provides the probabilities that the system will fall into each of the states after n transitions or steps, given the starting probabilities Z_0.

In certain cases, a Markov chain has a kind of stabilizing property, in the sense that the vectors Z_n will approach a limiting vector as n gets large. That this does not always happen can be seen from the example

$$P = \begin{pmatrix} 0 & 1 \\ 1 & 0 \end{pmatrix}, \qquad Z_0 = (1 \quad 0)$$

The reader can verify that

$$Z_1 = Z_3 = Z_5 = \cdots = (0 \quad 1)$$
$$Z_0 = Z_2 = Z_4 = Z_6 = \cdots = (1 \quad 0)$$

In this example, the state alternates between $(1 \quad 0)$ and $(0 \quad 1)$ indefinitely. On the other hand, let us say that a transition matrix P is *regular* if some integer power of P has all positive entries. For example, the matrix

$$P = \begin{pmatrix} 0 & 1 \\ .4 & .6 \end{pmatrix}$$

is regular since P^2 has positive elements. It can be proved that a regular transition matrix has the following properties.

1. There is a unique probability vector $X = (x_1 \, x_2 \cdots x_k)$ which has the property that $XP = X$. The components of X are all positive.
2. The sequence of matrices P, P^2, P^3, ..., P^n, ... tends to the matrix Q in which each row is the vector X.
3. If Z_0 is any probability vector, the sequence of vectors Z_0P, Z_0P^2, ..., Z_0P^n, ... tends to the vector X.

As a simple example, consider the transition matrix

$$P = \begin{pmatrix} \frac{3}{4} & \frac{1}{4} \\ \frac{1}{2} & \frac{1}{2} \end{pmatrix}$$

Since P is regular, there must be a vector $X = (x_1 \, x_2)$ such that $XP = X$. Since

$$XP = (x_1 \quad x_2) \begin{pmatrix} \frac{3}{4} & \frac{1}{4} \\ \frac{1}{2} & \frac{1}{2} \end{pmatrix} = (\tfrac{3}{4}x_1 + \tfrac{1}{2}x_2, \; \tfrac{1}{4}x_1 + \tfrac{1}{2}x_2)$$

the equation $XP = X$ is equivalent to the linear equations

$$\tfrac{3}{4}x_1 + \tfrac{1}{2}x_2 = x_1, \qquad \tfrac{1}{4}x_1 + \tfrac{1}{2}x_2 = x_2$$

or

$$-\tfrac{1}{4}x_1 + \tfrac{1}{2}x_2 = 0, \qquad \tfrac{1}{4}x_1 - \tfrac{1}{2}x_2 = 0$$

In addition, since X is a probability vector, $x_1 + x_2 = 1$. The sole solution of these equations is $x_1 = \tfrac{2}{3}$, $x_2 = \tfrac{1}{3}$. Thus $X = (\tfrac{2}{3} \quad \tfrac{1}{3})$. According to property 3, for any initial probability vector X_0, the vector $Z_0 P^n$ will be approximately equal to X for large values of n. For example, for $Z_0 = (1 \quad 0)$ the reader can verify that the successive values are $Z_0 P = (.75, .25)$, $Z_0 P^2 = (.6875, .3125)$, $Z_0 P^3 = (.6719, .3281)$, ...

The vector X represents an *equilibrium probability distribution* for the regular Markov chain. After a large number of transitions, there are well-defined probabilities x_1, x_2, ..., x_k that the system will be in the various states, and these are independent of the initial state of the system. Therefore, although we cannot predict what state the system will occupy at given times, we can predict the approximate proportion of time that it will spend in each state.

For a more thorough but elementary discussion of Markov chains, one can refer to any of a number of texts on "finite mathematics." The book by Kemeny and Snell (1960) is a thorough reference on theory, with representative applications. The book by Bartholomew (1973) contains a large number of applications in the social sciences, as well as a discussion of other types of stochastic processes.

Other kinds of stochastic processes have already been applied to the study of the distribution of settlements, as in Chapter 10 by Chadwick in this volume. Chadwick's basic assumption is that at the macro level, the place chosen for a new settlement can be regarded as random, since it depends on a large number of decisions taken at the micro level and on a large number of influences. In Chadwick's model I, the simulation started with a known distribution of settlements in Messenia in the Middle Helladic period. The region was then divided into a cell grid and an "environment surface" generated to reflect the desirability of individual cells as settlement sites. Then, 75 new sites were selected randomly and results compared with the actual settlement distribution in the Late Helladic period. Various features were added by Chadwick in subsequent versions of the model, representing, for example, the need for settlements to be spaced out from one another in order to have sufficient land, and in this way the effect of each such additional feature was examined. The dominant mode in these models is that of filling in empty sites, but other models can be based on "budding off" of new settlements from existing places.

Many other types of stochastic processes are potentially applicable to the description of social and historical processes working through time. Among these are *branching processes* (Harris 1963), *diffusion processes,* and *percolation processes* (Frisch and Hammersley 1963). Since lack of space prevents even a cursory description of all of these, we shall be content with a brief outline of the simplest stochastic model for the diffusion of an item of information or of an innovation throughout a population. In this model, there is a population of N units, which we shall call people, although in some applications these could be groups of people such as families or craft groups in different localities. Suppose that one person of the N becomes aware of a new piece of information, and then spreads the information to others. Persons who receive the information may become "spreaders" in their turn, and the process of diffusion continues until all N persons have received the information or until transmission ceases. Whether or not a person hears the news depends on the chance event of his coming in contact with someone already possessing the news, and on the probability that he is in a receptive frame of mind. Consequently, a probabilistic model is called for. Suppose that we let $n(t)$ denote the number of persons who have heard the news up to time t. In the simplest model, we assume that in any time interval Δt there is a probability $\alpha \Delta t$ of transmission of the news to any individual from a central source (such as a central authority or central place), and that there is a probability $\beta \Delta t$ of transmission between individuals. The latter is assumed to be the same for all pairs of individuals, implying that the population is homogeneously mixing. Now if there are n persons who have heard the news at time t, then there are $N - n$ who can first hear the news during the time from t to $t + \Delta t$. The probability of a new hearer from the central source is therefore $\alpha(N - n)\Delta t$. The probability of transmission between individuals is $\beta n(N - n)\Delta t$, since of all the possible pairs of persons there are $n(N - n)$ pairs which consist of one person who knows the information and one who does not. Combining these results, we find that the probability that the number of knowers increases from n to $n + 1$ during time Δt is

$$(N - n)(\alpha + \beta n) \, \Delta t$$

This model was proposed by Taga and Isii (1959), but is almost identical with the so-called simple epidemic model described by Bailey (1975). For this process, it is possible to give an explicit formula for the probability that $n(t)$ has any specified value, but a better understanding is perhaps achieved by examining the mean value $\bar{n}(t)$, or expected number of persons who have heard the news up to time t. For further details and extensions, see Bartholomew (1973, Chapters 9, 10). Among the extensions considered are some in which spatial dependence is considered, including the well-known work of Hägerstrand (1967).

It seems likely to the author that models of diffusion and percolation can be fruitfully applied to temporal and spatial patterns of settlement, trade, and exchange of information. Much remains to be done in this direction.

Another way to incorporate randomness in the mathematical description of change is provided by the theory of stochastic difference equations. An elementary introduction is provided in the mimeographed manuscript of Cobb (1976).

Optimization and the Mathematical Theory of Games

An important aspect of human cultural systems is their orientation toward achieving goals. To achieve these goals, societies devise organizations, behavioral strategies, and methods for making decisions. Various mathematical theories have been proposed to provide a framework for analyzing phenomena of this sort. Generally, these may be called *prescriptive* or *optimization* models, in contrast to *descriptive* or *predictive* models. In this section, we shall comment very briefly on some of the available mathematical formulations, in the hope that some may prove useful in modeling in archaeology.

Mathematical programming is the name given to the mathematical theory of how to allocate limited resources among different activities in an optimal way. In the special case in which all the mathematical functions are linear functions of their variables, the theory is known as *linear programming*. Since Chapter 16 by Keene in this volume contains an excellent introduction to linear programming, we shall merely list a few important aspects of the method. First, a well-defined goal must be specified, although in cultural modeling, it may not be easy to determine what optimization principle is operating, if any. Do some cultures optimize stability? resiliency? adaptiveness? strength vis-à-vis neighbors? In any case, in order to apply the mathematical theory, the goal must be defined as maximizing or minimizing (*optimizing*) a specified function of the variables, called the *objective function* or *cost function*. The choice of values for the variables in order to achieve the optimum is *constrained* by the availability of the various resources. In this theory, a single decision maker makes the allocation or choice of resources in a centralized way, and there is a single objective function. For example, in Chapter 16, the decision is assumed to be made by the hunter–gatherer group as a unit, and a single objective function is built up that combines considerations of search time, pursuit time, and risk. Linear programming is essentially static rather than dynamic, although, as Keene points out, various dynamic inferences can be drawn from the post-optimal analysis.

Dynamic programming (Bellman 1957; Dreyfus and Law 1977) is a theory of optimization under dynamic rather than static conditions. The essential feature of dynamic programming is that the process is envisioned as proceeding in a sequence of *stages*. At each stage, a decision is made as to the allocation of resources for this stage, based on the current state of the system. The goal is to optimize the performance over a specified period of time or number of stages. Thus, the problem is optimization in a *multistage decision process*. For example, the problem treated by Keene could be interpreted in this way, with successive months representing the successive stages. Dynamic programming introduces a dynamic element and permits decisions to be made on the basis of a current assessment of the situation at each stage. It also turns out to be fairly easy to introduce some chance or stochastic aspects. The theory presumes that there is a single decision maker and a single objective function.

The mathematical *theory of games* is another method for the study of decision making. In the theory of optimization as described earlier, there is a single decision maker who is trying to achieve a specified goal, in the face of specified constraints. In contrast, game theory applies to situations in which two or more individuals or groups are striving to achieve separate or antagonistic goals by conflict, cooperation, or both. Each individual must adjust his plans not only to his own goal and ability but also to the goals and capacities of others. The mathematical theory has been called game theory because certain games, such as poker and bridge, fit into this context, but the theory has been widely applied to conflict and bargaining situations of a military, economic, and political kind. Much of the terminology has been taken over from that used in games in the ordinary sense. Thus, the decision makers are called *players*, the rewards or values assigned to the outcomes are called *payoffs*, and the specifications of information available to the players, and the resources under the control of each player, are called the *rules* of the game.

In this section, some of the fundamental ideas of game theory are described, and references to applications in the social and behavioral sciences are given. One of the important basic concepts is that of a *game tree*. This is a type of mathematical graph in which the points or vertices represent choice points, and the lines or branches indicate alternatives. As a simple example, consider two players who are matching pennies. Player 1 chooses "heads" (H) or "tails" (T). Player 2, not knowing player 1's choice, also chooses "heads" or "tails." If the two players make the same choice, player 2 wins a penny from player 1, but if their choices are different, player 1 wins a penny from player 2. The game tree is shown in Figure 2.9. The bottom vertex, labeled $P1$, indicates that player 1 makes the first choice, and the two branches above $P1$ show these choices as H or T. On the next level up, player 2 makes the choice and the two vertices are labeled $P2$. Above each vertex $P2$ are two branches, H and T, for the two possible choices of player 2. Since the game terminates at this point, there are no more vertices or

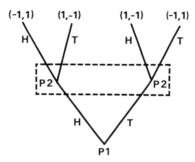

FIGURE 2.9 *Game tree of the game of matching pennies.*

branches. As can be seen, there are four paths from the bottom vertex to a topmost or terminal vertex, representing the four possible plays of the game. For each of these, the payoff to the two players is indicated. Thus if both players choose *H*, the payoff (−1, 1) means that player 1 loses one penny and player 2 gains one. If player 1 chooses *H* and player 2 chooses *T*, the play terminates at a point marked (1, −1), indicating that player 1 gains one penny and player 2 loses one.

When a game is depicted in this way by its game tree, it is said to be a game in *extensive form*. If a player always knows the actual choices made by all players who have already moved, then the game is called a game of *perfect information*. In such a game, a player who is about to move knows exactly to which branch point on the game tree the game has progressed. If this is not the case, the player will not know the exact branch point but only a set of possible branch points, called his *information set*. For example, in the game of matching pennies, player 2 does not know the initial choice made by player 1. Therefore, on the game tree, player 2's information set contains the pair of vertices labeled *P*2. This is indicated on Figure 2.9 by the dashed box enclosing these vertices.

It should be noted that in the game of matching pennies, it does not matter whether the players make their choices sequentially as described, or simultaneously, since in either case each player is ignorant of the choice of the other. However, if the game is played with perfect information, then clearly the second player will always win. In political and social applications, the situation often involves the sequencing of moves when there is partial information and the possibility of bluffing, bargaining, and so on.

A very important concept in the theory of games is that of a *strategy*. A strategy for a player may be thought of as a list indicating what choice he will make for every possible position in which he may find himself during the game. That is, for every one of his information sets, it must assign a branch to follow from any vertex in the information set. For example, in the matching game, player 2's strategy might be to follow the left branch (heads). His only other possible strategy is to follow the right branch (tails).

Once all players have chosen a strategy, play of the game is completely determined, provided there is no chance element in the game. A strategy, by definition, requires foreseeing all possible situations that may arise in the course of the game. In practice, a player usually chooses his moves at most a few moves in advance, since in all but the simplest games or situations the number of possible choices is too great to plan for every contingency. From a theoretical point of view, however, we can overlook this restriction.

The game of matching pennies is a two-person *zero-sum game*. By this is meant that for each outcome of the game, the sum of the payoffs to the players is zero. In other words, what one player wins the other player must lose. The theory of these games is very complete mathematically, and is facilitated by representing the games in a different form called the *normal form*. In this representation, one forms a matrix in which there are as many rows as there are strategies available to player 1, and as many columns as there are strategies available to player 2. The entry in position ij in the matrix contains the payoff to player 1 if he uses strategy i and player 2 uses strategy j. For a zero-sum game, it is unnecessary to give also the payoff to player 2, which is the negative of the payoff to player 1. For the game of matching pennies, the matrix is

$$
\begin{array}{cc}
 & \text{Player 2} \\
 & \begin{array}{cc} H & T \end{array} \\
\text{Player 1} \quad \begin{array}{c} H \\ T \end{array} & \left|\begin{array}{cc} -1 & 1 \\ 1 & -1 \end{array}\right.
\end{array}
$$

The most important theorem of the theory of two-person zero-sum games asserts that in every such game there exists a pair of strategies for the two players that are *in equilibrium*. (The notion of strategy has to be somewhat generalized from what has just been described in order for this to be true.) This means that if one player chooses such a strategy, then the other cannot do better than to choose his strategy from the equilibrium pair. There is a stability about strategies in equilibrium, for if player 2 knows that player 1 is employing such a strategy, there is no reason for player 2 to deviate from the equilibrium strategy.

Chess is an example of a two-person zero-sum game, and as such the result just described must hold. Of course, the number of strategies available to the players in chess, and in many other real games and conflict situations, is so great as to preclude actually listing all the strategies or finding best strategies. The theory of games is of little use in finding effective or best strategies. Rather, its principal value has so far been in leading to the classification of games, and the invention of precisely defined concepts in terms of which to analyze the structure of the games.

For two-person nonconstant sum games, the situation becomes more complex. It turns out that although there are still equilibrium strategies, it is possible in some cases that both players can obtain larger payoffs with strategies that are not in equilibrium. This requires that the players choose their strategies jointly, and therefore that they reach an agreement to do so. Moreover, there may be several favorable choices, some more favorable to one player and some to the other. Consequently, bargaining over the choice is necessary. Thus, the theory turns away from the study of "best" solutions or strategies to the study of what constitutes rational choice in such circumstances.

Still more complicated issues are raised in the study of *n-person games,* either constant sum or nonconstant sum. It becomes fruitful to concentrate attention on the possible coalitions that may form, if any are permitted. It is impossible here to give more details. The reader may refer to books on "finite mathematics" for more explanation at an elementary level, and to the books by Luce and Raiffa (1957), Owen (1968), Rapoport (1970), and Shubik (1964) for more complete information, examples, and references. The book by Buchler and Nutini (1969) contains interesting applications in the social sciences. The articles by Lucas (1971, 1972) survey recent advances.

Concepts from game theory may be useful in analyzing situations of political and economic conflict and change in early societies. Indeed, work has already been done on questions of voting power in legislatures, political equilibrium, guerrilla and tribal warfare, foreign policy, and so forth. The article by Southwold (1968), building on the theory of Riker (1962), attempts to describe struggles for the kingship in the African kingdom of Buganda in terms of *n*-person game theory. The theory leads, at least, to interesting observations about the intervals between rebellions, the amount of political information available to contestants for the throne, and the tendencies under some circumstances toward secession of tribes. The article by Taylor (1971) surveys mathematical political theory.

In conclusion, it should be pointed out that the mathematical literature contains discussions of other varieties of games. For example, the book by Owen describes games played in stages, and games with stochastic elements.

Acknowledgments

I wish to express my deep appreciation to Richard Bellman for his stimulation and encouragement of my attempts to bring mathematical thinking to bear on the problems of culture change.

The following have kindly written to signify their approval of reference to their work: Elliott W. Montroll and Gordon and Breach (publishers) for material on snowflake diagrams; Associated Book Publishers Ltd. and Methuen & Co. Ltd. for permission to extract from the article by D. H. Thomas (1972).

References

Bailey N. T. J., 1975, *The Mathematical Theory of Infectious Diseases,* Second edition, New York, Hafner.

Bartholomew D. J., 1973, *Stochastic Models for Social Processes,* Second edition, London, John Wiley and Sons.

Bellman R., 1957, *Dynamic Programming,* Princeton, University Press.

Bellman R. and Cooke K. L., 1963, *Differential-Difference Equations,* New York - London, Academic Press.

Brauer F., Nohel J. A., and Schneider H., 1970, *Linear Mathematics,* New York, W. A. Benjamin.

Braun M., 1975, *Differential Equations and Their Applications,* Applied Mathematical Sciences Vol. 15, New York - Heidelberg - Berlin, Springer-Verlag.

Buchler I. R., and Nutini H. G. (eds.), 1968, *Game Theory in the Behavioral Sciences,* Pittsburgh, University Press.

Clarke D. L., 1968, *Analytical Archaeology,* London, Methuen.

Cobb L., 1976, Stochastic Difference Equations with Sociological Applications, *Modules in Applied Mathematics,* Washington, Mathematical Association of America.

Cooke K. L. and Freedman H. I., A Model for the Adoption of a Technological Innovation, in preparation.

Dreyfus S. E. and Law A. M., 1977, *The Art and Theory of Dynamic Programming,* New York, Academic Press.

Driver R. D., 1977, *Ordinary and Delay Differential Equations,* Applied Mathematical Sciences, Vol. 20, New York - Heidelberg - Berlin, Springer-Verlag.

Fisher J. C. and Pry R. H., 1971, A Simple Substitution Model of Technological Change, in Cetron M. J. and Ralph C. A. (eds.), *Industrial Applications of Technological Forecasting,* New York, Wiley-Interscience.

Forrester J. W., 1968, *Principles of Systems,* Cambridge, Mass., Wright-Allen.

Forrester J. W., 1969, *Urban Dynamics,* Cambridge, Mass., The M.I.T. Press.

Forrester J. W., 1971, *World Dynamics,* Cambridge, Mass., Wright-Allen.

Frisch H. L. and Hammersley J. M., 1963, Percolation Processes and Related Topics, *Journal Soc. Indust. Appl. Math.* 11, 894–918.

Gandolfo G., 1971, *Mathematical Methods and Models in Economic Dynamics,* Amsterdam - London, North-Holland.

Goldberg S., 1958, *Introduction to Difference Equations,* New York, John Wiley.

Hägerstrand T., 1967, *Innovation Diffusion as a Spatial Process,* translation by A. Pred, Chicago and London, University of Chicago Press.

Harris T. E., 1963, *The Theory of Branching Processes,* Berlin - Gottingen - Heidelberg, Springer-Verlag.

Herman R. and Montroll E. W., 1972, A Manner of Characterizing the Development of Countries, *Proc. Nat. Acad. Sci. U.S.A.* 69, 3019–3020.

Hodder I. and Orton C., 1976, *Spatial Analysis in Archaeology,* Cambridge, University Press.

Jeffries, C., Klee V. and Van den Driessche P., 1977, When Is a Matrix Sign Stable?, *Canadian J. Math.* 29, 315–326.

Kemeny J. G. and Snell J. L., 1960, *Finite Markov Chains,* Princeton, New Jersey, Van Nostrand.

Klee V. and Van den Driessche P., 1977, Linear Algorithms for Testing the Sign Stability of a Matrix and for Finding Z-Maximum Matchings in Acyclic Graphs, *Numerische Mathematik* 28, 273–285.

Lucas W. F., 1971, Some Recent Developments in N-Person Game Theory, *SIAM Review* 13, 491–523.

Lucas W. F., 1972, An Overview of the Mathematical Theory of Games, *Management Science* 18, 3–19.

Luce R. and Raiffa H., 1957, *Games and Decisions: Introduction and Critical Survey*, New York, John Wiley.

MacDonald N., Time Lag in Systems Described by Difference or Differential Equations, *Int. J. Systems Science*, to appear.

Maybee J. and Quirk J., 1969, Qualitative Problems in Matrix Theory, *SIAM Review* 11, 30–51.

Montroll E. W. and Badger W. W., 1974, *Introduction to Quantitative Aspects of Social Phenomena*, New York - London - Paris, Gordon and Breach.

Owen G., 1968, *Game Theory*, Philadelphia, W. B. Saunders.

Rapoport A., 1970, *N-Person Game Theory: Concepts and Applications*, Ann Arbor, University of Michigan Press.

Rescigno A. and Richardson I. W., 1973, The Deterministic Theory of Population Dynamics, in Rosen, R. (ed.), *Foundations of Mathematical Biology*, Vol. III, New York, Academic Press, 283–360.

Riker W. H., 1962, *The Theory of Political Coalitions*, New Haven, Yale University Press.

Roberts F. S., 1976, *Discrete Mathematical Models*, Englewood Cliffs, New Jersey, Prentice-Hall.

Roberts F. S. and Brown T. A., 1975, Signed Digraphs and the Energy Crisis, *Amer. Math. Monthly* 82, 577–593.

Shubik M. (ed.), 1964, *Game Theory and Related Approaches to Social Behavior*, New York, John Wiley.

Smith J. Maynard, 1974, *Models in Ecology*, Cambridge, University Press.

Southwold M., 1968, A Games Model of African Tribal Politics, in Buchler and Nutini, 1968.

Taga Y. and Isii K., 1959, On a Stochastic Model Concerning the Pattern of Communication-diffusion of News in a Social Group, *Ann. Inst. Statist. Math.* 11, 25–43.

Taylor M., 1971, Review Article: Mathematical Political Theory, *British Journal of Political Science* 1, 339–382.

Thomas D. H., 1972, A Computer Simulation Model of Great Basin Shoshonean Subsistence and Settlement Patterns, in Clarke D. L. (ed.), *Models in Archaeology*, London, Methuen.

Zubrow E. B. W., 1975, *Prehistoric Carrying Capacity: A Model*, Menlo Park, California, Cummins.

3

RICHARD BELLMAN

Mathematics in the Field of History

Introduction

Galileo asserted that the language of science was mathematics, a dictum well substantiated over the intervening years. The outstanding success of this methodology in the physical sciences has held out the hope for many years that a number of aspects of human affairs could similarly be studied using these procedures. Many people, however, maintained that mathematics had no role in these areas because of the presence of so many qualitative rather than quantitative factors. They believed that mathematical reasoning can be fruitfully employed only in domains where numbers, formulas, and clockwork regularities abound. This belief is fortunately not correct as we wish to explain briefly in what follows.

Some of this pessimism stems from a basic misunderstanding of the nature of mathematics, some from the usual prejudice that impedes relations between cultures, and some from a fear instilled by Sunday supplement scientific propaganda frequently centering around computers. In this connection, let us note that it is sad that as a general rule mathematicians and scientists are far more familiar with the humanities than conversely.

In this chapter we wish to emphasize the symbol manipulation capacity of the digital computer. We shall give some examples to illustrate this. Finally, we wish to discuss kladistics, a theory connecting one event with another, a fundamental part of the field of history. And we shall give some references for further reading.

83

Transformations:
Mathematical Approaches to Culture Change

Mathematics

Let us describe mathematics as the study of conceptual structures, their transformations over time, and their interactions. If we replace the carefully chosen vague term *structure* by the equally vague term *system,* and speak of the study of human systems over time, we obtain a reasonably good quick definition of the field of history.

Accepting the fact that any human activity must possess structure, indeed many different types of structures, it is plausible that any field can profit by the use of mathematical thinking. This was a popular idea during the Renaissance with great influence upon art, architecture, and music. The interaction of mathematics with music goes back to the Greeks.

It is the function of the mathematician to discern and use this structure.

Classical Use of Mathematics

The classic use of mathematics is quite stylized. The structure (system, process, etc.) under consideration is first endowed with properties or qualities such as "position" and "velocity" which can be described in numerical terms. Some, but not all, of these can actually be measured. This modeling, as the activity is called, of course, requires intimate knowledge of the field and a great deal of trial and error.

No mathematical theories are intrinsic; all are superimposed. In order to appreciate the effort involved, it is essential to note that when we view existing approaches, we see only the successes. It is very difficult to estimate the ratio of successful to total attempts.

Next, certain rules are introduced to tell how these numerical quantities change over time. For example, there is the famous law of Newton, $F = ma$, force equals mass times acceleration. Acceleration is change of velocity; velocity is change of position. Using calculus, these statements translate into simple equations (usually differential equations) which can be applied by a scientist, or mathematician, to predict the future behavior of the system, that is, to predict the future given the present, and sometimes to discover the past. This usually requires an enormous amount of arithmetic, whence the great significance of the digital or analog computer. This device has been responsible for two scientific revolutions, but this is a story in itself.

We have spoken in terms of equations, which means using an analytic language. Mathematics, however, has many languages at its disposal. A geometric or topological language may be more useful and intuitive in many situations. Also, there is the technique of algebra. In describing structure, geometry and algebra will play a large role.

Basic Abilities of the Computer

When we use the term *computer* we are thinking of a device that possesses several remarkable properties. It can do arithmetic on a grand scale, it can store and retrieve numbers or data that can be translated into numerical symbols; it can follow instructions to perform these operations, and to display intermediate and final results. Thus, a digital computer can evaluate an arithmetic expression such as $1 \times 2 + 3 \times 4 + 5 \times 6 + 7 \times 8 + 9$ in the following steps:

$$1 \times 2 = 2; \text{ store } 2$$
$$3 \times 4 = 12; \text{ add } \quad 2 + 12 = \quad 14; \text{ store } 14$$
$$5 \times 6 = 30; \text{ add } 30 + 14 = \quad 44; \text{ store } 44$$
$$7 \times 8 = 56; \text{ add } 56 + 44 = 100; \text{ store } 100$$
$$\text{add } 100 + 9 = 109; \text{ answer}$$

The numerical solution of the equations of celestial mechanics requires nothing more than this conceptually, given the laws of motion, and little more than this arithmetically.

Presumably, these facts should greatly influence the presentation of scientific theories and make widely available the scientific heritage bequeathed by such scientists as Archimedes, Galileo, Newton, Euler, and Gauss. Unfortunately, those who have painfully acquired knowledge generally have little desire to share it, consistent with the medieval idea that "knowledge is power." This, however, is another digression.

Use of the computer is never routine. Although the basic ideas are simple, a great deal of skill is required to obtain numerical answers to numerical questions. One of the great advantages of the digital computer is that it never gets bored.

Before the development of the digital computer, it was impossible to treat the processes of the social sciences because of their complexities. There are so many interactions and variables to consider that a treatment by hand is impossible.

Symbol Manipulation

The foregoing arithmetic ability, important as it is, is only a special case of a more general skill of the computer, symbol manipulation. Thus, for example, the computer can deal with general nonnumerical symbols A, B, C, D, E, with the rules (algorithms): At each stage

1. A transforms into C

2. B into A
3. C into D
4. D into B
5. E into B

We may then ask the question: If we start with the set of symbols ADE, what set will we have after 100 stages, after 1000 stages?

We can answer this by hand, of course. Referring to the preceding transformation rules, at the end of one stage we have

$$ADE \rightarrow CBB$$

at the end of two stages,

$$CBB \rightarrow DAA$$

at the end of three stages,

$$DAA \rightarrow BCC$$

and so on. There are, as might be expected, more sophisticated approaches to questions of this type but this is of no matter here. These problems may be easily resolved by the use of matrix analysis.

The digital computer can carry through these operations in microseconds and either print out the final result, any desired intermediate results, or the entire sequence. Alternatively, it can display these results on a computer screen as desired. The investigator can, by pressing a few buttons, ask questions such as:

"What would have happened if we started instead with ABE?"
"What would have happened if the transformation rule was changed slightly, that is, A → D?"
"Could we ever end up with all A's, that is, could B, C, D, and E ever disappear?"

The computer frees us from the burden of elementary operations and permits us to spend our time instead thinking up significant questions, interpreting results, and improving models of real systems.

Chance Effects

The foregoing is an example of a deterministic process, much too rigid for most scientific and engineering purposes and certainly so for the social sciences. We could equally well, however, allow for chance effects, or in more mathematical terms, stochastic effects. Thus, we can allow rules of the following type:

1. There is a probability of $\frac{1}{2}$ that A transforms into C, a probability of $\frac{1}{2}$ that A becomes B.
2. There is a probability of $\frac{1}{3}$ that B becomes C, D, or A.

The computer can replicate this process in various ways, running through it a large number of times to determine average behavior or extreme behavior. Generally it readily allows an examination of a huge set of possible patterns. This is often called a Monte Carlo procedure.

One of the advantages of a digital computer here is that it is very difficult for the human mind to follow all possibilities. There is a great tendency to overlook certain paths. Again, many of these problems can be handled by matrix analysis.

Complexity

In many applications the transformation of a symbol depends on the presence of other symbols. Thus, the rules (algorithms) may read:

A transforms into C if B is present, otherwise into D, and so on.

We can combine this more complex algorithm with the stochastic behavior described earlier to obtain more realistic descriptions of processes.

It is essentially impossible for the human mind to perform an enumeration of cases systematically for a large number of stages in a process of this nature. The computer can, however, with the aid of simple programs (sets of computer instructions) carry out a thorough examination of cases and display the desired data in various ways.

It can, in addition, following another computer program, interpret the results, select significant data, alter hypotheses to fit the observed facts (as a good scientist or historian might), add relevant factors, and so on. How far it can go in an analysis depends on the trained and experienced human carrying out the investigation, that is, on the expert. Part of this training in expertise can now be furnished by computer studies of this nature, accelerated and motivated.

We can now study the fascinating "What if . . ." questions of history, and explore countless hypotheses.

A description of the abilities of the digital computer can be found in the book by Bellman (1978).

Music Generation

Viewed abstractly, we have a method of generating music by computer. This is one of the standard techniques that is used. We can do several things. First, we can take a particular composer and analyze his style and generate the kind of music that he would. Second, by the use of these methods, we can generate new music. Before the computer, this was done by Schillinger

(1946, 1948), for Tin Pan Alley composers who were out of ideas. The method was also used by Mozart (1947).

Simulation

The reader versed in the classical uses of mathematics in science will realize that there is nothing conceptually new so far despite the absence of numbers.

We do begin to encounter conceptually novel processes when we do not allow the luxury of specific symbolic description, the existence of explicit rules of transformation, or the presence of a criterion for behavior. Nonetheless, we insist upon decision making. This is typical of much political, economic, business, and military decision making. Although this kind of process can be studied fruitfully by simulation techniques, some new ideas are required which are discussed in another place (see Bellman and Smith 1973).

We have not discussed simulation here since it is discussed in other chapters in this volume.

A Simple Process

Suppose that we wish to study the process involved in a South American or African country changing from one form of government to another, say from a traditional military dictatorship to the traditional Communist dictatorship. We might begin by listing several qualities:

A: strength of Catholic church
B: economic level
C: strength of military
D: climate
E: strength of middle class
F: strength of revolutionary movement

In place of a single symbol, we might now use one, two, or three. Thus, A denotes weak influence of church, AA moderate influence, AAA strong influence; D denotes poor climate, DD moderate, DDD excellent, and so on. Thus, we might write some rules: F → FF if B, DDD, and A or AA, and so on. Each country will possess its own descriptions and its own transformation rules. We can then ask for some long-term trends and predictions.

Similarly, we can study the evolution of certain legal concepts from the Magna Carta to Holmes, the decline of feudalism, the decline and fall of the Roman Empire, and in general the workings over time of any indentifiable historical, economic, and political forces on a particular system.

It is essential to note that the computer here is a logic machine, exploring the consequences of the data and hypotheses that the experts furnish. Different experts, different predictions.

Fuzzy Systems

We have been using the theory of fuzzy systems, the creation of Lotfi Zadeh. The theory of fuzzy systems enables us to handle qualitative variables. It is also another approach to uncertainty where classical probability is replaced by grade of membership.

One of the features of the theory of fuzzy systems is the use of linguistic variables, as we have done previously.

There are many applications of the theory of fuzzy systems to history. For the way this theory can be used for decision making, see Bellman and Zadeh (1970). It is also true that many large systems possess their own logic, as is discussed by Bellman and Zadeh (1977). Many other references will be found in these papers.

Kladistics

A basic question in structural theory in all fields of culture concerns the reconstruction of evolutionary or kladistic trees on pathways by inferences from the characteristics of organisms, systems, or data surviving at the present time. Let us cite the fields of biology and anthropology, the use of fossils in the case of archaeology, and the domain of philology.

In recent years, methods have been developed for deducing trees which satisfy the condition of requiring a minimal number of evolutionary steps of changes in characters to explain the evolutionary history of the set of existing structures. These are outlined by Camin and Sokal (1965), Hendrickson (1968), Kluge and Farris (1969), Wagner (1961), Estabrook (1968), and Sankoff (1972). The principle of minimum evolution or "parsimony" is generally assumed in these papers as a suitable hypothesis in the absence of empirical laws of evolution. General algorithms for these "most parsimonious" trees have not been completely studied, although algorithms for close approximations called "Wagner trees" do exist. For ferns, see Farris (1970). Other conceptually related trees have been studied by Bellman, Cooke and Lockett (1970).

A very interesting algorithm for reconstructing phylogenetic relationships from protein amino acid sequence data under some restrictions about all distance measures is given by Beyer, Stein, Smith and Ulam (1973). A useful source of references is Bellman and Dreyfus (1962).

An excellent introduction to the subject in which many further references will be found is given by Marchi and Hansell (1973).

Conclusion

What we have tried to do herein is to sketch some of the ways in which mathematics can be used in history. There are many applications of mathematics to history, and we have made no attempt to cover all of them. What we wish to emphasize is how great an opportunity exists.

References

Bellman, R., 1978, *Introduction to Artificial Intelligence*, San Francisco, Boyd and Fraser.

Bellman, R., Cooke, K. L. and Lockett, J., 1970, *Algorithms, Graphs and Computers*, Academic Press.

Bellman, R. and Dreyfus, S., 1962, *Applied Dynamic Programming*, Princeton University Press.

Bellman, R. and Smith, C. P., 1973, *Simulation in Human Systems—Decision-Making in Psychotherapy*, John Wiley, New York.

Bellman, R. and Zadeh, L., 1970, Decision-making in a fuzzy enviroment, *Management Science*, 17, 141–164.

Bellman, R. and Zadeh, L., 1977, Local and fuzzy logics, in Dunn J. M. and Epstein G. (eds.) *Modern Uses of Multi-Valued Logic*, Dordrecht, Netherlands, D. Reidel.

Beyer, W. A., Stein, M. L., Smith, T. F. and Ulam, S. M., 1973, A Molecular sequence metric and evolutionary trees, *Mathematical Biosciences*, 17, 444–461.

Camin, J. H. and Sokal, R. R., 1965, A Method for deducing branching sequences in phylogeny, *Evolution*, 19, 311–326.

Estabrook, G. F., 1968, A general solution in partial orders for the Camin-Sokal model in phylogeny, *Journal of Theoretical Biology*, 21, 421–438.

Farris, J. S., 1970, Methods for computing Wagner trees, *Systematic Zoology*, 19, 83–92.

Hendrickson, J. A., 1968, Clustering in numerical cladistics: A minimum-length directed tree problem, *Mathematical Biosciences*, 3, 371–381.

Kluge, A. G. and Farris, J. S., 1969, Quantitative phyletics and the evolution of Anurans, *Systematic Zoology*, 18, 1–32.

Marchi, E. and Hansell, R. I. C., 1973, Generalizations on the parsimony question in evolution, *Mathematical Biosciences*. 17, No. ½, 11–34.

Mozart W. A., (1947), Musikalisches Würfelspiel, Anhang 294D, in *Chronologisch-thematisches Verzeichnis* by L. R. von Köchel, 3rd edn., A Einstein (ed.), Reprinted at Ann Arbor, J. W. Edwards, 1947, p. 909.

Sankoff, D., 1972, Matching sequences under deletion/insertion constraints, *Proceedings of the National Academy of Science, U.S.A.*, 69, No. 1, 4–6.

Schillinger, J., 1946, *Schillinger System of Musical Composition*, Carl Fisher, New York.

Schillinger, J., 1948, *Mathematical Basis of the Arts*, Johnson Reprint, New York.

Wagner, W. H., Jr., 1961, Problems in the classification of ferns, in *Recent Advances in Botany*, University of Toronto Press, Toronto, 841–844.

4

ROBERT ROSEN

Morphogenesis in Biological and Social Systems

Introduction

Morphogenesis, in its widest sense, is the generation of pattern and form in a population of interacting elements. It has been most extensively studied in the context of developmental biology, in order to understand how we can account for the marvelously detailed and intricate structures characteristic of an adult organism from a proliferating population of genetically identical individual cells. In the course of such studies, which are being most actively pursued at the present time, it has been recognized that (*a*) the basic morphogenetic mechanisms called into play in developing biological systems are actually of a much more general scope, and (*b*) these mechanisms may be formulated in broad mathematical terms, and their consequences studied in an entirely abstract way. Within biology itself, mathematical formulations originally developed in a developmental context are currently being applied to such diverse questions as the distribution of species in space, the propagation of polymorphisms in the "gene pools" of species, and the spread of epidemics. All of these, and many others, can be regarded as involving the time course of differentiation in a population of interacting individuals.

Now the relation of biology to the human sciences has always been extraordinarily close and rich. At the simplest and most reductionistic level, human societies are composed of biological organisms, so that we may expect the biological properties of the individuals in a population to play some role in the behavior of the population as a whole. More interesting,

Transformations:
Mathematical Approaches to Culture Change

however, are the *homologies* which appear to exist between the structure and behavior of human populations and those which appear in biology. A very old idea is that human (and animal) societies can be regarded as "superorganisms," whose individuals play the same role with regard to the society as individual cells play with regard to an organism (ranging from the philosophical speculations of Hobbes, Rousseau, and Hegel, among others, to the arguments of zoologists like Emerson (1939). In economics, schools as diverse as laissez-faire and Marxist socialism drew significantly from arguments resting on biological analogies. In economics and operations research, the concept of "adaptation" plays an important role; models in these areas look very familiar to physiologists and population biologists. Most recently, analogies have been drawn between biological structures and languages, which represent the most basic items of human currency.

Within the human sciences, similar analogies are constantly being drawn between different classes of systems. Probably the most influential recent example involves the *structuralism* postulated by the anthropologist Levi-Strauss, and the possibilities it offers for classifying and understanding cultural relationships.

With this kind of background, it is natural to explore the parallels that arise between morphogenesis in biological systems and cognate phenomena which arise at the level of the human sciences. In the present note, we shall consider two such processes: (*a*) the distribution of populations over a landscape, as ultimately manifested in "settlement patterns," and (*b*) the social differentiation that occurs within a society. At the most general level, both of these involve the generation of patterns in populations of interacting individuals. They appear initially different in that the first involves a differential distribution of a population in space, whereas the second involves an internal differentiation, in which the individuals of the population become progressively distinct from one another in cultural (i.e., functional) terms. However, as we shall see, at a sufficiently deep formal level, these differences disappear, and allow us to take a unified view of these and related problems.

We shall not be concerned with developing specific models for the detailed study of any particular morphogenetic process, but rather with developing a context in terms of which such specific models can be generated. Our approach is elementary, in that we shall develop the basic ideas in a stepwise fashion, stressing at each stage the intuitive meaning of every aspect of the formalism. We apologize to the reader who is familiar with the notions involved, but we feel that even such a reader may find something new in our development.

In the final section, we shall consider the role that general morphogenetic ideas may play in an integrated theory of human cultures and their emergence.

Population Distributions in Space

The basic problem to which we shall address ourselves in this section is the manner in which a population distributes itself on a surface ("landscape") under a variety of conditions. We shall, as already noted, proceed in a stepwise fashion, developing a succession of progressively more general models as we add new hypotheses.

Our basic initial supposition is that we are dealing with a population of identical individuals, whose distribution on a surface A may be represented by a continuous function defined on that surface. That is, if we assume that A has been given coordinates in some fashion, so that each point in A can be labeled uniquely by a pair of numbers (x, y), then the *density* of the population at (x, y) is a number $a(x, y)$ which depends continuously on (x, y). Indeed, we shall assume more than this, namely, that the density $a(x, y)$ of our population is a sufficiently differentiable function of x and y. Such an assumption represents, of course, a substantial idealization of a population consisting of a finite number of discrete individuals. We make it for two reasons: First, it allows the powerful tools of mathematical analysis to be brought to bear on the problem; second, experience with a wide variety of physical, biological, and social applications gives ample evidence that such an idealization works well in practice. We shall see some specific examples of this as we proceed.

In mathematical terms, the situation we are envisaging is that of a *scalar field*. We are dealing with a spatially extended system, whose state is determined when the value of the field quantity $a = a(x, y)$ is given for each point in the space we are considering (in this case, the surface A). Since the values of this quantity are numbers (scalars) the field we are considering is a scalar field.

Given $a = a(x, y)$, we can ask how fast the field quantity a is changing as we move from an initial point (x_0, y_0) in the surface. In general, rates of change are expressed in terms of *derivatives* of the quantity in whose change we are interested, evaluated at the initial point (x_0, y_0).

Now we can move away from (x_0, y_0) in arbitrary *directions* in the surface A. Therefore, such a displacement away from our initial point involves a *vector* $\mathbf{r}$, that is, a quantity with both magnitude and direction. Given our coordinate system in A, the vector $\mathbf{r}$ can be identified in this coordinate system as a *pair* of numbers which represent its coordinates in that system; this is shown in Figure 4.1. Suppose we want to know how fast our field quantity $a(x, y)$ is changing in the direction $\mathbf{r}$. From elementary calculus, we can write

$$\frac{\partial a}{\partial r} \, dr = \frac{\partial a}{\partial x} \, dx + \frac{\partial a}{\partial y} \, dy.$$

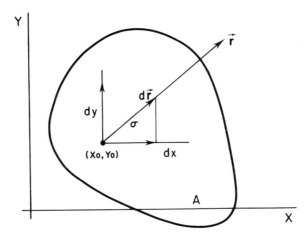

FIGURE 4.1 *The representation of a vector displacement as a pair of numbers in a coordinate system.*

Looking at Figure 4.1, we can see the geometric relations between the quantities appearing in this expression. In particular, since $dx = dr \cos \theta$ and $dy = dr \sin \theta$, we have

$$\frac{\partial a}{\partial r} = \frac{\partial a}{\partial x} \cos \theta + \frac{\partial a}{\partial y} \sin \theta \tag{4.1}$$

as the general expression for the rate of change of our field quantity a as we displace from an initial point (x_0, y_0) in an arbitrary direction **r**.

To a mathematician familiar with vectors and operations on them, this expression has a suggestive form. As we have seen, a vector for us is specified by a *pair* of numbers (u, v). Given two such vectors (u_1, v_1), (u_2, v_2), we can define a most important operation on them, called the *scalar product* or *dot product:*

$$(u_1, v_1) \cdot (u_2, v_2) = u_1 u_2 + v_1 v_2$$

The result of applying this operation between two vectors is a *number* (scalar). Looking at (4.1), we see that it is of this form; it appears to be the scalar product of two vectors. One of these vectors is $(\cos \theta, \sin \theta)$, which simply represents the *direction* of the displacement **r** in which we are interested. The other appears to be a vector whose components are the rates of change of the field quantity a in the directions corresponding to the coordinate axes. This vector, which we may denote by

$$\nabla a = \left(\frac{\partial a}{\partial x}, \frac{\partial a}{\partial y} \right)$$

is called the *gradient* of a, and is extremely important. In general, given any scalar field, we can define a *vector field* which is its gradient. When we do this, we can write the rate of change of the scalar field quantity a in any direction $\mathbf{r}$ in the simple form

$$\frac{\partial a}{\partial r} = \mathbf{r} \cdot \nabla a$$

We shall now consider how to introduce a *dynamical* element into this discussion. We want to consider the field quantity as *changing in time*, so that $a = a(x, y, t)$. Such a change in time amounts to a *flow* of our population in A, and we want to specify what such a flow will look like at an arbitrary point of A.

In order to do this, we must make some *hypothesis* about what drives the flow. The simplest and most general assumption we can make is that the flow in time will depend in some way on the gradient in space, and only on that gradient. The character of this dependence will ultimately depend on the details of the interactions between the individuals of the population with each other, and with the surface on which they are distributed.

One such hypothesis is that the individuals in the population "prefer" interactions with the surface to interactions with each other. Hence they will appear to repel each other, or to put as much surface between each other as possible. Intuitively, this will result in a flow from regions of high density to regions of low density on the surface. The simplest expression of this hypothesis in quantitative form is to say that, at any point in A, the flow in any direction $\mathbf{r}$ is proportional to the gradient of the field quantity in that direction:

$$\text{flow} = -D(\nabla a \cdot \mathbf{r})$$

Let us imagine a small square in the surface A, as shown in Figure 4.2, and

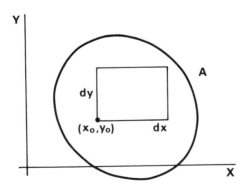

FIGURE 4.2 *Change in density of population within a small square in the surface A.*

ask how fast the density of our population is changing in that square under the hypotheses we have made.

Now the change in population inside the square is simply given by the difference between the number of individuals entering and the number leaving the square during an interval of time dt. We will assess this in two steps: the net change in the interval dt occurring through the vertical sides of the square, and the net change in that interval occurring through the horizontal sides.

Let us take the vertical sides first. Through the leftmost vertical side, we can say that the net number of individuals crossing that side in the interval dt is given by

$$-D \left. \frac{\partial a}{\partial x} \right|_{x_0} dy \ dt$$

where the partial derivative, evaluated at the point (x_0, y_0), expresses the hypothesis that the flow in the X-direction is proportional to the gradient in that direction. Likewise, the flow through the rightmost vertical side is given by

$$-D \left. \frac{\partial a}{\partial x} \right|_{x_0+dx} dy \ dt$$

where the derivative is evaluated at the point $(x_0 + dx, y_0)$.

This last expression can be simplified by the use of Taylor's theorem, which allows us to approximate the value of a function $f(x)$ in the vicinity of a point x_0 in terms of $f(x_0)$ and the derivatives of f at x_0. Specifically, we have

$$f(x_0 + h) = f(x_0) + hf'(x_0) + \text{higher order terms}$$

We now put $f = \partial a/\partial x$. We find

$$\left. \frac{\partial a}{\partial x} \right|_{x_0+dx} = \left. \frac{\partial a}{\partial x} \right|_{x_0} + \left. \frac{\partial^2 a}{\partial x^2} \right|_{x_0} dx$$

to a first approximation.

Now the total flow in the X direction is simply the difference between the flow through the leftmost and the rightmost vertical sides of our square. Putting our results together, we find that this is simply

$$D \left. \frac{\partial^2 a}{\partial x^2} \right|_{y_0} dx \ dy \ dt$$

Repeating this argument for the horizontal sides of our square, we find that the net flow in the Y direction is just

$$D \left. \frac{\partial^2 a}{\partial y^2} \right|_{y_0} dx \, dy \, dt$$

The total flow is just the sum of the two flows; that is, it is given by

$$D \left(\frac{\partial^2 a}{\partial x^2} + \frac{\partial^2 a}{\partial y^2} \right) dx \, dy \, dt$$

On the other hand, the total change of the population in the square during the time interval dt can also be written as

$$\frac{\partial a}{\partial t} dx \, dy \, dt$$

Equating these two expressions, we arrive at the partial differential equation describing the flow:

$$\frac{\partial a}{\partial t} = D \left(\frac{\partial^2 a}{\partial x^2} + \frac{\partial^2 a}{\partial y^2} \right) \tag{4.2}$$

This is the simplest form of the *diffusion equation;* it describes among other things the flow of heat in a conductor, the diffusion of chemical species in a solution, and the movement of simple biological populations in space.

The expression

$$\frac{\partial^2 a}{\partial x^2} + \frac{\partial^2 a}{\partial y^2} = \nabla^2 a$$

is called the *Laplacian of the field quantity a.* It can be shown (e.g., Hopf 1948) to have a simple physical interpretation: The Laplacian of a, evaluated at any point of A, is proportional to the deviation between the value of a at that point and the *average value* of a in a small neighborhood of that point. Thus, the diffusion equation (4.2) we have written down, which we recall embodies the hypothesis that the individuals in the population prefer interactions with the surface to interactions with each other, says intuitively that (in the absence of other forces) the population will spread itself uniformly over the surface; the flow will be away from regions of high density and toward regions of low density. This is, of course, in intuitive accord with our feelings about diffusion processes. We see explicitly, however, that this is a consequence of a tacit assumption about the properties of the individuals in our population, that is, about the manner in which they interact with each other and with the surface on which they are distributed. The reader may find it instructive to see how corresponding equations, embodying other assumptions, may be derived in a fashion analogous to that given herein.

In formal terms, we are often most interested in the *steady state solutions* of the diffusion equation (4.2). These are characterized by the fact that the flow is no longer changing in time, that is, that $\partial a/\partial t = 0$. In these circumstances (4.2) reduces simply to *Laplace's equation:*

$$\nabla^2 a = 0$$

one of the most familiar equations of mathematical physics.

We note explicitly that, if we have several *independent* populations a_1, ..., a_n arrayed on the same surface A, each of them will exhibit a flow, governed by a diffusion equation of the form (4.2), as if the others were not present.

We are now going to generalize our discussion, in two separate ways; we will then proceed to put these generalizations together.

GENERALIZATION I. We have tacitly assumed throughout the preceding discussion that the surface A is uniform (i.e., homogeneous and isotropic) in its properties. We are going to weaken this assumption and allow the properties of the surface to change from point to point. We shall do this by assigning another scalar field to A, governed by a quantity $\rho = \rho(x, y)$. Intuitively, we shall think of ρ as measuring an *affinity* of the point (x, y) for the individuals in the population; the larger the value of the affinity ρ at a point, the more "attractive" the individuals of the population find that point.

It is clear that this concept of "affinity" will result in flow characteristics that are opposite to those manifested by diffusion. Diffusion proceeds from regions of high density to regions of low density; affinities will cause a flow of the population from regions of low affinity to regions of high affinity. However, as before, the new flow will be proportional to the *gradient* of the affinity ρ. Consequently, it is a simple matter to adapt our previous arguments to the new situation; when we do so, we arrive at a generalized diffusion equation, which has the form

$$\frac{\partial a}{\partial t} = D_1\nabla^2 a - D_2\nabla^2\rho \qquad (4.3)$$

It should be recognized that we are tacitly assuming that the quantities D_1, D_2 are constants, independent of any particular point in the surface A. If this assumption is not satisfied, we obtain somewhat more complicated equations involving the spatial derivatives of D_1, D_2; however, we shall not require this added generality in the subsequent discussion.

We are also assuming that the scalar field $\rho(x, y)$ is not changing in time, that is, does not flow. This amounts to assuming that the character of the surface A (i.e., the "landscape") is fixed once and for all, and is independent of the population density. We can of course weaken this hypothesis, for instance by assuming a (slow) decay of ρ in regions of high population density:

$$\frac{\partial \rho}{\partial t} = -Ka\rho$$

Other forms of interrelationship between the two fields ρ and a may be imagined.

Systems described by equations of the form (4.3) arise in many contexts. One of the simplest is in the concept of a *template*, considered as a system which organizes a population of elements in a particular way. Perhaps the most familiar mode of template organization is in the synthesis of biological macromolecules, such as nucleic acids and protein. Variants of these equations also appear implicitly or explicitly in discussions of the role of "prepatterns" or "morphogenetic fields" in developmental biology, and the discussion of the origin of patterns through such mechanisms as chemotaxis, as for instance in aggregation of slime molds (Keller and Segal 1970). The characteristic feature of template activity is that the "information" which specifies the organized population does not inhere in the individuals in the population, but in the template. As we shall see, such considerations bear strongly on such questions as the distribution of biological species into "niches," or the availability of resources as a determinant of human population distribution patterns.

We remark that, just as we can consider a family of independent populations $(a_1, ..., a_n)$ diffusing on the same landscape, so we can consider a family $(\rho_1, ..., \rho_m)$ of distinct affinities. These enter additively into the relation (4.3) in the obvious fashion.

GENERALIZATION II. Let us retreat once more to the basic diffusion equation (4.2). A presupposition for the validity of this equation is that the number of individuals in our population is constant, or stated another way, that there are no sources or sinks for the population present in the system. Thus, in particular, if we want to consider a situation in which the population is *proliferating*, we need to remove this restriction.

It is easy to modify (4.2) to include the presence of sources and sinks. We do this by introducing a general "source term" or production term into the equation, so that it becomes

$$\frac{\partial a}{\partial t} = Q + D\nabla^2 a \qquad (4.4)$$

The production term Q can be regarded simply as another scalar field, or it can be a function $Q = Q(a)$ of the density of population at a particular point of the region A. If $Q > 0$, there is a net production of a; if $Q < 0$, there is a net consumption.

Equations of the form (4.4) represent the simplest form of *diffusion–reaction* equations. They arise, for example, in the study of chemical systems, in which the density (concentration) of a chemical species can change as a result of chemical reactions as well as by diffusion through an extended medium. Most generally, we consider a family $(a_1, \ldots, a_n)$ of interacting species, each of which diffuses separately; such a system is governed by a coupled set of n diffusion–reaction equations of the form

$$\frac{\partial a_i}{\partial t} = F_i(a_1, \ldots, a_n) + D_i \nabla^2 a_i \qquad (4.5)$$

The exact form of the reaction terms $F_i(a_1, \ldots, a_n)$ is determined by the specific chemical reactions occurring between the reactants $a_1, \ldots, a_n$. These equations also arise in the study of the interactions of biological populations (e.g., through predation) in space.

Reaction–diffusion systems governed by equations such as (4.4) or (4.5) are currently being extensively studied, mainly in connection with the generation of biological patterns during development through differentiation. Intuitively, their interesting properties arise through the coupling of diffusive processes, which as we have seen tend to homogenize the distribution of a population, with sources and sinks, which can tend to cause differential variations of population densities in a region A.

The usual mathematical approach to systems such as (4.4) or (4.5) is as follows. Rather than solving the equations completely (which is a difficult job), we proceed by *assuming* a spatially homogeneous steady state solution, that is, one for which the populations involved are distributed in a homogeneous manner over A, and are not changing in time. We then perturb this solution slightly. The fact that the perturbation is small allows us to replace the original functions F_i in (4.5), which may be arbitrarily complex, by simple linear expressions in the perturbed values. We then investigate the *stability* of the homogeneous situation by determining whether the simplified linear system will return to its unperturbed state, or whether it will depart further from this state. This is specified solely in terms of the *eigenvalues* of the linearized system in a familiar manner which we need not elaborate here. If the linearized system is *unstable*, it means that any random departure from homogeneity will be successively *amplified* by the system; the system will thus "drive itself" further and further from the homogeneous state. By definition, then, the system will autonomously accentuate small spatial inhomogeneities in population distributions. It is meaningful to regard the asymptotic (i.e., long-time) pattern so generated as representing the *adaptation* of the population to the initial perturbation.

It should be noted that, in contrast to the template situation considered previously, a diffusion–reaction system can be regarded as entirely self-organizing. The "information" for the generation of population distributions inheres entirely in the individuals of which the population is composed, and on the kind of perturbation from homogeneity initially imposed on the population.

It should also be noted that the coupling of reactions (sources and sinks) and diffusion can result in some surprising effects, such as the accumulation of populations *against* density gradients. Such "wrong way" flow is very common in biological systems; it is commonly termed *active transport*. In the past, biologists have tended to explain active transport by assuming the existence of specific "pumps" for moving populations uphill against their gradients. We see here, however, that such behavior can arise naturally through the appropriate coupling of diffusion with reaction.

Historically, the first to study the instability of the homogeneous steady states of diffusion–reaction systems, and suggest that biological forms could be generated in this way, was Rashevsky (1940). A decade later, the mathematician Turing (1952) proposed a much simpler embodiment of this idea, which could be studied in much greater detail. This work has become quite influential in modern theoretical biology and in theoretical physics; in the latter, it has been studied extensively by many interested in irreversible processes in open systems under the rubric of "dissipative structures" or "symmetry breaking" (e.g., Prigogine 1969). In recent years, a number of simple inorganic chemical systems have been discovered which actually exhibit striking pattern-generating capabilities (Winfree 1974; Tyson 1976); these provide an important empirical laboratory for the study of such systems. It is fair to say that the diffusion–reaction systems, with their capability of amplifying deviations from homogeneity, provide an archetypal morphogenetic mechanism.

Having now described two basic classes of generalizations of the simple diffusion system (4.2), it is natural that we put them together. In the simplest case to be discussed presently, we will envisage a population of identical individuals distributed in a region A such that (a) the individuals can *proliferate* at some net rate, and (b) the affinity ρ of the points of A varies according to some distribution $\rho(x, y)$. This situation represents a combination of the template idea, embodied in the affinity $\rho(x, y)$, with the diffusion–reaction schemes, embodied in the proliferation.

Intuitively, we wish to consider specifically the case of a human population distributing itself over a landscape. The affinity will represent the distribution of some fixed resource on the landscape (e.g., water, arable land, mineral resources). It is clear that the proliferation of the population will be favored by a high value of ρ, and will be inhibited by a high density.

This suggests that the proliferation term should be of logistic form:

$$Q = f(\rho)a - g(\rho)a^2$$

where f, g are two functions that specify the effect of the resource ρ on the stimulation and inhibition of proliferation, respectively.

Our model for the distribution of the population over the landscape A is then expressed by the differential equation

$$\frac{\partial a}{\partial t} = [a(f(\rho) - ag(\rho))] + D_1\nabla^2 a - D_2\nabla^2\rho \qquad (4.6)$$

The specific morphogenetic properties of this kind of model depend on the interplay between the three basic mechanisms it expresses: proliferation, diffusion, and environmental affinity. As we noted previously, diffusion tends to uniformize population distribution, whereas affinity and proliferation can tend to act against uniform distribution. We can therefore conclude already that such a system will necessarily exhibit *bifurcations,* that is, switch from one mode of distribution to another as the parameters of the system (such as D_1, D_2) are varied through certain critical values. Such bifurcations are the analogs of the *catastrophes* introduced by Thom (1974), and used by him as the point of departure for morphogenetic studies. Such bifurcations will also arise as the gradient of the affinity ρ changes, for example through depletion by the resident population; this too can result in rapid and marked changes of the pattern of distribution of the population.

In the application of equations of the form (4.6) to human population distribution patterns, it will be of interest to study not so much the stability of a uniform distribution, but to see how the population pattern changes in time from an initial distribution of a relatively small number of point sources. This involves finding full solutions of (4.6) with the appropriate initial and boundary conditions, and this is a generally difficult analytical problem. It should be much easier to study such situations through simulation techniques. Such techniques are readily applicable to empirically interesting situations; we would suggest that significant insights into population spreads in specific geographical areas could be obtained by utilizing the means we have described previously.

Cultural Differentiation

We have seen in the preceding section how a morphogenetic problem pertaining to human settlement patterns may be formulated, utilizing techniques originally developed for cognate problems in biology. As we pointed out, such models as a class have the capability to pass autonomously from a homogeneous situation to an inhomogeneous one, and thus can exhibit the basic phenomena of self-organization. In the situation considered previously, we dealt only with the problem of the distribution of a population of identical individuals over a landscape, and saw how inhomogeneities of the population in space could occur. There is in principle no reason why these same techniques cannot be applied to a different kind of morphogenetic problem, namely the emergence of *cultural* differentiation in a human population. This is the problem to which we shall address ourselves in the present section.

The problem here is to develop mechanisms for the manner in which a population of initially identical individuals can autonomously differentiate into a number of functionally distinct subsystems, especially as a function of population density. If we wish, we can regard such a differentiation as occurring at a single point in the landscape visualized in the preceding section. Just as before, the guiding idea will be to create a situation in which the homogeneous state may become unstable, so that random deviations from it will be successively amplified by the system.

To formulate the problem of cultural differentiation properly requires a number of new ideas, which did not appear in our earlier discussion. In that discussion, an individual in the population was treated as if it had no internal structure; its only characteristics were its position on the landscape at an instant of time, and (implicitly) its affinity for the landscape and for other members of the population. Obviously, this idealization will not suffice for a discussion of cultural differentiation; by its very nature, this kind of differentiation requires the individuals in the population to become different from one another in some functional aspect, and this in turn requires us to assign some notion of internal structure to the individuals themselves. It is this internal structure, assumed initially in the same state for every member of the population, that we desire to change in time as a consequence of belonging to the population. Therefore, the first order of business in attacking the problem is to assign some meaningful kind of internal structure to the individuals comprising our population.

In cultural terms, we may say that what distinguishes one individual from another are the kinds of activities in which he engages. Let us therefore suppose that we are given a spectrum of activities $\alpha_1, \ldots, \alpha_k$ in which a member of the population can possibly engage. In any convenient unit of time, a given individual will spend some fraction λ_1 of the interval engaged in activity α_1, a fraction λ_2 engaged in activity α_2, and so on. During that time interval, then, the individual in question can be characterized, as far as the culture is concerned, by the k-tuple $(\lambda_1, \ldots, \lambda_k)$. These numbers thus characterize the *cultural state* of the individual, and will be taken as the fundamental state variables for the subsequent discussion.

Our problem then becomes to start with a situation in which all the individuals in a population are in the same cultural state, and by virtue of reasonable dynamical considerations have the population pass to a situation in which these individuals come to be in a spectrum of different cultural states. It is then reasonable to say that the population has become *culturally differentiated* in an autonomous fashion.

In order to proceed, we have to consider what kinds of factors can cause an individual in a given cultural state to undergo a change of state. In general, there are three factors which can contribute to such a change of state:

1. Autonomous dynamical processes intrinsic to the particular individual
2. Interactions between the individuals in the population
3. Interactions with the environment

The reader will note that these three features also appeared explicitly in the discussion of the preceding section: The first was embodied there in the proliferation, the second in our formulation of diffusion, and the third appeared in the concept of affinity.

For the moment, let us concentrate on the second of these features, namely the interactions that can occur between the individuals in the population. Intuitively, an interaction between two individuals means at least that the *state* of one of them is capable of imposing a *change of state* on the other. By "state" we here mean "cultural state," which it will be recalled has been represented as a k-tuple $(\lambda_1, \ldots, \lambda_k)$ of numbers specifying the fraction of a unit time interval spent in each of the possible activities available to an individual. A change in state means a change in at least one of the λ_i, and thus a change in the distribution of activities exhibited by the individual in a unit time interval. In a suggestive language, we can say that an interaction between individuals in a population means precisely that the cultural state of one of the interacting individuals causes a modification in the *behavior* of another.

Now it is clear that, if the members of a population can interact, the state *of the population* is not uniquely determined by specifying simply the states of its members. This is because the very concept of state was invented to embody a causal dynamical intuition that the state of any system at an instant should uniquely determine the state of the system at subsequent instants. Obviously, we do not have enough information embodied in the state descriptions of individuals to do this. The "missing information" required to specify the states of the population in this sense involves, of course, a specification of the manner in which these individuals interact with one another, at a particular instant of time. Such a specification turns a population into a *network*, characterized by a particular "topology."

A simple example may make this clear. Let us suppose that our population consists of a number N of abstract "cells." Suppose that our cells are all

identical in structure, and that the states of each of them can be characterized by a single quantity x; thus at an instant t, the state of the ith cell can
be denoted by $x_i(t)$. Let us think of x as a diffusing chemical substance;
interaction between cells thus corresponds to diffusion of x between cells
which are physically contiguous. Consider Figure 4.3, which shows the sorts
of "networks" that can be formed from these cells. It is intuitively clear that
if internal reactions are present, the cell labeled i may assume quite different
states in these networks, even though the cells are all initially the same. The

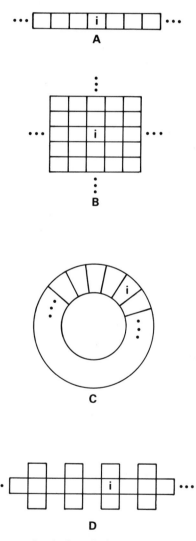

FIGURE 4.3 *Different networks which can be formed from a number of abstract "cells."*

only difference between these networks resides in the patterns of interaction imposed on the population.

In a certain sense, then, the imposition of an initial pattern of interaction upon such a population plays the role of a *template;* it supplies the "missing information" which allows the subsequent states of the population (and of each of the members of the population) to be determined when the initial states of the individual members are known. It is clearly a very special situation (tantamount to noninteraction) in which the dynamics of a population is independent of the initial specification of a configuration of interaction.

From this example, we see that the interactions posited between the individuals in a population correspond to imposing a "geometry" or topology on the population; two individuals "contiguous" in this geometry interact strongly, whereas individuals not contiguous interact weakly or not at all. This notion of "contiguity" may, although it need not, be related to spatial proximity; it is a functional, and not a spatial, relation between individuals. In other words, the geometry thus imposed on the population by specifying a network of interactions determines the "position" of each individual *within the population;* this may or may not be related to the distribution of the population itself in real space. Indeed, in the situation we are considering, in which the population is idealized as localized at a single point of real space, cultural differentiation can clearly have nothing to do with spatial distribution.

Once we have specified the initial configuration of interactions between the individuals in our population, we may write down the manner in which the states of the individual members of our population are changing in time. In general, let us suppose that the ith individual in the population is characterized by the k-tuple $(\lambda_{i1}, \ldots, \lambda_{ik})$. We have already seen that each of these state variables changes as a result of three distinct processes: (a) intrinsic dynamics; (b) interactions with other individuals; and (c) interactions with the environment. If then λ_{ij} is a typical state variable of the ith individual, then the following hold:

1. The intrinsic dynamics (a) of the individual contributes to a change in λ_{ij} which can be represented as

$$\frac{d\lambda_{ij}}{dt} = f_j(\lambda_{i1}, \ldots, \lambda_{ik}) \tag{4.7}$$

2. The interactions with other individuals contribute to a change in λ_{ij} which can be represented as

$$\frac{d\lambda_{ij}}{dt} = F_{ij}(\lambda_{i1}, \ldots, \lambda_{ik}, \lambda_{\mu_1 1}, \ldots, \lambda_{\mu_r k}) \tag{4.8}$$

where $\mu_1, \ldots, \mu_r$ denote all the individuals in the population with which the ith individual interacts.

3. The interaction with the environment contributes to a change in λ_{ij} which can be represented as

$$\frac{d\lambda_{ij}}{dt} = S_{ij}(t) \tag{4.9}$$

Putting these three processes together, we find that the total rate of change of λ_{ij} as a result of all the forces impinging on the ith individual is expressible in the form

$$\frac{d\lambda_{ij}}{dt} = f_i(\lambda_{i1}, \ldots, \lambda_{ik})$$

$$+ F_{ij}(\lambda_{i1}, \ldots, \lambda_{ik}, \lambda_{\mu_1 1}, \ldots, \lambda_{\mu_r k}) \tag{4.10}$$

$$+ S_{ij}(t)$$

We thus have one equation of the form (4.10) for each state variable λ_{ij}; hence, if there are N members of the population, we have a total of Nk equations in all. Equation (4.10) should be compared with Equation (4.6); the two kinds of equations are in fact formally very closely related. For if we consider the indices i and j of (4.10) as *continuously* varying instead of discrete [so that λ_{ij} can be written as $\lambda(i, j)$], then these indices take on the character of the variables x and y of (4.6); the three terms of (4.10) can then be regarded as generalizations of proliferation, diffusion, and affinity, respectively. Indeed, in this fashion the discrete state variables λ_{ij} become a single scalar field quantity $\lambda(i, j)$ defined on the manifold (i, j) of indices. Thus, although the *interpretations* we have given to (4.6) and (4.10) are very different, the actual underlying conceptual structure is very much the same, as indeed it must be, since we are concerned with general phenomena of morphogenesis.

In the case of cultural differentiation, we would want to proceed as indicated in the preceding section: to posit an initial homogeneous state for the members of the population as a whole, and see how this state responds to perturbations. That is, we would initially suppose that

$$\lambda_{1j} = \lambda_{2j} = \cdots = \lambda_{Nj}$$

for each $j = 1, \ldots, k$. A small perturbation from these values will convert the equations of (4.10) into *linear* equations in the perturbed values; the coefficients in these linear equations would embody the network structure initially imposed on the population. The stability of this linear system then tells us whether the perturbation autonomously amplifies (differentiation) or decays back to the homogeneous state.

Discussion

The development of the preceding sections was mainly intended to show that morphogenesis is a phenomenon that can occur in any population of interacting units under appropriate conditions. We have seen in the second section how such a population can differentially arrange itself in space, and in the third section how such a population can differentiate from a homogeneous state as a consequence of amplification of local deviations from homogeneity. We have indicated further a sense in which these two apparently different kinds of morphogenetic phenomena are in fact embodiments of the same underlying formal ideas.

Our discussion was deliberately kept at the most general level, to indicate the universality of the mechanisms responsible for the morphogenesis. Thus, our population could consist of physical particles, chemical molecules, biological cells or organisms, or individuals in a culture. This emphasizes the fact that the distinctions between these vastly different contexts are primarily of a *technical* character, and not of a conceptual one. They enter into our discussion (*a*) in our choice of description of the individuals and of the interaction between them, and (*b*) in our interpretation of the consequences of these choices. They do not enter into the character of the formalism itself, which is designed to describe *morphogenesis* in whatever specific context it appears.

There were two main reasons for proceeding in this fashion. One of these embodies a general strategic principle in dealing with behavioral phenomena, namely that it is of value to determine a set of *minimal* circumstances under which these phenomena are manifested. When one is dealing with individual systems of any complexity, such as individual organisms or individual human cultures, there is a tendency to utilize *all* the information at one's disposal in an attempt to understand particular behaviors of the system. Not only is this usually unnecessary, but it often serves actually to obscure the actual roots of the behavior, and the relations between the given system and others. For instance, a mathematician might prove a theorem about real numbers by utilizing all the rich structure present in the real number system: its several algebraic properties, its topological properties, its measure-theoretic properties. If it turns out that the theorem actually holds only because the real numbers are, say, an additive group, then the proof in question is a bad proof: It obscures the nature of the relations involved, and it does not generalize properly; it does not identify the class of systems in which the result actually holds. Thus, considerations of parsimony (i.e., minimal conditions for the manifestation of a behavior) are closely related to generality (i.e., the specification of the largest class of systems in which the same kind of behavior is actually manifested).

Second, if it turns out that two different systems manifest the same kind of behavior because they share common elements of organization in this sense, this implies that the differences between them are important, not for this behavior, but for others. Thus, the differences between two morphogenetic systems may not manifest themselves *morphogenetically* at all; this could not be recognized easily if one approached the morphogenesis in each by assuming that all of their individual properties must be manifested morphogenetically. On the other hand, if we proceed in the minimal fashion indicated, we are able to classify the functional effects of the differences between them much more effectively.

We pay for this kind of parsimonious approach by appearing to lose the details of an individual system in return for embedding the system in a context, a class of systems which behave similarly. Thus, it may seem a far cry from our general discussion of cultural differentiation in a population to any specific description of cultural differentiation in a particular place and time [as for example Renfrew's (1972) treatment of the rise of the Aegean civilization, which was in fact the point of departure for much of the foregoing]. Such a detailed description involves such things as patterns of settlement, descriptions of specific artifacts characteristic of particular periods, the emergence of social classes, and similar rich details of cultural differentiation. As Renfrew points out, however, the basic task is to *explain* these descriptions in some autonomous way: Why these particular patterns arose at this time and place and not elsewhere; why they evolved in the fashion they did.

Clearly the archaeologist deals with materials that have undergone many levels of selection, at each stage of which information has been lost. For instance, by its very nature, archaeology is restricted to materials that are "survivable," that can persist from the time of their creation to the present. This fact already very heavily skews what the archaeologist can observe of an ancient culture. Further, not every item which is "survivable" in this sense actually survives; this skews his picture still further. At each stage, he tends to lose precisely the information which would allow him to understand the causal historical relationships between the remains he actually sees. If he is to reconstruct these historical relationships, the information lost at each stage must be resupplied from somewhere. Since it cannot in principle come from the remains themselves, it can only come from embedding the given historical situation in a wider *context*, and utilizing the context itself as a source of information.

Now every way of developing such a context involves the recognition of a functional homology, or similarity, between the given specific situation and other situations. Such a recognition is at the root of any modeling relation; it involves an assertion that the situation in which we are currently interested is sufficiently like others so that we can learn about it by studying them. The phrase "sufficiently like" already tacitly involves a sacrifice of the details of any one specific situation, in exchange for the acquisition of a context consisting of a *class* of systems which are in some sense *similar*. Within that context, new information becomes available which can be used to illuminate the properties of any system within that class.

One such context for the archaeologist is provided by anthropology; we may hope to restore information lost in the remains of an ancient culture by studying modern ones. In the same way, the paleontologist, interested in the properties of extinct organisms, relies on a context created by the biology of surviving ones.

What we are suggesting is that the general properties of morphogenetic systems, which we have illustrated by the discussion of the preceding sections, provide another kind of context for the archaeologist (and for many others concerned with cognate problems). Explicitly, the context here is the class of populations which differentiate in time. Within this context, it is possible to evaluate explicitly the temporal consequences of *any* specific hypotheses about the nature of the individuals in the population, and their mode of interaction with each other and with their environment. Thus, information can come from this kind of context which it is difficult to imagine could come from any other. We can already see in the general properties of morphogenetic systems many of the kinds of resources postulated by Renfrew; as a specific example, we may cite his concept of the "multiplier effect," an autocatalytic amplification of deviations from homogeneity in such a system.

The ultimate utility of the general morphogenetic context in, say, archaeological investigations will depend on the art with which morphogenetic information can be interpreted in archaeological terms, and conversely. But the presence of such a new context, and the possible new insights which can be drawn from it, should not be ignored.

References

Emerson, A., 1939, Social coordination and the superorganism. *American Midland Naturalist* 21, 182–209.

Hopf, L., 1948, *Differential Equations of Physics* (W. Nef, trans.). New York, Dover Publications.

Keller, E. F., and Segel, L. A., 1970, Initiation of slime-mold aggregation viewed as an instability, *Journal of Theoretical Biology* 26, 397–415.

Prigogine, I., 1969, Structure, dissipation and life, in Marois, M. (ed.) *Theoretical Biology and Physics,* Amsterdam, North Holland, 23–52.

Rashevsky, N., 1940, An approach to the mathematical biophysics of biological self-regulation and of cell polarity, *Bulletin of Mathematical Biophysics* 2, 15–25.

Renfrew, C., 1972, *The Emergence of Civilization,* London, Methuen.

Thom, R., 1975, *Structural Stability and Morphogenesis.* (D. H. Fowler, trans.). Reading, Massachusetts, W. A. Benjamin.

Turing, A. M., 1952, The chemical basis of morphogenesis, *Philosophical Transactions of the Royal Society B,* 237, 5–72.

Tyson, J. J., 1976, *The Belousov-Zhabotinskii Reaction,* New York, Springer-Verlag.

Winfree, A., 1974, Rotating chemical reactions, *Scientific American* 230, 82–95.

II

HIERARCHY AND
SOCIAL SPACE

The rich man in his castle,
The poor man at his gate,
God made them high or lowly,
And order'd their estate.

Mrs. C. F. Alexander
All Things Bright and Beautiful

Hierarchical ordering is a characteristic feature of complex systems in general, and certainly of all the more closely integrated sociocultural systems. Yet it is only in recent years that the general features of hierarchical organizations have been analyzed (e.g., Pattee 1973). Many hierarchical structures can be summarized in tree form (Figure II.1), where the structure is analyzed into a number of successive levels, units at a higher level each dominating a number of often relatively uniform units at the lower level, and they in turn can dominate further units yet lower in the hierarchy. It should be noted that this branching tree structure, although superficially the same as the "family tree" of descent or evolution, differs fundamentally from it: The latter portrays a development in time without hierarchical implications; the former represents a structure at a given point in time.

Archaeological research into ranking, stratification, and hierarchical structures has followed three main approaches. In the first place there is the use of archaeological data to investigate personal ranking with an individual society (see Tainter 1977). Social ranking is a salient feature of all those societies which the anthropologist does not classify as "egalitarian" (Fried 1967). Ranking, however, can show a continuous grading from high to low, and need not imply a division into "levels": It is with stratified societies that the division into classes is seen. The use of cemetery data to provide information about social structure rather than simply about chronology and demography, initiated in effect by Binford (1971), has been systematically applied in a number of cases (e.g., Tainter and Cordy 1977; Shennan 1975).

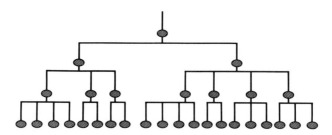

FIGURE II.1 Generalized hierarchical structure expressed in tree form. Higher level units dominate the lower subordinate units.

Second, the study of the flow of information in highly structured social systems has led to a perspective in which human social organization and spatial organization are regarded simply as aspects of human societies functioning as organizations for decision making (Wright and Johnson 1975; Johnson 1978).

The most obvious place for the archaeologist to look for hierarchical organization, however, is in the size and distribution of archaeological sites, especially settlements. Spatial analysis is now one of the best developed fields of archaeological theory (for a review see Johnson 1977) and it is widely recognized that the more obvious archaeological indicators of ranked or stratified societies may be spatial ones (Peebles and Kus 1977). Hodder in Chapter 5 of this volume contrasts the smooth and continuous frequency distribution of size for settlements, predicted by the rank–size rule, with the stepped distribution predicted by central place theory. He goes on to consider how far the former can be regarded as the result of random rather than highly structured processes, a topic discussed also by Chadwick in Chapter 10 of this volume.

Chapter 6 by Renfrew and Level and Chapter 7 by Alden consider spatial organization in relation to political organization, and so approach the important and neglected question of the relation between spatial and social structure. These two chapters are as concerned with analyzing structure at given points in time as with explaining processes of change—an inevitable situation when the study of social structure from archaeological data is a comparatively recent preoccupation. At the same time they look at successive stages along a time trajectory, and the analysis is relevant to the study of change in considering social space, and the interaction at a distance of settlement and societies.

The similarity in the basic approach of the three chapters in this part is no less striking than the diversity in the data examined.

A.C.R.

References

Binford L. R., 1971, Mortuary practices, their study and potential, *American Antiquity* 36, 6–29.

Fried M. H., 1967, *The Evolution of Political Society,* New York, Random House.

Johnson G. A., 1977, Aspects of regional analysis in archaeology, *Annual Review of Anthropology* 6, 479–508.

Johnson G. A., 1978, Information sources and the development of decision-making organisations, in Redman C. L. (ed.), *Archaeology as a Social Science,* New York, Academic Press, in press.

Pattee H. H. (ed.), 1973, *Hierarchy Theory,* New York, George Brazilier.

Peebles C. S. and Kus S. M., 1977, Some archaeological correlates of ranked societies, *American Antiquity* 42, 421–448.

Saxe A. A., 1970, Social Dimensions of Mortuary Practices, doctoral dissertation, University of Michigan, published by University Microfilms, Ann Arbor, 1976.

Shennan S., 1975, The social organisation at Brank, *Antiquity* 49, 279–288.

Tainter J. A., 1977, Modelling change in prehistoric social systems, in Binford L. R. (ed.), *For Theory Building in Archaeology,* New York, Academic Press, 327–351.

Tainter J. A. and Cordy R. H., 1977, An archaeological analysis of social ranking and residence groups in prehistoric Hawaii, *World Archaeology* 9, 95–112.

Wright H. T. and Johnson G. A., 1975, Population, exchange and early state formation in southwestern Iran, *American Anthropologist* 77, 267–289.

5

IAN HODDER

Simulating the Growth of Hierarchies

Introduction

For many samples of archaeological sites, the sizes of the sites have been estimated. For example, the area covered by surface spreads of pottery identified in surface surveys, or the area enclosed by defensive walls may have been calculated. The many limitations and problems of such data are discussed herein. But if some measure of site size or importance is available, then the sites can be ranked from largest to smallest and the relationship between rank and size can be studied. The aim of this chapter is to suggest to archaeologists that there is a value in developing the analysis and interpretation of rank–size relationships and in considering the sorts of processes which might have produced the relationships.

The underlying theoretical framework will concern the relationship between pattern and randomness. The basic contention from which the detailed work follows is that the aggregate effect of numerous variables acting on a system is to produce a "random" pattern which is not highly ordered or structured. The pattern thus contains little information for the onlooker about how the system functioned. Where a few forces act strongly to constrain choice, the end result of a process is highly structured and contains information. Such end results and patterns are nonrandom. For further discussion of this approach see, for example, Pred (1967, 307) and Cliff and Ord (1973).

117

Transformations:
Mathematical Approaches to Culture Change

Rank–Size Relationships

The rank–size rule (Zipf 1949) states that

$$P_n = P_1(n)^{-1} \qquad (5.1)$$

where P_n is the population size of the nth ranked settlement and P_1 is the population of the largest settlement. Knowing the population size of the largest settlement in an area, the size of the second largest can be predicted according to this rule. For example, if the largest settlement contains 100,000 people, then

$$P_2 = 100,000 \times \tfrac{1}{2} = 50,000$$

Archaeologists usually have to estimate population from settlement area, and a general relationship between the logarithm of settlement area and the logarithm of population size has been noted (e.g., Wiessner 1974). However, since the nature of this relationship varies from society to society, the archaeologist is forced to consider the situation in which settlement size (s) is substituted for population size:

$$s_n = s_1(n)^{-1} \qquad (5.2)$$

This substitution has an effect on the applicability of the rank–size rule since s does not equal P directly and consistently. But the underlying idea, that the size of the nth ranked settlement is some function of the $(n - 1)$th settlement, remains valid.

Given an observed relationship between rank and size it is possible to fit a regression line of the form

$$\log s_n = \log s_1 - b \log n \qquad (5.3)$$

in order to see how well the parameters agree with the predictions of the rank–size rule [where $b = -1$ in Equation (5.2)]. Such a procedure has been applied to a group of Welsh hillforts (Hodder and Orton 1976, 72). However, there has been little study in archaeology of the variation of such parameters, and some of the types of explanations which can be considered are to be discussed in this chapter.

A difficulty related to the use of the rank–size rule is that it is an empirical finding with no theoretical basis. If any set of sites is arranged from the largest to the smallest, it is likely that *some* curve could be found to fit the rank–size relationship. The choice of which curve to use is arbitrary without any theory behind the choice. Thus, if it is not known *why* the rank–size rule fits a particular set of data, and since other arbitrary curves could be found which fitted equally well, there is little value in the application of the rule.

However, some researchers have considered the types of processes involved in the growth of hierarchies and have discussed the rank–size relationships which result. For example, Curry (1964) uses the entropy model to determine expected rank–size relationships. He considers N people divided among Z settlements, so that each settlement has an equal chance of attracting a given population. Neglecting the spatial pattern, he then considers the total number of distinguishable ways in which people can be distributed among the settlements. Curry determines the entropy of such a system when the system is large, and considers the situation in which entropy is maximized. (Maximum entropy defines the most probable state of the system.) The most probable state for the rank–size relationship occurs when, given the size of the largest settlement, the population or size of the nth settlement is a constant ratio of the $(n - 1)$th settlement. The rank–size rule is just a special case of this.

Other stochastic processes may also be relevant to the production of settlements of different sizes. In the random splitting model (Cliff *et al.* 1974) the total summation of settlement sizes in a study area is shared out at random between the number (n) of settlements. The total area of settlements (S) is then like a stick which is broken up into n segments or shares at random, and the shares can be ranked from 1 (smallest in this case) to n (largest). $s_{(r)}$ is then defined as the size of the rth largest settlement, and $g_{(r)} = s_{(r)}/S$ (the size share of the rth largest settlement).

Whitworth (1934) has shown that, with random splitting, the expected share of the rth largest settlement is

$$E[g_{(r)}] = \frac{1}{n} \sum_{i=1}^{r} \frac{1}{n + 1 - i} \qquad (r = 1, 2, ..., n) \qquad (5.4)$$

However, there is usually a lower limit to the size of sites. For example, minute hillforts do not occur in Iron Age Britain. Cohen (1966) has, therefore, introduced a threshold minimum share size (Δ) into the random splitting model:

$$E[g_{(r)}] = \left\{ \left[\frac{1}{n} - \Delta \right] \sum_{i=1}^{r} \frac{1}{n + 1 - i} \right\} + \Delta \quad (r = 1, 2, ..., n) \qquad (5.5)$$

This model has been fitted by Chadwick (1977) to the rank–size relationship of Mycenaean sites in Messenia, Greece, where it gave a better fit to the data than the rank–size rule.

One difficulty with the random splitting model concerns the underlying hypothesis. It is reasonable to consider the division of a country into states or counties by a random splitting of the total country (S). But it may be thought less reasonable or less elegant to begin with a total abstract settlement acreage and divide it up into settlements of different sizes. This may be a reversal of the true process of development, and it is perhaps necessary to look to other stochastic processes to provide a more realistic picture.

Several studies have considered stochastic mechanisms operating through time in order to allocate individuals to settlements with attention focused on the "contagiousness" of numbers of people attracting further people. For example, Thomas (1967) has developed a stochastic model of this sort and examined the types of rank–size relationships which result. He starts out with a set of settlement sizes that are assumed to be normally or lognormally distributed. Thomas then moves the settlement pattern through a series of phases in which a very large number of factors (which he sees as independent variables) determine the changes in population and size of settlements. In any one phase, the increase in population is very small, but this increase is proportional to population size so that larger centers attract more people than smaller centers. The overall relative growth rate is seen as being stochastically independent from phase to phase. Thomas then asks what steady state is found after the addition of many small numbers of population as a result of many independent variables over a lot of short time periods. He shows that the result of such a stochastic process is a lognormal or loglognormal frequency distribution of settlement sizes.

Work by Chapman (1970) provides further insight into the generation of rank–size relationships by stochastic processes. For example, he chooses a series of random numbers normally distributed around a mean. He then ranks the numbers and shows that the entropy is very high, very near maximum entropy.

Up to this point, the special features of archaeological data have not been brought into the discussion. In many cases it may be difficult to estimate precisely the size of prehistoric sites, or only parts of the sites may have been inhabited at any one time, and some of the sites may not be exactly contemporary. Many of the sites, and perhaps many of a particular size range, may not have been found. So, any original rank–size relationship is blurred and distorted by the time it reaches the archaeologist. If this blurring and distortion result from a great variety of factors, it may be reasonable to equate the aggregate effect with random blurring.

Chapman (1970) found that simulation of the random blurring of rank–size relationships decreased the organization or order in the pattern, and entropy always increased. Beckman (1958) and Vining (1953) have also suggested that, if a clear stepped hierarchy is considered and random variation is allowed within each level, a total blurring of the steps and a continuum of settlement sizes occur. So it is likely that many archaeological rank–size relationships will have high entropy and a low information content because of the blurring effect of survival and recovery factors.

The foregoing discussion has described some theories about the forms of rank–size relationships produced by different stochastic processes. Such a background of theory enables the archaeologist to identify and measure the nonrandom, structured, and organized settlement system. It is necessary now to consider the types of deviation from "random" expectation that might be looked for.

Chapman (1970) has shown that greater variation in size among smaller numbers of sites relates to lower levels of entropy. Consider a situation in which rank has been plotted against size for a known sample of sites (e.g., Figure 5.2). The lower the overall gradient of the rank–size line (i.e., the flatter the curve), the higher is the entropy. Steeper curves and sharper gradients reflect greater organization and lower entropy.

One of the most interesting types of departure from the expectations of stochastic processes is the occurrence of a clear stepped hierarchy. In classical central place theory, each hierarchical level within a set of service centers has a fixed size in relation to the other levels (Berry and Garrison 1958; Haggett 1972; Morrill 1970), although this idealized situation rarely occurs in reality.

Berry (1961) has suggested that rank–size relationships have two extremes. One of these is the *rank–size* type with an exponential continuum of settlement sizes, and the other is the *primate* situation in which there is a stratum of small towns and settlements dominated by one or more very large centers, and with deficiencies in numbers of settlements of intermediate sizes (Figure 5.1, where the centers are ranked from smallest to largest). A number of intermediate situations were also considered.

In a study of 37 countries, Berry (1961) found that primate patterns occurred in smaller countries with shorter histories of urbanization, and simpler economic and political lives. In such systems fewer forces act, so that inhomogeneities and kinks occur in the rank–size pattern. But in the larger, more complex countries, the rank–size exponential curve was found. Here the aggregate effect of numerous forces in a complex society results in a "random" pattern with high entropy (Berry 1961 and Simon 1955). As shown in Figure 5.1, Berry suggested that early, simple societies had a primate rank–size pattern which developed, by a series of stages of infilling, into the rank–size exponential curve.

Crumley (1976) has attempted to develop Berry's results into a general model about the growth of early states. The move from primacy to rank–size reflects the process of urbanization, so that the type of changes seen in Figure 5.1 should be identifiable in the settlement patterns of early states. She suggests a possible example of this from the pattern of settlement around the city of Uruk on the Mesopotamian plain. In the late Uruk period (ca. 3300 BC) a primate situation is suggested, whereas in the Early Dynastic period (ca. 2800 BC) there is more of an even spread in size between small hamlets and towns, and Crumley suggests that this indicates a move toward the rank–size continuum.

There have been several other studies of the rank–size relationships of archaeological sites. The analyses of Iron Age hillforts and Mycenaean sites

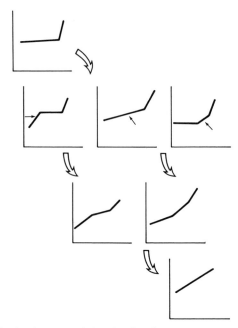

FIGURE 5.1 *The development of city size distributions according to Berry (1961, 583). The rank–size relationship (sizes ranked from smallest to largest) develops from "primate" (top left) via intermediate stages, to "rank–size" (bottom right).*

have already been mentioned, and Johnson (1972) has examined the hierarchy of Early Dynastic sites in the Diyālā Plains, Iraq. Rathje (1973) has studied cemeteries, the graves being ranked according to richness and artifact content, with an approach similar to that being developed in this chapter. He sees the rank-richness graph, in which there is a continuum of richness with a constantly decreasing exponential slope, as reflecting "the relative independent sorting of social identities and social identity symbols" (Rathj   749). But where there are marked levels of social status, there may be concentrations of social roles and their associated insignia so that a series of plateaus occurs in the rank–richness graph.

The aim of the remainder of this study is to examine the types of stochastic processes which can best be seen as generating a wide range of archaeological data, and to consider the nature and interpretation of deviations from expected patterns.

The Data

Twelve data sets were used in the analysis. These were chosen from available publications and represent a range of different types of site, different dates and areas, and different standards of data collection and fieldwork. In all cases the raw data were converted into size shares (p. 119). In interpreting the results of the analysis, discussion will focus partly on the nature of the archaeological sample. For this reason, an assessment of the data is included in the following descriptions.

The internal acreages of *Iron Age hillforts* in the southwest of Britain were measured on 6 in. Ordance Survey Maps. The precise region studied is that enclosed in Figure 3.9 of Hodder and Orton (1976), comprising mainly the Wessex area of Dorset, Hampshire, Wiltshire, and Somerset. Two types of hillfort have been considered separately. Multivallate hillforts, with more than one defensive bank and ditch, are thought to be especially characteristic of the later Iron Age in the area studied (see Harding 1974, 65), although several begin earlier. Many, such as Danebury and Maiden Castle, appear to enclose densely occupied sites. The more numerous univallate forts, on the other hand, cover a long period beginning in the Bronze Age. Their function probably varied from stock enclosure to small farmstead to large settlement. But any generalization about the function of hillforts is restricted by the lack of adequate excavation of their interiors. So one limitation of these data is that the nature of the sites is not fully understood, although it would probably be correct to say that the univallate hillforts comprise a wider range of functional types than do the multivallate. A further limitation of the data is that the hillforts are not all contemporary. But again the multivallate probably cover a shorter period of time than the univallate. The number of known hillforts will probably be added to in the future, many may have been destroyed, and the general lack of adequate excavation has already been noted. As far as one can assess, then, the hillforts provide relatively "bad" data, although the multivallate less so than the univallate.

Romano-British walled towns in lowland Britain in the third and fourth centuries AD provide a "better" sample. They cover a restricted date range and it is unlikely that large numbers of new sites will be found. In addition, the walled area can be measured fairly precisely in most cases, although occupation outside the walls is known. Epigraphic and literary evidence indicates that there is some relationship between town size and political, administrative and economic importance.

The distribution of *Romano-British sites in the Lincolnshire Fenlands* has been studied in detail by fieldwalking and air photography (Salway *et al.* 1970). As a result of the survey, an individual site was defined as "a scatter of ploughed domestic debris, often over an area of dark occupation soil (ibid., 49)." The sizes of these sites ranged from about 50 ft. long to 300 ft. by 400 ft. Such surface spreads in the plowsoil may represent farms that sometimes clustered into settlements. Sites were grouped by Salway *et al.* into the same "settlement" when separated by less than 500 ft. "Settlements" were then grouped into "complexes" if less than 1500 ft. apart.

One difficulty connected with these data is that it is difficult to be certain how much of a settlement or complex was in use at any one time, although Salway *et al.* do attempt to date the sites in each settlement individually. A further problem is that the area covered by pottery scatters may not accurately reflect the size of the site beneath the plowsoil. This is especially the case with sites which were under crop or grass so that no occupation material could be collected. Because of these problems, only one set of site dimension data was used in this study. These were the approximate dimensions of complexes in the late second century. Since the complexes were possibly not fully occupied at any one time, more reliable data can perhaps be obtained from the numbers of individual sites in the settlements and complexes at particular phases. The phases used were the late second century and the early fourth century AD. Salway *et al.*, however, make the point that these are minimal figures, including only discovered distinguishable dated sites. They undoubtedly underestimate the actual numbers of sites in many of the settlements and complexes. Problems of this sort limit the reliability of the Fenland data even though these result from very detailed and intensive field survey and analysis. The "better" data are the numbers of sites in settlements and complexes, since they do not involve a high level of measurement.

The distribution and size of *Early Dynastic I* sites from the Diyālā Plains, Iraq (ca. 2800 BC) have already been examined by Johnson (1972). The data used by Johnson are based on surveys by Adams, who points to several known or suspected biases (Adams 1965, 120). Oates (1977) has also provided a good discussion of the difficulties of using Mesopotamian survey data for locational studies. Specifically considering Johnson's (1975) study of earlier Uruk settlement, she points to the difficulty of providing accurate dates for sites. Site size is particularly difficult to assess because not all of a site may have been occupied at one time. Also, disturbance may cause the outward spread of shards from a mound. "Thus in archaeological terms overall distribution of settlement debris is a questionable criterion of site size, and an even more doubtful indicator of population (Oates 1977, 104)."

Johnson (1972) grouped the Diyālā sites subjectively into large towns (over 15 ha), towns (6–15 ha), large villages (3–5 ha), villages (1–3 ha), and hamlets (less than 1 ha) on the assumption that "areal size is . . . directly proportional to functional and population size (Johnson 1972, 770)." The following note was added: "This is most probably an erroneous assumption. It is, however, necessary due to the present lack of more detailed data." Indeed, Oates (1977, 106) gives numerous examples of where, among Assyrian capitals for example, documentary evidence shows that a correlation between size, importance, and the number of "service functions" cannot be made.

Similar problems affect the distribution of *Late Helladic I–IIIB sites in*

Messenia, Greece. The survey of surface indications of sites in this area was carried out by the University of Minnesota Messenia Expedition (McDonald and Hope-Simpson 1972). The sites have been divided here into those in the "near" province based on Pylos and the "far" province, following the provisional division made by Chadwick (1972, 1976). McDonald and Hope-Simpson point to several limitations of their data. For example, the size of the site is measured as the area strewn with surface pottery and other habitation debris. But "erosion and wash versus deep earth cover, the season and state of cultivation when the collection was made, the history and use of the site, and various other factors might make such observations [on size] meaningless or even misleading (Chadwick 1976, 126)." The lack of firm stratigraphic results from the area also makes dating from scatters of pottery very difficult, especially when the shards are scanty and worn. Not all sites said to be LH I–IIIB are, therefore, necessarily precisely contemporary, while the whole of the site may not have been occupied at the same time. As was found with the Mesopotamian sites, comments in the UMME catalog of sites in Messenia suggest that there may be no clear relationship between the political or administrative importance of sites and their size.

The final data set used in this study is of rather a different nature than the preceding. These are the lengths of *earthen long barrows* in southern England (Ashbee 1970). These neolithic burial mounds cover the period from the mid fourth millennium to the late third millennium BC. The spatial distribution of long barrow lengths has already been studied by Reed (1974). The data have been included in this study for two reasons. First, they provide a contrast to the settlement data. Second, they have played a part in Renfrew's (1973) hypothesis that the neolithic in Wessex saw the gradual development of social stratification, and that long barrows may have had a symbolic value for small social groups. If this is correct, it is possible that the lengths of the barrows could have been used to symbolize the relative importance of individuals or groups. If they were, and if the societies were ranked, some structuring would occur in the rank–size distribution. An analysis of the sizes of the long barrows, then, might provide a test for Renfrew's hypothesis. Ashbee (1970, 21) has already noted that "almost every group [of long barrows] has one or more extended or great mounds which on a size basis stand apart from their neighbours."

The actual data used in this study were the lengths of those earthen long barrows without evidence of sarsen stones or stone chambers in the south-west of England (Dorset, Hampshire, Wiltshire, Cranborne Chase, Stonehenge, and Salisbury Plain groups). The main limitation of these data is that no two barrows can be said to be precisely contemporary. They represent the residue of a process which continued over a very long period of time.

The data sets just discussed vary from relatively "good" (such as the

Romano-British walled towns) to the very "bad" (such as the Late Helladic sites). Indeed, it might be felt that many or all of them have too many limitations to make any analysis worthwhile. But any such feeling occurs because archaeologists have traditionally refrained from developing types of hypotheses which specifically consider the nature of the data. By using the approach outlined earlier as the basis for analysis, it is specifically assumed that marked but unstructured survival and recovery biases will blur and destroy any original structure in the data. According to this approach, there is very little that can be said about an unstructured "random" pattern. But if the survival and recovery biases have been acting in a structured, "nonrandom" way, this will be visible in the resulting pattern and the pattern can be interpreted accordingly. In some cases, however, no postdepositional factors may be found to explain the observed structure. Also, two sets of data (early and late Romano-British sites in the Fenlands, for example) may have been affected by identical survival and recovery factors, yet one data set may show a markedly more structured rank–size relationship than the other. In such cases, it is justifiable to consider whether any constraints and restrictions affected the processes which originally formed the data. This chapter aims to provide an approach for the identification of constraints whether in the original processes of data formation or in the survival and recovery processes. The basis of the analysis will be to compare the data sets with the end results of different simulated processes.

The Processes

This section describes the growth processes used to simulate rank–size curves that could be compared with the actual data. In each case the simulated curve was plotted by the computer (e.g., Figure 5.2). Also calculated in order to aid comparison of the actual and simulated data were (a) the sum of all the differences between actual and simulated sizes at each rank, (b) the square root of the sum of all the squared differences between actual and simulated sizes, and (c) the value obtained in (b) divided by n (the number of sites). In Table 5.1 the data sets have been arranged from smallest to largest n. The figures in the table show that the average difference (c—in parentheses in Table 5.1) is greatly affected by the number of sites so that the total squared differences between the actual and simulated curves (b—not in parentheses in Table 5.1) provide a better guide to the relative fit of the different processes to the data. Although there is also a relationship between (b) and n, marked exceptions and anomalies can be picked out in the table, and these are discussed presently. However, any measure of total or average differences between the simulated and actual data may hide specific and interesting variation. Visual comparison between the curves is essential.

A further warning should be made about comparing the fit of different simulation processes to any one data set. This is only possible where the size shares for each settlement have been defined in the same way. Where a growth process which has arbitrary size increments is concerned (see later) the results cannot be compared with the other procedures.

1. In the first process to be described, the same number of sites as in each data set was chosen from a normal distribution having the the same mean and standard deviation as the actual data. The sizes allocated to the n sites were then ranked in descending order. The whole process was repeated 20 times for each data set and average size values for each rank were obtained and plotted (Figure 5.2). There is no theoretical basis for expecting a normal rather than a skewed distribution such as the gamma for size distributions. But it is of interest to consider the simple situation of symmetrical variation around a mean.

The results of the random selection of site sizes from a normal distribution often provide better fits to those data sets with larger n (see earlier). However, the multivallate hillforts provide by far the worst fit even though they have only medium n. This is because of the markedly concave rank–size relationship of the actual data in which a few sites are dominant. The data sets providing the best fits are the two collections of information on site numbers from the Roman Fenlands in the earlier phase (late second century). Visual comparison (Figure 5.2) shows that both the simulated and actual curves for the Fenland data have little concavity.

2. Using the actual number of sites for each data set, the predictions of the random splitting model with [Equation (5.5)] and without [Equation (5.4)] a minimum share size were compared with the data sets. Figure 5.3 provides an example of the fit of this model and the results are shown in Table 5.1. As Cliff and co-workers (1974) found in their application of this model to modern data, the use of a minimum share size allows a better fit, although Table 5.1 shows that the difference is usually marginal. As was found for the first process, the late second century Fenland sites provide a relatively good fit to the model, in whatever form are the data. Both the Early Dynastic sites and the multivallate hillforts show relatively bad fits. The reasons for this are discussed later.

3. The third procedure simulates a growth process in which units of size are added to settlements over time in such a way that larger sites attract more units. The "contagiousness" of larger populations, attracting larger increments of population, has already been discussed.

The simulations began in phase 1 with the number of settlements observed in a data set. The sizes of these sites were chosen at random from a uniform distribution between 1.0 and 20.0. In a second series of simulations the sizes were chosen from a normal distribution of mean 10.0. Unit increments were then added to the settlements at random, but larger sites had a greater chance of attracting these increments. Thus, if a site had a 1/20th share of the total settlement area, it had a 1/20th chance of receiving an

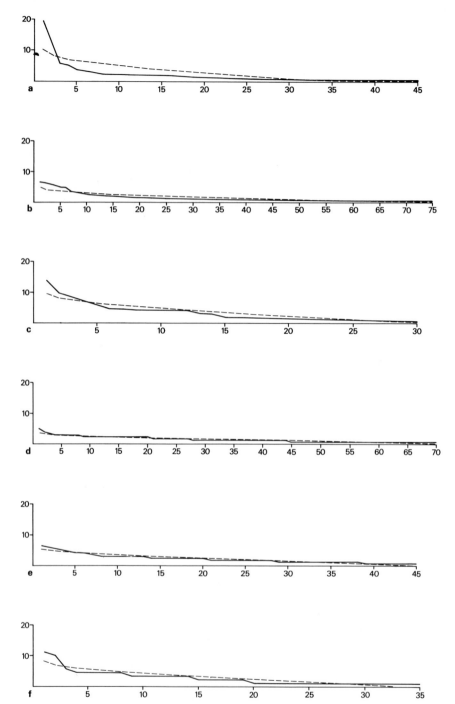

FIGURE 5.2 *The actual relationship between rank (horizontal axis) and size (vertical axis) for the 12 data sets. Sites are ranked from largest to smallest. The curves predicted as a result of allocating sizes from the normal distribution are also shown (dashed lines). (a) Multivallate Iron Age hillforts; (b) univallate Iron Age hillforts; (c) Romano-British walled towns; (d)–(h) Romano-British Fenland sites: (d) late second century* AD, *numbers of sites per*

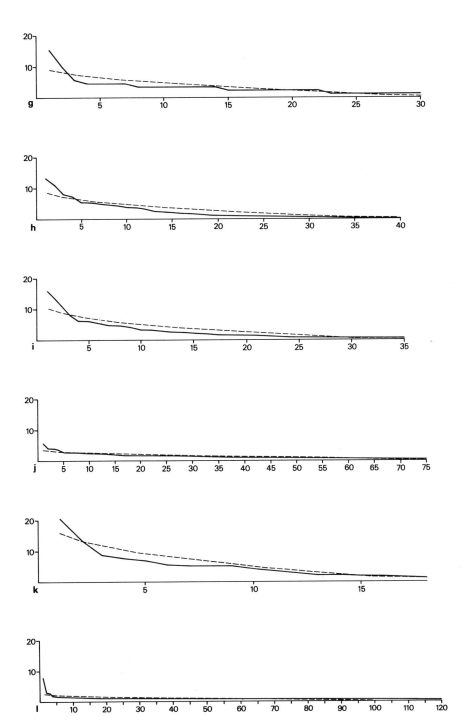

"settlement"; (e) late second century AD, *numbers of sites per "complex"; (f) early fourth century* AD, *numbers of sites per "settlement"; (g) early fourth century* AD, *numbers of sites per "complex"; (h) areal size of late second century "complexes"; (i) Early Dynastic sites from Iraq; (j) Late Helladic sites in the "near" province; (k) Late Helladic sites in the "far" province; (l) neolithic earthen long barrows.*

TABLE 5.1

The Fit of the Data Sets to the Rank–Size Relationships Produced by Different Procedures

Data set	*n*	Normal distribution	Random splitting model without minimum	Random splitting model with minimum	Central place theory		
					$K = 3$	$K = 4$	$K = 7$
Late Helladic "far"	19	7.9(.4)	31.0(1.6)	28.7(1.5)	10.8(.6)	13.2(.7)	16.3(.9)
Romano-British walled	32	6.4(.2)	24.8 (.8)	23.4 (.7)	11.6(.4)	13.4(.4)	15.8(.5)
Late Fenland complexes	32	9.0(.3)	23.9 (.7)	20.5 (.6)	9.6(.3)	11.1(.3)	13.4(.4)
Late Fenland settlements	37	6.6(.2)	21.5 (.6)	17.7 (.5)	11.8(.3)	13.1(.4)	14.7(.4)
Early Dynastic sites	39	9.3(.2)	26.5 (.7)	26.2 (.7)	11.3(.3)	13.1(.3)	15.7(.4)
Early Fenland areas	45	8.1(.2)	24.4 (.5)	23.8 (.5)	12.1(.3)	13.9(.3)	16.0(.4)
Multivallate hillforts	48	14.8(.3)	26.5 (.6)	25.7 (.5)	7.5(.2)	9.3(.2)	12.2(.3)
Early Fenland complexes	48	2.8(.1)	17.5 (.4)	14.6 (.3)	12.4(.3)	13.1(.3)	14.1(.3)
Early Fenland settlements	71	2.8(.0)	14.4 (.2)	10.8 (.2)	10.7(.2)	11.2(.2)	11.8(.2)
Univallate hillforts	77	5.9(.1)	16.9 (.2)	15.4 (.2)	11.5(.1)	12.2(.2)	13.2(.2)
Late Helladic "near"	79	3.2(.0)	14.2 (.2)	12.3 (.2)	9.7(.1)	10.3(.1)	11.1(.1)
Neolithic long barrows	122	6.3(.1)	12.3 (.1)	10.3 (.1)	5.9(.0)	6.5(.1)	7.3(.1)

increment. Six hundred units were added in this way, but the process was stopped at phases 2 (after 200 additions), 3 (400 additions), and 4 (600 additions). At each phase 20 separate simulations were carried out to produce average sizes for the *n*th ranked settlement. At each phase, also, the size shares of each site were reassessed, and the shares were ranked, plotted, and compared with the actual data.

The example in Figure 5.4 shows that through time, a more concave

FIGURE 5.3 An example of the predictions of the random splitting model with (dashed line) and without (dotted line) a minimum share size. The predictions are for the Late Helladic "far" province sites (continuous line).

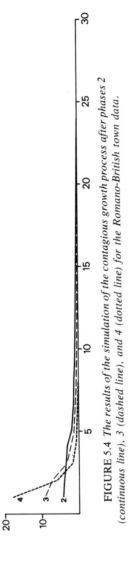

FIGURE 5.4 The results of the simulation of the contagious growth process after phases 2 (continuous line), 3 (dashed line), and 4 (dotted line) for the Romano-British town data.

rank–size curve is formed as the bigger sites increase relatively faster. This pattern would, of course, not occur if some maximum limit on size had been introduced. In the latter case the middle ranges of sizes would gradually have filled in the gap between large and small, producing a less concave curve. As noted earlier, Berry (1961) has obtained some evidence of greater concavity in the rank–size graphs of less-developed countries. In the process simulated here, greater concavity occurs as larger centers attract greater increments at the expense of smaller centers. Thus, greater concavity again relates to a more constrained, less random, situation.

Nine out of the 12 data sets consistently provide better fits at phase 3 than at phases 2 and 4 (Table 5.2). This suggests that most of the data sets reflect the play of some constraints, but that these constraints have not been severe. However, as has frequently been noted before, the multivallate Iron Age hillforts and the Fenland late second century sites indicate opposite and marked deviations from the general situation. The multivallate hillforts show a considerably better fit at phase 4 than in the previous two phases. This relates to the dominance of a few forts in this data set. The Fenland second century sites (site number data) show the opposite situation with the best fit found at phase 2. As is further discussed later, this period and area concern a rural situation with little development of centralized control and without a complex site hierarchy. As Salway *et al.* (1970) have pointed out, by the fourth century AD the population appears to have gathered into larger agglomerations. It is thus of interest that it is the later simulated phase (3) which provides a better fit for the fourth century data from the same area.

A major failing of the processes just discussed is that they do not take spatial factors into account. In reality the rate at which a settlement grows and attracts population depends partly on the size and number of neighboring settlements. The simulation procedures described previously have the advantage of being fairly simple so that the results can be relatively easily understood. By introducing a spatial element, the number or variables which can affect the results increases. For example, what is the effect of different spatial patterns of settlement, and in what precise way do nearby settlements affect each other? Because of the increased number of variables taken into account, the results of the simulations are less easy to interpret.

4. Morrile (1962) has examined the growth of a settlement hierarchy with a fairly formal spatial pattern. Rather less rigid rules were used in the fourth procedure followed in this study. As in the contagious growth process, the simulation for each data set began in phase 1 by choosing the actual number of settlement sizes at random from a uniform distribution between 1.0 and 20.0. These sizes were then ranked from largest to smallest and converted into shares. Each settlement was allocated a location at random within a 50 × 50 unit area, and the total size of settlements within a 10- or 20-unit (in different simulations) radius of each settlement was calculated. In phase 2, $10n$ new units had the chance of being allocated to the existing settlements in

TABLE 5.2
The Fit of the Data Sets to the Rank–Size Relationships Simulated by the Contagious Growth Processes

Data set	n	Beginning with uniform distribution			Beginning with normal distribution		
		Phase 2	Phase 3	Phase 4	Phase 2	Phase 3	Phase 4
Late Helladic "far"	19	20.3(1.1)	18.4(1.0)	20.7(1.1)	19.5(1.0)	18.6(1.0)	21.2(1.1)
Romano-British towns	32	16.7 (.5)	15.0 (.5)	17.1 (.5)	15.8 (.5)	15.1 (.5)	18.5 (.6)
Late Fenland complexes	32	16.1 (.5)	13.5 (.4)	15.6 (.5)	15.3 (.5)	13.4 (.4)	16.0 (.5)
Late Fenland settlements	37	14.1 (.4)	12.6 (.3)	15.7 (.4)	13.6 (.4)	12.8 (.3)	17.1 (.5)
Early Dynastic sites	39	19.0 (.5)	15.7 (.4)	16.3 (.4)	18.3 (.5)	15.4 (.4)	16.9 (.4)
Early Fenland areas	45	17.3 (.4)	14.8 (.3)	16.0 (.4)	16.7 (.4)	14.6 (.3)	16.4 (.4)
Multivallate hillforts	48	20.5 (.4)	16.2 (.3)	12.9 (.3)	19.7 (.4)	15.5 (.3)	12.9 (.3)
Early Fenland complexes	48	11.3 (.2)	11.6 (.2)	15.6 (.3)	11.0 (.2)	12.2 (.3)	17.0 (.4)
Early Fenland settlements	71	9.4 (.1)	9.7 (.1)	13.0 (.2)	9.2 (.1)	10.2 (.1)	14.5 (.2)
Univallate hillforts	77	11.5 (.1)	9.8 (.1)	12.0 (.2)	10.9 (.1)	9.8 (.1)	12.9 (.2)
Late Helladic "near"	79	9.3 (.1)	8.9 (.1)	11.7 (.1)	8.9 (.1)	9.2 (.1)	12.7 (.2)
Neolithic long barrows	122	8.9 (.1)	8.0 (.1)	8.3 (.1)	8.6 (.1)	7.9 (.1)	8.7 (.1)

such a way that settlements in locations where there was less competition from neighbors grew faster, while larger centers had a greater chance of attracting increments.

This procedure was achieved in the following way. If the size of settlement i divided by the size of settlements in the 10- or 20-unit radius was greater than 1.0 (or .5, 2.0 in different simulations), then that settlement had a .75 ($\frac{3}{4}$) chance of being allocated a new unit. If the size ratio was less than .5, the settlement had only a .5 ($\frac{1}{2}$) chance of receiving an increment.

The whole process up to this point was repeated five times and the average size for each settlement was obtained. The settlements were then ranked again, the differences between the actual and the simulated rank–size relationships were assessed, and the simulated data plotted. In phases 3 and 4, $10n$ new units again had the chance of being allocated to the settlements, these being ranked and plotted at the end of each phase.

The fit of the end results of this simulation procedure to the data is shown in Table 5.3 for the 10-unit radius and varying size ratios, and a plotted example with the size ratio at 1.0 is shown in Figure 5.5. The example and the tables show that the introduction of a spatial component into the growth process results in the stabilization of the rank–size relationships. Over time larger centers are prevented from dominating the rest by the occurrence of neighboring settlements and there is little overall change in the pattern of size shares. However, there are less constraints with the lower size ratio (.5) and all sites increase fairly evenly. With the higher size ratio (2.0) increments are more likely to be added only when a site is relatively large and/or remote. In the latter case there are stronger constraints on the growth process and it is of interest that higher size ratios always provide a better fit to the data than do lower ratios (Table 5.3).

5. A fifth procedure was included which provides a contrast to those just discussed. This was to predict site size according to central place theory. In Christaller's view, each rank of settlements has a fixed size in relation to the largest center, and there are a fixed number of settlements at each rank. There is thus a clear stepped hierarchy. For example, in the $K = 3$ (marketing) principle there are 1, 3, 9, and 27 central places in descending levels in the hierarchy, and if the size of the largest center is s, the size of a second level center is $s/3$, of a third level center $s/9$, and of a fourth level $s/27$. (Berry and Garrison 1958; Haggett 1972). Similarly, in the $K = 4$ (transport) situation there are 1, 4, 16, and 64 centers in the different levels, and in the $K = 7$ (administrative) principle, 1, 7, 49, and 343 centers. Thus the $K = 7$ situation describes the greatest hierarchical distance between large and small centers. It is a more "controlled" and "constrained" situation with fewer medium range centers.

The fit of the predictions of central place theory to the data shown in Table 5.1 (see also the example in Figure 5.6). The definition of size share in this case allows direct comparison with the results of the first simulation process (random allocation from normal distributions) and it is clear that the first process generally provides a better fit than the predictions of central place theory. However, this is not the case for the Iron Age multivallate hillforts, and it will be shown later that the nature of late Iron Age society indeed leads one to expect a constrained, nonrandom, settlement hierarchy.

TABLE 5.3
The Fit of the Data Sets to the Rank–Size Relationships Simulated by the Growth Process with a Spatial Component

Data set	n	Size ratio = .5			Size ratio = 1.0			Size ratio = 2.0		
		Phase 2	Phase 3	Phase 4	Phase 2	Phase 3	Phase 4	Phase 2	Phase 3	Phase 4
Late Helladic "far"	19	31.2(1.6)	30.1(1.6)	30.5(1.6)	28.2(1.5)	28.6(1.5)	29.1(1.5)	26.5(1.4)	27.8(1.5)	28.4(1.5)
Romano-British towns	32	38.5(1.2)	40.2(1.3)	38.1(1.2)	34.4(1.1)	34.1(1.1)	33.1(1.0)	32.9(1.0)	32.0(1.0)	30.7(1.0)
Late Fenland complexes	32	38.1(1.2)	37.9(1.2)	38.1(1.2)	34.7(1.1)	33.7(1.1)	32.8(1.0)	33.3(1.0)	32.0(1.0)	310(1.0)
Late Fenland settlements	37	38.2(1.0)	40.2(1.1)	38.5(1.0)	34.1(.9)	34.8(.9)	33.6(.9)	32.0(.9)	33.2(.9)	31.9(.9)
Early Dynastic sites	39	49.3(1.0)	41.5(1.1)	43.2(1.1)	35.6(.9)	36.1(.9)	37.5(1.0)	34.4(.9)	35.1(.9)	36.3(.9)
Early Fenland areas	45	42.8(1.0)	43.3(1.0)	41.7(.9)	39.1(.9)	39.9(.9)	37.8(.8)	37.0(.8)	38.4(.9)	36.8(.8)
Multivallate hillforts	48	45.0(.9)	44.3(.9)	43.0(.9)	40.6(.8)	41.1(.9)	40.2(.8)	39.1(.8)	40.3(.8)	39.2(.8)
Early Fenland complexes	48	42.2(.9)	42.0(.9)	41.1(.9)	37.7(.8)	36.9(.8)	36.3(.8)	35.9(.7)	35.6(.7)	35.0(.7)
Early Fenland settlements	71	48.9(.7)	48.4(.7)	49.8(.7)	43.6(.6)	43.1(.6)	44.4(.6)	42.8(.6)	42.2(.6)	43.5(.6)
Univallate hillforts	77	52.1(.7)	52.8(.7)	51.2(.7)	46.4(.6)	46.8(.6)	44.6(.6)	45.2(.6)	45.9(.6)	43.9(.6)
Late Helladic "near"	79	50.1(.6)	49.1(.6)	50.8(.6)	45.9(.6)	45.4(.6)	46.7(.6)	44.9(.6)	44.4(.6)	45.5(.6)
Neolithic long barrows	122	60.2(.5)	60.3(.5)	60.7(.5)	55.2(.5)	55.8(.5)	56.0(.5)	54.4(.4)	55.1(.5)	55.3(.5)

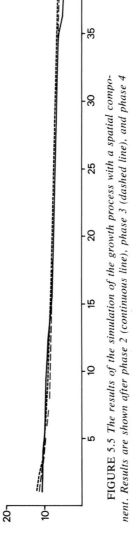

FIGURE 5.5 *The results of the simulation of the growth process with a spatial compo-nent. Results are shown after phase 2 (continuous line), phase 3 (dashed line), and phase 4 (dotted line) for the Romano-British town data.*

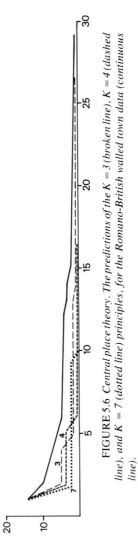

FIGURE 5.6 *Central place theory. The predictions of the K = 3 (broken line), K = 4 (dashed line), and K = 7 (dotted line) principles, for the Romano-British walled town data (continuous line).*

The only other case in which central place theory provides as good or a better fit than the random process is the neolothic long barrows (see later discussion). The greatest difference between the two processes is in the case of the Fenland second century AD sites. The good fit of these data to the first process has already been mentioned and they provide a particularly bad fit for central place theory. This is also the case for the areal size data from the same sites.

In general, then, the data sets show less contraints than envisaged in central place theory. Similarly, it is the $K = 3$ principle which always provides the best fit, and the $K = 7$ the worst. As suggested earlier, $K = 7$ implies greater constraints on the settlement hierarchy, and none of the data sets indicates this type of centralized administrative control.

Discussion of the Results

An important initial comment to make as a result of the simulations and procedures described earlier is that flatter, less concave, rank–size curves relate to the more unconstrained and purely random processes. More structured and constrained processes such as long-term contagious growth and central place hierarchies produce more concave rank–size curves. This finding corresponds well with work already discussed in this chapter (Chapman 1970). Lower gradients for rank–size curves indicate decreases in the "organization" or order in the settlement hierarchy, and increases in entropy. Berry (1961) has also seen the concave "primate" type of curve as being distinct from the less structured forms that result from less constrained processes.

But how does this difference between more and less organized rank–size relationships relate to the archaeological data? This is discussed by considering each data set in turn. Consideration of the relationship between the simulated and actual rank–size curves must take into account survival and recovery processes as well as the original formation processes. It will be shown that for the "bad" data, the less constrained processes which produce flatter rank–size curves provide better fits. For the "better" data, the more constrained processes provide better fits if restrictions and controls were imposed on the settlement hierarchy. In the latter cases the more concave rank–size curves are found.

Iron Age Hillforts

The multivallate hillforts provide a relatively poor fit to random processes such as choice from a normal distribution and random splitting. But they provide a relatively good fit to the predictions of the highly constrained central place theory, and to the end result of a contagious growth process. It has been shown that the multivallate hillforts comprise more reliable data than the univallate. Although the latter provide a slightly worse fit to the very unconstrained processes (1 and 2) than the other data sets with similar *n,* they do not provide as poor a fit as the multivallate or as good a fit to the more constrained situations. This difference between the two types of hillfort is probably related partly to the nature and survival of the data. But the difference may also be related to the original formation processes. The rank–size relationship of the multivallate forts has suggested a particularly highly constrained situation because of the presence of hillforts such as Ham Hill (210 acres) in an area in which the majority of the forts are below 25 acres (for a discussion of hillfort size, see Forde-Johnston 1976, 93–98). There is considerable evidence that the later Iron Age in Britain saw the growth of a strongly hierarchical society. Literary evidence relates the presence of strict social classes (Tierney 1960), whereas the archaeological evidence includes parade armor and highly valuable objects which must have symbolized and supported an elite. The southeast of Britain provides evidence of a hierarchy of centers dominated by *oppida,* but the lack of *oppida* in the southwest area studied here has meant that it has been difficult to determine the nature of the hierarchy. The evidence presented earlier, however, certainly suggests that in the southwest too a constrained situation had developed in the later Iron Age which led to the growth of some centers at the expense of others. However, it must also be borne in mind that few multivallate hillforts have been or are being extensively excavated. Until more refined chronologies and better understanding of the internal organization of these sites have been obtained, it remains possible that the structure in the rank–size relationship is an artifact of our present lack of knowledge.

Romano-British Fenland Settlement

In the discussion of the different simulations it was noted that the data for the Fenland ''settlements'' and ''complexes'' in the late second century AD stood out from the other data sets. A relatively good fit was found to processes 1 and 2. In addition, these data provided the only two cases in which a shorter period of contagious growth consistently led to a better fit. In contrast, the predictions of central place theory do not provide a good fit for the data. The data for the area sizes of the ''complexes'' in the late second century are less reliable because it is difficult to gauge whether the whole of the ''complex'' was in use at this time. For this reason the patterning in these data is less easy to see. However, this data set does show some of the greatest departures from the predictions of central place theory.

The data for the ''settlements'' and ''complexes'' in the early fourth century AD, however, show less similarities with the more unrestrained processes, but the data are not sufficiently structured to correspond with the central place theory predictions.

Salway *et al.* (1970) have described the changing settlement pattern in the Fenlands in the following way. In the first century AD, there was a pattern of single farms and small hamlets. In the second century all the existing settlements grow bigger and "new ones are added, often near an existing bunch" (Salway *et al*. 1970, 57). In the third and fourth centuries AD, the percentage of people living in agglomerations increased. This trend toward larger and more agglomerations is seen as being possibly related to the changing drainage patterns and wetter conditions.

The increasing agglomeration has been verified in this analysis in that the contagious growth simulations gave the best fit for the late second century data in phase 2 and the best fit for the early fourth century data in phase 3. In a peaceful rural situation in the second century it is possible that no marked constraints were in play on settlement formation and size. This is not the case in the fourth century when the worsening climate had perhaps caused agglomeration. The constraints here are environmental and, as shown earlier, the result is a less "random" pattern.

Other Data Sets

The analysis of the remaining data sets has shown that the rank–size graphs can be approximated by a variety of different processes. The Early Dynastic sites from the Diyālā Plain, however, show relatively bad fits to the normal distribution and to the random splitting model. These data are also among the worst fits to the end results of the contagious growth processes. Visual inspection of this rank–size graph (Figure 5.2) shows a relatively marked concavity. The play of some constraints is therefore suggested. It has been shown previously that these data are unreliable, and the nonrandom structure may be due to some data bias. But discussion of the data noted numerous effects on the survival and collection of the information and no systematic bias could be discovered which would have caused the structuring in the rank–size graph. The Early Dynastic settlement pattern is certainly the product of a fully developed state system with strong centralized control and authority. It is precisely in this type of system that deviations from "random" expectation are most likely to be found, even with inadequate data.

The Romano-British walled towns and the Late Helladic sites have size structures which are between what can be produced by very unconstrained processes and the highly constrained situation represented by classical central place theory. Their weakly concave rank–size graphs, therefore, do not reflect the play of any specially marked forces. In the case of the Romano-British walled towns it has been argued elsewhere (Hodder 1972) that the pattern is one of a hierarchy of service centers in which administrative, central government control, although important, did not play an overriding part. There were no strong forces causing inhomogeneities in the rank–size structure. The unreliable nature of the Late Helladic site data has already been discussed. Difficulties in the collection of the data, and in the dating of sites, and the apparent lack of correspondence between size and hierarchical status may have masked any original rank–size structure which may have existed. An ordered pattern would certainly have been expected in view of the highly centralized political and economic system evidenced in the Pylos area (Chadwick 1976). This structure is not reflected in the surviving settlement size hierarchy.

The neolithic long barrows are also poor data in that the barrows cannot be considered all contemporary within a broad period, and they cover a wide area in which, if Renfrew (1973) is correct, there may have been many separate hierarchical systems. It must also be remembered that it is only one possibility among many that the size of burial mounds reflects the social hierarchy, even if any such hierarchy existed. Perhaps as a result of these factors, the data correspond relatively well with the predictions of stochastic processes such as the random splitting model. That the data do not provide a better fit (see the relatively high deviation of these data from the normal distribution) is largely because of the presence of one very large barrow 1790 ft. long (Maiden Castle, Winterborne St. Martin) which well surpasses the rest. It seems unlikely that this barrow reflects the dominance by one group of the whole of the Wessex area, and the great size may relate to different or additional functions carried out here. The special nature of this barrow is supported by the evidence of exceptional burial practices (Ashbee 1970). Thus, further work on smaller areas, and perhaps with more closely dated sites, is necessary before Renfrew's (1973) suggestion of the development of neolithic hierarchies can be adequately tested against the distribution of barrow size.

Conclusion

The most marked differences from the end results of relatively unconstrained stochastic processes occur with the more reliable data sets in which there has been some constraint on the development of a hierarchy (e.g., the multivallate hillforts). Unreliable data sets such as the Late Helladic sites, the univallate hillforts, and the neolithic long barrows show less marked deviations from expectation and it cannot be known whether restrictions and constraints on the pattern ever existed. However, the closest similarities with simple stochastic processes occur with apparently reliable data in a purely rural situation (Romano-British Fenlands), where the probable lack of any constraints, at least in the formation and perhaps in the survival of the pattern, may be assumed. Only later, in the same area, did a deteriorating climate cause the constraints on settlement location and development which resulted in nonrandom rank–size patterns. The structure in each rank–size curve is the composite result of a complex balance between original forces and survival and recovery processes. The work described here provides an approach to the detection and initial interpretation of these structures.

References

Adams R. McC., 1965, *Land Behind Baghdad: A History of Settlement of the Diyālā Plains*. Chicago and London.

Ashbee P., 1970, *The Earthen Long Barrow in Britain*. London, Dent.

Beckman M. J., 1958, City hierarchies and the distribution of city size, *Economic Development and Cultural Change* 6, 243–8.

Berry B. J. L., 1961, City size distributions and economic development, *Economic Development and Cultural Change* 9, 573–88.

Berry B. J. L. and Garrison W. L., 1958, Alternate explanations of urban rank-size relationships, *Annals of the Association of American Geographers* 48, 83–98.

Chadwick A., 1977, Computer simulation of settlement development in Bronze Age Messenia, in J. Bintliff (ed.), *Mycenaean Geography*, Cambridge, British Association for Mycenaean Studies, 88–93.

Chadwick J., 1972, The Mycenaean documents, in W. A. McDonald and G. R. Rapp (eds.), *The Minnesota Messenia Expedition*, Minneapolis, University of Minnesota Press, 100–116.

Chadwick J., 1976, *The Mycenaean World*. Cambridge, Cambridge University Press.

Chapman G., 1970, The application of information theory to the analysis of population distributions in space, *Economic Geography* 46, 317–31.

Cliff A. D., Haggett P. and Ord J. K., 1974, *Elementary Regional Structure: Some Quantitative Approaches to the Spatial Organisation of Static and Dynamic Regional Systems*. Cambridge, Cambridge University Press.

Cliff A. D. and Ord J. K., 1973, *Spatial Autocorrelation*. London, Pion.

Cohen J. E., 1966, *A Model of Simple Competition*. Harvard, Harvard University Press.

Crumley C. L., 1976, Toward a locational definition of state systems of settlement, *American Anthropologist* 78, 59–73.

Curry L., 1964, The random spatial economy: an exploration in settlement theory, *Annals of the Association of American Geographers* 54, 138–46.

Haggett P., 1972, *Geography: a Modern Synthesis*. New York, Harper and Row.

Harding D. W., 1974, *The Iron Age of Lowland Britain*. London, Routledge and Kegan Paul.

Hodder I., 1972, Locational models and the study of Romano-British settlement, in D. L. Clarke (ed.), *Models in Archaeology*, London, Methuen, 887–909.

Hodder I., and Orton C., 1976, *Spatial Analysis in Archaeology*. Cambridge, Cambridge University Press.

Johnson G. A., 1972, A test of the utility of central place theory in archaeology, in P. J. Ucko, R. Tringham and G. Dimbleby (eds.), *Man, Settlement and Urbanism*, London, Duckworth, 769–85.

Johnson G. A., 1975, Locational analysis and the investigation of Uruk Local Exchange Systems, in J. A. Sabloff and C. C. Lamberg-Karlovsky (eds.), *Ancient Civilization and Trade*, Albuquerque, University of New Mexico Press.

McDonald W. A. and Hope-Simpson R., 1972, Archaeological exploration, in W. A. McDonald and G. R. Rapp (eds.), *The Minnesota Messenia Expedition*, Minneapolis, University of Minnesota Press, 117–47.

Morrill R. L., 1962, *Simulation of Central Place Patterns over Time*. Lund Studies in Geography, B, 24.

Morrill R. L., 1970, *The Spatial Organisation of Society*. Belmont, California, Wadsworth.

Oates J., 1977, Archaeology and geography in Mesopotamia, in J. Bintliff (ed.), *Mycenaean Geography*, Cambridge, British Association for Mycenaean Studies, 101–6.

Pred A., 1967, *Innovation Diffusion as a Spatial Process*. Chicago, University of Chicago Press.

Rathje W. L., 1973, Models for mobile Maya: a variety of constraints, in C. Renfrew (ed.), *The Explanation of Culture Change: Models in Prehistory*, London, Duckworth, 731–60.

Reed R. C., 1974, Earthen long barrows: a new perspective, *Archaeological Journal* 131, 33–57.

Renfrew C., 1973, Monuments, mobilization and social organisation in neolithic Wessex, in C. Renfrew (ed.), *The Explanation of Culture Change: Models in Prehistory*, London, Duckworth, 539–58.

Salway P., Hallam S. J. and Bromwich J. l'A., 1970, *The Fenlands in Roman Times*. Royal Geographical Society Research Series, 5.

Simon H. A., 1955, On a class of skew distribution functions, *Biometrika* 42, 425–40.

Thomas F. N., 1967, Additional comments on population size relationships for sets of cities, in W. L. Garrison and D. F. Marble (eds.), *Quantitative Geography*, Northwestern University Studies in Geography, 13, 167–90.

Tierney J. J., 1960, The Celtic ethnography of Posidonius, *Proceedings of the Royal Irish Academy* 60, C, 189–236.

Vining R., 1953, Delimitation of economic areas: statistical conceptions in the study of the spatial structure of an economic system, *Journal of the American Statistical Association* 18, 44–64.

Whitworth W. A., 1934, *Choice and Chance*. New York.

Wiessner P., 1974, A functional estimator of population from floor area, *American Antiquity* 39, 343–9.

Zipf G. K., 1949, *Human Behaviour and the Principle of Least Effort*. New York, Hafner.

6

COLIN RENFREW

ERIC V. LEVEL

Exploring Dominance: Predicting Polities from Centers

Sociopolitical organization is not the same as economic organization, and social space differs from the spatial ordering of markets and other spatial features of market economy. This chapter starts with a specific underlying problem in archaeology: the reconstruction or prediction (retrodiction) of sociopolitical organization from archaeological data. How can we use settlement remains, as documented archaeologically, to formulate the social and political configurations which helped to generate them, and were influenced by them?

The investigation hints at regularities in the spatial patterning of society which remain to be explored, and in particular in the absolute size of the political territory which an autonomous center of a given population size can expect to exploit. Such cross-cultural regularities, if documented, would have a significance well beyond the confines of archaeology.

The general background to the problem has been treated elsewhere (Renfrew 1978, 103–112) and six axioms developed:

1. The human social group is defined by the habitual association of persons within a territory.
2. Human organization is segmentary in nature: human spatial organization is therefore cellular and modular.
3. Basic social groups do not exist in isolation, but affiliate together into larger groups, meeting together at periodic intervals.
4. Human society is often hierarchical in nature: Human spatial organization is therefore stratified.

145

Transformations:
Mathematical Approaches to Culture Change

5. The effective polity, the highest order social unit, may be identified by the scale and distribution of central places.
6. Special interactions between polities undoubtedly take place, creating uniformities in artifact distribution: Such uniformities in themselves do not document societies or peoples.

Our aim in undertaking the work discussed here was to investigate the fifth of these in particular.

It should be stated clearly at the outset that our outlook owes little to classical central place theory of the geographers (Christaller 1933; Lösch 1954). It is an alternative approach to the question of human spatial organization, making none of the assumptions about "economic man" and his behavior (many of them no doubt entirely valid) underlying central place theory. It has much more in common with the perspective of Soja (1971).

The following assumptions are made:

1. Polities have continuous territorial jurisdiction over their domains, without intervening parcels of land.
2. A piece of land is normally under the jurisdiction of a single autonomous authority (and, where appropriate, its deputies within a hierarchical structure). This does not necessarily exclude areas of noman's land, where territorial authority is not exercised.
3. "Capitals," the autonomous administrative centers of independent sociopolitical polities, are in general the largest settlement or administrative sites within the territories of their polities. (Cases in which the "capital," the seat of administration of the polity, is not the largest settlement or administrative center, often reflect clearly identifiable special factors: Most of them are artificial creations, summer palaces, or federal capitals reflecting the rather sophisticated device of a voluntary association of states.)
4. There is some positive correlation between the size of the autonomous "capital" center (whether measured by area or by population) and the territorial area of the polity over which it has control.

We make no initial assumption about the precise relationship indicated in assumption 4 (or "hypothesis" 4). It should be particularly noted that we do *not* assume that settlements above a given arbitrary size all rank as autonomous centers whereas those below do not. On the contrary, we envisage that some centers which are autonomous capitals of polities in a given large region will have smaller populations than those which are not. In this respect our analysis differs fundamentally from that of most archaeologists using central place considerations, including Johnson (1972, 1975). Likewise the writings of Berry (1961) and Crumley (1976) concerning the primate city, although of very real interest and relevance, do not focus upon precisely the problem we consider.

Our investigation is limited at present to sedentary societies: The formulation, as stated here, is not applicable to nomadic or other mobile groups.

The model is applied in the first instance at a given time: It is static. But when successive time points in a settlement system are considered, and changing political configurations and boundaries predicted, it becomes dynamic. Indeed the model could be linked with some procedure to predict the growth of centers (not attempted here) to foretell changing political boundaries and the conflicts that accompany them.

Problems in Reconstructing the Territories of Polities

Consider the landscape of autonomous polities, each with at least one permanent settlement within its territorial boundary. The existence of some measure of territoriality is assumed, although the boundaries could well be "fuzzy" (for fuzzy sets cf. Zadeh 1965) with overlapping at territorial extremes (cf. Soja 1971, fig. 8). These polities may range from relatively simple acephalous societies whose principal settlement is a single village to highly complex nation states with populations measured in millions.

We imagine a settlement distribution (Figure 6.1) in which there are several settlements within the confines of each polity. In the archaeological case, let us suppose that no prior evidence remains for the political organization or the arrangement of territories (Figure 6.2). The problem is to reach some reconstruction of these.

If the archaeological sites were in contemporary use (and this is an important condition), a first approach might be to construct Thiessen polygons around each (Figure 6.3). Each piece of land would then be allocated to the jurisdiction of the settlement nearest to it. This ignores, rightly or wrongly, the size of the centers as well as any hierarchical arrangement among them. Several examples of such a procedure may be found in the

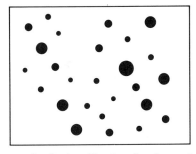

FIGURE 6.1 *A settlement distribution. The size of settlement is proportional to the area of the dot.*

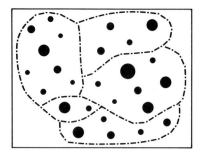

FIGURE 6.2 *Political divisions associated with the settlement distribution of Figure 6.1. Territorial boundaries are indicated by the broken lines.*

literature (e.g., Renfrew 1973, 133), all assuming, explicitly or implicitly, the absence of hierarchy.

This procedure can be modified, for instance by means of weighted Thiessen polygons, so that the territorial area is dependent on the size of the center (cf. Hogg 1971).

So far, however, no account is taken of *dominance*. For only in the most strictly acephalous societies are there no sites which are subordinate to others in the political or administrative hierarchy. But how are we to decide which sites dominate which? The opposite extreme to that seen in Figure 6.3 would be to assume that the largest center dominates all others, giving a single unified polity. The solution offered by some workers (cf. Johnson 1975) is to take sizes of centers in rank order, in the hope of finding some discrete separation between large (viewed as dominant, independent capitals) and small (seen as subordinate, second- or third-order locations). But in many cases, as envisaged earlier, this just does not work. To take an example from modern Europe, the population of Belgrade, the capital of Yugoslavia, is less than that of the seventh largest center in the United Kingdom. Standard geographical extensions of the rank–size rule are not in

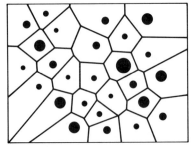

FIGURE 6.3 *Unweighted Thiessen polygons giving a notional territorial division for the settlement pattern of Figure 6.1. The archaeologist will often draw such a map as a provisional first attempt to reconstruct the territorial divisions of Figure 6.2 from settlement data.*

practice appropriate. What if there are no convenient breaks between first-
and second-order centers, nor any "primate" capitals, larger by an order of
magnitude than their nearest rivals within the polity?

The answer lies in considering dominance within a spatial context,
rather than in isolation in terms of size alone. It is necessary to assert some
relationship of size and distance, whereby the larger dominates the smaller if
the distance between them is sufficiently small, whereas the smaller retains
autonomy if that distance is great. In effect we assume some law of
monotonic decrement (cf. Renfrew 1977, 72) for political influence, and
hence for the dominance of capital centers. We assert that some such
relationship everywhere held until the development of near-instantaneous
communication methods (radio) and rapid, militarily effective air transport.

The XTENT Model

As a trial formulation, and nothing more is claimed here, we assume that
the influence of a center is proportional to a function of its size, and declines
linearly with distance:

$$I = f(C) - k \cdot d \; (I \geqslant 0) \tag{6.1}$$

where I is a measure of the potential political influence of a center at a
location x, C is a measure of the size of that center, d is the distance between
x and the center, and k is a constant.

Any location x will fall within the territorial jurisdiction of the polity
whose center exercises the greatest influence at x. In particular, if the
location x is the location of a center C_2, a neighboring center C_1 will dominate
location x and thus C_2 if $I_1 > I_2$ at location x; that is, if

$$f(C_1) - f(C_2) > k \cdot d_{1,2} \tag{6.2}$$

where $d_{1,2}$ is the distance between the two centers.

The position is seen in Figure 6.4. The influence of each center is
indicated on the y axis, and declines linearly with distance from the center,
reaching zero at the point where $f(C) = k \cdot d$. The second center, C_2, by virtue
of its position, is subordinate to C_1, while C_3, which is the same size as C_2,
remains autonomous. The more distant center C_4, although actually the
smallest in size, likewise remains autonomous. There is an area of no-man's
land between the territories of C_4 and C_5.

We have found it convenient to think of this as a "tent pole" model, the
dominance of a center being comparable to a radially symmetrical bell-tent
with the size of the center governing the height of the central pole (Figure
6.5). Those smaller settlements whose own tents can be pitched entirely

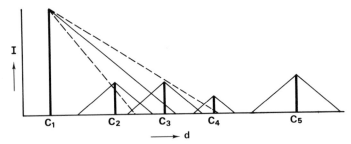

FIGURE 6.4 *The XTENT model, with influence of center as ordinate and distance as abscissa. Five centers are shown along a single line, the size of each indicated by a thick vertical line. The radius of dominance for each is given by the intersection of the solid line with the $I = 0$ axis (the dashed line indicates the effect of varying the slope). Note how C_2 is entirely dominated by C_1 whereas C_4, although smaller in size, has its own independent territory.*

within the bell-tent of their larger neighbor are dominated by that neighbor. Those whose central pole would protrude beyond the surface of the tent are the centers of autonomous polities.

This formulation, which we claim as the simplest conceivable approach to the problem of dominance, without the prior assumption of specific hierarchical levels, allows us to work with a single variable, k, the slope of the fall-off of influence (i.e., of the tent).

It is a central tenet of our approach that the value of k is not assumed, but is to be investigated empirically until general rules for its size can be formulated. It is at once inherently obvious that development in transport

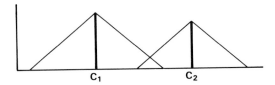

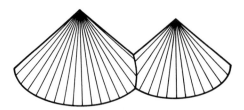

FIGURE 6.5 *The XTENT model, with (above) distance along a single line joining two centers (as in Figure 6.4) and (below) a three-dimensional sketch showing how the influence exerted by the two centers may be represented by two intersecting radially symmetrical bell-tents.*

facilities, such as the introduction of the horse or the railway, will reduce the value of k.

Distance d may be measured as simple linear distance, or *transformed* (for instance into travel time) to take account of varieties of terrain. Our initial formulation considers political control on land, and initially makes no distinction between terrestrial and marine distance. Further elaboration, using a suitable transformation for marine distance, would allow this over-simple assumption to be adjusted.

The approximate measure of "size" is a practical archaeological problem to be approached empirically in each case. If figures were available for population, this might be the best measure. Alternatively, area of settlement may be used, although this presents several practical problems familiar to archaeologists. Other possibilities would be the number of coins issued by a mint (if a polity may contain more than one mint center), the size of ceremonial monuments at the center, or any other plausible construct from the archaeological data. Clearly the validity of each measure has to be critically evaluated for each case.

The other element of choice, in addition to the value of k, concerns the function $f(C)$. We have worked with the formulation $f(C) = C^\alpha$, experimenting with different values of the exponent α, and measuring C in terms of either population (known) or area (estimated).

The most convenient allocation of territories to centers develops naturally from this model. Centers or settlements that have been "dominated" by others have no independent territory (at this level of analysis). Any location is assigned to the center whose influence upon it, as defined earlier, is greatest. If this location is not dominated by any center (i.e., the location does not lie under any tent), then it is left politically unassigned: The location is in "no-man's land."

Boundaries then occur in one of two ways. Either a boundary is a line of minimum influence between two centers, or else it is a line of division between "no-man's land" and a region under domination by some center. Thus the first type of boundary falls along the furrows created by the intersection of tents, whereas the latter type falls along the edges of tents where they meet the ground.

The model thus allows the creation of hypothetical political maps, using only the location and size of settlements (or other centers) as input information, and generating political divisions without any prior knowledge of them.

The Computer Program and Display

The computer utilized was the PDP 11/45 of the Institute of Sound and Vibration Research at Southampton University (with interactive-graphic facilities). This permitted both immediate interactive display and hard-copy graphic printout. The program, in FORTRAN, requires three data files for each case studied.

The first file, INPUT FILE (COORDS), lists the coordinates, in pairs, of all locations (settlements, centers, monuments, or whatever) under consideration.

The second, MAP OUTLINE FILE, gives in coordinate form the map boundary data which it is desired the computer should display. For instance, the simplified map of Europe, seen in Figure 6.9, is drawn by the computer from a file with coordinates for 283 points of coastline.

The third file, POP FILE, gives the measure for the size of different centers (which in the first case examined was the population, and in others area) in the same sequential order as their coordinates in INPUT FILE.

Using the data in the INPUT FILE and POP FILE, the program examines each center, checking it for dominance by neighboring centers. If a center is not dominated, it will have a boundary surrounding its political territory. The program marks such a center as autonomous, computes the boundary location, and draws it in.

If a center is dominated, it will not have a political boundary of its own since our model permits only autonomous centers to have independent political territories. The program marks such a dominated center as non-autonomous and omits it from any future calculations.

After all boundaries have been drawn, the autonomous centers are displayed with a given sign (in this case, a cross) and the dominated, subordinate centers falling within their territories by a square. Where appropriate the map outline is then automatically added from the MAP OUTLINE FILE.

A normalization factor is used, by which the sizes of all locations are divided: In general it is the size of the largest center in the series.

Various values of the exponent α were selected, in general between 1.0 and .125. A high value of α leads to the dominance of the entire area by the single largest center; a low value of α tends toward local autonomy by leveling out the size differences.

During the course of the investigation the program was modified to give with each hard-copy map a value for the number of autonomous centers, for the average nearest neighbor distance between autonomous centers, and for the average maximum radius of centers (i.e., the arithmetic average taking in turn the maximum distance attained between the boundary of each polity and its center).

Experiment 1: Malta

One of our first experiments involved the distribution of neolithic temples on the island of Malta (Evans 1971), dated to the approximate time range 3500 to 2500BC. Few prehistoric settlements have been found on Malta, but these impressive stone monuments are well known. The appropriate measure of size was taken to be the area enclosed by stones, for which $\frac{1}{2}\ell^2$ (with ℓ as the longest dimension) was taken as a convenient approximation. It had been suggested that groups of temples reflected some hierarchical organization, with territorial division by chiefdoms (Renfrew 1973, 154), and it was hoped that the model would offer some insights in this direction. Of course the assumption should be explicitly stated that the area occupied by the temple buildings reflects in some measure the power, influence, and size of the parent community, and that its location lies within the residential territory of that community. These assumptions are certainly questionable in this case, and so must be any conclusions about prehistoric Malta derived from the model. As a simple test case for the method, however, the example is a convenient one.

The computer was given (*a*) coordinate pairs for the locations of the 17 sites in question; (*b*) an estimate for the area of each, and (*c*) 221 pairs of coordinates read manually to give a digitized coastline for the islands of Malta and Gozo. This last is for display purposes only and plays no part in the computations, which take place as if the locations were on an isotropic plain.

For the first run, the exponent α was set at .5 (i.e., the computer worked with the square root of the area actually occupied by each site). This area in each case was first normalized by dividing by that of the largest temple: In effect, for convenience we start by adjusting the size of the largest location to unity. The slope parameter was then allowed to vary in steps of .01 from .05 to .01 (see Figures 6.6a–6.6d).

The computer then printed out autonomous and subordinate centers and territorial boundaries in each case. The greatest (i.e., steepest) slope corresponding to the sharpest fall-off in influence with distance, naturally produced the largest number of autonomous locations and the smallest number of "captures" by dominance. The relationship of the number of autonomous centers to the slope is seen in Figure 6.7. The linear relationship in Equation (6.1) postulated for distance means that boundaries, except where two territories touch, are circular in form. Outside the boundary the effect of the center in question is zero. This differs from the Thiessen polygon approach, where the entire region is divided up, influence being inversely proportional to distance. With weighted Thiessen polygons an inverse square relationship can be used, which in formal properties is related to Reilly's gravitation relationship (Hodder and Orton 1976, 188).

Gradual reduction in slope produces the assimilation of progressively more locations into larger political units, and offers a fascinating caricature for the evolution of a hierarchical political system from an egalitarian one. It should be noted that the initial hypothesis is strongly supported by the persistent association of several small groups of sites, including the group of

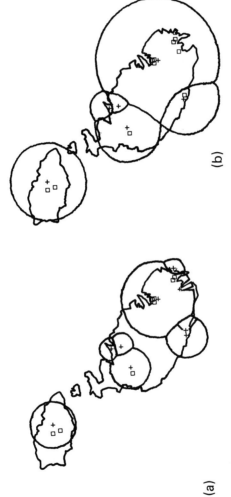

(a)

(b)

FIGURE 6.6 *Computer graphic map of territorial divisions in neolithic Malta. Temples are indicated by a cross when autonomous center, by a square when subordinate. The slope parameter varies: (a) .05, (b) .03, (c) .02, and (d) .01. The exponent α is .5 throughout.*

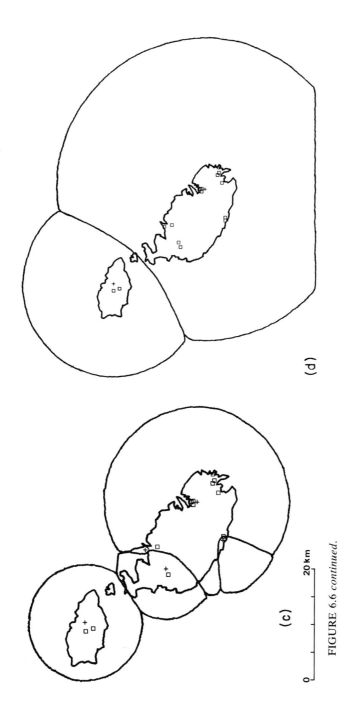

(d)

(c)

0   20 km

FIGURE 6.6 *continued.*

155

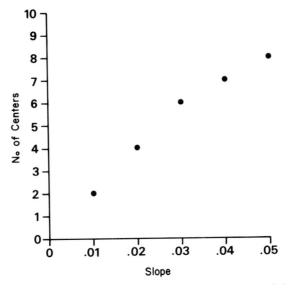

FIGURE 6.7 *Relation between the number of autonomous centers and the slope parameter for the Maltese temples.*

three on the northern island of Gozo, dominated by the great Ġgantija temple, the temples of Mgarr and Skorba in northwest Malta, and the grouping of the three Kordin temples in every case with the great center at Tarxien. An interesting feature of the model then is that varying the slope changes certain aspects of organization, while leaving others invariant.

As a second experiment, the slope parameter was now fixed at .05, using the same data set, and the exponent α varied, by a factor of 2 in each case, from 1 to .125 (Figures 6.8a–6.8d). An exponent of .125 implies that the eighth root of area is being taken for the magnitude of each site, the largest site (at Tarxien) being regarded throughout as unit size. The territorial sizes of smaller sites therefore increase with decreasing exponent, and when $\alpha = .125$ there are no fewer than 14 autonomous centers, since the eighth root of each is itself close to unity and they become effectively of almost equal size. But the map "looks wrong" because of the distortions, so that individual centers are no longer near the middle of their territories. Here perhaps the experiment suggests to us a criterion for selecting an appropriate value of α.

This and other experiments have shown, in a rather pragmatic way, that an exponent of 1 allows the larger centers to dominate the smaller to what seems an untoward extent, whereas an exponent of less than .25 produces what look like territorial distortions. No doubt both these statements require further substantiation. In most subsequent work we have used an exponent of .5. This has the consequence, when we use area as a measure of size for a center, that we are comparing linear measure for territory (radius) with linear measure for center (root area). The territorial area dominated by the

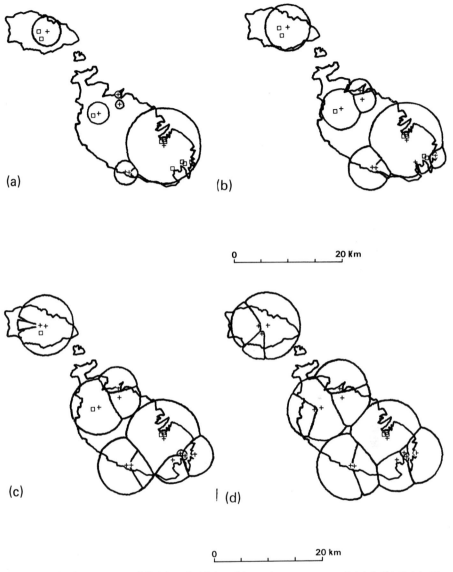

FIGURE 6.8 *Territorial divisions in Malta with varying exponent* α: *(a) 1.0, (b) .5, (c) .25, and (d) .125. The slope parameter is .05 throughout.*

site is thus proportional to the area actually occupied by the site itself. Likewise, when we use population, we are thinking of root population as proportional to radius of territory, and hence (by squaring) population as proportional to territorial area.

Experiment 2: Cities of Europe

In order to test the model against a case in which real political boundaries are accurately known, population sizes for the 117 cities in Europe in the year 1960 whose population exceeded 500,000 (Showers 1973, 260–286) were listed, together with their coordinates, and a digitized coastline for Europe. With an exponent of $\alpha = 1$, there were large areas of no-man's land between territories for all values of the slope greater than .1, and once again an exponent of $\alpha = .5$ was chosen as more appropriate. The resulting configurations for values of the slope parameter between .006 and .020 are seen in Figures 6.9a to 6.9d. The relationship between slope and number of autonomous centers is seen in Table 6.1. Each center of a given population size has a maximum radius of influence, determined by the slope, although naturally when centers lie close together their common boundary falls within their theoretical radii of influence. For a given slope, any city of population one million will have the same radius of influence. Moreover, when the exponent $\alpha = .5$, the radius of influence for a population of 10,000 will be precisely one-tenth of that for population one million. These figures are also seen in Table 6.1. Note that the figures given in the first column of Tables 6.1 and 6.2 and on the abscissa of Figures 6.7 and 6.10 are convenient parameters which are inversely proportional to the physical parameters listed in column 3 of the tables.

It should be noted that no distinction was made between distance over sea or over land. Had maritime distance been seen as an obstacle to effective domination, the jurisdiction of Paris would have extended in each case to the coast of the English channel.

A second apparent distortion is the tendency toward autonomy of a number of areas within the USSR. For instance, in the case in which the slope parameter is .006, Tbilisi, Baku, and Yerevan emerge as the capitals of autonomous provinces. But as so often in such cases, the exceptions prove interesting in themselves: The computer is mischievously predicting the autonomy of the Transcaucasian People's Republics of Georgia, Azerbaijan, and Armenia. This need not give comfort to separatist movements: It is a first instance among many on these maps where we appear to see a configuration appropriate to one time period appearing also at another.

Clearly the two maps approximating most closely to the actual political reality are those for which the slope parameter is .014 (36 autonomous centers) and .010 (19 autonomous centers). The relation between the slope parameter and number of centers is seen in Figure 6.10. In the latter case, London, Paris, Madrid, Lisbon, Rome, Athens, Istanbul, Moscow, Stockholm, Berlin, Budapest, Sofia, and Bucharest all acquit themselves appropriately (Istanbul since Ankara, lying outside Europe, is not included). The odd-men out, apart from the three Transcaucasian provincial centers, are Leningrad—a city whose former capital status is notable—and Odessa and Ufa in the USSR.

In the case in which the slope parameter α is .014, Belgrade, Vienna, Oslo, Copenhagen, and Warsaw are now among the territorial capitals, while Syracuse and Palermo recall earlier Sicilian autonomy, and indeed the short-lived Kingdom of the Two Sicilies, and Barcelona, the old independence of Aragon. An alarming number of localities in the southern USSR emerge as independent: Paradoxically this is because of their relatively small population size, or rather the late date at which this part of Europe became fully urban.

It is intriguing that when the slope parameter is .020, we see what approximates to a return to the Middle Ages (in western Europe) with separate status for former polity centers such as Naples, Valencia, Cordoba, and Sevilla. In effect the program is now including second-order centers, such as Glasgow and Belfast, and particularly notable is their manner of grouping themselves around the major, first-order centers which already emerge when the slope parameter is .006.

Turning now to the first of these maps, with slope parameter .006, we see indeed a Europe of great powers, reminiscent in some ways of the situation at the time of the Napoleonic wars, when Britain and France were the major competitors, yet with the retreat from Moscow clearly implied. Both Waterloo and the battlefields of the Peninsular War (in Iberia) are appropriately under British influence. Athens and Istanbul give us a hint of the Eastern question.

These comments, not all entirely serious, do reflect the important generalization already made in the case of Malta, that alteration in the slope for a given distribution may in some respects mimic the effect of the passage of time.

Experiment 3: Late Uruk Settlement

To illustrate the approach as applied to archaeological settlement data derived from survey, the program was applied to the Late Uruk settlement system in the Warka area of Mesopotamia. The settlement areas have been conveniently listed by Johnson (1975, 312–314), and location coordinates were measured from his map (ibid. 316). His data are derived from the survey by Adams and Nissen (1972) and we follow him in including 98 of the 118 sites listed by Adams and Nissen. It was necessary to assume an area for

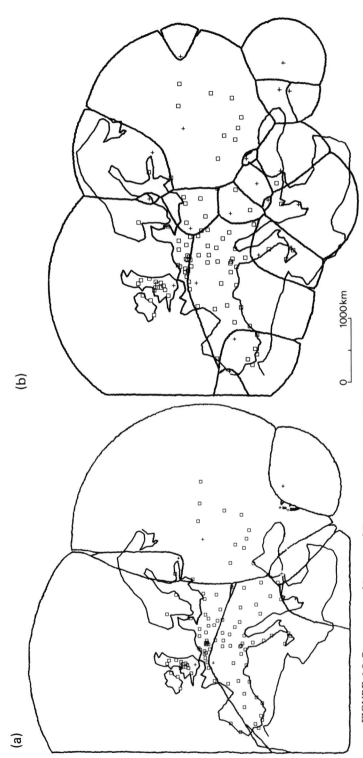

(b)

1000km

(a)

FIGURE 6.9 *Computer graphic maps of European polities in* AD 1960 *as predicted by the XTENT model. The exponent* α *is .5 throughout. The slope parameter varies: (a) .006, (b) .010, (c) .014, and (d) .020.*

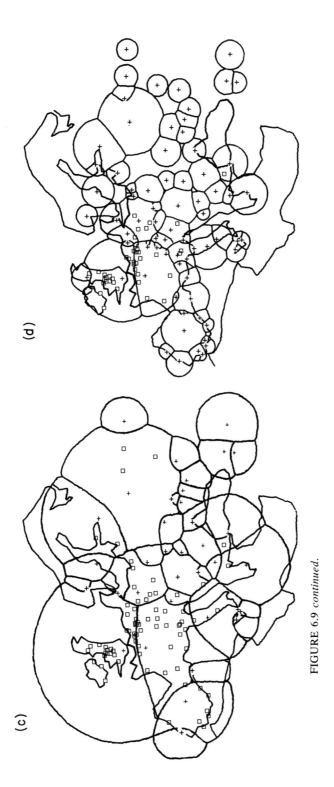

(d)

(c)

FIGURE 6.9 *continued.*

TABLE 6.1

The Effect of Varying the Slope on the Number of Autonomous Centers and on the Radii of Influence for the Cities of Europe in 1960[a]

Slope parameter	Number of autonomous centers	Radius (km)	
		For one million population	For 10,000 population
.006	9	1166	116.6
.008	15	875	87.5
.010	19	700	70.0
.012	29	583	58.3
.014	36	500	50.0
.016	45	437	43.7
.018	47	389	38.9
.020	53	350	35.0
.030	73	233	23.3
.040	86	175	17.5

[a] The exponent α is .5.

Warka itself, since this had not been estimated. In fact separate runs were undertaken for areas of 40, 60, and 80 ha, respectively, and the discussion here relates to that for an area of 60 ha.

The exponent α was held at .5 throughout, and the slope parameter was given successive values of .005, .01, .02, and .03. The results are seen in Table 6.2

As before, the computer determines which sites dominate others, in terms of their size and location, indicating the territory of dominant "capitals" and the locations of the subordinate settlements. As slope is decreased, all the settlements gradually become subordinate to larger centers, until only the largest is autonomous. As slope is increased, smaller and smaller centers emerge as "independent." In an egalitarian political situation the latter may approximate to the political reality. But when the administration is in reality hierarchical, the increase in slope leads to the appearance of subordinate second-order centers as autonomous.

Figure 6.11 shows the configuration with the slope parameter set at .01. The autonomous settlements are indicated by a cross. In addition we have used arrows to indicate the four centers which already emerge as autonomous when the slope parameter is .005. Here then we are in effect beginning to use an overlay of the configurations for different slopes to give an indication of internal, hierarchical structure within polities.

It is instructive to compare this with the configuration at which Johnson himself arrived (1975, 332) as a result of his locational analysis (Figure 6.12). By plotting a histogram for area of settlement he divided settlements into four size classes: large centers, small centers, large villages, and villages.

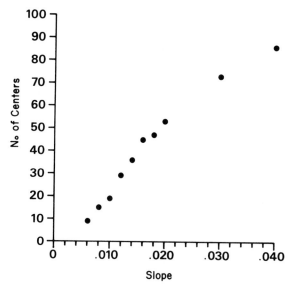

FIGURE 6.10 *Relation between the number of autonomous centers and the slope parameter for the European cities.*

Using classical central place theory concepts he regarded the settlement distribution as a modified hexagonal lattice (assigning special significance to sites at which ceramic wall cones have been found, considered as indicating a temple).

Of the five settlements classified as large centers by Johnson, four emerge as autonomous centers at slope parameter .005, and the resemblances between the two interpretations are obvious. Our program tends to grant autonomous status to middle-size settlements located far from others, and this has occurred with the two located at the southeast of the area. Likewise, our program underlines the potential significance of the center at the northwest (Johnson's "small center" No. 020). It is difficult to

TABLE 6.2
The Effect of Varying the Slope on the Number of Autonomous Centers and on the Radii of Influence for the Uruk Area in the Late Uruk Period[a]

Slope parameter	Number of autonomous centers	Radius (km)	
		For 1 ha	For 100 ha
.005	4	7.95	79.5
.01	18	3.97	39.7
.02	44	1.99	19.9
.03	62	1.32	13.2

[a] The exponent α is .5.

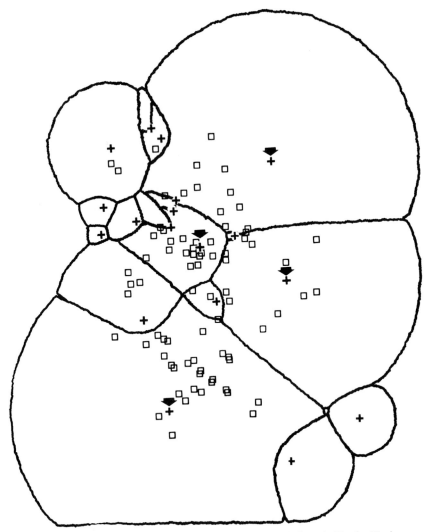

FIGURE 6.11 *Predicted political divisions for the Late Uruk period in the Warka area of Mesopotamia (exponent α = .5, slope parameter .01). Arrows indicate the four centers which emerge as autonomous with slope parameter .005. Compare with Figure 6.12, shown on the same scale.*

see why this was omitted from his lattice. Moreover, the six centers arranged between it and the two large centers to the south (Nos. 242 and 125) have very much the appearance of second-order locations in a settlement hierarchy and might well have responded to his central place approach.

Our program does not, in itself, tell us which of the alternative political configurations it produces (according to change in slope) is the most appropriate. This depends on the distance over which a center of a given size can

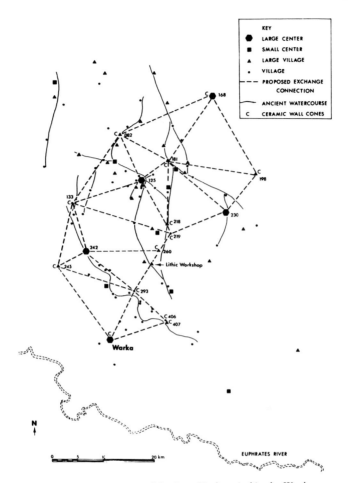

FIGURE 6.12 *Settlement structure of the Late Uruk period in the Warka area as analyzed by Johnson (1975, 332). Note the similarities with Figure 6.11, which is on the same scale.*

exert effective influence (see the last column of Table 6.2), which is inversely proportional to the slope. If a given distance (and slope) does effectively lead to a representation of the political reality, steeper slopes will give an insight into a structuring within polities, whereas smaller slopes predict supranational spheres of influence.

The XTENT Model as a Framework of Comparison

Our experiments, which included further examples not cited here, suggest that although a widely appropriate value of the exponent may be found ($\alpha \approx .5$), there is no easy or a priori means of judging the "right" slope.

We would claim, however, that the very concept of "slope" in this sense, expressed in absolute terms, may offer a conceptual advance. Accepting for the moment that the appropriate value for the exponent is agreed, we have in the slope a *single* variable which will uniquely determine the political landscape. For convenience we have spoken here using normalized values (such as .01, .02) without absolute units. But in Table 6.2 the appropriate absolute units were given for the Uruk pattern, and may be compared with those in Table 6.1 for European cities in 1960. Obviously direct comparison is possible only if we know the approximate population in Uruk times for a town whose area was 100 ha (or know the mean area for a town of 100,000 in modern Europe). But if we use, for the basis of argument, an urban population density of 100 ha^{-1} for Mesopotamia in the Uruk period, the last columns of the two tables become directly comparable. Indeed Figure 6.10 (Uruk settlement, with 100 ha seen as influencing a radius of 40 km) may be compared with Figures 6.8c and 6.8d (Europe 1960, with centers with a population of 10,000 influencing 50 and 35 km, respectively).

Such comparisons can at times be misleading. Transport factors, overall population density, and degree of urbanization must all have their effects. Moreover, although the exponent $\alpha = .5$ may be appropriate as a first approximation, it remains to be tested that a city with a population of one million has in fact a sphere of influence precisely 10 times the radius of a town of 10,000 population, or that town a radius 10 times the radius of a village of 100 ha.

Yet we would argue that these are precisely the questions that have to be asked. To what extent do the same parameters of distance and magnitude operate in the classic Maya lowlands as in Sumer, for instance, or in the Mississippian as in the European Iron Age? It may be that the XTENT model, and others like it, will offer a more rigorous framework for cross-cultural comparisons than has been available hitherto and hence open the way at last to a systematic and diachronic comparative study of human societies.

Acknowledgments

We are grateful to Dr. Colin Mercer of the Data Research Center, Institute of Sound and Vibration Research, University of Southampton, for access to its computer facilities, to Professor Kenneth Cooke for stimulation and encouragement, and to Professor Gregory A. Johnson for permission to reproduce Figure 6.12.

References

Adams R. McC. and Nissen H. J., 1972, *The Uruk Countryside,* Chicago, University Press.
Berry B. J. L., 1961, City size distribution and economic development, *Economic Development and Culture Change* 9, 573–587.
Christaller W., 1933, *Die zentralen Orte in Süddeutschland,* Jena.

Crumley C. L., 1976, Towards a locational definition of state systems of settlement, *American Anthropologist* 78, 59–73.

Evans J. D., 1971, *The Prehistoric Antiquities of the Maltese Islands, a Survey,* London, Athlone.

Hodder I. and Orton C., 1976, *Spatial Analysis in Archaeology,* Cambridge, University Press.

Hogg A. H. A., 1971, Some applications of surface fieldwork, in Jessen M. and Hill D. (eds.), *The Iron Age and its Hillforts,* Southampton University, 105–125.

Johnson G. A., 1972, A test of the utility of Central Place Theory in archaeology, in Ucko P. J., Tringham R. and Dimbleby G. (eds.), *Man, Settlement and Urbanism,* London, Duckworth, 769–785.

Johnson G. A., 1973, *Local Exchange and Early State Development in Southwestern Iran* (Museum of Anthropology of the University of Michigan Anthropological Papers 51).

Johnson G. A., 1975, Locational analysis and the investigation of Uruk local exchange systems, in Sabloff J. A. and Lamberg-Karlovsky C. C. (eds.), *Ancient Civilisation and Trade,* Albuquerque, University of New Mexico Press, 285–339.

Lösch A., 1954, *The Economics of Location,* Yale University Press.

Renfrew C., 1973, *Before Civilisation, the Radiocarbon Revolution and Prehistoric Europe,* London, Cape.

Renfrew C., 1977, Alternative models for exchange and spatial distribution, in Earle T. K. and Ericson J. E. (eds.), *Exchange Systems in Prehistory,* New York, Academic Press, 71–90.

Renfrew C., 1978, Space, time and polity, in Friedman J. and Rowlands M. (eds.), *The Evolution of Social Systems,* London, Duckworth, 89–112.

Showers V., 1973, *The World in Figures,* New York, Wiley.

Soja E. W., 1971, *The Political Organisation of Space.* (Association of American Geographers, Commission on College Geography, Resource Paper 8).

Zadeh L., 1965, Fuzzy sets, *Information Control* 8, 338–353.

7

JOHN R. ALDEN

A Reconstruction of Toltec Period Political Units in the Valley of Mexico

This chapter presents a definition of political interaction and uses it to derive an equation which estimates political interaction between pairs of sites from archaeological settlement pattern data. Nearest and second nearest interaction neighbors are determined and political units defined by isolating clusters of interacting sites. This model is tested and refined against a known situation, the Early Aztec period in the Valley of Mexico, and is shown to replicate the known political groupings and borders with considerable accuracy. It is then used to delineate political units for the Early and Late Toltec periods in the same region.

Previous interpretations of Toltec period prehistory are reviewed, and two statistics devised to estimate the degree of political disruption during each period. The early Toltec period seems to have been highly unsettled politically, whereas the Late Toltec period is seen as a time of stability when Tula had extended its political influence over the entire Valley of Mexico.

Political evolution involves changing patterns of political interaction among centers and between centers and their subsidiary sites. Yet political interaction has rarely, if ever, been clearly defined by archaeologists; as a consequence it has been impossible to determine the boundaries of political units and to deal concisely with problems involving political change through time. The conflicting reconstructions of Toltec period political organization in the Valley of Mexico (Parsons 1970; Charlton 1973, 1975; Blanton 1975) are an example of the disagreements that arise in the absence of a clear and quantifiable definition of political interaction. This chapter presents a new approach to the definition of political interaction, and applies that approach

169

Transformations:
Mathematical Approaches to Culture Change

toward a reinterpretation of Toltec period political organization in the Valley of Mexico.

I define political interaction as exchanges of information involved in making and implementing decisions by administrative hierarchies. These decisions might involve social, military, or economic matters but in all cases they are made and implemented through an administrative hierarchy. Within such hierarchies there are different levels of decision making, with only limited amounts of certain kinds of information moving between levels. For example, individuals might report that they are getting no irrigation water to a lower level administrator. This official reduces the complaints to a single message and reports to a higher level official that a canal seems to be broken. The higher level administrator, making a decision, directs a subordinate to see that the canal is repaired. That official selects a work party and fixes the canal. Each administrator distills the information that he passes up in the hierarchy and fills in the outlines of decisions handed down to him.

Using this definition it is possible to predict the amount of political interaction between pairs of locations if two assumptions are made.

ASSUMPTION 1. *There is a "cost" involved in transfers of information that is a function of the distance over which the information is transferred, and political hierarchies try to minimize these costs.*

This implies that, other considerations being equal, administrators will be located so that information can be gathered and decisions implemented most efficiently. The most efficient locations for minimizing costs are central locations for higher level officials and locations at the source of information for lower level officials. Thus, the edges of political units should show minimal evidence for the presence of administrators and areas with the most evidence of administrative functions should be the centers of administrative units.

ASSUMPTION 2. *The number of administrators at each level of a political hierarchy is directly proportional to the amount of information being processed, and the amount of information generated at a place is proportional to that place's population.*

Thus, if one person can deal with the problems of 100, then 10 people will be needed to deal with the problems of 1000. And if each lower level official reduces his information output to 10% of his information input, then one upper level administrator will be needed to coordinate the activities of 10 lower level administrators. Furthermore, if location A produces double the information of location B, then administrators from A will interact with their superiors at C twice as often as administrators from B.

It can be seen from these two assumptions that the political interaction between two places will be directly proportional to the product of the populations at each location and inversely proportional to some function of the distance between locations. Thus,

$$I = \frac{C(P_i \cdot P_j)}{f(d_{ij})} \qquad (7.1)$$

where I is political interaction, C is a constant, P_i is the population of location i, and d_{ij} is the distance between i and j.

How can this general formulation be made relevant for the archaeologist? First, the interaction model must be specified by defining both the function of distance to be used in the equation and a measure of the distance between sites. Second, the model must be tested using a data set that has comprehensive archaeological evidence on site locations plus historic or ethnographic information on political units and boundaries, and where historic and archaeological evidence overlap. Finally, the model must be applied to an archaeological situation where political units are not known, and the units predicted by the model used to reinterpret the archaeological situation. The remainder of this chapter deals with these problems.

Specifying the Interaction Model

The first step in specifying the model is selecting a function of distance that will reflect political interaction and fit known political data. An exponential function is chosen because this yields a variant of the gravity interaction equation. Geographers have found gravity models useful in dealing with many sorts of interaction in different areas of the world and in societies at different levels of complexity (Olsson 1965:43–46). The gravity interaction equation is directly analogous to the law of gravitation: the interaction between two locations is treated as directly proportional to the product of some measure of the "mass" of each location and inversely proportional to some power of the "distance" between locations. That is,

$$I = \frac{C(M_i \cdot M_j)}{(d_{ij})^a} \qquad (7.2)$$

This is just a more specific form of Equation (7.1). In gravity interaction models the measures of M and d depend on the type of interaction being modeled for. The empirically derived constant a affects the attenuation of interaction over distance, whereas C alters I linearly.

For the political interaction model established here, d is defined as directly proportional to the estimated travel time between sites. This seems to be a reasonable measure of the ease or difficulty of interaction between sites. The mass M of a site is defined as its estimated population, as derived for Equation (7.1).

Next, a set of data must be examined so that a value for a, the exponent of distance in Equation (7.2), can be empirically determined. Data from the Early Aztec period in the Valley of Mexico will be used for this test. This data set is chosen because the archaeological settlement data are adequate, there is sufficient ethnohistoric information to define political borders, and the ceramics used to define Early Aztec occupations can be clearly dated to the years discussed in the ethnohistoric sources. Also, the use of a data set from the same geographical area to specify the interaction model will eliminate possible effects on results derived through application of the model from many other variables such as ecological setting, subsistence patterns, and geographical constraints on settlement location.

Testing the Interaction Model

The Ethnohistoric Map

Political divisions in the Early Aztec period Valley of Mexico can be reconstructed from ethnohistoric records of settlements, conflicts, and alliances. As the term is used here the Early Aztec period begins about AD 1300 and ends with the death of Ixtlilxochitl and the extension of Tepaneca dominance over the Acolhuaque in 1418; ceramically this corresponds to the Aztec II period (Valliant 1938:554; MacNeish 1970:Fig. 153; but cf. Parsons 1971:26, where Aztec II is dated slightly earlier). The criteria for making the divisions subsequently noted and shown in Figure 7.2 are (*a*) warfare between cities or ethnic groups, (*b*) alliances between places, and (*c*) political dominance of one place over another. A single secondary criterion is considered, ethnic affiliation with a named tribal group. Unless otherwise referenced the information in this section is taken from Gibson (1964:10–19), for this author can make no pretense of controlling the extensive primary sources of ethnohistoric information on the Valley of Mexico. The following description of political units begins in the southwest part of the valley and proceeds counterclockwise, with site numbers from Figure 7.1 noted after site names.

The Culhuaque settled in Culhuacan (86) over a century before the Early Aztec era and they remained independent until about 1347, when they were conquered in the Tepaneca expansion from Azcapotzalco. While independent, Culhuacan included Ixtapalapa (83), Mexicalzingo (84), and Cerro de la Estrella (82) within its territory as well as Huitzilopocho, just west of the surveyed area. After 1347 the Culhuaque were part of the Tepaneca realm.

The territory of Xochimilco (92) was once very extensive, but by the fourteenth century it had been considerably reduced. The Xochimilca warred with the Culhuaque in the thirteenth century and with the Mexica and Tepaneca in the late fourteenth century. Ultimately Xochimilco was subdued by Nezahualcoyotl around 1430. During the Early Aztec period its western border was near the edge of the surveyed area; to the north and east Xochimilco was separated from Culhuacan/Tepaneca and Cuitlahuac.

Cuitlahuac (97), located on an island between Lakes Chalco and Xochimilco, never controlled much territory beyond the causeways connecting it with the mainland. The city fought against the Xochimilca, Tepaneca, Mexica, and Acolhuaque and was eventually conquered by the Mexica. However, during the Early Aztec period Cuitlahuac was politically independent. Its borders are drawn so that no other sites are included within its political sphere.

The Mixquica never controlled much beyond the edges of Mixquic (102). They fought with and fell under the influence of both the Chalca and the Xochimilca, were later defeated by the Tepaneca, attacked by the Mexica in 1403, and finally conquered by the Mexica about 1430. They seem to have been reasonably independent during most of the era considered here; therefore a border is drawn around Mixquic which includes the small sites between Mixquic and Cuitlahuac but nothing else.

The boundaries of Chalca territory are more difficult to define, particularly to the north, because frequent wars with their neighbors often resulted in changing borders. To the south, Amecameca (155) and Tlalmanalco (126) were always Chalca territory, as were Chalco Atenco (112) and Xico (109) before the reign of Montezuma I. To the north, Gibson suspects that Chimalhuacan Atenco (78) and Coatepec (67) were not taken from the Chalca until the fifteenth century, and after 1430 both of these towns and Ixtapaluca (73) were clearly within the Acolhua domain (Gibson, 1964:40). However, another source states that Chimalhuacan Atenco was established on land that had once belonged to Chalco (PNE 6:66). Since archaeological survey data show an Early Aztec occupation at Chimalhuacan Atenco, it appears that the Chalca had lost control of these territories before the end of the Early Aztec period. Following these considerations I drew the northern border of Chalca territory running between Chicoloapa (70) and Ixtapaluca (73).

As a result of intermittent expansion by the Acolhuaque during the entire Early Aztec period, all of the area surveyed to the north of Chalca territory was ethnically Acolhuaque by 1450. However, there was a break in this expansion between the death of Ixtlilxochitl in 1418 and the conclusion of the Tepaneca War around 1433, and during this time the Acolhuaque were subject to Tepaneca dominance. Changes made after this war and attributed to Nezahualcoyotl allow us to reconstruct the pre-1418 political situation.

First, Nezahualcoyotl subdivided the territory previously ruled by Teotihuacan (20), which had included Otumba (24), Tepeapulco, and Tlaquilpa. This area extends out of the surveyed area to the north and east. Second, he took control of Acolman (42), Tepexpan (43), and Tequicistlan (in the gap between the Teotihuacan and Texcoco survey areas) which had previously been independent of the Acolhuaque, of Teotihuacan, and of each other (Nuttall 1926:49–50). The location of the border between Acolhua and Teotihuacan territories is never specified, but the geographical division created by the Patlachique mountain range seems the most probable place for this boundary, and that is where it is drawn in Figure 7.2.

The political affiliation of Chiconautla (46) during the Early Aztec period is undetermined. However, its nearest interaction neighbors were probably sites outside of the survey area, and thus this site will not be considered in the model-fitting procedure. The only other situation in which boundary effects might present a problem is with the Culhuaque settlements, which might be clustered with Azcapotzalco if archaeological data on the location and population of that site were available. Since this would fit the ethnohistoric situation for the second half of the Early Aztec period, it cannot invalidate the results of the modeling procedure in any way.

The Archaeological Data

The next step is to map settlement patterns of the Early Aztec period and to assemble population estimates for each site in the survey area. First, a map of the continuous surveyed area of the Valley of Mexico was drawn, and all Early Aztec sites with estimated populations over 25 or with ceremonial–civic architecture were mapped. Sites with fewer than 25 inhabitants were not included because they would have drastically increased the time spent measuring site-to-site distances without improving the accuracy of the model-fitting procedure. For the Toltec periods all sites were mapped and measured.

Several problems were encountered during this step. First, site populations given by Parsons for the Texcoco (1971) and southern valley (in preparation) areas and by Blanton for the Ixtapalapa peninsula (1972) are given as maximum and minimum estimates. I took the midpoint of this range as the estimated population of a site. Second, only the southern valley report includes specific population estimates for the Early Aztec period sites. The Texcoco and Ixtapalapa reports note the presence and relative density of Early Aztec sherdage in their descriptions of Aztec sites, and Early Aztec populations in these areas are estimated from these data. The Teotihuacan Valley preliminary report (Sanders 1965) presented a more difficult problem. The only quantifiable data available are a series of maps showing site locations and sherd densities for the Aztec, Mazapan or Late Toltec, and

TABLE 7.1
Surface Sherd Density to Population Conversion

Sanders	Parsons	Parsons population estimate (persons/ha)	Population estimate used here (persons/ha)
Light	Light	5–10	8
Moderate	Light/moderate	10–25	18
Heavy	Moderate	25–50	38

Xometla or Early Toltec phases (Sanders 1965:Figs. 9–11). To estimate the populations of these sites I enlarged the published maps and measured the areas of sherd scatter at each site. Parsons, who participated in all the surveys cited here, provided the information in Table 7.1, which allows the conversion of Teotihuacan sherd density figures to the terminology used in all other surveys in the area. House mounds are estimated to represent a population of five. Finally, a correction factor is applied to change these estimates from Aztec populations to Early Aztec populations. This factor, .6, is the ratio of total Early Aztec to total Aztec population in the Teotihuacan Valley (Sanders 1965:Fig. 14). This correction involves the assumptions that (*a*) all later Aztec sites had been occupied during the Early Aztec period, and (*b*) all sites grew proportionately from Early to Late Aztec times. Although both assumptions are plainly oversimplifications, they are necessary if the survey data from Teotihuacan are to be used. Some sites had major structures, usually pyramidal mounds, but no evidence of permanent occupation. These are shown on the site distribution maps as ceremonial sites and are assigned populations of 10 so that their interaction neighbors can be calculated.

The next step was defining a measure of distance between sites that would be proportional to travel time. From Spanish comments about canoe travel (Cortés 1908:67–69; Gibson 1964:364) I concluded that travel over water was about 33% slower than travel over land. In other words, going a mile over water takes as much time as going 1.5 miles over land. From personal experience I estimated that changing altitude by 50 m, either up or down, is equivalent to walking 0.4 km over level ground in terms of travel time. Using these two figures an equivalent distance can be calculated for any route between two locations. That is,

$$t = C \text{ (total linear distance)} + .4 \text{ (number of 50-m contour lines crossed)} + .5 \text{ (distance over water)} = C(d) \tag{7.3}$$

where t is travel time, d is equivalent distance, and C is a constant. For convenience d is used as the distance between sites rather than assigning some value to C and calculating an estimated travel time. The order of interaction neighbors is the same whether t or d is used in the interaction equation.

Values of d were measured for several routes between pairs of sites, and the lowest value (corresponding to the fastest route) was put into a triangular matrix of intersite distances. This was a tedious procedure but the more accurate approximation of the travel time between sites resulted in a very close fit of the archaeological data to the ethnohistorically known patterns.

Finally, a series of interaction measures was calculated for the Early Aztec sites using a computer program written by Keith Kintigh. Computer runs were made using $1/d_{ij}$ and the equation $(P_i \cdot P_j)/(d_{ij})^a$ with 1, 1.3, 1.5, 1.7, 1.8, 1.9, and 2 as values of a to calculate estimated political interaction. When first and second interaction neighbors by these measures were plotted, an examination of the maps showed that the measure using $a = 1.9$ most closely approximated the ethnohistorically known borders. To summarize, the interaction equation that gave the best fit to the known political units is

$$I = \frac{(P_i \cdot P_j)}{(d_{ij})^{1.9}} \tag{7.4}$$

A systematic means of drawing borders around clusters was devised, so that the model could be applied to a period when political units were not known historically. First, site size categories were determined by drawing histograms of site population for each period and examining the histograms for natural breaks. These histograms and size categories are shown in Figure 7.7. Next, all sites in the two largest categories for each period were considered as potential centers of political units. The first boundaries were drawn by separating clusters that had no neighbor bonds to adjacent clusters (e.g., 42/43 from 63/64 on the Early Aztec maps). Then, clusters joined only by a row of border sites were separated. A border site is a site of the smallest size class or a ceremonial site that is joined to a central site of one cluster by its nearest neighbor bond and to a central site of another cluster by its second nearest neighbor bond. Two such borders exist for the Early Aztec period: between 42/43 and 20/21 and between 78 and 109/112. Boundaries were drawn so that the second nearest neighbor bond was broken, and these broken lines were not counted in the total neighbor bonds between clusters in the last step of the clustering operation. In this step a nearest neighbor line between two clusters was counted as three neighbor bonds and a second nearest neighbor line was counted as one neighbor bond. Clusters connected by more than six neighbor bonds were combined.

It is difficult to evaluate quantitatively the fit of the Early Aztec political clusters derived through the model to the historically known political pattern. However, an examination of Figure 7.2 indicates that the two patterns are quite similar, especially when all possible sources of distortion are considered. Over 95% of the sites are correctly assigned to political units, and 17 of the 19 sites in the two largest size categories are correctly assigned. Although the information that the model fails to duplicate is certainly significant, the good fit of the model to the ethnohistoric data indicates that the assumptions made here and the application of an interaction model to the definition of political clusters are in general justified.

A model has been devised for distilling political relationships from archaeological data in the Valley of Mexico. Now, that model will be used to predict political relationships for the Early and Late Toltec periods in the same region. This would seem to be a reasonable extension of the model in that it is being applied to an earlier time period but one in which factors such as the technology of communication, subsistence adaptation, ecological setting, and geological constraints on settlement location do not change. I would not argue that the model as derived here could be immediately applied to other societies or geographical settings—it *may* be applicable, but that remains to be demonstrated.

The process of measuring distances, calculating interaction neighbors, and delineating political clusters was continued for the Early and Late Toltec periods. Site population estimates for these periods were made by the same procedures followed previously, except that no correction factor needed to be applied to the Teotihuacan figures. One important problem was encountered in the Early Toltec period data—no occupation is shown for Teotihuacan (Sanders 1965:Fig. 9) although a significant occupation from this period is mentioned elsewhere in his report. I therefore used a population estimate of 4750, putting the site at the lower end of the largest size class. Larger estimates of the population of Early Toltec period Teotihuacan (Parsons, 1974:98) were rejected because they are based on interpolation between the Late Classic and Late Toltec populations of the site. A more accurate estimate must await the publication of surface survey data collected by the Teotihuacan Mapping Project on the density of sherdage of various periods within the city.

Tables 7.2–7.4 show for each period the sites, their nearest interaction neighbors, and their estimated population. Figures 7.1–7.6 show the site locations and the political clusters determined through the interaction model.

This new information permits a reinterpretation of the Toltec period in the Valley of Mexico. After the propositions of earlier researchers have been reviewed, a new interpretation of Toltec period political organization is suggested, and several testable implications of this interpretation are proposed.

TABLE 7.2
Early Aztec Period Sites, Their Nearest Interaction Neighbors Calculated by Equation (7.4), and Their Estimated Populations[a]

	Interaction Neighbors					Interaction Neighbors			
Site	1st	2nd	3rd	Population	Site	1st	2nd	3rd	Population
1	20	21	9	105	46	43	42	63	1720
2	20	21	9	90	47	63	64	43	10
3	20	21	9	10	48	63	64	43	10
4	20	24	21	45	49	63	64	20	1000
5	24	6	20	135	50	52	63	64	600
6	24	20	5	180	51	50	52	63	10
7	20	21	9	120	52	50	63	64	250
8	20	9	21	90	53	50	63	52	40
9	20	21	19	610	54	63	55	64	280
10	20	9	19	30	55	63	64	54	750
11	20	19	12	45	56	63	55	64	150
12	20	19	11	45	57	63	64	55	80
13	20	42	21	10	58	63	64	43	10
14	20	42	16	90	59	63	64	60	10
15	20	42	14	45	60	63	64	55	130
16	20	19	42	120	61	63	64	78	10
17	20	19	21	10	62	63	64	78	375
18	20	19	21	120	63	64	78	62	11250
19	20	21	9	690	64	63	78	67	8000
20	21	19	9	3900	65	64	67	63	10
21	20	22	19	1330	66	67	64	63	10
22	20	21	37	610	67	64	63	112	1875
23	24	37	20	135	68	67	63	64	15
24	20	37	21	1770	69	67	63	64	15
25	24	20	27	115	70	67	64	63	60
26	27	24	20	60	71	78	64	63	10
27	24	20	31	195	72	112	78	63	10
28	24	20	37	90	73	112	63	64	260
29	24	37	33	60	74	112	78	63	10
30	24	33	20	150	75	112	79	63	15
31	24	30	27	105	76	112	78	63	15
32	24	30	33	45	77	112	78	63	10
33	24	37	20	500	78	64	63	112	6000
34	37	24	35	105	79	78	63	64	10
35	36	49	37	380	80	78	112	63	30
36	35	37	49	310	81	78	112	63	35
37	24	20	22	990	82	83	86	92	10
38	20	49	63	10	83	86	84	92	1500
39	20	42	63	90	84	86	83	92	500
40	63	20	49	240	85	86	83	84	50
41	43	42	20	440	86	83	88	84	2440
42	43	41	20	1770	87	86	88	92	25
43	42	41	46	1860	88	86	83	92	120
44	43	42	46	30	89	86	92	88	40
45	46	42	43	10	90	92	86	83	10

Table 7.2 *(Continued)*

Site	Interaction Neighbors			Population	Site	Interaction Neighbors			Population
	1st	2nd	3rd			1st	2nd	3rd	
91	92	86	112	25	125	126	112	124	90
92	86	112	97	7500	126	155	112	125	2250
93	92	97	94	25	127	112	155	129	25
94	92	97	112	40	128	129	112	155	25
95	92	97	112	40	129	112	155	126	270
96	97	92	112	115	130	112	129	155	30
97	92	112	102	2250	131	112	155	132	150
98	92	97	112	40	132	131	112	155	55
99	102	112	97	150	133	134	112	131	150
100	102	97	112	190	134	133	112	155	300
101	102	112	109	120	135	134	155	112	40
102	112	101	97	1500	136	134	155	112	40
103	112	109	102	70	137	131	155	132	40
104	112	109	103	30	138	155	131	112	40
105	112	109	106	75	139	126	155	112	120
106	112	109	107	300	140	155	144	141	30
107	112	106	109	75	141	144	155	126	255
108	112	109	106	120	142	143	155	112	75
109	112	108	102	1350	143	155	142	144	210
110	112	109	108	60	144	155	141	112	410
111	112	109	113	60	145	146	148	155	25
112	109	113	63	9350	146	148	155	145	75
113	112	109	111	115	147	155	112	148	240
114	116	112	67	15	148	146	155	149	180
115	116	112	117	60	149	148	155	112	55
116	112	117	63	960	150	155	147	148	25
117	116	112	118	375	151	155	152	148	60
118	112	117	116	150	152	155	151	148	70
119	112	126	109	10	153	155	112	126	75
120	112	126	121	105	154	155	126	112	25
121	120	112	126	25	155	112	126	144	10500
122	126	112	123	25	156	155	157	112	45
123	112	126	122	60	157	155	156	112	40
124	126	112	125	45					

[a] Site numbers followed by zeros were not assigned to a site. An asterisk before an interaction neighbor indicates that the starred and following site had equal estimates of political interaction.

TABLE 7.3
Late Toltec Period Sites and Interaction Neighbors

| Site | Interaction Neighbors | | | Population | Site | Interaction Neighbors | | | Population |
	1st	2nd	3rd			1st	2nd	3rd	
1	50	46	4	85	50	51	54	45	1240
2	4	3	5	15	51	50	54	44	145
3	4	2	5	15	52	50	54	51	45
4	6	7	3	235	53	54	50	55	10
5	4	7	* 3	10	54	55	50	58	505
6	4	7	5	30	55	54	50	61	45
7	4	5	6	20	56	57	50	58	75
8	4	50	46	10	57	58	60	61	300
9	50	4	10	25	58	57	61	54	205
10	4	50	9	25	59	57	60	63	40
11	18	12	14	55	60	57	63	58	60
12	11	14	18	10	61	58	62	57	200
13	19	11	18	25	62	61	57	54	105
14	18	15	11	25	63	60	61	58	185
15	17	18	14	10	64	63	57	67	25
16	18	*17	14	15	65	63	57	64	15
17	18	15	14	25	66	67	63	57	30
18	17	50	24	225	67	66	63	57	90
19	20	23	13	30	68	63	57	67	25
20	19	23	21	10	69	70	93	41	25
21	23	19	22	10	70	69	93	41	25
22	23	44	21	30	71	50	57	63	10
23	22	50	19	40	72	32	18	31	105
24	18	50	32	25	73	93	81	85	25
25	31	28	32	35	74	32	31	28	40
26	27	28	32	10	75	93	85	76	25
27	28	26	31	10	76	77	93	85	25
28	27	25	31	40	77	76	93	85	25
29	28	32	30	10	78	93	98	104	25
30	29	32	28	10	79	* 0	* 0	* 0	0
31	32	25	18	60	80	93	85	81	25
32	31	72	18	105	81	93	85	*83	25
33	72	50	32	20	82	93	90	83	25
34	50	18	43	20	83	93	90	84	25
35	37	38	36	15	84	93	85	83	25
36	38	37	35	20	85	93	88	80	125
37	38	36	35	15	86	* 0	* 0	* 0	0
38	36	37	35	40	87	93	88	84	10
39	50	38	54	35	88	93	85	89	25
40	41	50	54	45	89	93	88	85	25
41	40	50	54	85	90	93	83	82	25
42	50	54	93	10	91	93	54	50	10
43	50	44	51	110	92	93	98	90	25
44	50	45	43	125	93	98	90	95	625
45	50	44	51	240	94	* 0	* 0	* 0	0
46	50	54	48	355	95	93	98	85	25
47	50	48	49	70	96	* 0	* 0	* 0	0
48	50	47	49	80	97	93	98	99	10
49	50	48	47	25	98	93	78	95	50

TABLE 7.3 *(Continued)*

	Interaction Neighbors					Interaction Neighbors			
Site	1st	2nd	3rd	Population		1st	2nd	3rd	Population
99	93	104	98	25	149	148	131	218	40
100	93	104	102	25	150	131	215	220	10
101	93	106	124	25	151	131	148	220	10
102	104	93	99	25	152	220	218	148	25
103	106	124	93	25	153	218	220	131	55
104	93	102	99	75	154	220	218	215	20
105	93	104	124	25	155	215	220	218	30
106	103	124	101	25	156	157	215	155	10
107	124	122	123	50	157	215	156	220	30
108	93	120	124	25	158	215	164	159	10
109	93	*120	110	25	159	164	215	158	25
110	93	109	114	25	160	161	162	131	225
111	112	93	113	25	161	160	162	131	150
112	115	113	93	25	162	161	160	131	125
113	116	115	93	25	163	162	161	160	30
114	93	110	85	25	164	215	131	166	135
115	*113	112	116	25	165	164	215	131	10
116	113	115	93	25	166	131	164	162	70
117	* 0	* 0	* 0	0	167	166	168	131	10
118	131	93	116	25	168	166	131	*169	15
119	* 0	* 0	* 0	0	169	166	168	131	10
120	93	108	109	25	170	131	171	166	10
121	131	93	124	25	171	172	176	177	45
122	123	124	107	50	172	174	171	173	15
123	122	124	107	100	173	172	174	171	10
124	125	123	107	225	174	172	171	176	10
125	124	123	122	25	175	176	177	171	10
126	123	124	131	50	176	177	175	171	45
127	124	125	131	10	177	176	175	171	40
128	131	160	161	300	178	176	177	131	35
129	131	160	128	180	179	180	131	178	20
130	131	128	160	10	180	131	179	178	90
131	128	160	137	1150	181	182	183	184	15
132	* 0	* 0	* 0	0	182	181	183	215	45
133	* 0	* 0	* 0	0	183	182	181	184	15
134	* 0	* 0	* 0	0	184	185	215	182	40
135	* 0	* 0	* 0	0	185	184	186	215	35
136	* 0	* 0	* 0	0	186	185	215	184	15
137	131	139	148	50	187	188	215	190	15
138	* 0	* 0	* 0	0	188	187	*190	189	15
139	131	137	148	25	189	190	188	215	10
140	131	148	141	15	190	189	188	215	10
141	148	131	218	20	191	215	185	184	25
142	131	218	220	15	192	194	193	*196	70
143	146	131	147	20	193	194	192	*196	25
144	147	146	131	10	194	192	193	*196	25
145	146	147	218	10	195	196	198	197	25
146	147	218	131	50	196	195	198	197	25
147	146	218	220	75	197	198	*196	195	25
148	149	131	220	115	198	197	*196	195	25

TABLE 7.3 (*Continued*)

	Interaction Neighbors					Interaction Neighbors			
Site	1st	2nd	3rd	Population	Site	1st	2nd	3rd	Population
199	200	197	198	25	251	249	248	250	10
200	199	202·	197	25	252	253	254	203	25
201	202	200	192	25	253	252	254	203	70
202	203	215	253	190	254	253	252	203	25
203	202	215	253	160	255	257	256	261	75
204	215	203	202	25	256	257	255	261	40
205	215	208	207	25	257	255	261	259	135
206	208	215	*209	25	258	257	259	261	15
207	215	208	206	25	259	261	257	260	60
208	209	215	206	160	260	259	261	263	30
209	208	210	215	25	261	264	262	259	180
210	208	215	209	25	262	261	264	266	30
211	215	208	212	25	263	264	261	260	45
212	215	211	208	25	264	261	263	259	110
213	215	212	208	10	265	266	261	262	10
214	215	208	*211	25	266	261	264	265	75
215	220	240	208	1200	267	264	261	257	150
216	215	240	208	50	268	271	270	266	15
217	220	219	218	45	269	270	266	271	10
218	220	222	221	570	270	269	271	266	40
219	220	222	218	110	271	270	266	268	40
220	218	222	219	570	272	273	275	242	25
221	*220	218	222	90	273	275	276	272	70
222	220	218	221	300	274	275	273	240	25
223	224	225	*220	45	275	273	276	240	125
224	223	225	226	25	276	280	275	278	60
225	226	223	227	25	277	275	276	280	10
226	225	227	218	25	278	280	276	275	45
227	226	225	223	25	279	280	276	278	15
228	218	220	223	25	280	278	276	281	80
229	218	220	233	30	281	280	278	275	125
230	218	220	232	10	282	281	280	275	25
231	218	220	222	10	283	281	282	275	25
232	233	218	220	10	284	285	281	283	10
233	222	220	218	150	285	281	284	275	25
234	233	257	220	30	286	287	281	289	25
235	220	222	215	50	287	286	281	289	25
236	215	237	220	10	288	289	291	290	25
237	240	215	238	100	289	291	290	292	50
238	240	237	215	25	290	292	291	289	52
239	240	215	243	25	291	292	290	289	25
240	239	243	215	250	292	290	291	289	70
241	240	243	237	25	293	292	*295	294	25
242	240	272	275	25	294	289	292	*293	25
243	240	215	275	50	295	292	296	293	25
244	245	240	215	25	296	298	297	292	75
245	244	246	240	25	297	296	298	292	25
246	215	240	245	90	298	296	297	292	25
247	248	250	249	25	299	296	298	292	25
248	250	247	249	25	300	296	299	298	25
249	251	248	253	25	301	296	292	281	25
250	248	247	249	10					

TABLE 7.4
Early Toltec Period Sites and Interaction Neighbors

Site	Interaction Neighbors			Population	Site	Interaction Neighbors			Population
	1st	2nd	3rd			1st	2nd	3rd	
1	120	31	35	40	49	46	48	78	55
2	120	13	12	180	50	46	48	51	10
3	120	31	35	110	51	46	48	50	10
4	120	31	35	15	52	46	53	57	65
5	120	31	35	10	53	46	57	54	275
6	120	31	35	20	54	53	46	55	15
7	120	31	35	85	55	46	53	57	60
8	120	31	35	60	56	46	79	53	10
9	120	31	10	20	57	46	58	79	490
10	120	31	35	195	58	57	46	79	90
11	120	12	31	90	59	46	57	60	25
12	120	11	31	320	60	59	46	57	10
13	120	35	31	505	61	67	57	65	10
14	120	12	31	45	62	46	57	67	10
15	16	120	35	25	63	64	65	67	25
16	35	31	120	180	64	65	63	67	30
17	18	120	35	15	65	67	64	66	90
18	21	19	35	135	66	67	69	65	390
19	18	35	120	90	67	66	46	79	2960
20	21	18	35	15	68	69	67	66	40
21	18	35	31	160	69	67	68	66	165
22	35	31	120	150	70	67	66	79	40
23	35	31	120	25	71	67	70	69	10
24	27	25	26	85	72	67	79	91	90
25	24	27	26	10	73	72	79	67	15
26	24	27	35	25	74	75	79	67	15
27	24	35	31	110	75	74	79	67	15
28	31	35	34	10	76	79	67	75	15
29	31	35	34	75	77	46	79	78	75
30	31	35	34	250	78	46	79	98	225
31	35	34	30	6000	79	98	46	96	3830
32	31	35	34	25	80	79	98	93	10
33	31	35	34	15	81	79	98	93	10
34	31	35	46	1200	82	67	83	84	60
35	31	34	46	5400	83	82	67	84	20
36	35	31	37	10	84	82	83	67	10
37	35	31	39	25	85	67	82	91	10
38	35	31	37	10	86	91	67	88	10
39	35	31	34	15	87	88	91	89	50
40	35	31	34	10	88	*89	87	91	200
41	35	31	120	15	89	88	91	87	50
42	35	31	46	250	90	91	88	89	35
43	46	35	45	450	91	88	90	93	580
44	46	43	53	10	92	93	91	79	50
45	46	43	53	150	93	79	91	92	530
46	48	35	31	9000	94	93	79	98	10
47	46	48	49	10	95	98	79	96	80
48	46	49	31	525	96	98	79	95	195

TABLE 7.4 (*Continued*)

Site	Interaction Neighbors			Population	Site	Interaction Neighbors			Population
	1st	2nd	3rd			1st	2nd	3rd	
97	98	79	96	85	109	104	106	98	375
98	79	96	97	1800	110	111	104	112	10
99	98	79	93	140	111	112	110	104	25
100	*0	*0	*0	0	112	111	104	98	75
101	102	104	103	75	113	114	104	109	10
102	104	101	103	215	114	115	104	117	55
103	104	102	101	75	115	114	116	117	15
104	105	106	107	1125	116	115	114	119	10
105	104	107	106	70	117	118	119	114	15
106	104	107	109	204	118	117	119	98	10
107	104	105	106	80	119	117	118	114	20
108	104	109	106	30	120	31	35	12	4750

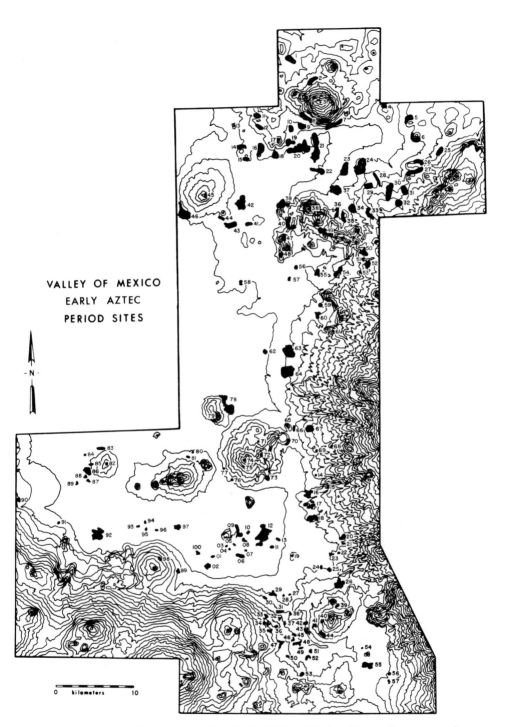

FIGURE 7.1 *Early Aztec period sites in the Valley of Mexico. Site numbers increase from top to bottom, and the first digit of three-digit site numbers is omitted.*

185

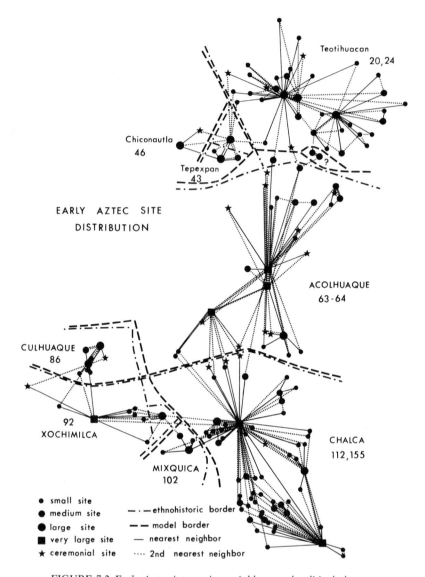

EARLY AZTEC SITE
DISTRIBUTION

FIGURE 7.2 *Early Aztec interaction neighbors and political clusters.*

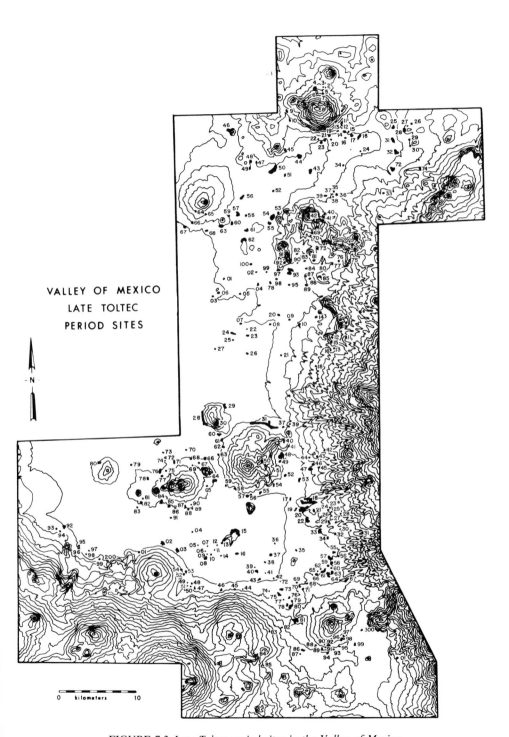

FIGURE 7.3 *Late Toltec period sites in the Valley of Mexico.*

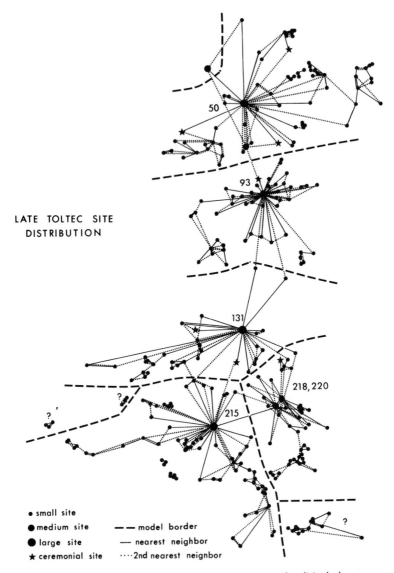

LATE TOLTEC SITE
DISTRIBUTION

● small site
● medium site
● large site
★ ceremonial site

— — model border
— nearest neighbor
····2nd nearest neignbor

FIGURE 7.4 *Late Toltec interaction neighbors and political clusters.*

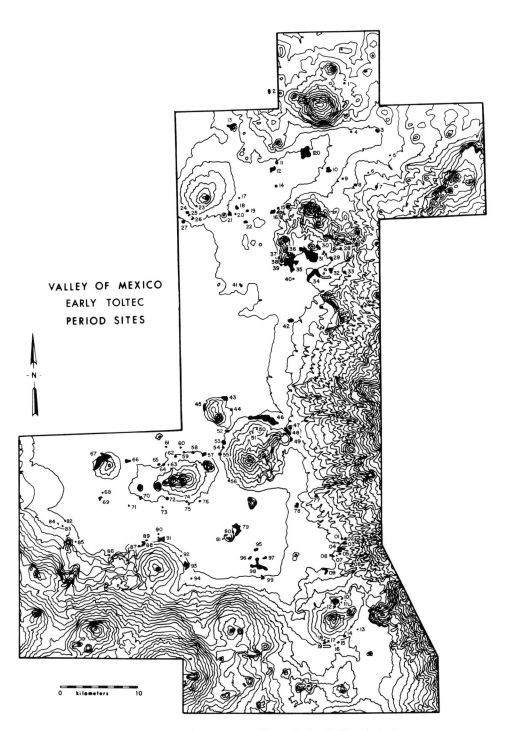

VALLEY OF MEXICO
EARLY TOLTEC
PERIOD SITES

FIGURE 7.5 *Early Toltec period sites in the Valley of Mexico.*

189

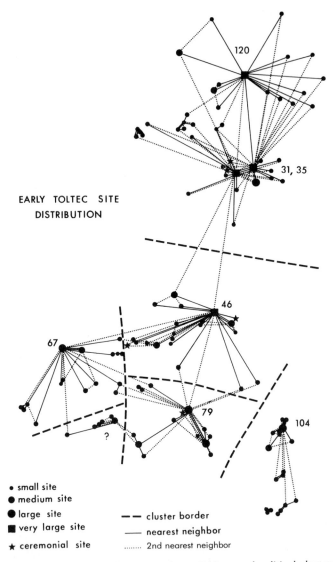

EARLY TOLTEC SITE
DISTRIBUTION

- small site
- medium site
- large site
- very large site
★ ceremonial site

—— cluster border
——— nearest neighbor
········ 2nd nearest neighbor

FIGURE 7.6 *Early Toltec interaction neighbors and political clusters.*

Previous Discussions of Toltec Political Organization

The first reconstruction of Toltec period political organization based on archaeological data was made by J. Parsons (1970:436–7):

> My present hypotheses to account for the main outlines of this Early Toltec settlement pattern are: 1) to regard the three major centers as populated primarily by large blocks of people moving outward from the decaying urban center at Teotihuacan into sparsely occupied lands; and 2) to regard the wide unoccupied central zone as the manifestation of a political frontier between new major centers at Cholula (to the southeast) and Tula (to the northwest)—a kind of no-man's-land, which offered little possibility for permanent residence, lying midway between the domains of two competing, militaristically-oriented states.

> The succeeding Late Toltec period is characterized by a substantial increase in numbers of sites, together with a marked population dispersal, a decline in community size and degree of nucleation, and an apparent decrease in overall population. I would suggest that these combined processes of demographic depression and ruralization are largely the product of two related processes: 1) an intensification of the hostile confrontation between Tula and Cholula (leading ultimately to the collapse of Tula as a major power center by the end of the Late Toltec period); and 2) the final erosion of the remaining vestiges of Teotihuacan's influence as a regional power center.

As evidence for this interpretation Parsons notes that during the Late Toltec period the Texcoco area seems to show two contemporaneous ceramic traditions, the northern distinguished by Mazapan red on buff and the southern marked by Aztec I (or Culhuacan variant) black on orange. Finally, he observes that if the dates of the native historical tradition embodied in the *Codice Xolotl* are pushed back several centuries, then those traditions might be interpreted as supporting this conflict hypothesis.

Charlton (1973) criticizes the conflict interpretation by reevaluating the same survey data that Parsons had considered. Charlton's primary assumption, which allows a quantitative evaluation of the survey data, is that the range of settlement types in an area reflects the degree of independence of that area.

For the Early Toltec period he suggests the presence of local Teotihuacan-derived states. This proposition accounts for the appearance of two Early Toltec settlement clusters in the Texcoco area; the area between these clusters was not settled, according to Charlton, because it was marginally less attractive agricultural land than the occupied areas to the north and south. Finally, these Early Toltec settlement clusters were nucleated rather than dispersed because of "the continued operation of Teotihuacan population centralization on the part of Teotihuacan derived local Early Toltec states (1973:419)."

For the Late Toltec Charlton states (1973:420):

> I suggest that the settlement pattern changes in the northern and central areas during the Late Toltec period (reduction in settlement types, ruralization, demographic depression,

population expansion into the central Texcoco region) may be understood as a result of the breakdown of the Early Toltec socio-political unit in the north (reflected in the reduction of variety of settlement types) and the incorporation of this unit and the northern and central Texcoco region into the newly dominant and expanding orbit of Tula. The ruralization of the population would result from a shift of cultural activities such as political and religious organization to the new center. At the same time, the northern and central areas began to participate in the marketing system which distributed pottery of the Mazapan complex.

It is probable that the southern area may have retained some socio-political independence as evidenced by the wider range of settlement types present in that area; however, it did begin to participate in the market system which distributed pottery of the Aztec I ceramic complex related ultimately to Cholula ceramics. . . . It is possible to suggest that economic and, perhaps, political boundaries between Cholula and Tula may have developed in the Late Toltec period.

These hypotheses, he adds, fit the traditions of the *Codice Xolotl* without requiring the redating of events described in that document.

Recently, Blanton (1975) and Charlton (1975) have suggested alternative interpretations of the Early Toltec settlement pattern. Blanton argues that the Early Toltec period was a time of "Balkanization" in the Valley of Mexico, when discrete, competing sociopolitical units were separated by zones of contested territory (1975:230). Charlton responds that aside from the gap in Texcoco area occupation there is no evidence for conflict (1975:233), and repeats his argument that a continuing tendency toward population nucleation and a policy of selecting certain environmentally favored locations best explain Early Toltec settlement patterns. Both authors agree that the Late Toltec period is best seen as a time when Tula had extended its influence over most of the Valley of Mexico, and use new survey data to show that no clear border between Mazapan and Aztec I ceramics existed in Texcoco during the Late Toltec period (Blanton 1975:230).

These interpretations can be criticized because they fail to define and explicitly deal with political interaction. Also, their analyses do nothing to delimit clusters of settlements in any systematic or replicable manner. Because their discussions of settlement patterns are impressionistic, they have difficulty describing changes in settlement patterns through time, and any observed diachronic changes cannot be attributed to changes in political organization. The analysis of political units and borders presented here deals with these objections and supports the reinterpretation of Toltec period political evolution which is presented in the following.

Interpretations and Results

Early Toltec societies were probably closely related to those of Teotihuacan. There is no evidence of continuity in population between Late

Classic Teotihuacan and any of the Early Toltec political clusters, but as a first estimation such a connection seems reasonable. The appearance of Early Toltec societies might be best evaluated, then, by studying the failure of the mechanisms integrating Teotihuacan as a city and as a society.

Fortunately, that study is being made (Millon 1973). Unfortunately, only very preliminary remarks about the collapse of Teotihuacan have been published. It appears that the political domain of Teotihuacan had been shrinking for some time before the city's fall. The Late Classic population of the city decreased even though the population of the Teotihuacan Valley became increasingly concentrated in the city. Decreased rainfall, Millon hypothesizes, may have contributed to the pressure on the political and economic mechanisms integrating Teotihuacan society, and hints of a shift to a more decentralized kind of ritual expression indicate that integrative religious ties may have also been strained. A major fire in the city signaled the end of the successful urban adaptation at Teotihuacan (Millon 1973:59–63). Early Toltec society somehow emerged from this collapse.

The evidence for simultaneous depopulation of Teotihuacan and re-population of other parts of the Valley of Mexico (Parsons 1974:98) implies that groups of people were moving out of the city. However, we know none of the factors that united the groups of emigrants and separated them from other similar groups. These could have included political allegiance to a ruling individual, kinship ties, *barrio* identification, economic specialization, class membership, or specific ritual or religious beliefs; one important question for future research is to identify which of these mechanisms integrated single Early Toltec political clusters and differentiated one cluster from another.

The apparent representation of ethnic identity during the Late Aztec period in the distribution of spindle whorl types (M. Parsons 1975:214) hints that patterns of stylistic variability in other classes of objects might show prehistoric patterns of "us" versus "them." Thus, propositions about ethnic or social identifications of different Early Toltec political clusters may be testable through analyses of stylistic variation in certain artifact classes.

Blanton suggested that the Early Toltec period was a time of conflict between political units in the Valley of Mexico. In order to test this proposition two measures of disturbance within the surveyed area have been devised. These measures reflect any deviation from the most efficient patterns of information flow and the distribution of subsistence products, and in the Early Aztec period are correlated with extensive militarism and a highly unsettled political situation.

The first measure of disturbance is the ratio of the standard deviation of cluster population to the mean cluster population, a measure reflecting the uniformity of political cluster sizes. This ratio may indicate the degree of competition between clusters, for when competition is intense certain clusters should expand at the expense of others and a synchronic record will

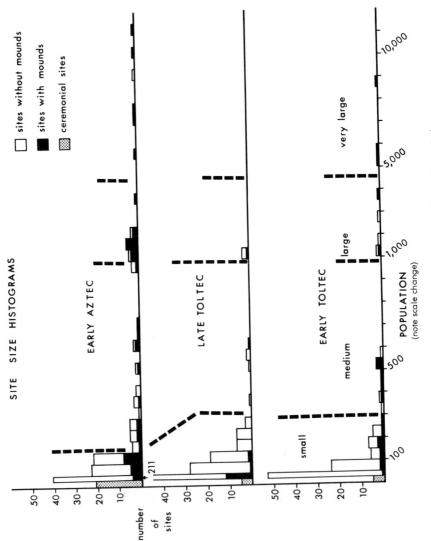

FIGURE 7.7 *Histograms of site population by period.*

show clusters having a broad range of sizes. This would result in a standard deviation that is high with respect to mean cluster population. When there is no competition between political units, as when they are administered by a single hierarchical superior, principles of efficiency in administration and distribution should tend to reduce the variation in cluster sizes. In such cases the ratio of standard deviation to mean cluster population would be low. During the Early Aztec period a high degree of competition between political units has been documented, and the standard deviation to mean population ratio is .83. This implies that intense competition was also a feature of Early Toltec political interaction, when the value of the ratio is .72, and that during the Late Toltec competition between clusters was much less intense (with a ratio of .32).

The variances in cluster populations for each period were tested to see if the differences between periods were statistically significant. An F-test was used, with the null hypothesis that there was no significant difference in the variances for each period (Table 7.5). The variances of the Early Aztec and Early Toltec periods were not significantly different, but both differed significantly from the Late Toltec variance in cluster population. Thus, the test supports the conclusions of the preceding paragraph about the similarities and differences among the three periods.

There is a second potential measure of the relative stability of political relations between clusters: the ratio of larger sites to the number of hamlets occupied during a period. According to Chisholm (1962:138–140), scattered hamlets tend to coalesce into larger, more central, and more easily defended settlements during times of disturbance. If the proposition that the Early Toltec period was less stable politically than the Late Toltec period is correct, then we would predict a lower proportion of hamlets (defined as sites with a permanent population of 50 or less) in the Early Toltec period. This prediction was tested using a χ^2 statistic and the null hypothesis that the Late Toltec and Early Toltec hamlet ratios are no different was rejected at a high level of confidence (Table 7.6). Thus, the suggestion that the Late

TABLE 7.5
F-Test Statistics Comparing the Variances in Political Cluster Populations between the Three Archaeological Periods

Period	Variance	df	$F(s_i^2/s_j)$	Reject H_0
Early Aztec	127,238,000	6	89.9	Yes*
Late Toltec	1,416,000	4	30.7	Yes**
Early Toltec	43,428,000	4		
		EA-ET	2.9	No***

*$p < .0005$.
**$p < .005$.
***$p > .10$.

TABLE 7.6

χ^2 Test of the Proportions of Hamlets in the Early and Late Toltec Periods[a]

	Hamlets	Larger sites	Total
Early Toltec	53	60	113
Late Toltec	211	71	282
Total	264	131	395

[a] $df = 1$; $\chi^2 = 27.12$; $p \ll .001$.

Toltec period was politically more stable, and also the interpretation of the standard deviation to mean cluster population ratio as a measure of disturbance, is supported.

Plotting the ratio of larger sites to hamlets (hereafter called the *disturbance index*), where a high value indicates unstable political conditions and a low value indicates greater stability, provides interesting results (Figure 7.8). First, disturbance seems to have been less severe during the Early Toltec period in the southern valley than in the valley as a whole. Second, a comparison of the Early Toltec and Early Aztec periods in the southern valley (the only survey area with good data on Early Aztec hamlets) indicates that political stability during both periods was almost identical. Thus, it would appear that political relations between clusters during the Early Toltec period in the southern valley were like those described earlier for the Early Aztec period—confused, shifting, and unstable. Third, the sharp increase in the proportion of hamlets during the Late Toltec shows an interesting pattern. In the northern valley the proportion of hamlets is higher, hinting that ruralization had developed for a longer time in that area. This may indicate that the northern area was the first to be brought under the control of an outside political power. It might also indicate that the northern

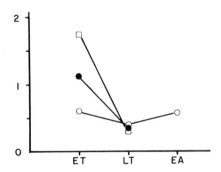

FIGURE 7.8 *The ratio of larger sites to hamlets, or* disturbance index, *during the post-classic periods in the Valley of Mexico. A higher index implies more disturbance, a lower index less.* ○, *southern valley;* □, *northern valley,* ●, *combined areas.*

valley was being systematically exploited for its agricultural production, as is suggested later.

Certain details of the Early Toltec political cluster pattern raise several other points. First, even if there are several small Early Toltec sites in the unsurveyed areas of the Texcoco plain, the gap between the northern and southern clusters (120/31 and 46, 67, etc.) is wider and more distinct than any gap between warring Early Aztec units. The proposition that this Early Toltec gap represents an unoccupied zone between warring political units (Blanton 1975:230) does not explain the noteworthy size of that gap. The suggestion that the Texcoco plain lacked the combination of environmental factors desired by Early Toltec peoples (Charlton, 1973, 1975) seems possible but as Blanton notes is not totally convincing, particularly without a quantitative analysis of settlement locations and environmental zones in the surveyed areas of the valley. I would suggest that this clear gap implies major social and ideological differences between the northern and southern political clusters, and that each cluster represents a faction of the population of Teotihuacan before its collapse. The competition between northern and southern Early Toltec clusters was perhaps related to the factors that caused the breakdown of social integration in Teotihuacan, and it does not seem impossible that Teotihuacan was burned by Teotihuacanos during a period of severe internal strife.

Second, the southern clusters seem more or less loosely connected even though they do not form a single political unit. The similarities of this Early Toltec pattern to the Early Aztec pattern and close parallels with the Mixteca Alta region (Spores, 1967:10, 92–101) are marked, and this indicates that there may also be parallels between the political organizations of these regions. On this basis, I would venture to suggest that the individual clusters within the southern group of Early Toltec units were ruled by semiautonomous members of a few intermarrying noble lineages, and that although these clusters competed for political advantage through raiding and marriage alliances, they were not attempting to dominate one another through systematic conquest.

The pattern of political clusters derived for the Late Toltec period is very different from the Early Toltec and Early Aztec patterns. The mean cluster population in the Late Toltec is only one-third that of the Early Toltec, and the standard deviation-to-mean cluster population ratio is .32—a significantly lower value. Also, the disturbance index for the Late Toltec period is lower, indicating a significantly more stable situation. Both of these features indicate a time of greatly reduced competition between political units. I concur with Blanton and Charlton that during the Late Toltec period the Valley of Mexico was incorporated into an expanding sphere of Tula-centered political control. I would speculate that as part of the incorporation process the ruling classes of the Early Toltec units were removed to Tula, and that many of the administrative and ceremonial functions of the previously independent clusters were incorporated by Tula. Thus, the Late Toltec political units may represent one hierarchical level of administration and information collection; decisions made in Tula were passed down to the lower level units that have been isolated in this study.

It is also possible that the lower population of the surveyed area during the Late Toltec period resulted from a deliberate policy of Tula. The Valley of Mexico may have served as an agricultural production zone for the Toltec center; craft production, such as obsidian blade manufacture or pottery making, may have been centralized at convenient locations in the valley and the distribution of craft and agricultural products administered by officials from Tula. This hypothesis would account for the regular size and spacing of Late Toltec political clusters (for administrative efficiency), the apparent population decline in the valley (resettlement of people in other areas), and the great increase in the number of hamlets in the survey area during this period (for intensive agricultural production). The appearance of scattered hamlets in the bed of Lake Chalco may indicate an expanding use of this potentially rich area which culminated in the Aztec *chinampa* system.

Possible tests of this interpretation are indirect and beyond the scope of this chapter, and thus they are only mentioned here:

1. Major agricultural storage facilities in the larger sites of the Late Toltec clusters might indicate the presence of an agricultural redistribution system.
2. A lack of home craft production tools in the hamlets could indicate that the residents of the hamlets were full-time agricultural specialists whose needs for craft items were filled through exchange or redistribution.
3. Low stylistic variability both within and between political clusters would imply that a production and distribution network was operating on a scale larger than a single political cluster.

Summary

This chapter has presented a quantitative analysis of Early and Late Toltec period settlement patterns that reveals units of political interaction. The patterning of these units is interpreted in terms of political and social processes. The Early Toltec period seems to represent a continuation of the conflicts that caused the collapse of Teotihuacan dominance over the Valley of Mexico. Blanton's interpretation of this period as a time of "Balkanization" in the Valley of Mexico is supported by two suggestive statistics: the ratio of standard deviation to mean cluster population and the disturbance index. It is also supported by parallels in settlement patterns to two ethnohistorically known times of political disruption, the Early Aztec period in the Valley of Mexico and the Mixteca Alta before Spanish contact.

The interpretation of the Late Toltec period as a time when Tula had extended its influence over the whole Valley of Mexico is also supported. It is suggested that the observed settlement pattern reflects an attempt to maximize administrative and distributive efficiency over what may have been an area of agricultural production, and several potential tests of these propositions are presented.

The analysis of archaeological settlement patterns presented in the first part of this chapter allowed a systematic examination of previous propositions about political organization and evolution in the Valley of Mexico during the Toltec period. It also allowed a series of tests of suggested interpretations to be devised. The interaction model of political organization, although not perfect, appears to be a powerful tool for examining certain archaeological situations where a degree of ethnohistoric control is available. It can generate specific questions for further research, and seems to be one of the most promising techniques for examining the relationships between political, economic, and social systems in complex societies where only archaeological data are available.

Acknowledgments

I wish to thank Kent Flannery, Jeff Parsons, and Henry Wright for reading and commenting on an earlier version of this chapter. Liz Brumfiel, Keith Kintigh, and Judy Nowack gave me substantive critical comments on the same version of this chapter, leading to improvements in both methodology and style. The interpretations and conclusions, however, remain my own responsibility.

References

Blanton, Richard E., 1972, Prehispanic settlement patterns of the Ixtapalapa Peninsula region, Mexico. *Occasional Papers in Anthropology 6*. Department of Anthropology, Pennsylvania State University.

Blanton, Richard E., 1975. Texcoco region archaeology. *American Antiquity* 40, 227–230.

Charlton, Thomas H., 1973, Texcoco region archeology and the *Codex Xolotl*. *American Antiquity* 38, 412–423.

Charlton, Thomas H., 1975, From Teotihuacan to Tenochtitlan: the early period revisited. *American Antiquity* 40, 231–235.

Chisholm, Michael, 1962, *Rural settlement and land use*. Hutchinson and Co., London.

Cortés, Hernan, 1908, *Fernando Cortés—his five letters*. Translated by F. A. MacNutt. The Hakluyt Society, Volume 11.

Gibson, Charles, 1964, *The Aztecs under Spanish rule*. Stanford University Press, Stanford.

MacNeish, Richard S., Frederick A. Peterson and Kent V. Flannery, 1970, *Prehistory of the Tehuacan Valley: Volume 3—Ceramics*. D. S. Byers (ed.) University of Texas Press, Austin.

Millon, Rene, 1973, *Urbanization at Teotihuacan, Mexico: Volume 1—the Teotihuacan map.* University of Texas Press, Austin.

Nuttall, Zelia, 1926, Official reports on the towns of Tequizistlan, Tepechpan, Acolman, and San Juan Teotihuacan sent by Francisco de Castañeda to His Majesty, Philip II, and the Council of the Indies, in 1580. *Papers of the Peabody Museum* XI, 45–86.

Olsson, Gunnar, 1965, Distance and human interaction—a review and bibliography. *Regional Science Research Institute Bibliography Series* 2, Philadelphia.

PNE, 1905–1948, *Papeles de Nueva España.* Francisco del Paso y Troncoso (ed.) Madrid and Mexico.

Parsons, Jeffrey R., 1971, An archaeological evaluation of the *Codice Xolotl. American Antiquity* 35, 431–440.

Parsons, Jeffery R., 1971, Prehistoric settlement patterns in the Texcoco region, Mexico. *University of Michigan Museum of Anthropology, Memoirs* 3.

Parsons, Jeffery R., 1974, The development of a prehistoric complex society: a regional perspective from the Valley of Mexico. *Journal of Field Archaeology* 1, 81–108.

Parsons, Jeffery R., in prep., Prehistoric settlement patterns in the southern Valley of Mexico.

Parsons, Mary H., 1975, The distribution of Late Postclassic spindle whorls in the Valley of Mexico. *American Antiquity* 40, 207–215.

Sanders, William T., 1965, The cultural ecology of the Teotihuacan Valley. Department of Sociology and Anthropology, Pennsylvania State University. multilithed.

Spores, Ronald M., 1967, *The Mixtec kings and their people.* University of Oklahoma Press, Norman.

Valliant, George C., 1938, A correlation of archaeological and historical sequences in the Valley of Mexico. *American Anthropologist* 40, 535–543.

III

SIMULATION AND THE MEASUREMENT OF CHANGE

Merely corroborative detail, intended to give artistic verisimilitude to an otherwise bald and unconvincing narrative.

W. S. Gilbert
The Mikado

Simulation implies the use of an explicit model to produce a representation, in some sense, of the real world. It often differs, however, from other forms of modeling by its considerable complexity, at least in the application, so that a computer is normally required to perform the requisite calculations.

A simulation thus starts from a general, often in some respects simple, model. From this an explicit algorithm is expressed in an appropriate computer language. Input data, which may be prolific, representing the initial conditions (often including environmental information) are supplied, and the computer following the algorithm carries out the prescribed sequence of operations to yield the output, either in numerical or in graphic form.

Often the input data are conceived as representing the state of a system at a given point in time, and the program proceeds by successive iteration along the time trajectory of the system so that successive states of the system are modeled or simulated. A common class of model of this kind is the system dynamics model (see Chapter 2 and Part IV) where the computer is used to calculate the complex interactions between the various components and subsystems of the system, and hence their successive states.

Another feature common to many simulations is the use of random or stochastic elements at different stages of the iteration, so that the outcome is not uniquely determined by the initial conditions. The use of stochastic models, including Monte Carlo methods and Markov chains (cf. Chapter 2; also Clarke 1968, 449) is now a standard simulation procedure. In such models only certain aspects of the final output state are directly determined by the regularity which is being modeled and much of the richness of the output comes from the controlled use of random effects. Spatial patterns are commonly simulated in this way, using a controlled combination of determined and random processes to build up a sequence of successive stages of growth of the pattern (e.g., Hägerstrand 1953, Morill 1962). Chadwick (Chapter 10, this volume; 1977) has used this approach to model settlement growth in bronze age Greece.

In each case the object of simulation is to generate an output which in some sense resembles, that is, is a *simulacrum* of, the real world. Successive runs, when a stochastic process is involved, may correspond either more or less closely to the observed reality. In some cases various features of the underlying model can then be varied in an endeavor to improve the goodness of fit.

But how good is good? The evaluation of the efficacity of the output is one of the most difficult problems involved in simulation. For although a statistical measure can often be found which will estimate the goodness of fit of one aspect of the simulacrum against the same aspect of the real pattern, there is no objective way of assessing the overall similarity of two complete spatial patterns.

A further fundamental difficulty is that very different assumptions and models can, in certain cases, generate closely similar patterns. This problem of equifinality (Hodder and Orton 1976, 239; Renfrew 1977, 83) has already been recognized in archaeological applications, but not yet seriously tackled.

Perhaps the chief danger of simulation procedures is that the complexity of the computing process can mask the underlying properties and weaknesses of the model, obscuring the very significant effect upon the output exercised by unobserved or superficially unimportant assumptions implicit within the model itself.

Simulation is not explanation: the explanatory power resides always within the underlying model, and the predictions of a model can certainly be compared with the real world without using any simulation procedure (e.g., Jochim 1976). Simulation is simply a technique for exploring the implications of a model in a manner which, without the computer, would be exceedingly tedious. In a sense, therefore, the real interest of the contributions that follow lies in the exploratory framework which they construct.

Many simulation models in archaeology (cf. Hodder, 1978) are spatial models, having as their end product a settlement pattern whose properties and structure may then be compared with the real pattern which is being simulated (cf. Thomas 1972). Such is the case with the chapters in this part by Chadwick, by Gunn and by Ammerman and Cavalli-Sforza, although the interest in each case transcends the simple comparison of real and simulated settlement patterns. But of course any observed pattern among data may be simulated: Among interesting examples are the work by Zubrow (1975) on population dynamics and by Wright and Zeder (1977) on trading patterns. Chapter 5 by Hodder in this volume simulates frequency distribution of size of settlement, without closely considering the two-dimensional configuration in space.

The chapters here by Eighmy and by Plog are not primarily concerned with spatial patterning, but with growth. Nor is a computer simulation needed to compare their data with the important general growth curves they hypothesize (see also Chapters 1 and 2).

Each of these chapters, however, is concerned with change, with its measurement, and with its quantitative prediction.

A. C. R.

References

Chadwick, A., 1977, Computer simulation of settlement development in bronze age Messenia, in Bintliff J. (ed.), *Mycenaean Geography*, Cambridge, British Association for Mycenaean Studies, 88–93.

Clarke, D. L., 1968, *Analytical Archaeology,* London, Methuen.

Hägerstrand, T., 1967, *Innovation Diffusion as a Spatial Process,* Chicago, University Press.

Hodder, I. (ed.), 1978, *Simulation Studies in Archaeology,* Cambridge, University Press.

Hodder, I. and Orton, C., 1976, *Spatial Analysis in Archaeology,* Cambridge, University Press.

Jochim, M. A., 1976, *Hunter Gatherer Subsistence and Settlement, a Predictive Model,* New York, Academic Press.

Morrill, R. L., 1962, Simulation of central place patterns over time, *Lund Studies in Geography, Series B, Human Geography* 24, 109–120.

Renfrew, C., 1977, Alternative models for exchange and spatial distribution, in Earle, T. K., and Ericson, J. E., *Exchange Systems in Prehistory,* New York, Academic Press, 71–90.

Thomas, D. W., 1972, A computer simulation model of Great Basin Shoshonean subsistence and settlement patterns, in Clarke, D. L. (1972). *Models in Archaeology,* London, Methuen, 671–704.

Wright, H. T. and Zeder, M., 1977, The simulation of a linear exchange system under equilibrium conditions, in Earle, T. K. and Ericson, J. E. (eds.), *Exchange Systems in Prehistory,* New York, Academic Press, 233–253.

Zubrow, E. B. W., 1975, *Prehistoric Carrying Capacity: A Model,* Menlo Park, Cummings.

8

JEFFREY L. EIGHMY

Logistic Trends in Southwest Population Growth

Understanding population dynamics has been a major issue in anthropology (Spooner 1972; Swedlund 1975), and an important contribution to this understanding is provided by the analysis of trends in population change. Apart from specific historical information, accurate diachronic records can provide data concerning the direction, rate, regularity, and form of population change. The advantages of trend analysis in prehistoric population research have been discussed several times (Cowgill 1975; Longacre 1970, 207; Zubrow 1971, 129), and archaeological time depth has naturally lent itself to consideration of diachronic trends in population change. Although archaeologists cannot count people, they have used indices of population size such as settlements, houses, habitation rooms, and roofed area to analyze prehistoric cultural developments (Gummerman 1970, 30; Plog 1974, 93; Schwartz 1956, 29).

For prehistoric times, trend analysis is made particularly important as a tool for studying population dynamics because it avoids the complicated attempt to convert material indices to rough estimates of population size Casselberry 1974; Cook and Heizer 1968; LeBlanc 1971; Plog 1974, 88–98). These conversion factors are apparently variable from one region to the next. For instance, LeBlanc (1971) and Cook (1972) found that one factor commonly used to estimate population, number of houses, is culturally and/or regionally variable. Still such indices do show that for a given population, architectural and settlement variables correlate well with population size. For example, data from the 1970 Mexican census (Mexico 1971, 400–406) show that for a rural section of Chihuahua the number of houses per

205

Transformations:
Mathematical Approaches to Culture Change

village and village population are correlated in a simple linear fashion with a squared correlation coefficient of .98. By looking at relative change in such indices within a given community, culturally or regionally variable parameters may be held constant, and an accurate representation of the diachronic trend in population size depicted. Cowgill (1975, 508) has recently suggested that some of the more specific implications of population theory can be tested diachronically using trends in the prehistoric record.

One idea Cowgill (1975, 508) suggests testing is whether growth is an inherent characteristic of sedentary human populations. If so, colonizing or agriculturally intensifying populations should increase in number until substantial stress is experienced. The growth trend for these sedentary communities should approximate an S-shaped growth curve (Cowgill 1975, 509). Although a substantial number of cases will have to be analyzed in order to understand the issue fully, this chapter applies Cowgill's test to several prehistoric communities in the American Southwest.

The theory behind an S-shaped or logistic population trend has been outlined by Pearl and Reed (1920). It begins with the fact that human populations have the potential to grow at an exponential rate if unchecked by environmental limitations. Normally, limitations such as space, food, and disease do affect population growth, and they affect growth in a density-dependent manner. That is, in the early stages of exploiting a new niche, when population size is small, the checks have little effect, and the population can grow at a nearly exponential rate. Growth is gradually slowed by subsistence or environmental resistance as the size of the population approaches the maximum supportable by the niche. Maximum population size is determined by the capacity of the subsistence strategy to support people. The rate of growth at any particular time is dependent on the density of the population at that time, and the trend in population growth resembles a lazy S shape.

Depicting Prehistoric Population Trends

The remainder of this chapter presents evidence from the prehistoric Southwest which suggests that the size of localized sedentary communities grows according to the expectations of a density-dependent model. The question of population change in the Southwest has already received special attention (Gummerman 1975, Longacre 1975, Plog 1974, Zubrow 1971). In fact, Reid (1973, 119–134) in analyzing a variety of data sources has come up with a density-dependent model for explaining pueblo growth which is a verbal complement to the mathematical model tested here. The excellent treatment population problems have received in the Southwest is due partially to the better time control in Southwest archaeology, and it is dendro-chronological dating control which makes the present analysis possible.

For the Southwest reliable indices to population growth trends can be obtained through dendrochronologically dated roof beams. Although logs used in roof construction may be extremely sensitive to population growth, they are not necessarily sensitive to population decline and abandonment. Therefore the remarks of this chapter are restricted to the growth periods of the communities considered. However, to derive even this portion of the total change record the assumptions which are necessary to relate log cutting to roof area growth and roof area growth to population growth need to be recognized and discussed.

Assumptions Relating Log Cutting to Roof Area Growth

It seems reasonable to expect that an adequate sample of roof beams from a site or group of related sites reflects the need for roofed space by a community. With a good record of the temporal distribution of cutting dates the trend in roof construction itself can be outlined. Although it is felt that this trend can be derived accurately, it does depend on the condition that the available logs reflect the total number of logs cut through time for domestic roofing by a prehistoric community. Four assumptions must be met in order to satisfy this condition. The first assumption is that only live trees were cut for construction purposes. Another assumption is that the logs cut for roof construction have not been carried off the site or destroyed (e.g., reused as firewood). This condition generally requires that a site or group of sites, to tell us anything meaningful about growth in a roofed area, probably should not have been occupied for a great length of time. With long occupations the chance that human activity will alter the growth record increases. Another obvious assumption is that the natural processes which form the archaeological record have not differentially destroyed roofing logs with respect to cutting dates (Schiffer 1976, 12–17).

The final assumption is that the cutting dates available (i.e., those logs with actual final rings) are a representative sample of all logs cut. There is no way to test this directly; however, in the following analysis only cases with a relatively large number of cutting dates were considered.

Assumptions Relating Increase in Roofed Area to Population Growth

Even if one is assured that the available sample of cutting dates is an index to roof area growth, extending the cutting dates to population growth is conditional on establishing a further link between increasing roofed area and population growth. All researchers agree (for a summary see Casselberry 1974) that roofed area and population size are related in a fairly simple positive way, but to infer population *growth* from an increase in roofed area requires three further assumptions.

First, it is necessary to assume that roofs are not abandoned during the growth period of a community's history, or, if it does occur, that abandonment is some fairly constant proportion of living space. If either is true, then the cutting dates of new logs for roof construction should indicate a growth in population size. This holds even if rooms are outgrown, destroyed, and rebuilt using old roof logs, for there would be no need to cut additional trees unless the population had actually increased. Thus, a good sample of roof beam cutting dates, regardless of whether or not the beams are over their original rooms, provides an index to a community's requirements for roofed space through time. Dean (1969, 197) has constructed population growth trends from trends in construction log cutting and finds no major violations of this assumption.

A second assumption is that the amount of roofed area per person does not change with increased population size. Unfortunately, the exact relationship among village area, roofed area, and population is far from established. Wiessner (1974) found that Bushman *village* area per person increased with an increase in population size, whereas Naroll (1962) found that actual *roof* area per person in largest cities decreased slightly with increasing population. However, the per person decrease in roofed area was so slight that Naroll felt archaeologists could use a simple formula, population equals one-tenth the floor area in square meters, which implies a fairly uniform correspondence between roofed area and population size. Casselberry (1974) also uses a simple linear function and Cook (1972) uses two linear functions—one for groups of less than six people and another for larger groups. These are the best estimates to date, but the correlations are probably weak. For example, Naroll's data only had an R^2 of .77. Thus, the relationship is still in question, and for purposes of this chapter the amount of roofed area per person is assumed not to change significantly as group size increases.

A third assumption is that the cutting dates available come from domestic roofs. Thus, dendrochronological dates from firewood, ceremonial rooms, etc., should not be and were not, when indicated, used.

To summarize this section, the crucial assumptions are that roofed space during the growth of a site is not abandoned and that roofing logs have not been differentially destroyed with respect to cutting dates by cultural or natural formation processes.

Method of Analysis

Southwest archaeologists routinely use frequency distributions of cutting dates to show periods of building activity, and good estimates of site settlement have been established based on these distributions (Dean 1969, 197; Harrell and Breternitz 1976, 386). These analyses also show considerable year-to-year variability in prehistoric tree cutting activity. An alternative way to treat these data is in a cumulative form. A cumulative distribution represents a running total of logs added for site construction. It indicates the number of logs in *use* each year rather than the number of logs *cut* each year. Cumulative distributions also tend to average out yearly variation in log cutting because, if an excess is cut one year, fewer will be cut the next, bringing the running total closer to a real representation of actual logs needed. Presenting data in a cumulative form is a common technique in social science for averaging out experimental error and secular variation. It often results in more descriptive precision (Hamblin, Jacobsen, Miller 1973, 7). Once cumulative distributions have been calculated, the next step in testing for the existence of density-dependent population growth is to see how well the empirical distributions conform mathematically to the expectations of a density-dependent growth model.

A number of mathematical functions produce S-shaped trends (Erickson 1975) but the logistic is found most useful in population research because it makes "theoretical sense" for population growth under certain conditions and because the parameters of the logistic can be easily interpreted. The function in its integrated form and parameters used to test the dendrochronological data are

$$Y = \frac{A}{1 + B^{-kt}}$$

where

Y is the cumulative number of logs
A is the absolute, intrinsic limit to the number of logs accessible (asymptote)
B is an empirically derived scaling constant
k is a growth rate constant
t is time

If all assumptions discussed earlier hold, then a cumulative trend in roofing logs which proves logistic implies density-dependent population growth. A could be converted by some factor to the intrinsic limit to population growth under given conditions and k represents the population growth rate constant.

The best logistic curves were then fit to the cumulative dendrochronological data in all available cases with adequate data. From the best fit, accurate estimates could be made of A, the absolute intrinsic limit to the number of logs accessible, B, the scaling constant, and k, the growth constant. The data were also tested for exponential growth patterns. A squared correlation coefficient, R^2, was used to estimate how well the data actually conformed to the logistic and exponential curves.

Results

Figure 8.1 presents the cumulative distribution of construction log cutting at Chetro Ketl from AD 989 to 1112 and the best fit of a logistic curve. The growth trend in Chetro Ketl roofing logs or roofing space is clearly logistic, fitting a logistic function with an R^2 of .96. The high R^2 suggests that log cutting at Chetro Ketl was controlled by an important and potent underlying density-dependent growth process. Such a statement, based on only one case, is hard to defend, particularly considering all the assumptions necessary in its extension. But when combined with the evidence from all other available cases with adequate data, it gains credibility (Table 8.1). In

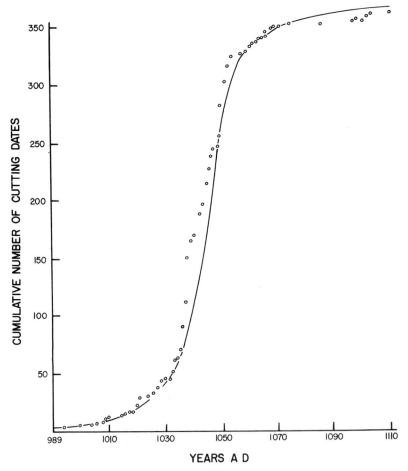

FIGURE 8.1 *Cumulative distribution of construction log cutting at Chetro Ketl, Chaco Canyon, New Mexico, AD 989–1112.*

TABLE 8.1
Data Summary: Southwest Logistic Trends

Site	Source	Total span tree cutting	Time span used	Usable logs	Logs used	$Y = \dfrac{A}{1 + B^{-kt}}$		
						A	k	R^2
Betatakin, Arizona	Dean 1969, 56–63	1234–1286	1246–1286	124	123	139	.20	.99
Kiet Siel, Arizona	Dean 1969, 104–112	1226–1286	1262–1286	91	84	82	.48	.97
Canyon Creek, Arizona	L. T-R. R.[a]	1226–1286	1300–1336	109	100	98	.17	.99
Chetro Ketl, New Mexico	Robinson, Harrill, Warren 1974, 16–24	989–1112	989–1112	354	354	385	.12	.96
Pindi, New Mexico	Robinson, Hannah, Harrill 1972, 36–40	1215–1381	1310–1381	36	24	23	.26	.99
Showlow, Arizona	Bannister, Gell, Hannah 1966, 39–47	1335–1384	1369–1384	61	46	57	.52	.95
Johnson Canyon I, Colorado	Harrill & Breternitz 1976, 387–389	1041–1161	1122–1161	40	28	28	.46	.97
Johnson Canyon II, Colorado	Harrill & Breternitz 1976, 387–389	1193–1231	1196–1231	48	48	44	.35	.99
Arroyo Hondo I, New Mexico	Robinson, Harrill, Warren 1973, 57–60	1315–1335	1315–1335	22	22	20	.81	.97
Arroyo Hondo II, New Mexico	Robinson, Harrill, Warren 1973, 57–60	1357–1410	1320–1410	135	131	133	.31	.95
Cerro Colorado, New Mexico	Bannister, Hannah, Robinson 1970, 18–21	604–737	642–695	66	43	45	.22	.97
M-3 Site, Utah	L. T-R. R.	1199–1265	1229–1261	40	37	40	.24	.96
Moon House, Utah	L. T-R. R.	1132–1267	1228–1267	36	34	46	.15	.97
Wupatki, Arizona	Robinson, Harrill, Warren 1975, 92–96	1106–1212	1106–1173	72	45	24	.15	.13

[a] L. T-R. R. is Laboratory of Tree-Ring Research Archaeological Data Reports, Laboratory of Tree-Ring Research, University of Arizona, Tucson, Arizona.

six additional cases (Betakin, Johnson Canyon II, Arroyo Hondo I & II, Moon House, and M-3 Site) the logistic function describes virtually the entire record of cumulative growth in tree cutting activity with an average R^2 of .97. In four additional cases (Pindi, Showlow, Johnson Canyon I, Cerro Colorado) the initial portion of the growth record is more complicated, and a logistic function does not describe the entire growth record accurately. However, when a few logs in the initial years of the available record are eliminated, the logistic function again depicts the major portion of the growth trend quite well. Arbitrarily selecting a starting point other than at the first date available does not necessarily violate the cannons of good curve-fitting procedure. Grilliches (1957, 504) regularly eliminated the early portion of a record of change. He pointed out that there was simply no sure way to know the starting point of a logistic process. As a result, Grilliches decided the process could be identified when 5% of the population had adopted a new innovation.

It is probably significant that the four additional cases (along with Arroyo Hondo I) are ones with relatively few data. The special treatment and lack of data make the logistic parameters generated for these cases highly tentative. An example of the four special cases is presented in Figure 8.2, Showlow Ruin. In the Showlow case, a logistic trend seems to be present only from about AD 1369 through 1384 when for some unknown reason the trend was terminated as it reached its natural asymptote. It is possible that the actual population trend at Showlow and other sites may be different in details from the trend indicated by the available construction log data.

In all but two cases the calculated asymptotes appear to be fairly close to the actual limits of site growth. In only two cases, Cerro Colorado and M-3 Site, did the time period used to generate the logistic curve not include the final logs cut. At Cerro Colorado, two logs were omitted, and, at M-3 Site, six logs were omitted.

To summarize, a logistic function describes 13 of 14 possible cases with an $R^2 \geq .95$. In only one case (Wupatki Ruin) where a large enough number of cutting dates exists to outline the growth trend is that trend not described well by a logistic curve. Notwithstanding the Wupatki case, the presence of logistic growth trends in construction log cutting seems well established. Since the trend, when evident, can be consistently described with a high squared correlation coefficient, the trend appears rather robust. Since the cases come from different types of sites (i.e., rock shelters, pueblos, and pithouse villages), from different time periods, from different areas in the Southwest, and from sites and localized groups of sites, density-dependent growth appears to be a common feature of site growth in the Southwest.

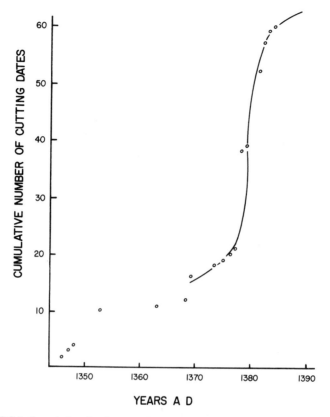

FIGURE 8.2 *Cumulative distribution of construction log cutting at Showlow Ruin, Showlow, Arizona,* AD *1369–1384.*

Discussion

All cases except Wupatki fit the density-dependent logistic model better than the density-independent exponential model (Table 8.2). However, three of the cases fit an exponential function fairly well, and they lead to a discussion of the possible density-related factors which could cause density-dependent growth in roofed space. An immediate reaction to the logistic pattern in roofed area growth is to suggest that it results from limitations on dwelling space. As a community runs out of room, such as a rock shelter, community growth might slow. The data, however, do not support this possibility. Three cases which are clearly limited by space,

TABLE 8.2
Comparison of Exponential and Logistic Fits (R^2)

Site	Exponential	Logistic
Betatakin	.93	.99
Kiet Siel	.72	.97
Canyon Creek	.87	.99
Chetro Ketl	.76	.96
Pindi	.42	.99
Showlow	.16	.95
Johnson Canyon I	.31	.97
Johnson Canyon II	.65	.99
Arroyo Hondo I	.52	.97
Arroyo Hondo II	.61	.95
M-3 Site	.93	.96
Moon House	.91	.97
Wupatki	.86	.13

Betatakin (Figure 8.3), M-3 Site, and Moon House (Figure 8.4) rock shelters, show the least tendency to density-dependent growth. In fact, they are the three cases which come closest to fitting the density-independent exponential model. It appears that dwelling space had very little influence as a density-related factor suppressing growth. Growth continued unabated until the community literally ran into rock walls. This does not mean that growth in these examples was independent of any constraints, for they still conform better to a logistic function. However, it does suggest that space is not the crucial density-related factor. Limited space truncated the location of dwellings in a particular rock shelter, but it did not define the limits to growth in the community's population which occupied the rock shelter (for interesting comparable trends see Erickson 1973, 1975). The location of the community's additional dwellings probably involved the branching out to adjacent rock shelters. Johnson Canyon I and II (Figure 8.5) and Canyon Creek, which all include a number of rock shelters, seem to bear out this interpretation. Growth in these rock shelter groups conforms more clearly to the pattern expected under conditions of density-dependent growth.

We are left, I believe, with the interpretation that density-dependent site growth results from density-dependent growth in the communities building those sites, in which case the data conform to the theoretical expectations outlined by Cowgill (1975, 508). Factors that might cause the population of localized communities to grow in a density-related manner include disease, predation, food supply, and availability of critical resources such as fuel and manufacturing materials. Many of these factors can either be subsumed under or are a function of what can be generally termed the subsistence strategy. Subsistence strategy is an admittedly ambiguous phrase, but an attempt to deal with its components is beyond the scope of this chapter.

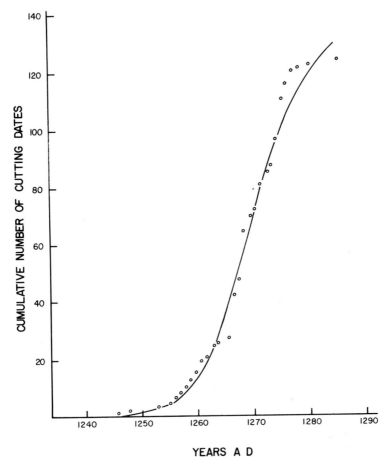

FIGURE 8.3 *Cumulative distribution of construction log cutting at Betatakin Ruin, Tsegi Canyon, Arizona,* AD *1246–1286.*

Suffice it to say that the subsistence strategy encourages growth in localized communities at low population densities while becoming an increasingly restrictive factor as population density rises. Apparently, in the past a subsistence strategy set the rate of population growth and presented real and significant limits to population size. In fact, a reoccurring feature seems to be the cessation of community growth altogether, at least for an observable period of time. This fact suggests that in many instances migration of Malthusian mechanisms may have been the more immediate concomitants of carrying capacity stress on community subsistence strategies than increasing intensification (Boserup 1969).

Cowgill (1975, 509) argues that the presence of logistic population growth would establish the inelastic tendency for sedentary communities to grow until restrained by environmental resistance. As such, the data confirm

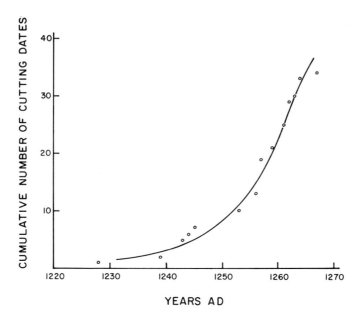

FIGURE 8.4 *Cumulative distribution of construction log cutting at Moon House, Grand Gulch, Utah,* AD *1228–1267.*

this tendency, at least for prehistoric Southwest communities. The main thrust of Cowgill's argument is, however, to question the inevitability of population growth, and the Wupatki case may be evidence that the tendency was avoided. Although demographers admit that a logistic trend may be the theoretical expectation for population growth when conditions remain constant, it has, in fact, seldom satisfactorily predicted population growth among modern, regional populations because rate of growth and regional carrying capacity have been regularly altered by human activity (Pollard 1973, 23; United Nations Population Division 1953, 34–35). Cowgill correctly cautions, therefore, that any simple theory of population growth must be investigated not only at the microlevel but also at the macrolevel before population dynamics can be understood fully. Regional data from the Southwest (Gummerman 1970, Plog 1974, Schwartz 1956) do, in fact, show major periods of actual population decline.

The possibility remains, however, that the growth tendency is a major feature of local colonizing or intensifying communities, and the question then becomes one of specifying where and how the human propensity for population growth will be expressed (Cowgill 1975, 521) and showing the relationship between growth trends in local communities and regional populations. Based on present evidence tentative hypotheses can be offered for future testing. First, it is suggested that prehistoric local communties after moving into a new niche either through colonization or subsistence intensification

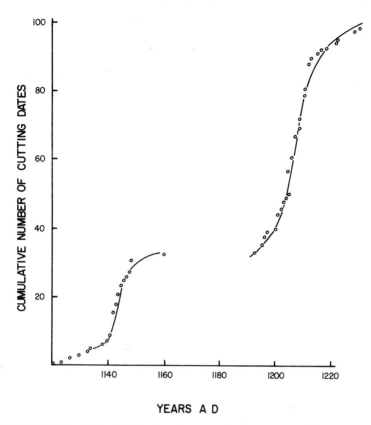

FIGURE 8.5 *Cumulative distribution of construction log cutting at Johnson Canyon I and II, Johnson Canyon, Colorado, AD 1133–1231.*

often grow rapidly in a density-dependent manner. Second, since the asymptotic ceilings to growth are often reached, local communities frequently stop growing as a result of natural limitations, thereby forcing emigration and/or Malthusian checks to limit further population growth within the community. In the Southwest, for example, it has been suggested that a succession of communities were settled, expanded, and abandoned because places still existed within the region to which a local community under stress could relocate (Mindeleff 1900, Reid 1973). Extending these suggestions one step further, it may be that it is recurrent stress at the community level caused by population pressure on the local subsistence strategy which eventually triggers a strategic evolution in regional subsistence practices resulting in a general rise in population potential. This evolution may occur before the regional carrying capacity is strained. If so, the logistic pattern may not show up in regional population trends.

Other interesting questions are raised by these data. Following the suggestions of Cowgill (1975, 508–509), it would be interesting to determine the temporal occurrence of migration, technological breakthrough, or agricultural intensification relative to periods when communities experienced asymptotic restriction. For example, is there evidence of changing subsistence strategies at Wupatki which interrupted a simple logistic trend in population growth? Macrolevel population trends need to be constructed accurately in order to identify the nature of long-term regional growth epochs. Finally, an interesting question concerns the conditions which set the parameter values A, the absolute, intrinsic limit to growth in a given case, and k, the growth rate constant.

Summary

This chapter reports trends in Southwest site growth as seen through addition of logs for roof construction. By making a number of assumptions, the addition of logs to a site can be seen as an index to growth in a prehistoric community's population size. A logistic function was fit to the available cases with good results implying that construction logs and, presumably, population size grew in a density-dependent manner. Based on a comparison of logistic and exponential fits of rock shelter data, it was argued that dwelling space was not the factor causing density-dependent growth patterns. The most likely cause of this logistic pattern is the effect of a subsistence strategy on population growth. The consistent logistic pattern suggests that the subsistence strategy at the community level was extremely important in determining community growth and setting ceilings on maximum population size. Finally, it was suggested that asymptotic restrictions resulting from relatively high population densities at the community level may be an important and overlooked feature in the evolution of regional subsistence practices.

Acknowledgments

I would like to thank Dr. J. Jefferson Reid and Allen E. (Gene) Rogge for helping clarify many points in this chapter and discussing ideas surrounding data interpretation. The paper also profited from comments by Dr. Jeffrey S. Dean, Dr. Robert McC. Netting, Dr. Jerry L. L. Miller, Randy A. McGuire, Eric B. Henderson, and John D. Meredith. Thanks are due Dr. Jeffrey S. Dean, Dr. William R. Robinson, and the Laboratory of Tree-Ring Research, The University of Arizona, for making it convenient to use the Laboratory of Tree-Ring Research Data Reports. Finally, I want to acknowledge the kindness of Dr. Douglas Schwartz and Dr. William Lipe for permission to use their unpublished tree-ring data from Arroyo Hondo and Grand Gulch.

References

Bannister, B., E. A. Gell, J. W. Hannah, 1966, Tree-ring dates from Arizona N-Q: Verde-Showlow-St. Johns Area. Tucson, Laboratory of Tree-Ring Research, University of Arizona.

Bannister, B., J. W. Hannah, W. J. Robinson, 1970, Tree-ring dates from New Mexico M-N, S, Z, Southwestern New Mexico area. Tucson, Laboratory of Tree-Ring Research, University of Arizona.

Boserup, E., 1969, *The Conditions of Agricultural Growth*. Chicago, Aldine.

Casselberry, S. E., 1974, Further refinement of formulae for determining population from floor area, *World Archaeology* 6(1), 117–122.

Cook, S. F., 1972, *Prehistoric Demography*. Reading, Addison-Wesley.

Cook, S. F. and R. F. Heizer, 1968, Relationship among houses, settlement areas and population in aboriginal California, in K. C. Chang (ed.), *Settlement Archaeology*, Palo Alto, National Press, 76–116.

Cowgill, G. L., 1975, On causes and consequences of ancient and modern population changes, *American Anthropologist*, 77(3), 505–525.

Dean, J. S., 1969, *Chronological Analysis of Tsegi Phase Sites in Northeastern Arizona*. Papers of the Laboratory of Tree-Ring Research No. 3, Tucson, University of Arizona Press.

Erickson, E. E., 1973, The life cycle of life styles: projecting the course of local evolutionary sequences, *Behavior Science Notes* 8(2), 135–165.

Erickson, E. E., 1975, Growth functions and culture history: a perspective on classic Maya culture development, *Behavior Science Research* 10(1), 37–61.

Grilliches, Z., 1957, Hybrid corn: an exploration in the economics of technological change, *Econometrica* 25(4), 501–522.

Gummerman, G. J., 1970, *Black Mesa: Survey and Excavation in Northeastern Arizona—1968*. Prescott, Prescott College Press.

Gummerman, G. J., 1975, Alternative cultural models of demographic change: Southwestern examples, in A. C. Swedlund (ed.), *Population Studies in Archaeology and Biological Anthropology: A Symposium, Memoir* 30, Society for American Archaeology.

Hamblin, R. L., R. B. Jacobsen, and J. L. L. Miller, 1973, *A Mathematical Theory of Social Change*, New York, Wiley and Sons.

Harrill, B. G., and C. D. Breternitz, 1976, Chronology and cultural activity in Johnson Canyon cliff dwellings: interpretations from tree-ring data, *Journal of Field Archaeology* 3(4), 375–390.

Laboratory of Tree-Ring Research, n.d., Archaeological data reports on file at the Laboratory of Tree-Ring Research. Tucson, University of Arizona.

LeBlanc, S., 1971, An addition to Naroll's suggested floor area and settlement population relationship, *American Antiquity*, 36, 210–211.

Longacre, W. A., 1970, *Archaeology as Anthropology, A Case Study*. University of Arizona Anthropological Papers No. 17, Tucson, University of Arizona Press.

Longacre, W. A., 1975, Population dynamics at Grasshopper Pueblo, Arizona, in A. C. Swedlund (ed.), *Population Studies in Archaeology and Biological Anthropology, A Symposium, Memoir* 30, Society for American Archaeology.

Mendeleff, C., 1900, Localization of Tusayan Clans, *Nineteenth Annual Report of the Bureau of American Ethnology*, Washington, Smithsonian Institution.

Mexico, Dirrección General de Estadistica, 1971, IX *Censo General de Población, 1970, localidades por entidad federativa y municipio con algunas caracteristicas de su población y vivienda*, Vol. 1, Aquascalientes a Guerrero. México, D. F., Secretariá de Industria y Comercio.

Naroll, R., 1962, Floor area and settlement population, *American Antiquity* 27, 587–589.

Pearl, R. and L. J. Reed, 1920, On the rate of growth of the population of the United States since 1790 and its mathematical representation, *Proceedings of the National Academy of Sciences* 6, 275–288.

Plog, F. T., 1974, *The Study of Prehistoric Change.* New York, Academic Press.

Pollard, J. H., 1973, *Mathematical Models for the Growth of Human Populations.* Cambridge, Cambridge University Press.

Reid, J. J., 1973, Growth and response to stress at Grasshopper Pueblo, Arizona. Ph.D. dissertation, Tucson, University of Arizona. Ann Arbor, University Microfilms.

Robinson, W. J., J. W. Hannah, B. G. Harrill, 1972, Tree-ring dates from New Mexico I, O, U, central Rio Grande area. Tucson, Laboratory of Tree-ring Research, University of Arizona.

Robinson, W. J., B. G. Harrill, R. L. Warren, 1973, Tree-ring dates from New Mexico J-K, P, V, Santa Fe-Pecos-Lincoln area. Tuscon, Laboratory of Tree-Ring Research, University of Arizona.

Robinson, W. J., B. G. Harrill, R. L. Warren, 1974, Tree-ring dates from New Mexico B, Chaco-Gobernador area. Tucson, Laboratory of Tree-Ring Research, University of Arizona.

Robinson, W. J., B. G. Harrill, R. L. Warren, 1975, Tree-ring dates from Arizona H-I, Flagstaff area. Tucson, Laboratory of Tree-Ring Research, University of Arizona.

Schiffer, M., 1976, *Behavioral Archeology.* New York, Academic Press.

Schwartz, D. W., 1956, Demographic changes in the early periods of Cohonina prehistory, in G. R. Willey (ed.), *Prehistoric Settlement Patterns in the New World.* New York, Wenner-Gren Foundation.

Spooner, B. (ed.), 1972, *Population Growth: Anthropological Implications.* Cambridge, Massachusetts Institute of Technology.

Swedlund, A. C., 1975, *Population Studies in Archaeology and Biological Anthropology: A Symposium,* Memoir 30, Society for American Archaeology.

United Nations, Population Division, 1953, History of population theories, *The Determinants and Consequences of Population Trends,* New York, United Nations.

Wiessner, P., 1974, A functional estimator of population from floor area, *American Antiquity* 39, 343–350.

Zubrow, E. B. W., 1971, Carrying capacity and dynamic equilibrium in the prehistoric Southwest, *American Antiquity* 36, 127–138.

Zubrow, E. B. W., 1974, *Population, Contact, and Climate in the New Mexico Pueblos,* University of Arizona Anthropological Papers No. 24, Tucson, University of Arizona Press.

9

FRED PLOG

Alternative Models of Prehistoric Change

In two earlier papers, I discussed basic problems in anthropological approaches to change (Plog, 1974, 1977). I will briefly summarize these and then illustrate potential solutions or at least routes to solutions.

Empirical Problems

A fundamental difficulty in change studies in anthropology is their reliance on patterns of *spatial* rather than *temporal* variation. Certainly, the two should be related. Yet, inferring temporal variability from spatial patterns necessitates a gigantic act of faith: the belief that every temporal process has a unique spatial correlate. Empirical difficulties with the assumption have been demonstrated when correlations have been attempted using independent data bases for defining spatial and temporal patterns (Graves, Graves, and Kobrin, 1969).

Nevertheless, the confusion of spatial and temporal variation remains substantial as indicated by two examples. First, archaeologists and anthropologists, to varying degrees, do associate unique spatial patterns with particular temporal processes. Since the heyday of "age–area" studies, the final pattern shown in Figure 9.1 has been taken to represent the spread of some innovation from a developmental center. Yet, the alternative pathways in Figure 9.1 show how such a pattern can result from several different developmental trajectories. Ceramic data from the southwestern United States indicate that such alternatives do occur (Martin and Plog 1973): Some

221

Transformations:
Mathematical Approaches to Culture Change

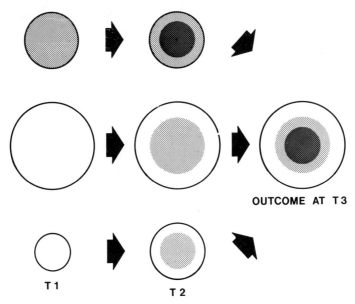

FIGURE 9.1. *Alternative temporal patterns that could lead to the same spatial pattern at T3.*

styles or types occur in low frequency over a broad area before they become predominant in a restricted area.

The use of reconstructed patterns of temporal variation by archaeologists results from similar behavior on the part of anthropologists. The latter are prone to base change records on the recollections of their informants. But all people conventionalize the past. To the extent that one wishes to study the nature of such conventionalizations, recollections are nonproblematical. As change records, however, recollections are inadequate. Bee (1974) argues that change studies are inevitably based on reconstruction. That they are invariably retrospective is a truism; one cannot know change save by observing that it has occurred. But retrospection and reconstruction are not the same. Reconstruction is necessary only in the absence of a set of temporally discrete and sequential observations on the basis of which patterns of temporal variation can be described. When phenomena are observed in the process of changing, and when records of past variation are available, reconstruction is unnecessary. Such records are admittedly rare, but they have rarely been sought.

Methodological Problems

Archaeologists make equally problematical assumptions concerning the aspects of temporal variation that deserve study and the manner in which such studies are undertaken. First, we assume that the number of observations necessary for analyzing change are nonproblematical. Many, if not most, change studies are based on "before" and "after" observations—only two well-defined points. Defining temporal variation over a series of stages is equally problematical because they are simply a series of befores and afters. Periods of relatively rapid change are generally consigned to the lines that divide the stages—there is change within the stages that is ignored; there is little or no record of the changing itself.

A second problem, an almost inevitable consequence of the first, is the tendency to assume linear patterns of temporal variation. Given only two temporally discrete observations (before, after), one has on choice but to assume a linear trajectory. Yet, whereas two points are sufficient to define a straight line, there are a very large number of different curves, temporal trajectories, that may have connected two points. Moreover, as I shall argue later, a linear trajectory is one of the more improbable.

Theoretical Problems

Anthropological change theories also reflect this before–after orientation in that they seek to connect triggering events on the one hand and outcomes on the other. Few theories seek regularities in the patterns of temporal variation or attempt to explain them. Yet, efforts to connect triggering events and outcomes assume a relatively radical position: That patterning in cultural and natural behavior involves a unique association of event and outcome. A century of searching by anthropologists has not demonstrated this case but its opposite; different triggering events can have the same outcome and the same triggering events can have different outcomes.

If one examines changes studies in other disciplines, the problem with such an approach is evident: Regularities are not found in events but in processes. For example, we would expect little success in attempting to formulate an explanation that linked circumstances under which matches are lit and the outcome of having lit a match. There are too many conditions under which people light matches and too many consequences of their having done so. By focusing on processes such as "ignition" and/or "combustion," abstractions of match-striking, the process of change involved in striking a match, real regularities covering many variables have been formulated.

In summary, archaeological studies of change are most likely to succeed if we focus on patterns of changing; undertake observations on the basis of which such patterns can be described; describe the patterns instead of making restrictive assumptions about them; and seek regularities in patterns of temporal variation.

An Alternative Approach

Solutions to some of these problems are proposed by Hamblin and co-workers in their book, *A Mathematical Theory of Social Change* (1973). Although it has been influenced by the ideas of other sociologists, anthropologists, and systems theorists, the book follows directly from James Coleman's efforts to understand change (e.g., 1968). This book was reviewed by Michael Burton (1976), an anthropologist. Because I believe that his comments reflect some of the problems I have described, I will structure my initial discussion of the book around his review.

First, Burton objects to the disparate data employed by the authors: "
. . . cigarette consumption, world altitude records, Gross National Product, adoption of hybrid corn, and PhD production (1976, 659).'' Although it is true that these data are employed, it is hardly fair to imply that the authors attempt a universal theory of change capable of handling variation in all of them. More accurately, they employ diverse data to provide independent tests of a number of specific models and theories, to ask if there are commonalities in change trajectories defined over different empirical phenomena and very different situations. Thus, it is not "PhD production" that is the subject of their tests, but limited aspects thereof. Yet, Burton's shock at the suggestion of even limited commonalities in disparate data is an illustration of the attitudes that discourage a focus on processes rather than events.

Second, Burton attacks the authors' focus on the shape of change curves and comments "two change processes can take the same mathematical form yet differ greatly in rate (1976, 659).'' The issue of rates of change is not ignored in the book. Burton's conception of rates of change is based on a before–after treatment of change processes; it is an average rate of change defined for the entire change episode. But, Hamblin *et al.* demonstrate that average rates of change are specific to particular phenomena and situations. It is in *change in rates of change,* variation in the rate of change during the change episode itself, that the strongest patterning occurs. Patterning and regularities are not identified in simple description of events, nor in the derivation of average rates of change, but in variation in the rate of change.

Finally, Burton is upset because the authors suggest that differential rates of change are explained by variability in reinforcement for adopting a particular innovation but fail to discuss the nature of the reinforcers. Again, the key point is missed. Hamblin *et al.* argue that specific reinforcers are not at issue—analytically *ceterus paribus* is invoked; empirically, reinforcers offset one another. Instead, the authors direct attention to the internal dynamics of the change process itself and suggest that situationally specific reinforcers are less important than the organizational and behavioral patterns that shape processes.

Although I question the utility of *A Mathematical Theory of Social Change* as a theory applicable to archaeological problems, it does contain important methodological insights that have equally significant theoretical consequences. For example, Hamblin and co-workers discuss four different temporal processes and what they have found to be typical curve forms associated with each social adaptation (power functions), binary adoption (logistic, decaying exponential functions), use diffusion (exponential functions), and innovation (logistic functions). Given the longer time spans and more variable situations with which archaeologists deal, these claims are simplistic. They do, however, provide a baseline from which specific arguments can be formulated.

The authors' major claim is both statistical and empirical—they are able to account for 90% or more of the temporal variation in most of the cases studied, which contrasts with about 10% of the variation accounted for by most "verbal" theories. Their final chapter is as exquisitely formulated a theory of succinct definitions, clear axioms, and carefully derived conclusions as one can find in the social sciences. To the extent that the flaws of their theories are evident, it is because of the clarity of their exposition; were most social theories reduced to 10 or so pages of clear definition, postulation, and deduction, their flaws would be equally manifest.

Given these suggestions, I want to return to some of the problems identified at the outset of this chapter. I will focus on the adequacy of temporal observations, the problem of assumed linearity, the analytical definition of patterning, and the connection of outcome and events, providing hypothetical and/or real illustrations of the manner in which following the suggestions of Hamblin, *et al.* proves to understand the past.

Observational Adequacy

I argued earlier that observations made at only two points in time are almost certainly inadequate for defining temporal variation. Given such an approach, change can only be linear. But how many points are necessary and how many are sufficient for adequately defining a pattern of temporal variation? Both abstract and concrete responses to this question can be made. The abstract answer is relatively simple: sufficient points, a sufficient density of observations, that some of the observations could be removed or found to be incorrect without affecting the description of the overall pattern of variability. To assume that each of a series of temporally separate observations is inevitably correct is to take a risk that few scientists would choose to afford. As Figure 9.2 illustrates, three observations are clearly insufficient. Only a single error in observation would produce a fundamentally different trajectory. But given that economy in research is necessary, it is desirable to know more specifically what number of observations results in a usable definition of temporal processes. Hamblin *et al.* conclude on the basis of their extensive analyses that 7 points are satisfactory and 11 desirable for

```
        O                           X       O                              O

X       X   ?   O           X           ?   O              X           ?   O

        O                               O                      X           O
_____          _____          _____
      TIME                      TIME                      TIME


        O                           O       X              X       O

X   ?   O   ?   X              ?   O   ?              ?   O   ?

        O                   X       O                      O       X
_____          _____          _____
      TIME                      TIME                      TIME


O                           O           X          O

O   ?   X       X           O   ?   X              O   ?   X

O                           O                      O               X
_____          _____          _____
      TIME                      TIME                      TIME
```

FIGURE 9.2. *Given two known points (X) and a single ambiguously defined point (O), significantly different patterns of change are possible.*

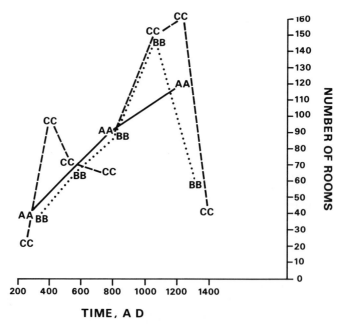

FIGURE 9.3. *Change in the number of rooms in Hay Hollow Valley using three (AA), five (BB) and seven (CC) points.*

minimally describing a given pattern of temporal variation. (This claim may, of course, prove specific to the relatively limited oscillation in the family of curves they consider.) Figure 9.3 shows important differences in demo- graphic changes (number of habitation rooms) in Hay Hollow Valley, Arizona, that result from employing 3, 5, and 7 points. The pattern defined over seven points differs from that defined over a greater number of points largely in respect to the steepness of the lines (increases and decreases) and their height. Thus, the 7 figure seems to have some validity at the level of overall pattern, and few gains in empirical detail occur after 11 points have been used (see Plog, 1974).

One suspects that such minima may be specific to particular phenomena. Moreover, one can use probabilistic models—those that assign probabilities either to the value associated with a particular point in time or to the temporal placement of a particular value. I have employed this approach in demographic reconstructions in two areas of Arizona (1975). It is, in any case, clear that most archaeological change studies have relied on too few observations for empirical reliability to be assumed. Inspired guesswork may, of course, have saved the day.

Assumed Linearity

One of the more serious and yet characteristic assumptions in ar- chaeological change studies is that the typical form of change curves or trajectories over time is a straight line. It is beyond the scope of this chapter to demonstrate the pervasiveness of this assumption. Let me simply give one archaeological example of its consequences.

When constructing seriograms archaeologists employ a record of change in ceramic types |or|styles. Although several or a large number are generally employed, seriations work because one type is replacing another at any given point during the period being studied. That is, although several types define the overall pattern, the relative distribution of two types is the basis of the relationship at any one point; the date assigned to a given site or stratum is usually based on the relative abundance of only two types.

Given this condition, the relationship can also be described in terms of variation from 0 to 100% of a given type as it appears and displaces another and is then replaced by still another. When such a pattern covers, for example, a 200-year period, dates between the two extremes are inferred on the assumption that change is linear. But Hamblin *et al.* suggest that a number of alternative trajectories are more probable than a linear one. If their argument is correct, the consequences for accurately estimating dates are substantial. Figure 9.4 shows a linear and several nonlinear models of variation between two points. Note the different dates associated with 50%

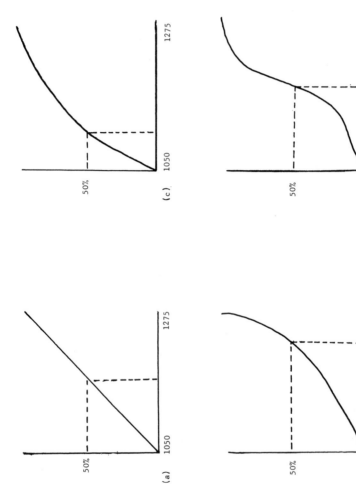

FIGURE 9.4. *Inferred dates differ widely, depending on which temporal process most accurately describes artifactual change.*

of two types in each chart. The bulk of the variance in one instance defines the earliest 150 years of the period (Figure 9.4b) whereas in another it defines the last (Figure 9.4c).

Table 9.1 summarizes data from the Chevelon drainage of Arizona indicating that the problem is a real one. We normally date sites occupied between about AD 1050 and 1275 on the basis of the relative percentages of Little Colorado and Cibola White Wares, a relationship that can simply be described in terms of the percentage of Cibola White Wares. Were the rate of change over this period a strictly linear one, the values shown in the second column would be expected. But, data from tree-ring and radiocarbon-dated sites support the existence of a curvilinear pattern as shown in the third column. This example is by no means the only one that can be cited. Much of the recent literature dealing with the correlation of radiocarbon and tree ring dates shows a similar relationship (Ralph *et al.* 1977; Refrew 1977), and the important consequences of ignoring curvilinearity.

The Locus of Patterning

A central, if not the central, argument presented by Hamblin and his colleagues concerns the locus of patterning in change. They argue that meaningful relationships are not found in simple descriptions of shifts in behavior patterns, nor in the incidence of behavior, nor even in the rate of change for a particular behavioral episode. Instead, they demonstrate that the strongest patterning is in variability in the rate of change *during* a change episode. The basis for this reasoning is indicated in Table 9.2. This table illustrates an observed pattern of change and the observations that might have been made if the rate of change were increasing, decreasing, or remaining the same through the episode in question. The factors that determine

Table 9.1

A Comparison of the Pattern of Change Expected in the Percentage of Cibola White Ware Given a Linear Pattern and the Observed Pattern

Date (AD)	Expected (%)	Observed (%)
1275	90	92
1250	80	88
1225	70	88
1200	60	70
1175	50	?
1150	40	10
1125	30	?
1100	20	00
1075	10	00
1050	00	00

Table 9.2

Change in the Number of Rooms in Hay Hollow Valley, Arizona[a]

Century	Observed	Linear	Decreasing	Increasing
1	91	91	91	91
2	41	99	105	94
3	115	107	117	97
4	69	115	127	103
5	65	123	135	111
6	65	131	141	121
7	91	139	145	133
8	131	147	147	147
9	152	155	148	161

[a] The first pattern is that actually observed. The next three are those that would have been observed given a linear, decreasing, and increasing rate of change in the number of rooms.

whether this rate is increasing, decreasing, or remaining constant are explored later. Here, I simply note that the alternative that occurs will or at least can have a powerful influence on observed data.

Theory

In the preceding sections, I have emphasized assumptions we make that constrain our observations and analyses. In this section, I carry the discussion to theory and present an illustration of the manner in which theoretical statements can ignore temporal variability.

The law of cultural dominance is generally stated as follows: "That cultural system which more effectively exploits the energy resources of a given environment will tend to spread in that environment at the expense of less effective systems (Sahlins and Service 1968:75)." I do not defend here the utility of formulating propositions in terms of energy, systems, and exploitation, but am instead concerned simply with the nature of the statement and the evidence that has been used in support of it. If one carefully examines the statement, it only claims that more effective systems will *tend to spread*. Although the statement certainly implies that, a certain percentage of the time, less effective systems will be replaced by more effective ones, the statement can be both valid and true in the absence of any such evidence. It is a statement about trends or tendencies, not about outcomes. Yet the bulk of the evidence marshalled in its support concerns outcomes of particular event sequences.

It is possible to identify at least one event sequence in which the statement is true when read as a statement of tendency and false when read as a statement of outcome. Coombs (1975) has described the replacement of indigenous hunting–gathering groups in California by Spanish colonists.

Measured over most energetic criteria and given local resources, the native hunter–gatherers more effectively exploited the environment than did Spanish agriculturalists. Yet the Spanish did replace local Indians. Proponents of the law of cultural dominance argue that this exception is attributable to Spanish military might and to coercion. But a careful inspection of relevant records fails to provide evidence of the use of either threat or force. More importantly, there is evidence that what occurred is consistent with the law when taken as a statement about trends, not outcomes.

Basically, the interaction between the Spanish and native populations of California resulted in transformations in the life-styles and subsistence practices of both. In the specific case of Santa Barbara mission (Coombs and Plog, 1974; 1978), the harvest was insufficient to support the native population and colonials. Such support was unnecessary, however, because missionaries arrived with a substantial supply of food, and, on this basis, proved more effective in supplying the needs of a *few* villagers than the villages were in supplying the needs of *all* their members. As a result, and in accordance with the cultural dominance hypothesis, the mission gained its first converts at the expense of the villages.

It is evident from related research (Coombs 1975: 141–174) that the majority of these initial converts were adolescents and young adults—village members of paramount economic and reproductive importance. This fact is critical for it set into motion the economic decline of the villages. *With a decline in the effectiveness of the village economies, the mission could continue to gain additional converts even if the mission itself declined in effectiveness.* That is, the mission could continue to gain converts so long as it remained *relatively* the more attractive alternative. Available evidence in fact suggests that the effectiveness of the villages was declining. Thus, the situation was as shown in Figure 9.5: The effectiveness of both populations declined, possibly even to the same extent. Thus, the interaction between two groups even in a stable environment may result in a less viable system than was there initially and the sequence of chance may be consistent with a law as long as it is a statement of tendency. The multiple laws that affect the occurrence of events in the real world condition outcomes, but all are statements of tendency.

Interpretation

The history of the Basket Maker–Pueblo concept in Southwest prehistory provides an excellent illustration of increasingly detailed definitions of change sequences. For the last 50 years, this concept has been used to refer simply to a cultural boundary between the Pueblo and ancestral Basket Maker peoples. To the extent that the concept was defined in greater detail, definitions focused on lists of largely technological traits. A few ar-

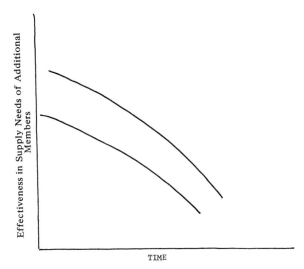

FIGURE 9.5 *Change in the ability of the mission and villages to satisfy needs of members.*

chaeologists attempted to view the phenomenon in somewhat more dynamic terms, suggesting that a transition of basic developmental process occurred. Recently (1974), I argued that at least for Hay Hollow Valley, Arizona, the concept refers best to a period of rapid change in technological, organizational, and demographic phenomena with quite understandable relationships to one another. Change over time in specific variables was measured using survey and excavation data. A number of significant changes were evident during the transitional period AD 700–1000: (*a*) the rates of increase in the number and density of sites and the number of rooms (inferentially, population) were at a maximum; (*b*) there was a substantial increase in the utilization of work space on nondwelling sites; (*c*) there was a substantial increase in the number of sites on which more than a single residence group lived and in the diversity of site sizes present at any one time; and (*d*) innovations in hunting and plant-processing and storage facilities occurred.

Some of the insights of Hamblin and co-workers can be applied to these same data. Rates of change for specific variables are shown in Table 9.3. These values and curves inferred from them are shown in Figure 9.6. A major problem is immediately apparent. Had there been only a single change episode, the number of observations would have been sufficient. But in most cases there appears to have been more than a single such episode. As a result, the number of observations is insufficient, and a great deal of guessing is necessary as to what the shape of the curve actually is. There is currently no way of resolving this empirical problem. I will, however, illustrate the interpretation of different curve forms in the manner of Hamblin *et al.*, assuming that the apparent patterns are the correct ones.

Table 9.3

Rates of Change in Selected Variables, Hay Hollow Valley, Arizona[a]

Date (AD)	Technology	Ratio of habitation to limited activity sites	Diversity of limited activity sites	Number of rooms	Density of sites	Incidence of large sites
250				1.3(+)	.10(+)	2.0(+)
350				1.0(+)	.23(+)	.8(+)
450	.1(+)	.2 (−)	.12 (−)	.5(−)	.78(+)	.5(−)
550	.1(+)	.03(−)	.12 (+)	.1(−)	.98(+)	.8(−)
650	.1(+)	1.3 (−)	.025(−)	.0	.06(+)	.8(−)
750	.6(+)	.5 (−)	.05 (−)	.4(+)	.18(+)	1.1(+)
850	.6(+)	.6 (+)	.48 (−)	.3(+)	.85(+)	.0
950	.2(+)	.2 (−)	.31 (−)	.2(+)	.23(+)	.2(+)
1050	.3(+)	.06(−)	.00	.0	.65(−)	.4(+)
1150	.3(+)	2.00(+)	.60 (+)	.2(−)	.98(−)	.1(+)
1250	.2(+)			1.7(−)	1.22(−)	1.0(−)
1350	.1(+)			1.0(−)	.82(−)	2.0(−)

[a] Rates are calculated $t_2 - t_1/(t_1 + t_2 \div 2)$.

1. Technology. This record describes both changes in the creation of storage facilities and the adoption of new types of manos and metates. It is best described as a single logistic (increasing then decreasing) process lasting from AD 450 to 1350 or as a pattern with little change prior to AD 750 and a decaying exponential process thereafter (most rapid at the outset, decreasing thereafter). Hamblin *et al.* suggest that these two curves forms are generally associated with the adoption of innovations, especially the replacement of some behavior or technological item by an alternative.

2. The organization of work. Changes in the organization of work are measured using the ratio of space on living to limited activity sites and in the diversity of limited activity site types. Change in the former is best described by a single decaying exponential process lasting from AD 650 to 1050; earlier and later points are difficult to incorporate in any pattern. Again, this curve form is typically associated with binary adoption, in this instance the replacement of a dwelling unit–temporary camp pattern by one involving a variety of functionally specific loci. Change in the diversity of limited activity sites is best described by a logistic process at about AD 850, reflecting experimentation and innovation in site locations.

3. Population. Population is measured by changes in the number of living rooms. Three episodes of change are evident, beginning at about AD 250, 750, and 1250. In each instance, the rates suggest a decaying exponential process. It is not reasonable to treat population in the terms of Hamblin *et al.* What the patterns suggest is that demographic change in the valley was not the product of a slow incremental process, but of two booms and a final

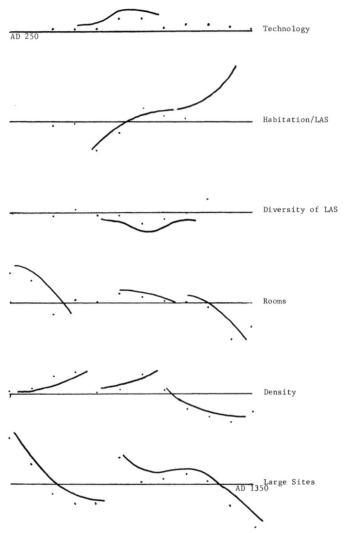

FIGURE 9.6. *Inferred patterns of change in Hay Hollow Valley.*

and equally rapid decrease. In all probability, this increase did not occur over the period of a century, which the figures seem to suggest, but over an even shorter interval. In the case of the first two epochs, alternatives such as migrations and significant innovations in productive processes, the adoption of agricultural subsistence strategies, and/or more intensified versions thereof must be explored.

Change in the density of sites also occurred in three episodes. Each is best described as an increasing exponential process, generally associated with social adaptation and use diffusion, major shifts in underlying organizational patterns, and their diffusion among related peoples. Since density reflects overall change in the utilization of the valley, the articulation with Hamblin *et al.*'s claims is again reasonable.

4. Social organization. The percentage of population living on sites with more than a single residence group is best described by an early and a late curve. The first is a decreasing exponential process, the second logistic. These patterns suggest that living arrangements are adopted as innovations and that slightly different circumstances may have underlain the two episodes of social change.

I wish to stress once again the very tentative and tenuous nature of these interpretations. More than anything else they underscore the need for a greater number of observations. It is interesting, nevertheless, that the strongest patterning, in most instances, occurs during the period of the transition. The very earliest and very latest points in the prehistory of the valley are the most difficult to fit to the curves, suggesting less regular change processes at these times. Technological change is minimal, ultimately no more than a slight increase in a rather regular process. The conjoint changes in population and the organization of work are simultaneous and far more dramatic. Their co-occurrence suggests that the best explanation of changes in the valley will prove to be intensification of production following the arguments of Boserup (1969) and Logan and Sanders (1975) rather than the argument I originally presented. In any case, a somewhat different explanation of the situation from my original one seems warranted and the need for additional and more refined data collection on which a tighter summary of events could be based is evident.

References

Bee, Robert, 1974, *Patterns and Processes*. New York, The Free Press.

Burton, Michael, 1976, Review of Hamblin, Jacobsen, and Miller: A mathematical theory of social change. *American Anthropologist* 78: 659.

Boserup, Ester, 1965, *The Conditions of Agricultural Growth*. Chicago, Aldine.

Coleman, James, 1968, The Mathematical study of change. In H. Blalock and A. Blalock (eds.) *Methodology in Social Research*. New York, McGraw-Hill. 428–478.

Coombs, Gary, 1975, Migration and adaptation: Indian Missionization in California. Unpublished PhD dissertation. University of California, Los Angeles.

Coombs, Gary and Plog, Fred, 1974, Chumash Baptism: An ecological perspective. In L. J. Bean and T. F. King, (eds.) ANTAP: California Indian political and economic organization. Ramona, California, Ballena Press, 137–154.

Coombs, Gary, and Plog, Fred, 1977, The Conversion of the Chumash Indians: An Ecological Interpretation. Human Ecology.

Hamblin, Robert, Jacobsen, R., and Miller, J., 1973, *A Mathematical Theory of Social Change*. New York, Wiley.

Logan, Michael and Sanders, Willam, 1976, The model. In E. Wolf (ed.) *The Valley of Mexico*. Albuquerque, University of New Mexico Press, 31–58.

Martin, Paul, and Plog, Fred, 1973, The archaeology of Arizona. New York: Natural History Press.

Plog, Fred, 1973, Diachronic anthropology. In C. Redman, (ed). *Research and Theory in Current Archeology*. New York, Wiley, 181–198.

Plog, Fred, 1974, *The Study of Prehistoric Change*. New York, Academic Press.

Plog, Fred, 1975, Demographic studies in southwestern prehistory. In A. Swedlund, (ed.) *Population Studies in Archaeology and Biological Anthropology. Memoir, Society for American Archaeology,* 94–103.

Plog, Fred, 1977, Explaining change. In J. Hill (ed.), *The Explanation of Prehistoric Change.* Albuquerque, University of New Mexico Press, 17–57.

Ralph, Elizabeth and Michael, Henry, 1974, Twenty-five years of radiocarbon dating. *American Scientist* 62, 553–560.

Sahlins, Marshall and Service, Elman, 1968, *Evolution and Culture.* Ann Arbor, University of Michigan Press.

10

A. J. CHADWICK

Settlement Simulation

A simulation model is a simplified representation of reality, or some theory about it, which works, that is, it changes state either progressively as in a dynamic model or in discrete steps as in comparative statics. It represents not a static picture of a system, but an attempt to replicate the processes involved in its evolution, in either a descriptive or explanatory fashion. As such it is only an aid to understanding the real world, not an end in itself. For this reason any simulation model needs to be firmly grounded in both theory and empirical data, and can never be better than the foundations these two elements can supply. Without a theory to interpret the general form and significance of the structural relationships the model is meaningless, and without an empirical base it cannot be tested against reality to discover its validity. This is not to deny that a priori models do not have a place, merely that care should be taken to treat them as such, until they have been tested. If these two factors are ignored, there is a danger that in a technique such as simulation, especially when a computer with its associated programming problems is involved, the model will become the all-dominating goal, and the original aims will become lost in a morass of equations and elegant algorithms to solve them.

The point of building a model of any sort is that it forces vague conceptualizations to be transformed into a concrete form. As Lowry (1965) points out in a paper specifically aimed at planners, although all potential modelers should read it, there is a world of difference between writing

$$Y = f(U, V, X, Z)$$

237

Transformations:
Mathematical Approaches to Culture Change

and writing

$$Y = \log U + a\left(\frac{V}{X}\right) - Z^b$$

The vague statement that Y is a function of U, V, X, and Z is often nothing more than formalized common sense, but the second formula explicitly states what the relationship is. This means that, given the limitations inevitably involved in simplifying a complex situation, a hypothesis can be tested and stand or fall on its explanatory power, and not have to be accepted as an act of faith. Nothing can ever be proved to be true, but it can at least be shown to be either false or inferior to an alternative. In model building there is, however, an inherent problem, that of equifinality. Just because a simulation model has been produced that appears to work, there is no guarantee that the hypothesized process was in fact the one operating, in the absence of any independent evidence. This is one of the many limitations of the method that have to be accepted.

There are a large number of ways of classifying models, as well as ideas about how one should go about such a modeling exercise (Chadwick, 1971; Chorley and Haggett, 1967; Clarke, 1972). In practice I suspect that most model builders proceed by methods that are distinctly ad hoc, and which do not have the conceptual elegance that is often implied after the event. As a result of experience a few general points can be made, although this is not to imply that they were followed in the work presented herein. The most important feature is to have a clear idea as to what the objective of the whole exercise is. This helps to concentrate attention on the important relationships, exclude the irrelevant, and prevent the emergence of an uncoordinated mass of disparate elements that do not fit together. The next stage is to read and study all the available theory and empirical data relevant to the objective. Otherwise there is the danger of falling into the trap, as Pred points out in the postscript to his translation of Hägerstrand's book (Hägerstrand, 1967), of gaining absolutely no "additional comprehension of the processes involved," and reproducing one's own ignorance. A number of systems dynamics models (Forrester, 1969) that have emerged are fine examples of this. This procedure should generate a number of specific hypotheses that can then be tested by appropriate means. Finally, the actual type of model selected should fit the problem, and only as a secondary consideration the available data, not vice versa. This includes a decision as to whether simulation is the most appropriate tool for the problem in hand. The key note of any model should be simplicity, for the simpler it is, the easier it is to understand, and the less arbitrary the calibration procedure needs to be. A simple linear regression:

$$Y = a_0 + a_i X$$

has at least two parameters to estimate, quite apart from the possibility of transforming the variables. In this case ordinary least squares could be used to calibrate the model, but as the number of variables and equations increases it becomes more difficult, as does the evaluation of the significance of the parameters. Hence the need to keep the model simple is evident, unless the data justify otherwise.

Empirical and Theoretical Background

The model of settlement described here could perhaps be better called an algorithm for the infilling of a settlement pattern under certain conditions. By itself it describes rather than explains the processes involved, hence the importance of a theoretical context within which to interpret it. The work was originally carried out as a geographical exercise (Chadwick, 1977), rather than an analysis of settlement, and hence tended to proceed with rather little consideration for empirical problems. It is hoped that some of the ideas will be found interesting, and possibly stimulate some thought. The model attempts to bridge the gap between two maps of settlement pattern for part of the Peleponnese (south Greece) in Mycenaean times. The data come from the report of the University of Minnesota Messenia expedition— UMME (McDonald and Rapp, 1972), which attempted by a synthesis of contributions from many different disciplines, to reconstruct the Bronze Age environment of the Kingdom of Pylos. For convenience the area UMME used will be called Messenia (Figure 10.1), although the modern *nomos* covers a much smaller area.

UMME conducted an extensive search for Mycenaean sites, dating them on the basis of surface finds of shards, using air photographs to identify potential locations, on certain assumptions about preferred locations (Hope Simpson, 1957). They provide a whole series of settlement maps, including Middle Helladic (ca. 1600 BC) and Late Helladic IIIb (ca. 1250 BC) (Figure 10.2). It is the gap between the 94 sites of the former and the 169 of the latter period, a difference of 75, that the model attempts to bridge. This involved making the fundamental assumption, which would apply to any simulation model based on archaeological data, that the maps were accurate, or at the very least representative samples. It will usually be possible to point out a large number of problems in using a particular data source, in this case the uncertainties of dating shards, and the possibility of bias alluded to earlier. Apart from trying to counteract known systematic sources of error, the only answer is to carry on regardless, provided the limitations of what is being done are appreciated and clearly stated.

One geographical idea on settlement that has seeped through into archaeology is that of central place theory. This is a static description of an expected pattern of relative location and hierarchy of settlement under a set

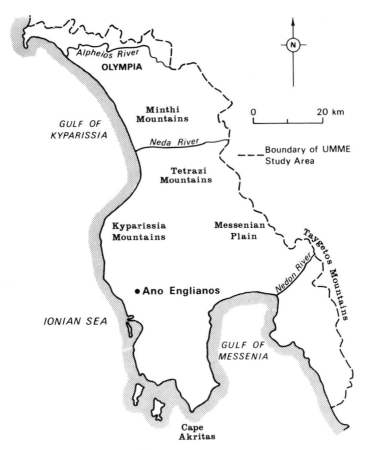

FIGURE 10.1 *The study area: Messenia.*

of restrictive assumptions which include an isotropic plain and a uniform distribution of population. The latter point is important because as a result the theory says nothing about the population of places, only their range of functions, that is the sorts of shops and services available. The total lack of any mechanism for growth means that the theory is of little direct use in looking at settlement processes, and generally any attempts to fit hexagons onto maps are doomed to failure. The theory does, however, focus attention, directly or indirectly, on the concepts of size, spacing, and evolution as necessary parts of any settlement theory. There are undoubted regularities across space and down the size hierarchy that have to be explained. It should be emphasized that attention is being concentrated on settlement at the macro scale, not the microlocational reasons why a particular place is exactly where it is.

An alternative view is that of Curry (1964), in what he calls the "random spatial economy." The basic hypothesis behind this is that at the macro level location in space is random, as a result of the large number of individual decisions taken at the micro level and subject to a multitude of influences,

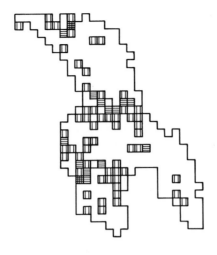

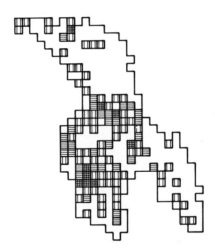

FIGURE 10.2 *Settlement patterns for the Middle Helladic (upper) and Late Helladic (lower) periods in Messenia (source, UMME). The intensity of shading indicates one, two, or three settlements, respectively, per 2 × 2-km cell.*

but restricted by certain overall constraints. These mean that not all locations are equally likely, the maximum entropy situation, since they impose a degree of organization on the system which in theory can range from none to complete determinism. Hudson (1969) provides a framework within which to view the operation of these constraints, drawing heavily on ideas of competition and survival from ecology. He envisages an *n*-dimensional space (a niche space) of orthogonal environmental factors, since he is thinking in physical terms, but this can be extended to include social, economic, and political forces. The various constraints, for example physical absolutes and the level of economic activity, operate to define the area in this space where settlement is favored, some parts being more optimal than others. Translated into physical space and a reasonably mature settlement pattern, this implies that the areas of densest habitation should mark the optimum under a given set of constraints, given sufficient relaxation time. Within this framework, actual site location, for the foregoing reasons, will be random, but influenced by the competition between places for limited resources. This provides a much more flexible way of looking at settlement, albeit less precise, than central place theory.

The idea that randomness provides a useful explanatory device, at this scale, can be taken further. An extensive literature was produced in the 1960s in geography concerned with the rank–size rule, which was originally noted by Zipf (Chorley and Haggett, 1967). He observed that in the United States the second largest city was half the population of the first, the third was one-third, and so on. Much effort was expended trying to fit various sorts of curve to empirical distributions, and trying to tie these up with a blurring of the central place hierarchy. An alternative approach is to imagine a stick of unit length, which is equally likely to break at any point. It is possible to calculate (Cliff, Haggett, Ord, Bassett, and Davies, 1975) the expected proportions that would be produced if it were split into n pieces, given a minimum threshold size for the smallest piece, d:

$$E[g_{(r)}] = \left\{ \left[\frac{1}{n} = d \right] \sum_{i=1}^{r} \frac{1}{n+1-i} \right\} + d \qquad (r = 1, 2, ..., n) \qquad (10.1)$$

where

$E[g_r]$ is the expected size of the rth largest share,
n is the number of pieces, and
d is the threshold size of the smallest piece.

UMME supplies population estimates for 131 sites, based on the areas of the sites insofar as they can be determined, times a constant multiplier. If these estimates are ranked from smallest to largest, the stepped curve in Figure 10.3 results; this curve has a general exponential shape. This can be compared with that generated by the random splitting model, in which d can be estimated from the empirical data using the formula

$$d = \frac{n^2 g_{(1)} - 1}{n(n-1)} \qquad (10.2)$$

where

$g_{(1)}$ is the largest share as a proportion of the total.

A statistical test supports the random splitting hypothesis, with an estimated d value of about 26 people. This implies that the distribution of settlement sizes, or at least archaeological estimates of their areal extent, follows the statistically most likely distribution. Given an estimate of the

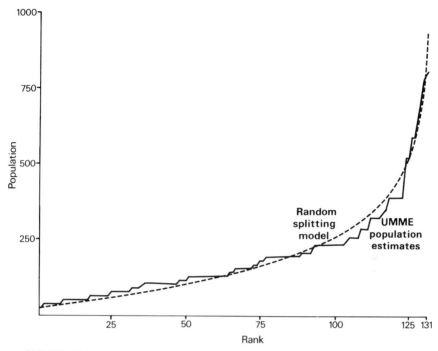

FIGURE 10.3 *Comparison of populations of sites in rank order (from the smallest) as predicted by the random splitting model and as observed in Messenia.*

kingdom's population from an independent source, for example the linear B tablets, it is possible to work out a possible number of sites. For example, a figure of 75,000 produces 215 settlements between the Neda and Nedon rivers, compared with the 138 found by UMME. This line of reasoning cannot be taken too far, but it does illustrate that a stochastic approach to settlement can produce plausible answers.

Attempts at simulating settlement (Haggett 1965) have been few and far between. Bylund (1960) produced a deterministic model of colonization in Swedish Lapland, in an attempt to explain why some of the poorer land was often exploited before the best. It operated on the principle of budding off from existing places, starting from an initial base on the coast, and assuming indigenous population growth and distance minimization. Bylund's results show a broad similarity with the patterns found in Lapland, but his ideas do not seem to have been exploited elsewhere. The stochastic approach is represented by Morrill (1962), but only within the confines of central place theory. Morrill was principally concerned with the migration of population according to a set of probabilities derived from an empirical distance decay found in southern Sweden. His results are interesting in showing how random disturbances through time can accumulate to give considerable variations in the populations of settlements. The model does not, however, help with the question of where places are founded, although it does say something about why.

The idea of a simulation model was derived initially from an interest in the work of Hägerstrand (1967) on the diffusion of agricultural innovations. There seemed no obvious reason why, in theory at least, a similar sort of approach could not be applied to settlement. His book is a painstaking example of the sort of detailed analysis that needs to be put into empirical data to produce a good model. As Pred says, to quote his postscript again, some subsequent studies "have fallen short of expectations because of inadequate research and/or a deficiency of rigor," a criticism that could well be leveled at this work. Hägerstrand's simplest model assumed that knowledge of an innovation, for example T.B. controls, would be general in the population, but initially would only be adopted by a few individuals distributed at randon. From these centers the innovation would be spread by face-to-face contact between adopters and nonadopters, in which the latter are convinced by the experience of the former. To model these contacts he placed a symmetrical 5×5 matrix of probabilities over each existing adopter, the information field derived from fitting a negative exponential curve to data about the frequency of telephone calls versus distance, and rotating it through $360°$. A random number was then chosen from a uniform distribution and used to locate the new adopter, and the procedure was repeated for each existing adopter. He went on to make the model more realistic by allowing for such factors as the barrier effects of lakes, the need for multiple tellings, and variations in the density of potential adopters.

Similar ideas can be applied to settlement. The receptive population, the land, has variable potential, and the random spatial economy provides a background within which to interpret the stochastic element. A "settlement field" also exists, not to give the neighborhood effect of the information field, but rather to space places out, not only from one particular settlement but from all others. Unlike the Hägerstrand model this says nothing about the forces that bring about the "demand" for a new settlement or how they operate, be they internal population growth or external migration. The notion of the spacing out of settlement stems from the need for each place to have some form of "territory" to exploit, to provide it with an economic base, which could be subsistence agriculture or a gold mine. This "territory" need not be defined in terms of a contiguous geographic space but rather the n-dimensional space mentioned earlier, and it should not be thought of as an exclusive zone, merely an area one place is more likely to exploit than any other. In terms of an agriculturally based community, as was found in Bronze Age Messenia, it seemed reasonable to assume that the territory could be defined as a continuous space around a settlement, due to the operation of distance constraints, as demonstrated for example in Von Thünen's model (Chorley and Haggett, 1967).

As a first stage in the analysis of the settlement patterns, Thiessen polygons (Haggett and Chorley, 1969) were constructed for both maps. These are regions drawn such that every point within them is closer to the settlement they surround than any other. This procedure defines a settlement's first-order neighbors, those places with contiguous polygons. Figure 10.4 gives the frequency distribution of the average first-order neighbor distances for Middle and Late Helladic, both giving curves that have a general lognormal shape. An analysis of the data, along with a visual inspection of the patterns, suggested that as an initial hypothesis the distributions consisted of a series of clusters, possibly generated by contagious growth from a series of original centers, the gap between the two periods being characterized by a process of infilling, rather than an extension of the settlement frontier.

Model Building

To test these ideas the two distributions were examined in two main ways, using nearest neighbor and quadrat analyses. The former compares the average of all linear distances from the ith settlements to their kth neighbors, against a theoretical value derived assuming a Poisson distribution (King, 1969):

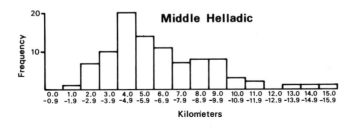

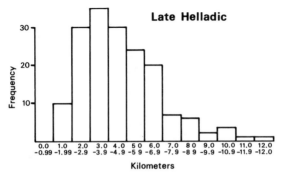

FIGURE 10.4 *Frequency distributions of average first-order nearest neighbor distances for (a) Middle Helladic and (b) Late Helladic Messenia.*

$$R = \frac{r_a}{r_e} \tag{10.3}$$

where

$$r_a = \frac{\sum_{i=1}^{n} r_i^k}{n}$$

r_i^k is the straight line distance from the ith place to its kth neighbors,
n is the total number of points,
$r_e = 1/p$, and
$p = n/(\text{total area})$.

The statistic R ranges from a value of 0, completely clustered, through 1.0, random (Poisson), to 2.1491, a dispersed pattern. The results are usually a little difficult to interpret, a problem not helped by the variations that can be produced by changing the definition of area in the equation. In this case it was defined as the study area as used by UMME, but given sufficient data to complete the maps along the land boundaries, the combined areas of the Thiessen polygons would provide a consistent definition. Table 10.1 gives the results for nearest, second nearest, average, and furthest first-order neighbors, the general message being that the patterns are random but with some evidence of clustering.

A more fruitful approach in providing some ideas on the mode of settlement was quadrat analysis (Rogers, 1974). In this the pattern to be analyzed is covered with a grid of equally sized cells, and the number of quadrats with 0, 1, ..., n occupants are counted. The resulting frequency distribution can then be compared with various theoretical ones generated by a variety of models. Accordingly the two maps were covered in a lattice of 1109 cells, each 2×2 km, and a cell count taken, the procedure being repeated for 4×4 and 6×6 km lattices formed by aggregation. This was done so the fit of the models could be tested for scale dependency (Harvey, 1968). The first to be calibrated was the Poisson:

$$P(x) = \frac{e^{-\lambda}\lambda^x}{x!} \qquad (x = 0, 1, ..., n) \tag{10.4}$$

TABLE 10.1
Nearest Neighbor Results on First-Order Neighbors

	Nearest	Second	Average	Furthest
Middle Helladic	0.54	0.79	1.00	1.54
Late Helladic	0.51	0.76	0.99	1.54

where the parameter can be estimated as

$$\lambda = \frac{\sum_{i=1}^{n} x_i f_i}{n}$$

x_i is the number of settlements in a cell, and
f_i is the number of cells with that number.

The fit of this model was tested using both χ^2 and Kolmogorov–Smirnov (Siegel, 1956). The latter is the more powerful test, but the former has the advantage of considering the deviations in all classes. The goodness of fit was best for the smallest cell size, but became significant, at the 99% level used throughout, on the 6×6-km cell grid. The 99% level was chosen with the aim of minimizing the risk of a type I error, rejecting the null hypothesis when it is true, with the aim of allowing the simulations a wide margin of error. As an alternative the negative binomial model was fitted (Williamson and Bretherton, 1964):

$$P(x) = \left(x + k - 1 \atop k - 1 \right) p^k (1 - p)^x \qquad (x = 0, 1, ..., n) \qquad (10.5)$$

where the parameters can be estimated from the mean, $\bar{x}$, and variance, s^2, of the observed distribution as:

$$p = s^2 \bar{x}, \qquad k = \frac{\bar{x}^2}{s^2 - \bar{x}}$$

This model gives a satisfactory fit for all three cell sizes, at both time periods, but it suffers from the problem that there is more than one possible generating process. Two of these are applicable to settlement, and it is possible to differentiate between them by analyzing the expected compared with the actual changes in the p and k parameters as cells are aggregated to form larger ones (Cliff and Ord, 1973). The result is to suggest that the two patterns are the outcome of a model like the Poisson given here; that is, they are essentially random. However, unlike the Poisson the chance of a cell receiving 0, 1, ..., n settlements is not fixed across the map since λ is allowed to vary. Cliff and Ord suggest that this can be interpreted as meaning that the probabilities are biased by a factor such as the quality of the underlying environment.

Before proceeding to model construction on the basis of these results, consideration must be given to what constitutes a good fit between a set of simulations and the actual Late Helladic pattern. The simulations were carried out using the 2×2-km cell lattice, but it seemed unreasonable to expect the model to be accurate to 2 km in the absence of any detailed information on the local microenvironmental characteristics. Accordingly the results were aggregated into the 4 × 4-km cell grid before being printed out and analyzed by the computer. The testing was done three different ways. First, by counting the cell frequencies and using χ^2 with the Late Helladic distribution, an aspatial test. Second, a residuals map was created by taking each simulation away from the observed pattern and testing the result for spatial autocorrelation. This is basically a test of whether or not the residuals are randomly located, significant clumping of positives or negatives indicating some form of systematic bias. The statistic used was

$$I = \frac{n \sum_{i=1_{i \neq j}}^{n} \sum_{j=1}^{n} w_{ij} x_i x_j}{\sum_{i=1_{i \neq j}}^{n} \sum_{j=1}^{n} w_{ij} \sum_{i=1}^{n} x_i^2} \tag{10.6}$$

where

n is the number of nonzero residuals,
x_i is the residual in the ith cell, and
w_{ij} are the elements of a weights matrix, in this case
$w_{ij} = 1$ if i and j touch at either a side or corner,
$w_{ij} = 0$ otherwise.

Full details of the standardization of this statistic and the appropriate test procedures can be found in the book by Cliff and Ord (1973). Finally the simulations were compared visually with the desired result, on the grounds that if it looks right, it is right.

Following the results of the quadrat analysis, model I was constructed on the assumption that the environment was the key determining feature, and nothing else. To handle this, an "environment surface" was constructed from a synthesis for each quadrat of the 2 × 2-km cell grid of the availability of water and the geomorphology, and taking into account the resource potential of the sea. Information for this was derived from maps in the UMME volume, and full details are given elsewhere (Chadwick, 1978). The aim was to produce a surface (Figure 10.5 shows a modified version) that gave a measure of the relative attractiveness of different areas. Model I operated by taking this surface and converting it into probabilities. The 75 new sites that are needed in addition to the Middle Helladic pattern were then located using random numbers from a uniform distribution. This assumes that settlement location is random, but biased by the environment and independent of existing places. For a population of 30 simulations the aspatial fit was good, but the test of the residuals produced outright rejection. Visually the model produced a wide dispersion of sites and insufficient concentration where required. This failure was not very surprising because of the model's assumption of independence—settlement does not take place in a vacuum.

```
*----+----1----+----2----+----?----+----4----+----5----+----6----+----7----+----8----+----9----+----1----+----1---+
ICC00000000REEE840+++++00        4E                                                                              I
IC0000000C EEEEE8000+ +000         EEE            +++.                                                            I
I00        0EEEEEEECC CCC +CCC CEEEEEEEEEEEEECCC++                                                                I
I00        EEEEE8000N++++++0CCC CEEEEEEEEEEEEEEECC+...                                                            I
+00        CCCCCCC0+++2+++CCCC CEEEEEE 5 EEC0++.......                                                            +
I          C0CC0++++++++++CCCCC C 8 EEEEEEEC00+++.....                                                            I
I          0C0++++++++++++++CCCCCEEEEEECCC+++++++++00C0 8 EEE                                                     I
1          ++++++++++++++++++CCCCCCCCCC0+++++++++00008 8 EEE                                                     1
I          +++++++++++++++++CCCCC+++++++C00 8 EEEEEE                                                             I
1          +++....1...++...+++++++CC000 8 EEE ■■■■■■■ EEE                                                         1
I          +++...+++...+.1..+..++++000 8 9985 ■ EEEEEEE                                                           I
I          +++++++++......+++++000E6888E ■ EEEEEEE88                                                             I
+          +++++++C002C0C++.......+++++++C000CEE C0CCC C0888                                                      +
I          +++++C8 8 84EC+...........++..++++0C00 NC C00000                                                      I
I          ++++CCE0C0+1.............1...++++++CCCC0CC0                                                           I
I          ++++CCCC+++..................++++++++                                                                 I
I          +++++++++....++++...........+++++++                                                                   I
2,         +++++++....1..++++++............                                                                       2
I          +++++++++++00C00+++...                                                                                I
I          +++++.+++C08 4 EE00C++.                                                                               I
I          +++....+++C8 8 EEEE00C++.                                                                             I
I          +++.......++C0000+++.....                                                                             I
+          +++.....1....++++.....                                                                                +
I          C0C++.                                                                                                I
I          CC++................++++                                                                              I
I          CCC++++...........++++++++++                                                                          I
3          8E0CC0+++++.+++++++++++....1....                                                                      3
I          ■EECC+++1+++++00CC+++.                                                                                I
I          ■ 8 ■ 88800+++++++..++08 4 E8C0++.                                                                    I
I          ■■■■■■■■ 8800++++...1+000000+2++++.                                                                   I
+          ■■■■■■■■ 8800++...+....++++++++++.....                                                                 +
I          88888888EEEEE0CCC+++++++.++++++++00CC+++++...1.                                                        I
I          CCCEEEEEEEECCCC+++++.......+++0000CC000++                                                             I
4          +·CC0C0C0000C00++++++........++00CCECOCC++.                                                          4
I          ++++CC0CE6CCCC++++++++.....+C0 8 EEEE80000++++.                                                       I
I          ..++CCC4 8 8C0++++++++2++....1...+C8 8 84EEEE000CC+++.                                                I
I          ....+CC000C++++..++++.........++000CC0 8 8 000000000++.....                                           I
I          ........++++++++++++.........+++++0++C0 8 EEECE8000C+++.............1                                 I
+          ...1....++2++++..1........+++++00000C0CC0++C0 8 EEEEE000C+++...........                                +
I          .++++++++...........++++C0000C00CCC00 8 8 80C0000++.....                                             I
I          .....++++*.........++C000 8 8 8 8 EE00CCC00 8 8 8 8 30C0800+++.......                                  I
I          ......++++*...++++++0000 8 88888888 8 8 0CC0 8 8 888846EEE00C++.......                                 I
5          +++++++++1..++++.++++0008 8 8 88888888 888CC0000000000000++....                                       5
I          +++++CCCCr0CCC0C0C0++++00C0 8 EEEEEEEEC0 8 8 00 8 0R0000++.........1.                                 I
I          CCCCCCCCr 8 8 EEE8000+++++0N 8 8888888888 80CC0+++++++++++++++++++C+++.....                           I
I          CC0+CC0CC ■ 8 EE4EE0C+++++++C00 8 8 EEEEEE0CC0++++++++++++++++2+3++.........                          I
+          ++2CCCEEEEEEEE80C++.....++000 9 888888 ■ A0CC+++++2++++++++++++++C+++.....                           +
I          CCEEEEEE ■ EEE0+........++000EEEE88880CCC+++++++++.......                                             I
I          ■ 5 ■■■■■■ ■ ■C++.1...++000E88EEE800CC++++                                                           I
I          ■■■■■■EEEE80C++..+++++000E84EE80000C++                                                                I
I          ■■■■■EEEEE C0G+++++++0C08 8 EEE800000+++                                                              I
I          EEEEEEEEE800++++++0000C000000+                                                                        I
6          EEEE4C0+++++++++++++++++                                                                              6
I          CCCCCC++1+++++++++1++++++++                                                                           I
I          +0C++++.........++.......++++++                                                                       I
I          ++++++++...............+++++                                                                          I
+          ..1....1......1.                                                                                      +
I          ++++....++++++++++++++++++                                                                            I
I          ++++2++++++++++++++++++++                                                                             I
7          +++3+CCCE8EC0000+++++++                                                                               7
I          ++++0CCCE ■■■■ EC0000C00++++++                                                                         I
I          C 3 0C00C 5 8C CC0000000C0+++++                                                                       I
I          ++++2+CC G00000000C0C0C++++                                                                           I
I          ++++++++0000000C0C00CC++                                                                              I
+          0000C0C0000CC                                                                                         +
I          00C00CC0000C                                                                                          I
I          0C000CCCCCCC                                                                                          I
+          ++++++++++                                                                                            +
I          +++++                                                                                                 I
*----+----1----+----2----+----3----+----4----+----5----+----6----+----7----+----8----+----5----+----1----+----1---*
-SYMAP
   3.44 SECONDS FCR MAP

TIME =   4.76
```

FIGURE 10.5 *Transformed environment surface for Messenia showing relative attractiveness of different areas for settlement (increasing attractiveness indicated* $\cdot$, $+$, 0, θ, ■).

Development

This lack of independence brings in the concept of the territory in two different ways. First, the attraction of a particular cell, only 4 km², will depend not only on itself but also on the surrounding area; second, there is a need for places to be spaced out from one another in order to have sufficient land. Model IIa was constructed by transforming the environment surface using a form of potential model, which has the general form of the summation of the product of the masses of the ith and all jth places, divided by some function of the distance between them. In this case the distance function was of the general form

$$Y = a_0 + a_i \log X \tag{10.7}$$

The parameters were derived by fitting the equation using ordinary least squares to the frequency distribution of the average distance to the sides of the Middle Helladic Thiessen polygons (Figure 10.6). The resulting surface is not that different from the old, so in retrospect this may have been unnecessary. A settlement field was generated by fitting to the Middle Helladic first-order average neighbor frequency distribution (Figure 10.4) a curve of the form

$$Y = a_0 + a_i \log X + a_{ii}(\log X)^2 \tag{10.8}$$

When rotated through 360°, entered in the cells of a 11×11 lattice, and converted to probabilities with the center cell left blank, the result is as shown in cross section in Figure 10.7. The resulting shape is perhaps best described as that of a lognormal doughnut. If the settlement field is centered over an already settled cell, a biased set of probabilities can be obtained by multiplying the field by the transformed environment surface and converting back. In practice this is achievable in one step using the equations

$$P_{ij} = A_i W_j f(d_{ij}) \tag{10.9}$$

$$A_i = \frac{1}{\sum_{j=1}^{n} W_j f(d_{ij})} \tag{10.10}$$

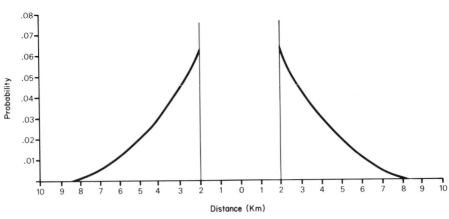

FIGURE 10.6 *Cross section of distance decay function used for transforming the environment surface (Figure 10.5). The figure for probability represents the chance of finding the boundary of a first-order neighbor's Thiessen polygon at the distance in question from the (already occupied) central cell.*

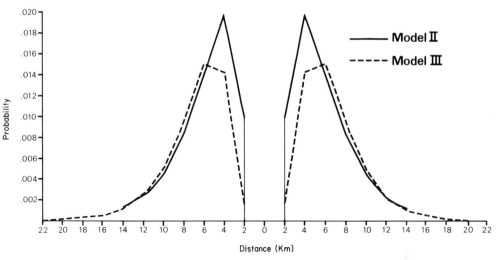

FIGURE 10.7 *Cross sections of settlement fields used for models II and III. (The probabilities are as for Figure 10.6, but they refer to the first-order neighbors themselves not to their boundaries.)*

where

P_{ij} is the biased probability of a first-order neighbor being in the jth cell,
W_j is the transformed environment surface value, and
$f(d_{ij})$ is a function of distance, the settlement field probabilities.

Model IIa operated by calculating these biased probabilities for all the cells around any occupied quadrat on the map. The values for each individual cell were then added and divided by the grand total to produce a set of probabilities for the whole of Messenia. Ten percent of the existing numbers of sites were then located using random numbers, the figure representing a compromise between the cost in computer time and the ideal of recalculating the probabilities after the location of each new site. Actual entry to a cell also depended on the number, if any, of current occupants. If it was empty, entry occurred immediately; with one occupant the chance of failure was 0.33, with two 0.66, and with three 1.0 since no Late Helladic cell has more than that number of sites. The model was stopped as soon as the Late Helladic total of 169 was reached starting from Middle Helladic's 94. The fit of this model was poorer than model I aspatially, but better spatially. The desired clumping of settlement was now occurring, but the peaks were too large and the remoter sites had been lost. One particular area showed consistent overestimation in all the simulations run of this model, and that was along the northern frontier of the study area.

Model IIb introduced two improvements, one of which was subsequently seem to have a negative effect. The value which each biased settlement field summed to was changed from 1.0 to the number of sites in a cell. This had the unfortunate effect of increasing the surrounding cells' probabilities excessively in the final map, which helped to exacerbate the peaking problem, although relatively few quadrats were involved. Second, model IIa treated all boundaries as reflective, which meant that the total value of the settlement field was concentrated in fewer cells, and hence again produced a disproportionate effect on the final probability map. Along the coast and the eastern boundary which is mainly mountain, this is reasonable enough, but along the northern frontier into Elis it is not, which explained why the piling-up problem was especially acute along the Alpheios. To correct this the northern boundary was made partially absorbent by repeating the top two rows of the transformed environment surface as two new rows along the top of the map. This allowed some of the settlement field, but not all, to be directed over the "border," providing for the fact that there are unknown places to the north affecting location in the study area. It must be admitted that this is very much an ad hoc solution, and that ideally the information required should have been obtained, and used to do the simulations, through applying the test procedures to a core area only. These changes resulted in another improvement in the spatial fit, but although less severe the problem of piling up remained.

Model IIIa attempted another approach to the overconcentration problem, by recalibrating the distance decay terms used in both transforming the environment surface and producing the settlement field. This was done by using the raw Middle Helladic first-order neighbor data rather than the average figure for each place, the basic effect of which is to give the distributions smaller peaks and longer tails. As a result the settlement field now fitted into a 17×17 rather than an 11×11 lattice, though still with the same basic shape, the dashed line in Figure 10.7. This gives the remoter sites more chance of being simulated, and helps to cut down the concentration effect produced by a series of settlement fields being piled up on top of each other. Figure 10.5 shows the transformed environment surface, though this is not significantly different from the previous version. These changes produced the best results so far, but still not good enough; peaking still occurred.

The final attempt, model IIIb, includes an element which up to now had been ignored, that of population. It would seem logical that the sites with larger populations would repel new settlement more than others, due to their greater presumed pressure upon local resources. Conversely, an underpopulated area, relative to the resources available, should be more attractive because of the unexploited potential. This seemed to be a good route by which to tackle the overconcentration problem, which results from the models Hägerstrandian origins, and is also the reason why the model deals with infill rather than extension of the settlement frontier. The UMME population estimates have already been mentioned, but these do not cover all sites; therefore, there is the problem of allocating numbers to the rest of the remaining sites, as well as to simulated places that should not "exist." In addition, the population ought to grow through time, and in so doing provide, in part at least, an explanation for the emergence of new settlements. As an alternative the transformed environment surface value for a cell was taken as a rather dubious surrogate for population. From this, taking into account the number of sites in a quadrat, an inverse index was created with a minimum of 1.0 for large "population" centers, and a maximum of 6.0 for small. The settlement field around each occupied cell was now made to sum to this value, so that it would have proportionally more or less effect on the final probabilities for the whole map.

As a result of running the model in this form it is possible to say at a 99% significance level that the observed Late Helladic site distribution in Messenia could just be a member of the simulated population of 49. Visually the fit looks much better, with a greater spread of sites (see Figure 10.8). Aspatially one of the simulations is significantly different, but most of the rest have very low χ^2 values. Model IIIb then suggests that the factors controlling the growth of the settlement pattern between Middle and Late Helladic were the environment, the spacing effect of the need for territory, population size, and a stochastic element. The environment provides the enabling framework within which the settlement process occurs, the geographical representation of the abstract n-dimensional space. This simple mapping into geographical space only applies because of the assumption that each settlement primarily depends on agriculture, and that the exploitation

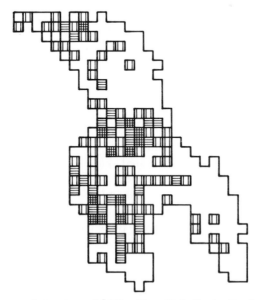

FIGURE 10.8 *A simulation (by model IIIb) of Late Helladic site distribution in Messenia.*

of resources is carried out on the basis of distance minimization. From the evidence of the linear B tablets (Chadwick, 1976) there was a significant economic element which has been ignored, although it could be argued that this has more to do with settlement size than location. Inside this framework the forces of competition are expressed through such factors as the settlement field and population size, which can be expressed in general terms as the pressure on resources at a given technological level. The stochastic element represents the inherent random nature of such a process to the observer at this scale. Quite apart from not having the information, there is a multitude of factors that could be involved, many of which may only have significance at one point in space and time.

The dominant process in this area at this period seems to have been one of infill, with an emphasis on continuity, not a growth through, for example, direct budding off from existing places as in the Bylund model. It would not, however, have been possible to do a similar exercise from Early Helladic since many of the sites present then disappear in Middle Helladic, only to reappear in Late Helladic. The forces involved in determining location could have been hypothesized a priori, but the building of the model has allowed them to be tested, insofar as that is possible. However, as mentioned earlier the model is only a description, and it says nothing about the processes that generated the need for new settlement, the most obvious being population growth. An obvious major development would be an attempt to build this in, something that would necessitate the introduction of the time dimension. At the moment the model says nothing about whether the new sites appear in 300 years or 10 min., the stochastic element being the only driving force. On a smaller scale the model could be improved, for instance, by an inversion of the way of looking at the spacing-out mechanism. At the moment the probability of a cell receiving a settlement is computed from the point of view of the existing sites, not the quadrat itself. An alternative would be to consider each cell as having a certain attractive power, and then subtract from this to allow for the relative location of existing places and their populations. This sort of approach would avoid the piling-up problem of the settlement fields, and allow explicit consideration of all, rather than just first-order neighbors. The major constraint on such developments is not the imagination of hypotheses to be tested, but the availability of data.

It is hoped that this chapter has been of use in pointing out some of the ways in which simulation can be useful and applicable to settlement studies. As emphasized at the beginning it is only a technique that may be of use in certain situations, most notably when suitable quantities of relevant data are either readily available or easily obtainable. The three interrelated steps of objective definition, theoretical and empirical analysis, and choice of technique, provide a guide to carrying out such an exercise. The value in trying to build any form of model is that it makes the ideas of the investigator more precise, and hence more easily refutable. It must be remembered, however, that any model represents only one way of looking at reality, and that there are a multitude of equally valid alternatives.

References

Bylund, E. (1960) Theoretical considerations regarding the distribution of settlement in inner North Sweden. *Geografiska Annaler* XLII, 225–231.

Chadwick, A. J. (1977) Computer simulation of settlement development in Bronze Age Messenia, in Bintliff, J. (Ed) *Mycenaean Geography: Proceedings of the Cambridge Colloquium*. Cambridge, Institute for Mycenaean Studies.

Chadwick, A. J. (1978) Settlement simulation, in Hodder, I. (Ed) *Simulation Studies in Archaeology*. Cambridge, University Press.

Chadwick, G. (1971) *A Systems View of Planning*. London, Pergamon.

Chadwick, J. (1976) *The Mycenaean World*. Cambridge, University Press.

Chorley, R. J., and Haggett, P. (1967) *Models in Geography*. London, Methuen.

Clarke, D. L. (1972) *Models in Archaeology*. London, Methuen.

Cliff, A. D. and Ord, J. K. (1973) *Spatial Autocorrelation*. London, Pion.

Cliff, A. D., Haggett, P., Ord, J. K., Bassett, K. A., & Davies, R. B. (1975) *Elements of Spatial Structure: a Quantitative Approach*. Cambridge University Press.

Curry, L. (1964) The random spatial economy: an exploration in settlement theory, *Annals of the Association of American Geographers*, 54, 138–146.

Forrester, J. (1969) *Urban Dynamics*. Boston, M.I.T. Press.

Hägerstrand, T. (1967) *Innovation Diffusion as a Spatial Process*. University of Chicago Press, with postscript by Pred, A.

Haggett, P. (1965) *Locational Analysis in Human Geography*. London, Edward Arnold.

Haggett, P., and Chorley, R. J. (1969) *Network Analysis in Geography*. London, Edward Arnold.

Harvey, D. W. (1968) Pattern, process, and the scale problem, *Proceedings of the Institute of British Geographers*, 45, 71–78.

Hope Simpson, R. J. (1957) Identifying a Mycenaean site, *Annual of the British School of Archaeology at Athens*, 52, 231–259.

Hudson, J. C. (1969) A location theory for settlement, *Annals of the American Association of Geographers*, 59, 365–381.

King, L. J. (1969) *Statistical Analysis in Geography*. New York, Prentice-Hall.

Lowry, I. S. (1965) A short course in model design, *Journal of the American Institute of Planning*, 31, 158–166.

McDonald, W. A., and Rapp, G. R. (Eds), (1972) *The Minnesota Messenia Expedition*. The University of Minnesota Press.

Morrill, R. J. (1962) Simulation of central place patterns over time, *Lund Studies in Geography*, Series B, No. 24, 109–120.

Rogers, A. (1974) *Statistical Analysis of Spatial Dispersion: the Quadrat Method*. London, Pion.

Siegel, S. (1956) *Nonparametric Statistics for the Behavioral Sciences*. New York, McGraw-Hill.

11

JOEL GUNN

Occupation Frequency Simulation on a Broad Ecotone

Introduction

Several archaeologists have demonstrated interest in modeling and simulating the behavior of bands. A partial list includes Birdsell (1973), Wobst (1974), Thomas (1974), Prewitt (1974), Yellen (1977), Hester *et al.* (1977), and Gunn (1977a, 1977b). The following study is directed toward the simulation of those processes which govern the distribution of camps–sites. The product of the simulation is to be a statistical probability surface whose properties resemble the distribution of sites in a survey area. The processes to be accounted for include climatic change, geomorphology, and cultural adaptation. The project is part of a culturally and ecologically oriented research program being implemented by staff members of the Center for Archaeological Research, The University of Texas at San Antonio. Current funding policies by various government agencies provide us with numerous small and large contracts in the south and central Texas region. Conceivably each archaeological effort could be executed in isolation. We feel, however, that given a common problem orientation, they will, over the years, provide a reasonably complete inventory of environmental and cultural phenomena in the area. A general ecological orientation was chosen because we thought data collected with this problem orientation in mind could best stand the test of time, that is, the coming and going of interests in the archaeological community.

To implement this orientation, members of the Center staff have agreed as a matter of policy to collect a specified set of ecological observations on

257

Transformations:
Mathematical Approaches to Culture Change

all sites for all projects regardless of additional, project-specific problem orientations. These observations report the relationships of sites to geomorphic transects and subsistence resources. We recognize that any number of models could be utilized in the analysis of these data and varying points of view are encouraged and duly published in the Center's Special Publication series. The following effort, then, is one person's attempt to synthesize an outlook within which this rather rapidly accumulating data base can be analyzed. Since the project is basically long term, this chapter is focused more on model refinement and the early stages of simulation than final model testing.

The assumptions explored in this chapter are illustrated in Figure 11.1. Adaptations are induced adjustments to global temperature change and to geomorphic landforms. They are evidenced by the frequency and intensity of sites on various landforms. Frequency and intensity of occupation of geomorphic landforms (microhabitats) reflects the more basic aspects of culture including subsistence strategy and social organization.

That adaptation is linked to climate is commonly understood. Climatic change at the global rather than local level is specifically suggested here. Geomorphic landform (and associated phenomena such as soil type) is taken to be a key environmental variable rather than local biota (pollen, etc.) because it is statistically independent of cultural variation. Treating biota as causally prior to culture, as is commonly done, results in a spurious analysis of adaptations since biotic and cultural adaptations are responses to common underlying causes, global temperature, and geomorphic microhabitats. Also, geomorphology is universally observable whereas paleobotanical observation often is difficult or impossible.

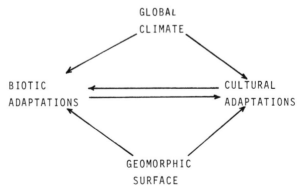

FIGURE 11.1 *Underlying assumptions explored in this chapter. Global climate and geomorphic surfaces control the biotic and cultural phenomena observable at any given location. Biota and culture are mutually effective. See Figure 11.5 for details.*

Environment

The structure of climate during the past is here understood as a permutation of present climate. The ecological structure of Texas is relatively simple and lends itself readily to such a treatment. It is arid in the west and very moist in the east. Bryson (1966) and Gunn and Mahula (1977) outline the general characteristics of weather systems affecting the area.

The classic work on biotic provinces produced by the weather system was published by Blair (1950) and is probably the most cited publication in the archaeological literature of the region. Blair compiled his assessment of Texas biotic provinces from various surveys of plant and animal life made in 1901, 1905, 1931, 1938 to 1940, 1942 to 1944, and 1946 to 1949. There was notable change in global temperatures during these five decades (National Academy of Sciences 1975; Matthews 1976, Wright and Gunn 1977, Bryson and Murray 1977:130). However, the bulk of the works referenced were researched in the 1930s and 1940s. The two decades from 1930 to 1950 were the warmest in terms of global temperatures during the present cold–warm–cold cycle. Being at the top of a cycle mitigates to some extent the problem of calibrating the present climatic regime with those of the past, and is, therefore, an ideal framework from which to work.

According to Blair (1950, 95–96),

A great area in central Texas, from the Pecos on the west to the western boundary of the Austroriparian forest on the east [see Figure 11.2], is principally a region of transition between the Sonoran and Austroriparian biotas. In this area the two major biota intermix

FIGURE 11.2 *Biotic provinces and supraprovinces of Texas. Provinces are from Blair (1950). Supraprovinces were determined by principal components (Valdez n.d.).*

or interdigitate. . . . Several obvious factors influence the distribution of plants and animals in the transition area, or great ecotone. These factors are principally edaphic or physiographic ones. Austroriparian species may be expected to range westward . . . where local conditions produce a more mesic environment than the regional average . . . The stream systems of Texas provide important routes for the westward distribution of Austroriparian species into comparatively arid, generally traceless environments. . . . Rock outcrops on dissected plateaus and on escarpments provides avenues for dispersal of . . . Chihuahuan province species . . . eastward.

During the 1931–1969 period Texas received an annual average of 1422 mm of precipitation in the east and 200 mm in the west (see precipitation transect, Figure 11.3). A study of Texas weather patterns suggests two sources of precipitation (Bielser and Gunn 1977). Spring and summer rain is predominantly from a monsoon effect which draws supersaturated air off the Gulf of Mexico and deposits moisture on land as rain, either due to cooling in the spring or convection cells during the summer. The effect of monsoon and convection circulation appears to spread westward during cooler global climates. Whether the effect is a product of changes in high pressure cells in the Gulf of Mexico, or simply an increase in effective moisture due to reduced evaporation is as yet unresearched.

The distribution of fall and winter precipitation is the product of a peculiar relationship to the mountains in western North America. A tributary of the jet stream called the "subtropical flow" and its accompanying westerlies draw moisture off the Pacific Ocean and carry it eastward across the continent. Warm global temperatures, probably through the medium of Pacific water temperatures, drive the subtropical flow northward to California where most of the moisture is combed out of the clouds over the Sierra Nevada Mountains and Rocky Mountains. Global cooling, however, generally moves weather systems southward (Sanchez and Kutzbach 1974). To the west of central and south Texas, the mountains of northern Mexico are relatively low and they allow moisture to pass into the southern plains. Here northern cold fronts collide with the moist westerlies causing spectacular increases in precipitation during colder winters. The winter of 1976–1977 was an example of the cooler pattern. California was dry and south Texas wetter than normal (Canby 1977).

Estimating how far changing global temperatures displace the monsoon circulation is an uncertain procedure now, though future research may reveal more definite information. Jose Enrique de la Peña (1975), who traveled with Santa Ana's army to the Alamo in the winter of 1836, reported a very hard journey due to weather conditions which do not resemble those in south Texas and northern Mexico today. He saw cypress trees in northern Mexico about 300 km west of their present range. Cypress trees grow in areas of greater than 700 mm of rainfall (Figure 11.3). This would effectively move the 700-mm rainfall line out to the present 400-mm line. The year 1836 was preceded by a half-century of lower than usual sunspot activity (Eddy

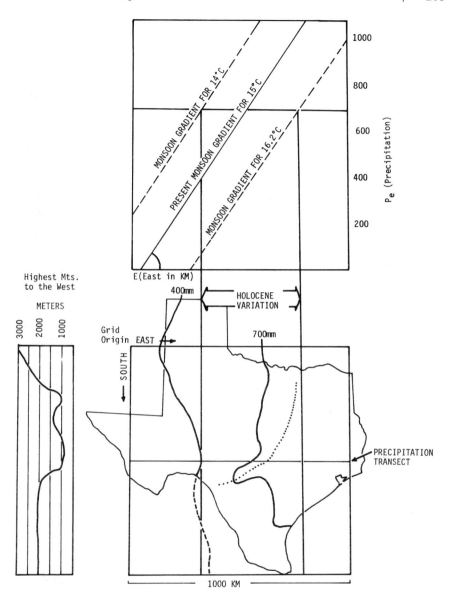

FIGURE 11.3 *Climatic variation during the Holocene.* Bottom right—*Map of Texas with 700- and 400-mm precipitation contours, estimated movement of the 700-mm contour (straight lines projected from above), and precipitation transect (see Top). Bottom left—Highest mountains to the west used to estimate effect of north–south movement of subtropical flow in response to changing global temperatures. Top—Estimated movement of precipitation gradient along precipitation transect and origins of projections for 700-mm contour movement. (From Gunn and Mahula 1977.)*

(a)   (b)

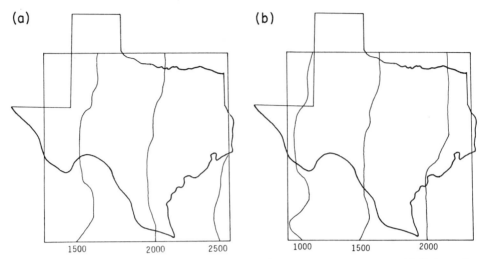

| 1500 | 2000 | 2500 | | 1000 | 1500 | 2000 |

FIGURE 11.4 *Simulated precipitation at various average temperatures.* (a) *Estimated precipitation during the Pleistocene (temperature 11°C). Note that the 700-mm precipitation contour is off the map to the west.* (b) *Estimate of precipitation at Holocene low (temperature 14°C). The 700-mm precipitation contour is further west than at present (see Figure 11.3 for present).* (c) *Estimate of precipitation at present (temperature 15°C). This map is included to give the reader a sense of the accuracy at which the climate simulation operates. Since elevational changes have not been incorporated into the calculations, the effect of the Balcones Escarpment (dotted line in Figure 11.3, bottom right) are not accounted for. Otherwise accuracy appears to be within a few percentage points.* (d) *Estimate of precipitation at Holocene highs (temperature 17°C). The 700-mm precipitation contour is nearly off the map to the east.*

1977), and judging by several graphs such as those published by the National Academy of Sciences (1975), the temperature of the northern hemisphere was probably depressed about 1.5°C. Until better evidence is found a figure of 200 km westward displacement per 1°C of global climatic change will be assumed (300 km ÷ 1.5°C).

Figure 11.3 illustrates the movement of the 700-mm precipitation contour based on this factor. Projections are made in the illustration for the warmest and coldest episodes of the Holocene, thus marking the range of variation of the prairie–forest ecotone during the present geological epoch. As can be seen, the model estimates a considerable range of climatic unrest over the last 10,000 years. These quantities can be manipulated mathematically through a series of equations (Gunn 1977a) and thus can be incorporated into a simulation of the affect of global climate on local weather systems and ultimately on culture.

Estimates were also made of the amount of movement caused in the subtropical flow by comparing the very cold winter of 1976–1977 with previous years. This vector of climatic change was also parametrized in a series of equations and incorporated into the simulation (Gunn 1977a).

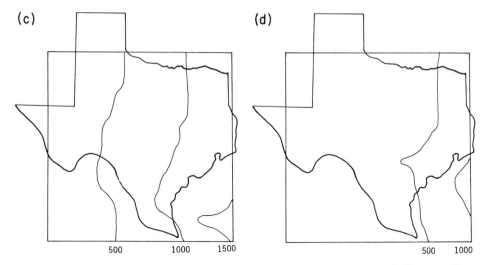

Figure 11.4 illustrates a series of runs of the climate simulation. Their presentation is intended to acquaint the reader with the implications of the weather system as it is now being modeled. Figure 11.4a is an estimate of Pleistocene conditions at an average northern hemisphere temperature of 11°C. Climate is much wetter as evidenced by the fact that the 700-mm contour does not appear on the map. The accuracy of the estimate is supported by work on paleosols by Sorenson, Mandel and Wallis (1976) and by the recovery of phytoliths indicative of pine forests from a Paleo-Indian site in San Antonio (Robinson, Gunn and Hester n.d.).

Figures 11.4b–11.4d illustrate maps for 14°C (Holocene low), 15°C (present conditions), and 17°C (Holocene high). West Texas becomes progressively drier as global temperatures rise. During the warmest point in the Altithermal maximum most of Texas is estimated to be arid.

Cultural Variability and Processes

Chronology and Analogy

The Central Texas Archaic has long been regarded as a very enduring and stable Holocene adaptation to a prairieland environment. Recent studies confirm that culture development in the normal sense of transformation from primitive to technologically complex is indeed absent. There is every reason to believe, however, that south and central Texas are environmentally unstable and required numerous adaptive responses on the part of the people who occupied the area prehistorically. Some of the evidence for this climatic instability is accumulated in the report by Gunn and Mahula (1977) and constitutes the empirical background for what follows.

Adaptive responses to climatic instability appear to range over the spectrum of culture typical of the North American Eastern and Western Archaic traditions. Weir (1976) analyzed systemically the Central Texas Archaic which he defines temporally as a period from 700 to 8000 BP. It is divided into five phases (Table 11.1). Weir's phases are bounded periods of relative systemic stability separated by episodes of relative instability and adaptive adjustment. The goal of the investigation was to study "the complexity of those subsystems that regulated stability and effected change in the five phases of the Central Texas Archaic (Weir 1976:5)." Each phase is a period of stability fostered by negative feedback.

Weir's systemization of group dynamics is developed in terms of Birdsell's demographic equilibrium processes including density, communications, and local group equilibria. The trajectory of culture change in central Texas is determined by Weir to move from unstructured, unspecialized groups in the earliest times to a highly structured and specialized cultural configuration in the Round Rock phase (2600–4200 BP) (Weir 1976:120). Subsequently, unstructured, unspecialized cultures return. The cultural trajectory appears to be heavily influenced by climatic change as it closely follows climatic variability from the Altithermal maximum to the Neoboreal minimum and finally the Roman–Medieval climatic maximum (Gunn and Weir 1976).

Until evidence is presented to the contrary, I would like to think that during periods of warmer global temperatures the ecotonal biotic provinces and accompanying cultural adaptations move eastward. During cooler periods eastern species and their adaptations move westward. To simplify the problems of dealing with these two contrasting trends the area will be treated as if it were composed of two biocultural zones. Analysis by Valdez (n.d.) shows that when the biota of Blair's zones (Figure 11.2) are reduced by multivariate procedures and plotted, the Austroriparian and Texan zones (wet provinces to the east) are very close together and form a set which contrasts strongly with the drier ectonal provinces to the west. Since the grosser characteristics of a cultural territory determine the nature of the

TABLE 11.1
Weir's Central Texas Phases

		Dates (BP)
	Late prehistoric	400–1500
Central	Twin Sisters	7000–2000
	San Marcos	1800–2800
Texas	Round Rock	2600–4200
	Clear Fork	4000–5000
Archaic	San Geronimo	4500–8000
	Paleo-Indian	7000–?

cultural adaptations to it, I will assume that Texas is composed of two culturally relevant biotic supraprovinces, the Humid and Arid zones (Figure 11.2).

Cultural adaptations to these zones are taken to be analogs of the Desert Archaic and the eastern Woodland Archaic traditions. Without being too specific, I suggest Steward's (1938) Great Basin Shoshone as an example of western nomadism and Winters' (1969) Riverton Culture as an example of the Woodland Archaic. Although both adaptations involve annual movement to subsistence resources, the Woodland adaptation is more of a transhumant process whereas the western tradition is clearly a nomadic seasonal round. Archaeologically the arid adaptation should be evidenced by numerous small sites of about equal size. The Woodland sites would be found to contrast in size between permanent settlements and seasonal, transhumant collecting stations. The analogy between microhabitats in ecotonal Texas and the Great Basin is quite close. The riparian zones along river valleys in Texas provide resources similar to those of the piñon–juniper forests of the basin. Intervening uplands are similar to more desertic basin environments.

Cultural Adaptations— Negative Population Equilibrium

The nomadic and transhumant processes associated with these analogs may be taken to imply different philosophical approaches to coping with the environment and the accumulation of goods resulting in striking differences in the amount of occupation debris and observability in the archaeological record. Relative to the desert tradition, recent anthropological studies of nomadic hunters and gatherers have virtually reversed everything that has previously been thought about them. Empirical studies such as those by Lee and Devore (1973) show that they are not hard-pressed victims of the food quest. Perhaps more important for the Western-biased observer of the archaeological record, Sahlins (1972) has demonstrated that they have an economic world view which is diametrically opposed to our own and which is founded in the realities of their technology, population density, and resource availability. That economic philosophy is most readily summed up as, "do as little as you can and carry as little as you can with you." This sounds like the Western definition of laziness but in nomadic cultures it is a viable strategy for survival which the most ambitious people cleverly follow. Sahlins thinks the concept of laziness was probably a Neolithic invention, perhaps the first Madison-Avenue-style advertising campaign to increase worker efficiency. Since it is a labor-inducing philosophy, it is more amenable to sedentary cultures where goods are brought to camp rather than the camp being taken to the goods.

Primitive philosophy implies a different attitude toward population density. It has always been assumed that primitive adaptive systems, like our own, are continually pressing against the carrying capacity of the land. No little effort has been expended in the search for an elusive formula which will estimate how much below carrying capacity primitives typically maintain themselves in order to avoid problems of overpopulation. Perhaps the effort is ill spent. In the light of the "least work" principle a number of recent studies make sense. For instance, Wobst (1974) has shown that the "magic number 25," which seems to be an almost ubiquitous band size, represents the minimum demographic unit which can be expected to survive stochastic fluctuations in demographic variables. The population level that primitives typically maintain, then, is as low as possible without getting caught by the "fickle finger" of stochastic, demographic fate. The reasons are quite tenable within the context of hunter–gatherer philosophy. The more people there are in a group, the harder everyone has to work. This is easily demonstrated by the fact that the more people there are in a band the sooner the resources are used up around a camp and the sooner everyone has to move to a new location. Therefore, there is reason in keeping population of the band to a bare minimum.

In the case of primitive cultures, then, the equilibrium is not between carrying capacity and population. The equilibrium is maintained between band demography and chance, a negative equilibrium. They gamble with the fate of the band rather than the fate of individuals who would starve if the carrying capacity were overrun. The gamble seems remarkably palatable when it is considered that bands are loosely organized and if a band proves inviable, its members simply make an extended visit to relatives in other bands. As Birdsell (1973) has pointed out, their loyalty is with the dialectic tribe rather than the band. Yellen's ethnoarchaeological observations among the !Kung strongly support a coherent dialectical tribe with very fluid band composition (1977:69–73).

It seems to me that his contrast between a strategic, negative population equilibrium for primitive cultures and a positive population equilibrium for developed cultures has the potential to bring some order to the chaos of thinking about primitive society. It also explains the relative scarcity of debris in arid-period location sites, and it suggests a relative constancy to the rate of accumulation since a lower bound is the controlling element.

Carrying Capacity and Organizational Complexity

Although this scheme tends to downplay the role of carrying capacity, it cannot be left out of the picture. We can surmise that high-carrying capacity for primitives increases the number of people that can be clustered in an area without causing more work for everyone.

The potential for increased density can be exploited in two ways, by logical analysis. The route taken distinguished between primitive and developed approaches to social organization and debris accumulation. Increasing density can be effected by packing bands closer together in smaller territories. This is the primitive approach, but since groups are still nomadic and small, no notable change in debris is apparent in a given site. The second alternative is by increasing the size of the band while keeping the area of the territory the same. This approach requires a distinctive philosophical outlook because a larger number of people in the same organization automatically implies a more complex social structure to maintain order in all aspects of life. As Flannery (1972) has pointed out, elaboration of the social structure requires that everyone pay overhead to ceremonialism or to those appointed to positions of power. The effect on archaeological sites is to increase the rate of debris accumulation both by sheer weight of numbers and by the increased use of material goods as symbols of status.

So far as we can determine, central Texas was generally occupied by people of the Western Archaic tradition except for periods of lower global temperature. During these times the eastern woodlands, and presumably eastern woodland-like people, spread westward. Exceptionally large sites containing quantities of elaborate lithic types during the cold and humid Round Rock phase of the Archaic support this presumption (Weir 1976; Prewitt n.d.; Gunn and Weir 1976) and by inference support a more "complex" cultural organization.

Operationalization

It is helpful to think of two zones and two types of cultural adaptations. As I have shown, the more evident functions of each system can be flow-charted to incorporate subsistence strategy, cognitive maps, monitoring variables, and so on (Gunn 1977a). However, it would facilitate the task of simulation if the two types were thought of as extremes of a spectrum and the differences between extremes defined as continuous variation on a set of variables. Yellen has pointed out that, rather than typologically, the difference between sites can be managed as a continuum from briefly occupied, one-task sites to more complex sites occupied for longer periods (1977:77–80). Nomadic–sedentary behavior, then, can be measured as an "occupation intensity index" with nomadism rating low and sedentism high. The longer a site is occupied the higher the probability any given task will be performed leaving the resultant debris.

In keeping with this principle a series of variables were defined which incorporate, as far as possible, most of the current theory on social organization and subsistence strategy of hunters and gatherers. Each variable is subject either directly or indirectly to climatic change and to feedback mechanisms. Ultimately the variables are combined to define the probability of camping at a given location in a study area.

The *environmental* variables are global climate, precipitation, and geomorphology. Global climate is an average temperature curve for the northern hemisphere during the Holocene adapted from one composed for the National Academy of Sciences (1975) from several indicators. From this curve precipitation is calculated as was explained earlier. Local climate is defined as humid if precipitation is above 700 mm/year, arid if below that figure.

A geomorphological transect from swamp to hilltop was defined in nine sections (Table 11.2). An area of 134 km² was selected for study from along the south bank of the Pedernales River in central Texas. The area was selected because it encompassed the Hop Hill locality, a site surveyed and excavated by the author under the auspices of the Texas Parks and Wildlife Department (Gunn and Mahula 1977). The study area was bounded on the east and west by perennial tributaries of the Pedernales and to the south by high hills. The area was gridded into 250-m² "camp sites." Each camp site was coded according to its location on a geomorphic transect. (Any study area could be entered.)

Although landforms remain the same through time, the microhabitats they support change with climate. It is at this point that environment overlaps with *subsistence strategy*. Here, subsistence strategy is defined in terms of how a group apportions its year among microhabitats (Table 11.2). This scheduling is apportioned according to some general perceptions of how ethnohistoric Texas Indians exploited the environment and may be refined later. Arid habitations are more generally in the uplands, apparently to gather the products of cactus and for visibility during the search for game. Humid occupations tend to be in valley floodplains where swollen streams provide rich aquatic and riparian resources.

Several variables were defined on the basis of research into the habits of Texas Indians by Campbell and analyzed by Gunn *et al.* (n.d.). Regression coefficients between precipitation and territorial size, population density,

TABLE 11.2
Codes for Campsite Cells

		Probabilities	
		Arid	Humid
1.	Swamp	.01	.02
2.	River floodplain	.15	.30
3.	Stream floodplain (perennial)	.15	.30
4.	Valley slope	.10	.02
5.	Upland margin	.30	.01
6.	Upland plain	.20	.30
7.	Creek (intermittent)	.01	.02
8.	Upland slope	.01	.02
9.	Hilltop	.07	.01

number of bands in a territory, and number of camps in a year are shown in Table 11.3. The expected number of camps a year is incorporated into the simulation as a part of subsistence strategy. Shorter terms of stay in arid regions are assumed to reflect scarcer resources. Territory and number of bands in the territory are used to define *social structure*. Also, since a study area will typically be only part of a band territory it is used to determine the probability of the band being in the study area during a given year.

Several *feedback* mechanisms are defined, mainly in terms of a cognitive map of the area. As more time elapses since a band occupied a camp, the probability of their remembering it goes down. If a band dies out, however, the simulation "forgets" the cognitive map and all remembrances of the area are lost until another band rebuilds its knowledge of the study area.

The variable "recovery" accounts for a period subsequent to a visit while the biotic resources recover their abundance. This process is generally slower in arid regions than humid ones. This, too, is calculated on the basis of years since the last visit.

To ensure occasional visits to the study area a "patrol" factor is maintained. It increases the probability of a chance visit as the length of time since a camp was established increases. The process is analogous to conservation procedures observed among North American Indian groups who visited parts of their territory only occasionally to allow time for game to replenish.

The interaction of the variables is illustrated in Figure 11.5 and the end product is to test the likelihood of a band occupying a camp, given its climate, landform, and history of habitation. Once a habitation is established the amount of debris accumulated is calculated on a relative basis as determined by the nomadic–sedentary characteristics of the adaptation. In this preliminary study it was estimated that a sedentary population would be responsible for 10 times the debris of a nonsedentary camp.

Since a full discussion of the distributional properties of the simulation variables is longer than the space available here, a fuller description will appear under another title (Gunn, Barbour and Wadington n.d.).

TABLE 11.3
Regression Estimates for Balcones Cultures Cline and Modeled Global–Local Climatic Relationships in Central Texas (Pedernales River)

Dependent variable	Independent variable	Regression coefficient	Intercept
Territory	Precipitation	−9.02	16,265.0
Population density	Precipitation	.87	495.0
Number of bands	Precipitation	−.0042	11.72
Number of camps	Precipitation	−.029	51.5
Precipitation	Global temperature	−272.7	4718.2

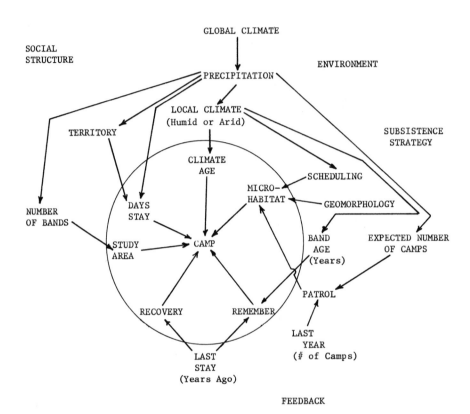

PROBABILITY OF A CAMP

(At a Given Location)

FIGURE 11.5 *Concepts and quantities which enter into the probability of a camp being occupied. Probabilities inside the circle are final products of concepts and calculations represented outside the circle. Probability of camp is the product of all the probabilities within the circle.*

Figure 11.6 shows the approximate character of the digitized landform surface submitted to the simulation. The Pedernales River flows from west to east across the top of the map. Valley slopes are shaded to distinguish the alluvial floodplain from the upland margins. High hills and upland slopes line the south end of the map. Between the hills and river are broad, flat uplands.

Figure 11.7 is the final probability surface from a 9500-year simulation run. The climate trajectory was that of the Holocene from 10,000 to 500 BP. During this time over 73,000 camps were made, leaving about 121,000 debris units. The average number of camps per year in the study area was 5.

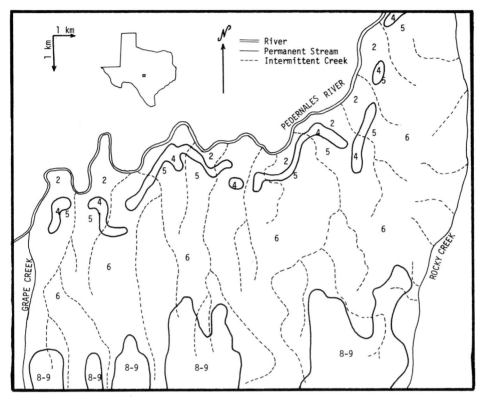

FIGURE 11.6 *Landform surface of the study area. The horizontal and vertical scales differ due to printer character and line size. The study area is divided into 2100 "camp sites" of 250 m². The numbers are landform types listed in Table 11.2.*

The area was visited by 110 bands or village groups. The average age of the bands at the time of their disappearance was 84 years. The probability surface suggests that perennial tributaries of the Pedernales and upland margins immediately behind the valley slopes received the highest concentration of density units. The second most popular habitats are the valley alluvium and the upland slopes.

Heavy occupation on the upland margins probably reflects the vast stretches of time during which nomads roamed the region. Relatively dense occupation in the river valley is a product of less frequent visits by transhumant groups who left much more dense concentrations of refuse. Few locations in the flat uplands escaped occupation or were only visited a few times; they were generally occupied a few hundred times.

It should be kept in mind that the probability surface reflects the density of occupation expected in camp sites, given the parameter setting explained earlier, and free of the effects of erosion. Erosion will eventually have to be

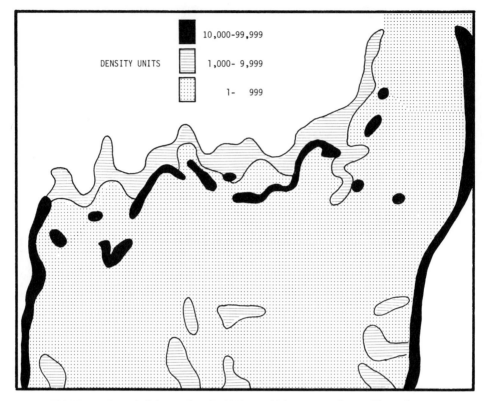

FIGURE 11.7 *Probability surface for 9500-year Holocene simulation. The various textures represent the frequency of density units. One density unit was accumulated for an arid adaptation site, 10 for humid sites; 73,000 sites produced 121,000 density units over the period of study.*

modeled for the simulation to reflect reality. The frequency of sites in upland environments after about 3000 BP and their infrequency before that time suggest a major erosional event.

Conclusion

The benefit expected from this exercise is that as our data accumulate from various projects in the area, we will be able to test the underlying model against distributions in limited study areas. The model will be adjusted until an acceptable fit is obtained between the characteristics of the simulated occupation probability surface and observed data. The ultimate version of the program should produce a surface which resembles a full space–time map of human occupation in the central Texas region. The model itself will be an explanation of prehistoric behavior and the products of the simulation may be valuable aids in reconstructing past settlement patterns, even in areas now archaeologically destroyed by construction, in projecting costs of survey and excavation, and in cultural resource management.

Acknowledgments

Thomas R. Hester, Colin Renfrew, Kenneth Cooke, T. N. Campbell, John Barbour, and James Wadington provided helpful suggestions on the content of this chapter. The University of Texas at San Antonio Computer Center provided time and facilities for development and running the simulation program which is written in Fortran IV. Jack Frost, Director of the Computer Center, was extremely helpful in providing advice on how to manage a program which takes about 4 hr of CPU time to wend its way through the Holocene.

References

Bielser, Sarah and Gunn, Joel, 1977, Atmosphere and Modern Climate, In: *Hop Hill: Culture and Climatic Change in Central Texas*. Center for Archaeological Research, The University of Texas at San Antonio, Special Report 5.

Birdsell, Joseph B., 1973, A basic demographic unit, *Current Anthropology* 4, 337–356.

Blair, W. Frank, 1950, The biotic provinces of Texas, *The Texas Journal of Science* 2(1), 93–117.

Bryson, Reid A., 1966, Air masses, streamlines, and the Boreal forest. *Geographical Bulletin* 8(3), 228–269.

Bryson, Reid A. and Murray, Thomas J., 1977, *Climates of Hunger*, Madison, University of Wisconsin Press.

Caldwell, Joseph, 1958, Trend and tradition in the prehistory of the Eastern United States, *American Anthropological Association* Memoir 88.

Canby, Thomas Y., 1977, The year the weather went wild, *National Geographic* 152(6), 799–828.

de la Pena, Jose Enrique, 1975, *With Santa Anna in Texas*. Translated and edited by Carmen Perry. Texas A & M University Press, College Station.

Eddy, John A., 1977, The case of the missing sunspots, *Scientific American* 236(5), 80–92.

Flannery, Kent V., 1972, The cultural evolution of civilizations, *Annual Review of Ecology and Systematics* 3.

Gunn, Joel, 1977a, An enviro-cultural system for Central Texas, In: *Hop Hill: Culture and Climatic Change in Central Texas,* Center for Archaeological Research, The University of Texas at San Antonio, Special Report 5.

Gunn, Joel, 1977b, Idiosyncratic chipping style as a demographic indicator, In: Hill, J. and Gunn, J. (eds.), *The Individual in Prehistory*, Academic Press, New York.

Gunn, Joel and Frank Weir, 1976, Took kit hypotheses: A case of numerical induction, *Lithic Technology* 5(3), 131–135.

Gunn, Joel and Royce Mahula, 1977, *Hop Hill: Culture and Climatic Change in Central Texas*. Center for Archaeological Research, The University of Texas at San Antonio, Special Report 5.

Gunn, Joel, John Barbour and James Wadington, n.d., A Probability Surface for Site Distributions of Nomadic Cultures. (In preparation.)

Gunn, Joel, and Thomas R. Hester, n.d., Ethnohistoric Texas Populations: Estimates from

Remnant Cultural Substrate in South Texas. Center for Archaeological Research, The University of Texas at San Antonio. (In preparation.)

Hester, Thomas R., *et al.*, 1977, *An Archaeological Survey of the Radium Springs Area, Southern New Mexico,* Thomas R. Hester (ed.), Center for Archaeological Research, The University of Texas at San Antonio, Archaeological Survey Report 26.

Lee, Richard B. and Irven Devore (eds.), 1973, *Man the Hunter.* Aldine Publishing Company, Chicago.

Matthews, Samuel W., 1976, What's happening to our climate? *National Geographic* 150(9), 576–615.

National Academy of Sciences, 1975, *Understanding Climatic Change: A Program for Action,* Washington, D.C.

Prewitt, Elton R., 1974, Late Archaic Occupations at the Loeve-Fox site, In: *The Texas Archaic,* T. R. Hester (ed.), Center for Archaeological Research, The University of Texas at San Antonio, Special Report 2.

Prewitt, Elton R., n.d., Roger's Springs: A Burned Rock Midden in Central Texas. (In press.)

Robinson, Ralph, Joel Gunn and Thomas R. Hester, n.d., Phytolith Analysis of Soils from Saint Mary's Hall Paleo-Indian Site. In: *Saint Mary's Hall* by Thomas R. Hester. (In preparation.)

Sahlins, Marshall, 1972, *Stone Age Economics,* Aldine-Atherton, Chicago.

Sanchez, W. A. and J. E. Kutzbach, 1974, Climate of the American tropics and subtropics in the 1960s and possible comparisons with climatic variations of the last millennium, *Quaternary Research* 4(2), 128–135.

Sorenson, Curtis J., Rolfe D. Mandel and John C. Wallis, 1976, Changes in bioclimate inferred from paleosols and paleohydrologic evidence in East-Central Texas, *Journal of Biogeography* 3, 141–149.

Steward, J. H., 1938, Basin-plateau aboriginal sociopolitical groups, *Bureau of American Ethnology, Bulletin* 120.

Thomas, David Hurst, 1974, An empirical test for Steward's model of Great Basin settlement patterns, *American Antiquity* 38(2), 155–176.

Valdez, Fred, n.d., *Biodistributions of Texas,* Center for Archaeological Research, The University of Texas at San Antonio. (In preparation.)

Weir, Frank A., 1976, *The Central Texas Archaic,* Unpublished Ph.D. dissertation, Washington State University, Department of Anthropology.

Winters, Howard D., 1969, The Riverton Culture, *Illinois Archaeological Survey, Monograph* 1.

Wobst, H. Martin, 1974, Boundary conditions for Paleolithic social systems: A simulation approach, *American Antiquity* 39(2), 147–178.

Wright, June and Joel Gunn, 1977, World Climatic Parameters, In: *Hop Hill: Culture and Climatic Change in Central Texas,* Center for Archaeological Research, Special Report 5.

Yellen, John E., 1977, *Archaeological Approaches to the Present,* Academic Press, New York.

12

ALBERT J. AMMERMAN
L. L. CAVALLI-SFORZA

The Wave of Advance Model for the Spread of Agriculture in Europe[1]

We first became interested in the wave of advance model in 1971 while working on the question of the spread of early farming in Europe (Ammerman and Cavalli-Sforza 1971; Ammerman and Cavalli-Sforza 1973). Since that time, we have extended our study of the model both in terms of its application to archaeological contexts and its implications for human biology (e.g., Menozzi *et al.* 1978). In this chapter we would like to review some of the developments along archaeological lines, especially as they related to the basic interpretation of the model. It is worth commenting briefly on the nature of models: as conceptual constructs, they provide us with a means of describing complex events in a concise and structured way. More specifically, they take as their premise a need to simplify complex events or situations in order to place them within a predictive framework. It is this framework, in turn, which offers a means for evaluating how well a given model—in terms of behavior expected under the model—fits observations drawn from events that have actually occurred. In the case of the wave of advance model, population growth and local migratory activity would be seen as producing a diffusionary process which takes the form of a population wave expanding outward at a steady radial rate. As explained subsequently, the model also specifies the set of quantitative relationships that are considered to hold among these three variables (i.e., the rate of growth, the variance of the migratory activity, and the velocity of the spread), thus establishing a predictive framework which can be used for evaluating the adequacy of the model.

[1] The research reported in this chapter was supported in part by grants from the N.I.H. (5 R01GM20467), N.S.F. (BNS76-15095), and E.R.D.A. (EY-76-03-0326).

275

It can be seen in retrospect that there was a major gap in the repertoire of models available to the archaeologist for explaining cases of diffusion involving population movements. Terms such as migration and colonization, which we now see as having been all too often invoked in the earlier prehistoric literature, tend to have connotations of movement over some distance, a planned expedition, and a basic change in cultural context. In addition, attention was usually directed more toward the "effects" of the colonists in taking up their new place of residence than toward the processes or "causes" at home that were responsible for their departure. There was really no adequate model for describing situations where movements were over short distances for the most part (e.g., taking the form of the relocation of settlements to adjacent, unoccupied land) and where the cumulative result of many such movements was a slow and continuous form of expansion. In such a case, it would be possible for those "moving" to maintain a continuity in their social contacts and also in cultural context. The wave of advance model makes its contribution toward filling this gap by suggesting how local processes such as population growth can produce what in some respects is a form of colonization without colonists.

The Original Problem

By the mid-1960s, a sufficient number of radiocarbon dates had become available so that there was the possibility of having an estimate of the time of "arrival" of farming in many parts of Europe. Various attempts were made at collecting these data (e.g., Clark 1965), but no real effort was made in terms of exploring this information in a more analytical way. The problem that we initially turned to was that of trying to measure the rate of spread of early farming in Europe. This was done with the thought in mind that a rate measurement, even as a first approximation, might provide some new insight into the processes involved in the spread. It is worth recalling that there is little or no evidence for the local domestication (which would imply the exploitation of wild forms of the plants at the start of the process) in different parts of Europe of cereals such as emmer wheat (*Triticum diococcum*) and barley (*Hordeum distichum* and *Hordeum vulgare*). These cereals are generally considered to have been domesticated first in the Near East (Zohary 1969; Renfrew 1969; Van Zeist 1976) and subsequently introduced into Europe, where they are regularly recovered at early farming sites. In the original analysis, which was based on some 50 dated sites, regression techniques were used for measuring the rate. A detailed account of this work is given in the article by Ammerman and Cavalli-Sforza (1971).[2] The results of

---

[2] Since calibration curves do not extend back far enough to cover the earlier dates in the analysis (Olsson 1970), the dates employed are those cited in years BP in *Radiocarbon*. Only

the analysis indicated that there appeared to be a fairly regular pattern to the spread over most of Europe and yielded a rate of about 1 km/year or 25–30 km per generation. It should be emphasized that these figures represent average values or central tendencies for the spread as a whole. A more refined technique for studying the pattern and rate of spread was developed in 1973 and 1974. This involved the drawing of a series of isochrons, lines representing equivalent times, on the map of Europe. The computer-generated lines were drawn on the basis of a fitting procedure that operated directly on a geographic array of dated sites. One advantage of this approach is that the attribution of centers of origin for the spread (something required by the regression approach) can be avoided. It also provides a better reflection of regional variations in the rate of spread: this can be seen in the pattern of spacing between the isochrons on the map with the lines, for example, running closer together when the rate is slower. The maps made in 1974 were based on some 80 dated sites and revealed much the same picture as the earlier study (Cavalli-Sforza 1974:88; Menozzi et al. 1978:790).[3] Perhaps the most striking finding is the slowness of the overall rate, which carries a number of implications for the interpretation of the spread. Another feature of interest, especially with regard to the application of the wave of advance model, is the suggestion of regularity—see in terms of the spacing between the isochrons in the mapping approach—in the spread over different parts of Europe.

In turning to explanations of how this spread occurred, two contrasting modes of interpretation have traditionally been advanced. One of these is stimulus diffusion which would involve the passing of domesticated strains and information about farming techniques from one group to the next without the geographic displacement of the groups. The other is what we have called demic diffusion where the spread of the new economy would be seen as linked with population movements of some kind. Without going into an extended discussion of these two lines of explanation and the range of models included under each one, it is worth noting that these two modes as hypotheses need not be regarded as mutually exclusive. In fact, one of the more productive research strategies here is probably that of trying to evaluate the relative importance of the two within a given regional setting. But what is needed before this can be attempted is the introduction of much

---

dates with a standard deviation of 200 years or less were used for the rate measurement. As more dates become available, it is probably best to avoid the use of dates from cave sites where contamination is more likely to occur and anomalous dates appear more often to be encountered.

[3] Recently, we have been able to generate an isochron map of Europe based on a set of some 40 Late Mesolithic sites serving as estimates for the "end" of a strictly hunting and gathering way of life in different parts of Europe. The patterns in this map are in agreement with and complementary to those seen in the spread of early farming map. The two areas of the farming map where further study would seem to be called for are the western Mediterranean and the eastern part of the Soviet Union.

more specific models, each having its own set of well-defined implications. This is the point at which a model such as the wave of advance model makes its entry. In addition to the rate measurement itself, another factor that was instrumental in directing our attention to the model was the observation that changes in population level or density are often held to be associated with the transition from an economy based on hunting and gathering to one based on food production. This is a subject that will receive further discussion in the section on population growth.

The Model

The wave of advance model is concerned with describing situations in which processes of diffusion and growth take place simultaneously. For most of us, it is far from obvious on intuitive grounds alone what form the outcome of such an interaction should take. The model was first put forward by Fisher (1937), who was interested in the problem of the spread of an advantageous gene and had the insight of describing the spread in terms of an advancing wave front (Figure 12.1). Fisher gave a solution for the stationary form of the wave front for the case of the diffusion of an advantageous gene in a one-dimensional habitat. D. G. Kendall (1948) subsequently gave, by another mathematical approach, a model for the spread of a population growing exponentially and with the diffusion process taking place in a two-dimensional space. This work was extended by Skellam (1951), who developed a formulation of the model in which population growth was treated in a logistic manner. Following Skellam's formulation, the rate of advance of the wave front ρ is given by

$$\rho = \sigma\sqrt{2\alpha}$$

where σ is the standard deviation of the local migratory activity and α is the growth rate in the exponential treatment of population growth or the initial growth rate in the logistic mode of population increase (for an outline of the mathematical formulation of the model see the appendix in Ammerman and

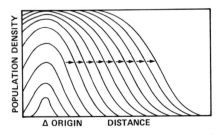

FIGURE 12.1 *R. A. Fisher's (1937) conception of the wave of advance.*

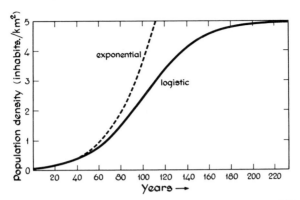

FIGURE 12.2 *Population growth curves. The same growth rate (α = .039) is used for both the exponential and logistic curves.*

Cavalli-Sforza 1973). It should be mentioned that this formula represents an approximate solution for the asymptotic velocity of the leading edge of the wave front. The analytical approach to the solution of the differential equation involved in the formulation of the model presents some difficulty.[4] More recently, Skellam (1973:79) indicates how the problem can be approached numerically by replacing the differential equation with an appropriate finite difference equation. Computer runs made using this approach offer support for the equation just given.

It is useful to comment on the treatment of the two components, population growth and local migratory activity, which determine the rate of spread in the model. In the case of a population growing exponentially, there would be a steady acceleration in population size N over time t. The rate of increase would be described by the equation $dN/dt = \alpha N$, where α is again the growth rate (see Figure 12.2). It is usually more realistic in ecological terms (at least as a first approximation) to consider that the pattern of growth in biological populations follows a sigmoid or logistic curve with the pace of growth being relatively high at the start and progressively slowing down as a saturation level in terms of the population numbers in an area is approached. Here the growth rate is given by the equation

$$\frac{dN}{dt} = \alpha N(1 - \frac{N}{N_{max}})$$

where N_{max} is the maximum population size or the carrying capacity. As far as the velocity of the wave front is concerned, the parameter of importance in the logistic treatment of growth is not so much the upper limit to popula-

[4] Aronson and Weinberger (1975) provide a recent discussion of the stationary properties of the wave front.

tion size as the initial growth rate or the rate applying in those areas in which the wave front is currently advancing. The potential for growth in human populations (excluding emigration) is about 4% per year as a maximum rate. A growth rate falling in the range between 1 and 2% would seem to be a more reasonable one to expect for actively growing human populations on the basis of what is known about fertility and mortality schedules from the study of contemporary populations (e.g., Keyfitz and Flieger 1971; Coale 1972). To gain a better sense of what such rates mean over time, it is helpful to translate them into the amount of time that it would take a population to double in size. A rate of 3% per year would imply, for example, a doubling time of 23 years, whereas a rate of 1% would require 69 years. It is also convenient to view increasing population size in the model in terms of changing population density. In fact, one way of defining the leading edge of the wave front is as the area in which dynamic changes in density are being experienced. Under the logistic treatment of growth, those areas well behind the advancing front would have at most moderate rates of growth and not experience major changes in density level over time. Most of the population growth at any one point in time would be taking place in what might be called the "growing fringe" or the pioneer zone where the wave front is passing.

For the migration component, the treatment follows the classical "random" one for diffusionary processes, which is mathematically the most tractable formulation to consider. The migratory activity is regarded as taking place continuously in time and space and with the distribution of migration distances conforming to a bidimensional "normal" or Gaussian surface, where the values of the z axis (see Figure 12.3a) give the probability that an individual located at the beginning at point 0 will reach a point having the coordinates (x_1, y_1) after a given time. It is usually more convenient for this distribution surface to be transformed into a distribution curve (Figure 12.3b) with the distances plotted along one axis. Here the distance of an individual from the starting point is given by $d = [(x_1^2 + y_1^2)]^{\frac{1}{2}}$. The shapes of the Gaussian surface and the transformed distribution curve are both

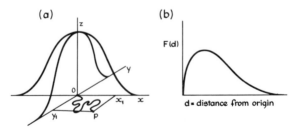

FIGURE 12.3 (a) Distribution of migration distances, assuming that migration is random in direction and occurs in a plane. For example, an individual starts his migration at the origin $(x = 0, y = 0)$, and after following an irregular path, arrives at point p (x_1, y_1) at a given time. The value $z = f(x, y)$ gives the frequency of individuals expected to be at point (x, y) at a given time t. (b) The distribution surface on the left has been transformed into a distribution curve (in one dimension), where distances from the origin are given by $d = [(x^2 + y^2)]^{\frac{1}{2}}$.

described by σ, the standard deviation of the "migration". Further consideration is given in a later section to the question of how well this mathematical treatment models what is actually happening in terms of migratory behavior in biological and cultural contexts.

It is of interest at this stage to indicate in a more tangible way what is meant by a migration distribution. In the case of living populations or situations for which good records on historical demography are available, we can construct frequency distributions of the distances between the places that people have lived at different points during their lifetime. One of the common ways of doing this involves a comparison of the residence of parents (where they were born) and their offspring (where their children were born). Such observed distributions, which refer to a basic time unit of one generation, can in turn be analyzed and compared with different models for migratory behavior such as the "normal" curve for random migration (Cavalli-Sforza 1962). Another example of the description of migration distributions, which is more directly related to the problem with which we are concerned, is provided by Stauder (1971) in his study of the Majangir, who practise a pioneer form of swidden agriculture in Ethiopa. Most of the movements are over distances of less than 10 miles and the migration distributions, which are broken down by age groups in the population, indicate that the older a person is, the further that person's residence is likely to be from his or her birthplace (Stauder 1971: 138).

In our case it is obviously difficult to obtain direct observations on this distribution of migration distances. There is, however, the possibility of estimating values of σ, the standard deviation of the distribution, indirectly from the formula for the velocity of the wave front by using the rate measurement for the spread and feasible values for the rate of population growth. By comparing such estimates of σ with observed estimates for contemporary and historical peasant populations, an indirect "test" of the model can be made in terms of internal consistency. Using a 2% per year rate for population growth, an estimate of 25 km per generation can be obtained for the standard deviation of the migration distribution (Ammerman and Cavalli-Sforza 1973:350). This compares favorably with estimates for recent peasant populations where values of σ fall mainly in the range between 10 and 20 km per generation. This suggests that there is a compatibility between these indirect estimates (drawn from ethnography) and the Fisher–Skellam model of population expansion. A more rigorous approach to testing the model will call for more direct estimates of parameters such as the rate of growth.

Population Growth

There has been extensive interest over the last decade in population growth and population pressure as variables in the explanation of cultural development and evolution. A recent review of this literature with a comprehensive bibliography is presented by Weiss (1976). From an ecological perspective, the shift from hunting and gathering economies to those based on food production permits higher levels of population density or a more efficient use of space in relation to population numbers. In demographic terms, population growth (excluding that due to the emigration of individuals from another population) depends on an increase in the net reproductive rate of a population. This may be the result of an improvement in mortality rates or an increase in fertility rates or a combination of the two. One possibility that has been regularly suggested is that increased food supplies made available by a farming economy (in contrast with the exploitation of seasonal resources under a hunting and gathering economy) may have reduced the mortality rates for some age classes in farming populations.[5] Another possibility is that changes in fertility patterns are associated with the transition from hunting and gathering to food production. Among populations of hunters and gatherers, a nomadic style of life which often involves the seasonal movement of campsites tends to encourage a relatively long spacing between births (e.g., Lee 1972). The more sedentary way of life under a farming economy permits a shorter birth interval, which implies that women can have more children during their reproductive years. There are many potential pathways between economic and social factors and vital events in a population (e.g., Hasan 1973) and the interactions between fertility and mortality schedules in situations in which growth is occurring can be complex (e.g., Coale 1972). If a choice between different alternatives is to be made, theoretical discussions of the different "mechanisms" of population growth have to be balanced with a more empirical orientation. This is clearly a demanding business in archaeology. In a recent paper (Ammerman *et al.* 1976), we have discussed various methodological aspects of the problem of estimating population growth in prehistory. Although this is not the place to attempt a summary of this work, it is worth commenting that growth is observed in several of the examples examined and that much can probably be done along the lines of describing growth patterns and estimating growth rates, once we have a better idea of the kinds of data required and an interest in developing more rigorous methods of analysis.

---

[5] Studies of comparative life expectation using skeletal data do not seem to reflect an improvement in mortality (Weiss 1973). However, one limitation here is that young children and potential changes in their mortality rates are not taken into consideration in the analysis. From a nutritional standpoint, this might be regarded as the age class that stands most to gain from the availability of cereals and possibly also milk products from domesticated animals. In the reconstruction of life tables using skeletal data, it is worth recalling a circular problem that is encountered as far as the study of growth rates is concerned. Assumptions about the growth rate of a population are required and the usual assumption made is that $r = 0$. If this convention is adopted in the case of a population that is, in fact, growing, the population will appear to have a worse mortality schedule than it actually has (Ammerman *et al.* 1976: Fig. 6).

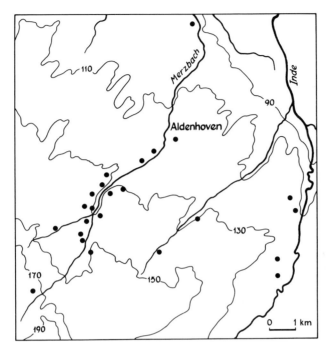

FIGURE 12.4 *Distribution of known Bandkeramik sites on the Aldenhoven Platte near Cologne. (After Eckert et al. 1971, 1972.)*

Instead of trying to estimate rates directly, another approach to the question of population growth involves looking at levels of population density. From the study of contemporary hunters and gatherers, it is held that the density levels of such populations are usually on the order of .1 persons per square kilometer or less (Lee and DeVore 1968). If substantially higher densities are indicated for early farming populations, then growth can be reasonably inferred. The best areas to explore this approach are those that have been systematically investigated on a large scale such as the Aldenhoven Platte near Cologne in Germany (e.g., Eckert *et al.* 1971, 1972; Farrugia *et al.* 1973). A large number of Bandkeramik settlements have been located here along a stream called the Merzbach (Figure 12.4). On the basis of some 160 Bandkeramik houses identified during excavations along a 2.5 km stretch of this stream, it is possible to make estimates of local population density on the order of 2–5 persons per km².[6] It is worth adding

[6] The following calculations can be carried out to obtain what amounts to a minimum average estimate of local density. A total of 160 houses were identified during the excavations at eight Bandkeramik settlements along a 2.5 km stretch of the Merzbach. If the assumption is made that a house was occupied on average for 25 years, some 4000 house-years would be represented in all. Taking the period of Bandkeramik occupation to last 700 years, this means

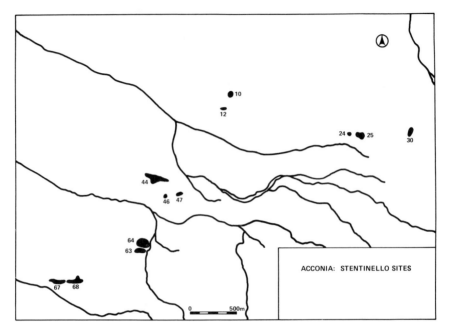

FIGURE 12.5 *Distribution of known Stentinello sites near the village of Acconia in Calabria. Stentinello is the name for the regional impressed ware pottery style found in Sicily and some areas of Calabria.*

that there is little archaeological evidence for Mesolithic or late hunter–gatherer settlement on the loess soils of the Aldenhoven Platte. Another example drawn from our own field work in Calabria in southern Italy is the dense pattern of early farming settlement observed in areas such as the one systematically surveyed near Acconia (Figure 12.5). What makes this example of particular interest is the occurrence of the settlements in a dune area, which would be considered a marginal area according to some ideas about the location and distribution of early farming sites in Europe (e.g., Jarman

that at any one time an average of 5.7 houses were being lived in. Assuming that each house was occupied by a family made up of an average of 5 people, there would be an average of 11.4 people living along each kilometer length of the stream. If the spacing between adjacent streams on the landscape is taken to be 6 km (i.e., there is a territorial band extending 3 km deep on each side of the stream), there would be an average density of 2 persons per square kilometer. The two main assumptions required for this calculation are the length of house life and the size of a household. If larger values would turn out to be more appropriate for either of them, the density would be correspondingly higher. In addition, it is unlikely that all of the houses were identified at the sites. If population growth is taking place during the period, then the density would be lower than the value cited during the early part of the period and somewhat higher during the latter half. If there is a pattern of cycling in occupation to allow for a fallow period (e.g., Soudsky and Pavlu 1972), then there would be periodic fluctuations in local population density with the values alternately rising above and falling below the one cited here.

and Bay-Petersen 1976: 185).[7] In the case of the Acconia area, it is likely from various lines of investigation that the light, sandy soils were actually the most suitable for early forms of subsistence farming. It is again worth noting that little evidence for Mesolithic settlement was encountered during the course of intensive survey work in the Acconia area, which would lend added weight to the interpretation of a major change in population level. Studies along these lines could provide us with a more detailed picture of settlement distributions and changes in population density in other parts of Europe.

Diffusionary Processes and Settlement Patterns

In the case with which we are concerned, movement basically takes place between settlements: these are the stepping-stones in the diffusionary process. As mentioned earlier, the treatment of migration in the model follows the classical one of so-called random diffusion. Although this is the most convenient formulation in mathematical terms, there are various questions that can be raised about how well this serves the purpose of describing what is happening in the prehistoric context. Several of these questions are briefly discussed under separate headings in this section. A fuller and more technical discussion of the relationship between the formulation of models and the interpretation of diffusionary processes in population biology is given by Skellam (1973).

1. The discrete treatment of time and space. In the mathematical formulation of the model, "movement" is considered to be taking place continuously in time and space. It is, however, evident in our case that a discrete treatment is more realistic. Individuals move from one settlement, which has a fixed location in space, to another settlement. With respect to time, movement does not go on continuously but occurs at intervals or periodically. Simulation studies provide one way of checking to see if there is a major divergence between what is found to occur under a discrete treatment and what is expected under the model with its continuous formulation. Such studies in which the same parametric values are employed in the two treatments indicate that a reasonable approximation is maintained. An example of a relatively simple simulation based on a discontinuous treatment

---

[7] In "site catchment" studies, dune areas are usually treated as being unsuited for farming or having nonarable soils (e.g., Vita-Finzi and Higgs 1970). The problem here would seem to be that the land classification scheme is a modern one where the outlook on production is market-oriented. Our own observations in Calabria suggest that cereals such as wheat, barley, oats, and maize can be grown quite easily (without irrigation) on dune soils: the yields are not high but they are sufficient for subsistence purposes and less work is required in the preparation of fields on these light soils. Reports on the survey work and excavations in the Acconia area are in preparation.

of time and space is shown in Figure 12.6 (Ammerman and Cavalli-Sforza 1973: 351-52). As one might expect, a somewhat larger value for the standard deviation of the migration distribution is required to achieve the same rate of advance under the discrete treatment, when the same rate of population growth is used. In the simulation work discussed by Skellam (1973: 79-81), it can be seen that a discrete treatment tends to "blunt" the leading edge of the wave front. The consequent slowing down of the velocity of the wave front can be interpreted as a stochastic effect in the zone that we have called the growing fringe. Due attention to stochastic effects in this zone is clearly needed in a realistic treatment of the diffusion process and the general implication is that the rate of advance is likely to be somewhat slower for a given pair of parameters (for the growth rate and the migration distribution) than would be expected under the continuous model.

2. Reflecting barriers.   In the mathematical formulation of the model, no direct consideration is given to barriers that might occur on the landscape. As Skellam (1973: Fig. 5) shows in an exercise where more than half of the area in the plane of movement was excluded by enclosing numerous small blocks within reflecting barriers, the large-scale results of diffusionary processes are independent of the fine texture of the "medium" in which diffusion occurs. In the case of large-scale barriers such as mountain ranges, constraints are placed on the plane of movement itself and local effects will depend in part on the configuration of the barrier.

3. Pattern of movement.   The classical treatment of diffusion relies on the assumption of statistical independence among the individual movements. For example, the direction of a given movement is not correlated with that of the preceding movement. In our case, there may well be a tendency toward outward or centrifugal movement, when the pattern of a large number of movements is examined. Skellam (1973: 68-70) discusses such a situation and describes how the properties of the diffusionary process are basically

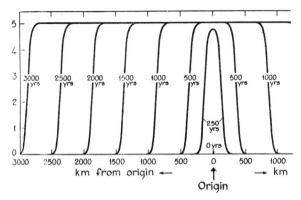

FIGURE 12.6 *Computer simulation of the wave of advance based on a discontinuous treatment of time and space (see Ammerman and Cavalli-Sforza 1973: 352).*

maintained but with an amplification of the variance of the migration component, which is linked with the degree of dependence exhibited. The implication here is that under the same frequency distribution of migration distances, a comparative increase in the velocity of the spread would be observed. An increase in velocity over what is expected on the basis of the standard deviation of the migration distribution can also occur in cases in which there is a departure from a normal distribution among the migration distances. An example would be distributions exhibiting leptokurtosis, which is a name used to describe the shape of a distribution having more items near the mean and at the tails than a normal distribution.

4. Induction of displacement.   The level of activity in a diffusionary process is influenced by the spatial framework in which the process operates. The underlying motivation for movement may involve either one of attraction or repulsion to certain places on the landscape or in the plane of movement. An archaeological example of a case in which repulsion operates would be that of swidden or slash-and-burn farming, where after a certain number of years of cultivation it is the practice to leave an area in a fallow state for a period of time before the land can be reoccupied. The people living at such a settlement are periodically subject to "repulsion" or forced to leave and in deciding on the place to relocate to may take account of which places are more or less attractive. In the case of permanent settlement or long-term occupation of sites, there would be a lower level of migratory activity (i.e., a lower proportion of the population would participate in moves during one generation). Another way of looking at the question of induction of displacement is in terms of heterogeneity in patterns of population density over the plane of movement, which represents a departure from the conditions envisaged under the general model. Density would tend to be low in places which are "repulsive" and high in those places considered "attractive" at a given time. The effects on the velocity of the diffusionary process will depend on the extent and degree of heterogeneity and can be incorporated in modified formulations of the process (Skellam 1973: 27-73).

Each of these topics calls attention to a potential line of divergence between the general model and its application in real world contexts. In some situations we may be able to adapt the mathematical model and make it more realistic. Some of the necessary conceptual extensions of the model may, however, be too complex for a mathematical formulation but will be amenable to study through the use of simulation techniques. A good starting point here is the careful study of settlement patterns. How sites are arrayed over the landscape conditions in a general way such things as the relative frequency of movements and the size of migration distances. We can obtain an intuitive sense of this if we contrast two kinds of settlement systems: (a) a dispersed one where there are many small sites (with only a few families living at each) which are located at relatively short distances from one another, and (b) a more aggregated system where many families live at any one site and the average distance between nearby settlements is larger (assuming roughly the same density level in the two cases). In the first case, population growth will take the form primarily of an increase in the number of new settlements. It will be difficult for a person living at a site to find a person that he or she can marry (i.e., a person of an appropriate age class belonging to the opposite sex, not having a consanguineous relationship, and not already married) at the same site. Marriage will usually require that one or both of the people change their residence. The level of migratory activity will be high in such a case. On the other hand, many of the movements will probably be over quite short distances. In some ways, archaeologists are not prepared on intuitive grounds to appreciate the fact that probably less than half of the people in such a settlement system experience their full sequence of vital events—birth, giving birth to and raising children, death—at a given site. This stems from a tendency to equate life histories with site histories. If we turn to the second system, there is likely to be much more in the way of equivalence between the two. Population growth can take the form of both an increase in the number of households at a settlement and an increase in the number of settlements on the landscape. In a large settlement, it is probably easier to find a mate within the same settlement and the level of migratory activity is subsequently lower. But when movement does occur, it will tend to be over longer distances. There is also a good chance that the shapes of the frequency distributions of migration distances will differ between the two kinds of systems. In the context of early farming in Europe, the settlement patterns of the Bandkeramik culture of central Europe would appear to reflect more the former system (Farruggia et al. 1973), whereas the mound sites of cultures going under various names in Greece and the Balkans would come closer to the latter. These two kinds of systems are put forward for purposes of exposition and represent in general terms two poles. There are no doubt other systems that can be identified and a much more detailed account of the two systems presented briefly here could be given. One of the ways of further exploring the details of such systems as they relate to economic, social, and demographic aspects of organization is provided by simulation studies.

Simulation Studies

In trying to work out the relationships between a model with a high degree of generality such as the wave of advance model and specific contexts, simulation studies serve in a sense as a heuristic middle ground. In the design and elaboration of a simulation study, our attention is drawn to assumptions implicit (yet often unrecognized) in the model and also to areas of prehistoric knowledge in need of further development. Simulation "runs" provide a chance to examine the patterns of interaction between variables in a given structural setting and thus a sense of the relative importance of the variables or their parametric values. Space is not available here to go into an extended discussion of the scope of simulation studies or to present a case study in any detail. It is perhaps most useful to present some examples of the output of simulation runs in order to illustrate the connections between this kind of work and the model. The examples are taken from a simulation study of Bandkeramik settlement patterns and more specifically from runs made using the so-called BANDK 2 simulation model, which is based on the concept of a shifting form of settlement occupation related to a swidden type of farming system (e.g., Soudsky and Pavlu 1972).[8] A detailed account of the design of this simulation study is given in a paper by Ammerman and Cavalli-Sforza (n.d.). The settlement pattern is considered to be characterized by a linear sequence of sites (as along a set of linked streams) with side branches at intervals to the main linear network. The site locations along the network take one of the three following states: (a) the location is occupied by a small village; (b) it is unoccupied and available for settlement; and (c) it is unoccupied and unavailable for settlement (i.e., the location was recently occupied and is now in a fallow state). At the start of a simulation run, several locations are occupied at one end of the network and the rest of the locations are available for occupation. The individual villages experience population growth according to a logistic treatment which is related to local levels of population density. The splitting off of a new village takes place whenever the growth of a given village reaches a certain size. A site location can only be occupied for a certain number of years and then passes through a fallow period of specified length. When the period of occupation comes to an end, relocation to a nearby available site location takes place.

Several examples of simulation runs using the BANDK 2 model are shown in Figure 12.7, where the position of the occupied settlement furthest from the starting end of the network is plotted against different times in the respective runs. Two main variables, the growth rate and the length of the occupation–fallow period, are allowed to vary in the four runs. It is evident that there is a faster rate of advance (rise in the curve) for the two runs based on the larger value for the growth rate, as we would expect according to the wave of advance model. A secondary effect related to the question of the

---

[8] More recently, we have been working on simulation studies based on the interpretation of Bandkeramik settlement patterns in terms of more permanent, single farmsteads that are periodically rebuilt (Farruggia et al. 1973). The topic of possible interactions between farming populations and local Mesolithic populations is not dealt with in this chapter (see Ammerman and Cavalli-Sforza 1973: 353). Newell (1970) discusses this question with regard to the typologies of lithic assemblages at Bandkeramik settlements in southeast Holland. Our knowledge of Late Mesolithic cultures and populations is unfortunately still quite limited for most parts of Europe.

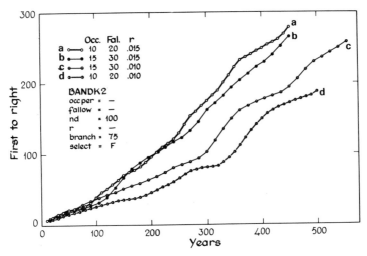

FIGURE 12.7 *Examples of BANDK 2 simulation runs. The position of the occupied site furthest from the starting end of the linear network (first to right) is shown for different times in the respective runs. The variables that are allowed to vary in the four runs presented here are the occupation period (Occ.), the fallow period (Fal.), and the growth rate (r). It is worth noting that the occupation period has the same ratio to the fallow period (1:2) in all four cases.*

discrete treatment of time is also suggested: the curves based on the longer combination of occupation and fallow periods run below those based on the shorter periods in which the same growth rate is used. This is probably due to the somewhat slower turnover time (or lower level of activity) of relocation in the former case. In Figure 12.8, migration distributions obtained during the course of a run (run c, based on the occupation period of 15 years and a growth rate of .010 in Figure 12.7) are shown for four different levels of local density, which is computed in terms of the relative proportion of site locations within a specific neighborhood of a given site location that are currently either occupied or in fallow. Distance is measured in terms of the number of site locations along the linear network that a village is required to move in making a relocation (with negative "distances" being in the direction of the starting point and positive ones in the direction of the advance). The pioneer zone would correspond to the area with a local density (ld) falling in the range between .00 and .25, where population growth is taking place most actively. It is interesting to note the progressive shifts in the migration distributions to shorter distances with an increasing level of local density. In the pioneer zone, the mode of the "positive" relocations is 9–10 site locations long. In those areas with high local densities (i.e., .76–1.00, where incidentally there is relatively little population growth), it is only 2–3 site locations long. One of the striking features of the four distributions taken as a whole is that only a relatively small proportion of the relocations are larger than 6 site locations in either direction. The examples presented in Figures

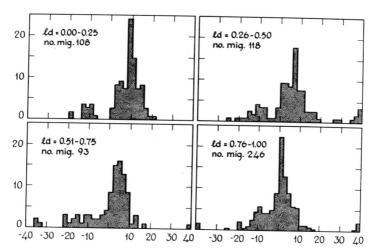

FIGURE 12.8 *Migration distributions for the third simulation run (Occ. = 15; r = .010) shown in Figure 12.7. The frequency distribution was accumulated over the period from time 316 through 451 during the run. The distributions are given in terms of relative frequencies for each of four levels of local density (see the text). Distance is measured in terms of the number of site locations along the linear network.*

12.7 and 12.8 indicate how an outward spread can be set up and maintained by local population growth and migratory activity operating within the context of a settlement system. Without going into the question of the evaluation of simulation models and the need for refining existing models and exploring new simulation models, it would seem to be clear that new insight into the general model and its application is provided by this line of investigation.

Acknowledgments

We would like to thank Juliana Hwang of the Department of Genetics at Stanford University for the preparation of the computer programs for the BANDK simulation study. We would also like to express our thanks to the University of Calabria and the Superintendent of Antiquities in Calabria for their collaboration with respect to the fieldwork conducted in Calabria.

References

Ammerman, A. J. and L. L. Cavalli-Sforza. 1971. Measuring the Rate of Spread of Early Farming in Europe. *Man* 6: 674–688.

Ammerman, A. J. and L. L. Cavalli-Sforza. 1973. A Population Model for the Diffusion of Early Farming in Europe. In *The Explanation of Culture Change*. Ed. C. Renfrew. London, Duckworth.

Ammerman, A. J. and L. L. Cavalli-Sforza. n.d. A Simulation Study of Bandkeramik Settlement Patterns. Paper given at the Symposium on Applications of Computer Simulation to Archaeology, Society of American Archaeology, San Francisco, May 1973.

Ammerman, A. J., Cavalli-Sforza, L. L. and D. K. Wagener. 1976. Toward the Estimation of Population Growth in Old World Prehistory. In *Demographic Anthropology: Quantitative Approaches*. Ed. E. Zubrow. Albuquerque, University of New Mexico Press.

Aronson, D. G. and H. F. Weinberger. 1975. Non-linear Diffusion in Population Genetics, Combustion, and Nerve Pulse Propagation. *Partial Differential Equations and Related Topics*. In Lecture Notes in Mathematics, vol. 446. Springer.

Cavalli-Sforza, L. L. 1962. The Distribution of Migration Distances: Modes and Applications to Genetics. In *Human Displacements* (Entretiens de Monaco en Sciences Humains, Première Session). Ed. J. Sutter. Monaco, Hachette.

Cavalli-Sforza, L. L. 1974. The Genetics of Human Populations. *Scientific American* (Sept.): 80–89.

Clark, J. G. D. 1965. Radiocarbon Dating and the Expansion of Farming Culture from the Near East over Europe. *Proceedings of the Prehistoric Society* 31: 57–73.

Coale, A. J. 1972. *The Growth and Structure of Human Populations*. Princeton, Princeton University Press.

Eckert, J., Ihmig, Jürgens, A., Kuper, R., Löhr, H., Lüning, J. and I. Schroter. 1971. Untersuchungen zur Neolithischen Besiedlung der Aldenhovener Platte. *Bonner Jahrbücher* 171: 558–664.

Eckert, J., Ihmig, M., Kuper, R., Löhr, H. and J. Lüning. 1972. Untersuchungen zur Neolithischen Besiedlung der Aldenhovener Platte II. *Bonner Jahrbücher* 172: 344–394.

Farruggia, J. P., Kuper, R., Lüning, J. and P. Stehli. 1973. *Der Bandkeramische Siedlungsplatz Langweiler 2*. Rheinische Ausgrabungen 13. Bonn, Rheinland Verlag GMBH.

Fisher, R. A. 1937. The Wave of Advance of Advantageous Genes. *Annals of Eugenics, London* 7: 355–369.

Hasan, F. A. 1973. On Mechanisms of Population Growth during the Neolithic. *Current Anthropology* 14: 535–542.

Jarman, H. N. and J. L. Bay-Petersen. 1976. Agriculture in Prehistoric Europe—the Lowlands. In *The Early History of Agriculture*. Philosophical Transactions of the Royal Society of London, Biological Sciences, vol. 275.

Kendall, D. G. 1948. A Form of Wave Propagation Associated with the Equation of Heat Conduction. *Proceedings of the Cambridge Philosophical Society* 44: 591–594.

Keyfitz, N. and W. Flieger. 1971. *Population: Facts and Methods of Demography*. San Francisco, Freeman.

Lee, R. B. 1972. Population Growth and the Beginnings of Sedentary Life among the !Kung Bushmen. In *Population Growth: Anthropological Implications*. Ed. B. Spooner. Cambridge, The MIT Press.

Lee, R. B. and I. DeVore (eds.). 1968. *Man the Hunter*. Chicago, Aldine.

Menozzi, P., Piazza, A. and L. L. Cavalli-Sforza. 1978. Synthetic Maps of Human Gene Frequencies in Europeans. *Science* 201:786–792.

Newell, R. R. 1970. The Flint Industry of the Dutch Linearbandkeramik. In *Linearbandkeramik aus Elsloo und Stein*. Ed. P. J. R. Modderman. Nederlandse Oudheden 3. 'S-Gravenhage, Staatsuitgeverij.

Olsson, I. U. (ed.) 1970. *Radiocarbon Variations and Absolute Chronology*. New York, Wiley.

Renfrew, J. M. 1969. The Archaeological Evidence for the Domestication of Plants: Methods and Problems. In *The Domestication and Exploitation of Plants and Animals*. Eds. P. Ucko and G. Dimbleby. London, Duckworth.

Skellam, J. G. 1951. Random Dispersal in Theoretical Populations. *Biometrika* 38: 196–218.

Skellam, J. G. 1973. The Formulation and Interpretation of Mathematical Models of Duffusionary Process in Population Biology. In *The Mathematical Theory and Dynamics of Biological Populations*. Eds. M. Bartlett and R. Hiorns. London, Academic Press.

Soudsky, B. and I. Pavlu. 1972. The Linear Pottery Culture Settlement Patterns in Central Europe. In *Man, Settlement and Urbanism*. Eds. P. Ucko, R. Tringham and G. Dimbleby. London, Duckworth.

Stauder, J. 1971. *The Majangir*. Cambridge Studies in Social Anthropology 5. Cambridge, Cambridge University Press.

Van Zeist, W. 1976. On Macroscopic Traces of Food Plants in Southwestern Asia. In *The Early History of Agriculture*. Philosophical Transactions of the Royal Society of London, Biological Sciences, vol. 275.

Vita-Finzi, C. and E. S. Higgs. 1970. Prehistoric Economy in the Mount Carmel Area of Palestine. Site Catchment Analysis. *Proceedings of the Prehistoric Society* 36: 1–37.

Weiss, K. M. 1973. *Demographic Models for Anthropology*. Memoir 27, Society for American Archaeology, Washington, D.C.

Weiss, K. M. 1976. Demographic Theory and Anthropological Inference. *Annual Review of Anthropology* 5: 351–381.

Zohary, D. 1969. The Progenitors of Wheat and Barley in Relation to Domestication and Agricultural Dispersal in the Old World. In *The Domestication and Exploitation of Plants and Animals*. Eds. P. Ucko and G. Dimbleby. London, Duckworth.

IV

SYSTEMS AND SUBSYSTEM INTERACTION

What might have been is an abstraction
Remaining a perpetual possibility
Only in a world of speculation.
What might have been and what has been
Point to one end, which is always present.

T. S. Eliot
Burnt Norton

A system may be thought of as a number of parts which interact together to form a whole. Systems theory is concerned with the often complex consequences of these mutual interactions. Stated thus baldly the approach may seem neither promising nor rich. Yet it has proved illuminating in modeling a whole range of behaviors among different complex units ranging from mechanical devices to biological organisms. Human organizations have been modeled in this way, and increasingly past social units, or parts of them, are being analyzed as complex interacting systems.

Systems modeling become possible through the improved electronic technology associated with the development of the computer (Wiener 1948; Ashby 1956; Beer 1959). Some of the basic ideas were implicit in mechanical control mechanisms and governing devices, where the behavior of the mechanism was constrained to lie within an accepted range. If the variable in question (e.g., temperature in the case of a thermostat) began to move outside the accepted range, the device would act automatically in a self-regulating way, that is, homeostatically, to counteract the change. Cybernetics, which started as the study of artificial control mechanisms, is thus fundamentally concerned with feedback: the device whereby the output of the mechanism—its behavior—also forms part of its input, thereby influencing its further behavior. Self-regulation, which involves movement to counteract excessive change, depends on negative feedback.

The power of systems theory lies in its ability to consider simultaneously and systematically both the behavior of the constituent parts and of the whole complex unit which they form. Indeed the approach has proved of such widespread relevance, so many different kinds of complex organization can be analyzed in an analogous way, often showing comparable behaviors, that general systems theory (von Bertalanffy 1968) has emerged as a discipline in its own right, concerned with the general behavioral regularities which different systems in different areas of experience display.

The analysis of a complete sociocultural complex into systems and subsystems (which may themselves be further analyzed in like manner) can already give a number of insights, even before any attempt is made to formalize a concrete and quantitative model (see Clarke 1968, chapter 3; Renfrew 1972, chapters 2, 3 and 21). Good discussions of the fundamentals of systems theory, with a critical appraisal of applications in disciplines close to archaeology, have been given by Buckley (1967), Harvey (1969, chapter 23), and Langton (1972); see also Chapter 2 in this volume.

The potential value of the approach to archaeology has been discussed by a number of writers, including Munton (1973), Wood and Matson (1973), and Klejn (1973), and applications by Flannery (1968) and Rathje (1973) were among the earliest in this field.

The two chapters in this part of the volume use systems theory in an approach toward modeling the entire sociocultural system. The treatment is in many ways analogous to the system dynamics modeling of Forrester (1971), the limitations of which are discussed briefly in Chapter 14 by Cooke and Renfrew. Recently Hosler and co-workers (1978) have applied this approach in an interesting consideration of the Maya collapse.

Underlying all these treatments, as well as that of Plog (1974), is the analysis or breakdown of the total culture system into its constituent subsystems (Figure IV.1). The behavior of the system is determined by the interaction of its subsystems (as well as by the environment), and the behavior of the system at a given point in time (i.e., the state variables for the subsystems, and the level of interaction between them) can be predicted from these

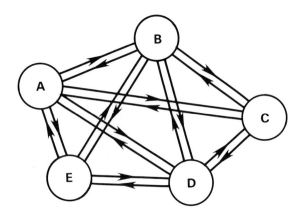

FIGURE IV.1. *Breakdown of the culture system into mutually interacting subsystems.*

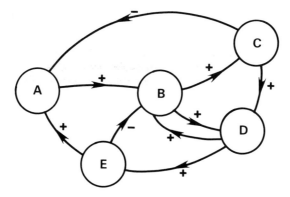

FIGURE IV.2. *Causal chain with feedback loops. An analysis of the significant interactions within the culture system.*

values at an immediately preceding point in time. The trajectory of the system can thus be predicted—that is, simulated—by a process of iteration, each successive state of the system determining the next state.

Often the interaction diagram (Figure IV.1) is written rather in the form of a causal chain, with a number of positive or negative feedback loops (Figure IV.2; see also Figure 2.7). But although this at first sight appears more explicit than the previous figure, it is merely a special case of it. Both can be represented by the matrix of interactions seen in Figure IV.3. And Figure IV.2 differs from Figure IV.1 only in that a number of the interactions have zero value. It should be noted that the formulation used by Gérardin allows the possibility of a time delay (or "viscosity") for each interaction in addition to a measure of its strength.

↙	A	B	C	D	E
A	•	O	–	O	+
B	+	•	O	+	–
C	O	+	•	O	O
D	O	+	+	•	O
E	O	O	O	+	•

FIGURE IV.3. *Matrix of interactions within the culture system, formally equivalent to both Figures IV.1 and IV.2.*

Such models may yet prove to be of real value in modeling past culture systems. Maruyama (1963) has stressed the importance of positive feedback where growth is concerned, identifying "the second cybernetics" as the study and application of deviation-amplifying mutual positive feedback networks. But the problem, discussed in Chapter 1, of modeling the emergence of entirely new properties—a feature of all sustained growth that is anything more than mere increase in scale—has yet to be overcome.

A. C. R.

References

Ashby, W. R., 1956, *An Introduction to Cybernetics*, New York, Wiley.

Beer, S., 1959, *Cybernetics and Management*, London, English Universities Press.

Bertalanffy, L. von, 1968, *General System Theory*, New York, George Brazilier.

Buckley, W., 1967, *Sociology and Modern Systems Theory*, New York, Prentice Hall.

Clarke, D. L., 1968, *Analytical Archaeology*, London, Methuen.

Flannery, K. V., 1968, Archaeological systems theory and early Mesoamerica, in Meggers, B. J. (ed.), *Anthropological Archaeology in the Americas*, Anthropological Society of Washington, 67–87.

Forrester, J. W., 1971, *World Dynamics*, Cambridge, Mass., Wright-Allen.

Harvey, D., 1969, *Explanation in Geography*, London, Edward Arnold.

Hosler, D., Sabloff, J. A., and Runge, D., 1978, Simulation model development, a case study of the Classic Maya collapse, in Hammond N. (ed.), *Social Process in Maya Prehistory*, New York, Academic Press.

Klejn, L. S., 1973, Marxism, the systemic approach and archaeology, in Renfrew 1973, 691–710.

Langton, J., 1972, Potentialities and problems of adopting a systems approach to the study of change in human geography' *Progress in Geography* 4, 125–179.

Maruyama, M., 1963, The second cybernetics, *American Scientist* 51, 164–179.

Munton, R. J. C., 1973, Systems analysis, a comment, in Renfrew 1973, 685–690.

Plog, F. T., 1974, *The Study of Prehistoric Change*, New York, Academic Press.

Rathje, W. L., 1973, Models for mobile Maya, a variety of constraints, in Renfrew 1973, 731–760.

Renfrew, C., 1972, *The Emergence of Civilisation, the Cyclades and the Aegean in the Third Millennium B.C.*, London, Methuen.

Renfrew, C. (ed.), 1973, *The Explanation of Culture Change, Models in Prehistory*, London, Duckworth.

Wiener, N., 1948, *Cybernetics*, New York, John Wiley.

Wood, J. J., and Matson R. G., 1973, Two models of sociocultural systems and their implications for the archaeological study of change, in Renfrew 1973, 673–684.

13   LUCIEN A. GÉRARDIN

A Structural Model of Industrialized Societies: Evolutions, Stability, Policies, Governability

In order to describe cases of societal evolution, we need some kind of models for the studied phenomena. Systems analysis offers a possible approach in this respect. Structural modeling is the simplest available technique. Very often, social structures are actually complex and not merely complicated (whether weakly or strongly complicated). Some mechanical aid is therefore required to explore the intricate mesh of interacting parts.

Complex systems often cross the threshold of internal stability, which should not prevent one from defining their governability in accordance with given policies. Technological systems do not usually present very difficult problems concerning the definition of strategies to be followed to implement a given policy. The actors at work are more or less in agreement regarding the objectives. The problem is quite different in the case of socioeconomic or/and sociocultural systems. The actors at work most usually prefer different objectives corresponding to different policies and therefore strategies. The question then arises of finding out how diverging strategies can coexist without prejudicing survival. Here also the help of the computer is very fruitful in searching for conflicts behind the evolutions.

Societies as a Complex System

Life in society is by its very nature problematical inasmuch as several potential solutions always appear in any aspect of societal life, whether cultural, religious, artistic, political, or ethical, as well as relating to indus-

299

Transformations:
Mathematical Approaches to Culture Change

trial production and consumption, that is, economical. Past history and present experience show that at least three ways of controlling all these problems are known so that the minimum coherence necessary to life in society does exist. Those three ways are constraint (religious or ideological), unanimity, and mutual discussion. Traditional societies were (and are) ruled by some kind of constraint summarized in religious myths that always yield one answer each time an existential question arises. Yet it can happen that a traditional society is suddenly faced with so fundamental a new problem that the myths can no longer provide the adequate existential answer. The outcome can then be fatal and bring about the collapse of the corresponding culture, unless a prophetic man proposes new myths that will make old rules evolve toward new rules. Unanimity seems possible only in the case of small communities. The third possibility, mutual discussion, is of relatively recent origin.

The Greek and Roman republics were not really liberal democracies, but rather traditional aristocratic societies. Elaborated by the "philosophers" of the eighteenth century, and politically implemented in the nineteenth century, liberal society implies the paramount role of mutual discussion and consequently accepts the inevitability of living in a permanent state of conflict. When discussing this point in a symposium about "The Terrors of the Year 2000," Jean Baechler (1976, 175) points out these foundations of the liberal society:

> Conflicts were born from the plurality of alternatives and of the different choices made by individuals and groups. How could a stable and satisfactory order result from the free development of conflicts? A first liberalism that was prevailing in the XIXth century answered in this way. First this axiom: "the plurality of choices is not an irreducible fact, but rather the result of stupidity and superstition. Plurality is irrational. There is one perfect order, because it is rational, and men have the knowledge to find and found it." This theorem follows: "to make reason overcome, we only have to enlighten interests and opinions and let them enter into competition. If no exogenous event alters the game, competition necessarily leads to a point of equilibrium where the antagonistic forces cancel one another." The "invisible hand" makes the rationality of whole society triumph over the particular irrationalities.

Nowadays, we understand that the optimism of the theologians concerning the free market, with equilibrium reached through automatic processes, was excessive. We must admit another axiom and another theorem that Jean Baechler (1976, 176) expresses as follows:

> The plurality of possibilities is an irreducible fact. The choice between possibilities is not irrational but arbitrary, which results in everybody being right. In other words, several solutions are always possible, and they are equivalent. It follows that any solution is both good and bad, and men have to find out a realistic bargain. Choice cannot be rational but can be rationalised. Confrontation of alternative projects leads to a state which appears to be the least inadequate solution. There is no guarantee that the result will be marvellous, but it is impossible that it will become extremely bad. It might be tolerable for society, considering human nature and the human condition.

Meanwhile, owing to the increased artificiality of the industrialized society, the *laissez-faire* classical equilibrium rule must be replaced by some kind of rationalized planning of development. By rationalization, we mean some matching of available resources against goals and/or long-term objectives, according to some norms and/or values (i.e., economic efficiency, or citizens' participation, or self-fulfillment of human beings, and so on).

A knowledge of myths is sufficient for a traditional society to perpetuate itself without too much difficulty. The continuous development of a liberal society requires that the underlying structures be better understood so as to define acceptable ways of growth. Systems analysis appears quite naturally as a possible solution for this necessary preliminary understanding. Munton (1973, 686) has explained the usefulness and also the possible pitfalls of systems analysis:

> All systems represent an abstraction of that part of the real world under investigation, but this kind of simplification does not return system analysis to that form of reductivism referred to earlier. System analysis accepts the complexity of the real world and needs to investigate it in its own right, and employs models that attempt to account parsimoniously for as much of that complexity as possible. A system therefore represents only a conceptual framework for the investigation of a particular problem and should not be accorded a real existence of its own.

The definitions of what a system and a structure are appear numerous. Now is not the time for discussion of this point. Let us simply say that a system is *an holistic organization of things that are mutually interacting. The influences between neighboring things are carried via processes. The totality of the relations modeling processes constitutes the structure.* On account of its relative time stability, any society can well be modeled in formal systems that are homeomorphic to the world of phenomena. The difficulties begin to arise when attempting to build a particular formal system concretely.

The practical case described here has been carried out for the benefit of the VIIth French National Plan (Gérardin 1975). We first aim at obtaining a better understanding of the complexity of interrelated things under study. The subject, in the case described here, is "industry and society in France." The methodology described remains very general.

Characteristics of Structural Modeling

The objectives in studying societal development and cultural changes are various. We can, for instance, try to outline very long-term evolutions, with revolutionary discontinuities. On the other hand, we may wish to study the detailed aspects of development in the 2 or 3 years to come. Finally, we could wonder what the possibilities of change are in the next 10–15 years. The first type of study must allow that the processes can be strongly nonlinear. This approach is, for instance, that of René Thom (1972). His *Theory of Catastrophies* has been rather widely applied (see Chapters 18 and 20 by Poston and Zeeman, respectively, in this volume). This approach supplied interesting information but it is not possible to define a meaningful nonlinear structure. The best known short-term detailed study remains the dynamic modeling of Professor J. Forrester (1969a). Dynamic modeling has been used for long-term studies (Forrester 1969b, 1971a), but because of the lack of precision of data on the one hand, and of the modifications through time of interaction processes on the other, the supposed accuracy of the output results is simply a delusion. *"Garbage in, garbage out!"*

In the field of sociotechnological and/or socioeconomic systems, practical experience shows that it is quite impossible to assess precisely all the numerical data necessary to elaborate a relevant dynamic model. Yet, it would be disastrous to make this a pretext for neglecting important variables or for leaving the matter to mental models alone. The systematic analysis of a complex of interwoven things always leads to a better understanding, even if it does not result in a fully quantitative model.

Structural modeling as developed, for example, by John Warfield (1973, 1976) offers a relatively simple procedure, appropriate to the imprecise or qualitative estimation of many socioeconomic and sociocultural data. In brief, it is a linearization of dynamic modeling. It thus retains all the advantages of dynamic modeling and in particular the possibility of studying complex systems with many mutually interacting loops. Structural analysis offers the major advantage of a great simplicity as the whole of the studied system is represented by a square matrix (or matrices) on which both the features of the system ("parts") and the interaction between these things ("processes") are the basic ingredients of the model. This matrix (these matrices) is (are) equivalent to a graph or to a directed graph or to a weighted directed graph (as data are more and more accurate). Structural analysis matches the new philosophy of systems analysis which, in contrast to the conventional analytic Cartesianism, gives priority to the complexity of problems, to holistic viewpoints, and to the teleology of processes.

Defining the constituent "parts" and their mutual influences is not an easy task, especially when the studied structure is actually complex and not simply complicated. By complex, we mean a structure with many closed loops between interacting parts. By complicated, we mean either a simple hierarchical structure (weakly complicated) or a hierarchical structure with circuits of influences (strongly complicated). Figure 13.1 explains these categories by simple examples of five parts T_1 to T_5. In Figure 13.1b, there are circuits such as T_1, T_2, T_3, but no loops with all arrows pointing in the same direction.

The design of a model requires many discussions within a multidisciplinary group, gathering experts with divergent and complementary views on the problem studied. In the practical case described here, the numerous

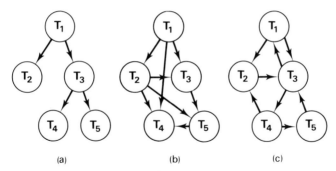

FIGURE 13.1. *Complicated and complex structures: (a) weakly complicated; (b) strongly complicated; (c) complex.*

discussions that took place during the study led us to retain 12 parts (or variables) only. That particular number has nothing magical whatsoever. It could have been reduced to 6 or 8 variables, for instance. Or alternatively, we might have preferred a more elaborate analysis relating to 15–20 variables. But limiting oneself is necessary so as to be able to summarize complex organizations in a correct manner. The selected number of variables prevents getting lost in details (the analysis would then get too intricate), while bringing about a complexity which already completely defies an intuitive judgment. A model should always be midway between a tree and its leaves, so that we do not take the leaves for the tree or in a reverse manner the tree for the leaves. Figure 13.3 enumerates concisely the names of these variables. Naturally, each of them is the subject of a detailed description that specifies its many aspects. In this connection, for instance, structural unemployment due to maladaptation of workers against evolving industrial processes is an aspect of variable 1: *sharing of the work benefits,* while causal unemployment due to loss of adequate matching between production and consumption is an aspect of variable 5: *working conditions at the employment level toward more stability and security or toward more mobility and insecurity.*

The list of the selected variables enables us to elaborate a square matrix that sums up the processing structure. We indicate in the box at the crossing of row i and column j whether or not an influence is exerted by variable i on variable j. Other structural models, such as KSIM used by Professor J. Kane (1972), describe this influence the other way around, from column j toward row i. In Chapter 14 of this volume, K. L. Cooke and C. Renfrew have adopted the KSIM approach. Taking into account the linear characteristic of structural models, each influence operator links two variables and only two. For each pair of variables V_i and V_j, we will ask ourselves the two following questions: Does V_i exert an influence on V_j? Does V_j exert an influence on V_i?

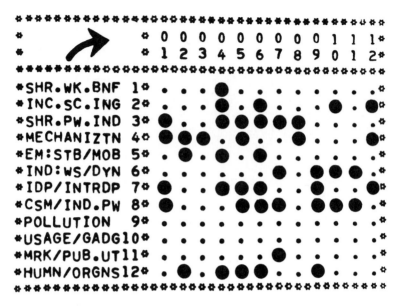

FIGURE 13.2. *Influences at work indicated by a structural matrix.*

When the answer is yes, the influencing mechanism should be specified in detail. Once the complete list of operators has been established, the structural model is elaborated. Figure 13.2 shows the result for the practical case studied here: industry and society in France.

This kind of structural matrix summarizes the structure of the studied system. It is equivalent to a directed graph (for the theory of digraphs, see Harary 1965). A detailed descriptive list of all the variables and a detailed descriptive list of all the processes must accompany the matrix. In the case described here, this represents some 50 pages. It is not possible to reproduce them here due to the lack of available space (for the complete description, see Gérardin 1975).

From Graph to Weighted Digraph

The structural matrix allows one to estimate the direct consequences of a given action, as well as the second-order consequences. Therefore, it helps in formulating strategies corresponding to a given policy. After analyzing a specific question, a strategy consists of establishing a rationalized behavior through logical deductions. This rationalized behavior is directed toward a goal (or a set of goals) that constitutes a "policy." The meaning of rationalization should be kept in mind, that is, a matching of available resources with goals according to some norms. The set of norms, the "value system," constitutes the rationale of a society.

Whenever technological problems are to be solved, the goal is a unique aim, relatively well defined: increase wages, reduce rate of discount, offer an income credit or propose a lower age for retirement, and so on. In the case of bargaining between antagonistic actors, the goal is rather a fuzzier objective.

So as to assess plausible strategies, it is necessary to define the structural model better, after specifying the main possible trends of evolving variables. For the sake of simplicity, let us consider in the present case two well-defined and opposite sets as a first analysis. Figure 13.3 summarizes such a dichotomy. For the convenience of subsequent computations, the two opposite directions are referenced by the letters C and M.

Evolutions leading to type M objectives tend to be situated in the scope of a free-market liberal society ruled by a *laissez-faire* ideology inherited from the heroic ages of the nineteenth century. Evolutions leading to type C objectives tend to be situated in the scope of a "cooperative" and rather "socialist" (in the idealized meaning of the word) society.

Processes (operators) between variables either enhance (+) or inhibit (−). We ask ourselves questions in order to define these signs. After completing this second step, the digraph becomes a *"signed" digraph*. We go a step further by assessing a weight to each influence operator. To do this, it is

	C *(onviviality)*	M *(arket)*
	IF THE EVOLUTION IS MORE IN FAVOR OF :	
1 − SHARING OF WORK BENEFITS	WORKERS AND MIDDLE MANAGEMENT	CAPITAL, FINANCE AND TAXES
2 − INCOME AND SOCIAL INEQUALITIES	GREATER EQUALITY AND EQUITY	GREATER INEQUALITY AND INEQUITY
3 − SHARING OF POWER WITHIN CORPORATIONS	GREATER PARTICIPATION OF WORKERS	GREATER AUTHORITY OF CAPITAL OWNERS
4 − SUBSTITUTION OF WORK BY CAPITAL	MORE EMPLOYMENT AND LESS TOUGH MECHANIZATION	MORE CAPITAL USE AND MORE TOUGH MECHANIZATION
5 − EMPLOYMENT : STABILITY/MOBILITY	STABILITY AND SAFETY	RISK AND INSECURITY
6 − INDUSTRIAL POLICY : WAIT AND SEE/DYNAMISM	MORE WAIT AND SEE AND DAILY ROUTINE	MORE DYNAMISM AND TOUGH BUSINESS
7 − INDEPENDENCE/ INTERDEPENDENCE	MORE INDEPENDENCE AT NATIONAL LEVEL	MORE INTERDEPENDENCE AND WORLD TRADE
8 − CONSUMERISM/ INDUSTRIAL POWER	CONSUMERS AND LOCAL COLLECTIVITIES	INDUSTRIAL POWER AND ESTABLISHMENT
9 − POLLUTION BY INDUSTRY	POLLUTION PREVENTION AND INTERNALIZATION OF COSTS	"LAISSEZ-FAIRE" AND EXTERNALIZATION OF COSTS
10 − REAL USAGE/ GADGET	MORE REAL USAGE OF PRODUCTS	LESS REAL USAGE AND MORE "GADGETRY"
11 − PRIVATE MARKET/ PUBLIC SECTOR	PUBLIC UTILITIES AND COLLECTIVE SERVICES	MERCHANT SECTOR AND INDIVIDUAL GOODS
12 − HUMAN LEVEL/ BIG ORGANIZATIONS	HUMAN SCALE AND DECENTRALIZATION	LARGE ORGANIZATIONS AND CENTRALIZATION

FIGURE 13.3. *Variables and their possible evolutions toward either type M (market) or type C (cooperative) objectives.*

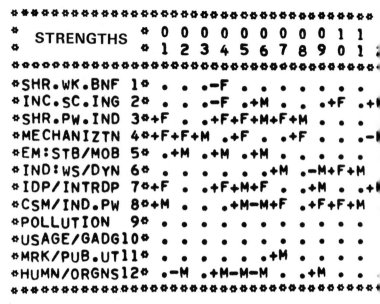

FIGURE 13.4. *Strength and delay for influences at work expressed as weighted digraph for the "industry and society in France" model.*

necessary to define units in order to measure each variable. To avoid a lot of difficulties, the simplest way is to normalize all the variables and therefore to have the same scale from −1 to +1 for each variable. Because the available information is often very approximate, it is not realistic to quantify the strength of processes in a very precise manner. Only two values are used in the described case of industry and society in France. These values are either strong (F for *fort,* in French) or medium (M). It might be possible to use a more detailed scale with three or five or more values. We prefer to put letters instead of numbers to indicate the strength of process operators because numbers could give a false idea regarding the accuracy of the available information.

Very often it takes time for influences to have effect through the operation of processes. Therefore the relative viscosities are summarized on another matrix. In the present case, we have used a three-level scale. The viscosity is either low (I for instantaneous), medium (R for *retarde,* in French), or high (T for *tardif,* in French). Roughly speaking, I means 1 year or less, R equals 3 years as an average, and T, 5 years. Here also, it might be possible to use a more detailed scale, with 5 or 10 or more levels.

Group discussions between experts make it possible to assess the strength and viscosity for each process. The simple model of Figure 13.2 evolves to give the more accurate (or less crude) matrices of Figure 13.4. The signed digraph becomes a *weighted signed digraph.*

DELAYS	01	02	03	04	05	06	07	08	09	10	11	12
HR.WK.BNF 1	•	•	•	R	•	•	•	•	•	•	•	•
NC.SC.ING 2	•	•	•	R	•	T	•	•	•	I	•	T
HR.PW.IND 3	I	•	•	I	I	I	R	I	•	•	•	•
MECHANIZTN 4	I	R	R	•	I	•	•	R	•	•	•	T
M:STB/MOB 5	•	T	•	I	•	T	•	•	•	•	•	•
ND:WS/DYN 6	•	•	•	•	•	•	R	•	T	T	T	•
OP/INTROP 7	R	•	•	I	I	R	•	•	I	•	•	T
SM/IND.PW 8	I	•	•	•	I	T	R	•	I	R	R	•
OLLUTION 9	•	•	•	•	•	•	•	•	•	•	•	•
USAGE/GADG 10	•	•	•	•	•	•	•	•	•	•	•	•
RK/PUB.UT 11	•	•	•	•	•	•	I	•	•	•	•	•
UMN/ORGNS 12	•	T	•	T	I	T	•	•	R	•	•	•

Associated Graphic Presentation

Although convenient for analysis, the square matrix (matrices) of mutual influences is (are) not self-explanatory. It appears necessary to convert it (them) to sketch out the complexity of the studied system. To this end, a diagram can be used summarizing "proximities" between variables, bearing in mind the complexity of mutual influences. How are we to estimate these proximities? If the studied system is actually complex, many closed-loop processes (i.e., subsets of influences closing on themselves) are at work. It is useful to give a concrete example for illustrative purposes. The emphasis put on international exchanges (variable 7 evolves toward an M objective) brings about dynamism in industry (variable 6 also evolves toward an objective). This evolution toward more industrial dynamism brings about the obligation to emphasize the exchanges directed toward the outside world in order to export the extra production. This implies an evolution of variable 7 toward an M objective, which reinforces the effect of the initial shift. The whole brings about a "snowball" process (Figure 13.5): The initial action is multiplied by the inherent game of economic forces at stake. Such snowball processes are typically those of growth in our industrialized societies.

Another case exists. For instance, the evolution toward more mechanization and automation (variable 4 evolves toward an M objective) brings about the overqualification of a restricted number of workers and simultaneously the disparity between incomes (variable 2 evolves toward an objec-

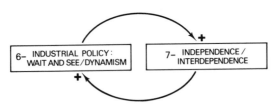

FIGURE 13.5. *Snowball process.*

tive also of type M). It also brings about some amount of structural unemployment which strengthens the economical disparity of a social rejection. This evolution toward greater inequality (variable 2 toward M) brings about an opposite effect on the evolution of variable 4. When increasing low wages, and consequently reducing some inequalities, one induces an acceleration of mechanization so as to make savings on those increased low wages. However, maintaining inequalities does not favor turning toward an increased mechanization. This kind of closed-loop process gives a natural stabilization (Figure 13.6), or rather a "resistance to change" quite favorable to societal coherence.

A third type of closed-loop process exists that turns out to be very dangerous for societal coherence. Let us examine the case of variables 4, 12, and 5. If variable 4 evolves toward an M objective (more mechanization), it leads to a fragmentation of tasks, encouraging claims by small groups outdistancing traditional worker unions. Therefore, variable 12 evolves toward a C objective. Yet, these small groups are not powerful enough and their action increases instability in employment conditions (variable 5 evolves toward M). On the opposite side, the existence of large unions does favor safety in employment. Therefore evolutions in variable 5 in one direction or another entail evolutions of variable 4 toward similar ends. Increased security in employment restrains mechanization, since it is difficult to dismiss workers who become maladapted to new working conditions and vice versa.

The closed-loop process (4, 12, 5) is an accelerating one. We find a snowball effect again, except that two interacting variables (4, 12) evolve in opposite directions, thereby accelerating the initial contradiction. Therefore this kind of process leads to exacerbation of internal tensions, and potentially to the collapse of society (Figure 13.7).

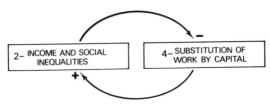

FIGURE 13.6. *Stabilization process.*

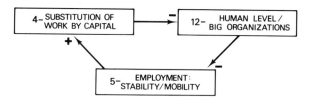

FIGURE 13.7. *Collapse process.*

The industry and society in France system thus modeled is so complex that there are always interactions between many closed-loop processes, a factor that greatly complicates the intuitive search for the direct and second-order effects resulting from a given action. Moreover, we must take into account process viscosities. We have therefore developed a computer program in order to compute all closed loops within a given complex system. The method for automatically computing all these loops is very simple. We consider the structural matrix as a Boolean matrix. We raise this Boolean matrix to its successive Boolean powers. If several ones appear in main diagonal boxes, then the corresponding variables are concerned with a given closed loop, the length of which is the corresponding matrix power. The algorithm removes possible ambiguities (Gambrelle 1974). The computer prints the list of all closed loops of length 2, length 3, and so on. Each closed loop is described by its strength and its delay. The first parameter is the product of individual strengths of constituent processes (with the quite arbitrary numerical translation: 5 for F, 3 for M). The second parameter is the sum of individual delays of constituent processes (with the following numerical translation: 1 for I, 3 for R, 5 for T).

Figure 13.8 is an excerpt of the printed list of closed loops of length 3. The first line depicts a collapsing process (4, 12, 5); the second line depicts a growing snowball process (5, 6, 7); and the third line depicts a stabilizing process (6, 7, 12). The table shown in Figure 13.9 gives the number of closed loops of a given total length for the system described here.

The balance between accelerating (snowball effect) and stabilizing closed-loop processes appears at first sight quite satisfactory. Collapsing processes are fortunately very few in number.

STRENGTHS	**+**	45	4---	12	--	5	++	4
DELAYS		7	T	I		I		
STRENGTHS	**+**	27	5 ++	6	++	7	++	5
DELAYS		9	T	R		I		
STRENGTHS	**–**	45	6 ++	7+++	12	--	6	
DELAYS		13	R	T		T		

FIGURE 13.8. *Example of closed-loop processes.*

Length of closed-loop processes	2	3	4	5
Number of processes	7	14	25	46
Accelerating loops	3	7	13	19
Stabilizing loops	4	5	10	19
Collapsing loops	0	2	2	8

FIGURE 13.9. *Closed-loop processes for industry and society structural model.*

The program also prints the constitution of strongly connected subgraphs of successive powers. For example, variables 1, 2, 4 are strongly connected by closed loops of length 2 with strength $F \times F$. If we lower the strength of processes to $M \times M$, variables 1, 2, 3, 4, 5, 12 are strongly connected by closed loops of length 2. This also holds for variables 6 and 7, as shown in Figure 13.10.

By considering on the one hand the strongly connected subgraphs and on the other the many interwoven closed-loop processes, we can sketch the diagram of Figure 13.11 by a trial and error process. The thickness of lines connecting interacting variables depicts their "proximity." This strength is directly related to the number of closed-loop processes concerned by the corresponding line, weighted in a reverse way by the increasing lengths of the loops and by process viscosity. The "hard core" of the industry and society in France complex system described here is clearly the strongly connected subgraph of variables 1, 2, 3, 4, 5, 12. This conclusion is supported by common sense, which helps to validate the designed model.

Pulse and Value Evolutions

Whenever technological problems are to be studied, the goal of a given policy is a unique aim relatively well defined: for example, designing nuclear power utilities, constructing a mass-transit system for urban commuters, developing a new computer-aided learning system. In the case of societal problems, the goal is much fuzzier, more like a long-term objective: decreasing social inequalities and or inequities, improving quality of life, giving people more freedom and choices for self-development. In this latter case, the main problem is to balance adequately the short-term and long-term effects of actions. It is first necessary to have adequate short-term effects following a given action, especially for a liberal democracy with regular

```
1  2  3  4  5  12          GROUP
6  7                       GROUP
```

FIGURE 13 10. *Example of strongly connected subgraphs of length 2.*

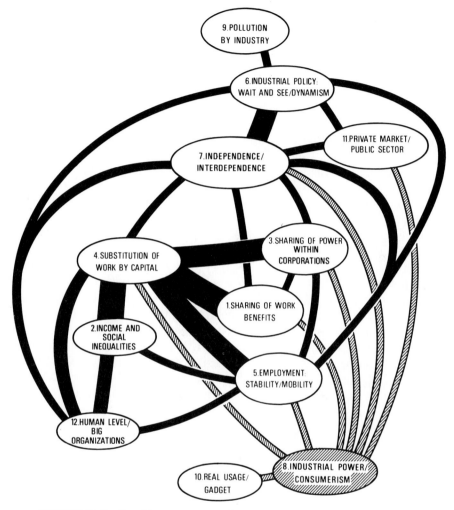

FIGURE 13.11. *Graphic presentation of industry and society in France model.*

approval by citizens. A societal strategy will be defined as stable if the long-term evolution of variables does extend the initial short-term evolutions in the desired direction.

As far as dynamic models are concerned, a structural model is equivalent to a set of first-order differential equations or, more precisely, finite difference equations. The actual computation of time evolution will always be made by a step-by-step process, with an evaluation at each step of increments (positive and/or negative) acting on each variable, taking into account the previous step variations of influencing variables.

We can focus our attention on those increments $P_i(t)$ that describe the discrepancies relating to a known evolution. We will then say that we make a pulse estimate of system evolution. On the other hand, we can focus our attention on the $V_i(t)$ value of the variables. We will then say that we make a value estimate of system evolution. Variables and increments are linked through the vectorial relation:

$$V_i(t_N) = P_i(t_N) + V_i(t_{N-1}) \tag{13.1}$$

Knowledge of the initial value $V_i(0)$ at the initial time $t = 0$ is required in order to perform this value estimate computation.

In both cases, it is interesting to introduce auxiliary variables that will permit us always to have a unit delay in processor viscosities (Erdmann 1977; Lombard, 1977). Thus, if for example variable V_2 influences variable V_3 through a process operator, the viscosity of which has an R value (conventionally equal to three delay units), we will introduce two auxiliary variables V_k and V_m so that the (V_2, V_3) arrow of the initial graph becomes the set of arrows (V_2, V_k), (V_k, V_m), (V_m, V_3) of the auxiliary graph, as indicated in Figure 13.12. If the process viscosity had been I, we would not have introduced any auxiliary variable. Finally, if the viscosities had been T, we would have introduced four auxiliary variables. It might be very easy to generalize this rule for a more (or less) detailed viscosity scale. This use of auxiliary variables translates the two (strength and delay) structural matrices M into only one strength matrix M^*, the size of which is greater than the size of the starting matrices. This entails an increased use of memory storage in the computer, but the computation is greatly facilitated. In the end, the computation cost is lower.

Let us consider a given initial state of the value vector $V_i(0)$ of the variables at the starting time $t = 0$ are given vectorial sets $P_i^{(\circ)}(t_j)$ of actions made at successive times t_j through variables V_i. The pulse estimate evolution of those variables is given by

$$P_i(t_N) = \sum_{j=1}^{N-1} P_i^{(\circ)}(t)M^* + P_i^{(\circ)}(t_N). \tag{13.2}$$

It is interesting to differentiate between positive and negative increments by considering separately the positive component $M^*_{(+)}$ and the negative component $M^*_{(-)}$ of the structural auxiliary matrix M^*:

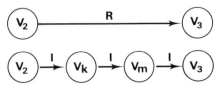

FIGURE 13.12. *Interacting variables.*

$$P_i(t_N) = P_{i(+)}(t_N) + P_{i(-)}(t_N) + P_i^{(\circ)}(t_N) \tag{13.3}$$

with

$$P_{i(+)}(t_N) = \sum_{i=1}^{N} P_i^{(\circ)}(t_j)M^*_{(+)}$$

$$P_{i(-)}(t_N) = \sum_{j=1}^{N} P_i^{(\circ)}(t_j)M^*_{(-)} \tag{13.4}$$

Combining relations (13.1) and (13.2) permits the computation of the vectorial value estimate evolution:

$$V_i(t_N) = V_i(0) + P_i^{(\circ)}(0) \sum_{\tau \sim 0}^{N} (M^*)^\tau + \cdots + P_i^{(\circ)}(t_{N-1})M^* + P_i^{(\circ)}(t_N) \tag{13.5}$$

In the author's research group, a package of programs has been developed which is called STRINGDALE (for STRuctural modelING DAta LanguagE). It allows us to enter the data easily and to make the computations that are summarized in the vectorial and/or matricial equations (13.3) to (13.5), as well as other computations that will be described in the following paragraphs. STRINGDALE makes it possible to present the output in a very convenient manner.

It is possible to use structural matrices in several other ways to estimate the evolution of the variables. The study presented in Chapter 14 by Kenneth L. Cooke and Colin Renfrew in this volume gives an illustration. These authors assume that the value of each variable evolves naturally according to an S growth curve of the Gompertz type. The mutual interactions indicated by the structural matrix modify these natural evolutions.

The Search for Intrinsic Stability

The study of the time evolutions immediately raises the problem of the intrinsic stability of the system modeled by a structural matrix. The problem is a conventional one because a structural model equals a system of linear differential equations. Very numerous mathematical studies exist in this field. The very special case of structural modeling has been studied in depth by F. Roberts (1972, 1976) who makes a distinction between *pulse-stable* and *value-stable* systems. A value-stable system is, by definition, also pulse stable but the reverse is not true.

The actual computations of stabilities have been greatly improved by J. Lombard in the case of weighted digraphs with process viscosities. Theoretically, it should be sufficient to solve the secular equation associated with the matrix to determine the value stability. It is well known that this is practically impossible to do by hand when more than two or three variables are involved since a secular equation is found to be of too high a degree for formal solution. Fortunately, computer programs exist permitting one to find the roots (either real or imaginary) with an excellent accuracy. The main difficulty is formally to elaborate by hand the secular equation when the size of the auxiliary matrix M^* is great. J. Lombard (1977) has shown that the coefficients of this equation are related in a very simple way with the number of closed-loop processes and pseudo-closed-loop processes. Figure 13.13 explains the meaning of the latter term. No vertices are common between closed-loop components of a pseudo-closed loop.

Computer solving by the Bairstow method of the industry and society in France secular equation shows that the system is intrinsically unstable, because of the four following imaginary roots:

	Modulus
$1.0820 \pm .2996j$	1.1227
$.8882 \pm .6288j$	1.0883
$.0612 \pm 1.0139j$	1.0157
$.8546 \pm .7485j$	1.1361

J. Lombard (1977) proposes another way of studying the short- and long-term instabilities. He directs attention to Equation (13.5). Variable values are linearly linked to the successive powers of the auxiliary matrix M^*. These successive powers give a valuable idea of the intrinsic stability of the modeled system. If all coefficients are less than 1, the system is pulse stable, which is a sufficient condition. Unfortunately, the continuous growth of the coefficients of these matrices $(M^*)^\tau$ does not necessarily mean that the corresponding system is value unstable. It is possible indeed to have some kind of balancing between positive and negative successive powers. In any case, the set of successive matricial powers is not very expensive to compute and gives valuable information on long-term stability or instabilities.

The tabulation in Figure 13.14 shows some stability results concerning the industry and society in France structural model described here. In order

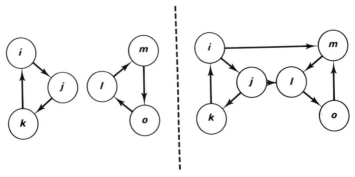

FIGURE 13.13. *Definition of pseudo-closed-loop processes of length (6, 3).*

```
************************************        ************************************
*                 *  0  0  0  0  0  1*     *                 *  0  0  0  0  0  1*
*  STRENGTHS      *  1  2  3  4  5  2*     *  STRENGTHS      *  1  2  3  4  5  2*
************************************        ************************************
*                 *                 *      *                 *                 *
*SHR.WK.BNF  1*  .  .  .-F  .  .*            *SHR.WK.BNF  1*  .  .  .-F  .  .*
*INC.SC.ING  2*  .  .  .-F  .+M*            *INC.SC.ING  2*  .  .  .-F  .+M*
*SHR.PW.IND  3*+F  .  .+F+F  .*             *SHR.PW.IND  3*+F  .  .+F+F  .*
*MECHANIZTN  4*+F+F+M  .+F-F*               *MECHANIZTN  4*+F+M+M  .+M-F*
*EM:STB/MOB  5*  .+M  .+M  .  .*            *EM:STB/MOB  5*  .+M  .+M  .  .*
*HUMN/ORGNS12*  .-M  .+M-M  .*              *HUMN/ORGNS12*  .-M  .+M-M  .*
*                 *                 *      *                 *                 *
************************************        ************************************
```

```
POWER   : 5                                 POWER   : 5
.............                               .............

 .00   .00   .00  -.50   .00   .00           .00   .00   .00  -.25   .00   .00
 .00   .00   .00  -.50   .00   .50           .00   .00   .00  -.25   .00   .50
-.25   .50   .25  -.25  -.25   .00          -.37   .25   .25  -.44   .06   .00
-.25   .50   .25   .25  -.25 -1.00          -.44   .12   .12   .25  -.22 -1.00
 .25   .50   .00  -.12   .25   .00           .25   .50   .00  -.22   .25   .00
-.12  -.75  -.12   .50  -.12   .00          -.06  -.62  -.12   .50  -.03   .00

POWER   :10                                 POWER   :10
.............                               .............

1.37   .25   .12   .00  1.37   .50           .73   .22   .22   .12   .37   .25
1.31  -.12   .06   .25  1.31   .50           .70  -.09   .16   .37   .35   .25
-2.00 -1.37  -.62   .03 -2.63   .50         -1.01  -.27  -.30   .11 -1.12   .56
-1.50   .37   .00  -.16 -1.62   .00          -.95   .33  -.06   .06  -.87  -.19
-.47  -.56  -.34  -.66  -.59   .37           .02  -.06  -.18  -.41  -.02   .47
 .16   .12   .09   .64   .09  -.87           .12   .02   .03   .27   .05  -.81

POWER   :15                                 POWER   :15
.............                               .............

1.72  1.25   .41 -1.20  2.53   .12           .39   .35   .29   .06   .65  -.02
1.80  1.31   .45  -.88  2.58  -.31           .45   .36   .30   .19   .67  -.42
-.07 -1.77  -.10  2.89  -.95  -.72          -.20  -.95  -.11   .52  -.60  -.25
 .60   .39   .60  1.86   .48   .34          -.41  -.37  -.03   .47  -.55   .10
 .47 -1.02  -.27   .72   .14   .37           .43  -.25  -.01   .07   .18   .38
-1.48   .46  -.01  -.46 -1.43  -.58          -.64   .32  -.12  -.36  -.34  -.26

POWER   :20                                 POWER   :20
.............                               .............

-1.05   .01  -.60 -3.21  -.60  1.83          -.71   .45   .12  -.40  -.13   .12
-1.79   .24  -.60 -3.44 -1.31  1.54         -1.03   .61   .06  -.59  -.30  -.01
1.29  2.86  1.49  1.85  1.85 -3.77           .99   .24   .41   .41   .78  -.99
2.74  3.28  1.61   .44  3.82 -1.66           .77  -.13   .20   .49   .53  -.66
1.64   .94   .53   .63  2.00 -1.23           .75   .21   .31   .32   .71  -.19
-1.73 -1.02  -.29   .92 -2.41   .69          -.62  -.28  -.24  -.16  -.71   .52
```

FIGURE 13.14. *Long-term instabilities of original and modified structure.*

to reduce the price of the computation, we have only taken into account the six variables of the hardcore (1, 2, 3, 4, 5, 12).

It is very interesting to study the sensitivity of instability to structural modifications of a specific process. The two cases shown in Figure 13.14 are first (left-hand side) the actual state with "wild automation" and second (right-hand side) a more "cooperative" state with "humanized automation." In the latter case, the strength of both operators (4→2) and 4→5) has been lowered from F to M. The cooperative structure is less unstable, a conclusion which is supported by common sense. In both cases, the long-range instabilities of the model suggest designing policy actions in order to stabilize the industry and society in France system voluntarily.

Governability and the Search for Strategies

As long as we go no further than the short-term scale and remain on a casual level, intuition can be fairly useful since the network of influences in cascade is of little consequence. It might be quite different when we want to anticipate long-term evolutions of a subset of variables on a causal and/or a structural level. The elaboration of strategies must make allowances for the addition and/or subtraction of the multiple effects of loops bringing to each variable the product of all influences at work, taking into account the viscosities of processes. How can we actually set up this search for governability? According to the definition of strategies, it is a matter of setting up a rational behavior aimed at carrying into effect a specific policy.

In the present case, a policy consists of selecting given objectives (C or M types) to which a given societal actor would wish to have the variables evolve, and assessing the relative weights of results. The definition of a strategy consists first of selecting the variables through which this actor will act and then of ordering sequentially the required actions. The latter point appears to be very important. Christmas is neither the 26th nor the 23rd of December. If we attempt to do everything at the same time, we incur the greatest incoherence. The results may even be opposed to those which intuition would suggest. This counterintuitive effect results from the complex created by the many interrelated influences (Forrester, 1971b).

The STRINGDALE package contains a module with which to search heuristically for these strategies. We try to define perhaps not the best strategy but at least one that is not too bad. Each societal actor can define his own policy and therefore search for his own strategy. Let us first consider the establishment as societal actor. It wants, for example, to exert power inside enterprises (evolution toward M for variable 3), to increase the industrial power facing consumerism (also M for variable 8), and to emphasize the role of the market (always M for variable 1). Figure 13.15 displays this policy with the relative weights given to the three desired objectives. The establishment fixes as its time horizon $t_N = 7$ (years). This actor can act mainly through variables 1, 3, and 4 toward either C or M objectives. Figure 13.16 proposes a possible strategy. The state evolution of the system is shown in Figure 13.17. The target objectives are reached at period 7. We see the many side effects of the strategic actions. The French word *periodes* stands for time, and it indicates the successive years (in the present case). The amplitude of value evolution is shown on a three-level scale: M, MM, MMM (or, if more, +M+) or C, CC, CCC (or, if more, −C−). This is in agreement with

```
****************************
*SHR.WK.BNF  1*  ###  *
*INC.SC.ING  2*  ###  *
*SHR.PW.IND  3*   MM  *
*MECHANIZTN  4*  ###  *
*EM:STB/MOB  5*  ###  *
*IND:WS/DYN  6*  ###  *
*IDP/INTRDP  7*  ###  *
*CSM/IND.PW  8*   MM  *
*POLLUTION   9*  ###  *
*USAGE/GADG10*  ###  *
*MRK/PUB.UT11*    M   *
*HUMN/ORGNS12*  ###  *
****************************
```

FIGURE 13.15. *Establishment policy.*

the poor accuracy of input data. The use of numerical figures might give a false feeling of accuracy. In short, each successive column in Figure 13.17 describes one of the successive states of the evolving system.

Another societal actor, such as unions of workers (highly politicized in France of course!), can design a different policy: better salaries and more power inside factories and industrial plants. Figure 13.18 summarizes this policy with the relative weights of the target objectives. The time horizon is 7 years as in the establishment case.

```
*****************************************************
*  PERIODES  *  1 * 2 * 3 * 4 * 5 * 6 * 7 * 8 * 9 *10 *
*****************************************************
*SHR.WK.BNF  1*                                          *
*INC.SC.ING  2*                                          *
*SHR.PW.IND  3*MMM  MMM  MMM  MMM  MMM  MMM              *
*MECHANIZTN  4* M                                        *
*EM:STB/MOB  5*                                          *
*IND:WS/DYN  6*                                          *
*IDP/INTRDP  7*                                          *
*CSM/IND.PW  8*                                          *
*POLLUTION   9*                                          *
*USAGE/GADG10*                                           *
*MRK/PUB.UT11*                                           *
*HUMN/ORGNS12*                                           *
*****************************************************
```

FIGURE 13.16. *Establishment strategy.*

```
✿✿✿✿✿✿✿✿✿✿✿✿✿✿✿✿✿✿✿✿✿✿✿✿✿✿✿✿✿✿✿✿✿✿✿✿✿✿✿✿✿✿✿✿✿✿✿✿✿✿
✿  PERIODES  ✿ 1 ✱ 2 ✱ 3 ✱ 4 ✱ 5 ✱ 6 ✱ 7 ✱ 8 ✱ 9 ✱10 ✿
✿✿✿✿✿✿✿✿✿✿✿✿✿✿✿✿✱✱✱✱✱✱✱✱✱✱✱✱✱✱✱✱✱✱✱✱✱✱✱✱✱✱✱✱✱✱✱✿✿✿✿✿
✿SHR.WK.BNF 1✿      M    M    MM   MM  MMM  +M+  +M+  +M+✿
✿INC.SC.ING 2✿                M    M    M   MM   MM  MMM  +M+✿
✿SHR.PW.IND 3✿ M    M    M    MM   MM   MM   MM   MM  MMM  MMM✿
✿MECHANIZTN 4✿ M    M    M    MM   MM   MM  MMM  MMM  +M+  +M+✿
✿EM:STB/MOB 5✿      M    M    MM   MM  MMM  +M+  +M+  +M+  +M+✿
✿IND:WS/DYN 6✿      M    M    M    M    M   MM   MM  MMM  MMM✿
✿IDP/INTRDP 7✿                M    M    MM   MM  MMM  MMM  +M+✿
✿CSM/IND.PW 8✱      M    M    M    M    MM   MM  MMM  MMM  +M+✿
✿POLLUTION  9✿           M    M    M    MM   MM  MMM  MMM  +M+✿
✿USAGE/GADG10✿                M    M    MM   MM  MMM  +M+✿
✿MRK/PUB.UT11✿                M    M    M    M    M   MM✿
✿HUMN/ORGNS12✿                     C    C    C   CC   CC✿
✿✿✿✿✿✿✿✿✿✿✿✿✿✿✿✿✿✱✿✿✱✱✱✱✱✱✱✱✱✱✱✱✱✱✱✱✱✱✱✱✱✱✱✱✱✱✱✱✱✿✿✿✿✿✿
```

FIGURE 13.17. *System evolution corresponding to strategy (Figure 13.16).*

The possible acting variables are also different. Figure 13.19 displays a possible strategy for unions and Figure 13.20 the result on system evolution. The target objectives are reached at the prescribed time. Here also we notice the many side effects.

How do we compute the strategies? The algorithm designed by P. Erdmann (1977) works briefly as follows. Value evolutions corresponding to all elementary actions are computed. The elementary action that gives the result closest to the designed policy is selected. This difference is decreased by repeating the first step and so on. The computation ends when the

```
✿✿✿✿✿✿✿✿✿✿✿✿✿✿✿✿✿✿✿✿✿
✿SHR.WK.BNF 1✿ CCC  ✿
✿INC.SC.ING 2✿  CC  ✿
✿SHR.PW.IND 3✿  CC  ✿
✿MECHANIZTN 4✿ ###  ✿
✿EM:STB/MOB 5✿ CCC  ✿
✿IND:WS/DYN 6✿ ###  ✿
✿IDP/INTRDP 7✿ ###  ✿
✿CSM/IND.PW 8✿ ###  ✿
✿POLLUTION  9✿ ###  ✿
✿USAGE/GADG10✿ ###  ✿
✿MRK/PUB.UT11✿ ###  ✿
✿HUMN/ORGNS12✿ ###  ✿
✿✿✿✿✿✿✿✿✿✿✿✿✿✿✿✿✿✿✿✿✿
```

FIGURE 13.18. *Union policy.*

```
0000000000000000000000000000000000000000000000000000000000
*  PERIODES  * 1 * 2 * 3 * 4 * 5 * 6 * 7 * 8 * 9 *10 *
0000000000000000000000000000000000000000000000000000000000
*SHR.WK.BNF  1*          CC                                *
*INC.SC.ING  2*                              C            *
*SHR.PW.IND  3*CCC   CC CCC              C                 *
*MECHANIZTN  4*                                           *
*EM:STB/MOB  5*                                           *
*IND:WS/DYN  6*                                           *
*IDP/INTRDP  7*                                           *
*CSM/IND.PW  8*                                           *
*POLLUTION   9*                                           *
*USAGE/GADG 10*                                           *
*MRK/PUB.UT 11*                                           *
*HUMN/ORGNS 12*                                           *
0000000000000000000000000000000000000000000000000000000000
```

FIGURE 13.19. *Union strategy.*

difference is smaller than a given error (e.g., 10 or 5%) or when the number of computation steps is greater than a given number (in order to avoid excessive computer time, and therefore prohibitive cost.)

Internal Tensions and Conflicts at Work

The pulse or value evolution of each variable is the result of opposite effects (in the present case C and M) carried through many processes' very often associated on closed loops. Therefore, it is possible to have a small

```
0000000000000000000000000000000000000000000000000000000000
*  PERIODES  * 1 * 2 * 3 * 4 * 5 * 6 * 7 * 8 * 9 *10 *
0000000000000000000000000000000000000000000000000000000000
*SHR.WK.BNF  1*     C    C   CC   CC   CC  CCC  -C-  -C-  -C-*
*INC.SC.ING  2*                    C    C   CC   CC   CC  CCC*
*SHR.PW.IND  3* C   C    C    C    C   CC   CC   CC   CC   CC*
*MECHANIZTN  4*     C    C   CC   CC   CC   CC   CC   CC   CC*
*EM:STB/MOB  5*     C    C   CC   CC  CCC  CCC  -C-  -C-  -C-*
*IND:WS/DYN  6*     C    C    C    C    C    C   CC   CC  CCC*
*IDP/INTRDP  7*               C    C   CC   CC   CC   CC  CCC*
*CSM/IND.PW  8* C   C    C    C   CC   CC   CC   CC  CCC*
*POLLUTION   9*          C    C    C    C   CC   CC  CCC  CCC*
*USAGE/GADG 10*               C    C   CC   CC  CCC  CCC*
*MRK/PUB.UT 11*          C    C    C    C    C   CC*
*HUMN/ORGNS 12*                              M    M    M'   M *
0000000000000000000000000000000000000000000000000000000000
```

FIGURE 13.20. *System evolution corresponding to the strategy of Figure 13.19.*

resulting effect as the balance between great positive and negative increments (here C and M). This kind of situation indicates a strong potential
tension associated with the corresponding strategy. It is therefore interesting
to display this kind of balance.

Figure 13.21 shows this information for the case of the establishment
strategy in Figure 13.16 and Figure 13.22 shows similar information for the
case of unions' strategy in Figure 13.19. In both cases, potential conflicts
appear as very limited. True conflicts arise when societal actors choose
opposite policies and therefore play a game of conflicting strategies.

This is the case, for example, when the establishment plays the strategy
shown in Figure 13.16 and the unions play the strategy shown in Figure

```
◊◊◊◊◊◊◊◊◊◊◊◊◊◊◊◊◊◊◊*◊◊◊*◊◊◊◊◊◊◊◊◊◊◊◊◊◊◊◊◊◊◊◊◊◊◊◊◊◊◊◊◊◊◊◊◊◊◊* ─ ─ ─ ─ ─ ─
◊  PERIODES  ◊ 1 * 2 * 3 * 4 * 5 * 6 * 7 * 8 * 9 *10 ◊
◊◊◊◊◊◊◊◊◊◊◊◊◊◊◊*◊◊*◊◊*◊◊*◊◊*◊◊*◊◊*◊◊*◊◊*◊◊*◊◊*◊◊*◊◊*◊◊*◊◊*◊◊*◊◊*◊
◊SHR.WK.BNF  1◊      M    M    M    M    MM   MM   MM   MM   MM◊
◊INC.SC.ING  2◊                M    M    M    M    M    MM   MM◊
◊SHR.PW.IND  3◊ M    M    M    M    M    M    M    M    M    M ◊
◊MECHANIZTN  4◊ M    M    M    M    M    MM   MM   MM   MM   MM◊
◊EM:STB/MOB  5◊      M    M    M    MM   MM   MM   MM   MM   MM◊
◊IND:WS/DYN  6◊      M    M    M    M    M    M    M    MM   MM◊
◊IDP/INTRDP  7◊                M    M    M    M    MM   MM   MM◊
◊CSM/IND.PW  8◊      M    M    M    M    M    M    M    MM   MM◊
◊POLLUTION   9◊           M    M    M    M    M    MM   MM   MM◊
◊USAGE/GADG10◊                M    M    M    MM   MM   MM◊
◊MRK/PUB.UTI11◊               M    M    M    M    M    M ◊
◊HUMN/ORGNS12◊                                    M    M ◊
◊◊◊◊◊◊◊◊◊◊◊◊◊◊◊◊◊*◊◊*◊◊*◊◊*◊◊*◊◊*◊◊*◊◊*◊◊*◊◊*◊◊*◊◊*◊◊*◊◊*◊◊*◊◊◊◊
```

```
*◊*◊*◊*◊*◊*◊*◊*◊*◊*◊*◊*◊*◊*◊*◊*◊*◊*◊*◊*◊*◊*◊*◊*◊*◊*◊*◊*◊*◊*◊*◊◊◊
*  PERIODES  * 1 * 2 * 3 * 4 * 5 * 6 * 7 * 8 * 9 *10 ◊
*◊*◊*◊*◊*◊*◊*◊*◊*◊*◊*◊*◊*◊*◊*◊*◊*◊*◊*◊*◊*◊*◊*◊*◊*◊*◊*◊*◊*◊*◊*◊◊◊
*SHR.WK.BNF  1*                                              ◊
*INC.SC.ING  2*                                              ◊
*SHR.PW.IND  3*                                              ◊
*MECHANIZTN  4*                C    C    C    CC   CC   CC*
*EM:STB/MOB  5*                                              ◊
*IND:WS/DYN  6*                          C    C    C    C ◊
*IDP/INTRDP  7*                                              ◊
*CSM/IND.PW  8*                                              ◊
*POLLUTION   9*                          C    C    C    C ◊
*USAGE/GADG10*                                              ◊
*MRK/PUB.UTI11*                                              ◊
*HUMN/ORGNS12*                      C    C    C    C    C ◊
*◊*◊*◊*◊*◊*◊*◊*◊*◊*◊*◊*◊*◊*◊*◊*◊*◊*◊*◊*◊*◊*◊*◊*◊*◊*◊*◊*◊*◊*◊*◊◊◊
```

FIGURE 13.21. *Potential conflicts associated with the establishment strategy of Figure
13.16.*

PERIODES	1	2	3	4	5	6	7	8	9	10
SHR.WK.BNF 1		C	C	C	C	C	C	CC	C	C
INC.SC.ING 2					C	C	C	C	C	C
SHP.PW.IND 3	C	C	C		C	C	C	C	C	C
MECHANIZTN 4		C	C	C	C	C	CC	C	CC	CC
EM:STB/MOB 5		C	C	C	C	C	C	CC	C	CC
IND:WS/DYN 6		C	C	C		C	C	C	C	C
IDP/INTRDP 7				C	C	C	C	C	C	CC
CSM/IND.PW 8		C	C	C	C	C	C	C	C	C
POLLUTION 9			C	C	C	C	C	C	C	C
USAGE/GADG10					C	C	C	CC	CC	CC
MRK/PUB.UT11					C		C	C	C	C
HUMN/ORGNS12									C	C

PERIODES	1	2	3	4	5	6	7	8	9	10
SHR.WK.BNF 1										
INC.SC.ING 2										
SHR.PW.IND 3										
MECHANIZTN 4					M	M	M	M	M	MM
EM:STB/MOB 5										
IND:WS/DYN 6							M		M	M
IDP/INTRDP 7										
CSM/IND.PW 8										
POLLUTION 9							M		M	M
USAGE/GADG10										
MRK/PUB.UT11										
HUMN/ORGNS12							M	M	M	M

FIGURE 13.22. *Potential conflicts associated with the union strategy of Figure 13.19.*

13.19. There is hardly any difference between the absolute values of totally opposed results shown in Figures 13.17 and 13.20. Therefore, the resulting balance is nil. The strength of the conflicts between the two opposite potential states is very strong, however, which is in agreement with common sense.

A criticism widely leveled against system analysis (and consequently against structural modeling) is its inherent conservatism, which arises because of the invariance of structures. Yet the simplicity of structural modeling permits us to conduct many structural sensitivity studies in order to gain a better understanding of complex societal problems under study. It is possible to refine by taking into account the interactions (casual and/or structural) between the system and its environment. Both past and present history clearly show the paramount influence of discrete events. It is therefore possible to try to model the system environment as a set of discrete events with given probabilities of occurrence through time. The actual occurrence of a given event and its effects on different evolutionary paths may be observed. In a reverse manner, the evolutions of values of variables can be seen to react on probabilities of occurrence of events. The structural matrix very easily permits this kind of fruitful generalization (Gérardin 1976).

Conclusion

The industrial society of the nineteenth century was characterized by objectives of the M type. After 100 years of economic growth, liberal industrialized society is now characterized by a mixture of M and C objectives. To take up an actual illustration, the President of France, Valéry Giscard D'Estaing, has given in his booklet "Democratie Française," a description of what he calls ""société libérale avancée." It is possible to summarize his proposal with the use of STRINGDALE language as shown in Figure 13.23. The time horizon is quite naturally 7 years, which is the length of time of the French presidential mandate. Figure 13.24 proposes a possible strategy, and Figure 13.25 shows the corresponding system state evolutions. Some second-order consequences are perhaps unexpected. In any case, they are not taken into consideration in the President's booklet.

As in the case of all examples given here, these results concerning

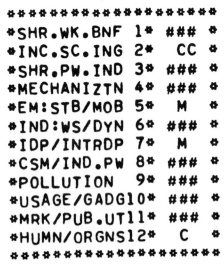

FIGURE 13.23. *"Democratie Française" proposed policy.*

PERIODES	1	2	3	4	5	6	7	8	9	10
SHR.WK.BNF 1	M									
INC.SC.ING 2	CC	CC	CC	CC	CC	CC	CC			
SHR.PW.IND 3			MM	MM						
MECHANIZTN 4										
EM:STB/MOB 5										
IND:WS/DYN 6										
IDP/INTRDP 7	CC	CCC		M	M	M	M			
CSM/IND.PW 8										
POLLUTION 9										
USAGE/GADG10										
MRK/PUB.UT11	C		M	M	M	M				
HUMN/ORGNS12										

FIGURE 13.24. *"Democratie Française": possible strategy.*

evolutions, stability, governability, and conflicts between antagonist societal actors are all implicit within the input data of the structural matrix. Mechanical help is needed for converting these input data into output results, especially if the system structure is actually complex. The main point remains the selection of what are considered the main features (variables) of the system under study, and also the main process operators describing proximity between these features. The resulting qualitative evolutions of the system state, possible strategies, and information on potential conflicts do not pretend to be accurate forecasts. The simulation results can act to stimulate creative thinking on alternative possible futures. Nothing more!

PERIODES	1	2	3	4	5	6	7	8	9	10
SHR.WK.BNF 1	M	M	C	C	C	C	M	MM	MM	MMM
INC.SC.ING 2	C	C	C	C	CC	CC	CC	CC	CC	C
SHR.PW.IND 3			M	M	M		M	M	M	M
MECHANIZTN 4		C	C	C	C	M	MM	MM	MMM	MMM
EM:STB/MOB 5		C	C	C	C		M	MM	MM	MMM
IND:WS/DYN 6				C	C	C	C	C	C	
IDP/INTRDP 7	C	C	C	C	C	M	M	M	C	C
CSM/IND.PW 8			M			C	C	C	M	MM
POLLUTION 9		C	C	C	C	C	C	C	C	M
USAGE/GADG10		C	C	C	C	CC	CC	CC	CC	CC
MRK/PUB.UT11	C	C		M	M	M	M	M		C
HUMN/ORGNS12						C	C	C	C	C

FIGURE 13.25. *System evolution corresponding to the strategy of Figure 13.24.*

In any case, the discussions conducted with the aid of systems analysis are always very fruitful, for they provide a better understanding of the complex organization underlying the societal and cultural problems studied.

Note

Owing to the lack of available space, it has not been possible to describe the algorithms in detail. Those who would like more details should apply to the author at the following address: Lucien A. Gérardin, Research Director, Future Studies Group, THOMSON, 49bis Avenue Hoch, 75362 Paris Cedex 08, France.

Acknowledgments

I acknowledge with pleasure the valuable work of some members of my research group for designing and writing the programs, in particular J. M. Gambrelle (loops and proximity graph), P. Erdmann, and J. Lombard (stability and governability). My secretary, D. Ardiet, aided by my sister-in-law, Marie-France Noiré (Mira Devi), accomplished the difficult task of translating my original mixture of English and French.

References

Baechler, J., 1976, La solution libérale est-elle en crise? in *Les Terreurs de l'An 2000,* (actes du colloque international tenu à Jouy-en-Josas, September, 27–30, 1975), Paris, Hachette 175–203.
Erdmann, P., 1977, *Contribution de l'Analyse de Système à la Prospective. Modélisation et Gouvernabilité d'un Système* Ph.D Thesis, GRASCE, University of Aix-Marseille.
Forrester, J., 1969a, *Principles of Systems,* Cambridge, Wright Allen Press.
Forrester, J., 1969b, *Urban Dynamics,* Cambridge, M.I.T.
Forrester, J., 1971a, *World Dynamics,* Cambridge, Wright Allen.
Forrester, J., 1971b, Counterintuitive Behaviour of Social Systems. *Simulation* (U.S.A.), February, 1971.
Gambrelle, J. M., 1974, Etude des processus d'évolution par la recherche de bouclages dans un graphe, *Revue Technique THOMSON-CSF* 6, 635–645.
Gérardin, L. A., 1975, *L'Industrie et la Société, des problèmes en masse et un noeud de conflits,* Rapport au Commissariat au Plan, Paris.
Gérardin, L. A. 1976. Un modèle événements-tendances pour intégrer l'imprévu dans l'analyse de systèmes des organisations complexes, in Billeter E., Cuenod, M., and Klaczko, S. (ed.), *Overlapping Tendencies in Operation Research System Theory and Cybernetics,* Proceedings of an International Symposium, University of Fribourg (Switzerland), Birkhauser Verlag, Basel (Switzerland), 34–47.
Harary, H. N. R. Z., and Cartwright 1964, *Structural Models: An Introduction to the Theory of Directed Graphs,* New York.
Kane, J., 1972, A primer for a new cross-impact language: KSIM, *Technological Forecast and Social Change,* 4, 129–142.
Lombard, J., 1977, *Contribution de l'Analyse de Système à la Prospective, Modélisation et Stabilitè d'un Système.* Ph.D. Thesis, GRASCE, Univèrsity of Aix-Marseille.

Munton, R. J. C., 1973, Systems analysis: a comment, in Colin Renfrew (ed.) *The Explanation of Culture Change: Models in Prehistory,* London, Duckworth.

Roberts, F. S., 1972, *Building an Energy Demand Signed Digraph II: Choosing Edges and Signs and Calculating Stability.* RAND Corp. R-927/2-NSF Report, May, 1972.

Roberts, F. S., 1976, *Discrete Mathematical Models,* Prentice-Hall, New Jersey.

Thom, R., 1972, *Stabilité structurelle at Morphogenèse, Essai d'une theorie génétique des modèles,* EdiSciences, Paris.

Warfield, J. N., 1973, *An assault on complexity,* (Battelle Monograph no. 3,) April 1973, Battelle, Columbis (Ohio).

Warfield, J. N., 1976, *Societal Systems: Planning, Policy and Complexity,* John Wiley, New York.

14

KENNETH L. COOKE
COLIN RENFREW

An Experiment on the Simulation of Culture Changes

The problem of the long-term analysis of culture change for specific cultures has long been discussed by philosophers of history such as Spengler (1918) and Toynbee (1947), although the resulting insights have usually been expressed as a series of rather vague generalizations.

The development of systems theory has for some years suggested the possibility that the simulation of the historical trajectories of culture systems might be undertaken using a quantitative approach, although the complexity of any real culture system is clearly very great.

This chapter describes a preliminary and largely unsuccessful attempt to apply this approach. We believe, however, that the attempt is an interesting one, illustrating as it does a simple interaction model, and the various practical decisions which have to be made in applying it. The outcome was not a successful, even if crude and oversimplified, representation of change of a prehistoric culture. Instead we were able to recognize, and then analyze, the manner in which the form of the model, whatever the nature of the actual data used as input, came to determine the "predicted" behavior of the system. Comparison with the well-known "world model" used for the study *The Limits to Growth* (Meadows *et al.* 1972) led in an illuminating way to an analogous conclusion: that at this stage criticism of its assumptions about the present state of the world (i.e., about input data) are largely irrelevant. The nature of the output of that model, like our own, is best appreciated after critical examination of its structure, and of the range of outputs of which it is in fact capable.

The object of this chapter is therefore to describe an experiment in

327

Transformations:
Mathematical Approaches to Culture Change

systems modeling during which we gained some valuable experience of the real problems involved. The work arose out of discussions at the Center for the Study of Democratic Institutions, Santa Barbara, California, in which a number of approaches to the use of mathematical modeling, systems theory, and simulation in tracing culture trajectories were discussed by various participants including Wilkinson and co-workers (1973), Rosen (1973), and the authors of the present chapter (cf. Cooke 1973).

The Interaction Model

The problem for which this model was formulated is the explanation of the emergence of complex societies in the Aegean in the third and second millennia BC (Renfrew 1972). The approach is one of very general application, however, and with just a few modifications can be applied to the early development of any complex society (see also Gérardin, Chapter 13, this volume).

The fundamental theoretical proposition sustaining the model—with which few will disagree—is that the changes and developments in the cultures in question (in this case the Aegean) were brought about by complex interactions of components in the society. As it stands this asserts no more than the rejection of very simple migrationist or diffusionist views, and naturally leaves room for the assessment of the effects within the society of contacts with other areas.

In the language of systems theory, the society is a system, its components being the members of the society, all the artifacts they made or used (including nonmaterial ones), and all objects in nature with which they came in contact. In this view, there is an essential coherence or conservatism of cultures due to negative feedback. That is, the system acts to counter disturbances. Innovations in society, on the other hand, are due to "deviation-amplifying mutual causal systems," that is, positive feedback.

In order to use these concepts, it is necessary to decompose the society or system as a whole into a number of subsystems, and then to analyze in detail the interactions among these subsystems. A large part of the work cited (Renfrew 1972) is devoted to this identification of subsystems and their interactions. The subsystems are briefly defined as follows:

1. Subsistence subsystem. The interactions which define this system are actions relating to the exploitation of food resources. Man, the food resources, and the food units themselves are components of the subsystem.
2. Metallurgical technology.
3. Craft technology. The metallurgical and craft subsystems are defined by the activities of man which result in the production of material

artifacts. The components are the men, the material resources, and the finished artifacts.

4. The social subsystem. This is a system of behavior patterns, where the defining activities are those which take place between men.
5. The projective or symbolic subsystem. Here we are speaking of all those activities, notably religion, art, language, and science, by which man expresses his knowledge, feelings, or beliefs about his relationship with the world.
6. The external trade and communication subsystem. This is defined by all those activities by which information or material goods are transferred across the boundary of the system between human settlements or over considerable distances.

Population does not strictly rank as a subsystem within the framework described here, not representing a class of activity, but a parameter relevant to the description of the system.

This brief description does not begin to describe adequately the analysis of the system into its component subsystems. Nor is it claimed that the subsystems defined represent the only or the best such breakdown. For most cultures, for instance, it would not be desirable to distinguish the metallurgical and craft technology subsystems. What is essential to this approach, however, is some such analysis into subsystems, and an evaluation of the extent to which they interact, so that growth and development in one favors or inhibits development in another to an extent which can be made explicit. Such interactions have been considered in some detail for the Aegean (summarized in Renfrew 1972, 488–494). The matrix of interactions (Table 14.1) is thus of particular importance. The projection and quantification of such a matrix is a necessary step in an analysis of this kind (cf. Plog 1974, Tables 6.1 and 13.1).

Any causal chain, using this framework of analysis, can be illustrated diagramatically as a number of feedback loops, where the subsystems which interact strongly are seen as linked (with a sign to indicate whether feedback is positive or negative). The values (or functions) in the matrix indicate the strength (or the variation) in the feedback for each pair of subsystems. Likewise any matrix of interactions can be represented diagrammatically (Figure IV.1, p. 296 of this volume): When weak or zero linkages are omitted from the diagram the complex web of interactions is more easily seen as a series of feedback loops.

The Simulation: Objectives and Technique

In all simulations, one wishes to gain insight into the structure of the system by tracing out its performance under a variety of suppositions concerning that structure and under a variety of conditions. Thus, in the experiments we have underway, we are interested in the evolution of culture when the subsystems interact as in Table 14.1, as well as when alternative interaction matrices are assumed.

Methods for bringing this system within the compass of concrete mathematical technique have been suggested by Cooke (1973) and Rosen (1972, 1973). Here we shall report on experiments with a version of Rosen's method. As in most systems analysis, we must first identify the variables. For us, the variables are the six subsystems listed earlier plus population. Of course, it would be possible to break each subsystem down into smaller parts, for purposes of greater detail, but in this formative stage it has seemed preferable to use a simple, highly aggregated model.

Some comment on "population" as a variable is required. We mean to measure here the actual size of the population and to ignore all other demographic factors. It could well be argued that population density, age distribution, genetic factors, and so on, are of importance. However, it is convenient for the present discussion to restrict our application to Crete during the Early Bronze Age. Since the land area is thus fixed, there is no need to distinguish between population and population density. Moreover, there is no persuasive evidence of significant racial or genetic change during this period. Also, the available data could be interpreted to indicate an overall regularity of population growth, making it unnecessary to postulate important fluctuations in age distribution, and so on. Thus, population is the chosen variable. Incidentally, we make the usual convenient assumption in deterministic mathematical models that population can be treated as a real variable in the mathematical sense, rather than as an integer variable.

It is now necessary to decide what values the other variables shall be allowed to take. Although there is a possibility of using discrete or qualitative values, we have here elected to allow each variable to take real values.

Finding an appropriate real variable as an indicator for a concept is an important and difficult task. In our case, we seek a variable descriptive of the state of each of the subsystems. One of the ways in which this can be done is to regard each variable as an *index* of the level of sophistication of the subsystem it measures. We have adopted this approach here. It should of course be noted that for the purposes of analysis the state of each subsystem is here regarded as adequately described by a single index. Thus we define x_i to be a numerical variable whose values represent a scale for this variable. In our case, we let $x_i(t)$ be the measure of the ith subsystem at time t, where the subsystems corresponding to $i = 1, 2, 3, 4, 5, 6$, are those indicated earlier, in the order given. We also let Cx_7 be the number of persons in the population, where C is a scaling constant to be chosen for convenience.

In archaeological terms the precise choice of the measure used to give a value for each of the variables is of course a crucial one, and in practice the behavior of the system will be in part determined by the measure chosen. In each case several approaches are possible. The following formulations are set out simply to show that the problems, although of major theoretical significance to archaeology, do not prevent the selection of indices whose values can in principle be estimated from the archaeological record. For example, we may define the indices as follows:

x_1 (subsistence). The number of persons fed by the food-gathering–food-producing activities of one person.

x_2 (metallurgy). The number of metal artifacts produced within the territory of the society per head of population per year.

x_3 (craft). The range of specialist products in the society, measured in terms of artifact types.

x_4 (social). The number of well-defined roles distinguished in the society.

x_5 (projective). *Either* the number of abstract concepts in use in the society relating to measure (including units and numerals) *or* the number of man-hours per head per year spent in religious observances or in facilitating them (e.g., by building temples).

x_6 (external trade). Proportion of the GNP exported beyond the confines of the system.

Because of the mathematical formalism to be adopted here, it is necessary to *normalize* each variable so that its value lies between 0 and 1. This can be done in various ways. As an example, suppose that x_1 is defined as just suggested, and suppose that it is estimated that x_1 takes values between 1.05 and 1.8 for the class of cultures under study. Then if we let $\bar{x}_1 = x_1/3$, the values of $\bar{x}_1$ lie between .35 and .6. These values are certainly between 0 and 1, and values near 1 represent a better developed subsistence system than values near 0. The population variable is normalized by choice of the constant C. For example, we might estimate that the population of Crete was 12,600 in the Middle Neolithic period. If we choose $C = 630,000$, then $x_7 = .02$ at this time. Subsequent population increases correspond to increasing values of x_7.

We shall henceforth assume that all variables have been normalized, and that measures have been selected for the variables in such a way that the expert in cultures is able to correlate these numerical values with his qualitative perceptions.

A second alternative interpretation of the variables has been suggested by Rosen (1973). Roughly speaking, $x_1(t)$ is regarded as a measure of the percentage of time spent by all members in the population on subsistence-related activities, $x_2(t)$ is a measure for metallurgy-related activities, and so on. (Consequently, the sum of x_1–x_6 must equal 1 at all times.) This interpretation has not been adopted here, for reasons explained at the end of this section.

The next stage in the simulation is to adopt a procedure for changing the values of the variables. The key to this is the matrix of interactions, which is reproduced in Table 14.1.

The matrix is to be interpreted in the following way. Growth in a subsystem y in the left column is favored by growth in a subsystem x in the top row through the mechanism indicated in the matrix. The key to the mechanisms $A_1, A_2, \ldots, G_7$ may be found in the work cited. As suggested by Rosen, we replace this matrix by the matrix of *signatures*, as follows. Wherever no interaction is indicated, we place a 0. Wherever a favoring mechanism appears, we place $+1$. Wherever an inhibiting mechanism appears, we place -1. Thus, we obtain a matrix, which we name A, as follows:

$$A = \begin{bmatrix} 0 & 1 & 1 & 1 & 1 & 1 & 1 \\ 0 & 0 & 1 & 1 & 0 & 1 & 0 \\ 1 & 1 & 0 & 1 & 1 & 1 & 1 \\ 1 & 1 & 1 & 0 & 1 & 0 & 1 \\ 0 & 0 & 1 & 1 & 0 & 1 & 1 \\ 1 & 1 & 1 & 1 & 1 & 0 & 0 \\ 1 & 0 & 1 & 1 & 1 & 0 & 0 \end{bmatrix}$$

Later, we shall discuss possible changes in the matrix A.

The procedure we have adopted for using the signature matrix has been suggested by Kane (1972) and Kane *et al.* (1972, 1973). First, a choice of the

TABLE 14.1

Matrix of Interactions between the Subsystems of the Culture System (with Population) [a]

						x	
y	Subsistence	Metallurgy	Craft technology	Social systems	Projective and symbolic systems	Trade and communication	Population
Subsistence	—	B_1	B_5	B_2, B_3, B_4	B_7	B_6	B_8
Metallurgy		—	C_1	C_2, C_3, C_4		C_5	
Craft technology	D_1	D_4	—	D_2	D_5	D_6	D_3
Social systems	E_1	E_2, E_3, E_4	E_2, E_3	—	E_5		E_6
Projective and symbolic systems			F_1, F_5	F_2, F_3	—	F_4	F_6
Trade and communication	G_1	G_2, G_3	G_4, G_5	G_6	G_7	—	
Population	A_1		A_4	A_2, A_5	A_3		—

SOURCE. After Renfrew (1972, 488).

[a] Growth in subsystem y favored by growth in subsystem x through the mechanism indicated in the matrix (cf. list in Renfrew 1972, 489–94).

initial state of the system is made. That is, values are assigned to the variables at time $t = 0$, corresponding to an estimate of the stage of development of the subsystems. Next, a sequence of subsequent states (i.e., values of the variables) is calculated by mathematical iteration. Consider a system with any number m of variables. (In the application previously described, $m = 7$.) If h denotes one unit of time, the values are determined from the equation

$$x_i(t + h) = x_i(t)^{p_i} \qquad (i = 1, 2, \ldots, m) \qquad (14.1)$$

where t is given the successive values $t = 0, h, 2h, \ldots$, and where the p_i are exponents calculated as follows:

$$p_i = \frac{q_i}{r_i} \qquad (14.2)$$

$$q_i = 1 + \tfrac{1}{2}h \sum_{k=1}^{m} (|a_{ik}| - a_{ik})x_k(t) \qquad (14.3)$$

$$r_i = 1 + \tfrac{1}{2}h \sum_{k=1}^{m} (|a_{ik}| + a_{ik})x_k(t) \qquad (14.4)$$

If we let

$$a^-_{ik} = \begin{cases} |a_{ik}| & \text{if } a_{ik} < 0 \\ 0 & \text{if } a_{ik} \geq 0 \end{cases} \qquad (14.5)$$

$$a^+_{ik} = \begin{cases} 0 & \text{if } a_{ik} \leq 0 \\ a_{ik} & \text{if } a_{ik} > 0 \end{cases} \qquad (14.6)$$

then

$$q_i = 1 + h \sum_{k=1}^{m} a^-_{ik}x_k(t) \qquad (14.7)$$

$$r_i = 1 + h \sum_{k=1}^{m} a^+_{ik}x_k(t) \qquad (14.8)$$

If A^+ denotes the matrix with entries a^+_{ik}, A^- denotes the matrix with entries a^-_{ik}, and x denotes the vector with entries x_i, then we may write

$$q_i = 1 + h(A^-x)_i, \qquad r_i = 1 + h(A^+x)_i \qquad (14.9)$$

where $(\ )_i$ denotes the ith component of a vector.

From Equations (14.1) we can generate values of the variables x_i at successive time points $t = 0, h, 2h, \ldots$. The equations are nonlinear, but have certain useful features. First, if $0 \leq x_i(t) \leq 1$ for all values of i, then q_i and r_i are both positive, as can be seen from (14.7) and (14.8) or (14.9).

Consequently, p_i is positive and therefore $0 \le x_i(t + h) \le 1$. That is, the region $0 \le x_i \le 1$ $(i = 1, 2, \ldots, m)$ is invariant (variables automatically remain in the prescribed domain). Thus, the equations are suitable for use with variables scaled to lie between 0 and 1. We note also that if $x_i(t) = 0$ or 1 for some value of i, then $x_i(t + h) = 0$ or 1. The exponent p_i incorporates the time step h in order to adjust the time scale. Another important property of these equations is that positive feedbacks $(a_{ik} > 0)$ increase the number r_i but do not contribute to q_i, and negative feedbacks $(a_{ik} < 0)$ increase the number q_i but do not contribute to r_i. It follows that positive feedback tends to make p_i small and negative feedback tends to make p_i large. If $0 < x_i(t) < 1$, we see from (14.1) that $x_i(t + h) > x_i(t)$ when $p_i < 1$ and $x_i(t + h) < x_i(t)$ when $p_i > 1$. Thus, a preponderance of positive feedback will result in increasing values of x_i and a preponderance of negative feedback will result in decreasing values. More precisely, if

$$\sum_{k=1}^{m} a^+_{ik} x_k(t) > \sum_{k=1}^{m} a^-_{ik} x_k(t) \tag{14.10}$$

then $p_i < 1$ and $x_i(t + h) > x_i(t)$ [unless $x_i(t) = 0$ or 1]. Additional discussion of the mathematical properties of (14.1) is given later.

Underlying this procedure is the assumption that a complex interacting system can be adequately described by a set of binary interactions between pairs of variables—that is, that the influence of x_k on x_i is independent of the values of all variables other than x_k. This assumption is frequently made in modeling schemes based on the concept of feedback loops.

It will now be explained why it is not convenient to interpret $x_i(t)$ as a measure of the percentage of time spent by all members of the population on activities related to the ith subsystem. To be more precise, Rosen suggested that for each subsystem i, and each person p in the population, we let $f_i(p)$ denote the proportion of time or degree of involvement of p with activity i; thus $0 \le f_i(p) \le 1$ and $\sum_{i=1}^{m} f_i(p) = 1$. Then, summing for all persons p in the population, we let

$$u_i = \sum_{p=1}^{N} f_i(p)$$

Finally, define $x_i = u_i/N$, where N is the total number of persons in the population, so that $0 \le x_i \le 1$. Now clearly we have

$$\sum_{i=1}^{m} x_i = \frac{1}{N} \sum_{i=1}^{m} u_i = \frac{1}{N} \sum_{i=1}^{m} \sum_{p=1}^{N} f_i(p) = \frac{1}{N} \sum_{p=1}^{N} \sum_{i=1}^{m} f_i(p) = \frac{1}{N} \sum_{p=1}^{N} 1 = 1$$

That is, the normalized variables x_i must sum to 1. However, if we start with variables x_i at time $t = 0$ which sum to 1 and apply formula (14.1), the new values x_i [i.e., $x_i(h)$] will not, in general, sum to 1. Thus, the use of Equation (14.1) is incompatible with this interpretation of the variables x_i.

Initial Trial Runs

A number of trials were first made to test the behavior of our system. Simulations were carried out on the computer at Claremont using a program in APL. Visual interactive facilities were used, allowing progressive experimentation with input parameters. All the figures have been redrawn from Polaroid photographs of the screen display. Figures 14.1a and 14.1b show the growth pattern of the variables when the signature matrix A given in the preceding section is used, with two different choices of the initial conditions. In the first case, all variables are started with initial values of .1. In the second, variables 2 and 3 (metallurgy and craft technology) are started with values of .01. Figure 14.2 shows the growth when the initial values are all .1 but the signature matrix is changed by arbitrarily placing zeros in all entries in the fourth column to simulate the hypothesis that there is no positive feedback from the social subsystem to other subsystems.

Examination of these graphs shows that in all cases, the variables follow an S-shaped growth curve. That is, there is slow growth at first, then approximately exponential growth, and then leveling off toward the maximum possible level. Certain curves tend to lie above the others, notably the graph of x_1 (subsistence). However, little can be inferred from this at this time, since no *calibration* of the numerical scales has been adopted.

An implicit assumption in the use of signature matrices of this kind is that the feedbacks are all of equal strength. Whatever the significance of the numerical values, whatever their scalings, this seems unlikely to be true. In fact, there is no reason to restrict the entries to being 1, 0, or -1. The mathematical formulas allow any real numbers. By calling on panels of experts, one can assign different weights to different influences. The following matrix was suggested, as a guess at appropriate weightings of influences, by E. Elster and S. LeBlanc:

$$B = \begin{bmatrix} 0 & .5 & .5 & 1.0 & .25 & .75 & .75 \\ 0 & 0 & .75 & 2.0 & 0 & 1.0 & 0 \\ .5 & .75 & 0 & .5 & .5 & .25 & .25 \\ .25 & .75 & .5 & 0 & .1 & 0 & .5 \\ 0 & 0 & .25 & .75 & 0 & .25 & .5 \\ .25 & 1.0 & .75 & .35 & .1 & 0 & 0 \\ .75 & 0 & .1 & .85 & .1 & 0 & 0 \end{bmatrix}$$

The program was run with initial values

$$.3, \quad .01, \quad .1, \quad .1, \quad .1, \quad .2, \quad .1$$

and the results are shown in Figure 14.3. The chosen initial values reflect an assumption that subsistence and trade were at a higher level than the other subsystems at the beginning of the Early Bronze Age.

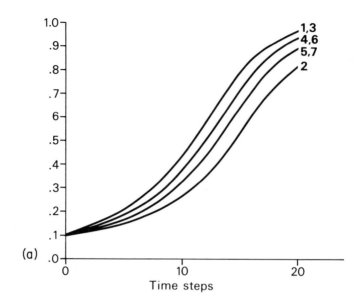

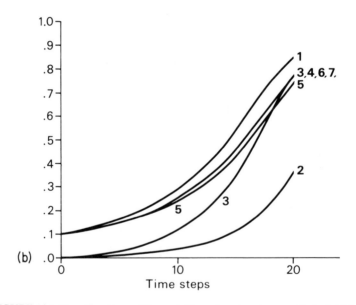

FIGURE 14.1 *Growth pattern of the variables using signature matrix A. Initial values: (a) all at .1; (b) variables 2 and 3, .01, remainder .1.*

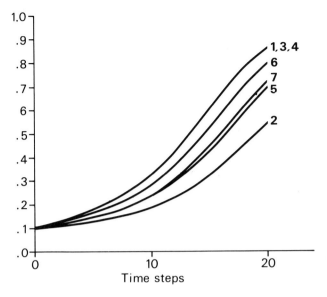

FIGURE 14.2 *Growth pattern of the variables using matrix A with zero for all entries in the fourth column.*

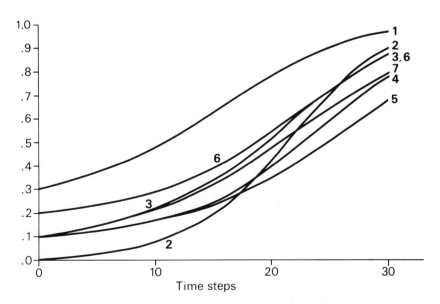

FIGURE 14.3 *Growth pattern of variables using matrix B and initial values between 0 and .3.*

The choice of a weighting matrix B such as the one given here again raises questions about the scaling. For example, if we consider any row of the matrix, the sum of its entries in some sense indicates the total influence of all variables on the subsystem associated with that row. The row sums for the B matrix are as follows: subsistence 3.75, metallurgy 3.75, craft 2.75, social 2.1, projective 1.75, trade 2.45, population 1.8.

It will be noted from Figure 14.3 that a large row sum tends to make the corresponding variable increase rapidly but, because of secondary effects, the relationship is not strict.

Each column in B represents the total effect of one subsystem on all others. For the matrix given here, these column sums are 1.75, 3, 2.85, 5.45, 1.05, 2.25, 2. This gives the impression that the influence of the social subsystem is being weighted far more heavily than the influence of any other subsystem.

A problem that arises in interpreting these simulations is the determination of the scale of the time variable. What is the period of time to be assigned to the arbitrary step h, the interval between successive states of the iteration?

In any real case some approximate estimate for the rate of change can be reached for most of the variables, and from this the length of the time step may be established. To take one example, estimates exist for the population of Crete at successive time periods. For instance, it has been suggested, although the figures are hypothetical, that the estimated population of Crete rose from 12,600 to 75,000 in about 1500 years. Therefore, x_7 increased by a factor of 6 in 1500 years. Consulting Figure 14.1a we see that x_7 increased from .1 to .6, that is, by a factor of 6, in about 14.4 time steps. Therefore we can assume that one time step represents about 1500/14.4, or 104 years. The same calculation applied to Figure 14.1b results in a time step of $h = 86$ years, and Figure 14.2 in 84 years. Of course it must be emphasized that this calculation depends on the assumption that the growth curve produced by the model represents the actual growth curve to within acceptable accuracy, and that the estimates in question make a suitable basis for calculation. Any other variable could be used in a similar manner.

As we have observed, all the results so far show steady growth of all subsystems. In fact, in all the experiments described so far, all entries in the matrix are positive. Therefore, (14.10) holds and all variables must increase at every time step. When all feedbacks are positive, we have a pure growth model. When all feedbacks are negative, we have a pure decay model. Moreover, in the pure growth model, since each variable is increasing, and yet cannot exceed 1, it must level off either at 1 or possibly at some value less than 1. In the following section, we show that only in exceptional cases can the variables approach equilibrium values less than 1. Consequently the expected behavior is for all variables to follow an S-shaped growth leveling off at 1.

It is clear that no culture system behaves in such a way that all variables increase to some high notional value, and remain indefinitely at this high level. Indeed, as used up to this point, the model, although adequately simulating growth, fails to reflect adequately the property that is most characteristic of all successful culture systems: homeostasis.

A preliminary experiment was to insert some negative values for the indices in one subsystem. Here "piracy" was imagined as operating negatively on a number of subsystems. (The projective system was omitted in this instance.) The Matrix C is as follows:

	Subsistence	Metallurgy	Craft	Social	Trade	Population	Piracy
Subsistence	0	.5	.5	1.0	.75	.75	−2.0
Metallurgy	0	0	.75	1.0	1.0	0	−.2
Craft	.5	.75	0	.5	.25	.25	.3
Social	.25	.75	.5	0	0	.5	.5
Trade	.25	1.0	.75	.35	0	0	−2.0
Population	.75	0	.1	.85	0	0	−.5
Piracy	.5	.75	.75	.5	1.0	.5	0

All variables were given initial values of .3. The results are graphed in Figure 14.4. The negative interactions in this case slow down growth of some variables but do not cause a collapse of the system.

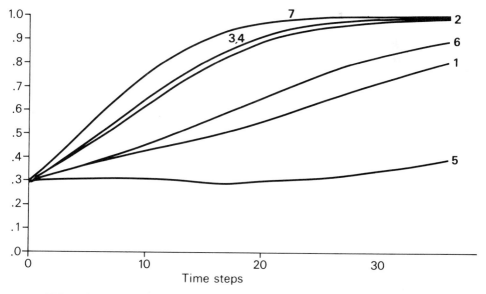

FIGURE 14.4 *Growth pattern of the variables with some negative values for the indices (matrix C). All variables have initial value .3.*

Range of Behavior of the Iterates

After a number of trial runs such as the foregoing, it became apparent that a more thorough examination of the properties of the system was required. What behavior, other than steady growth and steady decay, is possible for the mathematical iteration given by Equations (14.1)–(14.9)? In attempting to answer this question, we have proceeded in two ways. On the one hand, we have used theoretical means to locate all possible equilibrium points of the iteration. On the other hand, we have used computer experiments to demonstrate that sustained periodic oscillations can occur.

We begin by describing our results concerning equilibrium states. We let x denote the column vector with components x_i, and write $p_i(x, h)$ instead of p_i to emphasize the dependence on x and h. Let

$$f_i(x, h) = x_i^{p_i(x,h)} = \begin{cases} \exp[p_i(x, h) \log x_i] & \text{if } x_i > 0 \\ 0 & \text{if } x_i = 0 \end{cases} \tag{14.11}$$

and let $f(x, h)$ be the vector with components $f_i(x, h)$. Then the iteration (14.1) has the form

$$x(t + h) = f(x(t), h) \qquad (t = 0, h, \ldots) \tag{14.12}$$

Suppose that $x(t)$ tends to a constant vector $\hat{x}$ as $t \to \infty$. Then from (14.2)–(14.4) we see that $p_i(x(t), h)$ tends to $p_i(\hat{x}, h)$. If $\hat{x}_i > 0$, we also have $\log x_i(t) \to \log \hat{x}_i$ and therefore $f_i(x(t), h)$ tends to $f_i(\hat{x}, h)$. If $x_i(t) > 0$ and $x_i(t)$ tends to $0 = \hat{x}_i$, then $p_i(x(t), h)$ tends to a positive constant and $f_i(x(t), h)$ tends to zero. Therefore, from (14.11), (14.12) we deduce that

$$\hat{x} = f(\hat{x}, h) \tag{14.13}$$

in either case. That is, $\hat{x}$ is a *fixed point* of the iteration defined by (14.12). The following theorem shows how to find all such fixed points.

THEOREM 1. *Consider the iteration defined by (14.1)–(14.4):*

(a) *If $x(t)$ has all components $x_i(t) \geq 0$ and if $x(t)$ tends to a constant vector $\hat{x}$ as $t \to \infty$, then (14.13) is satisfied.*

(b) *If $\hat{x}$ has all components $\hat{x}_i \geq 0$ and if $\hat{x}$ satisfies (14.13), then*

$$\sum_{j=1}^{m} a_{ij}\hat{x}_j = 0 \qquad \text{for all } i \text{ for which } \hat{x}_i \neq 0 \text{ or } 1 \tag{14.14}$$

Conversely, if $\hat{x}$ is a vector for which $\hat{x} \geq 0$ and for which (14.14) holds for every i for which $\hat{x}_i$ is neither 0 nor 1, then $\hat{x}$ satisfies (14.13).

Proof. Part (a) has already been proved, and we turn to part (b). Assume that $\hat{x}_i \geq 0$ and $\hat{x}$ satisfies (14.13). If $\hat{x}_i \neq 0$, $\hat{x}_i \neq 1$, then from (14.13) and the definition of f_i, we deduce $p_i(\hat{x}, h) = 1$. Hence $q_i = r_i$ and

$$\sum_{k=1}^{m} a^{-}{}_{ik} \hat{x}_k = \sum_{k=1}^{m} a^{+}{}_{ik} \hat{x}_k \qquad (14.15)$$

From this equation, (14.14) follows. Conversely, let $\hat{x}$ be a vector with $\hat{x}_i \geqslant 0$ for which (14.14) holds. For any i for which $\hat{x}_i \neq 0$ or 1, we have (14.15). Therefore, $p_i(\hat{x}, h) = 1$ and $f_i(\hat{x}, h) = \hat{x}_i$. For any i for which $\hat{x}_i = 0$ or 1, we have $f_i(\hat{x}, h) = 0$ or 1 by definition, and again $f_i(\hat{x}, h) = \hat{x}_i$. Thus, (14.13) holds. This completes the proof.

An important conclusion to be drawn from Theorem 1 is that every equilibrium state (fixed point) of the iteration must have all its components equal to 0 or 1, unless the matrix A satisfies certain linear relations (14.14). In particular, if $\hat{x}$ is a fixed point with $0 < \hat{x}_i < 1$ for every i, then (14.14) must be satisfied for every i. This is equivalent to $A\hat{x} = 0$. Such an $\hat{x}$ therefore exists if and only if A is a singular matrix. This proves the following corollary.

COROLLARY. *The iteration has a fixed point $\hat{x}$ with $0 < \hat{x}_i < 1$ for every i if and only if* det $A = 0$.

In general, we expect that the matrix A will be nonsingular, since the set of singular matrices is of "low dimensionality" or "probability" among the set of all matrices. Consequently, we can interpret the result as stating that the only equilibrium states $\hat{x}$ possible for the model are those in which at least one component $\hat{x}_i$ equals 0 or 1. That is, some subsystem variable must tend to its minimum or maximum allowable value. The fact that it is impossible to have an equilibrium of the system with all limits $\hat{x}_i$ strictly between 0 and 1 (unless A is singular) seems to indicate that these equations, in their present form, are inappropriate for models in which equilibrium states are expected. In the following section suggestions are made for extensions that may be more useful in simulation of behavior over a long time span.

It is possible to analyze the local stability (local attractivity) of the fixed points. However, we omit this discussion here.

We shall now describe a numerical experiment which seems to reveal the presence of periodic behavior of the iteration. For this purpose it was thought best to simplify by reducing the number of variables. Initially a system was formulated with only three variables (conceived as population, subsistence, and craft technology) controlled by the matrix

$$D = \begin{pmatrix} 0 & .5 & -.9 \\ .4 & 0 & .2 \\ .5 & -.1 & 0 \end{pmatrix}$$

Figure 14.5 shows two runs, each made with a time step $h = .2$, and with respective initial values (a) .23, .95, .52; and (b) .1, .1, .1. For this matrix, there is an equilibrium state with $\hat{x}_1 = \frac{2}{5}, \hat{x}_2 = 1, \hat{x}_3 = \frac{5}{9}$. In both runs, $x_2(t)$

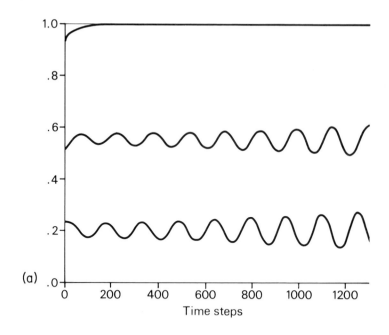

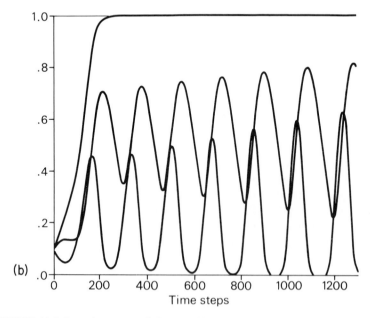

FIGURE 14.5 *Growth pattern of the variables, using three variables with interactions indicated in matrix D, and initial values (a) .23, .95, .52 and (b) .1, .1, .1.*

quickly tends to 1, and $x_1(t)$ and $x_3(t)$ oscillate around the values $\frac{2}{5}$ and $\frac{5}{9}$, with apparently increasing amplitude.

Figure 14.6 shows runs made with the slightly altered matrix

$$E = \begin{pmatrix} -.01 & .5 & -.9 \\ .4 & 0 & .2 \\ .5 & -.1 & -.01 \end{pmatrix}$$

There is an equilibrium state $\hat{x}_1 = 1900/9002, \hat{x}_2 = 1, \hat{x}_3 = 4980/9002$. The runs were made with respective initial values (a) .05 + 1900/9002, 1, 4980/9002; (b) .01, .5, .01; and (c) .98, .98, .05. In all three runs, $x_2(t)$ tends to 1. In (b), $x_1(t)$ and $x_3(t)$ appear to approach periodicity, and in (c) they seem to fall to zero. In any event, fairly complex oscillatory behavior seems to be possible for iterations of the form under consideration, presumably due to the non-linearity of the governing equations.

Extensions and Alterations of the Model

A number of extensions of the model may be considered.

Interaction Coefficients Varying with Value of Variable

As described earlier each entry a_{ij} in the matrix A is fixed once and for all during an experiment. Although this assumption may be reasonable during the first simple stage of model building, it is clearly inappropriate in any real case in which long-term behavior is considered. It may often be the case that an influence is present for small values of a variable but absent for larger values. In some cases the influence could become negative for large values, suggesting some kind of negative feedback. In general, then, the numbers a_{ij} should be allowed to be *state dependent* (i.e., functions of the values of some or all of the variables). In other words, the linear forms in Equations (14.7) and (14.8) should be replaced by

$$q_i = 1 + h \sum_{k=1}^{m} a^-_{ik}(x)$$

$$r_i = 1 + h \sum_{k=1}^{m} a^+_{ik}(x)$$

where $a_{ik}(x) \equiv a_{ik}(x_1, x_2, \ldots, x_m)$ is an arbitrary function of the variables x_1, $x_2, \ldots, x_m$, and where $a^+_{ik}(x) = a_{ik}(x)$ for $a_{ik}(x) > 0$ and $a^-_{ik}(x) = |a_{ik}(x)|$ for $a_{ik}(x) < 0$. In practice, one might begin by taking $a_{ik}(x)$ to be a quadratic function of x_k only, for example,

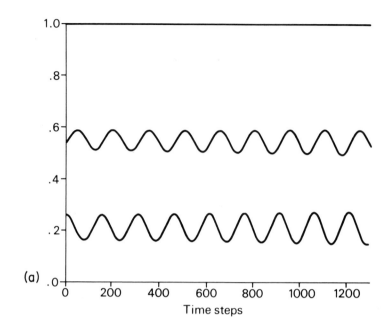

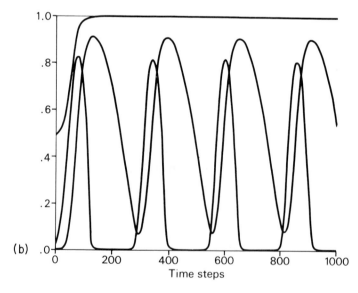

FIGURE 14.6 *Growth behavior pattern of the variables, with interactions indicated in matrix E, and with the initial values (a) 0.05 + 1900/9002, 1, 4980/9002; (b) .01, .5, .01; (c) .98, .98, .05.*

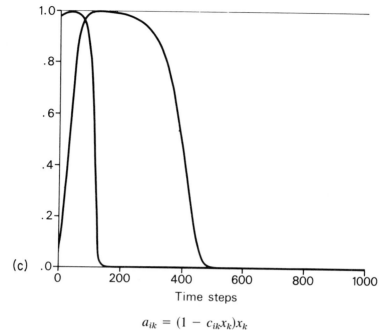

$$a_{ik} = (1 - c_{ik}x_k)x_k$$

No investigation of such models has been undertaken so far by us, although one can readily visualize that, with suitably formulated relationships, the stability of the system could be attained.

Interaction Coefficients Varying with Rate of Change of Variables

The difficulties in achieving a steady rate, or a number of steady states, with a linear dependence of q_i and r_i upon the value of the variable suggested the idea that in some cases these may depend rather on whether the variable in question is increasing or decreasing. For instance, if we are considering the influence of population on subsistence production, a stable, nonchanging population might be thought to induce no change in the subsistence system. Indeed, when we are trying to set up a homeostatic system, some formulation of the following form may be appropriate

$$q_i = 1 + \tfrac{1}{2}h \sum_{k=1}^{m} \left\{ \left| a_{ik} + \frac{b_{ik}}{x_k} \frac{dx_k}{dt} \right| - \left(a_{ik} + \frac{b_{ik}}{x_k} \frac{dx_k}{dt} \right) \right\} x_k$$

$$r_i = 1 + \tfrac{1}{2}h \sum_{k=1}^{m} \left\{ \left| a_{ik} + \frac{b_{ik}}{x_k} \frac{dx_k}{dt} \right| + \left(a_{ik} + \frac{b_{ik}}{x_k} \frac{dx_k}{dt} \right) \right\} x_k$$

Equations of this kind have been suggested by Kane, Thompson, and Vertinsky. We have not yet investigated such models. In a discrete time simulation, the derivatives dx_k/dt can be approximated by finite differences. A listing of a large FORTRAN program for systems of this type has been published by Thompson, Vertinsky and Kane (1974).

Time Lags

In many systems, changes in the present are determined not by the current values of variables but by their values some time in the past. This can easily be built into the model by allowing q_i and r_i to depend not only on $x_k(t)$ but also on x_k a given number of time steps earlier.

Alternative Forms of Equation (14.1)

Although the iteration equations (14.1)–(14.4) have certain convenient features, a number of other formulations in terms of differential and difference equations are possible. Some of these may be more useful by allowing "physical" interpretation of the parameters and by allowing the insertion of equations which reflect the supposed interactions more realistically and in more detail. A number of different mathematical formulations should be tried and compared.

Sensitivity Analysis

In evaluating a model such as the one described here, it is usually important to conduct a sensitivity analysis. That is, one endeavors to see how great the variation is in various performance measures when the parameters of the model are varied by a designated amount. We have not carried out such an analysis for the present model since we feel that the whole structure of the model is still under investigation.

Further Outlook

In the present early stage of development, the model proposed cannot be regarded as simulating in any meaningful sense the early development of Aegean civilization. That specific cultural context has simply been used as the starting point for the formulation of a much more general model, and the exploration of some of its properties.

Indeed, the foregoing discussion allows us to consider more clearly what sort of behavior would be required of such a model in order that we should feel its behavior modeled satisfactorily some aspects of the behavior of the real world. At least four may be suggested:

1. The rate of change and behavior of the variables should be consonant

with that of the limits in the range of real behavior which they represent.

2. The model should display homeostatic behavior, in the sense not of absolutely stable steady states, but of periods of very gradual change.

3. The model should display sustained growth under certain circumstances.

4. Ideally it should also display threshold effects—that is, periods of sustained and fairly rapid growth between periods of relative stability.

We suggest that this approach brings out in an informative way a number of the difficulties inherent in models of system dynamics. In particular it suggests that lengthy discussions of input (or output) data can usefully be deferred until the range of behavior of the model, when subjected to a wide variety of input data, has been examined and found plausible. Already this approach has led us to consider more closely the mechanism of homeostasis within the culture system. And already it has led us to feel more acutely the danger of ascribing to the real world aspects of model behavior which instead arise from the constraints built into the model. We were particularly struck by the difficulty in simulating homeostatic behavior with this model when the values of the coefficients were constant. Indeed it occurred to us to wonder whether this is not a limitation which applies also, although for different reasons, to the model, based on the work of Forrester, used for the study *The Limits to Growth* (Meadows *et al.* 1972). It is apparently the case that not one of the variables studied there in a number of different simulations reaches a steady state within the time span considered, until the population is artificially and externally held constant (ibid. 160).

The aim of the present work is indeed to arrive at (approximately) steady states, but these should arise from the interactions of the variables rather than be imposed quite arbitrarily from the outside.

Acknowledgment

We are grateful to Mr. Eric V. Level for his assistance with the computer simulations for this project.

References

Binford, L. R. and Binford, S. R. (eds.), 1968, *New Perspectives in Archaeology,* Chicago, Aldine.

Clarke, D. L. (ed.), 1972, *Models in Archaeology,* London, Methuen.

Cooke, K., 1973, A model of urbanization and civilization, University of Southern California, Dept. of Elect. Engr., Tech. Report No. RB 73–34.

Kane, J., 1972, A primer for a new cross-impact language - KSIM, *Technological Forecasting and Social Change,* 4, 129–142.

Kane, J., Thompson, W., Vertinsky, I., 1972, Health care delivery: a policy simulator, *Socio-Economic Planning Sciences,* 6, 283–293.

Kane, J., Vertinksy, I., Thompson, W., 1973, KSIM: a methodology for interactive resource policy simulation, *Water Resources Research,* 9, 65–79.

Meadows, D. H., Meadows, D. L., Randers, J. and Behrens, W. W., 1972, *The Limits to Growth,* London, Pan.

Plog, F. T., 1974, *The Study of Prehistoric Change,* New York, Academic Press.

Renfrew, C., 1972, *The Emergence of Civilization,* London, Methuen.

Renfrew, C., (ed.), 1973, *The Explanation of Culture Change: Models in Prehistory,* London, Duckworth.

Rosen, R., 1972, The simplest dynamical models, Occasional paper, Center for the Study of Democratic Institutions, Santa Barbara.

Rosen, R., 1973, A framework for "retrospective futurology," Occasional paper, Center for the Study of Democratic Institutions, Santa Barbara, 4 October 1973.

Spengler, O., 1918, *The Decline of the West.*

Thompson, W. A., Vertinsky, L., and Kane, J., 1974, KSIM - Policy simulation: User's Manual, *International Technical Cooperation Centre Review,* 3, 57–81.

Toynbee, A. J., 1947, *A Study of History, Oxford, University Press.*

Wilkinson, J., Bellman, R., Garaudy, R., 1973, The Dynamic Programming of Human Systems, Occasional paper, Center for the Study of Democratic Institutions, Santa Barbara.

V

THE DECISION NEXUS AND EARLY ECONOMIES

You argue by results, as this world does,
To settle if an act be good or bad.
You defer to the fact. For every life and every act
Consequence of good and evil can be shown.

T. S. Eliot
Murder in the Cathedral

Archaeology, and especially prehistoric archaeology, is rarely able to yield much information about the individual. Patterns of activity show more clearly in the record than different events or aspects in the life of any identifiable person. Yet the "atomic" level of analysis (see Chapter 1) is in many ways the most natural one, since ultimately most decisions are in fact taken by a human individual.

With the development of linear programming (Dantzig 1963; Keene, Chapter 16, this volume), Monte Carlo methods (Hammersley and Handscomb 1964), game theory (Chapter 2, this volume; von Neumann and Morgenstern 1947; Luce and Raiffa 1957) and dynamical programming (Bellman 1952), a cluster of methods are now available which together constitute decision theory, and substantially extend the range of classical microeconomics, with its traditional emphasis upon supply and demand, price and profit. They are reviewed in Chapter 2 of this volume. Yet anthropologists and archaeologists have, until very recently, and with a few exceptions (e.g., Joy 1967), been slow to use these new approaches.

Progress in this direction has, I think, been considerably hampered through lengthy wrangling by economic anthropologists of different persuasions, partaking in what these protagonists like to think of as a "great debate" (e.g., Pearson 1957; Cohen 1967). On the one hand the followers of Karl Polanyi, including Dalton (1961) and Sahlins (1965), quite validly reasserted the old criticism that since small-scale societies and indeed early state societies had no monetary currency and, they argued, no markets, the application to these societies of the traditional concepts of economics, geared to a monetary and market-orientated economy, could hardly be appropriate. Out of this "substantivist" school has come some of the most interesting economic anthropology of recent years (see Adams 1974 for a critical review).

On the other hand, the "formalists" continue to hold that the differences between "primitive" and industrial economies are of degree rather than of kind, and that there are valid economic principles of wide application which merit serious study (Firth 1965; Herskovits 1952). In some ways neo-Marxist anthropologists (Godelier 1972; Terray 1972; Meillassoux 1964) stand closer to the former than to the latter, with their concentration upon the "embeddedness" of the economy in its social matrix, and their insistence on Marx's fundamental distinction (Marx 1964) between capitalist and precapitalist social formations.

The three chapters in this part, together with recent papers by Reidhead (1977) and Limp (1977) and the original and important study by Jochim (1976), represent a significant new departure for archaeology. Keene and Schiffer are concerned with the alternatives open to the human individual, and in their rational assessment in terms of costs and rewards. Reynolds discusses the related problem when the decision is taken by a small group or band operating together. In a refreshing way all six studies avoid the soul-searching and philosophical agonizing of the "great debate." It should be noted that in doing so they make a number of important assumptions, and that so far the application is restricted to a limited field.

The first basic assumption is that the individuals concerned are capable of assessing rationally the utility (or attractiveness) of the various possible decisions, and of associating with them probabilities for the consequences. It is implicit in the analysis that concepts such as risk and cost are appropriate, although it is not argued that they are explicitly or consciously formulated by the actors. Studies of decision making in animals (McFarland 1977) are able to make similar assumptions without employing the concept of "economic man." The second important assumption is that the behavior is optimizing, seeking maximum results for minimum cost and minimum risk. Optimality principles are of considerable importance in biology (Rosen 1967) and economic anthropology (Burling 1962) as well as in other fields (cf. Zipf 1949), and raise a number of issues which have not yet been fully clarified.

All these chapters are so far restricted to a consideration of what amounts to a single subsystem (primarily the subsistence subsystem) of the total culture system. It is in this way that they escape the passions of the great debate. With the consideration of exchange, which is as much a social as an economic activity (and hence impinges on several subsystems simultaneously), the position is likely to become more difficult. Yet there is perhaps no reason why costs and risks in different fields (different subsystems) should not be modeled in different dimensions: If social as well as economic constraints are adequately considered, there should be less risk of "substantivist'' disapproval. The phenomenon of bimodal behavior—the sudden switch from one strategy to another—has already been explored by catastrophe theory (Zeeman 1976; Isnard and Zeeman 1976; Wilson 1976; see Part VI). And aspects of decision and choice have been considered in similar terms with reference to the archaeological record of innovation (Renfrew 1978).

Of course the archaeologist will never have much direct evidence about the actual reasoning of the prehistoric individual, or be able to observe the process of decision making. But he frequently has excellent data bearing on the consequences of the decisions. Models for decision making are thus eminently testable, and the archaeologist is consequently well justified in making models about the decision behavior of the individual, even if the individual himself remains invisible.

A.C.R.

References

Adams, R. M., 1974, Anthropological perspectives on ancient trade, *Current Anthropology* 15, 239–258.

Bellman, R., 1952. *Dynamic Programming,* Princeton, University Press.

Burling, R., 1962, Maximization theories and the study of economic anthropology, *American Anthropologist* 64, 802–821.

Cohen, P. S., 1967, Economic analysis and economic man: some comments on a controversy, in Firth R. (ed.), *Themes in Economic Anthropology* (A.S.A. Monographs 6), London, Tavistock, 91–118.

Dalton, G., 1961, Economic theory and primitive society, *American Anthropologist* 63, 1–25.

Dantzig, G. B., 1963, *Linear Programming and Extensions,* Princeton, University Press.

Firth, R., 1965, *Primitive Polynesian Economy* (2nd edition), London, Routledge.

Godelier, M., 1972, *Rationality and Irrationality in Economics,* London.

Hammersley, J. N. and Handscomb D. C., 1964, *Monte Carlo Methods,* London, Methuen.

Herskovits, M. J., 1952, *Economic Anthropology,* New York, Knopf.

Isnard, C. A. and Zeeman, E. C., 1976, Some models from catastrophe theory in the social sciences, in Collins L. (ed.), *The Use of Models in the Social Sciences,* London, Tavistock, 44–100.

Jochim, M. A., 1976, *Hunter-Gatherer Subsistence and Settlement, a Predictive Model,* New York, Academic Press.

Joy, L., 1967, An economic homologue of Barth's presentation of economic spheres in Darfur, in Firth R. (ed.), *Themes in Economic Anthropology* (A.S.A. Monographs 6), London, Tavistock, 175–189.

Limp, W. F., 1977, The economics of agricultural dispersal, Paper presented at the 42nd Annual Meeting of the Society for American Archaeology, New Orleans.

Luce, R. and Raiffa, H., 1957, *Games and Decisions: Introduction and Critical Survey,* New York, John Wiley.

Marx, K., 1964, *Pre-Capitalist Social Formations,* London, Lawrence and Wishart.

Meillassoux, M., 1964, *Anthropologie Économique des Gouro de Côte d'Ivoire,* The Hague, Mouton.

McFarland, D. J., 1977, Decision making in animals, *Nature* 269, 15–21.

Neumann, J. von, and Morgenstern O., 1947, *Theory of Games and Economic Behavior,* Princeton, University Press.

Pearson, H. W., 1957, The secular debate on economic primitivism, in Polanyi K., Arsneberg C. M. and Pearson H. W. (eds.), *Trade and Market in the Early Empires,* New York, Free Press, 3–11.

Reidhead, V. A., 1977, Labor and nutrition in food procurement: did prehistoric people optimize?, Paper presented at the 42nd Annual Meeting of the Society for American Archaeology, New Orleans.

Renfrew, C., 1978, The anatomy of innovation, in Green D. R., Haselgrove C. C., and Spriggs M. J. T. (eds.), *Social Organisation and Settlement* (British Archaeological Reports, Supplementary Series 47), 89–117.

Rosen, R., 1967, *Optimality Principles in Biology,* London.

Sahlins, M. D., 1965, On the Sociology of primitive exchange, in Banton M. (ed.), *The Relevance of Models for Social Anthropology* (A.S.A. Monograph no. 1), London, Tavistock, 139–236.

Terray, E., 1972, *Marxism and "Primitive" Societies,* New York, Monthly Review.

Wilson, A. G., 1976, Catastrophe Theory and urban modelling: an application to modal choice, *Environment and Planning A,* 8, 351–356.

Zeeman, C. E., 1976, A mathematical model for conflicting judgments caused by stress, *British Journal of Mathematical and Statistical Psychology* 29, 19–31.

Zipf, G. K., 1949, *Human Behaviour and the Principle of Least Effort,* New York, Hafner.

15

MICHAEL B. SCHIFFER

A Preliminary Consideration of Behavioral Change

This chapter aims to present a materialist conceptual scheme for the nomothetic study of behavioral change and to raise the possibility (largely by implication) that the paradigm archaeologists seem to be assembling for explaining change requires a fundamental overhaul (see Reid 1973). This chapter aspires to advance beyond a cautionary tale by furnishing specific suggestions as to how the laws of behavioral change might be sought. Regrettably, no principles are provided here, but a framework is developed that may help investigators to formulate appropriate nomothetic questions and to design research for answering them. The discussion begins with a general treatment of behavioral systems and change from the standpoint of "activity analysis." Elementary postulates are proposed and some of their implications for understanding change processes are explored. On the basis of these considerations, an analytic decision-making model is presented for organizing the study of behavioral change. A partially completed example illustrates the use of this framework. It is concluded that discovery of the laws of change will require that new directions of inquiry be pursued using diverse sources of data.

Behavioral Systems and Behavioral Change

A behavioral system articulates a human group to its natural and social environment. Such systems are formed by sets of activities which process energy, matter, and information (Miller 1965a,b). An *activity* consists of the

353

Transformations:
Mathematical Approaches to Culture Change

patterned behavior of one or more *elements* (animate and inanimate objects), at least one of which is an *energy source*. Energy sources, which carry out work and thus make behavior possible, are usually human beings, but they may also be animals, machines, wind, water, and the sun. The *social unit of activity performance* designates the individual or individuals who participate in the activity.

All elements, including energy sources, have morphological and behavioral characteristics that are crucial to a specified activity. These are referred to as *conjunction parameters*. For example, in the activity of bipolar flaking (Spears 1975), the cobble hammerstone must be of adequate toughness to withstand repeated hard blows. It must also be of a size sufficient to create the momentum for fracturing a core. The knapper (a noninfant person) needs to have some manual dexterity, at least one arm, and familiarity with the fracturing properties of the material being worked. However, the color and precise shape of a hammerstone are not relevant for bipolar flaking. Thus, conjunction parameters are only those properties that elements must possess in order to behave appropriately in a particular activity.

Elements that participate in more than one activity, particularly human elements, naturally have a set of conjunction parameters for each. These sets may overlap to varying degrees. As it applies to human elements, this formulation can eventually dovetail with status–role theory.

A consideration of the degree to which elements may replace each other in activities allows recognition of an important cause of behavioral change. Given that elements may have many conjunction parameters (with respect to an activity) and that many elements have conjunction parameters for many activities, it is unlikely that the conjunction parameters of any two elements would be totally isomorphic. The expectation that elements tend toward uniqueness in conjunction parameters is termed the *irreplaceability postulate*. Intuitively it is apparent why a shotgun cannot replace a tape dispenser in the activity of dispensing tape, but it is less obvious why a shotgun cannot replace in all respects a rifle for deer hunting. Conjunction parameters such as accuracy at a distance, minimum time elapsed between firings, and severity of the wound inflicted (holding constant distance from the hunter) would differ. Similarly, a 1965 Mercedes can perform the same transportation duties as a Mercedes of more recent vintage, but it conveys different information about the status of the owner.

The irreplaceability postulate applies also to energy sources and even to human elements. Clearly, individuals differ in a variety of characteristics that make them capable of performing some activities but not others. Most people, for example, can run a mile, but only a few can run it fast enough to compete in the Olympics. And although many native-born American adults are greater than 35 years of age, relatively few people possess the motivation, stamina, and social relationships required to mount and sustain a campaign for the presidency of the United States. Thus differences in motor habits and physical abilities, creativity, knowledge, experience, motivation, attitudes, and social relationships affect the fit between an individual and the requirements of an activity.

However, it does not follow from the irreplaceability postulate that *substitutions* will not occur. Indeed, that elements are substituted for one another frequently—despite only partial identities in conjunction parameters—leads to sometimes far-reaching behavioral changes. Because substitutions are seldom *replacements* (since the latter entail an isomorphism of conjunction parameters), one can expect *element disjunctions* to arise—situations in which the fit between the substituted element and the activity may be sufficiently different to alter the characteristics of activity performance. It is to a description of the latter that I now turn.

There are many ways to describe activities. In the present framework it is necessary to concentrate only on those features that illuminate the relationships between elements and activities, between activities and other activities, and between activities and the system's environment.

Activity–state parameters are those characteristics of activities most useful for examining element–activity relationships (in addition, of course, to conjunction parameters—which deal primarily with element–element relationships). Activity–state parameters include a listing of the elements, the nature of their interaction, and the rate and location of activity performance. Some of these have previously been termed "components" (Schiffer 1975:109, 1976:49). Another important activity–state parameter is the net energy expenditure. The latter is the amount of energy spent per unit of activity, above the basal metabolic rate, by the social unit of activity performance and any expenditures by other energy sources. The latter would be treated separately in many analyses. Additional activity–state parameters remain to be designated.

Activity performance results in the expenditure of energy and the alteration of elements. The latter wear out, break, become crippled, die, or are otherwise modified so that their conjunction parameters change. In the case of human elements, some of these changes, related to aging, are directly time dependent; whereas others, such as accidents resulting in disablement or death, and most changes in other elements, are time dependent only indirectly: They are a probabilistic function of the performance rate of an activity (see Sullivan 1978). When the characteristics change to the extent that conjunction parameters are altered and activity performance is impaired, replacement elements are obtained (unless there is substitution or activity change). In addition, food and/or fuel must be supplied to maintain the operation of the energy sources. Thus, if activity performance is to continue unchanged over some nontrivial period of time, a regular flow of replacement durable and consumable elements and energy sources must occur within the system. Moreover, the raw materials out of which elements are fashioned (or elements themselves) derive ultimately from the system's environment.

The matter and energy (and information) flows with reference to any activity are described by a set of *coupling parameters,* of which there are two kinds. *Intrasystemic* coupling parameters detail the flows between an activity and other activities of the system, whereas *direct* flows between an activity and the environment are specified by *extrasystemic* coupling parameters. Naturally, all activities are coupled, indirectly through other activities, to the environment. Coupling parameters are expressed, insofar as possible, as rates of material flow per instance of activity performance or unit of time (Schiffer 1976; Hildebrand 1978). Coupling parameters are often estimated only as rough probabilities, while in some instances—perhaps when flow rates are high—fairly accurate quantities may be specifiable. If a coupling parameter describes a flow from the environment or another activity, it is called an *input;* if the flow begins with the reference activity and goes outward, it is an *output.* For the sake of convenience, the matter, energy, and information flows delineated by coupling parameters are referred to herein as *material flows.*

Material flows establish patterned relationships among activities. This is stated formally as the *interdependence postulate:* In a behavioral system all activities are connected or related to all other activities by material flows. Direct and indirect, connections are always present.

The modern activity of an individual fishing on a riverbank can—with sufficient imagination on the part of the reader—illustrate some of the concepts developed so far. For the sake of simplicity, the activities of cleaning and dressing fish and transportation are excluded. It is assumed that fishing occurs for an indefinite period of time, and all figures are contrived. Fishing—the activity of procuring fish—involves the following elements: an individual (energy source and social unit of activity performance), cane pole, line, sinkers, floats, hooks, live minnows, tackle box, food, beer, clothing, insect repellent, sunglasses, and fish. The precise interactions between elements need not be treated, for the reader can surely envision the more specific acts, such as eating, casting, and raising the line. The location of fishing is on a riverbank at a place where the bottom is deeper and the current slower than average. Fishing occurs 40 times per year, for an 18-hr period.

First are considered the inputs. Extrasystemic coupling parameters might include 200 fish per year, 200 chiggers per year, 160 mosquitoes per year, and 20 snakes per year. Intrasystemic coupling parameters (the material flows for replacing lost, broken, worn-out, and dead elements) are 1000 minnows per year, 200 yards of line per year, 80 hooks per year, 80 sinkers per year, 80 floats per year, 2 cane poles per year, .2 tackle boxes per year, 80 sandwiches per year, 240 cans of beer per year, .002 fishermen per year, plus the rates for assorted packaging materials, clothing, insect repellent, sunglasses, and so on. Outputs can now be listed. Extrasystemic coupling parameters (in this case describing outputs of lost and discarded materials to the natural environment—i.e., archaeological context) include 1000 minnows per year, 80 sinkers per year, 80 hooks per year, 80 floats per year, 2 cane poles per year, 240 beer cans per year, 2000 oz. urine per year, 1.0×10^{-9} fishermen per year (drowned and lost), plus various rates for sweat, heat, food waste, packaging materials, clothing, sunglasses, insect repellent, containers, and so on. Intrasystemic coupling parameters, of course, consist of 200 fish per year coupled to the next activity of cleaning, .002 fishermen per year die, and assorted values for snake, chigger, and mosquito bites couple them to maintenance activities for the human element.

In the determination of flow rates for coupling parameters, as in other aspects of the activity analysis framework, a great deal depends on careful specification of the scale of the analysis. Behavior is a continuum that must be segmented into usable activity units depending on the problem at hand (see Harris 1964 for another general treatment of the behavior stream). For some purposes, the analysis might be carried out on the most fine-grained activities imaginable (e.g., placing a minnow on a hook, casting, drinking a beer) while other problems dictate the use of activities even more inclusive than fishing.

The nature of the relationship between any two activities is determined by the activities that lie between them and the intervening coupling parameters. These linkages are described in a variety of ways. For example, one can examine the *coupling distance,* that is, the number of intermediate activities, using the shortest path for calculation. Relationships may be direct, as when activities are coupled by a complementary pair of input and output parameters (the same 200 fish per year are output from fishing and input to cleaning) or very indirect and dependent on a series of complex linkages (e.g., crude oil procurement, transport, sale, chemical feedstock manufacture, sale, transport, plastic float manufacture, wholesaling, retailing, fishing). For some problems it may be helpful to devise indices of *coupling strength,* or the degree to which the performance of one activity depends on the performance of another. For example, if a family's only source of fish is what they catch, then (ignoring intermediate activities) fish eating depends greatly on fish procurement. On the other hand (and again without consideration for intermediate activities), if a fisherman sells fish to 100 families, fishing depends on the eating activity of each family only to a small extent. It should be possible in the future to employ simple ratios of input and output coupling parameters in the construction of coupling strength indices. Another potentially useful variable is *coupling variety:* the number of activities (taking separately inputs and outputs) to which the reference activity is coupled. And finally, a measure of *coupling redundancy* could be based on the number of linkages above a specified strength that exist between the activities. Other descriptions of activity relationships remain to be formulated, particularly those dealing with transitivity (see also Krause and Thorne 1971; Sullivan 1978). Of particular importance is the opportunity of establishing general patterns of covariation among these variables and other systemic properties (see Plog 1977).

It now becomes possible to formulate the *stability postulate:* Unless there is a change in one or more coupling parameters, the nature of an activity (i.e., the activity–state parameters) will remain constant. For example, fishing will continue unmodified unless there is a change in a coupling parameter, such as a greater rate of pole loss, inability to acquire bait, lack of replacement fishermen, or a lower rate of success. Change processes in a system are initiated by altered values of one or more extrasystemic coupling parameters. If there is a departure of a value from its normal range, change processes will be set in motion. For several reasons, behavioral changes are seldom confined to the originally affected activity. That can happen only if an activity and its substitute have identical coupling parameters. The vanishingly small probability that this will occur makes it possible to propose the postulate of *functional nonequivalence:* The substitution of activities usually involves a nonisomorphism in coupling parameters. This is called an *activity disjunction*. Differences in coupling parameters may be small or large, but they can be expected generally. Element disjunctions, of course, are a major source of altered coupling parameters. Because of the reticulate network of linkages between activities (as specified by the interdependence postulate), one can expect that an activity disjunction will set in motion additional activity changes. This we can term the *postulate of linked changes*. Thus, although change processes have their ultimate origin outside the system, the nature, extent, and persistence of change are *in part* determined by linkages within the system (the remaining determinants also are within the system and we shall turn to them later). As a result of the postulate of linked changes and regardless of the stability of extrasystemic coupling parameters, it is likely that most systems are undergoing behavioral changes most of the time.

Activity changes may be far reaching or localized, depending on the nature of the interdependence relationships and available substitutes (and other processes to be discussed later). For example, if a system disposes of refuse in an abandoned well that eventually fills up, the response may be simply to move the dumping activity elsewhere. On the other hand, if a staple food resource cannot be obtained or a plague drastically reduces a group's population, changes may be considerable. Among other implications, the postulate of linked changes leads to predictions about how sometimes unexpected consequences of behavioral change take place. For example, if the high cost of gasoline causes an individual to substitute bicycle travel for automobile travel, one might envision an increase in bicycle maintenance, decrease in automobile maintenance, changes in eating patterns, changes in personal cleansing habits, and so on. Each of these activities in turn can modify coupling parameters of still other activities. If many people begin bicycling, extensive changes may occur in a variety of different activities in response to very small but cumulative changes in the coupling parameters (e.g., those dealing with bicycle and accessory manufacture and distribution). This can be termed the *threshold effect*. It depends on the fact that a minute change in a coupling parameter might not affect an activity, but a larger one, perhaps made up of small contributions from a score of weakly coupled activities, will. The relevance of catastrophe theory (Renfrew 1978) for handling these changes should be explored.

Even though change processes may be initiated by altered values of extrasystemic coupling parameters, the immediate causes of most activity change should lie in modifications that occur in directly coupled activities (activity disjunctions). For example, a decrease in population size may lead to fewer purchases of luxury products. Fewer purchases of luxury products may result in lower rates of luxury product manufacture, which in turn may give rise to less procurement of exotic materials—and this eventually could reduce the amounts of long-distance trade. It is important to note that each of these causal links has a probability of less than 1 since alternatives are conceivable—and perhaps even likely—in response to each disjunction. Thus it can be seen that, although an investigator may "explain" reduced trade by invoking reduced population, the assumed law upon which that explanation rests (a one-to-one relationship between trade and population) is dubious. Clearly, other causal paths can also lead to a lessening of trade (e.g., changes in the distribution of wealth and status, higher cost for exotic trade goods), and population reduction may not always lead to less trade, since alternatives are available for increasing trade product usage in order to maintain important trade relationships. It is for similar reasons that "population pressure" (whatever it may be in behavioral terms) cannot account for changes (see Cowgill 1975; Hassan 1978); the linkages between population and, for example, subsistence activities are simply assumed to be invariant when they probably are not. Population pressure will lead to other behavioral changes and the change in question may be produced by other causes (cf. Plog 1976). Viewed from this perspective, the structure of causality in behavioral systems is not circular, as many maintain, but multilinear, even reticulate. Thus a good place to seek some laws of change is not in correlations between weakly and distantly coupled parts of the system, but in the *general patterns* of proximate causality that follow from the postulate of linked changes. If linked changes are to be understood, it is necessary to consider the processes whereby disjunctions are translated into specific activity changes from among the available alternatives. Activities are added, deleted, and modified and relationships between activities are changed in the context of decision-making processes. It is inevitable, then, that decision making has to be taken into account (for a useful anthropological treatment of decision-making processes in connection with adaptation, see McGuire 1975).

Decision-Making Processes

The treatment of decision-making processes begins with an alteration in the value of a coupling parameter of an activity. Information on this disturbance is received and assessed by the decision maker (an individual, household, task group, or other social unit), and alternative responses are enumerated. *Alternatives* are then compared in terms of their possible consequences or *outcomes* and the *probabilities* and *costs* (in the broadest sense) of each. The choice is made on the basis of a decision *criterion* or *rule*. There are many potential criteria, especially for making decisions under conditions of uncertainty (Luce and Raiffa 1957, 278–288)—which, as is shown later, characterizes situations of behavioral change. It is important to note that the decision maker need not be consciously aware of the rule that is used. Decision theorists have found it fruitful to assume merely that a rule can be found that will account adequately for choices—although the decision maker may be totally ignorant of it (see Luce and Raiffa 1957:31), as well as other features of the decision-making process. It is also assumed that the decision maker behaves rationally, that is, decisions conform to the rule (Luce and Raiffa 1957:55). In this (tautological) sense, the assumption of rationality does not preclude faulty decisions resulting from imperfect knowledge (Luce and Raiffa 1957:55).

Although the decision-making process can be reduced to a general structure, each component of that structure may vary independently and affect the choice to a significant extent. It is worth considering how decision processes vary and what the causes may be.

In the first place, for any decision only a subset of potential alternatives is considered (McGuire 1975). This is probably a result of (*a*) early deletion of unfeasible alternatives and (*b*) lack of knowledge of alternatives. Thus the actual repertoire of alternatives probably reflects in some sense the extent that the change situation presents new problems for which experience is at best an uncertain guide. Inventions of course can occur; but they, too, have probabilities and costs. Which material conditions determine the set of "plausible" alternatives is a question that demands urgent attention. Ironically, diffusion theory laid far too much stress on the knowledge variable and understandably collapsed after ethnographic and archaeological analyses demonstrated that knowledge of an alternative was a necessary but never a sufficient cause of change. It is entirely possible, nevertheless, that some factors identified by diffusionists as influencing the distribution of knowledge and invention probabilities, such as population size, age distribution, and interaction rates, may have a role to play in an expanded materialist framework.

Second, no decision takes into account all of the outcomes that may result from each alternative. Alternatives, thus, tend to have unforeseen consequences. The question is, under what material conditions do decisions rest upon an increasingly exhaustive treatment of outcomes? Another way to phrase this question, which underscores the magnitude of the problem facing the decision maker, is, what factors influence the extent to which decision makers can predict the consequences of behavior? Because change situations are novel, accumulated experience can take the decision maker only so far, and that may not be far enough. One hopes that this topic will receive serious attention, for such research will lead to a greater understanding of an important source of variability in change processes.

Third, rarely can precise probabilities and costs be assigned to all outcomes. Although many archaeologists glibly assume that probabilities and costs were readily calculable by decision makers, it seems more defensible to treat this degree of knowledge as a variable subject to material causation. For example, in the context of the nuclear energy debate, present-day decision makers are having a great degree of difficulty in determining the environmental costs of thermal pollution, probabilities of serious reactor accidents, costs of reactor maintenance and disassembly, health hazards of small doses of radiation, probabilities of terrorist appropriation of fissionable material, and the costs of safely maintaining a facility for long-term (100,000 years or more) storage of nuclear wastes. If an advanced industrial nation with its vast array of computers and Phds cannot acquire accurate data to determine the probabilities and costs of *outcomes that have never transpired,* then one might expect that in many other change situations decision makers had to act—perhaps quickly—with somewhat less than perfect knowledge. A fruitful research area is to investigate the material conditions under which decision makers are able to estimate closely probabilities and costs of outcomes and when they are not.

As a hypothesis I propose that the accuracy of cost estimates varies directly with the frequency of the event (see Erasmus 1961). For example, if one were considering the substitution of alternative tools in a frequently performed activity, information on the costs of use might be obtained easily by actual trials and the experience of others. Maintenance costs might be more difficult to learn and, if the tool's use life is very long, estimates of procurement and disposal costs may be quite inaccurate (holding constant the number in use, of course). One might further hypothesize that, if use costs are easier to estimate, an alternative having lower use costs might be favored initially (given a least-cost rule). Later, as other costs become known from experience, the tool might be rejected (cf. Erasmus 1961). Nuclear energy plants in the United States are perhaps undergoing a similar rejection process now.

Fourth, there are no grounds for assuming, as many archaeologists do, that all or even most decisions conform to just one rule. A more reasonable assumption is that decision rules vary systematically in response to situational factors. Thus, instead of continuing to invoke one or another criterion in the mistaken belief that its use is universal in decisions, we should be striving to identify empirically the decision rules in use and the material causes of variability in those rules (see Wood 1978). The regularities we should seek are those which determine when particular rules will be used. In this way, it may be possible for archaeologists to contribute to the science of decision theory, as they discover higher level principles.

Hopefully this excursion into decision making has demonstrated that for too long archaeologists have been taking as assumptions the kinds of statements that should have been hypotheses (see Sullivan and Schiffer 1978). It is convenient to assume that knowledge of alternatives does not affect decisions; it is convenient to assume that knowledge about possible outcomes and their probabilities and costs is irrelevant; and it is convenient to assume that all decisions conform to a single rule. There is, however, ample reason for believing that in addition to being convenient, these assumptions are false. It is time to abandon them decisively, if the principles of change are ever to be established by archaeological investigation. Admittedly, the magnitude of the research tasks becomes substantially greater, but at least there is the prospect of learning something.

It remains in this chapter to show how the postulates and implications of activity analysis may be integrated with a consideration of decision-making processes in order to facilitate the study of change.

The Study of Change

Archaeologists have available several independent sources of data that can be used for testing lawlike hypotheses about change processes. I propose that archaeological, historical, and ethnoarchaeological data will have to play complementary roles in our nomothetic investigations. For example, ethnoarchaeologists now study groups experiencing rapid change. Comparative study of these ongoing decision-making processes will provide initial clues as to what *general* variables may be responsible for differential knowledge of alternatives, outcomes, and the probabilities and costs attached to them, as well as employment of various decision rules. Historical data can be used to study rates of technological adoptions and to formulate additional hypotheses. And archaeological data can test the long-term diachronic implications of our ideas about the causes of variability in decision-making processes.

In order to evaluate hypothetical principles on actual change processes, it is necessary to devise a general analytic framework that encompasses variability in decision making. Indeed, a serious deficiency in past studies of decision making (especially those of sociocultural anthropologists) has been the failure to erect a sufficiently broad framework for evaluating how closely decisions are in accord with specific rules. One can frequently find case studies naively claiming to demonstrate that a decision departs from expectations under a least-effort or minimax rule. For example, in one study of a New Mexican community that had at first adopted, then rejected, an "improved" high-yield variety of maize, despite the availability of markets for disposing of surplus, the investigator concluded that idiosyncratic factors of taste had led to the rejection (Apodaca 1952). It is clear, however, that the analyst failed to consider how, during the trial period, the decision makers acquired information (previously unavailable) on the costs of planting, growing, harvesting, preparing, and cooking the new grain. Perhaps if all of the *relevant* costs were taken into account *and properly quantified*, both the initial acceptance and ultimate rejection might indeed be found to conform to a least-cost or minimax rule.

Activity analysis serves as a comprehensive and systematic framework for investigating change processes because its postulates allow the analyst to follow the consequences of alternatives in specific cases. By pursuing the outcomes, sometimes far down the line, we can at least be confident that knowledge available to the decision maker is not overlooked in our deliberations. We can thus be spared the embarrassment of discovering that the native decision-making model is far more sophisticated than our analytical model!

It will not be possible to develop the present discussion very far, nor to articulate the strategy for using activity analysis at its most general level. Instead, a partial framework, dealing with a technomic element, is presented.

Let us imagine that a band of hunter–gatherers, dependent in part for subsistence on large game procured with a thrusting spear, finds that hunting is becoming a great deal more difficult. Because the group maintains contacts with other societies, the men are aware of alternative weapons, such as the atlatl and bow and arrow. On the assumption that these are the only alternatives under consideration, the postulates of activity analysis can be employed to show how it might be determined if the decision arrived at is consistent with, for example, a least-cost criterion. Because suitable data on outcome probabilities and costs are unavailable, this example cannot be worked through to a conclusion.

The first comparison that might be made among the alternatives concerns the way that hunting itself will be affected. On the basis of the irreplaceability postulate, it is expected that differences in the conjunction parameters of alternative weapons will affect the activity–state and coupling parameters of hunting. For example, if the thrusting spear, atlatl, and bow and arrow differ in accuracy and killing power at a given distance from the hunter, one might expect different success probabilities. But additional outcomes can be anticipated as well, for it is unlikely that the alternatives would differ in only a few conjunction parameters. Other differences might include: (*a*) suitability for use on the run, (*b*) the rapidity with which each can be used again (given a miss), (*c*) ease of use during ambush, (*d*) likelihood of accidentally dispatching another hunter, and (*e*) capabilities for symbolizing social unit affiliation. It is very likely that experimental and ethnoarchaeological research would permit quantification of such differences in conjunction parameters.

Now, consider further the effects altered conjunction parameters might have on the activity–state parameters of social unit of activity performance, location, and net energy. Alternative weapons may, for example, give rise to preference for larger or smaller groups of hunters; demand a different positioning of the hunters with respect to the game and features of the natural environment; require the hunters to possess different motor skills; involve significant variations in net energy expenditure; and may alter the rates at which different animals are killed. Needless to say, it would be difficult to assign probabilities and costs to these outcomes at the present time, but such calculations are within the realm of possibility.

Systematic examination of coupling parameters leads to additional forecasts about probable differences in outcomes. First, let us take the extrasystemic outputs. It is likely that the alternative weapons will vary greatly in loss probabilities. In addition, some weapons and parts of weapons would have higher breakage and discard rates than others. And differences might also be demonstrable in the rates of wounded animals that escape. If success rates differed, then so too would the extrasystemic input of game. Alterations in intrasystemic outputs might arise, for example, if the alternative hunting patterns led to variations in injury and death probabilities for hunters, and if the rate of animals procured differed. As a result of differential loss, breakage, and discard probabilities, one would anticipate intrasystemic inputs to vary also. In particular, replacement rates of tools would differ, as might rates of personnel replacement. Not only would replacement rates vary, but so too would the specific elements replaced. In short, there is every reason to expect that differences in the weapons used for hunting could bring about many changes in activity–state and coupling parameters.

Our comparisons need not stop here. By the postulates of interdependence and linked changes, we can expect that altered coupling parameters in one activity (hunting) will produce changes in other activities. A systematic treatment of each affected coupling parameter will lead to additional predicted outcomes and will indicate which probabilities and costs may need to be included in the analysis. If replacement rates are modified, then the closely and strongly coupled activities of tool manufacture will also change. A higher rate of manufacturing activity, for example, may in turn lead to higher rates of raw material procurement (e.g., chippable stone, wooden shafts, binding materials). The use of new materials (e.g., feathers, vegetable fiber) will perhaps require new manufacturing activities which, of course, will lead directly to different procurement activities. One can almost envision such change processes ramifying throughout the system endlessly. For example, as procurement rates increase, so too will the discard, replacement, and ultimately manufacture rates of the tools used in procurement activities (e.g., knives, hammerstones). The proliferation of new activities requiring different skills will lead to changes in enculturation activities (e.g., new games, sports). The latter may result in the production of new elements (e.g., toys, models). Higher rates of raw material procurement and procurement of new materials from a distant source could lead to the establishment of a trading network.

Additional examples of potential outcomes brought about by different coupling parameters of hunting (associated with different weapons) could go on indefinitely. It should be obvious that only under some circumstances would decision makers take such outcomes into account or be able to estimate, even coarsely, the probabilities and costs of each. Nevertheless, long periods of experimentation and observation of other groups in which similar changes have occurred previously may permit some decisions to be based on more knowledge than the present-day analyst might suppose was available. For example, a group's failure to adopt technological "improvements" is often attributed to "cultural conservatism." In such cases, outcomes and costs of tool substitution, sometimes far down the line, may have been included in decision-making processes. This perspective raises the hope that eventually many changes (or lack of changes), formerly considered to be intractable to materialist explanation, can be handled convincingly.

Given the interdependence postulate it is possible to maintain that since change can be viewed as a process that creates other changes, it is not possible to delineate any sort of natural boundary, of time, space, or activities, within which to assess the consequences of change. This creates some rather sticky problems for the analyst, since there are no signposts for drawing boundaries around the analysis. If an analysis is prematurely terminated or too inclusive, it could give erroneous results with respect to the criterion being assessed. Thus the results obtained in attempting to measure the extent that a decision is in conformity with a particular criterion will be largely conditioned by the boundaries placed on the analysis. These boundaries are termed the *frame of reference*. Deciding what frame of reference to employ in analyzing particular change situations is one of the most difficult problems ahead, one that has been inexplicably overlooked in virtually all previous studies. Attempts to deal with this problem will be increasingly successful as the laws of decision making are learned.

Suppose that a point is reached, some time in the distant future, when it is possible to specify most laws of behavioral change. Examples may be found where the change cannot be readily explained. Shall we then have to invoke cultural caprice, whim, or fancy? I think not. Within the present framework otherwise inexplicable cases of change or nonchange may be approached by a treatment of additional social and psychological variables from a materialist standpoint. Let us see how this might come about.

In any behavioral system the participants become skilled in the performance of the many activities that they carry out on a regular basis. They come to expect that activities will take place in certain locations, with certain objects and people, and in certain ways. Repetitive behaviors give rise to activity-maintaining attitudes and values that also are costly to modify, *because they were costly to instill in the first place.* Thus departures from activities and new ones are in many instances resisted. In such cases the additional effort required to unlearn one behavior pattern and learn another needs to be considered. The appropriate question is, what variables determine the amount of effort that must be spent to "reprogram" a social unit of activity performance for a new behavior pattern? I suggest that the most promising variables are rooted in material conditions, such as group size, age structure, previous experience with change situations, and the original costs of programming the attitudes and values. It may be found, for example, that enculturation activities are among the most costly of any carried out by some kinds of systems. Resistance to change in these circumstances may make considerable sense.

The use of activity analysis postulates and concepts has permitted development of a partial framework for generating expectations about outcomes that may occur as a result of decisions to substitute elements and activities. It is hoped that future research will lead to refinements and further generalization of the framework.

Conclusion

A framework called activity analysis (and its postulates) has been proposed to help isolate the sources of behavioral change and to orient nomothetic research. It has been found useful to downplay the role of extrasystemic, distant causes of change in favor of a focus on the nature of change processes from the perspectives of element–activity and activity–activity interactions. Thus, a conclusion reached is that much behavioral change occurs in response to disjunctions created by element and activity substitutions. Activity changes take place also in the context of decision-making processes, and variation in those processes needs to be understood. It is perhaps the case that most changes result from attempts to cope with the unanticipated consequences of previous decisions.

If the laws of change are to derive from archaeological research, there must be a firm commitment to pursue nomothetic studies which creatively integrate ethnoarchaeological, historical, and archaeological data and which establish dialogues with other behavioral sciences. A dialectic process must arise whereby hypotheses about the determinants of variability in decision-making processes, acquired from ethnoarchaeological and historical study, give rise to long-term diachronic implications that can be tested using archaeological evidence. These results can in turn feed back and modify the hypotheses causing new ethnoarchaeological and historical data to be gathered and analyzed. Archaeological data, by itself, can reveal *macroprocesses,* those grand regularities that seem to recur frequently and are probably based on the working out, slowly and inevitably, of the long-term (probably unanticipated) consequences of sometimes small initial activity changes (see Plog 1976). Identification of the networks of apparently strongly coupled activities that change in tandem despite environmental variability will provide more insight into those processes than uncritical appeals to "initial kicks," "positive feedback," and remote original causes. Study of these relationships may disclose a powerful set of laws. Eventually archaeologists may find ways to integrate the large-scale regularities and the more fine-grained principles into a unified science of behavioral change.

Acknowledgments

For insightful critiques of various drafts of this chapter I thank Merrilee Salmon, Neal Ackerly, Fred Plog, Richard Wilk, Albert Goodyear, Norman Yoffee, Jeffrey Eighmy, Stephen Perlman, Colin Renfrew, Michelle Behr, and John Hanson. For helpful discussions of issues treated herein I thank Stephen Perlman, Merrilee Salmon, Albert Goodyear, Norman Yoffee, Thomas McGuire, Alan Sullivan, David Wilcox, and Fred Plog. None of these persons necessarily agrees with anything in this essay. For providing vital assistance during the formative period of this chapter's development, I thank the staff of the Institute of Archeology and Anthropology, University of South Carolina, Samuel D. Shiner, and Barney T. Bass.

References

Apodaca, Anacleto, 1952, Corn and custom: the introduction of hybrid corn to Spanish American farmers in New Mexico. In Spicer, E. H. (ed.) *Human problems in technological change*, Wiley & Sons, New York, 35–39.

Cowgill, George L., 1975, On causes and consequences of ancient and modern population changes. *American Anthropologist* 77, 505–525.

Erasmus, Charles J., 1961, *Man Takes Control: Cultural Development and American Aid.* Bobbs-Merrill, Indianapolis.

Harris, Marvin, 1964, *The Nature of Cultural Things.* Random House, New York.

Hassan, Fekri, 1978, Demographic archaeology. In Schiffer, M. B. (ed.) *Advances in Archaeological Method and Theory, Volume 1.* Academic Press, New York, 50–103.

Hildebrand, John A., 1978, Pathways revisited: A quantitative model of discard. in Schiffer, M. B. (ed.) Contributions to archaeological method and theory. *American Antiquity* 43:274–279.

Krause, Richard A. and Thorne, Robert M., 1971, Toward a theory of archaeological things. *Plains Anthropologist* 16, 245–257.

Luce, R. Duncan and Raiffa, Howard, 1957, *Games and Decisions: Introduction and Critical Survey.* John Wiley & Sons, New York.

McGuire, Thomas, 1975, Choice and adaptation: The economic and ecological consequences of bounded rationality. Written preliminary examination, Department of Anthropology, University of Arizona. Manuscript on file, Arizona State Museum Library, Tucson.

Miller, James G., 1965a, Living systems: basic concepts. *Behavioral Science* 10, 193–237.

Miller, James G., 1965b, Living systems: structure and process. *Behavioral Science* 10, 337–379.

Plog, Fred, 1976, Alternative models of prehistoric change. Paper read at the 75th Annual Meeting of the American Anthropological Association, Washington, D.C.

Plog, Fred, 1977, Modeling economic change. In Timothy K. Earle and Jonathon E. Ericson, (ed.) Academic Press, New York, 127–140.

Reid, J. Jefferson, 1973, Growth and response to stress at Grasshopper Pueblo, Arizona. Ph.D dissertation, University of Arizona, Ann Arbor: University Microfilms.

Renfrew, Colin, 1978, Trajectory discontinuity and morphogenesis: the implications of Catastrophe Theory for archaeology. In Schiffer, M. B. (ed.) *Contributions to archaeological method and theory, American Antiquity* 43:203–222.

Schiffer, Michael B., 1975, Behavioral chain analysis: Activities, organization, and the use of space. In *Chapters in the prehistory of eastern Arizona,* IV. *Fieldiana: Anthropology* 65, 103–119.

Schiffer, Michael B., 1976, *Behavioral archeology.* Academic Press, New York.

Spears, Carol S., 1975, Hammers, nuts and jolts, cobbles, cobbles, cobbles: experiments in cobble technologies in search of correlates. In Baker, C. M. (ed.), The Arkansas Eastman Archeological Project, *Arkansas Archeological Survey, Research Report* 6, 83–116.

Sullivan, Alan P., 1978, Inference and evidence in archaeology: a discussion of the conceptual problems. In Schiffer, M. B. (ed.) *Advances in archaeological method and theory, Volume 1,* Academic Press, New York.

Sullivan, Alan P. and Schiffer, Michael B., 1978, A critical exmination of SARG. In Euler, R. and Gumerman, G. (ed.), Investigations of the Southwestern Anthropological Research Group: An experiment in archaeological cooperation, Museum of Northern Arizona, Flagstaff, 168–175.

Wood, John J., 1978, Optimal location in settlement space: A model for describing location strategies. In Schiffer, M. B. (ed.) Contributions to archaeological method and theory, *American Antiquity* 43:258–270.

16

ARTHUR S. KEENE

Economic Optimization Models and the Study of Hunter–Gatherer Subsistence Settlement Systems

Introduction

In this chapter I will address three basic questions about the economic behavior of prehistoric hunter–gatherers: (*a*) What factors influence the subsistence decisions of hunter–gatherers? (*b*) What variations in these decisions are necessary in response to specific perturbations? (*c*) How will these behaviors be manifest in the archaeological record? These questions force us to consider a number of auxiliary problems, such as the following: What factors affect the stability of hunter–gatherer subsistence settlement systems; what are the limits on productivity in foraging societies; what are the precise effects of territory size, resource seasonality, resource diversity, and so on, on patterns of human adaptation; and how will a change in a single aspect of an economic system affect other components of the system?

Previous approaches to prehistoric economy have often attempted to deal with these questions on a subjective level. Most quantitative models were limited to consideration of only a few variables such as carrying capacity, biomass, or energy value of resources. But in considering the preceding questions, it becomes abundantly clear that hunter–gatherer societies are complex cultural systems which cannot be accurately studied on an intuitive level or described by simple two- and three-variable models. The problems at hand are multivariate and thus require multivariate methods.

One multivariate method well suited for addressing such problems is linear programming, a technique frequently employed by economists in

369

Transformations:
Mathematical Approaches to Culture Change

problems of allocation. In this chapter I use linear programming to construct models of traditional economy and changing subsistence patterns among the Netsilik Eskimo with the aim of developing a general model which can deal with the questions raised at the outset.

Jochim (1976) has approached similar problems from an emic perspective, that is, he has considered resource decisions in terms of criteria consciously employed by contemporary hunters and gatherers. This examination is more etic in nature. Rather than concentrate on the conscious criteria used by the decision maker, I have focused on the needs of the population and the decisions that must be made to satisfy them. This allows for the incorporation of nutritional criteria which, although not necessarily consciously recognized by a given population, must still be satisfied for a given subsistence strategy to succeed.

Assumptions

The models are based on the following assumptions (see also Keene in press):

ASSUMPTION 1. *Economic activities among hunter–gatherers are organized.*

ASSUMPTION 2. *The primary goal among hunter–gatherers is to provide the basic nutritive and other raw materials necessary for the survival of the population. The needs of the population will be satisfied whether or not they are perceived by the decision makers.*

ASSUMPTION 3. *When faced with a choice between two resources of equal utility, the one of lower cost will be chosen. Hunters and gatherers attempt to satisfy their basic needs at minimum cost. Therefore, economic behavior is both satisfying and optimizing.*

ASSUMPTION 4. *There are limits to the amount of a given resource which can be exploited within a given amount of time.*

ASSUMPTION 5. *Any alterations to the subsistence settlement system can be modeled in terms of changes in costs or limits of resource exploitation.*

Mathematical Programming Models

Programming is the mathematics of allocating limited resources among competing activities in an optimal manner. A program is simply a plan or schedule of activities which best satisfies a specified goal among all feasible alternatives. The goal is defined in terms of maximizing or minimizing a function of several variables which are subject to constraints, such as maximizing production or profit or minimizing cost or losses, subject to the availability of capital, raw materials, labor, time, and so forth. Programming involves construction of a mathematical model to describe the problem of concern. In *linear programming,* all mathematical functions contained in the model must be linear. The model is phrased as a series of linear equalities or inequalities which are solved simultaneously, usually with the assistance of a computer algorithm. Linear programming is a well-accepted method frequently employed in economics, agriculture, and industry to deal with a variety of resource allocation problems (Wagner 1975; Hillier and Lieberman 1974; Spivey and Thrall 1970; Dorfman, Samuelson and Solow 1958). Linear programming models have rarely been employed in anthropological studies, although Joy (1967) and Clarke (1968:496) have suggested their potential value. Heyer (cf. Schneider 1974:90) used linear programming in her study of the Kamba of Kenya; and Reidhead (1976), in perhaps the first archaeological application, used the technique to test hypotheses of nutritional and labor optimization among the prehistoric inhabitants of the Middle Ohio Valley.

In this chapter I will demonstrate the value of linear programming models to the study of hunter–gatherer subsistence settlement systems by modeling resource decisions made by a group of Netsilik Eskimo under varying conditions. These models focus on the area occupied by the Arviligjuarmiut, a branch of the Netsilik who inhabit the region of Pelly Bay along the northwest arm of the Gulf of Boothia. Two linear programming models are presented:

1. A model of the annual subsistence cycle of a small Arviligjuarmiut band (50 persons) using traditional hunting techniques. Input for the model comes from data describing the wildlife, environment, and human nutritional requirements for the area. Then, to test their accuracy, the predictions are compared to ethnographic accounts of traditional Netsilik economy.
2. A model of a change in the annual subsistence cycle which results from a change in technology, specifically the introduction of the rifle. Again, model predictions are compared to the empirical case.

Linear programming models are well suited to problems such as these, in which the large number of variables and constraints are difficult to control using more traditional methods. However, the use of linear programming is subject to the following conditions (cf. Daellenbach and Bell 1970:5; Reidhead 1976:18):

1. One must make explicit the conditions that must be satisfied and the factors that limit choices.
2. One must specify an *objective function,* or outcome, which the deci-

sion maker desires to achieve, for example, minimize cost or maximize profit.

3. It must be possible to state the objective function and constraints algebraically. This requires that variables be quantifiable.
4. The relationship between variables and objective function must be linear. This means that a change in one will cause a proportional change in the other.

A simplified example of a linear programming problem is presented at this time so that the reader may better understand the nature of the method and how it applies to the problem at hand.

Example of Linear Programming— The Diet Problem

A simplified example of the "diet problem" is offered as an illustration of linear programming (cf. Dorfman *et al.* 1958:9; Spivey and Thrall 1970:39). The problem is quite famous in the literature of linear programming as the first economic problem solved by explicit use of the method (cf. Stigler 1945).

The problem is to provide a basic satisfactory diet at the least possible cost. Consider the problem of minimizing the cost of a diet that must satisfy m nutritional requirements from n available foods, each possessing a specific quantity of a given nutrient. The problem can be viewed as a matrix. Let the column vectors represent the available resources or foods and the row vectors the various nutrients (cf. Table 16.1). For example, element a_{ij} in Table 16.1 represents the amount of the ith nutrient in the jth resource. Two additional vectors must be considered. The far right-hand side column, or b vector, indicates the constraints, or minimum requirement for each nutrient. The bottom row, or c vector, indicates the cost of acquisition for each resource. The problem can be stated algebraically as follows:

$$\text{minimize } z = \sum_{j=1}^{n} c_j x_j \qquad (16.1)$$

$$\text{subject to } b_i = \sum^{n} a_{ij} x_j \qquad (i = 1, 2, 3, ..., m) \qquad (16.2)$$

$$\text{and } x_j \geq 0 \ (j = 1, 2, 3, ..., n) \qquad (16.2)$$

where z is the total cost of production, c_j is the cost of one unit of resource j, and x_j is the amount of resource j acquired. In order to simplify this explanation I will calculate an optimum diet composed of two hypothetical foods, I and II, and three nutritive elements, vitamins Q, R, and S. Numerical data appear in the second part of Table 16.1. Each gram of food I contains 2 mg of

TABLE 16.1
Sample Linear Programming Model—The Diet Problem

	Symbolic notation						
Nutritive element (i)	Nutrients per unit of food (j)						Nutritional requirement
	1	2	3	4	5 ...	n	
1	a_{11}	a_{12}	a_{13}	a_{14}	a_{15}	a_{1n}	b_1
2	a_{21}	a_{22}	a_{23}	a_{24}	a_{25}	a_{2n}	b_2
3	a_{31}	a_{32}	a_{33}	a_{34}	a_{35}	a_{3n}	b_3
m	a_{m1}	a_{m2}	a_{m3}	a_{m4}	a_{m5}	a_{mn}	b_m
Costs	c_1	c_2	c_3	c_4	c_5	c_n	$z = c_j x_j$

	Numerical data		
Nutritive element = vitamin	Nutrients per unit of food		Nutritional requirement
	I	II	
Q	2	1	60
R	2	4	120
S	—	4	40
Cost	5	6	Minimum = ?
Amount of food available	100	70	

vitamin Q, 2 mg of R, and none of S. Food II has 1 mg of Q, 4 mg of R, and 4 mg of S. One gram of food I costs five arbitrary cost units, and food II costs six cost units per gram. We must satisfy the nutritional standards of at least 60 mg of vitamin Q, 120 of R, and 40 of S with a diet of minimum cost.

In other words, our problem is to minimize an objective function (total cost of the diet) of several variables (foods I and II) subject to certain constraints (the nutritional requirements). Or, in algebraic terms;

$$\text{Variables:} \quad x_I \text{ and } x_{II}$$
$$\text{Cost:} \quad z = 5x_I + 6x_{II} = \text{minimum}$$
$$\text{Constraints:} \quad 2x_I + x_{II} \geqslant 60 \qquad \text{(for } Q\text{)}$$
$$2x_I + 4x_{II} \geqslant 120 \qquad \text{(for } R\text{)}$$
$$4x_{II} \geqslant 40 \qquad \text{(for } S\text{)}$$

Since we cannot acquire a negative amount of a given food, we establish the additional constraints that

$$x_I \geqslant 0, \qquad x_{II} \geqslant 0$$

The maximum amount of each food accessible is

$$x_I \leqslant 100, \qquad x_{II} \leqslant 70$$

These inequalities are graphed in Figure 16.1. Points on or above line A represent all possible combinations of foods I and II which will satisfy the requirement for vitamin Q. Points on or above line B represent combinations satisfying the constraints of R, and points on or above C satisfy S. The shaded area on the graph represents all points which will satisfy all constraints. The point representing the diet of minimum cost will be found at one or more of the intersections of the lines which delineate the area of feasible solutions (points W, V, Z). In this case, the optimal solution is represented by point Z. At point Z,

$$x_I = 20, \qquad x_{II} = 20$$

Thus, the optimum diet satisfying the hypothetical requirements consists of 20 gm of food I and 20 gm of food II. The cost of this diet would be $5(20) + 6(20) = 220$ cost units.

The graphic method is, of course, only applicable to a two-variable problem. For three variables, a third dimension would be needed, and so on. This example illustrates the basic procedure involved in solving an optimiza-

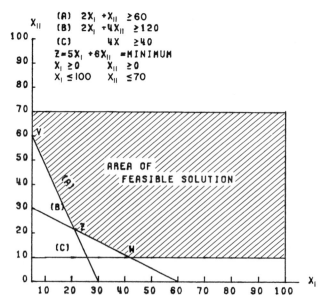

FIGURE 16.1 *The diet problem solved by linear programming. The solution for minimum cost is represented by point Z, indicating 20 gm of food I and 20 gm of food II.*

tion problem, and the solution is reached in essentially the same way regardless of how many variables are added. When the problem consists of more than three variables, a computer algorithm is often used to plot the intersects of the lines that define the area of feasible solutions (Spivey and Thrall 1970:62; Cooper and Steinberg 1974:8; Reidhead 1976:29). The most commonly used algorithms for such problems are known as the *simplex* and *revised simplex* methods. These have been discussed extensively in numerous texts, so I will not describe them in detail here (for particularly good documentation, the reader is referred to Dantzig 1963; Gale 1960; Spivey and Thrall 1970; Cooper and Steinberg 1974; Wagner 1975).

The Netsilik Models—Matrix Setup

The format of the Netsilik models is similar to that of the diet problem. The column vectors represent resources. There are 12 resources, each represented by 12 column vectors (one for each month of the year, since the nutritional value of a resource and the cost of acquiring it may vary considerably from month to month). There are also 12 row vectors, or constraint equations, representing 10 nutrients, one nonfood value, and a cost of acquisition. The 10 nutrients considered are energy, protein, fat, carbohydrate, calcium, vitamin A, thiamine, riboflavin, vitamin C, and iron. These obviously do not include all of the important nutrients necessary for an adequate diet. Rather, they represent nutrients most commonly quantified in the literature. Nonfood value is measured in terms of animal hides. Some column vectors for a given resource are absolutely identical to others for the same resource. For example, ringed seal in November through January shows exactly the same values for all 12 row vectors (cf. Keene in press). Thus, no choice between these vectors is possible unless additional decision criteria are introduced. For this reason, completely identical column vectors for a given resource have been collapsed to form single column vectors. This process of combining vectors reduces the size of the matrix from 12×145 to 12×85.

Although the value of a resource will vary from month to month, it is assumed that the minimum nutritional requirements of the population will be relatively invariant throughout the year.[1] These requirements are calculated in terms of minimum annual required intakes. The algorithm simultaneously solves for the best resource mix (adequate diet at minimum cost) for the entire year from data characterizing individual months. The solution is expressed as the amount of each individual resource harvested in each

---

[1] This assumption may not pertain to a few nutrients not used in this study. For example, the requirement for vitamin D, which can be synthesized from sunlight, would be higher during the dark season in the Arctic.

month, thereby providing a characterization of monthly resource scheduling. At present, I have chosen to use this simultaneous annual solution rather than a month-to-month interactive model to provide a general model of annual subsistence activities. It is possible to solve such problems on a monthly basis with the results of one month providing the input for the next (cf. Throsby 1962; Reidhead 1976:318–320), and these models can be refined to accommodate such a dynamic approach.

Costs

The key to the solution of the modeled problems lies in the establishment of a reliable measure of cost. Cost in subsistence economies is a complex function of work effort and risk, and quantification is not a simple procedure. Ecological studies on animal feeding strategies have generally divided the food acquisition process into two stages, search and pursuit (Norberg 1977; Schoener 1971; Emlen 1966; MacArthur and Pianka 1966). Search time (T_s) can be regarded as the time invested in locating a resource. Pursuit time refers to the time from detection of the prey until the time that capture is completed.

Search time is often calculated as an inverse function of the density (d) of food available (Norberg 1977:514; Schoener 1971:377), or

$$T_s \propto d^{-1} \tag{16.3}$$

Search time would be expected to decrease as overall resource density increases, since higher resource density would increase the probability of encounter.

When search is not random and when predator and prey are mobile, mobility must also be taken into consideration. Mobility is actually a multicomponent attribute (cf. Jochim 1976:27). One component relates to absolute mobility or degree of movement, and another refers to regularity of spatial behavior or localizability of a resource. If the location of a resource can be predicted, search time is reduced. Likewise, search time would be less for more sedentary resources. In this study, mobility is measured as the seasonal range of a prey species. Minimum and maximum mobility values are set at 1 and 100 km², respectively. When a resource is highly localizable, that is, when hunters can predict points of interception such as caribou crossing places, the mobility figure is reduced. When resources are highly inaccessible, the mobility figure is increased. Since data on home range are not always available, some estimates have been made. The important consideration is that the mobility values accurately express relative differences in this multicomponent attribute.

Pursuit time (T_p) is often estimated as the amount of time necessary to run down a prey and is calculated as a function of predator speed, prey speed, predator field of vision, and prey field of vision (Schoener 1971:378).

Human predators generally rely on technology rather than speed to capture prey. The majority of pursuit then is invested in stalking the prey (cf. Marks 1976:117; Nelson 1969; Stefansson 1944:452; Laughlin 1968:308). Stalking time can be approximated in terms of a critical distance (q) where q is the distance at which predator is perceived, minus the distance from which the hunter can successfully strike.[2] We would expect pursuit time to increase as critical distance increases. Pursuit time would decrease as resource aggregation size increases, since higher aggregations increase the probability of successful pursuit and also the probable yield per hunt. In addition, some animals such as caribou become much less wary in the presence of a large herd (Banfield 1973:385; Nelson 1968:199).

In summary, search time decreases as prey mobility decreases and as density increases, or

$$T_s \propto m/d \tag{16.4}$$

Pursuit time decreases as critical distance decreases and as aggregation size increases, or

$$T_p \propto q/a \tag{16.5}$$

A third factor to consider in the construction of a cost measure is the concept of risk. Inherent to risk are two separate components. The first involves risk to the personal well-being of the decision maker. The pursuit of certain species of animals, such as polar bear, or the utilization of certain hunting areas, such as the edge of an ice floe, may entail specific hazards for the hunter which can figure into the decision process. Nelson (1969:377) notes:

> The Eskimos seem to have an unspoken concept of "percentage risk." Thus a certain activity might be done without danger eight out of ten times, but because of this twenty per cent risk, the Eskimo seldom carries on the activity as long as it can be avoided.

Another important aspect of risk concerns the security of a resource or the risk of coming home empty-handed. Lee (1968) demonstrates that the !Kung emphasize gathered vegetable foods in their diet because these items are so readily accessible and so reliable. Among the !Kung, hunting is a relatively high-risk, low-return activity in terms of energy production, whereas gathering is a relatively low-risk activity and provides a high return. Jochim (1976:50–53) and Wilmsen (1973:6–10) have shown that resource security is a primary factor in the determination of site location and group composition.

Security can be partially evaluated in terms of resource stability. Highly stable resources whose numbers, movements, and location change little from year to year would be regarded as relatively secure. Less secure would

[2]This critical distance figure would not be pertinent to animals that are trapped. In this case, q is replaced in the cost equation by a constant k which has been set at a value of 50 for this study.

be resources susceptible to regular or periodic fluctuations in population size or that undertake mass migrations. These resources would not be consistently available, but the decision maker would have some idea of when a shortage was imminent. Even less secure would be those resources subject to erratic fluctuations in numbers, range, and location.

We would thus expect the cost of acquisition (c) to decrease as total risk decreases. Arviligjuarmiut resources were classified as low, moderate, high, or very high risk according to these criteria and were assigned risk coefficients of 1, 1.25, 1.5, or 2, respectively. Because of the risk inherent to travel during the dark season in the Arctic, as well as the increased difficulty in hunting due to diminished visibility (Stefansson 1944:68; Sonnenfeld 1960), risk was increased by .1 for activities during months of maximum darkness.

The cost measure used in this study is represented by the following formula:

$$c = (T_s + T_p)r \tag{16.6}$$

or

$$c = (m/d + q/a)r \tag{16.7}$$

This cost coefficient is an artificial measure. It cannot be converted into hourly labor input, caloric expenditure, or any other absolute value. However, it should accurately express relative differences in acquisition cost.

One additional point about costs should be mentioned. The reader is probably aware that in reality the cost of any resource is constantly increasing at the margin. That is, the cost of acquiring a second, third, or fourth unit of a given item is successively higher than the preceding one.[3] Cost is actually a curvilinear function (cf. Limp 1977). Optimization problems containing curvilinear functions can be solved through the use of separable programming (Hillier and Lieberman 1974:171–180; Wagner 1975:562) which breaks down a curvilinear function into small linear segments that can then be solved routinely with the simplex method. However, one is still faced with the problem of defining the function precisely. I have accommodated the linearity requirements of the model (see page 372) by employing an *average cost* figure, a common practice in optimization modeling (Driebeek 1961:61; Reidhead 1976).

Limits of Exploitation

Assumption 4 states that the amount of any resource available for harvest is limited. The upper exploitation limit of a resource is often calculated as the equivalent of the recruitment rate (Smith 1975:21–26). Recruit-

---

[3]This is true except when group capture is possible. Then the major cost is associated with taking the first animal in the group, and the cost for the others from the same group is considerably lower. However, the marginal cost will still increase for each successive hunt.

ment refers to the number of animals added to the breeding population each year and also represents the maximum sustainable (safe) yield. It is usually asserted that hunters manage their resources to the extent that these safe limits are not exceeded (Paine 1973:303; Feit 1973:122). Paine (1973) and others argue that when a prey population is depleted beyond a critical level, the predator will switch to an alternate resource, allowing the first prey species to recover its losses. This switching is explained as a response to increased search time caused by depletion of the prey population, and is related to the concept of marginal cost discussed earlier.

However, one cannot always assume that there will be an increase in marginal cost sufficient to force a predatory population to switch prey. There is historic evidence of hunters, following a sudden technological upgrading, grossly overexploiting animal populations far beyond safe recruitment levels (Kelsall 1968; Horne 1935; Balikci 1964; Zeissberger 1910). An additional problem with calculating recruitment rates is that even conservative estimates may far exceed the exploitation capabilities of a hunting population. This may be particularly true when territory is large, predator population is small, and prey population is migratory. The limiting factor in this case is not reproductive success of prey species, but rather technology, size of predator population, and access time to prey. Only a limited number of animals can be captured in a finite amount of time with a rudimentary technology. As technology improves and access time increases, harvest volume should also increase, potentially beyond the limits of safe exploitation. The problem with using maximum sustainable yields to set the upper bounds of the model is that (*a*) they may not realistically portray exploitation limits in terms of a group's procurement capabilities, and (*b*) they do not permit consideration of potential overexploitation of resources. In this study, technology, population size, and resource seasonality are regarded as the critical factors for setting the upper bounds of the model.

Data

Resource attributes used in the calculation of cost coefficients are quantified in Table 16.2. Demographic parameters of the model and data on nutritional requirements and nutritional composition of resources are presented and discussed by Keene (in press).

Interpreting the Models

The reader will recall that the basic programming problem approached in this investigation is the selection of an optimal schedule of resources which will satisfy a set of nutritional requirements and one nonfood requirement at a minimum cost. The results are presented in Tables 16.3 and 16.4. Table 16.3 describes the column vectors. The optimal solution to the prob-

TABLE 16.2
Resource Attributes

Resource	Jan.	Feb.	March	April	May	June	July	Aug.	Sept.	Oct.	Nov.	Dec.
Caribou[a]												
Density (/km²)	.031	.031	.031	.289	.289	.145	.145	.289	1.04	.145	.031	.031
Agg.	5	5	5	30	30	10	10	10	40	5	5	5
Cr. Dist.	370	370	370	370	270	170	170	170	170	270	370	370
Mob.	50	50	50	100	100	50	50	80	15	80	50	50
Risk	1.35	1.25	1.25	1.25	1.25	1.25	1.25	1.25	1.25	1.35	1.35	1.35
Musk-ox[b]												
Density	.08	.08	.08	.08	.08	.08	.08	.08	.08	.08	.08	.08
Agg.	20	20	15	15	10	10	15	18	15	15	20	20
Cr. Dist.	395	395	395	395	395	395	395	395	395	395	395	395
Mob.	30	30	30	30	50	50	30	30	30	50	30	30
Risk	1.1	1	1	1	1	1	1	1	1	1.1	1.1	1.1
Ringed seal[c]												
Density	3.1	3.1	3.1	6.25	11.6	11.6	6.25	6.25	6.25	3.1	3.1	3.1
Agg.	1	1	1	1	3	3	1	1	1	1	1	1
Cr. Dist.	50	50	50	50	197	197	197	197	197	150	50	50
Mob.	25	25	25	25	5	5	25	25	25	25	25	25
Risk	1.1	1	1	1	1	1	1.5	1.5	1.5	1.1	1.1	1.1
Bearded seal[d]												
Density	.2	.2	.2	.2	.2	.5	.5	.5	.5	.2	.2	.2
Agg.	1	1	1	1	1	1	1	1	1	1	1	1
Cr. Dist.	293	293	293	293	293	293	293	293	293	293	293	293
Mob.	35	35	35	35	20	20	35	35	35	35	35	35
Risk	1.1	1	1	1	1	1	1.5	1.5	1.5	1.1	1.1	1.1

	.01	.01	.01	.01	.01	.01	.01	.02	.02	.01	.01	.01
Polar bear[e]												
Density	.01	.01	.01	.01	.01	.01	.01	.02	.02	.01	.01	.01
Agg.	1	1	1	1	1	1	1	1.25	1.5	1.5	1.5	1.25
Cr. Dist.	397	397	397	397	397	397	397	397	397	397	397	397
Mob.	40	40	40	80	80	100	100	80	80	80	80	80
Risk	2.1	2.1	2.1	1.5	1.5	2	2	1.5	1.5	1.5	1.5	1.5
Fish[f]												
Density	30	30	30	30	40	40	30	30	30	30	30	30
Agg.	1	1	5	10	25	40	10	5	1	1	1	5
Cr. Dist.	5	5	5	3	3	3	3	5	5	5	5	5
Mob.	15	15	15	15	15	2	7	15	15	15	15	15
Risk	1.6	1.6	1.35	1.25	1.25	1.25	1.25	1.25	1.5	1.5	1.5	1.5
Birds[a]												
Density	.39	.39	.77	3.9	4.6	5	4.6	3.9	.77	.39	.39	.39
Agg.	1	1	1	5	10	10	10	5	1	1	1	1
Cr. Dist.	75	75	75	75	75	25	75	75	75	75	75	75
Mob.	10	10	10	10	10	1	15	15	10	10	10	10
Risk	1.35	1.35	1.35	1.25	1.25	1.25	1.25	1.25	1.25	1.25	1.25	1.25
Hare[a]												
Density	12.4	12.4	12.4	12.4	12.4	12.4	12.4	12.4	12.4	12.4	12.4	12.4
Agg.	4	4	4	4	4	4	4	4	4	4	4	4
Cr. Dist.	50	50	50	50	50	50	50	50	50	50	50	50
Mob.	5	5	5	3	3	3	3	3	3	5	5	5
Risk	1.6	1.6	1.6	1.5	1.5	1.5	1.5	1.5	1.5	1.5	1.5	1.5
Wolf[a]												
Density	.008	.008	.024	.024	.024	.024	.024	.008	.008	.008	.008	.008
Agg.	4	4	4	4	4	4	4	4	4	4	4	4
Cr. Dist.	50	50	50	50	50	50	50	50	50	50	50	50
Mob.	100	100	100	100	100	100	100	100	100	100	100	100
Risk	1.1	1.1	1.1	1	1	1	1	1	1	1	1	1

TABLE 16.2 (Continued)

Table 16.2 (*Continued*)

Resource	Jan.	Feb.	March	April	May	June	July	Aug.	Sept.	Oct.	Nov.	Dec.
Lemming[j]												
Density	1000	1000	1000	1000	1000	1000	1000	1000	1000	1000	1000	1000
Agg.	5	5	5	5	5	5	5	5	5	5	5	5
Cr. Dist.	50	50	50	50	50	50	50	50	50	50	50	50
Mob.	1	1	1	1	1	1	1	1	1	1	1	1
Risk	1.35	1.25	1.25	1.25	1.25	1.25	1.25	1.25	1.25	1.35	1.35	1.35
Squirrel[k]												
Density	400	400	400	400	400	400	400	400	400	400	400	400
Agg.	2	2	2	2	2	2	2	2	2	2	2	2
Cr. Dist.	50	50	50	50	50	50	50	50	50	50	50	50
Mob.	1	1	1	1	1	1	1	1	1	1	1	1
Risk	2.1	2	2	2	1.5	1.5	1.5	1.5	1.5	2.1	2.1	2.1
Fox[l]												
Density	3	3	3	3	3	3	3	3	3	3	3	3
Agg.	2	2	2	2	1	1	1	1	1	1	1	1
Cr. Dist.	50	50	50	50	50	50	50	50	50	50	50	50
Mob.	16	16	16	16	16	16	16	16	16	16	16	16
Risk	1.6	1.5	1.5	1.5	1.5	1.5	1.5	1.5	1.5	1.6	1.6	1.6

[a] Balikci (1964), Burch (1972), Foote (1965), Kelsall (1968).
[b] Balikci (1964), Horne (1934), Stefansson (1914), Tener (1957, 1965).
[c] Banfield (1973), McLaren (1958a), Nelson (1969), Smith (1973), Villiers (1968).
[d] McLaren (1958b), Mansfield (1963), Villiers (1968).
[e] Banfield (1973), Harrington (1964), Perry (1966).
[f] Andrews and Lear (1956), Balikci (1964), Ross (1835), Scott (1954), Sprules (1952), Steigenberger *et al.* (1974), Villiers (1968).
[g] Godfrey (1966), Hørring (1935), Kortright (1942), MacPherson and Manning (1959), Manning *et al.* (1956), Ross (1835), Sutton (1932).
[h] Banfield (1973), Dergebøl and Freuchen (1935), McLulich (1937).
[i] Kelsall (1968), Mech (1970), Walker (1964).
[j] Banfield (1973).
[k] Banfield (1973), Dergebøl and Freuchen (1935), Mayer (1953), Rasmussen (1931).
[l] Banfield (1973), MacPherson (1969), Vibe (1967).

TABLE 16.3
Model of Traditional Netsilik Economy—Column Vectors

Resource	Month	Column activity	Upper bound	Cost	Shadow price	Maximum cost	− Range (%)	+ Range (%)
Caribou	Dec.–Jan.	0		2,277.3	1,938.3	339.0	85	
	Feb.–March	0		2,108.6	1,916.3	192.3	91	
	April	0		447.9	255.6	192.3	57	
	May	0		443.8	256.9	186.9	58	
	June	0		452.3	265.4	186.9	59	
	July	0	90	452.3	260.0	192.3	57	
	Aug.	90	90	367.3	−120.1	487.4		33
	Sept.	90	90	23.3	−464.1	487.4		1990
	Oct.	0	90	817.7	330.3	487.4	40	
	Nov.	0	90	2,277.3	1,791.6	485.7	79	
Musk-ox	Nov.–Jan.	0	15	434.2	14.0	420.2	3	
	Feb.	5	5	394.7	−25.5	420.2		6
	March	5	5	401.3	−18.9	420.2		5
	April	0	5	401.3	127.8	273.5	32	
	May	0	5	664.5	391.0	273.5	59	
	June	0	5	664.5	537.6	126.9	81	
	July, Sept.	0	10	401.3	274.4	126.9	68	
	Aug.	0	5	396.9	270.0	126.9	68	
	Oct.	0	5	716.5	443.0	273.5	62	
Ringed seal	Nov.–Jan.	70	70	63.9	−117.7	181.6		184
	Feb.–March	60	60	58.1	−123.5	181.6		212
	April	30	30	54.0	−127.6	181.6		236
	May	30	30	66.1	−112.8	178.9		171
	June	0	30	66.1	34.5	31.6	52	
	July	0	20	301.5	269.2	32.3	89	
	Aug.	0	30	301.5	193.3	108.2	52	
	Sept.	0	10	301.5	119.9	181.6	40	
	Oct.	20	20	173.8	−7.7	181.5		4

Table 16.3 (*Continued*)

Resource	Month	Column activity	Upper bound	Cost	Shadow price	Maximum cost	−Range (%)	+Range (%)
Bearded seal	Oct.–Jan.	4	5	514.8	34.2	514.8	0	0
	Feb.–March	0	10	468.0	246.6	221.4	53	
	April	0	5	468.0	252.2	215.8	54	
	May	0	5	393.0	177.2	215.8	45	
	June	0	5	333.0	117.2	215.8	35	
	July–Sept.	0	15	544.5	29.7	514.8	5	
Polar bear	Dec.–Jan.	0		9,233.7	8,733.6	500.1	94	
	Feb.	0		12,476.4	11,972.1	504.3	96	
	March	0		12,397.0	11,891.2	505.8	96	
	April	0		6,397.0	5,891.2	505.8	92	
	May	0		6,476.4	5,970.6	505.8	92	
	June	0		20,794.0	20,434.9	359.1	98	
	July	0		20,794.0	20,581.6	212.4	99	
	Aug.	0		12,595.5	12,383.1	212.4	98	
	Sept.	0		12,595.5	12,089.7	505.8	96	
	Oct.	0		9,233.7	8,727.9	505.8	94	
	Nov.	0		9,233.7	8,729.5	504.3	94	
Fish	Nov.–Jan.	0	100	8.80	2.65	6.15	30	
	Feb.–April	0	100	8.25	2.09	6.16	25	
	May	200	200	1.88	−4.27	6.15		227
	June	200	200	.66	−5.49	6.15		832
	July	800	800	.16	−5.99	6.15		3740
	Aug.	800	800	.62	−5.53	6.15		892
	Sept.	400	400	1.00	−5.15	6.15		515
	Oct.	200	200	2.03	−4.12	6.15		203

Species	Period						
Birds	Nov.–Jan.	0		135.9	135.4	.5	99+
	Feb.–March	0		125.8	125.3	.5	99+
	April	0		110.0	109.5	.5	99+
	May	0		23.6	22.8	.8	97
	June	0		13.5	12.4	1.1	92
	July	0		3.4	2.2	1.2	65
	Aug.	0		12.1	11.0	1.1	91
	Sept.	0		21.9	20.8	1.1	95
	Oct.	0		118.8	118.0	.8	99
Hare	Nov.–Jan.	0		20.6	14.6	6.0	71
	Feb.–March	0		19.4	13.4	6.0	69
	April	0		19.1	13.1	6.0	68
	May–June	0		19.1	13.5	5.6	71
	July–Sept.	0		19.1	13.1	6.0	68
	Oct.	0		20.6	14.6	6.0	71
Wolf	Nov.–Jan.	0		13,763.8	13,672.0	91.8	99
	Feb.–March	0		12,512.5	12,420.7	91.8	99
	June–Sept.	0		4,179.1	4,087.3	91.8	98
	Oct.	0		4,597.0	4,505.2	91.8	98
Lemming	Oct.–Jan.	0		13.5	13.5	0	100
	Feb.–Sept.	0		12.5	12.5	0	100
Squirrel	Jan.	0		52.5	37.4	15.1	71
	Feb.–April	0		50.0	34.9	15.1	70
	May, Nov.–Dec.	0		37.5	22.4	15.1	60
	June–July	0		37.5	22.4	15.1	60
	Aug.	0		37.5	22.4	15.1	60
	Sept.	0		37.5	22.4	15.1	60
	Oct.	0		52.5	37.4	15.1	71
Fox	Oct.–Jan.	0	20	88.5	43.0	45.5	48
	Feb.–April	12	15	45.5	3.2	45.5	0
	May–Sept.	0	25	83.0	81.5	1.5	98

TABLE 16.4
Model of Traditional Netsilik Economy—Row Vectors

Name	Annual requirement	Row activity	Surplus	Activity Minimum	Activity Maximum	Shadow prices Minimum	Shadow prices Maximum
Cost		59,588.9				−293.4	293.4
Nonfood (hides)	300.0	300.0	Binding	298.3	300.0	−293.4	293.4
Energy (kcal × 10³)	47,486.5	71,197.1	23,710.6	70,604.3	73,165.1	.04	0.03
Protein (kg)	1,069.7	4,630.8	3,561.0	4,623.3	4,655.4	3.0	2.2
Fat (kg)	340.8	5,699.1	5,358.3	5,640.4	5,893.9	.4	.3
Carbohydrate (kg)	124.0	346.3	222.3	337.5	375.5	2.5	1.8
Calcium (gm)	10,074.0	10,074.0	Binding	10,055.6	10,135.2	−6.0	6.0
Vitamin A (IU × 10³)	86,140.0	226,300.0	140,160.0	220,997.7	227,897.2	.01	.01
Thiamine (mg)	23,178.0	26,051.1	2,873.1	25,943.6	26,407.9	.2	.2
Riboflavin (mg)	24,711.0	73,121.7	48,410.1	72,974.4	73,610.8	.1	.1
Ascorbic acid (gm)	631.0	1,534.0	903.0	1,493.1	1,546.4	1.3	1.8
Iron (gm)	240.0	731.4	491.4	729.3	738.5	10.3	7.6

lem is presented in the first five columns of this table. With this information we know the optimal resource schedule for the Eskimo of Pelly Bay given the constraints imposed. These results are summarized in Figure 16.2.

POSTOPTIMAL STATEMENTS

Most linear programming packages provide a wide range of reporting optimons in addition to the optimal solution. These commonly include sensitivity or range analyses, which indicate the sensitivity of the model to discrete changes in the input values (costs, requirements, etc.). This supplemental information is known as *postoptimal analysis*. The last four columns of Table 16.3 provide postoptimal statements.

Shadow prices, shown in column 6, are statements of marginal cost or value. At their most fundamental level, they indicate how much it will cost (how much it will alter the objective function) to increase production of a resource by a single unit. For unused resources, shadow prices indicate the cost reduction necessary before a resource will be utilized. For expended resources (resources exploited to the upper limits of the model), they indicate how much extra the decision maker would be willing to "pay" to acquire additional units of that resource. For example, June birds, which were not used in the optimal solution, show a cost of 13.5 and a shadow price of 12.4. This indicates that if the decision were made to utilize birds in June, the total cost of production would increase by 12.4 cost units for every bird taken that month. A logical extension of this concept is that if the cost of birds in June could be decreased by 12.4, the resource would be incorporated into the optimal production schedule. Now consider April ringed seal which shows a cost of 54 and a shadow price of −127.6. Table 16.3 indicates that all ringed seal available in April were included in the optimal solution. The shadow price tells us that if additional ringed seal were available in April, the total cost of production would decrease by 127.6 for every additional seal taken. By extension, it would be worth investing as much as 127.6 cost units above the stated cost to acquire another seal. The maximum cost a resource can attain without altering the optimal solution is shown in column 7 of Table 16.3.

Typically, in formulating a linear programming problem, it is necessary to estimate some of the input parameters, much as I have done with cost. Thus, for any of the input values of the model, we would like to know over what range they can vary without affecting which variables enter into the optimal solution. If this range is narrow, the solution is sensitive to small fluctuations or errors in estimation. However, if the range is large and if the current input value is near the center of this range, we can be fairly sure that the solution is relatively insensitive to fluctuations or errors in estimation. Models that are highly sensitive to small changes or errors can be regarded as unstable; those that can tolerate a wide range of variation may be regarded as stable (Reidhead 1976:339; Cooper and Steinberg 1974).

A good deal can be learned about the sensitivity of costs from an examination of shadow prices. For example, winter musk-ox (November–January) shows a cost of 434.2 and a shadow price of 14.0 and is unused in the optimal solution. This means that a cost decrease of 14.0, only 3.2% of the original cost, would result in the inclusion of musk-ox into the winter production schedule. This resource can be regarded as highly sensitive to errors in cost estimation, and this factor must be considered in the final interpretation of the results. August caribou, on the other hand, would require an error in estimation of over 400% before the optimal solution would be affected.

The sensitivity analysis is summarized in columns 8 and 9 of Table 16.3. Column 8 indicates the percentage of decrease of the cost value necessary for an unused resource to be included in the optimal solution. The last column reveals the percentage that the cost of an expended resource may increase without changing the final solution.

ROW VECTORS

The row vectors in Table 16.4 can be interpreted in the same fashion as the column vectors in Table 16.3. The optimal solution is contained in the first four columns. Column 3 indicates row activity, or the amount of nutrient actually acquired, and column 4 gives the surplus acquired beyond the minimum annual requirement. The remaining columns provide postoptimal information. Column 5 shows the lowest possible row activity that can occur without changing the set of variables which compromise the optimal solution. Column 6 indicates the maximum possible activity of a given constraint before a change in this set of variables is necessary. Shadow prices, in columns 7 and 8, indicate the cost of eliminating or acquiring one unit of a given nutrient, respectively. These shadow prices can be used to measure the sensitivity of the model to minor modifications in dietary requirements. Columns 7 and 8 indicate that the model is extremely sensitive to small changes in calcium and nonfood requirements and least sensitive to changes in vitamin A requirements. I will elaborate on this point later.

Model of Traditional Subsistence Patterns: Summary of Results

The predicted annual subsistence cycle of the Netsilik can be interpreted from Tables 16.3 and 16.4 and is summarized graphically in Figure 16.2. The model predictions appear largely congruent with the ethnographic and historic accounts of Rasmussen (1931), Balikci (1964, 1970), Ross (1835), Boas (1888), and Brice-Bennett (1976) (cf. Figure 16.3), but there are some discrepancies. For example, in the modeled economy, fish productivity is overestimated in early spring and fall; and small game, which are generally taken throughout the year, are scheduled only for late winter. Traditionally,

TRADITIONAL NETSILIK ECONOMY:MODELED

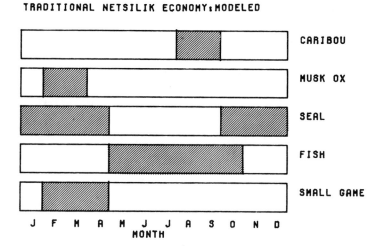

FIGURE 16.2 *Optimal resource schedule for traditional Netsilik economy as modeled.*

small game were a marginal or supplemental resource. Shadow prices imply the same, that small game would not be a critical staple, but might be utilized when more valuable resources did not fully meet the population's needs. Although small game were not incorporated into the optimal solution of the model, small changes in their cost relative to other resources would probably lead to their utilization.

There is really little value in attempting to confirm the absolute accuracy

TRADITIONAL NETSILIK ECONOMY:OBSERVED

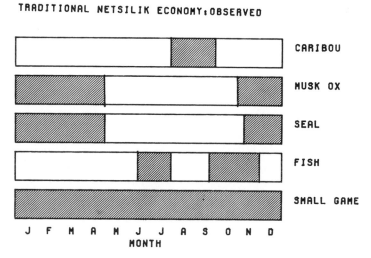

FIGURE 16.3 *Resource schedule for traditional Netsilik economy as ethnographically observed.*

of the quantitative predictions of the model. The quantitative solution is of limited value unless it is considered in conjunction with the postoptimal analyses. The reader may pursue more detailed comparisons between the predicted and observed subsistence patterns. The discussion that follows will touch on some of the salient features of the results.

NUTRITIONAL RESULTS

A number of important points can be made regarding nutrition and nonfood value of resources. The models indicate that in satisfying all 11 requirements, a considerable surplus was acquired for all but two: calcium and hides (cf. Table 16.4). In some cases this surplus was substantial. For example, in the case of energy (measured in kilocalories), an average surplus of 1300 kcal per person per day was acquired (compare with an average daily requirement of approximately 2300 kcal). For protein, the average surplus exceeded three times the average daily requirement. These are not unreasonable figures since they closely parallel ethnographic observations of consumption patterns among Arctic hunters (Krogh and Krogh 1914; Stefansson 1914; Foote 1965; Murdoch 1892; Weyer 1969).

Those nutrients which are not in surplus are called the *binding* constraints of the model. It is these constraints which ultimately determine the composition of the optimal solution. They represent the *limiting nutrients* since they are the most costly and least abundant (Odum 1971:106). Traditionally, evaluations of prehistoric diet have been based solely on energy requirements (kilocalories). Prehistoric carrying capacity or population estimates have generally been based on the amount of potential energy provided by available biomass (Casteel 1972; Zubrow 1975; Jochim 1976). Occasionally, both protein and energy have been considered (Hall 1971; Denniston 1972). Table 16.4 indicates that, if applied to the Netsilik, this approach would result in gross overestimation of carrying capacity and population size. Clearly, neither energy nor protein is the limiting factor in the Netsilik diet. A diet that barely satisfies the minimal energy or protein requirements would result in serious deficiencies in calcium, ascorbic acid, and possibly other nutrients. It would also not satisfy the population's nonfood requirements.

Nonfood value is of special interest because the annual cost of production is highly sensitive to changes in hide requirements. Successive programs were run with the nonfood requirement initially set at 100 and then increased by increments of 50. A surplus of hides is produced through the 250 requirement. When the nonfood requirement is set at 300, it becomes a limiting constraint, and the annual cost of production increases by 13%. At 350, there is a 61% increase over the original cost; when the requirement is 400, the increase is 137%; and at 450, the increase is 286%. This illustrates that nonfood materials will often figure significantly in determining the composition of diet and the structure of economic activities. Foote (1965) notes that there was a conscious effort on the part of the Alaskan Eskimo to "combine the search for food with the proper species and season which would yield the maximum amount of byproducts." Similar observations have been expressed by others (Laughlin 1968:310; Jochim 1976:23; Petersen 1973:153).

In the intermediate runs of these programs, it was impossible to predict intuitively how a change in a single requirement, hides, would alter the optimal solution. There was not necessarily a one-to-one correspondence between a change in one input value and a change in another. The interrelationship of numerous factors had to be considered. Linear programming models allow this simultaneous consideration of multiple factors.

UTILIZED AND NONUTILIZED RESOURCES

Table 16.3 shows that most of the resources in the optimal solution have been exploited to their maximum allocated levels. This can partially be attributed to the method by which bounds were established; but more realistically, it is a function of a small population inhabiting a large territory stocked with resources of quite diverse cost and minimal differences in utility. In the Netsilik case, necessary resources are available, but the population is constrained from utilizing them more extensively by manpower, mobility, and technology. The model indicates that if these constraints were removed, the Eskimo would subsist for almost the entire year on two or three resources, with the majority of production coming in May through October. Empirically, this is very nearly what happens following the introduction of the rifle, which removes the aforementioned constraints (see later), to some of the Central Eskimo groups.

Looking at the model again, we see that there are certain resources that will never be incorporated into the optimal solution. Polar bear, for example, is far too costly and would never be pursued under the stated conditions of the model. Yet, empirical evidence of polar bear consumption would not invalidate the model. The implications of this are particularly important in a archaeological application. Shadow prices for polar bear indicate that a cost reduction of almost 95% would be required before the decision to hunt polar bear would be made. This suggests that polar bear would not have influenced the planning of seasonal economic activities. However, if in the course of sealing, a group of hunters encountered fresh bear tracks, the search time, the major component in bear cost, would be so drastically reduced that bear would probably be taken (see also Reidhead 1976:334–336; Nelson 1969:185). This is confirmed ethnographically. Northern hunters do not deliberately search for exceptionally costly resources, but may pursue them when they are accidentally encountered (Nelson 1969; Feit 1973). Consequently, archaeological middens may not be accurate indicators of planned economic patterns. The mere presence of polar bear, for example, in Eskimo middens does not necessarily imply that this resource was pursued regularly or that it figured significantly into the annual economy. Likewise, the absence of specific fauna from middens may not reflect patterns of exploitation as much as patterns of consumption, butchering, and preservation. This is supported by recent ethnoarchaeological work (e.g., Yellen 1974). The models can thus serve as important complements to information derived from archaeological deposits since they permit a broader perspective of prehistoric economic behavior than can be attained from the archaeological record alone.

IMPLICATIONS FOR SETTLEMENT PATTERN STUDY

Although the problem of settlement pattern is not dealt with in this chapter it can be noted that the models also lend insight into the timing of seasonal population movements. The optimum solution tells us the quantity of each resource taken in any given month. This enables us to break the year into seasons based on changes in patterns of exploitation and consumption. This, in turn, has bearing on the location of seasonal camps, since most economic activities are associated with a specific location in which they are best carried out.

CONCLUSIONS

The critical point concerning diet and economy is that oversimplification, or reduction of a model to a few variables, can result in serious misconceptions. The data necessary to build more rigorous nutritional models are available for many contexts of they can be derived. When they are not at hand, it is important for the investigator to evaluate those factors which might be limiters in diet and economy.

The problem of limiting factors in diet and economy is by no means restricted to the Eskimo case. In fact, it may be less pronounced in the Arctic, where most of the resources are of the animal variety, and therefore are relatively complete nutritionally. The need for dietary complements is more pronounced in societies where gathering or horticulture make a significant contribution to the diet (Davidson *et al.* 1975). In such cases, foods may often be rich in only a few key nutrients and a number of different foods must be selected in the proper combinations to maintain an adequate diet.

Dynamic Applications

As archaeologists, we are concerned not only with synchronic aspects of economic systems, but also with how these systems behave through time, responding to perturbations of varying kind and degree. Linear programming models are well suited for dynamic analyses since one can easily alter the input coefficients and instantly view the effects of these changes. Specific input coefficients may be altered systematically or stochastically over a series of runs in order to simulate the behavior of the system through time. The choice of dynamic components within a model depends on the questions being investigated. For example, in the Eskimo model, I did not simulate the effect of cyclical and stochastic fluctuations in Arctic resources on resource decisions. This type of information is implicit in postoptimal analysis, since we know which components of the model are sensitive to changes and therefore can predict the behavior of the system in response to this sensitivity.

Of greater concern is the response of the system to major perturbations, such as resource depletion, climatic change, or technological innovation. Most conceivable disturbances can be characterized in terms of changes in some of the resource attributes which characterize this model, such as resource density, mobility, and aggregation. For example, we can view any technological change as in some way altering man's access to resources. Technology may reduce the mobility of the resource relative to man, and it may provide access to resources that were previously inaccessible. It may reduce the required labor input or increase the maximum potential yield. Consequently, it may alter the costs or bounds (i.e., the limits of exploitation) of a given resource. I have modeled the introduction of the rifle to Netsilik economy by considering these two factors.

In caribou hunting, the rifle decreases pursuit time by reducing the critical distance; hence, cost is lowered. Although a hunter with a bow might produce fatal results at a distance of 30–50 m (Stefansson 1914:96; Sonnenfeld 1960), the hunter with a rifle could be highly successful at a distance of 300 m or more (Stefansson 1944:475; Sonnenfeld 1960). In addition, the hunter with a rifle is able to exploit a larger portion of a single aggregation at one time. Thus, the maximum catch of caribou will increase. A similar, possibly more dramatic, effect would be realized with musk-oxen, which tend to cluster together and form a defensive ring when threatened. This is quite effective defense against wolves (Tener 1957), but is of little use against a man with a rifle.

The effects of the rifle on sealing can be equally striking. Although significant change in the efficiency of the breathing hole technique would not be expected (Rasmussen 1931:151; Boas 1888; Sonnenfeld 1960), the introduction of the rifle increases productivity and reduces cost of sealing in other seasons. Ice edge sealing (cf. Nelson 1969:246) becomes less risky as access to seals in the water improves, and sleeping seal hunting (Nelson 1969:310; Sonnenfeld 1960; Stefansson 1944:452) becomes much less costly as critical distance decreases. If boats were used, we would expect cost to decrease even further, since retrieval would be simplified and territory expanded.

However, the introduction of the rifle would not have such dramatic effects on all available resources. For instance, the overall effect on birds would be minimal (unless shotguns were employed), and no change would be expected in the cost of fish. In addition, the major cost for many resources lies in the search, and a decrease in pursuit time would have little effect on cost in these cases. Changes in resource attributes for the model of postrifle Netsilik economy are presented in Table 16.5.

Model of Postrifle Economy

The model of postrifle Netsilik economy is presented in Table 16.6 and summarized in Figure 16.4. The model predictions are actually more congruent with the empirical case (cf. Figure 16.5) than the figures appear to indicate. Final interpretation of the model must be made in conjunction with the postoptimal analysis.

The introduction of the rifle at Pelly Bay resulted in increased exploitation of seal and caribou. Harvest of caribou intensified to the point of overexploitation. Balikci (1964) and Kelsall (1968:215–222) describe mass slaughter of caribou ambushed at crossing places. Seal hunting intensified in the spring as the ice edge became a viable productive hunting zone. Exploitation of seal and caribou was thus intensified in the postrifle period, whereas fishing and small game hunting decreased. The model indicates that harvest of fall caribou and winter and spring seal will increase as exploitation limits increase. In fact, an unbounded model predicts subsistence based entirely on fall caribou and spring seal.

Change is, of course, a continuous process. At this stage, the model does not provide a continuous characterization of change; rather, it offers a description of the results of discrete events. Although these models may not explain the processes of innovation and adoption (cf. Limp 1977), they do provide important insight into the immediate ramifications of various perturbations to a subsistence settlement system.

One can model other technological changes in the same manner. Of course a change in technology may not be limited solely to altering the costs or bounds of the models. A change in food preparation technique, for example, would alter the nutritional value of the food as well. This becomes a significant consideration among the Eskimo when they switch from oil lamps to hotter gas stoves. The ramifications of any change, though, should be describable in terms of the variables and parameters which define the model, and as long as this is the case the consequences of any perturbation can be modeled.

Archaeological Application

For any context, regardless of the quality of the archaeological data, we need four types of information to begin to develop these models: (a) knowledge of the basic environmental conditions at the time under consideration;

TABLE 16.5
Changes in Resource Attributes for Model of Postrifle Economy

Resource	Jan.	Feb.	March	April	May	June	July	Aug.	Sept.	Oct.	Nov.	Dec.
Caribou												
Critical distance	200	200	200	200	100	1	1	1	1	100	200	200
Risk	1.35	1.25	1.25	1.25	1.25	1.5	1.5	1.25	1.25	1.35	1.35	1.35
Musk-ox												
Critical distance	200	200	200	200	200	200	200	200	200	200	200	200
Risk	1.1	1	1	1	1	1	1	1	1	1.1	1.1	1.1
Ringed seal												
Critical distance		NO CHANGE			25	25	125	125	125	150	NO CHANGE	
Risk					1	1	1	1	1	1.1		
Bearded seal												
Critical distance	225	225	225	225	150	150	225	225	225	225	225	225
Risk	1.1	1	1	1	1	1	1	1	1	1.1	1.1	1.1
Polar bear												
Critical distance	200	200	200	200	200	200	200	200	200	200	200	200
Risk	1.6	1.25	1.25	1.25	1.25	1.5	1.5	1.25	1.25	1.6	1.6	1.6

TABLE 16.6
Model of Postrifle Netsilik Economy—Column Vectors

Resource	Month	Column activity	Upper bound	Cost	Shadow price	Maximum cost	− Range (%)	+ Range (%)
Caribou	Dec.–Jan.	0		2,231.4	2,059.0	172.4	92	
	Feb.–March	0		2,066.1	2,007.3	58.8	97	
	April	0	90	440.9	382.1	58.8	87	
	May	0	90	436.7	379.6	57.1	87	
	June	0	90	431.1	374.0	57.1	87	
	July	0	90	431.1	372.3	58.8	86	
	Aug.	0	90	346.1	59.4	286.7	17	
	Sept.	180	180	18.1	−268.5	286.6		1483
	Oct.	0	180	771.8	485.2	286.6	63	
	Nov.	0	90	2,231.4	1,945.3	286.1	87	
Musk-ox	Nov.–Jan.	0	30	423.5	157.4	266.1	37	
	Feb.	0	10	385.0	118.9	266.1	31	
	March	0	10	388.3	122.2	266.1	31	
	April	0	10	388.3	235.9	152.4	61	
	May	0	5	645.0	492.6	152.4	76	
	June	0	5	645.0	606.2	38.8	94	
	July, Sept.	0	10	388.3	349.6	38.7	90	
	Aug.	0	5	386.1	347.4	38.7	90	
	Oct.	0	5	702.1	549.7	152.4	78	
Ringed seal	Nov.–Jan.	70	70	63.9	−60.5	124.4		95
	Feb.–March	60	60	58.1	−66.3	124.4		114
	April	30	30	54.0	−70.4	124.4		130
	May	60	60	8.8	−114.8	123.6		1300
	June	60	60	8.8	−.9	9.7		10
	July	0	60	129.0	119.1	9.9	92	
	Aug.	0	60	129.0	61.5	67.5	48	
	Sept.	0	10	129.0	61.5	67.5	48	
	Oct.	0	20	85.2	17.6	67.6	21	

Species	Month							
Bearded seal	Oct.–Jan.	0	20	440.0	145.0	295.0	33	
	Feb.–March	0	10	400.0	332.4	67.6	83	
	April	0	5	400.0	334.1	65.9	84	
	May	0	5	250.0	184.1	65.9	74	
	June	0	5	250.0	184.1	65.9	74	
	July–Sept.	10	15	295.0	120.9	295.0	0	0
Polar bear	Dec.–Jan.	0		6,720.0	6,429.5	290.5	96	
	Feb.	0		10,200.0	9,908.2	291.8	97	
	March	0		10,166.7	9,874.5	292.2	97	
	April	0		5,166.7	4,874.5	292.2	94	
	May	0		5,200.0	4,907.8	292.2	94	
	June	0		15,300.0	15,121.4	178.6	99	
	July	0		15,300.0	15,235.1	64.9	99+	
	Aug.	0		10,250.0	10,185.1	64.9	99+	
	Sept.	0		10,250.0	9,957.8	292.2	97	
	Oct.	0		6,720.0	6,427.8	292.2	96	
	Nov.	0		6,720.0	6,428.2	291.8	96	
Fish	Nov.–Jan.	0	100	8.80	6.92	1.88	79	
	Feb.–April	0	100	8.25	6.37	1.88	77	
	May	15	200	1.88	.17	1.88	0	0
	June	200	200	.66	−1.22	1.88		185
	July	800	800	.16	−1.72	1.88		1075
	Aug.	800	800	.62	−1.26	1.88		203
	Sept.	400	400	1.00	−.88	1.88		88
	Oct.	0	200	2.03	.15	1.88	7	
Birds	Nov.–Jan.	0		135.9	135.8	.1	99+	
	Feb.–March	0		126.0	125.8	.2	99+	
	April	0		110.0	109.8	.2	99+	
	May	0		23.6	23.4	.2	99	
	June	0		13.5	13.2	.3	98	
	July	0		3.4	3.0	.4	88	
	Aug.	0		12.1	11.8	.3	98	
	Sept.	0		23.6	23.2	.4	98	
	Oct.	0		118.8	118.6	.2	99+	

Table 16.6 (*Continued*)

Table 16.6 (*Continued*)

Resource	Month	Column activity	Upper bound	Cost	Shadow price	Maximum cost	− Range (%)	+ Range (%)
Hare	Nov.–Jan.	0		20.6	17.4	3.2	84	
	Feb.–March	0		19.4	16.2	3.2	84	
	April	0		19.1	15.9	3.2	83	
	May–June	0		19.1	16.0	3.1	84	
	July–Sept.	0		19.1	15.9	3.2	83	
	Oct.	0		20.6	17.4	3.2	84	
Wolf	Nov.–Jan.	0		13,763.8	13,701.3	62.5	99+	
	Feb.–May	0		12,512.5	12,450.0	62.5	99+	
	June–Sept.	0		4,179.1	4,116.6	62.5	98	
	Oct.	0		4,597.0	4,534.5	62.5	99	
Lemming	Oct.–Jan.	0		13.5	13.5	0	100	
	Feb.–Sept.	0		12.5	12.5	0	100	
Squirrel	Jan.	0		52.5	26.0	26.5	50	
	Feb.–April	0		50.0	38.5	11.5	77	
	May, Nov.–Dec.	0		37.5	26.0	11.5	69	
	June–July	0		37.5	26.0	11.5	69	
	Aug.	0		37.5	26.0	11.5	69	
	Sept.	0		37.5	26.0	11.5	69	
	Oct.	0		52.5	41.0	11.5	78	
Fox	Oct.–Jan.	0	20	88.5	53.9	34.6	61	
	Feb.–April	0	15	45.5	10.9	34.6	24	
	May–Sept.	0	25	83.0	82.5	0.5	99	

POST RIFLE NETSILIK ECONOMY:MODELED

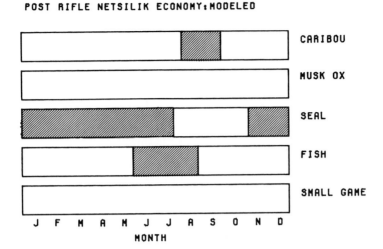

FIGURE 16.4 *Optimal resource schedule for postrifle Netsilik economy as modeled.*

(*b*) knowlege of which food resources were available; (*c*) quantification of the critical attributes of the model; and (*d*) a basic assessment of the technology available. With these data, one can develop the basic optimization models which predict the quantity and time of utilization of individual resources. Beyond pure reconstruction, the information provided in the postoptimal analysis is critical to the anthropologist concerned with culture processes. Postoptimal information provides an understanding of the stability and flexibility of the prehistoric economic systems and of those compo-

POST RIFLE NETSILIK ECONOMY:OBSERVED

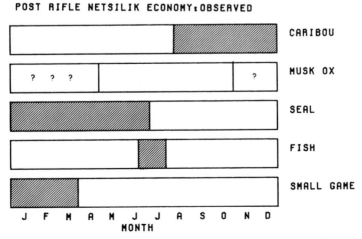

FIGURE 16.5 *Resource schedule for postrifle Netsilik economy as empirically observed.*

nents most sensitive to change. Essentially, any of the complex relationships depicted in the ethnographic models can be illustrated for an archaeological case as well.

Evaluation

In the preceding pages I have provided a set of comprehensive models of Netsilik Eskimo subsistence settlement systems. These models, in reality, represent only a first approximation. Numerous "bugs" still exist, foremost among which is the problem of cost. Since the cost coefficient used in this chapter is calculated partially from other artificial coefficients or estimates (e.g., mobility and risk), a sizable margin of error is possible. Future work should seek to replace these manufactured data with more reliable measures.

Another problem concerns the simultaneous annual solution. Because some vectors represent more than a single month, it is difficult in some cases to define the timing of harvest precisely. For instance, with November through January ringed seal, no criteria are available to determine whether the 70 seals allocated to this vector by the model represent 3 months' work, or whether they were caught in a single month. Empirically, the seal season begins around December. This is one possible interpretation of this vector, though others are also possible. Clearly, more precise criteria are needed to discriminate between months. A more dynamic, month-to-month procedure might be preferable.

The aforementioned problems must be addressed before such models can attain their maximum effectiveness as tools in prehistoric research. Yet even at this stage, the utility of the approach is clear. In a deductive framework, these models can be used to test hypotheses. Reidhead (1976), for instance, used linear programming models to test hypotheses of labor minimization among the prehistoric inhabitants of southeast Indiana. In addition, linear programming models could be used to generate hypotheses. In cases in which archaeological data are scant, these models would tell us what type of economic system we might logically expect. But perhaps the value of such models is not best seen in a purely hypothetico-deductive framework. They are, as are most models, heuristic devices; they do not necessarily prove anything or make predictions to specific degrees of accuracy. Their major value is that they force us to recognize the actual complexities inherent in band level economies and to focus on important interrelationships between variables.

Certainly, a good deal of refinement is needed, particularly in the way some of the input parameters are quantified. But these problems do not diminish the utility of the models. The problems also have heuristic value. Reidhead (1976:449) summarizes well:

When we approach complex problems relating to the economics of food production and nutritional utilization in a general non-quantitative fashion, the areas in which our data are weak are not so obvious. But when we attempt to apply such a simple and long accepted quantitative method as linear programming, the inadequacies of our data suddenly glare out at us in such a stark fashion as to become obvious. This alone would make the present application of linear programming valuable.

The major value of the linear programming approach is that it forces us to focus on important interrelationships among variables. Joy, in his introduction of the method to the anthropological literature (1967:180), stressed that the linear programming approach can be extremely valuable regardless of the accuracy of the quantitative data because the method forces the investigator to ask relevant questions:

> Conceptually, the chief advantage is that with this method, one can more readily trace potential implications of postulated relationships. One is required to undertake an explicit formulation of activities and constraints and to ask whether a coefficient is zero, positive, or negative. Therefore, one is required to make explicit the nature of the interrelationships in the system.

The models presented offer a general framework in which we can study prehistoric hunter–gatherer subsistence settlement systems. Perhaps they have raised more questions than they have provided answers, but with further refinements to the structure of the models and to the methods of quantification the answers should be forthcoming.

Acknowledgments

I thank the following individuals for comments and criticisms on earlier versions of this chapter: Pat Beirne, Kent V. Flannery, Richard I. Ford, Mary Hodge, Karl L. Hutterer, John W. Rick, John Speth, Jerry Voss, and Robert E. Whallon, Jr. Special thanks are extended to Van Reidhead for his valuable suggestions and encouragement.

References

Andrews, C. W. and Lear, E., 1956, The biology of the arctic char in Labrador. *Journal of the Fisheries Research Board of Canada.* 13, 33–60.

Balikci, Asen, 1964, Development of basic socio-economic units in two Eskimo communities. National Museum of Canada Bulletin no. 202.

Balikci, Asen, 1970, *The Netsilik Eskimo.* Garden City, N.Y., Natural History Press.

Banfield, A. W. F., 1973, *The Mammals of Canada.* Toronto, University of Toronto Press.

Boas, Franz, 1888, *The Central Eskimo.* Bureau of American Ethnology, Annual report, 6th, 1884–1885.

Brice-Bennett, Carol, 1976, Inuit land use in the East-Central Canadian Arctic, in *Inuit Land Use and Occupancy Project.* Ottawa, Dept. of Indian and Northern Affairs, Canada. v. 1, p. 65–81.

Burch, E. S., 1972, The caribou/wild reindeer as a human resource. *American Antiquity.* 37, 339–368.

Casteel, Richard W., 1972, Two static maximum population density models for hunters and gatherers: A first approximation. *World Archaeology.* 4, 19–40.

Clarke, David L., 1968, *Analytical Archaeology.* London, Methuen.

Cooper, Leon and Steinberg, David, 1974, *Methods and Applications of Linear Programming.* Philadelphia, Saunders.

Daellenbach, Hans G. and Bell, E. J., 1970, *Users Guide to Linear Programming.* Englewood Cliffs, N.J., Prentice-Hall.

Dantzig, George B., 1963, *Linear Programming and Extensions.* Princeton, N. J., Princeton University Press.

Davidson, Sir Stanley *et al.*, 1975, *Human Nutrition and Dietetics.* 6th ed. Edinburgh, Churchill Livingstone.

Denniston, Glenda B., 1972, Ashishik Point: An economic analysis of a prehistoric Aleutian community. Ph.D. thesis, University of Wisconsin—Madison. Ann Arbor, University Microfilms.

Dergebøl, Magnus and Freuchen, P., 1935, Mammals. *Report of the 5th Thule Expedition, 1921–1924.* Copenhagen, Gyldendal. v. 2, no. 45.

Dorfman, Robert, Samuelson, P. A., and Solow, N., 1958, *Linear Programming and Economic Analysis.* New York, McGraw-Hill.

Driebeek, Norman J., 1969, *Applied Linear Programming.* Reading, Mass., Addison-Wesley.

Emlen, J. Meritt, 1966, The role of time and energy in food preference. *The American Naturalist.* 100, 611–619.

Feit, Harvey, 1973, The ethno-ecology of the Waswanipi Cree: or how hunters can manage their resources. In Cox, B. (ed.) *Cultural Ecology,* Toronto, McClelland and Stewart. p. 115–125.

Foote, Don Charles, 1965, Exploration and resource utilization in northwestern arctic Alaska before 1855. Unpublished Ph.D. thesis, McGill University.

Gale, David, 1960, *The Theory of Linear Economic Models.* New York, McGraw-Hill.

Godfrey, W. Earl, 1966, The birds of Canada. National Museum of Canada Bulletin, no. 203, Biological series no. 73.

Hall, Edwin S., Jr., 1971, Kangiguksuk: a cultural reconstruction of a 16th century Eskimo site in northern Alaska. *Arctic Anthropology.* 8, 1–101.

Harrington, C. R., 1964, Polar bears and their present status. *Canadian Audubon Magazine.* Jan. 1964. 3–10.

Hillier, Frederick S. and Lieberman, Gerald J., 1974, *Operations Research.* 2d Ed. San Francisco, Holden-Day.

Horne, Edith, 1934, The present status of the musk ox. Special Publication of the American Committee for International Wildlife Protection, no. 5.

Hørring, R., 1935, Birds. *Report of the 5th Thule Expedition, 1921–1924.* Copenhagen, Gyldendal. v. 2, no. 6.

Jochim, Michael A., 1976, *Hunter-Gatherer Subsistence and Settlement: A Predictive Model.* New York, Academic Press.

Joy, Leonard, 1967, An economic homologue of Barth's presentation of Economic spheres in Darfur. In Firth, R. (ed.) *Themes in Economic Anthropology,* London, Tavistock, 175–190.

Keene, Arthur S., (in press), Models for the study of prehistoric diet. In Gilbert, R. I. and Mielke, J. H. (eds.) *Techniques for the Analysis of Prehistoric Diets,* Oxford: University Press of Mississippi.

Kelsall, J. P., 1968, *The Caribou.* Ottawa, Dept. of Indian Affairs and Northern Development, Canadian Wildlife Service.

Kortright, Francis H., 1942, *The Ducks, Geese and Swans of North America*. Washington, American Wildlife Institute.

Krogh, August and Krogh, Marie, 1914, A study of the diet and metabolism of Eskimos. *Meddeleser Om* Grønland, 51, 1–52.

Laughlin, William S., 1968, Hunting: An integrating biobehavior system and its evolutionary importance. In *Man the Hunter,* ed. R. B. Lee and I. DeVore. Chicago: Aldine. p. 304–320.

Lee, Richard B., 1968, What hunters do for a living, or how to make out on scarce resources. in Lee, R. B. and DeVore, I. (eds.) *Man the Hunter,* Chicago, Aldine. 30–48.

Limp, W. Frederick, 1977, The economics of agricultural dispersal. Paper presented at the 1977 meetings of the Society of American Archaeology, New Orleans, La.

MacArthur, Robert H. and Pianka, Eric B., 1966, On the optimal use of a patchy environment. *American Naturalist.*

McLaren, Ian A., 1958a, The biology of ringed seal in the eastern Canadian Arctic. Fisheries Research Board of Canada, Bulletin 118.

McLaren, Ian A., 1958b, Some aspects of growth and reproduction of the bearded seal, *Erignathus barbatus* (Erxleben). *Journal of Fisheries Research Board of Canada.* 15, 219–227.

McLulich, D. A., 1937, Fluctuations in the numbers of varying hare (*Lepus americanus*). University of Toronto Studies, no. 42.

MacPherson, A. H., 1969, The dynamics of Canadian arctic fox populations. Canadian Wildlife Service, Reprt series 8.

MacPherson, A. H. and Manning, T. H., 1959, The birds and mammals of Adelaide Peninsula, N.W.T. National Museum of Canada Bulletin no. 161.

Manning, T. H., Hohn, E. O., and MacPherson, A. H., 1956, The birds of Banks Island. National Museum of Canada Bulletin, no. 143.

Mansfield, A. W., 1963, Seals of arctic and eastern Canada. Fisheries Research Board of Canada, Bulletin, no. 137.

Marks, Stuart A., 1976, *Large mammals and a brave people*. Seattle, University of Washington Press.

Mayer, W. V., 1953, A preliminary study of the Barrow ground squirrel. *Journal of Mammology.* 34, 334–345.

Mech, David L., 1970, *The Wolf: The Ecology and Behavior of an Endangered Species.* Garden City, N.Y., Natural History Press.

Murdoch, John, 1892, *Ethnonological Results of the Point Barrow Expedition.* Bureau of American Ethnology, Annual Report, 9th.

Nelson, Richard K., 1969, *Hunters of the Northern Ice.* Chicago, University of Chicago Press.

Norberg, R. Åke, 1977, An ecological theory on foraging time and energetics and choice of optimal food searching method. *Journal of Animal Ecology,* 46, 511–529.

Odum, Eugene P., 1971, *Fundamentals of Ecology.* 3d Ed. Toronto, Saunders.

Paine, Robert, 1973, Animals as capital: Comparisons among northern nomadic herders and hunters. in Cox, B. (ed.) *Cultural Ecology,* ed. B. Cox. Toronto, McClelland and Stewart.

Perry, Richard, 1966, *The World of the Polar Bear.* Seattle, University of Washington Press.

Petersen, Robert, 1973, On the variation of settlement patterns and hunting conditions in three districts of Greenland, in G. Berg (ed.) *Circumpolar Problems,* Wenner Gren International Symposium series no. 21. p. 153–162.

Rasmussen, Knud, 1931, The Netsilik Eskimos. *Report of the 5th Thule Expedition.* Copenhagen; Gyldendal. v. 8, no. 1–2.

Reidhead, Van A., 1976, Optimization and food procurement at the prehistoric Leonard Haag site, southeast Indiana: A linear programming approach. Ph.D. thesis, Indiana University. Ann Arbor, University Microfilms.

Ross, Sir John, 1835, *Narrative of a Second Voyage in Search of the Northwest Passage.* London.

Schneider, Harold, 1974, *Economic Man.* New York, Free Press.

Schoener, Thomas W., 1971, Theory of feeding strategies. *Annual Review of Ecology and Systematics.* 366–404.

Scott, W. B., 1954, *Freshwater Fishes of Eastern Canada.* Toronto, University of Toronto Press.

Smith, Bruce D., 1975, *Middle Mississippi Exploitation of Animal Populations.* Ann Arbor, University of Michigan Museum of Anthropology, Anthropological papers, no. 57.

Smith, Thomas G., 1973, Population dynamics of the ringed seal in the eastern Canadian Arctic. Fisheries Research Board of Canada Bulletin, no. 181.

Sonnenfeld, J., 1960, Changes in Eskimo hunting technology: An introduction to impliment geography. *Annals of the Association of American Geographers.* V. 50, no. 2.

Spivey, W. A. and Thrall, R. M., 1970, *Linear Optimization.* New York: Holt, Rinehart and Winston.

Sprules, William M., 1952, The arctic char of the western coast of Hudson Bay. *Journal of the Fisheries Research Board of Canada.* 9, 1–15.

Stefansson, V., 1914, *The Stefansson-Anderson Expedition: Preliminary Ethnological Report.* Anthropological papers of the American Museum of Natural History, v. 14.

Stefansson, V., 1944, *Arctic Manual.* New York, Macmillan.

Steigenberger, L. W. *et al.*, 1974, Northern Yukon freshwater fisheries studies 1973. Task Force for Northern Oil Development, Environmental-Social Committee. Report no. 74–20.

Stigler, George J., 1945, The cost of subsistence. *Journal of Farm Economics.* 27:303–314.

Sutton, George M., 1932, The birds of Southampton Island. *Memoirs of the Carnegie Museum.* 12, 1–275.

Tener, J. S., 1957, The distribution of muskoxen in Canada. *Journal of Mammology.* 39:398–408.

Tener, J. S., 1965, *Muskoxen in Canada: A Biological and Taxonomic Review.* Ottawa, Dept. of Northern Affairs and Natural Resources.

Throsby, C. D., 1962, Some notes on dynamic linear programming. *Review of Marketing and Agriculture Economics.* v. 30, no. 2.

Vibe, Christian, 1967, *Arctic animals in relation to climatic fluctuations.* Copenhagen, Reitzel.

Villiers, D., 1968, *The Central Arctic: An Area Economic Survey.* Ottawa, Industrial Division, Northern Administration Branch, Dept. of Indian Affairs and Northern Development.

Wagner, Harvey M., 1975, *Principles of Operations Research.* 2d Ed. Englewood Cliffs, Prentice-Hall.

Walker, Ernst P., 1964, *Mammals of the World.* Baltimore, Johns Hopkins Press.

Weyer, Edward M., 1969, *The Eskimos: Their environment and folkways.* New York, Archon.

Wilmsen, Edwin N., 1973, Interaction, spacing behavior and the organization of hunting bands. *Journal of Anthropological Research.* 29 (1), 1–31.

Yellen, John E., 1974. The !Kung settlement pattern: An archaeological perspective. Unpublished Ph.D. thesis. Harvard University.

Zeisberger, David., 1910, David Zeisberger's history of the North American Indians, (eds.) A. B. Hulbert and W. N. Schwarze. *Ohio Archaeological and Historical Quarterly.* 19, 1–189.

Zubrow, Ezra B. W., 1975, *Prehistoric Carrying Capacity: a Model.* Menlo Park, Cummings.

17

ROBERT G. D. REYNOLDS
BERNARD P. ZEIGLER

A Formal Mathematical Model for the Operation of Consensus-Based Hunting–Gathering Bands

Introduction

For most of man's two million years on earth, he has lived as an egalitarian hunter–gatherer. The nature of the consensus-based hunting–gathering band has been a subject of great archaeological interest, since it is the baseline from which all subsequent cultural evolution has taken place. Numerous economic and geographic models have been designed for band societies and for the transition from bands using wild resources to bands practicing primitive agriculture. Unfortunately, most of these models make underlying assumptions about "maximization" which are not appropriate for band societies. In addition, as pointed out by Flannery (1972), they frequently concentrate on exchanges of matter and energy while ignoring exchanges of information. The result is that many models for the origins of agriculture view it as a way of increasing energy per unit of land, often as the result of some postulated human "population pressure."

In this chapter, we will examine a formal mathematical model which suggests that consensus-based, egalitarian hunter–gatherers (especially those living in mosaic environments such as those of the Near East, highland Mesoamerica, or the Andes) could not have "maximized" resource exploitation even had that concept been part of their ideology. By concentrating on problems of information exchange, we will also suggest that agriculture could have arisen in some areas as a solution, not to population problems, but to the predictable problems of resource search and scheduling encountered by any group without a decision-making hierarchy.

Transformations:
Mathematical Approaches to Culture Change

Hunter–Gatherer Information Processing

Broad comparisons have been drawn (Maruyama 1963) between the information processing capabilities of band societies and relatively more complex forms of social organization such as tribes, chiefdoms, and states. Yet there have been few attempts to characterize specifically the information processing capabilities of even hunter–gatherer groups in a formal fashion. In particular, it is of interest to see how the nature of the communication links (channels) between members affects the group's ability to evaluate and modify its resource procurement strategies. Each such strategy implements a set of group policies concerning portions of its environment (Flannery 1972). Thus changes in resource exploitation policies over time are related to corresponding changes in resource exploitation strategies. Our principal concern is to investigate in a formal way how these latter changes are facilitated (or retarded) by the presence of certain types of communication links between individuals. Since evidence for the presence of particular strategies can be obtained archaeologically, we might then, on the basis of observed changes in the archaeological record, be able to make inferences regarding associated changes in the communication structure. In particular, we want to demonstrate theoretically that to implement certain sets of resource procurement strategies which allow the exploitation of specific aspects of the environment, the presence of a certain communication structure within the group is a minimal requirement. By establishing such a correspondence, we can provide benchmarks through which to induce more precisely the social structure of a group from its archaeological remains.

In this chapter, we examine in an exploratory way the information-processing aspects involved when a group of individuals makes decisions about how best to utilize a two-dimensional distribution of resources. The pertinent factors are (a) the ability of each member to collect and process information about the resource distribution; (b) the extent to which information is shared among members; (c) the specific sets of decisions available for each member to make; and (d) the way in which the individual decisions are integrated to produce a group decision.

In this context, it is formally demonstrated that constraints on the communication between individuals impose limitations on the utilization which any egalitarian group can make of the spatially distributed resources accessible to it.

Our basic model of group decision making is that of the "linear threshold" or "voting" type which demands only minimal communication facility by its members. By relating our model to the perceptrons[1] studied by Minsky

---

[1]A simple pattern-recognizing scheme in which the model's components vote on the presence or absence of a particular pattern. The final decision is a weighted linear sum of the components' individual decisions.

and Papert (1969), we are able to employ some of their fairly deep results on the limitation of perception recognition in our own context.

Our specific aim here is to characterize formally certain aspects of egalitarian decision-making systems, and to demonstrate within the context of the model that it is hard for such a group to answer certain questions about its environment. In particular, we will demonstrate that the group's ability to decide on the direction to take for maximum resource exploitation is strongly limited by the information gathering of its individual members and *not* by the number of individuals in the group.

More concretely, let the area searchable by an individual be bounded by some constant M. Then no matter how large the group, or how complex the information processing power of the individual (limited of course to the search area), there is a maximum region of size N, determined by M, in which the group can decide the following question: In which region is the largest supply of resources concentrated? We stress that this is not a trivial limitation due to limited accessibility (since with a sufficient number of individuals an area of any size can be fully searched) nor to individual processing capacity, but a genuine limitation imposed by the structure of the decision-making process.

We show that by augmenting the basic group model with a *centralized decision maker* so that the structure is now of the *pandemonium* form (see Minsky and Papert 1969), the limitation on maximum region disappears. In fact, very little in the way of information collection capacity is required of the individual members to solve the "best direction" problem, though mental capacity by the decider for perception and comparison of directional proposals is now necessary.

Some Preliminaries—The Modeled Environment

We begin by providing a formal characterization of the environment with which our several decision-making models must deal.

DEFINITION. *Let R represent an arbitrary set of cells in the standard two-dimensional cellular space, that is, a planar region divided into R discrete subregions (cells) of unit area.*

Here it will be convenient for us to think of R as the catchment area, or current set of locations about which the group can acquire information. Each location i will refer to a particular cell in the two-dimensional space. With each cell in this space is associated a finite set of properties or attributes. At this point it is best to think of these properties as being resources of interest to the group. For our purposes all we need to know is whether a certain resource is present (coded here as 1) or absent (coded as 0) in a specific location at a certain time T. No assumption is made about the nature of these properties except that they can be recognized by an individual scanning the location. Therefore, if resource Z is present at location i, then an individual looking for property Z at location i will observe it.

The subset of all locations in which a resource Z is found at time T exhibits a certain distribution over the space R, as does the set of all locations at which it is not found. We denote by Z_T the subset of cells in R at which resource Z is found at time T. Since time will play no role in our current discussion, we drop the T subscript and refer directly to distributions as subsets Z of R.

In order to exploit a resource distribution Z, a group must be able to categorize it in various ways. The most fundamental categorization is of the binary kind in which the subset Z is determined to have some property P (such as being empty) or not have that property.

DEFINITION. *A configurational predicate is a function which assigns to each subset of the catchment set R one of two possible values.*

If the distribution of cells in R that possess resource Z is characterized by a property S, then $\psi_S(Z)$ takes the value of 1, otherwise it has the value of -1.

There are essentially two general classes of predicates:

1. Position-dependent predicates, where the predicate is defined precisely with reference to specific points in R. For example, the query "Are there nut crops in the canyon on the south side of the river?" is defined relative to a particular subarea within R.

2. Position-independent predicates are concerned with the recognition of general classes of patterns independent of where they occur within the region R. One example would be the predicate $\psi_{connect}$ defined previously which serves to identify the class of all connected regional distributions. Another position-independent predicate which might be of concern is whether any grove of trees within its territory, R, has ripe fruit, or is there any potential predator within the region R.

We now specify what it means for a group to *recognize potentially* a distributional predicate.

DEFINITION. *A distributional predicate is potentially recognizable by a group if there exists a decision-making algorithm or procedure executable by the group whereby it can decide with absolute certainty whether or not the predicate is true for any given distribution.*

The Group Theoretic Framework

In the preceding sections we developed a formalism in which to phrase both the distribution of resources and the properties of these distributions over the space R. Now we develop our basic model in which each individual is able only to vote for or against a particular question that is posed to the group. *He is not, however, able to express to the rest of the group the specific information used to form his opinion.*

The following assumptions are made about the behavior of any member:

1. The region of interest, R, is larger than the area over which the member can collect data. This is certainly a reasonable assumption when one is concerned with hunter–gatherers, where walking is the principal form of transportation.
2. Also it is assumed that if an observable resource is present at a cell, then an individual looking there will observe it.

Although the latter assumption is particularly optimistic, since more realistically some erroneous data might be collected, the presence of this assumption in the model serves a good purpose. We shall show that even these hypothetical groups composed of error-free individuals cannot recognize certain types of distributions without some additional processing. More realistic models with the same decision-making structure but employing error-prone individuals can at best only hope to do as well. With this in mind, we express the data collection activities of any one individual, X, as δ_X, a predicate whose domain of reference is a subset of points in R. This subset of points is termed the *support* of the local predicate δ_X.

For example, suppose an individual X searches a subregion S_X at time T in order to check whether there are any cells containing a resource Z. Formally, if $S_X \cap Z$ is not empty, $\delta_X(Z) = 1$, otherwise $\delta_X(Z) = -1$. The support of δ_X is then the subset of locations within R that are checked by an individual.

Local predicates of this kind, called masks, are basic to perceptron studies, but the theory is not limited to their use.[2] Supports of local predicates can overlap, so a location may be checked by more than one individual. Moreover, the support of a local predicate need not consist of contiguous cells. The requirement of contiguity is a natural one in our context, but since we are interested in showing limitations of the group decision model under even the most optimistic circumstances, we do not restrict supports to contiguous sets nor local processing to the mask type.

---

[2]The restriction to masks turns out not to limit perceptron capabilities according to a theorem of Minsky and Papert (1969).

It now remains for us to discuss how the several individual decisions are woven together by the group to produce an overall decision.

The Decision Function

As already indicated, we initially consider the case in which an individual can only communicate his opinion, either favorable or not, with respect to a question (predicate) posed to the group.

First we take the localized predicate δ_X which symbolizes the individual's decision based on his particular experience. With each individual X is associated a weight W_X that reflects the relative influence his/her opinion has on the group's decision about the particular class of problems. Every member is able then to vote on the matter, with some opinions counting more than others, and some counting not at all ($W_X = 0$).

Now the group decision ψ_{group} can be expressed as a weighted linear function of the individual decisions where

$$\psi_{\text{group}}(Z) = \begin{cases} 1 & \text{if} \quad \sum_{X \in \text{group}} W_X \delta_X(Z) > \theta \\ -1 & \text{otherwise} \end{cases}$$

The constant θ represents a certain level of confidence that must be attained before consensus is reached. If the sum of the weighted individual opinions taken together exceeds this level, a positive consensus is attained. Otherwise the consensus is a negative one. Note that the threshold θ is problem specific. It can therefore take small values for unimportant questions and larger values for more important ones.

We shall refer to these models as *voting groups*. Such models belong to the class of linear threshold devices and are formally isomorphic to the one-level perceptrons of Minsky and Papert (1969).

A predicate ψ is potentially recognizable by a group if there are weights $W_X, X \in$ group, and a threshold θ such that for each subset Z of R, $\psi_{\text{group}}(Z) = \psi(Z)$.

Individual Capabilities

An individual can recognize a class of position-dependent predicates, namely those whose reference cells fall within his support. If his domain is relatively small, this class of predicates is correspondingly restricted. Moreover, in such a case, the individual is incapable of recognizing any nontrivial translation-invariant predicates. A translation-invariant predicate is a special type of position-independent predicate in which the defining property is preserved under all spatial translations.

THEOREM. *An individual searching a maximum area, L, within a sufficiently large region R, cannot recognize any nonconstant translation-invariant regional predicates.*

Proof. Suppose ψ is a translation-invariant predicate on R which is recognizable by X. Then any two distributions which agree on L are ψ equivalent, that is, assigned the same ψ value. Let R be large enough so that a translation L' of L can be found disjoint from L. Let d_{empty} be the distribution of all zeros in R. Let d_L consist of any arbitrary assignment of zeros and ones to L' and zeros everywhere else. Translate d_{empty} and $d_{L'}$ so that L' is placed over L. Since d_{empty} and $d_{L'}$ agree on L they are ψ equivalent, and since ψ is translation invariant their translates are also ψ equivalent. Thus ψ assigns the same value to all distributions over L and hence to all distributions over R, that is, ψ is a constant predicate (ψ_{TRUE} or ψ_{FALSE}). Q.E.D.

With our intuition concerning the limits of individual capability thus reinforced we turn to group decision capabilities.

Recognition Capabilities of Voting Groups

Minsky and Papert (1969) have established certain capabilities and limitations of perceptron models. In our context, the most relevant strength of perceptrons is their ability to do certain kinds of counting and their ability to perform certain kinds of numerical comparisons. To make this precise, we need to introduce the notion of *order*. The order of a local predicate δ_X is the size of its support, that is, the number of cells at which it looks. The order of a perceptron or voting group employing a set of predicates $\{\delta_X \mid X \in \text{GROUP}\}$ is the maximum of the orders of its local predicates. Finally, the order of a predicate ψ_R on region R is the smallest order of all the perceptrons that can recognize ψ_R.

We have just now purposefully emphasized that a predicate always refers to a particular region. The reason is that even though this is true, we often think of the same predicate being applied to any arbitrary region. Technically, such a "predicate" is really a predicate scheme, that is, a rule which associates to each region R a particular predicate ψ_R. For example, the predicate scheme $\psi_{everywhere}$ assigns to any region R the predicate $\psi_{everywhere}$, where $\psi_{everywhere}(Z) = 1$ if and only if Z is a distribution on R and $Z = R$.

With this in mind, we can define the order of a predicate scheme to be the smallest of the orders of all the predicates defined by the scheme. If this order is finite, all the predicates, no matter what the size of the underlying region, are recognizable by perceptrons of this order or less; if the order is infinite, then the order of perceptrons needed to recognize the predicate ψ_R grows without bound as the size of the region increases.

We summarize some results of Minsky and Papert (1969) in Table 17.1. Let us interpret the table in terms of the voting group model. Our hunter–gatherer group can decide whether or not a region has any resource. To do this, it need only have enough individuals to cover the entire region with each individual examining a subset of cells for the presence of the resource. The weights can be all -1 for ψ_{empty} and all $+1$ for $\psi_{somewhere}$, with thresholds $|R|$ and $-|R|$, respectively ($|R|$ is the size of R). More usefully it can decide whether one region is more profitable than a second to utilize. It can recognize $\psi_{A \geqslant B}$ by weighting individuals sampling A by $+1$ and those sampling B by -1. All the results above the dashed line in the table are variations on this theme except for $\psi_{=N}$. This last result has an interesting implication in our context:

OBSERVATION. *The predicate $\psi_{A=B}$ (regions A and B contain the same number of resource cells) is of order 2. Moreover, at least one local predicate must have support in both A and B.*

Proof. $\psi_{A=B}$ is true if and only if $\psi_{A \geqslant B}$ and $\psi_{B \geqslant A}$ are both true or both false, that is, $\psi_{A=B} = \psi_{A \geqslant B} \cdot \psi_{B \geqslant A}$. By substitution of the linear forms, or by Theorem 1.5.4 of Minsky and Papert (1969), the order of $\psi_{A=B}$ is seen to be no greater than 2. If the order were 1, then the order of $\psi_{=N}$ would also be 1, since we could set up a distribution of N cells in A and recognize when any distribution in B had this same number of nonempty cells using $\psi_{A=B}$.

Now suppose $\psi_{A=B}$ is recognizable with predicates having supports restricted to either A or B but not both. Then the sum in the linear form splits

TABLE 17.1
Predicate Schemes and Their Order

Predicate	Definition	Order
ψ_{empty}	No resource in region	1
$\psi_{somewhere}$	Some resource in region	1
$\psi_{everywhere}$	Resource found everywhere	1
$\psi_{>N}$	At least N cells have the resource	1
$\psi_{<N}$	No more than N cells have the resource	1
$\psi_{=N}$	Exactly N cells have the resource	2
$\psi_{A>B}$	Subregion A contains at least as much resource as subregion B	1
$\psi_{A>C,B>C}$	Subregion C has less resource than A and B separately	∞
ψ_{parity}	An odd number of cells have the resource	∞
$\psi_{connected}$	The resource distribution is connected	∞

into two disjoint parts. By a familiar argument, we can show that the following four situations lead to a contradiction:

1. $|A \cap Z| = |B \cap Z| = 0$
2. $|A \cap Z| = 1, |B \cap Z| = 0$
3. $|A \cap Z| = 0, |B \cap Z| = 1$
4. $|A \cap Z| = |B \cap Z| = 1$ Q.E.D.

Thus to check the equality of resources in two disjoint regions at least one member of the group must sample both regions, in effect doing a comparison himself. In fact, in the realization with order 2, many individuals make elementary comparisons of pairs of cells.

From Table 17.1, we see that counting modulo 2 (ψ_{parity}) is not easy for perceptrons. In fact, Minsky shows that *all* cells must be examined by at least one individual in the group (meaning that he must be smart enough to make the calculation himself!). Also noteworthy is the fact that $\psi_{\text{connected}}$ is not of finite order, so that for any group of individuals there is a largest region in which the group (voting model) can handle the concept of connectivity. A more meaningful limitation is that of the infinite order of the minimization predicate $\psi_{A>C,B>C}$. This implies that deciding which of more than two alternative regions is best is hard for our voting model. But to see this requires that we formulate the notion of choice of direction for our model.

Group-Directional Decision Making

Although we have so far formulated our decision problem in binary form, much field observation (see Discussion) suggests that hunter–gatherer groups are very concerned with directional choices. Finding itself located at some point in a large region with which its members have some experience, the group must decide, among the diverse proposals, in which direction to move. The essence of this problem, we feel, is capturable by our voting model extended as follows to enable directional decisions.

Let a point in a region R be designated as the origin of a rectangular coordinate system (this is to represent the group's current position). Let QUAD designate the set of quadrants represented counterclockwise by the points $(1, 1)$, $(-1, 1)$, $(-1, -1)$, and $(1, -1)$, respectively.

DEFINITION. *A directional function ψ is a mapping from the subsets of R to QUAD. Thus ψ assigns to each distribution Z an element $\psi(Z)$ in QUAD which represents a direction in which to move.*

Our primary example is the maximization function ψ_{max} defined as follows: $\psi_{\text{max}}(Z) = (i^*, j^*)$ where (i^*, j^*) represents the quadrant having the largest number of resource cells. Formally,

$$|Q_{(i_*, j_*)} \cap Z| = \max_{(i,j) \in \text{QUAD}} |Q_{(i,j)} \cap Z|$$

where $Q_{(i,j)}$ is the quadrant represented by (i, j). (If there is a tie for the most profitable quadrant, we allow an arbitrary choice.) Although we shall work with four directions, our results are easily extendable to an arbitrary number of directions.

We now extend our voting model to enable directional decision making.

DEFINITION. *A vector voting model specifies a linear threshold directional function:*

$$\psi_{\text{group}} = \text{quad}(\sum_{X \in \text{group}} W_X \delta_X(Z))$$

where each δ_X is a local directional function mapping Z into $QUAD \cup \{(0,0)\}$ and quad maps the region R into quadrants, namely

$$\text{quad}(x, y) = (\text{bin}(x), \text{bin}(y))$$

where

$$\text{bin}(x) = \begin{cases} 1 & \text{if } x > 0 \\ -1 & \text{otherwise} \end{cases}$$

Our vector voting model is truly an extension of the basic voting model. In the vector model each individual can propose a direction based on the region he has explored. Each direction is treated as a unit vector, the associated weight gives a magnitude to the vector, and then the vectorial sum is taken. The resultant vector is then categorized according to the quadrant in which it lies. No generality is lost by not including a threshold explicitly since this may be included as one of the local functions. In these terms the basic voting model is a one-dimensional version of the extended model of the form

$$\psi_{\text{group}} = \text{bin}(\sum_{X \in \text{group}} W_X \delta_X(Z))$$

DEFINITION. *A vector voting model computes a directional function ψ if $\psi_{\text{group}} = \psi$.*

We now establish the promised limitation on the vector model's directional decision capabilities.

THEOREM. *The directional function ψ_{max} is not of finite order in the class of all vector voting models.*

Proof. Suppose to the contrary that the directional function is of finite order M. Let R be an arbitrary region with designated origin and let a vector model of order M compute ψ_{max}:

$$\psi_{\max}(Z) = \text{quad}\left(\sum_{X \in \text{group}} W_X \delta_X(Z)\right)$$

$$= \text{quad}\left(\sum_{X \in \text{group}} W_X(\delta_X^1(Z), \delta_X^2(Z))\right) \quad \text{(where } \delta^1 \text{ and } \delta^2 \text{ are the projections of } \delta \text{ on the first and second coordinates, respectively}$$

$$= \text{quad}\left(\sum_{X \in \text{group}} W_X \delta_X^1(Z), \quad \sum_{X \in \text{group}} W_X \delta_X^2(Z)\right)$$

$$= \left(\text{bin}\left(\sum_{X \in \text{group}} W_X \delta_X^1(Z)\right), \quad \text{bin}\left(\sum_{X \in \text{group}} W_X \delta_X^2(Z)\right)\right)$$

$$= (\psi^1_{\text{group}}(Z) \; \psi^2_{\text{group}}(Z))$$

where ψ^1_{group} and ψ^2_{group} are of order M (the projections have the same order as the original functions).
Thus

$$\psi^1_{\text{group}}(Z) = 1 \Leftrightarrow \psi_{\max}(Z) = (1, 1) \quad or \quad \psi_{\max}(Z) = (1, -1)$$

Now restrict ψ^1_{group} to quadrants $(1, 1)$, $(-1, 1)$, and $(-1, -1)$. Then

$$\psi^1_{\text{group}}(Z) = 1 \Leftrightarrow \psi_{\max}(Z) = (1, 1)$$
$$\Leftrightarrow |Q_{(1,1)} \cap Z| = \max\{|Q_{(1,1)} \cap Z|, \; |Q_{(-1,1)} \cap Z|, \; |Q_{(-1,-1)} \cap Z|\}$$
$$\Leftrightarrow |Q_{(1,1)} \cap Z| > |Q_{(-1,1)} \cap Z| \quad \text{and} \quad |Q_{(1,1)} \cap Z| > |Q_{(-1,-1,)} \cap Z|$$

Thus it is possible to decide which of three quadrants has the largest concentration of resource. But be defining $\bar{\psi}(Z) \times \psi^1_{\text{group}}(\bar{Z})$ where $\bar{Z}$ is the complementary distribution to Z, we then have

$$\bar{\psi}(Z) = 1 \Leftrightarrow |Q_{(1,1)} \cap Z| < |Q_{(-1,1)} \cap Z| \quad \text{and} \quad |Q_{(1,1)} \cap Z| < |Q_{(-1,-1)} \cap Z|$$

and thus the minimization predicate $\psi_{A>C, B>C}$ is of finite order M, a contradiction.

Q.E.D.

We conclude that for every vector voting group there is an upper bound on the size of the region in which the group can decide in which direction to go to find the largest concentration of resources. This upper bound is determined by the area sizes accessible to group members.

Decision Capabilities of Groups with Central Decision Maker

Consider now the vector model augmented with a maximizer D. The direction function computed by such a pandemonium structure is

$$\Phi(Z) = (i^*, j^*) \quad \text{where} \quad \text{MAG}_{(i_*, j_*)}(Z) = \max_{(i,j) \in \text{QUAD}} \text{MAG}_{(i,j)}(Z)$$

where

$$\text{MAG}_{(i,j)}(Z) = \left| \sum_{\delta_x(Z)=(i,j)} W_x \right|$$

In other words, the output direction is the one in which the magnitude of the associated vector is largest. Note that this requires that proposals of each of the members be classified into directional categories, the strength in each category totaled, and the results be perceived by the decider D who selects the category with greatest strength. Clearly much more in the way of intra-group communication is required to realize this structure.

It is easy to see, however, that pandemonium models can compute the maximization function with finite-order local functions. Indeed, let each cell (x, y) in R be scanned by a first-order local function

$$\delta_{(x,y)}(Z) = Z(x, y) \cdot \text{quad}(x, y)$$

that is, if resource is present at cell (x, y), then a proposal is made for motion toward the quadrant in which it lies. Using unit weights the resultant proposals in the four alternative directions are equal to their respective concentrations of resources. The maximizer thus selects the most promising direction.

Although we have shown how a group making decisions in the manner described by our model can theoretically compute a number of spatial predicates and functions presented to them by the environment, there is no guarantee that it will. In terms of the model, the following criteria must be met in order for a model computable function to be actualized.

1. There must be a set of expected values for the pertinent variables corresponding to locations within the environment.
2. The search areas must be coordinated so that all cells in the space necessary to the recognition of the pattern are scanned.
3. There must be coordination of weights for individual opinions regarding a problem with the individuals' experience and the level of consensus needed to obtain a group decision.

Note that point 2 requires that there be a sufficient number of members in the group so that the region is covered. Our limitation results show that *even* if this is the case, there are limitations on the group's decision-making ability. It is conjectured here that the coordination of weights is fostered by the presence of a relatively fixed set of social niches or roles that group participants might play. Such roles are often structured with respect to age and sex in egalitarian societies. Therefore, if a conflict between members arises and the one is able to displace the other, the principal effect is merely to change roles. If each role is characterized by an associated set of weights in the decision-making process, then the group, by ensuring the presence of a certain set of roles, is maintaining an associated set of weights as well. This increases the likelihood of a good decision being duplicated in the future, even though the individuals who made the initial decision may no longer be present.

Predictions and Open Questions

Our results suggest that the size of the region in which resources may be maximally exploitable by hunter–gatherer groups that do not possess centralized decision making is strictly limited by the individual's abilities to gather information. In semiarid environments where the distribution of resources is mosaic, with these patches scattered over a large area, this limitation could be an important one. In such an environment, variability in the amount of collected resources stems from at least three factors:

1. Variability in yield from one year to another
2. Variation in distribution of plant and animal resources over time
3. The ability of the group to identify and exploit maximum concentrations of existing resources

Our results suggest that this third factor will be important, since there is a region of maximum size beyond which an egalitarian group cannot always make such decisions. *There are, however, at least two ways by which the group could reduce the importance of the third factor.* First, it could alter the distribution of available plant resources by means of agriculture, guaranteeing that certain plants would be found in predictable areas. Second, as we demonstrated earlier, it could remove the constraint of maximum area by adding a central decision maker, that is, creating a hierarchy in the decision-making apparatus. These alternatives need not be mutually exclusive and might both be employed by a group. Indeed, examples of each alternative can be found in the ethnographic literature. For example, the Indians of the Pacific Northwest Coast of the United States and Canada developed a ranked society with a decision-making hierarchy but no agriculture (Drucker 1955). The Indians of Mesoamerica, on the other hand, developed agriculture thousands of years before hereditary ranking (Flannery 1972, 1973). We can now suggest that neither phenomenon is necessarily the result of "maximization" or population growth, but rather a solution to the search strategies and communication policies described herein.

References

Drucker, Philip, 1955, *Indians of the Northwest Coast,* New York, The Natural History Press.

Flannery, Kent V., 1972, The cultural evolution of civilizations. *Annual Review of Ecology and Systematics,* 3, 399–426.

Flannery, Kent V., 1973, The origins of agriculture. *Annual Review of Anthropology,* 2, 271–310.

Maruyama, Magoroh, 1963, The second cybernetics: Deviation amplifying mutual casual processes. *American Scientist,* 51, 164–179.

Minsky, M. and Papert, P., 1969, *Perceptrons.* New York, Prentice-Hall.

VI

HOLISTIC BEHAVIOR AND CATASTROPHE THEORY

There is a tide in the affairs of men
Which, taken at the flood leads on to fortune:
Omitted, all the voyage of their life
Is bound in shallows and in miseries.

William Shakespeare
Julius Caesar

One obvious path toward the understanding of an organism is through an analysis of its parts: From a close study of their working and interactions the behavior of the complex as a whole may be predicted. Such is the perspective of systems theory, whose application to the studies of human societies or human sociocultural systems was considered in Part IV. Analysis by reduction, at the atomic level, also underlies the work reviewed in Part V, where the behavior of the groups is analyzed in terms of decisions by individuals.

A diametrically opposite approach is to regard civilizations, cultures, or societies (or whatever sociocultural units are identified for the purposes of discussion) as units whose behavior can be discussed and compared, without a reductionist division into a series of supposed components. This approach is by far the older. Already in *Der Untergang des Abendlandes* in 1918 Oswald Spengler was predicting the decline of Western civilization on the ground that each culture has a comparable life cycle, with barbaric youth, stiff "archaic" adolescence, classical florescence, autumnal decadence, and barbaric, vulgar aftermath, in which category (perhaps not without reason) he situated the contemporary West. The massive work of Arnold Toynbee (1947), although less rigorously prescriptive, follows an analogous, if more ambitious, program of comparing the growth of civilizations. Something of the same vision of a natural sequence of events, a life cycle, can be seen in Steward's (1949, 178–209) "trial formulation of the development of early civilizations." Indeed I have always found the terminology of stages (archaic, formative, classic, postclassic), now standard in American archaeology (cf. Willey and Phillips 1958, *passim*), with its apocalyptic Spenglerian overtones, decidedly more misleading than our innocent European neologisms (Paleolithic, Neolithic, etc.).

Yet despite the pitfalls of a unilinear evolutionary approach, most scholars have felt that cultures or civilizations, even when they transcend the bounds of a single political unit, have a certain coherence in their behavior which merits study. Kroeber (1917) named this quality "the superorganic," and despite the mysticism which such terminology can provoke at the hands of a visionary, such as Teilhard de Chardin, the basic insight remains a valid one.

Three current archaeological approaches may be identified in which this basic insight is employed that sociocultural units may profitably be studied and compared without a decomposition into their constituent parts.

The first, already very familiar to archaeologists and anthropologists, is the so-called neoevolutionary approach of Service (1962) and Sahlins (1958). Using the simple and basic taxonomy of band, tribe, chiefdom, and state, human societies may be classified and compared. Other features, such as the mode of exchange commonly practiced (reciprocity, redistribution, etc.) show some correlation with these categories. Although some critics (e.g., Tringham 1974) have wrongly seen this "evolutionary sequence" as implying a necessary succession, the adoption of this terminology (e.g., Flannery 1972) remains in my view one of the most valuable recent advances in comparative archaeology. But of course a taxonomy is not in itself an explanation.

The second, very much newer approach, and not yet fully explored, takes as its starting point the idea of ecological succession (cf. Odum 1969). Gall and Saxe (1977), Athens (1977), and Cherry (1978) consider the development of complex societies in a deliberately analogous manner, employing the idea of developmental stages of the ecosystem, and applying the ecologist's categories of study (e.g., community energetics, community structures, life history, selection pressure, overall homeostasis) to human societies, each considered as an adaptive system. This has the great benefit of bringing into the discussion concepts of energy, information, and structure which, as we have seen in Part II, will be essential to any informative treatment. It opens the way, also, to the notion of "predatory expansion" (Sahlins 1961), where one sociocultural form is in some circumstances better adapted than, and prevails over, alternative adjustments within the ecological niche in question. These interesting ideas have yet to be fully worked out. Their predictive content has yet to be documented, and (just as important) it has to be demonstrated also that they do not share the capacity for erroneous prediction displayed by unilineal evolutionary theories.

The third approach, with which this part is principally concerned, is catastrophe theory. It deals with the behavior of very complex systems without any attempt at identifying all the parts or unraveling their complex interactions. Catastrophe theory falls within the field of differential topology, where the mathematics is effectively inaccessible to the nonspecialist, but the aims of the subject are clear enough. In the words of Chillingworth (1976, 1):

> The particular aim is to study the *global qualitative behaviour of dynamical systems*. A dynamical system is some system (economic, physical, biological, . . .) which evolves with time. Given a starting point, the system moves within a universe of possible states according to known or hypothesised laws, often describable locally by a formula for the "infinitesimal" evolution, namely a differential equation. The *global* theory is the theory of all possible evolutions from all possible initial states, together with the way these fit together and relate to each other. *Qualitative* theory is concerned with the existence of constant (equilibrium) behaviour, periodic or recurrent behaviour, and long-term behaviour, together with questions of local and overall stability of the system. Global qualitative techniques, mainly stemming from the work of Henri Poincaré (1854–1912), are important both because precise quantitative theoretical solutions may in general be unobtainable, and because in any case a qualitative model is the basis of a sound mental picture without which mechanical calculation is highly dangerous.

Catastrophe theory, the creation of René Thom (1975), is in particular applicable where gradually changing forces produce sudden effects, termed catastrophes on account of their discontinuous nature. It is concerned with conditions which are structurally stable, and this is appropriate to the real world, where the forms which we observe generally possess structural stability (see Poston, Chapter 18, this volume). The theory suggests insights not only into discontinuities with respect to time, but into the differentiation of forms as the result of bifurcations—that is, morphogenesis. One of its greatest strengths is that it shows that, under certain circumstances, the discontinuous behavior (and hence the genesis of form) of very complex systems can be classified in a small number of relatively simple ways.

This is not the place for an introductory account of catastrophe theory. Perhaps the best such treatment is by Zeeman (1976; for a fuller version Zeeman 1977, 1–64), and I have tried elsewhere to indicate some of the implications for archaeology (Renfrew 1978a). Another clear and simplified account of the mathematics has been given by Amson (1975), and a whole series of applications have been reviewed by Zeeman (1977) and Poston and Stewart (1978). Isnard and Zeeman (1976) have outlined a number of applications in the social sciences, and further papers are available treating stock-exchange collapse (Zeeman 1974), evolutionary change (Dodson 1975; 1976), innovation (Renfrew 1978b), and cycles of pig rearing and feasting in New Guinea (Thompson, in press). This example, the first in the field of anthropology, may interestingly be compared with the dynamic systems model by Shantzis and Behrens (1972) for much the same phenomena.

The chapters that follow can be fully understood only with some prior acquaintance with catastrophe theory. Yet immediately they convey some impression of the range of potential applications. Poston's introductory chapter gives a clear account of the underlying simplicity of catastrophe theory, and the chapter that follows is an explicit application to the problem of sudden settlement shift. Zeeman's discussion of ideologies is an imaginative and illuminating treatment, an example of the way catastrophe theory can advance our thinking even in fields which are extremely difficult to quantify. In the last chapter an attempt is made to show how the development of these ideas can offer new possibilities for more systematic work in comparative archaeology.

The application of catastrophe theory has not been without its critics (Zahler and Sussman 1977), and some applications have lacked rigor. Yet they have opened the way to the more serious and systematic treatment of such subjects as the rise and fall of civilization, which have hitherto been tackled in an almost entirely subjective manner. Such was the ultimate goal of Thom's remarkable book (1975). Certainly catastrophe theory constitutes one of the most interesting recent applications of mathematics to the study of change in the world.

A.C.R.

References

Amson J. C., 1975, Catastrophe theory: a contribution to the study of urban systems?, *Environment and Planning B*, 2, 177–221.

Athens J. S., 1977, Theory building and the study of evolutionary process in complex societies, in Binford L. R. (ed.), *For Theory Building in Archaeology*, New York, Academic Press, 353–384.

Cherry, J. F., 1978, Generalisation and the archaeology of the state, in Green D. R., Haselgrove C. C. and Spriggs M. J. T. (eds.), *Social Organisation and Settlement*, (British Archaeological Reports, Supplementary Series 47), 411–438.

Chillingworth D. R. J., 1976, *Differential Topology with a View to Applications*, London, Pitman.

Dodson M. M., 1975, Quantum evolution and the fold catastrophe, *Evolutionary Theory* 1, 107–118.

Dodson M. M., 1976, Darwin's law of natural selection and Thom's theory of catastrophes, *Mathematical Bioscience* 28, 243–274.

Flannery K. V., 1972, The cultural evolution of civilisations, *Annual Review of Ecology and Systematics* 3, 399–426.

Gall P. L. and Saxe A. A., 1977, The ecological evolution of culture: the state as predator in succession theory, in Earle T. K. and Ericson J. E. (eds.), *Exchange Systems in Prehistory*, New York, Academic Press, 255–268.

Isnard C. A. and Zeeman E. C., 1976, Some models from catastrophe theory in the social sciences, in Collins L. (ed.), *The Use of Models in the Social Sciences*, London, Tavistock, 44–100.

Kroeber A. L., 1917, The Superorganic, *American Anthropologist* 19, 163–213.

Odum E. P., 1969, The strategy of ecosystem development, *Science* 64, 262–270.

Poston T. and Stewart I. N., 1978, *Catastrophe Theory and its Applications*, London, Pitman.

Renfrew C., 1978a, Trajectory discontinuity and morphogenesis, the implications of Catastrophe Theory for archaeology, *American Antiquity* 43, 203–244.

Renfrew C., 1978b, The anatomy of innovation, in Green D. R., Haselgrove C. C., and Spriggs M. J. T. (eds.), *Social Organisation and Settlement,* (British Archaeological Reports, Supplementary Series 47), 89–117.

Sahlins M. D., 1958, *Social Stratification in Polynesia,* Seattle, University of Washington.

Sahlins M. D., 1962, The segmentary lineage, an organisation of predatory expansion, *American Anthropologist* 63, 322–345.

Service E. R., 1962, *Primitive Social Organisation,* New York, Random House.

Shantzis S. B. and Behrens W. W., 1972, Population control mechanisms in a primitive agricultural society, in Meadows D. L. and D. H. (eds.), *Towards Global Equilibrium, Collected Papers,* Cambridge, Mass., Wright-Allen, 257–288.

Steward J. H., 1949, Development of complex societies: cultural causality and law: a trial formulation of the development of early civilisations, *American Anthropologist* 51 (reprinted in Steward J. H., 1955, *Theory of Culture Change,* Urbana, University of Illinois, 178–209).

Thom R., 1975, *Structural Stability and Morphogenesis,* Reading, Mass., Benjamin (translation by D. H. Fowler of the French edition, published 1972).

Thompson M., in press, The geometry of confidence, an analysis of the Enge *te* and Hagen *moka,* a complex system of ceremonial pig-giving in the New Guinea highlands, in Thompson M., *Rubbish Theory,* London, Paladin, in press.

Toynbee A. J., 1946, *A Study of History,* (abridgment by D. C. Somervell), Oxford, University Press.

Tringham R., 1974, Comments on Prof. Renfrew's paper, in Moore C. B. (ed.), *Reconstructing Complex Societies* (Supplement to the Bulletin of the American School of Oriental Research no. 20), 88–90.

Willey G. R. and Phillips P., 1958, *Method and Theory in American Archaeology,* Chicago, University Press.

Zahler R. S. and Sussmann H. J., 1977, Claims and accomplishments of applied catastrophe theory, *Nature* 269, 759–763.

Zeeman E. C., 1974, On the unstable behaviour of stock exchanges, *Journal of Mathematical Economics* 1, 39–49.

Zeeman E. C., 1976, Catastrophe Theory, *Scientific American* 234, 65–83.

Zeeman E. C., 1977, *Catastrophe Theory, Selected Papers 1972–1977,* Reading, Mass., Addison-Wesley.

18

TIM POSTON[1]

The Elements of Catastrophe Theory or The Honing of Occam's Razor

. . . as soon as Lavoisier had reduced the infinite variety of chemical phenomena to the actions, reactions, and interchanges of a few elementary substances, or at least excited the expectation that this would speedily be effected, the hope shot up, almost instantly, into full faith, that it had been effected.

Samuel Taylor Coleridge, 1848

Catastrophe theory, in the broadest sense, may be thought of as a new point of view for judging and comparing "simplicity." This has obvious bearing on any activity that uses Occam's Razor in the celebrated form "of all explanations that fit, pick the simplest."

The shift in viewpoint amounts to deserting individual, apparent simplicity in favor of circumstantial or "by association" simplicity: "You can tell a thing that's simple by the company it keeps." An example may help to make this clear.

Consider water flowing down a slope. A traditionally "simplest" case is the flow of a thin even layer of water down an exact inclined plane. This is indeed simple to analyze, on the hypotheses that the layer *is* even, and the slope exactly a plane; for this reason it occurs early in hydrodynamics texts. An approximation to it often appears in a sufficiently carefully man-made weir (Figure 18.1). But Nature has her own view of what is simple (if you will forgive the gynomorphic shorthand of saying Nature "chooses" simple systems): it is never seen wild.

Leave off maintenance for a while, and you will see something more like Figure 18.2. If there is some measurable unevenness in Figure 18.1, you may be able to make some predictions as to just where erosion will make channels and join them. The more even the initial weir, the less prediction is possible. Around the "perfect" system of the texts cluster infinitely many

[1] This work was supported by Fonds national suisse de la recherche scientifique Grant No. 2.461.0.75.

Transformations:
Mathematical Approaches to Culture Change

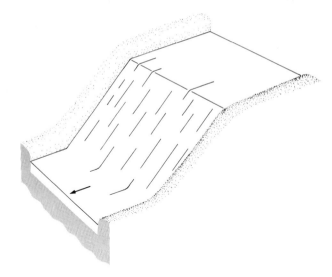

FIGURE 18.1 *Complicated.*

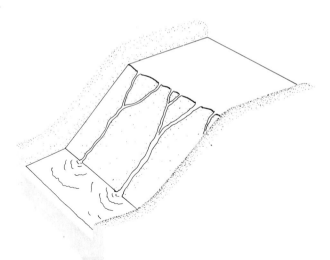

FIGURE 18.2 *Simple.*

possibilities into which the real system may develop, and the definition of perfection excludes the existence of data that imply which it will take. In this sense the system is infinitely complicated; it will never happen exactly, and the range of possibilities following from inexactness defies complete description. Even statistical estimates are very difficult.

In the same sense, Figure 18.2 is simple. All nearby possibilities look just like it. A *little* more water coming downstream will leave its form intact, as will any other small disturbance. (A larger disturbance or a sufficient length of time will, however, change it.) If change of form is what we consider significant, the effect of any small variation is nil, and the problem of predicting such effects becomes a simple one. A system poised at a branch between two possibilities (like Buridan's ass) is more complicated—but it is still much simpler than Figure 18.1.

The extreme of simplicity, in this sense, is known also as *structural stability:* perturb it a little and nothing changes. It should be emphasized that this idea thus depends crucially on (*a*) what kinds of perturbations are to be considered; (*b*) which of these are "little"; and (*c*) what constitutes a "change" (equivalently, what systems are "the same"). Different choices at any of these points give different results. At one extreme "the origin is forgotten, and all dharmas become one" so that everything is simple; at another each thing is unique and unrepeatable, hence complicated by the variety of its neighbors—unless it is considered a monad that *has* no neighbors, hence simple again. Thus all of the foregoing becomes empty philosophizing until appropriate choices are made, and many different choices may be defended. Much of the book by Poston and Stewart (1978) is concerned with the delicate interplay between the definition of "the same" natural to a given science, and the definition about which one can prove useful results. Here, finally, is the appearance of catastrophe theory as a part of science rather than philosophy. Using particular decisions for these choices, for a wide range of systems it has recently become possible to prove structural stability where it is present, and analyze the possible perturbations of less simple systems. Examples in which this leads to quantitative information in ship stability, laser physics, plate buckling, polymer flow, ecological frontiers, rainbow intensities, and so on are discussed in the necessary detail by Poston and Stewart (1978), and cannot be summarized here without the mathematical background set up in the early parts of the book. The mathematics is more general than any particular use of it, so what follows is an *example* of interpreting the mathematics as describing "things," not a prescription of the unique method. (The common statement that catastrophe theory "applies only to gradient systems" arises from this being the easiest setting for the introduction of its ideas. Similarly, children start to learn by counting particular things, but should not deduce that arithmetic applies only to oranges—-or that it applies to oranges in only one way!)

Consider then a statement like "the amount of diamonds nearby depends on where you are," which can be put equally as "the density x of diamonds is a function of position p." Often, one wishes to know what *determines* x (p) for various p. Now, if p takes values in a wilderness, this question is purely one of geological history: but if each p is in Holland, it means not only "how did so many diamonds get to Amsterdam?" but "why do so many stay there?" A common answer is in terms of an *equilibrium* value, with many other factors entering the equation. Equilibrium values generally change with time (London's high 1870s density of Italian paintings and Greek statues is clearly far above the 1970s commercial equilibrium, hence frequent appeals to "save for the nation" such foreign treasure) but most of the time the change is continuous. Catastrophe theory is most concerned with the points at which the change is *sudden*.

To permit concentration on such *dis*continuities, the mathematics ignores *smooth* variation with position p or time t. If Figure 18.3 shows the equilibrium density $x(p, t)$ of diamonds at position p and time t, we would read it as saying, "There was an immense but brief concentration A of wealth at p_1 at time t_1, and at p_2 a lesser concentration B which started at the same time but lasted much longer, until t_2" and attempt many conclusions. But because all the changes in the equilibrium value are smooth, by the transformations permitted in catastrophe theory they may be transformed away. Figure 18.4 is from this viewpoint "the same" as Figure 18.3. This is rather like increasing the contrast in a photograph; much information (about smooth changes) is lost, but sometimes interesting features are emphasized.

The key point here is that once $x(p)$ is considered as "the equilibrium value at p" rather than, say, "the value that x happens to have at p," only a mental habit implies that x will still be a function of p in the mathematical sense—that for each p there will be a *unique* equilibrium value. For most real systems this is not true in general. Mathematically it can be proved (and often is), but only from hypotheses such as "convexity of the utility function" which are very hard to justify. They are much used, however, because they make the mathematics easier for economists, who would rather not believe in multiple equilibria anyway. These suggest that the right "invisible

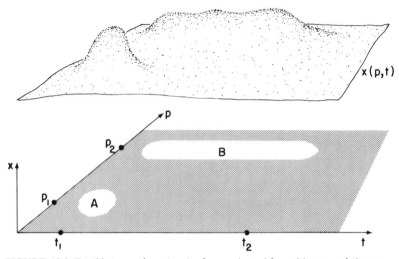

FIGURE 18.3 *Equilibrium value $x(p, t)$ of x varying with position p and time t.*

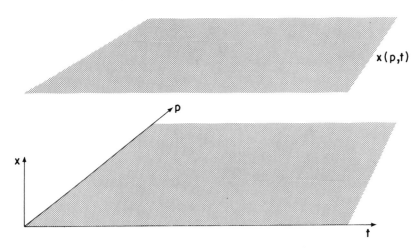

FIGURE 18.4 *Equilibrium value x(p, t) constant in time and space.*

hand of the market'' does not know what the left is doing. Once we face the possibility of multiple equilibria, we can expect, for instance Figure 18.5, which is not "the same" as Figure 18.4 even by the very broad range of transformations catastrophe theory uses.

Now, for many purposes Figure 18.3 is *not* the same as Figure 18.4 any more than molten gold is the same as gold ingots. But even for such purposes it is important to know that both are gold, the same element transformed but preserved. Figure 18.5 (or lead) will not transform into Figures 18.3 and 18.4 (or gold in any form, respectively), unless we widen much further the kind of transformation considered.

This analogy is strengthened by Thom's discovery that for such geometries of equilibria, as for chemical compounds, we indeed have irreducible, classifiable *elements* like those of chemistry. He christened these the *elementary catastrophes* to capture their association with discontinuity and sudden change (though the associated mathematics is often far from elementary in the schoolbook sense). Figure 18.5 becomes, in this view, a "molecule" consisting of two points, A and B, around which the geometry may be reduced to the star ard *cusp* form (Figure 18.6), and two curves, C, D, around each point of which it may, *locally*, be reduced to a standard *fold*.

Analogous to the periodic table, we have the classification of elementary catastrophes, of which the first two are the fold and the cusp. This classification has been systematized and vastly extended by Arnol'd (1972), who has listed all possible *simple* local forms. Simple, here, has now a precise technical meaning—that perturbations which are sufficiently small (in a sense requiring more calculus than I wish to use here) can produce only finitely many different results (where "different" means "not the same up to the transformations we have been discussing"). Moreover, we can be much

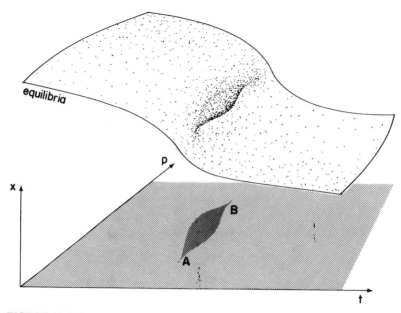

FIGURE 18.5 *For most positions p at most times t, x has only a single equilibrium value [given by the point of the surface above (p, t)]. But for (p, t) in the shaded region, several equilibria (stable and unstable) exist.*

more precise about the idea that "Nature chooses simple systems," in a sense made exact by Thom.

Two "general" curves in the plane will meet each other (and themselves) only in isolated points (Figure 18.7). Two general curves in three dimensions (Figure 18.7b) will fail to meet entirely. (For instance, a curve "in general position" in (x, y, z) space will miss the z axis.) Thom gave this a rigorous formulation, generalization, and proof, involving a translation of "most things are like this" into mathematical terms. This allowed in turn a precise statement and proof that with up to five "external" parameters like p and t in Figures 18.3–18.5, only simple points will typically be encountered, however many "internal" parameters like x the system has. (It is important to notice that the ideas of "most," "typical," etc. here rest on exactly the "general position" assumptions natural and traditional but implicit in, for example, physics, like "more equations than unknowns means no solutions." These ideas have simply been systematized and made more powerful; catastrophe theory stands in the same relation to their traditional forms as coordinate geometry does to that of the Egyptians.) Moreover these simple points will typically be met in even simpler ways; perturb Figure 18.5 a little and it will still have two points, near A and B, around which it reduces to Figure 18.6. In fact the perturbed version will be transformable back

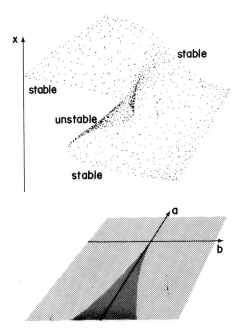

FIGURE 18.6 *The standard cusp catastrophe. Around A or B in Figure 18.5, the function whose minima define stable equilibrium (change sign for maximized quantities such as utility) can be given locally the form $x^4 + ax^2 + bx$ by suitable (a, b) coordinates in the (p, t) plane and a (p, t)-dependent change of x variable.*

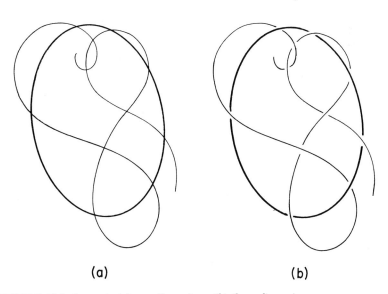

(a)   (b)

FIGURE 18.7 *Curves in (a) two dimensions, (b) three dimensions.*

exactly to Figure 18.5, which is thus as simple as possible. It is *structurally stable*.

In particular, with up to four external parameters there are exactly seven typically occurring stable local forms: Thom's famous *seven elementary catastrophes*. I will not list here their algebraic expressions (for which various choices are possible) for the same reason that in outlining chemistry at this level I would omit the Periodic Table. To know that the word "copper" appears on the list, even with its atomic number 29, is only meaningfully informative in the whole theoretical framework that relates "reddish, bendy stuff" to "beautiful blue crystals." Contrary to the common assertion that "it is possible to apply Thom's theorem without understanding the proof," I would suggest that it is *im*possible to apply it effectively without understanding its context—and a major part of its context is, exactly, its proof. You cannot "apply" the Periodic Table without knowing enough chemistry to be able in principle to reconstruct it. (Indeed, "applications" of the table *alone* are even rarer than successful applications of Thom's theorem *alone*. But each has a central part to play.) This is not to say that all scientists must learn the language of "ideals in the ring of germs at 0 of functions $R^{n+r} \to R$, considered as modules over the ring of germs at 0 of functions $R^n \to R$", and the "Whitney C^∞ topology". But at least an appreciation of the kind of transformation involved, and the way in which for suitable systems these lead via geometric "general position" arguments to the universality of the elementary catastrophes, is required for avoiding serious error. (A pictorial—as distinct from technically rigorous—account of this is in Poston and Stewart 1978. An account for the more mathematically expert is included in Zeeman 1977.) In particular, note the phrase "for suitable systems", just used. What systems are "suitable"?

I could give a technically precise answer to this question, by giving a technically rigorous statement of the hypotheses and implications of Thom's theorem. But the reader to whom the terms involved are immediately meaningful is ipso facto able to read the details of the exact proof. To give others informally an intuitive grasp of their meaning would require many examples and much discussion of what these hypotheses mean "in action." The best and most illuminating examples occur, exactly, in the proof—or in applications that use the ideas of the proof. (Readers familiar with statistics should consider the analogy with knowing when one can or cannot reasonably use the law of large numbers.) Just so does *use* of the Periodic Table in studying some mineral sample involve the same ideas as work on *establishing* it.

However, it is probably useful here to point out some of the things that the theorem does *not* say, but (on the basis of popular accounts) has been presumed to, in published "applications" in the social sciences.

First is the point that even among extremizing systems which usually *achieve* local equilibrium most of the time (the setting of the earliest applications), the seven elementary catastrophes exhaust only the *interior* stable possibilities; other things happen stably at a boundary point like "production is nonnegative." For more on this, see Renfrew and Poston (1978).

Second, if local equilibrium is not usual, much more complicated things can happen. An elementary account of a very simple model where two agents, each attempting to maximize profit, stably produce "chaos," is given at the end of Poston and Stewart (1978) to emphasize this point. The onset of such phenomena is not reducible to the setting in which Thom's theorem applies, though the mathematical tools and philosophy *behind* the theorem remain informative.

Third, the theorem says that in certain dimensions for the external parameters, typically *only* certain forms *locally* happen. It does not say that they *must* happen. (Figure 18.3 has the right dimensions to include a cusp, but *stably* does not. It would take a substantial perturbation to put one in.) It does not say, either, that the global geometry is reducible to *one* catastrophe. (Figure 18.5 stably has *two* cusps.) Analogously, the periodic table does not say that matter occurs in pure-element samples. Living matter, in particular, is an immensely complex *composite* of elements; insofar as its dynamics accede to elementary catastrophe theory, it is clearly compound in this as well. The most detailed work on this area, collected in the book by Zeeman (1977), involves multiple cusps in a testable gastrulation model. Thus a (published) geographical example which reasons essentially

> I have chosen 4 external variables and reduced the behavior variables [illegitimately] to 1, *therefore* by the classification my system is described by a *single* butterfly catastrophe

is multiply illegitimate in its argument. (Though this need not invalidate the *model*—a point to which I shall return.)

Finally, recall the range of transformations involved in reduction to these seven "elements." Geometries reducible, globally, to the standard cusp may take the detailed forms shown in Figure 18.6 or 18.8 (as "oxygen," O may occur as O_2 that we breathe, as O_3—ozone—that is a poison, as part of H_2O, etc. etc.). In particular Figure 18.8 shows that if cusp geometry is combined with a uniform lowering of equilibrium position with b, "large negative a" no more implies "there is an *inaccessible middle range* of x where no stable minima exist" than "here we have oxygen" implies "here is a gas". [For those at home with formulae, $(x + 4b)^4 + a(x + 4b)^2 + b(x + 4b)$ is easily reducible by a *b-dependent* change in x variable to the standard cusp form $x^4 + ax^2 + bx$, whose equilibria for the different values of a and b give the standard Figure 18.6. To those less at home than this, catastrophe theory is reluctantly not recommended.] Thus a feature of the standard cusp—and of many physical examples of it—should not carelessly be treated as this one often is, as a *consequence* of the presence of cusp geometry in general. (Though it can be a reasonable additional hypothesis to explore, being a *common* result of cusp geometry.)

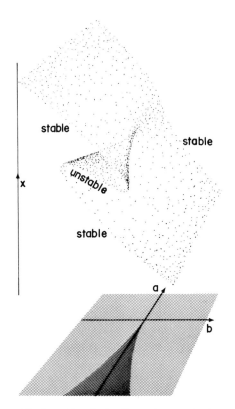

stable

stable

unstable

x

stable

a

b

FIGURE 18.8 *A stable form "equivalent" to the standard cusp but with significant "qualitative" differences from it.*

Most of these remarks are specializations to catastrophe theory of very general points about the application of mathematics, to the social sciences in particular. Much numerical work in sociology, psychology, and so on, consists of fitting data to a very few standard forms, such as linear relationships and bell-shaped curves. (I have known psychologists design experiments to produce two distinct populations, then so parametrize the data as to produce *one* normal distribution—thus destroying the bimodality under investigation.) Addition of the elementary catastrophes to the forms used is pure gain. They do represent the simplest forms which essential discontinuity in the geometry of equilibria may take, and many systems are indeed governed by varying equilibria.

The general hypothesis of behavior governed by local extremization is not invariably true, but is often reasonable; particularly as a working hypothesis rather than dogma. Given this, the general arguments of catastrophe theory, and a great wealth of concrete examples, show that irreducible discontinuity is commonly to be expected and that it may commonly be expected to appear in certain forms. (Thus to postulate a cusp catastrophe model, for instance, has greater explanatory content than simply to postulate a threshold. In one case a reasonable general mechanism is supposed, even if its details are inaccessible, and the hypothesis added that one of its frequent consequences applies in this case; in the other, there is a discontinuity at the threshold because there is a discontinuity—with no mechanism for its cause suggested even in principle. "Threshold" is a *name* for discontinuity, not an explanation, though thresholds *with* explanations do exist in physics. Often the explanation is a catastrophe.) The catastrophe geometry governing settlement pattern in the model of Renfrew and Poston (1978) illustrates how easily such discontinuities may arise in social systems. Particular examples are more convincing if *derived* from separately defensible hypotheses, as in the settlement pattern model and many physical examples; but many successful physical theories do essentially "postulate a catastrophe" and apply oscillatory integral theory, renormalization group, or whatever is physically appropriate to deduce measurable numbers from this *Ansatz*. It is not unreasonable to attempt the same in the social sciences, provided Thom's theorem is not regarded as a substitute for evidence. The general theory gives a guide to the forms that many systems *typically* (and many more, *often*) take, the information that these forms are insensitive to small adjustments, and an informed approach to many phenomena whose essential character is completely obscured by hypotheses of linearity or unimodal statistics. Thus to model the dynamics of city growth by a butterfly catastrophe, for example, is as legitimate as to hypothesize (and *test*) a Poisson distribution for farm sizes or ellipses for planetary orbits. Later developments may derive the butterfly, Poisson, or ellipse from lower level hypotheses—though the very way that theory shows many distinct processes to yield these forms can make decision between rival underlying theories difficult—but Kepler's work was not unscientific for not including Newton's It would have been less scientific if it *had* obtained the ellipses from an inverse square law of gravitation, but had *not* included careful comparison with the mass of observational data built up by Tycho Brahe (which Kepler had to purloin from Brahe's heirs). Kepler obtained a better fit, to excellent data, than did the cycles and epicycles of Ptolemy and Copernicus, and with a far simpler model. A merit of catastrophe theory is that the simplicity (in the sense discussed earlier) of its models is a theorem. But close concern with the data is needed as well: Occam's razor chooses the simplest among the explanations *that fit*.

References

Arnol'd, V. I., 1973, Normal Forms for Functions Near Degenerate Critical Points. The Weyl Groups of A_k, D_k and E_k and Lagrangian Singularities, *Functional Analysis and Applications* 6 (1973) 253–72 (trans. from *Func. Anal. i Priložen* 6 (1972) 3–25).

Poston, T. and Stewart, I. N., 1978, *Catastrophe Theory and its Applications,* Pitman, London. Includes Bibliography of some 450 items, so I feel absolved from attempting completeness here.

Poston, T. and Stewart, I. N., 1976, *Taylor Expansions and Catastrophes,* Research Notes in Mathematics 7, Pitman, London. A briefer account of the mathematics in the same informal style as the above, without applications.

Renfrew, and Poston, T., Endogenous Discontinuity in Settlement Pattern, this volume, Chapter 19.

Thom, René, 1972, *Stabilité Structurelle et Morphogénèse,* Benjamin (complete around 1968, but Systems Collapse was walking the publishing world): English translation by David Fowler, *Structural Stability and Morphogenesis,* Benjamin 1975. Not easy reading but repays informed effort; founded the subject.

Zeeman, E. C., 1977, *Readings in Catastrophe Theory,* Addison-Wesley. Collected papers, ranging from 10-dimensional geometry through naval architecture to detailed embryology and a theory of prison riots. Essential.

19

COLIN RENFREW
TIM POSTON

Discontinuities in the Endogenous Change of Settlement Pattern

Introduction

The simplest reasonable hypotheses on the economic use of land in agriculture and on the benefits of living in aggregated communities among differently dispersed nonurban populations are used to generate a model which predicts sudden shifts between a landscape of scattered farmsteads and one of nucleated villages as a result of smooth changes in such factors as soil fertility and farming technique.

Evidence for such shifts is to be found in the archaeological record, and has generally been interpreted as indicating changes of population in response either to sudden environmental change or to invasion. The analysis here offers instead an explanation of discontinuous change in terms of continuously changing variables. The approach can be extended beyond the analysis of settlement size to that of shifts in settlement location (e.g., valley versus hilltop). It suggests the possibility of a chain or cascade of catastrophes, each triggered by its logical predecessor.

The model brings out the importance of a class of stable phenomena not listed in Thom's theorem, since the theorem's hypotheses do not apply. These are the *constraint catastrophes*, governing stable bifurcation at a boundary for nonlinear optimization problems which are constrained by inequalities. Problems of this kind are universal in the social sciences (population, production, etc., being inherently positive quantities) and important for the programming methods they require. The bifurcation behaviors possible are significantly different from the "seven elementary catastrophes" but may be classified and analyzed by the same methods.

437

Transformations:
Mathematical Approaches to Culture Change

Settlement Discontinuity

In many regions of the world archaeological research has yielded evidence for marked and sudden change in settlement pattern. Often patterns of great stability come to a seemingly abrupt end with the modification or disappearance of the dominant settlement form, usually accompanied by the appearance of new forms often located in different topographical situations. Sometimes a first assessment of the evidence suggests to the observer a rapid change in population density, either substantial depopulation or sudden increase.

Within the traditional paradigm of archaeology (Sterud 1973) substantial change in the archaeological record of an area, and especially sudden change, is most readily explained by a change of "culture" which can generally be related to a change of "people." This is the invasionist or migrationist hypothesis. More gradual change is frequently explained on that paradigm in terms of "diffusion." Such an approach has been greatly criticized in recent years (Binford 1968; Clark 1966; Neustupny 1976; Renfrew 1969a; 1974), and such explanations in ethnic or cultural historical terms contrasted with those in processual ones (Flannery 1972), where the working of factors within the culture system including the results of external contact form a more appropriate field of explanation.

Change in settlement pattern, wherever possible accompanied by evidence of "destructions," has often been seen as the very strongest evidence to support ethnic as against processual arguments (cf. Childe 1950; Gimbutas 1965, passim), and instances can be found from the archaeological literature of every region of the world.

A good instance of such change and of such interpretation is offered by the decline in tell settlement at the end of the Late Neolithic or Chalcolithic in Bulgaria, Romania, and north Greece in the centuries prior to 3000 BC. The Late Neolithic settlement pattern of the area is one of nucleated villages, with great settlement stability leading to the formation of *toumbas* or *moghilas,* which are the counterpart of the tells of the Near East. Villages in the form of a cluster of some 20 or so huts are documented by excavations at Tell Azmak or Cascioarele, and the artifacts document incipient craft specialization (including early copper metallurgy) and a range of ritual forms organized on a village basis (ct. Childe 1957, Ch. VI; Renfrew 1969b; Theocares 1973). Yet in the space of a few centuries many of the tell sites were abandoned, evidence of settlement of any kind less frequently recorded by the archaeologist, and in some areas settlements are now found on higher ground and sometimes fortified. Survey in the Plain of Drama, for instance, documented eight sites in the *floruit* of the tell-village settlement phase, corresponding to Sitagroi phase III (Renfrew 1971), with only three sites in the succeeding settlement phase (Sitagroi V) and more numerous sites later (nine well documented), none of them at the location of the former tell villages and most of them on higher ground. These changes at the end of the southeast European Chalcolithic have traditionally been linked by many scholars with the "coming" of the Indo-Europeans.

At this point the obvious yet important archaeological principle should be stressed that in the absence of very systematic survey it is easier to detect and identify large archaeological sites than small ones, especially if they conveniently take the forms of mounds rising above a level plain. Many traditional techniques of archaeological survey and research will readily detect the remains of nucleated village settlements, while altogether failing to recognize the very much smaller and archaeologically less substantial sites of a dispersed settlement pattern, except in special circumstances. It is notable, for instance, that there is little direct evidence of dwellings in the Neolithic or Early Bronze Age of south Britain except as revealed beneath the large mounds or "barrows" erected for funerary and ritual purposes. Yet hardly a barrow is excavated without the original ground surface yielding indications of settlement or of use (e.g., plow marks) as an unexpected bonus to the excavator. Very small settlement units are simply less obvious than very large ones, especially in circumstances of geomorphological change, whether erosion or aggradation. Indeed were it not for the evidence of burial in cemeteries or otherwise prominent graves there are whole periods in the prehistory of several regions of Europe where we would have very little indication of human occupation at all.

An example is offered by the Late Aeneolithic of Central Europe, around 2500 BC (Shennan 1977, 165). The Middle Aeneolithic settlement includes nucleated hilltop sites amply documented in the archaeological literature (Pavelčik 1973). In the Late Aeneolithic period these sites are no longer occupied, and evidence for settlement units is very sparse. However, at this time cemeteries are found containing the characteristic pottery of the Corded Ware culture and the Beaker culture. Inevitably these have generally been interpreted in ethnic terms, and predictably both groups have at times been hailed as the first Indo-Europeans of the area, although alternative explanations are now being considered (Lanting and van der Waals 1976). The point here is that a marked change in settlement pattern has occurred, an apparent discontinuity which has inevitably led to suggestions of population change. This is an instance, moreover, where settlement evidence alone might have led to suggestions of marked depopulation, had it not been for the funerary evidence. The possibility is now emerging of explaining the new burial assemblage (Shennan 1976) as well as the new settlement pattern in processual terms, by a consideration of continuous and locally operating factors.

Sudden shifts in settlement pattern are not only from nucleated to dispersed. There are instances in the record also of relatively sudden nucleation. Such a shift is seen in the Cycladic Islands of Greece around 2200 BC. Toward the end of the Cycladic Early Bronze Age, toward the end of the duration of the Keros-Syros culture, prominent nucleated settlements are observed (Doumas 1972) and this becomes the characteristic settlement form for the Middle Bronze Age. The shift has been documented in detail for the island of Melos, where site survey under the direction of Mr. John Cherry has given evidence of a number of small and scattered sites in the earlier part of the Bronze Age, where around 2200 BC settlement was concentrated in the single "town" of Phylakopi with a population of perhaps around 600–1000. Once again the larger nucleated settlements have long been known, whereas the smaller, dispersed ones, until the recent introduction of highly systematic site survey with appropriate sampling strategies, have been known primarily through their associated funerary remains.

Many other instances could be given of relatively sudden shifts in settlement pattern, whose explanation is of great interest to the archaeologist. Such rapid shifts, because of their apparent discontinuity, have proved to be among the most difficult phenomena to explain in processual terms. But first the concepts of nucleated and dispersed settlement need more careful examination.

Nucleated and Dispersed Settlement

Amid the great diversity in settlement form and distribution among traditional farming communities of the world, two opposing extremes of what may be a continuous spectrum can be discerned. The first is dispersed settlement, the population living in small homesteads, farmsteads, or compounds, the home of a single extended family, although naturally linked by various ties of kinship and solidarity into larger communities. But spatially and residentially they are isolated units. In the extreme case there are no large and permanent settlements, although often there are "parish" or territorial shrines (e.g., Goody 1967, 91), burial places (Emory 1947), and defended refuges (Groube 1967, 17) for periodic or occasional assembly. The settlement pattern of much of Africa (Allan 1972) and of the Pacific has traditionally been of this kind, and even in the centralized societies of Central America and Southeast Asia the rural population was often distributed in this way, with a small "urban" population at the ceremonial and administrative centers (cf. Bray 1972).

At the other extreme the agricultural population is entirely agglomerated into large nucleated villages or compounds, agricultural "towns" from which the inhabitants go forth daily to work their fields. Apulia in southern Italy has a pattern of this kind, the towns with an average population of 6700 inhabitants accommodating 93% of the total population (Chisholm 1968, 114). It seems possible that Çatal Hüyük in central Anatolia circa 6000 BC was an agricultural town of this kind. With an area of 13 ha it may have housed some 5000 people. The great Pueblos of the American southwestern states in the eleventh century AD appear to have accommodated an essentially agrarian population with no supporting hinterland of rural population, although smaller settlement units are also found (Vivian 1970). Agricultural "towns" of this kind are common in different parts of Africa today (cf. Morton Williams 1971, 884).

Such large size of settlement for an essentially agricultural population with no rural hinterland of smaller settlements, is much less common, however, than a compromise between the two extremes in the form of the small farming village of between 50 and 1000 inhabitants. This represents the dominant settlement pattern in most agricultural areas and is abundantly documented by the archaeological record (Flannery 1972).

Geographers have long been aware of these contrasting settlement patterns (Brunhes 1920, 1952; Demangeon 1946; Aurousseau 1920). In his discussion of the dispersal and concentration of population, the "fundamental seed bed of human settlement," Brunhes contrasts maps illustrating settlement in Flanders (maximum dispersal) and in the Strasbourg region (nucleation in large villages)' stressing that both forms may be found together in the same region (Brunhes 1920, ch. XV). Demangeon (1946, ch. IX) draws the same distinction, dividing rural Frrance into two major areas, the northeast (characterized by villages) and the southwest (where very small settlements—hamlets—predominate), although he stresses the variation within the two areas. The *département* Manche, for example, has 32 settled localities per 10 km² whereas the Marne *département* has only 2 per 10 km².

Just what governs the ultimate equilibrium point of size in each area and period is much less clear. There is a natural tendency for settlement size to be larger in areas of very high population density, and vice versa, so that intensive exploitation may be associated with agricultural towns (although if it is labor intensive rather than land intensive, transport costs will be significant). And at the other extreme, systems with very long fallow periods, which are generally associated with much lower settlement density, often show very much smaller settlement units. Indeed swidden cultivators often have to change their place of residence altogether, when the long fallow necessitates the abandonment of all the fields around the village or homestead, to which they may return later if a cyclical system is practiced. There is then some tendency to dispersed settlement among swidden cultivators, but no simple linear relationship emerges (Harris 1972, 248–51).

Any analysis must proceed to balance the transport costs arising from nucleated settlement against the various social benefits that nucleation brings. And it is clear that in a single ecological zone very different settlement patterns may exist side by side. Brookfield and Hart (1971, 224) illustrate this graphically for New Guinea, and Schmieder (quoted Flannery

1972, 47) makes the same point for the nucleated Aztec and Zapotec and dispersed Mixe in Mexico. The same has frequently been noted for rural France (Demangeon 1946 ch. IX).

It is important here to distinguish between mean settlement size, in a spectrum running from dispersed to highly nucleated, and the question of central places. Confusion between the two has obscured many discussions of early urbanism. Classical central place theory has brought out very clearly the economic rationale behind the emergence of hierarchies of places, where places of higher order are needed to offer services which it is not economic to provide at lower order places with a much smaller population catchment (cf. Garner 1967). In general there is a close correlation between urban size and position in the hierarchy of places, but it does not follow that "big" means "central place," or vice versa. The special functions of a central place can be offered by a location with a very small resident population, as some of the organizing and ceremonial centers of the Maya civilization document (Bray 1972). Societies that are not at the state level of socio-economic integration offer similar examples through the functioning of periodic central places. And the periodic markets in China (Skinner 1964) and Africa (Hodder 1962) as well as in Europe offer examples of a location temporarily taking on a central place function without itself being of great population size. The converse also holds, so that agricultural towns such as those already cited may offer services to no one but their own resident population, and do not qualify as centers in any settlement hierarchy. It is thus perfectly possible for a settlement of several thousand individuals not to be a central place in this sense, whereas a settlement of just a few hundred can be.

In the discussion that follows our concern is with the size and spacing of settlement—horizontal arrangement, rather than the vertical arrangement implied by settlement hierarchy. For simplicity, therefore, the treatment is restricted to settlement patterns lacking any hierarchy of central places, but with some modifications it could be applied to the lowest level in a settlement hierarchy. Indeed if the expression P were generalized to refer to transport costs and distance decay factors of all kinds, the discussion might be applied to each level in turn of a central place hierarchy. In a modern urban context, it can be applied to the site and distribution of shopping centers (Poston and Wilson, 1977).

Factors Regulating Settlement Size

For convenience we shall assume that the residential units in our hypothetical study area are all of the same size, at the centers of congruent territories. In any real instance there will of course be variations both in space and time, which (as in statistical Newtonian physics) it is appropriate to take as random, superimposed on any general spatial or temporal pattern.

Our concentration in what follows on optima rather than averages, with implicit identification of the two, and the assumption of homogeneity correspond exactly to a "Landau theory" approach to the ordering of matter. Although this has its defects (see Poston and Stewart 1977, ch. 14 for a discussion in catastrophe theoretic terms), it is the natural approach here. The "exact" statistical methods involve passage to the limit of infinite samples.

It is assumed that there is no settlement hierarchy: All the settlements are primarily agricultural, and there are no interactions between settlements. Such specialist facilities as they possess are offered exclusively to their own inhabitants. Let the population density be B. We take B as essentially fixed in the short term, by the carrying capacity of the land with a given mix of crops and farming techniques: sudden changes are of course possible (e.g., by plague), but our concern here is with sudden alterations in settlement pattern arising from *gradual* changes in all other factors. Thus taking the variation of B as slow is less a hypothesis supposed always to hold than an indication of the case we wish to consider, in a demonstration that sudden causes are not a necessary condition for sudden effects. Let N be the number of persons per settlement. Let R be the distance from the settlement to the furthest point on the edge of its territory. It follows that

$$N = kR^2B \tag{19.1}$$

where k depends on the geometry of the territory. (For the closest—hexagonal—packing of settlements k is $\frac{3}{2}\sqrt{3}$, for others it is smaller—for example, square territories give k as 2.) When N is very small there will be numerous small settlements (farmsteads) and R is likewise small. N_{min} will be the number in a minimal family for which a figure as low as 3.5 has been proposed (Russell 1956, 52), although in practice N_{min} is not likely to be much less than 10. The pattern is as seen in Figure 19.1. When N is very large there will be just a few widely spaced nucleated settlements (agricultural towns). The maximum size of N is determined by the maximum distance from which land can productively be worked by residents of the settlement. This varies with the nature of the agriculture and available transport, but in practice is not normally greater than about 5 km, so that N varies up to the order of $100B$. The pattern is as seen in Figure 19.2.

We shall assume that for a given mix of crops and production methods, the productivity $p(r)$ of a member of the settlement working on a field at distance r from home is a linear function of r with slope $-a$, depending on the mix:

$$p(r) = C - ar \tag{19.2}$$

Since the amount of land at distance r grows with r (except in the essentially one-dimensional case of cultivable land restricted to a riverbank or narrow

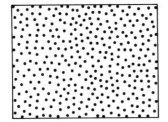

FIGURE 19.1. *Dispersed settlement pattern (N* small).

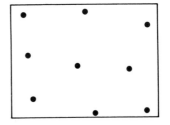

FIGURE 19.2. *Nucleated settlement pattern (N* large).

valley), we must integrate over the territory to find a mean productivity per member:

$$P(R) = C - \kappa aR \qquad (19.3)$$

where κ is a constant depending on the territory's shape. (For the one-dimensional case κ is $\frac{1}{2}$, for most reasonable place shapes it is greater.) We may absorb it by setting $A = \kappa a$, so that mean productivity becomes

$$P(R) = C - AR \qquad (19.4)$$

In essence this assumption simply follows the principle of economic rent of Ricardo and von Thünen (Chisolm 1968, 25) where the price of produce falls off in a linear manner with distance from the consuming center as a result of transport costs (Figure 19.3). In our own treatment labor costs as well as transport costs rise with distance from the settlement, since that is where the labor is located, and it is not suggested that a money economy is in operation. This is of course the fundamental principle of location, with the minimization of transport and other costs conforming to the law of least effort (Zipf 1949). Chisholm, in an extended discussion of this principle in relation to agricultural production (1968, chapter 4), cites studies in Finland

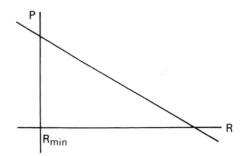

FIGURE 19.3. *Assumption: the mean productivity per member (P) declines linearly with mean territory size (R).*

where the net output per hectare falls to 25% as distance of land from the settlement increases from .1 to 3.0 km.

Clearly the value of A, the slope of the line, is governed by the labor requirements of the crop under the agricultural system in question. For labor-intensive systems, such as most irrigation systems, A is high and the falloff is steep. For a multicrop agricultural economy the falloff depends also on the spatial arrangement of the various crops, hence the circular zones of production in von Thünen's model, with labor-intensive crops near the center. The linear falloff suggested here is a very simple approach to the economics of location, but it is a tenable first approximation. Observe that for large enough R, P becomes negative: This is realizable only temporarily and in the presence of substantial stores, since it represents net loss of utility (e.g., workers consuming more calories than they bring home from their distant fields), but is certainly more correct than, for instance, setting P to be zero for R greater than C/A. The loss is real. We shall further assume that the "perceived rewards arising from communal life," S, follow a typical saturation curve (Figure 19.4) with a one-humped derivative (Figure 19.5) positive at $R = R_{min}$. [Our parametrization by R rather than N is via Equation (19.1) and thus depends on a particular quasi-fixed B.] The notion of S is difficult to express in quantitative terms, but it assumes that various kinds of peaceful human interaction bring advantage. The opportunities for such contact are of course increased by increase in population size of the settlement unit (with increasing R). It is clear that even for R_{min}, where the settlement unit is simply the extended family, the rewards are positive.

The two features of this curve from which we shall wish to argue (shown in fact by a much wider class than saturation curves: we could allow a slower-than-linear infinite rise, or a fall back to zero) are as follows:

1. The initially increasing positive slope, at R_{min}
2. The decrease toward zero of the slope, for larger R

The first could be deduced from a wide range of models for the benefits involved. For example, the effort saved in distributing the work of a specialist potter will be roughly proportional to R^2, for small R. Equally,

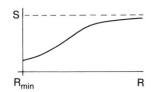

FIGURE 19.4. *The perceived rewards arising from communal life (S) are assumed to follow a typical saturation curve with respect to mean population of settlement, and hence mean size of territory.*

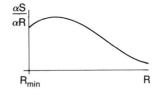

FIGURE 19.5. *The saturation curve for S is assumed to have one-humped derivative.*

there is a common human pleasure in richness of social pattern (as long as the complexity does not become incomprehensible to the point of anxiety) and as long as the settlement is small enough for all members to know each other the number of pairwise relationships grows as $\frac{1}{2}N(N - 1) \sim R^4$. The detailed elaboration of such models must depend on technological and/or social features of the particular society considered, but it is clear that feature 1 must hold in very many cases.

Feature 2 is in fact commonplace, except where it conflicts with convexity hypotheses adopted for reasons of mathematical convenience or ideology (such as the desire that the "invisible hand" of the market should always yield, as it sometimes does in practice, a unique equilibrium price). For example, once a potter has as many customers on his doorstep as he can supply, there is no further saving in grouping potters together unless they become more productive by cooperation, which would imply a change in technology. Social benefits will show similar saturation effects, or even diminish for large R. It has been suggested (Brookfield and Hart 1971, 226), for instance, that in some cultures disputes are difficult to contain when N rises above a certain threshold: "Beyond a certain size fissiparous tendencies are hard to control. The inherent instability may lead to sharp inversion in the 'curve of benefits.' "

More complicated functions could be proposed for S, for instance the sum of two saturation curves, one for the interactions arising from small social gatherings (saturating early) (cf. Forge 1972, 375) and one for the benefits arising from craft specialization within the agricultural community. This would lead to a more elaborate geometry, and we return to it later.

The next step is to combine the two functions P and S. Many ways of doing this might be proposed, but the simplest is to add them. This is particularly reasonable where S is a comparatively "objective" function of R, such as transport saving in distributing the products of specialists, and can be measured in units directly related to those used for P. We have examined more complicated "total benefit" functions $f(P, S)$; again, it is easy to add more catastrophes to the geometry that follows, hard with reasonable functions to remove them. For present purposes, then, we shall take the total benefit associated with a given R as

$$F(R) = P(R) + S(R) = C - AR + S(R)$$

and consider optimization of F.

These ideas have been well expressed, although not topologically analyzed, by Brookfield and Hart (1971, 226):

"But why should people tolerate distance when they can virtually eliminate it by living in scattered and if need be mobile homesteads? People aggregate because there are advantages in so doing, whether for common work, co-ordination of efforts in the raising of prestations, in defence, or for the company and social security enjoyed in a group. Such benefits will increase up to a certain group size, but in the absence of division and specialization of labour will not continue to increase in direct proportion to growing group size. If we can conceive of a "curve of benefits" arising from aggregation, the point at which this curve peaks represents optimal group size. If while still rising it intersects a curve expressing toleration of distance, the intersection will represent a sub-optimal maximum size."

The shape of the "total benefit" curve F varies dramatically with the agricultural parameter A; Figure 19.6 shows its form, and that of its derivative, for various values. Clearly for small A (low penalty for distance from the fields) the unique maximum is found at a large value of R, which is associated with nucleation into substantial settlements. Large A, on the other hand, gives a clear optimum at R_{min}, with maximum dispersal. The intermediate cases are our concern in the following section.

The Dynamics of Change: Catastrophe Theory

The analysis has so far been a static one, with fixed values for the parameters, but these parameters may vary in time or space. Both C and A, in particular, may change, through variations in soil productivity due to exhaustion or environmental change, or in the mix of crops and agricultural or transport methods used. (For the moment, treat the function S as fixed.) The constant C does not affect the positions of maxima or minima of the curve F but A clearly does: it is evident from Figure 19.6 that these occur where the slope of the S curve equals A. It is convenient to sum up the relationship as in Figure 19.7. This shows above each value of A the value(s) of R at which $C - AR + S(R)$ has a local maximum (solid curves) or minimum (dashed curves), gathering together the essential information of Figure 19.6 in one picture. It is clear by reference to Figure 19.6 that the "fold" occurring at $A = A_2$, $R = R_t$ is a consequence of the existence of a maximum for dF/dR, which in turn follows from the features 1 and 2 of S argued earlier.

Now it is reasonable to suppose that when F has a unique maximum, as for $A < A_1$ (giving a curve like Figure 19.6a) or for $A > A_2$ (as in Figure 19.6d), this will determine the settlement pattern. For people in a nonoptimal pattern will observe the improvements resulting from small random changes in the right direction (toward a town of optimal size for $A < A_1$, toward dispersal for $A > A_2$) and consolidate them; similarly, they will tend to reverse changes seen to be disadvantageous. In a fairly short time, this will bring them close to the maximum. But what happens when $A_1 < A < A_2$ is more problematic.

Suppose now that A starts at a value above A_2, with dispersed settlement, and is decreased by gradual improvement in agricultural technique, crops, rainfall, or transport (anything that frees more time for travel to

A large

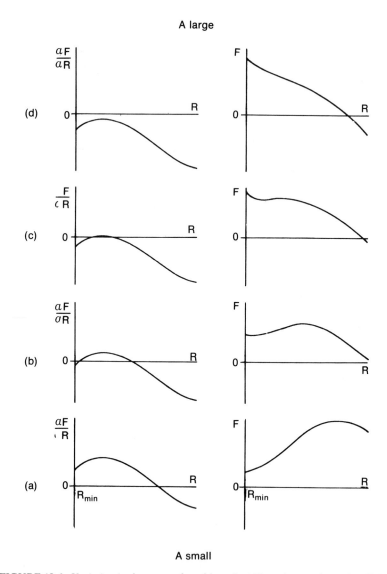

A small

FIGURE 19.6. *Variation in the curve of total benefits (F) against territory size (R) and its derivative as A (steepness of productivity falloff with distance) increases.*

distant fields, or makes the travel easier). As A passes A_2, there is no cause to consider change; dispersal remains the absolute optimum. But at some value A_3 between A_1 and A_2, the "nucleated" optimum at R_3 in Figure 19.8 will offer benefits equal to those of dispersal, and for $A < A_3$ it will offer more. If the people follow the simple rule "choose the absolute maximum of F", R becomes the discontinuous function of A shown as a heavy line in

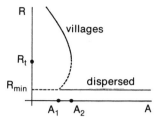

FIGURE 19.7. *The values of R (territorial size) against A (productivity falloff with distance) for which total benefits (F) are locally maximized (solid curves) or minimized (dashed curves).*

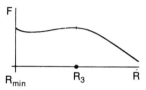

FIGURE 19.8. *As A (initially high) decreases, the benefits (F) for a spacing given by R = R_3 come to equal those accruing from dispersed settlement.*

Figure 19.9. If they do not perceive instantly the appearance of a new absolute maximum, or if (like many people in many cultures) they consider any contemplated large change as automatically a bad thing, there will be some range of values between A_1 and A_2 for which either dispersed or nucleated settlement may exist and continue, depending on past history.

Many things will affect the durability or otherwise of particular *metastable states,* as we may call local but not absolute maxima. Water may be carefully cooled, still liquid, below freezing point; but the introduction of an ice crystal then causes sudden loud change. Similarly, the appearance of one town in a region of dispersed settlement with $A < A_3$ could trigger the rapid appearance of many by the new visibility of the advantages. On the other hand, diamonds in the human environment are likewise metastable (and statistical mechanics suggests that they will *some day* turn to graphite and

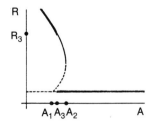

FIGURE 19.9. *Change in settlement pattern with changing A if people follow the rule: "Choose the absolute maximum of F."*

not often turn back, so that in the average over infinite time metastable states do not exist) but in practice "a diamond is forever." Extreme rigidity of landholding and inheritance arrangements, for example, could maintain a metastable settlement pattern for archaeologically long periods of time.

Another factor is the size of random fluctuations (the "thermodynamic noise" of the system). If new couples go to live in an existing house, as in many patrilocal or matrilocal cultures, such fluctuations will be less than in a culture with neolocal residence patterns where houses are regularly built at new locations without a detailed preliminary cost–benefit analysis. It is also important (particularly for the change, with increasing A, from nucleation to dispersal) whether land is held individually or with rights assigned by the community. Someone tied to a block of working land near the edge of the town's territory (rather than working in a number of dispersed plots) might go to live by it, initiating the disappearance of the town more readily than under a system of communal or dispersal tenure. Whole communities adopt drastic change, in general, less quickly than individuals.

In the language of catastrophe theory (cf. Chapter 18, this volume), we have a spectrum of possibilities ranging between the extremes of *Maxwell convention* and *perfect delay*. It is perfectly clear, however, that no reasonable dynamic which most of the time keeps F *at least* locally optimal, for F of the shape we have derived, can give *gradual* change between dispersed and nucleated settlement. (For no value of A in Figure 19.7 does any maximum lie between R_{min} and R_t.) We have shown that hypotheses which should be satisfied by a wide range of detailed models imply sudden change as a consequence of smooth variation in local factors such as climate or soil, or of endogenous or diffusion-carried smooth change in agriculture. Ethnic hypotheses "multiply entities beyond necessity" in the words of Occam's razor, unless supported by other types of evidence. (Notice that the general character of the model gives a particular "natural size" for nuclei, for a given homogeneous environment and aggregation–benefit curve S. This supports, in a not entirely circular fashion, our original hypothesis of roughly equal settlements and territories. A more sophisticated approach, with one or another more detailed model of the economic dynamics, could well generate this homogeneity as a theorem instead of a hypothesis. Such models tend to be hard to solve analytically, but computer studies would be interesting.)

Suppose, on the other hand, that conditions vary in space (e.g., if the culture is established in a wide plain across which soil fertility smoothly varies) but are steady in time. One would expect the boundary between an area of nucleation (where soil fertility is high, A low) and an area of dispersal to settle to a smooth curve along which A takes the equal-benefit value A_3, since people near this curve and in less than absolute optima would have the example of the better way nearby.

Variation in the Perceived Benefits of Aggregation

So far we have considered a fixed curve of benefits of aggregation, S, against R (Figure 19.4). This of course, implies a maximum possible value of S, which we shall call T: the value to which S tends as R increases.

In practice, however, the scale of the benefits curve will vary from culture to culture as well as with time (accompanied by social and technical change) within a single culture. For instance, if craft technology develops, and with it more sophisticated production techniques, specialists may require a wider market to dispose of the wares which, at maximum efficiency, they are producing. Equally, religious developments may take desirable and effective gatherings of a greater number of participants—or, conversely, domestic cults may be accentuated, with a turning away from group assembly, and a consequent fall in the scale of the saturation curve. The developments need not necessarily imply a change in the *shape* of the saturation curve, but simply in the value of T, the saturation value of S, and consequently in the value of N (and of R) at which S begins to show saturation effects in approaching the level T (Figure 19.10).

We now have curves approaching saturation values T_1, T_2, T_3 with points of inflection at R_1, R_2, R_3 as marked, representing the form of S as it grows through time. The initial assumptions of positive dS/dR at R_{min} and of a one-humped derivative remain unaltered. The hypothesis has been added that for low T the hump is at a value of R less than R_{min}, whereas for high T it moves into the domain of R greater than R_{min}. Thus hypothesis 1 is satisfied only for large T. Under these conditions the behavior is described by Figure

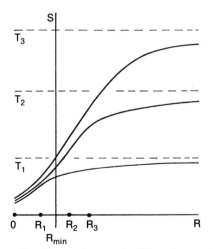

FIGURE 19.10. *Assumption: The maximum value (T) on the curve for benefits of aggregation (S) against territorial size (R) can vary.*

19.11. There is bimodality for (A, T) in the region M. The usual cusp divergence is seen: Slightly higher or lower A, as T increases, can give the "steady growth of towns" as T increases or "no change." The behavior with a fairly large and (even approximately) constant value of T is precisely that described in the preceding section, except that small variations of T may cause corresponding variations in the positions, though not the geometry, of the catastrophe points.

We can now follow several trajectories and grasp the relationships which result in sudden change in R. Take first time t_1 (point 1), with a relatively high value for A and low value for T. R is initially constrained to take on the value of R_{min} which corresponds to maximal dispersal. As A decreases, R begins to increase, taking on an intermediate value corresponding to settlement in medium-sized villages (point 2).

Social developments, reflecting either a limited measure of craft specialization within the settlements or increased adherence to a communal religious cult, lead to an increase in T (point 3). But now the agricultural system is obliged to make use of more labor-intensive methods, perhaps through a decline in soil fertility through overexploitation. This moves the control point, and hence the stable value of R, toward the edge of the fold (point 4). Slight further increase in A brings it to the catastrophe set, and there is no longer an even locally optimal large value of R, and an optimising dynamic must make it fall abruptly (point 5). At this stage the settlement pattern undergoes a striking change, from nucleated to dispersed. Settlement

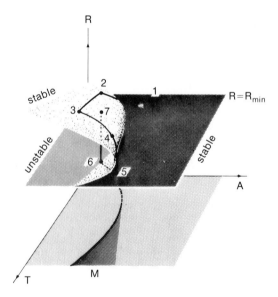

FIGURE 19.11. *Catastrophe surface giving the values of R for which total benefits will be a maximum (or minimum) for different values of A and T.*

fission occurs. (Again, less than a perfect delay could make it occur earlier, but the suddenness is independent of this.)

This is the phenomenon that looks so striking in the archaeological record, that a sudden exogenous change is usually adduced to account for it. On the other hand, a reduction of A, perhaps through some innovation such as the improvement of transport, coupled with any moderate change in T (in the diagram, a decrease), can take us to point 6 where the local optimum at R_{min} disappears. Settlement fusion takes place with the integration of the population of several dispersed units into larger settlement nuclei at point 7. This is a process related to that of urbanization, but one which *ex hypothesi* does not result in any hierarchy of settlement. The discussion so far assumes that the form of the saturation curve S remains as originally postulated in the preceding section. The situation may not, however, remain as simple as that.

If an advantage of a new kind becomes prominent (Figure 19.12), Figure 19.7 may be replaced by a picture like Figure 19.13, with two locally optimal nucleation sizes co-existing for some values of A. Even if less than absolutely

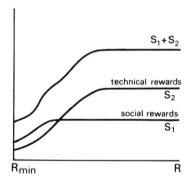

FIGURE 19.12. *A more complicated saturation curve for S against R than that assumed in Figure 19.4 is possible: The saturation curve is here the sum of two simple saturation curves.*

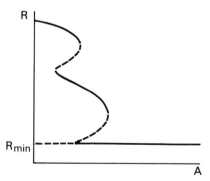

FIGURE 19.13. *The assumptions of Figure 19.12 give a settlement pattern with two locally optimal nucleation sizes coexisting for some values of A.*

optimal in internal economics, some town of the larger size could easily be stabilized by the addition of even a fairly minor central place function, and we would see a well-defined two-tier size structure.

Such richness of possibility means that elaboration of the general theory beyond this point requires close analysis of the economics of particular cases. The more complex a model becomes, the more justification is needed from data and subsidiary theories for its hypotheses, and the harder it is to test its conclusions.

Thus far we have treated the benefits of aggregation as a function S of R. But it is directly a function of population $N \sim R^2B$, so that if the density B increases the same benefits become available for smaller R. At the same time, a denser population must usually farm more intensely, which increases A—perhaps enough to exceed the new value of A_2, particularly if the law of diminishing returns becomes important. If there is still a locally optimal nuclear settlement, it will be a town of roughly similar population to before, but farming more intensively a smaller territory. Suppose that this optimum is pursued (rather than, say, the population pressure resisted by abortion, infanticide, or folk contraception). As the existing towns thus draw their skirts in, the excess population settles in the resulting gaps. Since this involves new housing location choices, new nuclear or dispersed settlement is likely to emerge according to strict maximization of F, after notable fluctuations. If the optimum found is dispersed settlement, it can act as an example to bring about the dissolution of the towns. Thus an end to the more obvious relics of human occupation may easily be associated with an *increase* in population density.

What is the role of catastrophe theory in all this? The preceding four sections did not use any calculus beyond a British syllabus for 15-year-olds, so where is the deep mathematics of Thom's celebrated theorem? (We could appeal to the deep machinery to establish that the model is *structurally stable*, and hence that small perturbations of P and S do not alter its topological features. But for the features of interest here, this is clear by far more elementary reasoning and for larger perturbations.)

First, it is the kind of argument exposure to catastrophe theory leads one to think up. Given the *topological* hypotheses (1) and (2) argued for earlier, and the supposition that the dynamics will not permit a long stay in a state that is not near at least a local maximum for F, a topological conclusion rigorously follows: transition between dispersed and nucleated settlement cannot be gradual. One can argue as precisely from qualitative assumptions valid in numerous cases as from quantitative ones which hold, approximately, in rather few, and catastrophe theory teaches this kind of thinking.

Secondly, the recognition of the fold catastrophe in Figures 19.7 and 19.13 means more than yet another confirmatory instance cf the almost omnipresence predicted by Thom's theorem. The data here do not allow a test of the consequences of its possessing in some coordinates a particular canonical local algebraic form, as they do for the rainbow and for ecological frontiers (see Poston and Stewart 1978), which is a pity. But the useful point is precisely that here is something that catastrophe theory makes familiar. The tendency in many theories to cling to convexity hypotheses (however unrealistic) which guarantee a unique optimum stems from the feeling that outside that well-tilled mathematical clearing is a jungle full of maneating plants, beasts with seven heads, and unclassifiable monstrosities generally. Catastrophe theory provides a taxonomy of the phenomena to be expected, at least within certain broad categories, and one can go into the jungle as a systematic botanist rather than a mythic hero seeking the chimera.

Finally, this example has led to developments in the mathematical theory itself, with implications beyond any one science, discussed in the following section.

Constraint Catastrophes

The point in the original model at which increasing A leads to the dissolution of towns (supposing delay convention) is recognizable as an example of Thom's *fold catastrophe*. But the catastrophe by which dispersal becomes a utility minimum (so that nucleation should occur) corresponds to nothing on Thom's list. It is nevertheless something that can stably, "typically" occur with one control variable, as a little thought makes clear. Since Thom's theorem is supposed to list "everything that can stably occur with up to four controls," have we found a counterexample? In reality our example could be in contradiction only with the most naive account of the theorem derived from popularizations. By its hypotheses, Thom's theorem describes singularities typical on a domain without boundary, and thus does not apply to our example where a smooth function may have an *extremum* at R_{min} without having *zero gradient* there. Indeed, to have both is unstable; Figure 19.14b may easily be perturbed into Figure 19.14a or 19.14c, distinct from 19.14b and each other.

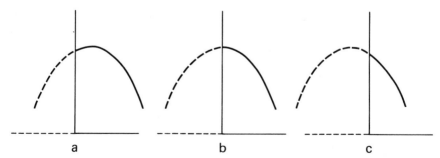

FIGURE 19.14. *Constraint catastrophe: The simplest catastrophe in the presence of a boundary.*

However, precisely the same mathematical techniques that yield Thom's list for the "interior" case may be applied in the presence of a boundary. Stimulated by precisely this case, the necessary algebra for finding standard forms to which such boundary phenomena may typically be reduced with any given number of control variables has been worked out (Pitt and Poston n.d.). This classification in turn led to explicit recognition of the geometrical form in Figure 19.11 (and its dual, with the same shape but maxima and minima interchanged) as among the four stable phenomena in codimension 2 added to the cusp (and *its* dual) of Thom's list, when boundaries are considered. Its relevance to the settlement analysis then became clear.

Such boundaries are evidently omnipresent in the social sciences (incomes cannot be below a certain level without removing people from the system, and certainly not negative; transport systems can carry only so much; dairy herds have positive numbers of cows; and so on), and not uncommon in the physical sciences. Indeed, a transformation assuming certain symmetries gives exactly Figure 19.11 for intensities in a phonon-assisted laser transition. The mathematical techniques for finding coordinate transformations to reduce particular examples to standard form, proving stability statements, finding when stability is "typical", and the like are very much as for the established theory, with technical differences in the results. (For instance, the list of possibilities becomes infinite, and stability no longer typical, with four controls instead of six.)

More discussion of these geometries may be found in Poston and Stewart 1978 (canonical polynomial forms are listed in Table 1 for up to three controls) and Pitt and Poston (n.d.); too much space in establishing vocabulary would be needed here. The important general point is that one should not be misled by the extent to which the statement of Thom's theorem appears simpler than its proof. It remains a mathematical theorem, that is to say a relation between certain hypotheses and certain conclusions. It is not necessary to know the connection—that is, the proof—in rigorous detail to apply it, but *some* understanding of the thinking involved is needed for a clear perception of what the hypotheses and conclusions actually are. Otherwise one may be tempted (as may be abundantly documented) either to claim conclusions that do not hold or to misunderstand and attack conclusions that do. Indeed, although there are a number of papers claiming to "apply Thom's theorem" that contain substantial mistakes, none are so wholly in error as the "critique" of Sussmann and Zahler (1977), summarized by Zahler and Sussmann (1978). For a refutation of their main claim of systematic mathematical error, see Poston 1978.

Likewise, one may miss opportunities to apply Thomist methods validly (as we would claim, given our hypotheses, to have done earlier) in conditions such as the presence of a boundary, or symmetry, or more general dynamics, which make unthinking application of Thom's *Theorem* inappropriate. Without some, even nonrigorous, notion of why such claims should be true (a bare minimum is probably represented by Poston and Stewart 1978), attempts to apply them look rather like applications of the multiplication table by someone not quite sure about what multiplication is. Suitably rephrased, however, the basic ideas of the arguments show as far closer to the traditional mathematical thinking of the sciences, and hence more accessible to the nonspecialist, than either technically rigorous presentation or complete popularization has tended to suggest.

Settlement Location and Catastrophe Cascades

A closely similar approach to the preceding may be applied to the question of settlement location. Let us now consider settlements no longer in a homogeneous plain but in a landscape with an altitude range. The land in the valley bottom is the most agriculturally productive, and that high up the slopes is less so. Let x now be the distance of the settlement from the riverside at the valley bottom, transverse to slope. The relation of P, productivity, to x is as seen in Figure 19.15. At the same time, there are rewards to be had from a defensible location, and defensibility also varies with x (Figure 19.16). This situation, which may in part describe the situation in the Plain of Drama mentioned earlier, would in practice be complicated by other factors, such as the convenience of access to upland pastures. The parameters will vary through time, and it is possible that the value of P_a might decrease through overexploitation of the more fertile arable land. At the same time the value of D_a might increase if population reached the carrying capacity of the region, resulting in competition between communities for land, or indeed if that carrying capacity were decreased through reduced productivity. It is not necessary here to make reference to the threat of hostility from forces outside the region: hostility between neighboring communities is itself sufficient to make very real the benefits of a defensive situation.

Once again, the curve of benefit against distance may be treated for first analysis as the sum of these two factors;

$$F(r) = P(R) + D(R)$$

It should be noted that this analysis is comparable to that put forward by Wagstaff (1978) where our benefit (D) is equivalent to "attractiveness," and Wagstaff's distance variable x relates to location within a region.

Again, examination of appropriate curves shows that there is no reasonable way for the community to drift gradually up the hill. The defensive advantages of a hill site are more obvious before a move than the economic benefits of aggregation discussed earlier, so one would expect a jump closer to the time at which the hill comes to represent an absolute utility maximum.

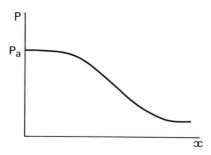

FIGURE 19.15. *Variation in productivity of land (P) against distance from valley bottom (x).*

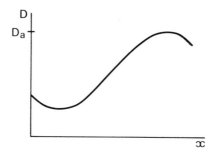

FIGURE 19.16. *Variation in defensibility (D) against distance from valley bottom (x).*

This is difficult to test ("threat perceived" by long-dead communities, which affects the value attached to defensibility, is hard to measure), but again we have a clear prediction of a sudden change at *some* point, easily produced endogenously by smooth variation of local factors which one expects to change with time. Again, hypotheses of outside influence require separate evidence, as does any claim that such influence was sudden.

It is worth remarking that the identification of "sudden" with "exogenous" is common also in areas of social interaction where data are far less sparse than in archaeology. It is particularly popular with those in authority. No revolt, whether of slaves, prisoners, students, or parliamentarians, is complete without claims of "outside agitation." Where these have any merit at all, the outsider often acts like an ice crystal in supercooled water, triggering rather than causing the phenomenon. Anyone who has tried to bring about rapid change in a social group not in such a metastable state will agree that to transform it requires at least what traditional archaeology has often assumed for all cases: an army. History is full of cases where a *successful* invasion made remarkably little difference to the basic social structure.

Cascades

In any real situation, a number of different problems have to be solved simultaneously. For instance, size and location of settlement will be governed by the two sets of arguments outlined here, in addition to others. Discontinuous behavior arising from continuous change in the variables in one of these frameworks can radically affect the variables in the other.

To take a hypothetical example, let us imagine that developments in craft specialization, such as the inception of metallurgy, increased the potential rewards of living in nucleated settlements. Metal tools and weapons could most efficiently be produced by full-time craft specialists supported by agricultural members of the community, which would thus have to be large enough in scale to make this economically viable. (Alternative devices, such as traveling craftsmen, could of course be introduced as in prehistoric temperate Europe in the Bronze Age, but that does not negate the validity of the argument.) The gradual development of this technology could produce a shift to nucleated villages or townships as described in the section on the dynamics of change.

We must now imagine settlement in the valley bottom undergoing rapid transformation from dispersed to nucleated. But this very change in the size of settlement unit will immediately affect the rewards of defensibility D in our second discussion. For D, the rewards of effective defense, must increase as the capital value of the facility defended (the settlement) increases. If portable material wealth per capita, in the form of metal objects, and stock value per capita, in the form of the installation for producing these, increase, so do the rewards of effective defense.

A sudden shift in settlement size is in this way likely to shift the maximum of the benefit curve for location. In the archaeological record the two changes will occur almost simultaneously, thus increasing the appearance of drastic change and the likelihood of an explanation in terms of sudden outside influence. Just such changes as these are observed in the Cycladic Islands of Greece at the end of the third millennium BC, and an explanation in terms of external agencies has been offered. But a cascade of catastrophes, the state variables of one acting as control variables of the next so as to produce a sequence of changes—a domino effect, to use the political jargon of the 1960s—will often result when the variables are coupled in a network of feedback systems.

In this chapter we have deliberately concerned ourselves with independent, autonomous communities, ignoring the interactions between them. In particular, the "towns" have not been allowed to act as central places for the dispersed settlements: There has been no settlement hierarchy. Such an approach seems appropriate when considering *le semis fondamental du peuplement* (Brunhes 1920), the variation between nucleated and dispersed settlement in rural communities. But to approach the problem of hierarchically ordered settlement systems within the same framework, it will of course be necessary to relax this assumption so as to deal with the central place functions of the larger settlements, and the flow to them of agricultural produce from the smaller ones which sustain them. We hope that the discussion of rural settlement given here prepares the ground for such a treatment.

References

Allan, W., 1972, Ecology, techniques and settlement patterns, in Ucko P. J., Tringham, R. and Dimbleby, G. W. (eds.), *Man, Settlement and Urbanism*. London, Duckworth, 211–226.

Aurousseau, B., 1920, The arrangement of rural population, *Geographical Review,* 1920.

Binford, L. R., 1968, Some comments on historical versus processual archaeology, *Southwestern Journal of Anthropology* 24, 267–75.

Bray, W., 1972, Land use, settlement patterns and politics in prehispanic Middle America, a review, in Ucko, P. J., Tringham, R. and Dimbleby, G. W. (eds.), *Man, Settlement and Urbanism*. London, Duckworth, 909–26.

Brookfield, H. C. and Hart, C., 1971, *Melanesia*. London, Methuen.

Brunhes J., 1920, *Geographie Humaine de la France* (Histoire de la Nation Francaise I). Paris, Plon.

Brunhes, J., 1952, *Human Geography*. London, Harrap.

Childe, V. G., 1950, *Prehistoric Migrations in Europe*. Oslo, Aschehoug.

Childe, V. G., 1957, *The Dawn of European Civilisation*. London, Routledge, 6th edn.

Chisholm, M., 1968, *Rural Settlement and Land Use*. London, Methuen, 2nd edn.

Clark, J. G. D., 1966, The invasion hypothesis in British archaeology, *Antiquity* 40, 172–89.

Demangeon, A., 1946, *La France: France Economique et Humaine* (Geographie Universelle, VI). Paris, Colin.

Doumas, C., 1972, Early Bronze age settlement patterns in the Cyclades, in Ucko P. J., Tringham, R. and Dimbleby, G. W., *Man, Settlement and Urbanism*. London, Duckworth, 227–30.

Emory, K. P., 1947, *Tuamotuan Religious Structures and Ceremonies* (Berenice P. Biship Museum Bulletin 191).

Flannery, K. V., 1972, The origins of the village as a settlement type in Mesoamerica and the Near East, in Ucko, P. J., Tringham, R and Dimbleby, G. W. (eds.), *Man, Settlement and Urbanism* London, Duckworth, 23–54.

Forge, A., 1972, Normative factors in the settlement size of neolithic cultivators (New Guinea), in Ucko, P. J., Tringham, R. and Dimbleby, G. W. (eds.), *Man, Settlement and Urbanism*. London, Duckworth, 363–76.

Garner, B., 1967, Models in urban geography and settlement location, in Chorley, R. J. and Haggett, P. (eds.), *Models in Geography*. London, Methuen, 303–360.

Gimbutas, M., 1965, *Bronze Age Cultures in Central and Eastern Europe*. The Hague, Mouton.

Goody, J., 1967, *The Social Organization of the LoWiili*, Oxford, International African Institute.

Groube, L. M., 1967, Models in prehistory: A consideration of the New Zealand evidence, *Archaeology and Physical Anthropology in Oceania* 2, 1–27.

Harris, D. R., 1972, Swidden systems and settlement, in Ucko, P. J., Tringham, R. and Dimbleby, G. W. (eds.), *Man, Settlement and Urbanism*. London, Duckworth, 245–62.

Hodder, B. W., 1962, The Yoruba rural market, in Bonhannan, P. and Dalton, G. (eds.), *Markets in Africa*. Northwestern University Press, 103–117.

Lanting, J. N. and van der Waals, J. D. (eds.), 1976, *Glockenbecher Symposium Oberried 1974*. Bussum, Fibula.

Morton-Williams, P., 1972, Some factors in the location, growth and survival of towns in West Africa, in Ucko, P. J., Tringham, R. and Dimbleby, G. W. (eds.), *Man, Settlement and Urbanism*. London, Duckworth, 883–90.

Neustupny, E., 1976, Paradigm lost, in Lanting, J. N. and van der Waals, J. D. (eds.), 241–8.

Pavelčik, J. 1973, Befestigte Industriezentren der Träger der Badener Kultur und ihr Platz in der gesellschaftlich-ökonomischen Entwicklung des ostlichen Teiles Mitteleuropas, *Musaica* XIII, 41–50.

Pitt, D. H. And Poston, T., n.d., Determinacy and unfoldings in the presence of a boundary.

Poston, T., and Stewart, I. N., 1978, *Catastrophe Theory and its Applications*, Pitman, London.

Poston, T., and Wilson, A. G. 1977, Facility Size vs. Distance Travelled; Urban services and the Fold Catastrophe, *Environment and Planning A*, 9, 681–686.

Poston, T., 1978, On deducing the presence of catastrophes. To appear in *Mathématiques et Sciences Humaines*.

Renfrew, C., 1969a, Trade and culture process in European prehistory, *Current Anthropology* 10, 151–69.

Renfrew, C., 1969b, The autonomy of the south-east European copper age, *Proceedings of the Prehistoric Society* 35, 12–47.

Renfrew, C., 1971, Sitagroi, radiocarbon and the prehistory of south-east Europe, *Antiquity* 45, 275–82.

Renfrew, C., 1974, British prehistory, changing configurations, in Renfrew, C. (ed.), *British Prehistory, a New Outline*. London, Duckworth, 1–40.

Russell, J. C., 1958, Late Ancient and mediaeval population, *Transaction of the American Philosophical Society*, New Series, 48 part 3, 1–152.

Shennan, S., 1976, Bell Beakers and their context in Central Europe, in Lanting and van der Waals, 231–40.

Shennan, S., 1977, Bell Beakers and their context in Central Europe; a new approach. Unpublished Ph.D dissertation, University of Cambridge.

Skinner, G. W., 1964, Marketing and social structure in rural China, *Journal of Asian Studies* 24.

Sterud, G., 1973, A paradigmatic approach to prehistory, in Renfrew, C. (ed.), *The Explanation of Culture Change*. London, Duckworth, 3–18.

Sussmann, H. J., and Zahler, R. S., 1978, Catastrophe Theory as applied in the social and biological sciences: A critique, preprint Rutgers University, *Synthèse* 37, 117–217.

Theochares, D., 1973, *Neolithic Greece*. Athens, National Bank of Greece.

Vivian, R. G., 1970, An inquiry into prehistoric social organization in Chaco Canyon, New Mexico, in Longacre, W. A. (ed.), *Reconstructing Pueblo Societies*. Albuquerque, University of New Mexico Press, 59–83.

Wagstaff, J. M. 1978, A possible interpretation of settlement pattern evolution in terms of "catastrophe theory", *Transactions of the Institute of British Geographers*, 3, 165–178.

Zahler, R. S., and Sussmann, H. J., 1977, Claims and accomplishments of applied catastrophe theory, *Nature* 269, 759–763. (Also correspondence *Nature* 270, 381–384 and 658).

Zipf, G. K., 1949, *Human Behaviour and the Principle of Least Effort*. Cambridge, Harvard University Press.

20

E. C. ZEEMAN

A Geometrical Model of Ideologies

Introduction

How do we place different ideologies in relation to one another? In this question the word *place* implicitly calls for some form of geometrical answer. For instance, we might specify which ideologies are close to one another and which are further apart—in other words, impose some form of topological structure upon the set of ideologies. Alternatively, we might impose an ordering upon the ideologies, by specifying which of any pair was further to the left and which further to the right; in other words, we would be placing the ideologies along the traditional one-dimensional political spectrum running from left to right. This immediately raises the questions: Why a one-dimensional spectrum? Why should they be ordered at all? Why not a two-dimensional array? Or would not a multidimensional array be more appropriate in view of the evident complexity of sociology? Moreover, in the traditional spectrum the extreme left and extreme right seem in some ways to be closer to each other than either is to the center; does this mean that we ought to impose a metric upon the spectrum that bends it round into the shape of a horseshoe? And where does the ideology of anarchy fit into the spectrum? Why do some ideologies embrace revolution while others prefer evolution? We answer all these questions by means of a geometrical model using catastrophe theory (Thom 1975; Zeeman 1977), and based upon a notion of conflict between certain basic underlying aims. We compare the model with experimental measurements of Eysenck (1954). At the end of the chapter we discuss the dynamic aspects of governmental change envisaged by different ideologies.

463

Transformations:
Mathematical Approaches to Culture Change

Basic Aims

We take as basic underlying aims the four ideals of *liberty, equality, fraternity,* and *opportunity.* These aims are important ingredients of the ideologies of modern industrialized societies, and we suggest that they may probably be important in most societies. The first three comprise the slogan of the French Revolution, and we add the fourth because one of the main arguments for technological advance is that it will eventually provide everyone with the opportunity of fulfilling themselves. We must begin to clarify our usage of the words.

These four basic aims fall, to some extent, into two conflicting pairs, for there is an economic conflict between equality and opportunity, and a political conflict between liberty and fraternity, between political freedom and political power. Belonging to a fraternity may result in loss of individual liberty, whereas individual freedom without restrictions may be disadvantageous to society as a whole. Similarly, the seizing of opportunity by a few may produce an elite and the loss of equality by the rest, whereas insistence upon egalitarianism for all may deny opportunities to the able and the industrious.

Different individuals in a society will place different emphasis upon the underlying aims, and we suppose that this emphasis can be measured using two independent continuous parameters (a, b), each scaled to lie between 0 and 1. The parameter a is an economic parameter measuring the relative emphasis placed on opportunity versus equality. The parameter b is a political parameter measuring the relative emphasis placed on fraternity versus liberty, on political power as opposed to political freedom. Each individual's emphasis is represented by a point $p = (a, b)$ in the unit square, which we call the parameter space P (Figure 20.1). Summarizing our assumptions, we obtain

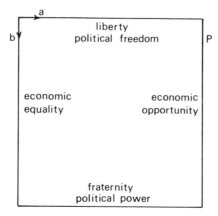

FIGURE 20.1. *The parameter space P.*

HYPOTHESIS 1. *Individuals can be plotted as points in P.* At first sight this hypothesis may appear too vague and oversimplified to be useful. However, in the section on the opinion space *X*, we shall allow for the complexity of all possible shades of opinion. Our eventual objective is to proceed through this complexity back to the simplicity of a surface *M* lying over *P*, upon which we can place the ideologies. The surface is illustrated in Figures 20.3 and 20.5, and contain a cusp catastrophe having *a* as normal factor and *b* as splitting factor. The surface in turn will further clarify our usage of the words.

Conflict Lines

The mathematical use of continuous parameters in the preceding section represents the possibility of gradual individual shifts of emphasis between the aims. We now want to introduce appropriate mathematical concepts to represent the additional idea of sociological conflict between the aims. First we introduce symbolic *conflict lines* L_1, L_2 in *P* to locate where the conflict lies, and then in the section on the shape of *M*, we shall enlarge these lines into conflict regions N_1, N_2 with specific mathematical definitions, sociological meaning, and potential measurability. There is no need to formulate a hypothesis about the conflict lines at this stage, since their purpose is merely to guide the location of our subsequent hypothesis about the conflict regions.

The first conflict line L_1 (see Figure 20.2) is a horizontal line running right across the square *P*, symbolizing the conflict between liberty and fraternity, between the individual and politics. The second conflict line L_2 is a vertical line running from the bottom of the square to a point *K* below the horizontal line; this symbolizes the increasing economic conflict between

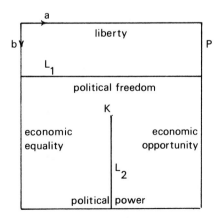

FIGURE 20.2. *Conflict lines.*

equality and opportunity under increasing emphasis upon political power, and the resolution of this conflict as sufficient emphasis is placed upon political freedom.

The Opinion Space X

The next objective is to plot the opinions of the individuals of a society in a multidimensional space X. We do this by means of the following thought-experiment which is not unreasonable since it is not dissimilar to actual experiments (Eysenck 1954). Send a questionnaire to all members (or to a representative sample) of the society. The questionnaire contains n questions about politics, such as what do you think about censorship, dissidents, free speech, freedom of travel, freedom to strike, free enterprise, unions, public ownership, comprehensive schools, and socialized medicine. The questionnaire should be appropriate to the society and its time, because what we want to find out is not the difference between different societies but rather the differences within each society that are common to all societies. Each question is phrased so that the answer can be plotted along an axis. For example we do not ask the bare question "Do you prefer A or B," but rephrase this as "Please indicate your position on the following scale":

Strongly prefer	Prefer	Neutral	Prefer	Strongly prefer
A	A		B	B

The number of questions, n, may be large, hundreds or thousands. The n axes define an n-dimensional space X, in which the set of answers of each individual determines a unique point x. Meanwhile Hypothesis 1 states that we can determine directly or indirectly, each individual's emphasis on the basic aims by means of a point p in the two-dimensional parameter space P. Therefore, each individual is represented by a point (p, x), which we call the opinion point, in the $(2 + n)$-dimensional space $P \times X$. We want to examine the shape of that great cloud of opinion points in $P \times X$, corresponding to all the different individuals in the society, and so we now introduce some hypotheses that will enable us to describe its shape.

HYPOTHESIS 2. *The distribution of opinion points follows a smooth probability distribution F on X parametrized by P.* In other words, for each point p in P, there is a probability distribution F_p on X such that the opinion points near $p \times X$ cluster near the maximum (or maxima) of F_p.

The sociological meaning of Hypothesis 2 is that communication between individuals who share a similar emphasis p upon the four basic aims will tend to bring their opinions closer together, and hence cause their opinion points to cluster sufficiently closely for the density to be approximately measurable by a smooth function, F_p.

HYPOTHESIS 3. *F is locally stable.* This is meant in the technical sense of catastrophe theory (Wasserman 1974). The mathematical justification for Hypothesis 3 is that locally stable F's form an open-dense set in the space of all F's (Markus 1977; Zeeman 1977). Therefore, any F given by experiment can be approximated arbitrarily closely by a locally stable F. Thus, within the margins of experimental error, there is no restriction in requiring F to be locally stable. Furthermore local stability ensures that qualitative properties of our subsequent constructions are robust, in other words, are preserved under sufficiently small perturbations of F.

The Surface M

Define $M = \{(p, x), F_p$ has a local maximum at $x\}$
$S = \{(p, x), F_p$ has a critical point at $x\}$

Here a critical point means a point x at which the slope of F_p is zero in any direction: It can be a local maximum, minimum, saddle point, or more complicated. Therefore,

$$M \subset S \subset P \times X$$

Let $\chi: S \to P$ denote the projection of S onto the parameter space P induced by the projection $P \times X \to P$. By Hypothesis 3 and the classification theorem for elementary catastrophes (Thom 1975, Zeeman 1977), S is a smooth two-dimensional surface in the $(n + 2)$-dimensional space $P \times X$; furthermore, the only singularities of the projection χ are fold curves and cusp points, and M is a subsurface of S bounded by fold curves.

The sociological significance of M is that it is the core of the cloud of opinion points. One should imagine the cloud as clustered about M, thinning out away from M, and thinning out near the boundaries ∂M of M. The more communication there is in the society, the closer will the cloud cluster about M, and the more significant will be the meaning of M.

The mathematical advantages of M are twofold: First it reduces the n-dimensional opinion space of X (which is impossible to visualize because n is too large) to a two-dimensional surface M, upon which we shall place the various ideologies, and which we shall be able to visualize as a whole embedded in three-dimensional space. Second, the limited nature of the types of singularity enables us to replace the abstract conflict lines given earlier by a more concrete hypothesis about the singularities.

The Shape of M

Suppose p is a parameter point on a conflict line. We translate the sociological notion of "conflicting opinions at p" into the mathematical notion of bimodality of F_p; in other words, we assume F_p has two local maxima, and so M is two-sheeted over a neighborhood of p. Now globalize this notion by assuming that F is bimodal over neighborhoods N_1, N_2 of the two conflict lines L_1, L_2, and is unimodal otherwise. We call N_1, N_2 the *conflict regions;* they are shown shaded in Figure 20.3. As we leave either side of a conflict region one of the two modes is preserved and the other has to disappear; we assume, further, that one of the modes is preserved on one side and the other on the other side. Therefore S has an S-shaped fold over N_1. Meanwhile L_2 terminates in the point K, and by Hypothesis 3 the only

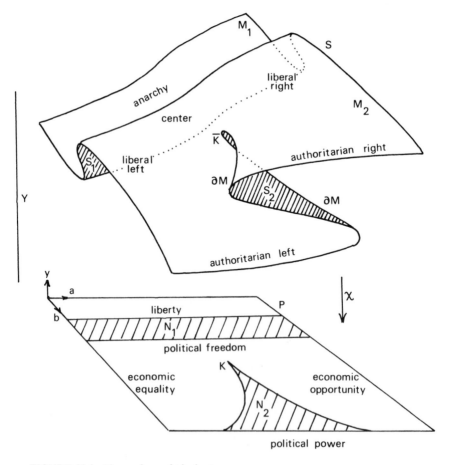

FIGURE 20.3. *The surface of ideologies.*

way an S-shaped fold can terminate is in a cusp (Markus 1977; Zeemon n.d.); therefore, S has a cusp singularity at K. Summarizing our assumptions and deductions into a single hypothesis we obtain

HYPOTHESIS 4. *The projection* $\chi: S \to P$ *has fold curves and a cusp singularity as shown in Figure* 20.3. The reader will observe that we have drawn S in Figure 20.3 as if it were sitting in three dimensions rather than in the $(2 + n)$-dimensional space $P \times X$. We justify this in a later section. Meanwhile notice that our discussion of folds and cusps is independent of the ambient space in which S happens to be sitting. The following deductions from Hypothesis 4 are also independent of the ambient space. M has two components M_1 and M_2, whose projections overlap on N_1. The projection of M_2 overlaps itself on N_2. The complementary subsurface $S-M$ has two components S_1, S_2 shown shaded in Figure 20.3, that project onto N_1, N_2; however, the components S_1, S_2 are sociologically meaningless because they represent saddle points of F, around which no opinion points cluster.

Remark. Hypothesis 4 appears to be far more drastic than Hypotheses 2 and 3. However, philosophically it is analogous to the conventional procedures of statistics. For, given a non-conflict-point p not in the closures of N_1 or N_2, choose a small neighborhood of p not meeting N_1 or N_2, and let m_p, v_p denote the mean and variance of the subcloud of opinion points lying above that neighborhood. Then the normal distribution with the same mean and variance is a candidate for F_p, and is unimodal at m_p. The way we have generalized this conventional statistical procedure is to introduce the parameter space P, so that as p varies in P the mean m_p traces out the surface M over P. The only subtlety we have allowed is to admit the existence of conflict regions above which the cloud splits in two, and where the bimodal average of two normal distributions gives a better fit than a single unimodal distribution. At the same time we have acknowledged the underlying continuity by requiring F to be smooth and locally stable. Of course with experimental data from a particular society it might be possible to give a better fit at conflict points by using a multimodal distribution, thereby making M multisheeted, and giving a finer resolution of ideologies; however, our objective is to present the simplest possible model consistent with the conflict lines of Figure 20.2, in order to discover qualities common to all societies. Therefore we have assumed the coarsest possible F with fewest possible modes, subject to the condition of having more than one mode on conflict lines. If we assume, further, that χ has the simplest possible bifurcation set, in the sense of having fewest components, cusps, and crossings, (namely 3, 1, and 0), then it can be proved (Zeeman n.d.) that χ is differentiably globally equivalent to the map shown in Figure 20.4. The logic of our development is rooted in our initial choice of the four basic aims; given the drastic oversimplification of Hypothesis 1, then Hypothesis 4 follows on naturally as a relatively mild addition.

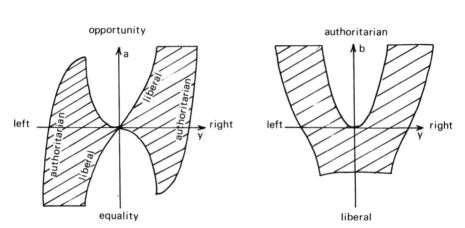

FIGURE 20.4. *Projection of* M_2 *onto the* (a, y) *and* (b, y) *planes.*

Ideological Interpretation of M

An ideology is an abstraction of ideas and opinions. In our model is would be nice to define an ideology as a connected region of the cloud of opinion points, except that strictly speaking a cloud of points cannot have "connected regions." However, M is the core of the cloud, and so let us define an ideology to be a connected open subset of M. Thus we can label the various sheets and different parts of M in Figure 20.3 with various ideologies: In this way we answer the question at the beginning of the chapter by "placing" the ideologies in relation to one another.

First observe that M has two components. The component M_1 represents opinions that place extreme emphasis upon individual freedom at the expense of society as a whole and tend to reject the ideal of government, and so we have labeled that sheet with the ideology of *anarchy*. The component M_2 represents opinions that admit the need of some form of government with varying degrees of emphasis, running from the *liberal* ideologies that place greater emphasis on the individual, to the *authoritarian* ideologies that place greater emphasis on the centralization of power. The liberals demand political freedom for the people, whereas the authoritarians demand political power for the representatives of the people.

The interesting feature of M_2 is its cusp singularity at the point $\bar{K}$ vertically above K. The question arises as to what the vertical axis in Figure 20.3 is. We shall deduce in the following section that the existence of the cusp (given by Hypothesis 4) implies the mathematical existence of a unique vertical axis Y (with vertical coordinate y). Therefore, Y must have sociological meaning. In fact it turns out to be none other than the traditional political spectrum, with the lower half corresponding to the political *left* and the upper half corresponding to the political *right*:

Authoritarian left	Liberal left	Center	Liberal right	Authoritarian right

y

We have deduced the existence of a one-dimensional spectrum of ideologies from our Hypotheses 1–4, but we must now justify our identification of it with the traditional political spectrum by deducing several consequences that agree with observation, and explain certain paradoxes.

1. There is a correlation between Y and the economic a axis: The left demands economic equality for the people; the right demands economic opportunities for the people; and the center demands equal opportunities for people. In fact "equal opportunities" often refers to education because as soon as people realize those opportunities they tend to be no longer equal.

2. When the left and right authoritarians are projected into Y they are furthest apart, but when they are projected into P they overlap—this explains the paradox of the apparent similarity of the extremes. Since the authoritarians overlap on the economic axis, there are some left-wingers who paradoxically place greater emphasis on opportunity, for instance certain intellectuals and managers, and similarly there are some right-wingers who paradoxically place greater emphasis on equality, for instance those who undertake responsibility for the underprivileged. The more authoritarian they are, the more the roles can be reversed. Paradoxically this enables each authoritarian ideology to transcend a greater range of economic emphasis than its liberal counterpart; hence it is liable to develop left and right wings within itself, as can be commonly seen in various authoritarian regimes today.

3. If M_2 is projected into the (b, y) plane as in Figure 4.20b, we obtain the anticipated horseshoe shape. Although the authoritarians may overlap on the economic a axis, nevertheless the empty interior of the horseshoe reveals that many opinions in X are inaccessible to them, especially those held by the center.

4. In a later section we shall discuss the dynamics of individuals changing their opinion. Changes of economic emphasis can cause conversions between left and right. Conversions of liberals may be gradual, but conversions of authoritarians are liable to be catastrophic. The more authoritarian, the longer the delay may be before conversion, the more dramatic it will be, and the more stable will be the resulting convert. Another interesting prediction of the model is that if the economic emphasis is kept fixed and the emphasis on political freedom is increased, then conversions between left and right can occur among those who are paradoxically placed in the sense

of item 2. On the other hand, if the emphasis on political power is increased this does not induce conversions, but tends to move individuals toward the extremes, and can induce divergence between liberals in the center who were previously close (Zeeman 1977, 17).

5. When we come to define Y, we find that the projection of M_1 onto Y is not mathematically uniquely determined and is therefore sociologically meaningless; in other words, the ideology of anarchy does not fit into the political spectrum. On the other hand, the projection of M_1 into P is meaningful, and this expresses the fact that in its emphasis upon liberty anarchy is closer to liberalism than to authoritarianism; but the most striking feature of anarchy is that it lies on a separate component, and is therefore disconnected from all other ideologies. As in item 2, we can have the paradox of a liberal placing more emphasis on political freedom than does an anarchist, and if that anarchist increases his emphasis on political power, he may be converted to an ideology more authoritarian than most liberals. The paradoxes all arise from the folds of S, which in turn arose from the bimodality of F, which represented the sociological conflict of opinion between the basic aims.

Embedding M in Three Dimensions

We now define the vertical axis Y and the mathematical embedding of M in the three-dimensional space $P \times Y$ illustrated in Figure 20.3.

By definition M is contained in the $(2 + n)$-dimensional space $P \times X$. The boundary ∂M_2 includes the fold curve containing the cusp point $\bar{K}$. Define Y to be the tangent to ∂M_2 at $\bar{K}$. The projection $P \times X \to P$ maps the line Y to the point K. Therefore, $Y \subset K \times X$. Let $\pi: K \times X \to Y$ denote orthogonal projection of the n-dimensional space $K \times X$ onto Y. Define $\pi: P \times X \to P \times Y$ by $\pi(p, x) = (p, \pi(K, x))$. At first sight π looks a very drastic map because it crushes hundreds of dimensions together, crushing the $(2 + n)$-dimensional space $P \times X$ down onto the three-dimensional space $P \times Y$. However, we have carefully arranged it so that π does not crush the two-dimensional tangent plane to S at $\bar{K}$. Therefore there is a neighborhood V of $\bar{K}$ in S which π embeds in $P \times Y$. Furthermore, since χ immerses (locally embeds) M_2 in P, π immerses M_2 in $P \times Y$. However, outside V this immersion might not be an embedding because where they overlap the upper and lower sheets of M_2 might bend together and intersect. We avoid this with another hypotheses:

HYPOTHESIS 5. *The immersion* $\pi: M_2 \to P \times Y$ *is an embedding.* Sociologically Hypothesis 5 is not unreasonable since it expresses a consistency between P and X. Y is the unique factor (the unique linear combination of answers to the questionnaire) that best detects the correlation between increasing bimodality and small shifts of emphasis toward more political power. Hypothesis 5 is satisfied if Y continues to register this correlation for large shifts of emphasis in the same direction.

We now turn to the anarchy sheet M_1. Although it follows from Hypothesis 4 that π embeds each of M_1 and S_1 in $P \times Y$, their images may intersect each other and may intersect the image of M_2; the folds on either boundary of S_1 may fold upward at some points and downward at other points. However, we can modify π on a neighborhood of $M_1 \cup S_1$ in S to give an embedding $\pi': S \to P \times Y$, whose image is similar to Figure 20.3, and whose composition with projection onto P continues to give $\chi: S \to P$ as desired. The penalty of such modification is that the composition

$$M_1 \xrightarrow{\pi'} P \times Y \xrightarrow{\text{projection}} Y$$

is no longer uniquely determined, and therefore sociologically meaningless. Therefore anarchy is not fitted into the political spectrum.

Experimental Testing

Since the projections of M_2 onto P and Y are sociologically meaningful, so also are the projections of M_2 onto the two vertical planes, the (a, y) plane and the (b, y) plane, as shown in Figure 20.4. We have rotated the projections so that the y axis now runs horizontally from left to right. One should think of the cloud of opinion points mapped down onto the shaded area, thinning out across the boundaries. Although we have drawn the shapes from the canonical cusp catastrophe, we would not necessarily expect M_2 to be canonical, and so we should expect the shapes given by experimental measurement to be deformations roughly preserving the quality.

It is interesting to compare Figure 20.4 with the experimental results of Eysenck (1954). Using the same axes as Figure 20.4b, Eysenck suggested that it would be a common sense hypothesis to place the spectrum of British political parties in a U-shape similar to our shaded area (1954, Figure 16, page 111), and his general experimental conclusions confirm this hypothesis (1954, 266, §4). What our model does is to give an underlying explanation of why it should be U-shaped.

When Eysenck comes to detailed experimental measurements of authoritarian versus liberal, he uses the James T-factor measuring tough-mindedness versus tender-mindedness. We suggest that the T-factor may in fact be correlated with our a axis measuring economic emphasis on opportunity versus equality, in which case our model predicts that the measurement of attitudes concerning various political issues could produce a distribution shaped like the shaded area in Figure 20.4a. Sure enough, Eysenck obtains such distributions (1954, Figures 23 & 27), and registers his surprise (1954,

170). Indeed it is a surprising shape unless one knows the classification of catastrophes and the geometry of the projections of the cusp catastrophe. At present statistical methods are biased toward linearity, and do not adapt readily to take account of the intrinsic nonlinearities that can occur stably in parametrized probability distributions.

Eysenck goes on to suggest a hypothesis that the T-factor is "the projection onto the social attitude field of a set of personality variables," but he does not explain the empty areas, why the variation in T-factor should be exhibited only by the extremists and not by the moderates in between. Our model unfolds his projection and explains the empty areas. The surface M_2 in effect predicts a subtle nonlinear correlation between the three variables a, b, y, which it would be interesting to test by a technique similar to Eysenck's experiment.

Dynamics of the Opinions of Individuals

We conclude the chapter with a discussion of some dynamic aspects of the model. So far the model has only been static; in the language of Zeeman (1977, 66) it has been at structure level 1. Dynamics enter in three ways: the dynamics of individual opinions, of governmental change, and of the ideologies.

First, since individuals may change their opinions, we should imagine the cloud of opinion points not clustered statically about M but more like a swarm of bees buzzing around M. A bee may sometimes pause on M, or crawl along M, or buzz around near M, or may sometimes make a relatively swift flight from one sheet of M to another. Some bees may exceptionally stray away from M, but the further away the smaller is the probability of finding any.

If an individual is gradually shifting his emphasis p between the basic aims, then his opinion point (p, x) will move correspondingly in $P \times X$, and will most likely follow M. If, however, p enters and crosses a conflict region, then as p leaves the other side of the conflict region (p, x) will cross ∂M and leave M; therefore the opinion x will become less and less likely unless the individual makes a catastrophic switch onto the other sheet of M, which represents the other mode of the conflict region. In other words, he will make large changes in many of his answers to the questionnaire because his previous answers have become inconsistent, representing an increasingly untenable position. For instance, as we have observed in the section on the ideological interpretation of M, a gradual shift of economic emphasis might cause an individual to switch between left and right. An individual may not necessarily wait until he reaches ∂M before switching: For instance, if p lies inside a conflict region, it is possible to switch from one sheet to another without changing p. An individual may do this for rational reasons: For instance, if he is minimizing a risk function based on gradually changing beliefs about future probabilities and gradually changing utilities, then he will switch his decision and opinions as the risk function crosses a Maxwell point (Smith, Harrison and Zeeman, n.d.).

Although the questionnaire may remain a valid test of opinion in a society for a decade or more, and although the resulting parametrized probability distribution F, and its modal surface M, may remain constant during that time, nevertheless we have incorporated into the model the volatility of individual opinions, the allowability of exceptional opinions, the permissibility of large or small, fast or slow, shifts in individual opinions, and the possibility of large-scale drifts of opinion across M. We now consider how such drifts may induce changes of government.

Dynamics of Governmental Change

In this section we discuss how the individual opinions in a particular society or country may affect its choice of government. Let μ be the measure on M defined by the density of opinion points, with $\mu M = 1$. If an ideology I is represented by an open subset I of M, then the voting strength of the ideology is μI. If a government is to be elected by democratic vote, then that ideology will gain power if $\mu I > \frac{1}{2}$. If the supporters of an ideology want to gain power, they can increase μI by either increasing μ or increasing I. Increasing μ means recruiting supporters by persuading individuals to shift their opinion point into I; increasing I means tolerating a greater variation of opinion within the ideology. The danger of too great a tolerance is that the ideology may then embrace contradictory opinions, which could weaken it and cause fragmentation into subideologies. We express this constraint mathematically by assuming that in $P \times X$ the center of mass M_I of I with respect to μ lies on M (or within the neighborhood of M defined by the standard deviations of the modes of F). For example, this would not be the case if I were to straddle both left and right extremes, for then m_I would lie in between two sheets of M.

Define $G_t = m_I$ if the government at the time t is controlled by the ideology I. As t varies the point G_t traces out a path G that describes the change of government. The path G may sometimes remain stationary for a period if, for instance, there is a fixed ideology controlling the government; or may move gradually if, for instance, the center of mass of that ideology is gradually shifting due to changing conditions; or may make a small discontinuous switch if, for instance, a nearby ideology wins an election; or may sometimes make a big catastrophic switch if, for instance, there is a revolution.

Changing political and economic perceptions in a society may produce very varied shifts of emphasis between the basic aims in different individuals, but at the same time may cause a gradual drift of the whole flock of opinion points in a particular direction across M, inducing the path G to follow in that direction. For example, an increasing density of population might induce a gradual shift of emphasis toward political power. Conversely, a movement of population to less populated regions might induce a shift of emphasis toward political freedom. A perception of increasing abundance of resources due to technological advance might induce a shift of emphasis toward economic opportunity. Conversely, a perception of increasing scarcity due to limited resources and population growth might induce a shift of emphasis toward economic equality. Although the general drift of opinion may be gradual, nevertheless the shape of M may force the induced path G to suffer catastrophic switches. In other words, the gradually changing conditions may produce a gradual shift of emphasis in individuals, which in turn may cause a sociological conflict of opinion and eventually induce catastrophic changes of government and social structure.

Dynamics of Ideologies

In this section we consider ideologies both within a society and transcending several different societies or countries. Each ideology within a society tends to envisage itself as an attractor for the path G. We must therefore model an ideology not only as a static subset I of M, representing a static subcloud of opinions, but also by a dynamic flow on M toward m_I, representing the dynamic conversion of recruits and the dynamic takeover of government. The geometry of the surface M gives an insight into the different types of dynamics embraced by various ideologies. Figure 20.5 illustrates the dynamics on M_2; we have omitted the anarchy sheet M_1 and the sociologically unimportant components of $S-M$.

The liberal ideologies envisage themselves as attractors of smooth flows, and therefore believe in evolution: The liberal left envisages an evolution from the liberal right, and vice versa. Both believe in gradual devolution from their authoritarian counterparts, devolving power from central to local government. For societies in which there are two dominant stable liberal ideologies, L and R say, we can define the majority of μ_t of L over R at time t by

$$\mu_t = \mu L - \mu R$$

The word *stable* in this context means that as time progresses μ_t oscillates between positive and negative, like the pendulum of a clock. If democratic voting is formally restricted to periodic intervals, then the path G will respond like the escapement of the clock, clicking back and forth between m_L and m_R. The stability of the system depends on the continuity of M between m_L and m_R, because this allows individual opinions to oscillate

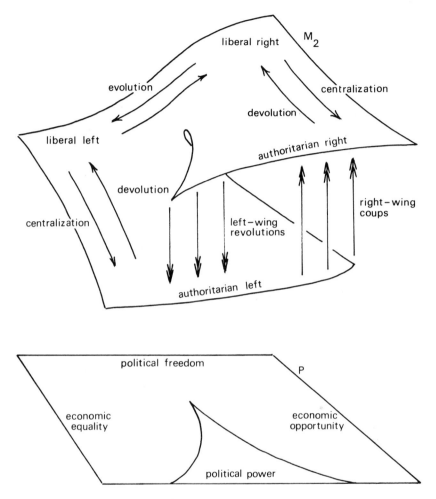

FIGURE 20.5. *Dynamics of ideologies.*

freely between *L* and *R* independent of the escapement, without constraint or catastrophic switches.

By contrast the authoritarian ideologies envisage themselves attractors of two quite different types of dynamic, one smooth and the other catastrophic. Both left and right authoritarians envisage a smooth evolution from their liberal counterparts by centralization and gradual accumulation of political power. At the same time each envisages the possibility of a catastrophic switch from the opposite extreme. Both agree that, given sufficient economic drift in their direction, and given a democratic vote, then this catastrophic switch would take place at the Maxwell point (Zeeman 1977,

306), as soon as the majority had swung in their favor. However, such upheavals resulting in large sociological change are usually resisted by the government in power, and so the catastrophe is liable to be delayed beyond the Maxwell point. The majority then argue that since the catastrophe will inevitably have come by the time G has reached the bifurcation point on ∂M, it is both sensible and justifiable to preempt the inevitable by the use of force. Thus the authoritarian left envisages a left-wing revolution to wrest power from the authoritarian right, and conversely the latter envisages a right-wing coup to wrest power from the authoritarian left. Once the principle of a catastrophic dynamic has been established as an integral part of the ideology, then it becomes logical for those who foresee an inevitable economic drift in their direction to use the revolutionary technique to anticipate the Maxwell point. Therefore after the revolution it becomes necessary to suspend democratic votes until the desired sociological changes have been effected, and the anticipated drift has caught up sufficiently to guarantee subsequent majority support. However, such practice is liable to induce a secondary drift of emphasis toward political freedom, and so authoritarians are obliged to incorporate into their ideologies a promised future devolution of power away from themselves, in order to recruit and maintain support. This places them in the paradoxical position of having to present themselves as simultaneously attractors and repellors of their own ideological flows: In principle they will eventually relinquish their power, but in practice they tend to entrench it. A good example is provided by Marxism. Marx and Engels (1848, 105) predicted in *The Communist Manifesto*:

> When, in the course of development, class distinctions have disappeared, and all production has been concentrated in the whole nation, the public power will lose its political character. . . . In the place of the old bourgeois society, with its classes and class antagonisms, we shall have an association, in which the free development of each is the condition for the free development of all.

Later Engels (1880, Vol. 19, 224) went further and coined the classic phrase:

> The state will not be abolished, *it will wither away*. (Der Staat wird nicht "abgeschafft," *er stirbt ab.)*

He predicted that after the transitional stage of the revolution (1884, 284):

> They [the classes] will fall as inevitably as they arose at an earlier stage. Along with them the state will inevitably fall. The society that will organise production on the basis of a free and equal association of the producers will put the whole machinery of state where it will then belong: into the Museum of Antiquities, by the side of the spinning wheel and the bronze axe.

In fact the authoritarian ideology appears to survive beyond the class structure, since in most Marxist regimes of today the state shows no signs of withering away but remains authoritarian; and like other authoritarian ideologies of both left and right, Marxism continues to embrace the revolution as a natural method of securing power, in contrast to the preference for evolution shown by most liberal ideologies. The appearance and disappearance of classes is a separate phenomenon that can also be modeled using catastrophe theory, but, we suggest, is a more transient phenomenon than that represented by the shape of M.

In summary, we propose that the shape of M and the dynamics on M are sociological invariants of human society, and that changing perceptions of population and resources may induce shifts of emphasis favoring particular ideologies at different times, but that there is no preferred dynamic on M—in other words, no historical law specifying some particular evolutionary sequence of ideologies to be more likely than any other.

References

Engels F., 1880, Die Entwicklung des Socialismus von der Utopie zur Wissenshaft, *Marx Engels Werke,* Dietz Verlag, Berlin, 1962.

Engels F., 1884, *The origin of the family, private property and the state,* Foreign Languages Publishing House, Moscow, 1954.

Eysenck H. J., 1954, *Psychology of politics,* Routledge and Kegan Paul, London.

Markus L., 1977, Extension and interpolation of catastrophes, *Proc. Symp. N.Y. Acad.* (to appear).

Marx K. and Engels F., 1848, *The Communist Manifesto* Penguin, London, 1967.

Smith, J. Q., Harrison P. J. and Zeeman E. C., n.d., The analysis of some discontinuous decision processes (to appear).

Thom R., 1975, *Structural stability and morphogenesis,* (Trans. D. H. Fowler) Benjamin, New York.

Wasserman G., 1974, *Stability of unfoldings,* Lecture Notes in Maths, 393, Springer, Berlin.

Zeeman E. C., 1977 *Catastrophe theory, Selected Papers 1972–1977,* Addison-Wesley, Reading, U.S.A.

Zeeman E. C., n.d., An extension problem involving cusps, (to appear).

21

COLIN RENFREW

Systems Collapse as Social Transformation: Catastrophe and Anastrophe in Early State Societies

The Mycenaean polity never really recovered from the onslaughts made on it at the end of the thirteenth century. The elaborate administration that had maintained its power disintegrated, its trade which was its life blood was disrupted and the fabric of its society decayed to an inglorious end. We are on the threshold of the Dark Ages.

Lord William Taylour
(1964, 178)

Introduction

Many writers in different areas have described, quite independently, the archaeological evidence in their region which clearly documents the sudden collapse of an early state society. Suddenly, and without any very obvious cause, a brilliant and flourishing society with a highly structured, central administrative organization disappears from the archaeological record. The immediate aftermath is always less clearly understood, because the range of archaeological evidence is much less adequate. Sometimes literacy is lost; always written records (if any) are notably fewer. The early state society fragments into a whole number of smaller units which (if they can be defined at all) are at a much lower level of sociopolitical integration. There is a decline in many activities, including craft-specialist production and trade, and often of population.

The overwhelming impression is one of discontinuity, and it is natural that in every case archaeologists have sought the cause of the collapse in some overwhelming cataclysm, either a natural disaster or a destruction through invasion. Yet, except in rare cases where a sudden natural cataclysm such as a volcanic eruption is evidently the cause, the precise explanation of the collapse remains elusive.

Further research generally shows that although the organizational structure did indeed disappear, there are elements of continuity with the succeeding period, the "dark age." Almost invariably the progress of research makes that Dark age less dark, and reveals a pattern of less highly structured

481

Transformations:
Mathematical Approaches to Culture Change

societies showing some of the organizational features recognized in the early developmental phases of the state society many centuries (or even millennia) earlier. Often the first, obvious explanation for the collapse, that it was brought about by the irruption of invaders or destroyers, proves difficult to substantiate. Frequently other monocausal explanations show themselves equally inadequate.

In each case the society has "relaxed" or "relapsed" organizationally with striking discontinuity, although continuity of certain other elements persists (usually, for example, there is no immediate language change). The collapse of central power is followed by competition among various small power groups inside the former territory and on its borders. The new central organization which in many cases develops in the same area often after a few centuries traces its origins back to one of these small groups. Indeed the new administration may seek to legitimatize its authority either by claiming direct lineal descent from the previous state, or alternatively by claiming to have overthrown it by heroic force of arms, a claim often all too readily accepted by later historians.

This scenario has deliberately been expressed in very general terms, and I think it will be recognized by archaeologists in many parts of the world. It seems to represent a rather general pattern, a type of change widely distributed in space and time among early state societies. It is this kind of diachronic pattern which I have sought to characterize (in Chapter 1 of this volume) as an allactic form.

Before giving specific examples, it may be worth setting down more precisely some of the very general characteristics which specific instances of this allactic form often display. It then becomes pertinent to seek an underlying explanation for these repeated patterns, and here catastrophe theory can help form our thinking. The following section owes much to a discussion by Adams (1973,22) of the Classic Maya collapse, and rather more to descriptions of the Mycenaean Dark Ages (e.g., Snodgrass 1971, Desborough 1975), like that which is quoted at the beginning of this chapter.

General Features of System Collapse

Collapse

1. Collapse of central administrative organization of the early state:

   a. Disappearance or reduction in number of levels of central place hierarchy

   b. Complete fragmentation or disappearance of military organization into (at most) small, independent units

   c. Abandonment of palaces and central storage facilities

    d. Eclipse of temples as major religious centers (often with their survival, modified, as local shrines)

    e. Effective loss of literacy for secular and religious purposes

    f. Abandonment of public building works

2. Disappearance of the traditional elite class:

    a. Cessation of rich, traditional burials (although different forms of rich burial frequently emerge after a couple of centuries)

    b. Abandonment of rich residences, or their reuse in impoverished style by "squatters"

    c. Cessation in the use of costly assemblages of luxury goods, although individual items may survive

3. Collapse of centralized economy:

    a. Cessation of large-scale redistribution or market exchange

    b. Coinage (where applicable) no longer issued or exchanged commercially, although individual pieces survive as valuables

    c. External trade very markedly reduced, and traditional trade routes disappear

    d. Volume of internal exchange markedly reduced

    e. Cessation of craft-specialist manufacture

    f. Cessation of specialized or organized agricultural production, with agriculture instead on a local "homestead" basis with diversified crop spectrum and mixed farming

4. Settlement shift and population decline:

    a. Abandonment of many settlements

    b. Shift to dispersed pattern of smaller settlements

    c. Frequent subsequent choice of defensible locations—the "flight to the hills"

    d. Marked reduction in population density

Aftermath

5. Transition to lower (cf. "earlier") level of sociopolitical integration:

    a. Emergence of segmentary societies showing analogies with those seen centuries or millennia earlier in the "formative" level in the same area (only later do these reach a chiefdom or "florescent" level of development)

    b. Fission of realm to smaller territories, whose boundaries may relate to those of earlier polities

    c.   Possible peripheral survival of some highly organized communities still retaining several organizational features of the collapsed state

    d.   Survival of religious elements as "folk" cults and beliefs

    e.   Craft production at local level with "peasant" imitations of former specialist products (e.g., in pottery)

    f.   Local movements of small population groups resulting from the breakdown in order at the collapse of the central administration (either with or without some language change), leading to destruction of many settlements

    g.   Rapid subsequent regeneration of chiefdom or even state society, partly influenced by the remains of its predecessor

6.   Development of romantic Dark Age myth:

    a.   Attempt by new power groups to establish legitimacy in historical terms with the creation of genealogies either (*a*) seeking to find a link with the "autochthonous" former state or (*b*) relating the deeds by which the "invaders" achieved power by force of arms

    b.   Tendency among early chroniclers to personalise historical explanation, so that change is assigned to individual deeds, battles, and invasions, and often to attribute the decline to hostile powers outside the state territories (cf. 5f)

    c.   Some confusion in legend and story between the Golden Age of the early vanished civilization and the Heroic Age of its immediate aftermath

    d.   Paucity of archaeological evidence after collapse compared with that for preceding period (arising from loss of literacy and abandonment or diminution of urban centers)

    e.   Tendency among historians to accept as evidence traditional narratives first set down in writing some centuries after the collapse

    f.   Slow development of Dark Age archaeology, hampered both by the preceding item and by focus on the larger and more obvious central place sites of the vanished state

Diachronic Aspects

7.   The collapse may take around 100 years for completion (although in the provinces of an empire, the withdrawal of central imperial authority can have more rapid effects).

8.   Dislocations are evident in the earlier part of that period, the underlying factors finding expression in human conflicts—wars, destructions, and so on.

9. Boundary maintenance may show signs of weakness during this time, so that outside pressures leave traces in the historical record.

10. The growth curve for many variables in the system (including population, exchange, agricultural activity) may take the truncated sigmoid form seen in Figure 21.1.

11. Absence of single, obvious "cause" for the collapse.

These criteria seem sufficient to document a social allactic form in much the same way as, for example, astronomers recognize that different stars in the sky are, on the basis of their short-term behavior, to be classed as supernovas. Likewise, vulcanologists classify volcanic eruptions on the basis of behavior through time as well as their geochemistry, into eruptive types, of which Plinian eruption is familiar to archaeologists for its destructive effects upon human settlement. It is claimed here that early state collapse ranks with supernova formation and Plinian eruption as an allactic form—all three classes of allactic form sharing a behavior of sudden change after a much longer period of quiescence.

It is interesting to speculate whether early state collapse may in some cases be cyclic in nature—as Plinian eruption is—while supernova formation is not.

Space does not allow different specific cases to be presented in detail. I hope to present elsewhere a consideration of the end of Mycenaean civilization in these terms. One feature that does emerge from such a comparison, however, is the remarkable extent to which not only the symptoms of the collapse are often comparable, but also the *explanations* which have been offered for them by scholars working quite independently in different areas (compare Sabloff 1973, 36 with Rhys Carpenter 1966).

Among specific cases that I would claim as instances of the more general allactic form whose characteristics have just been outlined are the following:

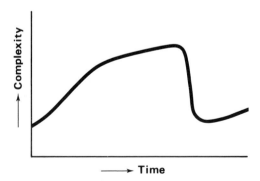

FIGURE 21.1 *System collapse: The sudden decline observed in several early state societies.*

1. *The Mycenaean civilization.* A paradigm case for a "Dark Age" in the Old World (see Desborough 1975, 663; Snodgrass 1971; Ålin 1962).

2. *The Minoan palaces.* Around 1450 BC, toward the end of the Late Minoan Ib period, nearly all major administrative sites in Crete, whether palaces or villas, were destroyed (Hood 1973; Marinatos 1939; Page 1970). Sometimes an explanation for this decline has been sought in the volcanic eruption of the nearby island of Santorini (cf. Ninkovich and Heezen 1965), but this simple explanation may not be sufficient. Invasion by mainland Mycenaeans is another recognized possibility, but there is at present little evidence to suggest whether this was immediately prior to or after the destruction of the Minoan palaces. Curiously the demise of Minoan civilization at this time, some three centuries before the Mycenaean quietus, has not often been treated together with the latter as an instance of systems collapse.

3. *The Indus Valley civilization.* The great cities of the Indus Valley civilization, notably Mohenjo-daro and Harappa, flourishing round 2000 BC, were destroyed some time around 1800 BC (Piggott 1950; Wheeler 1968; Allchin and Allchin 1968). The explanations offered focus either on some specific and radical environmental change or on the supposed invasion of Aryans from the north and west.

4. *The Hittites.* The Hittite empire of central Anatolia ended around 1200 BC. The great Hittite capital of Bogazköy was destroyed, other important sites such as Alaca and Alishar were likewise destroyed by fire, and in the central area of the empire, literacy ended (Akurgal 1962, 75). This pattern is conventionallly accounted for the the activities of Phrygian barbarians who "overthrew" the Hittite empire but whose military success diminished further south.

5. *Egypt: First Intermediate period.* At the end of the Sixth Dynasty of Egypt, "the central power was too weak and divided to hold back the surging tide of anarchy, and the civilization of the Old Kingdom was swept away with the political system which had created it (Aldred 1961, 100)." Literacy was, however, uninterrupted, and the continuity of Egyptian culture was not totally ruptured. This may therefore be a doubtful case of systems collapse, but the period is certainly seen as a Dark Age by Bell (1971).

6. *The Classic Maya.* The paradigm case for early state collapse in the New World. The whole subject has been reviewed in *The Classic Maya Collapse,* edited by Culbert (1973).

7. *Tiahuanaco.* There is evidence that the state organization centered on Tiahuanaco in the Titicaca area of southern Peru underwent a striking and perhaps sudden decline in the twelfth century A.D. The Wari empire of the Southern Highlands collapsed at about the same time, and pan-Andean unity dissolved into a series of regional traditions (Lumbreras 1974, 159; cf. Sanders and Marino 1970, 80). This may provisionally be considered a possible case of early state collapse.

8. *Other cases.* Collapse has been claimed for China in the "Warring States" period, and no doubt other cases can be documented. A rather different phenomenon, certainly related to system collapse as defined here, is the withdrawal of central, imperial power from a province of empire formerly held under strong military rule. Britain at the end of the fourth century AD offers a well-known example, and the "Dark Ages" of Britain conform in most respects to the description given earlier, although it is difficult to regard the collapse in Britain as entirely endogenous.

The discussion here focuses on the collapse of early states, where the similar trajectories followed constitute the allactic form which we have sought to define. But it is relevant to note that relatively sudden collapse seems to be a feature of other societies with a degree of centralized organization. One of the best documented and most interesting cases is the sudden decline of the Anasazi town sites in the southwestern United States in the thirteenth century AD (cf. Vivian 1970). Various cataclysmic explanations have been offered (Martin, Quimby and Collier 1947, 146), including "a great epidemic of some virulent but unknown disease." A multicausal explanation of the kind offered here for early state collapse may prove more satisfactory.

Stability and the Growth of Systems

Before turning, in the following section, to catastrophe theory, I would like to focus here on two very simple insights relating to complex societies. The first relates to hyperdevelopment, and the second to stability and growth.

Before the Crash: The Options Narrow

To adapt too well, too fully, and too effectively to present conditions may be to restrict the flexibility of response available to cope with a future change in those conditions. This is a truism of evolutionary biology, where high specialization can prove highly adaptive for a species in the short term but fatal in the long. Perhaps too it holds for many cases of system collapse.

In many early state societies there was a high degree of specialization among craftsmen and even among agriculturalists, coordinated by a central bureaucracy. Efficiency of production per capita was greatly increased by this specialization, but the price was a very high measure of interdependence. A craftsman (e.g., a potter) working full time could produce far more of his product and of far better quality than could five farmers each devoting one-fifth of his time to making the same product. In favorable conditions, then, it is very sound strategy for a society to maximize specialization through the agency of a central redistributive organization. In this way it is possible, through economies of scale, to support a very much larger population than would be the case if each individual family or village had to be largely self-supporting, producing all the commodities which it used.

The danger may come, however, if the external circumstances become less advantageous, so that it becomes difficult to support the existing population. The option of becoming less specialized is not open to the society or to its decision-making agency at the center. For although this would meet the change in external circumstances, it would mean a decrease in productive capacity, at least temporarily, and hence starvation for some of the community, which might in turn endanger the stability of the whole.

The only alternative is to increase productive efficiency by further increasing specialization. To specialize in this way, instead of to diversify, seems a natural homeostatic adjustment. If, however, external circumstances worsen, the situation may cross the homeostatic limits of tolerance of the system which simply cannot manage any longer and breaks down. That is to say that even further specialization and an increased work load cannot prevent a fall in production, with consequent starvation and perhaps unrest which will endanger the survival of the central bureaucracy.

Systems of this kind which, by virtue of their high specialization, depend heavily on the central bureaucracy to distribute the necessaries of life, are highly vulnerable. For if the central bureaucracy is disrupted and the distribution of products ceases, there is a sudden drop in efficiency and those specialists who are not actually producing food risk starvation. One imagines very much of this situation for the palace-centered polities of Mycenaean Greece, whose administrative archives have been preserved at Pylos and in part at other centers. The collapse of a central polity there might well prove irreversible, and there are special factors, such as the very long time needed to cultivate young olive trees before achieving effective production should the olive groves be destroyed, which reinforce this effect.

This phenomenon is what Rappaport (1978) has termed "oversegregation" or overcentralization, and is related to Flannery's (1972) "hypercoherence" or "hyperintegration." The system has adapted to existing diversity in the environment by specializing and centralizing: This makes it very effective for limited changes, but in the face of sustained change it may simply collapse.

Betancourt (1976) has written illuminatingly in similar terms about the Mycenaeans, and Willey and Shimkin (1973, 490) analyze the Maya collapse as follows:

> The success of the system produced growths of population and of competing centers which led to increasing rigidity in the system as it was subjected to internal stresses and external pressures. The system failed through inadequate recognition of these stresses and pressures and through inappropriate responses to them. The economic and demographic bases of the society were weakened; the consequences were the collapse of the

system, the decimation of the population, and a retrogression to a simpler level of sociopolitical integration.

It is worth noting that several "crash" phenomena in human society are of this general kind, where the only available response to a severe deficiency of strategy is to work more intensively at the same strategy. A sure way for a gambler to avoid loss may be to keep betting on the same number, doubling the stake at each throw. But if he is unlucky assets will run out before his number comes up. Stock exchange crashes are sometimes caused by an analogous "overheating" effect. The attraction to speculators of a rising index favors speculative buying, thus pushing share prices still higher. Profits can be realized only by selling: The price falls and the crash comes. The crisis of confidence which results in bankruptcy can arise when a financial organization becomes "overstretched" in a similar manner.

The Dangers of Zero Growth

For some human societies, stability (in the sense of peace and prosperity) is assured only by continued growth. Zero growth does not for them represent a stable state, and negative growth can accelerate to disintigration.

It is generally argued that stability and long-term survival in a system are assured through homeostasis. There is some resistance to any innovation, and such change as comes about is regarded as a response to outside stimuli, by way of a mininal adjustment to them. But when we are talking of culture change we are concerned with sustained growth, which somehow overcomes the negative feedbacks of the homeostatic controls. Sustained growth comes about through positive feedback effects, not only within individual subsystems but between subsystems—the multiplier effect (Renfrew 1972).

It is possible, therefore, to model growth by constructing a system with strong positive feedback loops which can outweigh in their effect the homeostatic, negative feedback loops (Cooke and Renfrew, chapter 14, this volume). Yet if there is an external factor tending to reduce growth or even induce negative growth, the rate of growth of the system may ultimately become zero. And a system with strong positive feedback loops and zero growth will usually be in an unstable or metastable situation, for a small negative growth will be reinforced during the growth phase and magnified, giving an increased rate of decline. A crash can easily be modeled in this way (see Hosler, Sabloff and Runge, 1977).

There are, moreover, indications that some subsystems of society can become adjusted to a steady positive rate of growth in such a way that this same rate can be peacefully sustained over a long period, whereas a reduction to a smaller (but still positive) rate will have disruptive effects. In many modern Western economies, for instance, a positive rate of growth is considered the norm, and if wage rates do not increase, in real terms, by a positive amount each year, there is dissatisfaction.

If a society is to adjust to zero growth after a prolonged period of positive growth, it must disconnect the positive feedback loops which made that growth possible. Such an adjustment may not be easy, and if it is not brought about, the multiplier effect may produce collapse. Bryan Feuer (1974) has fruitfully applied this model to the collapse of Mycenaean civilization.

The Cusp Catastrophe

A general description of the process of early state collapse can by given using the cusp catastrophe (Amson 1974; cf. Poston, Chapter 18, this volume; Thom 1975; Zeeman 1977). Limitations of space prevent a full discussion of the model employed, which has been concisely set out elsewhere (Renfrew 1978), but the outline is given here to sustain the new ideas in the two succeeding sections.

The sociopolitical system under consideration, the early state, can be described by a number of variables whose values represent the circumstances, the states, of its various subsystems. We shall choose a single variable, which could be one of these subsystem variables or some function of them, to represent in outline the general behavior of the system as a whole. Its value will change suddenly, for instance, when the system collapses.

For our model of early centralized society, we shall define this behavior variable, *degre of centrality D,* which is represented as a coordinate in the behavior space X. This is some measure of actual control of territory by a central authority through a pronounced hierarchical structure. High values will be reflected archaeologically by a hierarchy of central places, by insignia of kingship, by the maintenance of bureaucratic records, and by the other epiphenomena of state society. But degree of centrality refers as much to the software, the social reality, as to the hardware, the stock of palaces and temples. It can change rapidly, indeed no longer than it takes to cut a few throats. Indeed it should be thought of as some measure of the information-carrying capacity and effectiveness of the administration.

We visualize also a control space $C,$ or parameter space, as a horizontal plane with coordinates a and b. The choice of control variables is crucial to the model, as is a decision as to the number of control variables necessary. At first, to present the simplest possible example, the case with two control variables is chosen. Later four control variables are considered. The proposed control variables are $I,$ accumulated investment in charismatic authority, and $N,$ net rural marginality.

Charismatic authority refers to the structured organization in society which results in adherence to the polity which the center symbolizes. It is not a measure of popularity or belief but of the energy assigned to cultural devices used to promote adherence to the central authority. The second control variable, net rural marginality, relates to the economic balance for the rural population. On the income side of the account are the fruits of their agricultural or craft endeavor. On the debit side are the material contributions, in goods or labor, required of them by the central state authority as the price of citizenship and to escape punishment.

The idea of marginality is designed to give simultaneous consideration to productivity on the one hand, and the level of taxation or levy on the other. A given level of taxation may be entirely acceptable at one stage, but if productivity per capita decreases (perhaps through increase in population) the same burden is heavier to bear and marginality is high.

The notion of a model, of any explanation, implies that there is a relationship between the state and control variables, although we do not always need to know precisely what it is. We suppose that the evolution (the dynamics) of the system is governed by a family of functions f_c, $c \in C$, from the state space X to the real numbers: $f_c: X \rightarrow R$. To each point c contained in space C we have a real-valued function f_c defined on X, the state space, which we may think of as a generalized potential function. The stable states of the system under consideration are represented by maxima or minima of this function. In this case we may think of f_c as representing a measure of the viability or stability of the culture system. Another way of looking at this is to think of f_c as representing the "attractiveness" of the system for the given value of x. The main hypothesis required for a catastrophe theory treatment is that the system in general acts so as locally to maxmize f_c (when the function represents viability or attractiveness or benefit, or alternatively to minimize f_c when this is a potential function). The other important hypothesis is that of structural stability (genericity), discussed in detail by Thom (1975, ch. 3).

Let the graph M denote the maxima, minima, and so on, of f_c. We want to study the way these turning points of f_c change so we plot the set

$$M = \{(c, x) \in C \times X \mid X \text{ is a maximum, minimum turning point, etc., of } f_c\}$$

This is simply a graph: Given a point c in C we can read off the set of points in the manifold M lying over it, that is, any points x such that $(x, c) \in M$.

Thom's theorem, crudely paraphrased and assuming structural stability, states that if the number of control variables is no more than five, any singularity (or specially twisted region of the map which underlies the discontinuities in observed behaviour) is equivalent to one of a finite number of types called elementary catastrophes (Thom 1975; 9; Poston, chapter

18). In particular when there are only two control variables the only singularities of *M* are fold curves and cusp points.

The cusp catastrophe has the form seen in Figure 21.2. A discussion of its properties is given by Zeeman (1977) and Amson (1974), and is not repeated here. The attractiveness function has the form

$$f_c = \frac{1}{4}x^4 - \frac{1}{2}bx^2 - ax$$

For the manifold *M*,

$$\frac{\partial f_c}{\partial x} = 0,$$

so that *M* is the cubic surface in R^3 given by the equation

$$x^3 = a + bx$$

We can now use the properties of the cusp surface *M*, and in particular those of discontinuity and divergence, to help us grasp the anatomy of system collapse. For instance, if we start with high values of *a* and *b* (in control space *C*), the corresponding point in state space *X* is on the upper sheet of the cusp surface *M*. *x* has a high value. But if the value of *a* steadily diminishes, while *b* holds steady with a high value, the movement of the control point *c* in *C* brings the point (*c*, *x*) along this upper surface toward the

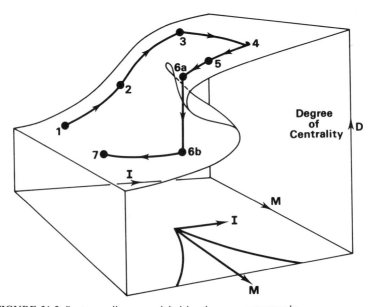

FIGURE 21.2 *System collapse modeled by the cusp catastrophe.*

edge of the fold. When c enters the area of C enclosed by the bifurcation curve B, there are two values of x for each pair of values (a, b) corresponding, respectively, to the upper and lower sheets of M. If the system *locally* maximizes f_c, it will stay as long as possible without sudden change (following the delay rule), that is, until c reaches the other side of the region of bimodal behavior, enclosed by the bifurcation set B. At this point there is suddenly only a single maximum of f_c, on the lower sheet of M, and x will undergo a sudden change of value. As a continues to decrease (if it does), change in x will now be smooth and steady again. It is this sudden change in x, corresponding to a discontinuous crash in the system, which represents for us the system collapse.

We therefore postulate a function $f_{I,M}(D)$ that expresses in some appropriate form the stability and viability of the system, reflected in the well-being of the rural population. The rural population, indeed the system at large, acts in such a way as locally to maximize the viability f, taking into account the various constraints implied by I and M. D, the degree of centralization, is here seen as reflecting the success or failure of the central authority in commanding or attracting the adherence of the rural population to the central system and hence ensuring its viability and survival.

Let us now follow a typical systems collapse time trajectory, as it might be for the Maya or Mycenaean civilization. The story starts at point one representing t_1. Marginality is low, and so is investment in charismatic authority. The degree of centrality is low. This is a prosperous noncentered society, which may well be egalitarian. I increases, through points t_2 and t_3, so that D increases: The state develops. But marginality is now increasing: It is no longer easy for the rural population to increase the per capita yield further in order to make the required contributions to the central administration. As population increases, or fertility decreases, or the tax burden is augmented, marginality now increases, with increase in I also to point 4.

But now the system is under stress, with high M, and I decreases slightly to point 5. There is now also a low value of D (on the lower sheet with the same values of I and M) for which efficiency is also a maximum. But the delay rule (representing the inertia of the system through its complex feedbacks) means that not until t_6, when the local maximum vanishes altogether, does the value of D change suddenly (point 6b on Figure 21.2). This very rapid change, the collapse of central government, will bring in its wake many other changes. In particular, the central personnel, no longer exercising control or imbued with the charisma that accompanies it, can no longer command I, the investment in charismatic authority. The instantaneous collapse of D (the rupture of centralized control) is followed by the rapid but slower diminution of I to point 7. The administrative population, with its specialist officials and craftsmen, either die or emigrate (or return to rural cultivation), and marginality is reduced (point 1).

This formulation, it should be noted, can take account of sudden changes in the external circumstances, caused for instance by a natural cataclysm, which can of course result in sudden changes in the control variables. These in turn may result in the catastrophic collapse of the system.

Acephalous and Centered Societies: Anastrophe

The cusp catastrophe model described in the preceding section was set up in order to seek some general explanatory formula for the very widespread phenomenon of system collapse. Like all models, however, it brings with it certain further properties and implications which were not envisaged in the initial formulation (Braithwaite 1953). These are themselves very interesting, and underline the fruitfulness of the approach.

Divergence

An important property of the cusp and higher order elementary catastrophes is bifurcation. If two systems start off at L with identical initial conditions (with identical values for the control variables and for the state variable), they can end up with identical values for the control variables yet in very different final positions M_1 and M_2 (with different values for the state variable D). The final value of D depends not only on the values of the control variables a and b at that point, but on the *past history* of the system, that is, on the trajectory between L and M. This is an important property of culture systems.

This property is illustrated in Figure 21.3. Two systems start off at point L. The first undergoes a slight increase in a (the normal factor) before being subject to substantial increase in b (the splitting factor); the second undergoes slight decrease in a before b increases. After the increase in b the value of a returns for each to the same initial figure. Yet one is now on the upper surface of the cusp surface, with high D, and the other on the lower, with low D. Of course if a were to decrease markedly, the first would undergo catastrophic decrease in D and both systems would again be in the same state. But there is no reason to expect this to occur. M_1 and M_2 are both stable states of the system or systems.

If now we consider a whole series of systems, starting off at or near L, with comparable initial conditions, as their subsequent varied histories, we can predict that some will end up on the upper sheet and some on the lower sheet. At a given time, if b should be low, they may show a fairly continuous distribution in terms of D (Figure 21.4, upper). But if b should be high, the distribution will be a bimodal one, with many on the upper sheet (high D) and many on the lower sheet (low D) and very few with intermediate values of D (Figure 21.4, lower).

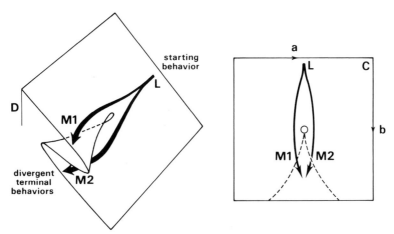

FIGURE 21.3 *Divergence: Two societies with analogous social organization which start off at the same starting point* (L) *can finish with centralized authority* (M₁) *and acephalous structure* (M₂), *respectively, in the same environmental conditions.*

Now returning to the variables used in the preceding section, we can imagine a number of separate polities in a given region in similar environmental conditions. Initially the population density is low and other factors may work to keep marginality low. Some of these polities will invest in charismatic authority to some extent, others much less so. As population increases, and perhaps other factors operate to increase marginality, a situation will develop in which some societies will show a pronounced degree of centralization, and others very little. If marginality is high, there

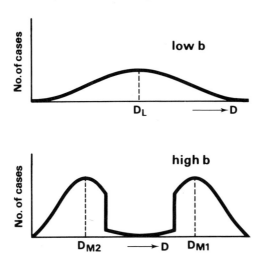

FIGURE 21.4 *Frequency distribution of social forms (variable* D, *degree of centrality) when splitting factor* b *is low (above) and high (below) as predicted by the cusp catastrophe (see Figure 21.3).*

will be few intermediate forms, although with low marginality the spectrum of centrality will be a continuous one.

It is interesting that this effect is precisely what some observers have recognized for traditional African societies. To quote Fortes and Evans-Prichard (1940, 5):

> It will be noted that the political systems described in this book fall into two main categories. One group, which we refer to as Group A, consists of those societies which have centralised authority, administrative machinery and judicial institutions—in short a government—and in which cleavages of wealth, privilege, and status correspond to the distribution of power and authority. This group comprises the Zulu, and Ngwato, the Bemba, the Banyankole, and the Kede. The other group, which we refer to as Group B, consists of these societies which lack centralised authority, administrative machinery, and constituted judicial institutions—in short which lack government—and in which there are no sharp divisions of rank, status or wealth. This group comprises the Logoli, the Tallensi, and the Nuer. Those who consider that a state should be defined by the presence of governmental institutions will regard the first groups as primitive states and the second group as stateless societies.

Some writers have sought to correlate the distinction with population density, and the foregoing analysis would tend to support the correlation, although it should be noted that population density is only one component of marginality, since environmental and social factors are also relevant. It has been argued recently that the distinction between group A and group B, between centered and acephalous, is very much an artifact of the observer, and that in reality the distribution is very much a continuous one. Inadequacies of observation or categorization by the anthropologist are not, however, to be ascribed to the model itself: It simply predicts that, given the underlying assumptions and with a fairly high marginality, there will be a bimodal distribution corresponding to societies of group A and group B.

One of the features of African political organization, however, which has particularly excited comment (e.g., Richards 1960) is that both centered and acephalous societies appear to exist in the same ecological region, often in close proximity, without apparent good reason to explain their coexistence or determine which form will be stable in a particular case. But this is exactly what our model predicts: that there should be stable states at M_1 and M_2, with a high and a low value of D, respectively, corresponding to centered and acephalous polities (high and low D) in precisely the *same* environmental conditions and indeed with certain similarities in their internal functioning (represented by the same values of a and b—in terms of our model of I and M).

Clearly this observation merits much closer study, but it is exciting that the model appropriate for the analysis of system collapse should make predictions which go some way toward clarifying what has hitherto seemed a paradox of political organization.

State Formation: Anastrophe

After the collapse of an early state, we have predicted that feedback among the variables, and in particular from X to C, will reduce the marginality fairly quickly. Subsequently further investment in charismatic authority may lead to increase in degree of centrality. Increasing marginality and further changes could then ultimately lead to a further collapse, so that the behavior might be cyclical (Figure 21.5).

Yet there is nothing in the model to suggest that the feedback on the lower sheet necessarily always works to reduce marginality. Instead it is tempting to consider the circumstances in which a system on the lower surface, with low D, might undergo a sudden "upward collapse" onto the upper surface, rapidly becoming a highly centered polity with high D. Within the context of the present discussion I propose to designate this phenomenon of "upward collapse" by the term *anastrophe* (Figure 21.6). It is the counterpart, therefore, of the catastrophe of system collapse. From the mathematical standpoint, of course, sudden increase of D, like sudden decrease, is simply a discontinuous change of the state variable: Both are catastrophes (in the sense of Thom) with only the relatively trivial matter of a change of sign to distinguish between them. While recognizing this, however, the distinction in the applied case does not appear trivial at all. So anastrophe will here refer to the discontinuous increase in the state variable D (which represents degree of centrality), and catastrophe to discontinuous decrease.

Continuous decrease of the normal variable a (in this case investment in charismatic authority), when the splitting variable b (in this case marginality) is held at a constant high value, produces a catastrophic decrease in D

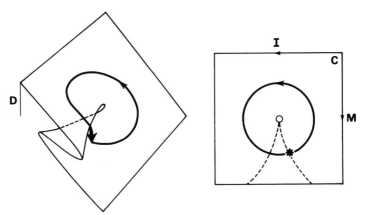

FIGURE 21.5 *Cyclical state formation (gradual) and collapse are possible (left) as the control variables change (right). Catastrophe.*

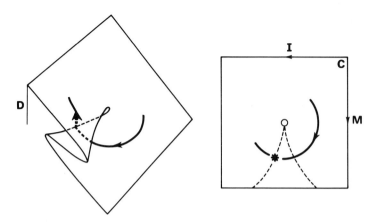

FIGURE 21.6 *Anastrophe: If the control variables follow a path close to the reverse of that seen in Figure 21.5, right, sudden state formation can occur.*

(degree of centrality). As we have seen, the system acts so as locally to maximize f_c with the operation of the delay rule and the switch to the lower sheet is deferred until the last possible moment. The model predicts that for an acephalous society, when marginality is high, steady increase in investment in charismatic authority will produce an anastrophe, a discontinuous rise in D. The model is here predicting for us another allactic form, the rapid formation of this state. If we define D by the size of territory or population, the anastrophe will entail the fusion of a number of acephalous polities to yield a single centered society (state formation by amalgamation). Alternatively, if D is defined in terms of levels of hierarchical organization without reference to scale, the anastrophe entails the sudden emergence of new structures of authority and administration by the insertion of a new hierarchical level, without any necessary change of scale (state formation by intensification). In practice sudden state formation will usually involve both these processes.

It is important to recognize that the model in itself, as formulated, tells us nothing of the nature of state organization, and a fuller analysis would undoubtedly require a deeper insight into the hierarchical structure and communication network implied by high centrality. Nor does it tell us that state formation implies any discontinuity. When marginality is low, investment in charismatic authority and degree of centrality can increase smoothly together, just as has been envisaged in Figure 21.5. What the model does do is to suggest that in certain conditions the state formation will be sudden, and to offer some suggestion as to what those conditions may be.

I suggest that the formation of the Zulu state may have been of this kind (see Gluckman 1960), and likewise the emergence of a centralized Saxon kingdom with a state organization in Britain in the ninth century AD.

The model itself does not indicate whether the anastrophe comes about as the result of war or by peaceful means. When an acephalous society is threatened by attack from outside, one response may well be to increase investment in charismatic authority, in the form of war leadership. But the change can also be a peaceful one: The formation of the Iroquois confederacy may be a change with elements of both.

The model here harmonizes with, and I think helps to sharpen, the insights of Robert Netting writing of political adaptation in Africa (1972, 332 ff):

> Let me suggest that political development in many cases takes place internally and voluntarily rather than by imposition or wholesale borrowing from neighbouring groups, and that the main lines of development and channels for change are prefigured in existing institutions and patterns of behaviour.

In his discussion (1972, 233) he stresses the role of charismatic leadership in the genesis of state organization:

> I would claim that on the road to statehood, society must first seek the spiritual kingdom, the essentially religious modes of focussing power are often primary in overcoming the critical structural weakness of the state. . . . The overwhelming need is not to expand existing political mechanisms (they are in certain respects radically inelastic) but literally to transcend them.

The model propounded here suggests that increasing marginality, whether arising from increased population, circumscription or whatever, may be one of the preconditions for the sudden anastrophic formation of a state society. Intriguingly it is likewise a necessary condition for the catastrophic collapse of the highly centered political system. I find it illuminating that a model conceived to describe the latter process should also prove relevant to the former.

Chiefdoms and the Butterfly Catastrophe

The model propounded in the section on the cusp catastrophe is appropriate to describe the sudden transition from a centered to a noncentered society. And as seen in the preceding section the formulation predicts a bimodal distribution of polities seen in terms of degree of centrality (Figure 21.4, lower). That corresponds closely with the group A/group B dichotomy of Fortes and Evans Pritchard, and to the distinction between egalitarian society and hierarchical society recently formulated by Service (1971, 157).

Many commentators, however, see a fundamentally trimodal distribution of polities among traditional and relatively simple agrarian societies. (In this discussion we omit consideration of hunter–gatherer bands at the one extreme, and of very complex political entities such as empires at the other.) This has been expressed by Morton Fried (1967) as a trichotomy between egalitarian, rank, and stratified societies, and by Service (1962) as a distinction between tribe, chiefdom, and state. This basic division into three has been widely accepted, although the term tribe is sometimes replaced by "segmentary society" (cf. Renfrew, 1976). The literature on the subject is extensive (cf. Sahlins 1968) and the desirability and appropriateness of the taxonomy cannot be argued here. Instead I propose to follow the procedure adopted in the section on the cusp catastrophe: first, to bring into discussion another of Thom's "magnificent seven" elementary catastrophes, and then to suggest its application.

The Butterfly Catastrophe

We have already discussed the operation of a system in which a state variable x, under the influence of two control variables a and b, is governed by a family of functions f_c, each conceived as a generalized potential function. Thom's theorem indicates that, given structural stability, the only singularities of M, (the graph of the maxima, minima, and so on, of f_c) when there are two control variables, are fold curves and cusp points.

The theorem goes on to state that where we have a single state variable x under the influence of four control variables (a, b, c, and d) the only singularities are the fold, cusp, swallowtail, and butterfly catastrophes.

A canonical form for the potential of butterfly catastrophe is given by

$$f_c(x) = \tfrac{1}{6}x^6 - \tfrac{1}{4}dx^4 - \tfrac{1}{3}cx^3 - \tfrac{1}{2}bx^2 - ax$$

where (a, b, c, d) are the control variables in the state space $X{\to}R$.

The associated catastrophe surface M is the four-dimensional surface given by

$$x^5 = a + bx + cx^2 + dx^3$$

The surface M is contained in R^5 and the bifurcation set B is contained in R^4, so that these cannot be readily illustrated graphically. Instead two-dimensional sections are drawn of B to show how it generates a cusp with an additional pocket indicating trimodal behavior. A fuller and more adequate description of the butterfly catastrophe is given by Zeeman (1977,29-32), Amson (1974), Isnard and Zeeman (1976), and Poston and Stewart (1976), and my description is drawn from these sources.

The four control factors are as follows;

a = normal factor
b = splitting factor
c = bias factor
d = butterfly factor

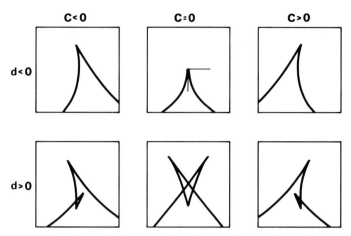

FIGURE 21.7 *Two-dimensional sections for the control space* C, *each drawn for* (c, d) *equal to a constant, for the butterfly catastrophe. This illustrates how variation in* d *(and* c) *governs the formation of the "pocket of compromise"—in this case chiefdom society.*

In Figure 21.7 various two-dimensional sections are drawn of the control space C. Each is an (a, b) plane drawn for (c, d) equal to a constant, and illustrates what the bifurcation set looks like in that section.

The effect of the butterfly factor d, when $d > 0$, is to bifurcate the cusp into three cusps as seen in Figure 21.7, lower. The effect of the bias factor c is to bias the position of the cusp. The normal and splitting factors operate very much as those of the cusp catastrophe seen in Figure 21.2.

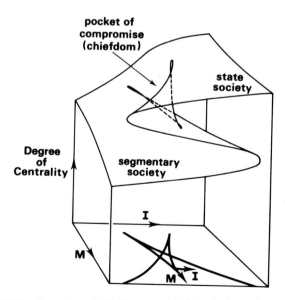

FIGURE 21.8 *The formation of chiefdoms modeled by the butterfly catastrophe.*

Figure 21.8 illustrates a section of the butterfly catastrophe, with the same variables *a, b,* and *D* as discussed for the cusp catastrophe earlier. The choice of the remaining control variables, *c* and *d,* is now discussed.

The Application

Once again we postulate a function $f_c(D)$ that expresses the viability of the system as reflected in the well-being of the rural population. We shall define the state variable *D* (degree of centrality) and the normal and splitting variables (investment in charismatic authority and net rural marginality) exactly as before.

But now, if we take a high value for *M* and a fairly high value for *I,* set the bias factor at 0, and give the butterfly factor a high value, the allegiance response and viability of the system against *D* gives a trimodal curve (Figure 21.9) instead of the bimodal curve associated with the cusp catastrophe. This implies that under certain conditions (given values of *a, b, c, d,*) there are stable states of the system for three different values of *D,* which we interpret in some cases as corresponding to segmentary society (egalitarian, tribe), chiefdom (ranked), and state (stratified). Under other conditions only one or two of these states will be possible.

At this stage it is necessary to give a meaning to *d,* the butterfly factor, and *c,* the bias factor. When *d* is negative the behavior is bimodal and a chiefdom is not possible; when *d* is positive the behavior is trimodal. I propose that *d* is to be regarded as a measure of the extent to which relations and rank in the society are determined by kinship, and that the butterfly factor be termed kinship ranking, and be represented by *K*. The underlying idea is that what makes a society a chiefdom where in other similar circumstances it might have been a state, is the extent to which relations within the

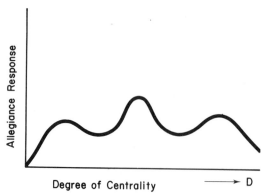

FIGURE 21.9 *Trimodal curve for allegiance response. For a given set of control values there can be three values of* D, *the degree of centrality, for which the allegiance response will be locally a maximum. These correspond to segmentary society, chiefdom society, and (early) state society, respectively.*

society are still determined by kin relationships, the result of birth or marriage, rather than be ascribed roles and statuses, or by membership of a class. The status of each individual is determined by his personal position in a complicated hierarchy of kin relationships, and often by his distance, in terms of kinship, from the individual of highest status in the group (the chief). Perhaps the simplest measure of this in a living society is simply the average of the number of relatives which members of the group can claim on the basis of detailed genealogical description. (In such a case a low number of relatives would give a large negative value for K, and a high number a high positive value.) In an archaeological situation the estimation of K is much more difficult, but perhaps not impossible. One is seeking to measure the extent of ranking, yet without counting stratification (which implies the division of society into a number of discrete classes). For the bias factor c we shall take the intensity of external threat to the system, denoted by T.

Figure 21.8 shows different changes in behavior with change in I and M where K is positive.

Space does not allow a more detailed discussion here, but some experimentation with the control variables will readily show how sudden, catastrophic change or gradual and continuous change can be effected from segmentary society (SS) to chiefdom, SS to state, chiefdom to state, state to chiefdom, state to SS, and chiefdom to SS.

Transformations

What started as an analysis of systems collapse has taken us far further, toward an analysis, or at least a description, of the transformations by which polities change their nature. At the outset the notion of allactic form was put forward, of which systems collapse is one of the most clearly recognizable examples.

Yet one of the first lessons which the discussion underlines is that the sudden collapse of an early state society is simply one of a number of possibly rapid changes of state of relatively simple agrarian societies. The preceding section reminded us that there are six conceivable discontinuous transformations among the three social forms considered: segmentary society, chiefdom, and state. There is of course no reason why these should have to be discontinuous, and indeed by following another path along the manifold the same changes can be effected without discontinuity.

The most obviously discontinuous, or at least very rapid, changes in the archaeological record are collapses, catastrophes to use Thom's term. But the discussion reminds us that sudden formations, sudden increases in organizational complexity and centrality, here termed anastrophes, can also occur.

There is little doubt, also, that the analysis holds several more insights which I have not spelled out, or which I have not seen. For instance, it would seen to be true that the well-known cases of systems collapse entail a catastrophic switch from early state society to segmentary society without stopping at the intermediate level of centrality, the chiefdom, on the way. Why is this? Is it that the level of marginality has to be so high before collapse ensues that it has already exceeded the limits of tolerance of a chiefdom society (cf. Figure 21.8)?

The property of divergence allows us to see how it is that discrete social forms may be observed, without intervening variants, rather than a complete spectrum of societies. This is indeed one of the most interesting aspects of catastrophe theory, that it generates thresholds and hence different forms. Further applications are likely to cast some light upon similar sociopolitical dichotomies, among which the Highland Burmese distinction between *gumsa* (ruled by chiefs) and *gumlao* (repudiating hereditary class difference) is particularly well known (Leach 1964, chapter VI).

In this chapter I have tried to bring out the features which arise from the mathematics of catastrophe theory and those which arise from my own specific formulation. Undoubtedly the problems raised here could be formulated differently, although the use of a different vocabulary sometimes masks the reality that the same distinctions are in fact being drawn. This is to some extent true, I feel, of Friedman's recent repudiation (Friedman 1974) of a systems terminology in favor of a neo-Marxian one. But without arguing that issue it is pertinent to remark that the notion of "trajectory" is very much at home within the context used here, and that transformations between different system states or social formations in the sense of radical, possibly discontinuous changes are not only permitted but required by catastrophe theory. Indeed the terms transformation and catastrophe (or anastrophe) are in most cases interchangeable. It is not of course surprising that the study of structural stability and morphogenesis should illuminate "structuralist" argumentation, but the underlying explanation or description of the transformations observed rests, in the case of catastrophe theory, on a much surer basis than an appeal to the altogether nebulous concept of "contradictions" (Friedman 1974, 465). The approach outlined here could, I feel, be translated into Marxist-structuralist thought (and language) to the benefit of the latter.

It must be admitted that many of the observations here do not derive directly from catastrophe theory: I do not claim to have "proved" anything in the mathematical sense. Yet the theory has worked as a valuable heuristic tool. For archaeologists badly need a framework of thought that will allow changes to be studied and compared. The classification of elementary catastrophes encourages the hope that allactic forms, as defined in Chapter 1, may indeed be recognized so that the analysis of cross-cultural regularities can be set on a more sound and formal basis, without encountering the objections which many anthropologists seem to hold for ethnographic analogies. Naturally each culture at a particular time is unique, and the sequence of events will from one perspective be unique also. A model of this kind can describe only those features with which its limited level of complexity allows it to deal. My argument here is that there are certain underlying regularities which it is useful to discern and to analyze. Such a procedure can in itself allow us to define more closely the special or unique features of the individual process, but it will never predict the infinite complexity and variety of each individual case. In the words of René Thom (1975, 320):

> It is tempting to see the history of nations as a sequence of catastrophes between metabolic forms; what better example is there of a generalised catastrophe than the disintegration of a great empire like Alexander's! But in a subject like mankind itself, one can see only the surface of things. Heraclitus said, "You could not discover the limits of the soul, even if you travelled every road to do so; such is the depth of its form".

References

Ålin P., 1962, *Das Ende der mykenischen Fundstätten auf dem griechischen Festland,* Lund (Studies in Mediterranean Archaeology I).

Adams R. E. W., 1973, The collapse of Maya civilisation: a review of previous theories, in Culbert T. P. (ed.), *The Classic Maya Collapse,* Albuquerque, University of New Mexico Press, 21–34.

Akurgal E., 1962, *The Art of the Hittites,* London, Thames and Hudson.

Aldred C., 1961, *The Egyptians,* London, Thames and Hudson.

Allchin B., and Allchin R., 1968, *The Birth of Indian Civilisation,* Harmondsworth, Penguin.

Amson J. C., 1974, Equilibrium and catastrophic models of urban growth, in Cripps E. L. (ed.), *Space Time Concepts in Urban and Regional Models* (London Papers in Regional Science 4), Pion, London, 108–128.

Bell B., 1971, The Dark Ages in ancient history: 1. The first Dark Age in Egypt, *American Journal of Archaeology* 75, 1–26.

Betancourt P. P., 1976, The end of the Greek bronze age, *Antiquity* 50, 40–47.

Braithwaite R. B., 1953, *Scientific Explanation,* Cambridge, University Press.

Carpenter R., 1966, *Discontinuities in Greek Civilisation,* Cambridge, Unviersity Press.

Culbert T. P., (ed.) 1973, *The Classic Maya Collapse,* Albuquerque, University of New Mexico Press.

Desborough V. R., 1975, The end of Mycenaean civilisation and the Dark Age, the archaeological background, in Edwards I. E. S., Gadd C. J., Hammond N. G. L., and Sollberger E. (eds.), *Cambridge Ancient History* (3rd edn.), II, ch. 36, 658–677.

Feuer B., 1974, An explanatory model for the collapse of the Mycenaean civilisation, unpublished seminar paper, California State University, Long Beach.

Flannery K. V., 1972, The cultural evolution of civilisations, *Annual Review of Ecology and Systematics* 3, 399–426.

Fortes M., and Evans-Pritchard E., 1940, *African Political Systems,* Oxford, University Press.

Fried M. H., 1967, *The Evolution of Political Society,* New York, Random House.

Friedman J., 1974 Marxism, structuralism and vulgar materialism, *Man* 9, 444–469.

Gluckman M., 1960, The rise of a Zulu empire, *Scientific American* 202, (April), 157.

Hood M. S. F., 1973, *The Minoans,* London, Thames and Hudson.

Hosler, D. H., Sabloff J. A. and Runge D., 1977, Simulation model development: a case study of the Classic Maya collapse, in Hammond N. (ed.), *Social Processes in Maya Prehistory,* London, Academic Press, 553–590.

Isnard C. A. and Zeeman E. C., 1976, Some models from catastrophe theory in the social sciences, in Collins L. (ed.), *The Use of Models in the Social Sciences,* Tavistock Press, London, 40–100.

Leach E. R., 1964, *Political Systems of Highland Burma,* London, Athlone Press (London School of Economics Monographs on Social Anthorpology no. 44).

Lumbreras S., 1974, *The Peoples and Cultures of Ancient Peru,* Washington, Smithsonian Institute Press.

Marinatos S., 1939, The volcanic destruction of Minoan Crete, *Antiquity* 13, 425–439.

Martin P. S., Quimby G. I. and Collier D., 1947, *Indians before Columbus,* Chicago, University Press.

Netting R. M., 1972, Sacred power and centralization: aspects of political adaptation in Africa, in Spooner B. (ed.), *Population Growth, Anthropological Implications,* Cambridge, Mass, M.I.T. Press, 219–244.

Ninkovich D. and Heezen B., 1965, Santorini tephra, *Colston Papers* 17, London, Butterworths, 413–453.

Pittott S., 1950, *Ancient India,* Harmondsworth, Penguin.

Poston T. and Stewart I. N., 1976, *Taylor Expansions and Catastrophes,* (Research Notes in Mathematics 7), London, Pitman.

Rappaport R. A., 1978, Maladaptation in social systems, in Friedman J. and Rowlands M. J. (eds.), *The Evolution of Social Systems,* London, Duckworth, 49–72.

Renfrew C., 1972, *The Emergence of Civilisation, the Cyclades and the Aegean in the Third Millennium B.C.,* London, Methuen.

Renfrew C., 1976, Megaliths, territories and populations, in De Laet S. J. (ed.), *Acculturation and Continuity in Atlantic Europe,* (Dissertationes Archaeologicae Gandenses 16) Brugge, De Tempel, 198–220.

Renfrew C., 1978, Trajectory discontinuity and morphogenesis, the implications of Catastrophe Theory for archaeology, *American Antiquity* 43, 203–244.

Richards A. I., 1960, Social mechanisms for the transfer of political rights in some African tribes, *Journal of the Royal Anthropological Institute* 90, 175–190.

Sabloff J. A., 1973, Major themes in the past hypotheses of the Maya collapse, in Culbert T. P. (ed.), *The Classic Maya Collapse,* Albuquerque, University of New Mexico Press, 35–42.

Sahlins M. D., 1968, *Tribesmen,* Englewood Cliffs, Prentice Hall.

Sanders W. T. and Marino J., 1970, *New World Prehistory,* Englewood Cliffs, Prentice Hall.

Service E. R., 1962, *Primitive Social Organisations,* New York, Random House.

Service E. R., 1971, *Cultural Evolutionism,* New York, Holt Rinehart and Winston.

Snodgrass A. M., 1971, *The Dark Age of Greece,* Edinburgh, University Press.

Taylour W., 1964, *The Mycenaeans,* London, Thames and Hudson.

Thom R., 1975, *Structural Stability and Morphogenesis,* Reading, Mass., W. A. Benjamin.

Vivian R. G., 1970, An inquiry into prehistoric social organisation in Chaco Canyon, New Mexico, in Longacre W. A. (ed.), *Reconstructing Prehistoric Pueblo Societies,* Albuquerque, University of New Mexico Press, 59–83.

Wheeler R. E. M., 1968, *The Indus Civilisation,* Cambridge, University Press, 3rd edn.

Willey G. R. and Shimkin D. B., 1973, The Maya collapse, a summary view, in Culbert T. P. (ed.), *The Classic Maya Collapse,* Albuquerque, University of New Mexico Press, 457–502.

Zeeman E. C., 1977, Catastrophe theory, in *Catastrophe Theory, Selected Papers 1972–1977,* Reading, Mass., Addison-Wesley, 1–64.

Index